D0953587

INTERPERSONAL DIAGNOSIS AND TREATMENT OF PERSONALITY DISORDERS

DIAGNOSIS AND TREATMENT OF MENTAL DISORDERS
Allen Frances, *Series Editor*

INTERPERSONAL DIAGNOSIS AND TREATMENT OF PERSONALITY DISORDERS

LORNA SMITH BENJAMIN
University of Utah

Foreword by Allen Frances

THE GUILFORD PRESS
New York   London

This book is for clinicians "in the trenches" who have grown weary with emergency phone calls, extra appointments, frequent hospitalizations, verbal bashings, frayed personal relationships, and uncollected accounts. It is also, in equal measure, for those who suffer from these chronic maladaptive patterns and hope to find new options.

©1993 The Guilford Press
A Division of Guilford Publications, Inc.
72 Spring Street, New York, NY 10012

Printed in the United States of America

This book is printed on acid-free paper.

Last digit is print number: 9   8   7   6   5   4   3   2

Library of Congress Cataloging-in-Publication Data

Benjamin, Lorna Smith.
    Interpersonal diagnosis and treatment of personality disorders/
Lorna Smith Benjamin; foreword by Allen Frances.
        p.   cm. — (Diagnosis and treatment of mental disorders)
    Includes bibliographical references and index.
    ISBN 0-89862-990-X
    1. Personality disorders.   2. Interpersonal relations.   I. Title.
II. Series.
    [DNLM: 1. Personality Disorders—therapy.   2. Personality
Disorders—diagnosis.   WM 190 B468i 1993]
    RC554.B45   1993
    616.85'8—dc20
    DNLM/DLC
    for Library of Congress   93-194
                                                                CIP

Foreword

The essence of being a mammal (and, most essentially, we are mammals) is the need for, and the ability to participate in, interpersonal relationships. The interpersonal dance begins at least as early as birth and ends only with death. Virtually all of the most important events in life are interpersonal in nature and most of what we call personality is interpersonal in expression. Indeed, psychotherapy can be defined as a specialized interaction designed to support or change someone whose ambient interpersonal behaviors and relationships have been insufficient, off the mark, or toxic. There are very few human activities, including psychotherapy, that are not best considered and defined from within an interpersonal model.

Given all the above, it is remarkable there has been so relatively little systematic theory and research on the ways in which people interact with one another, in life and in psychotherapy. Perhaps the major reason for this inattention is that the interpersonal is the prose we speak without being aware of it, and tends to be lost in the shuffle of more abstract model building or research. Personality theorists have often been more interested in describing drives, regulatory mechanisms, or cognitive structures while ignoring the interpersonal context in which each of these is developed and expressed. Psychotherapists have often been excessively technique conscious and give scant attention to the fact that any technical intervention will be understood by the patient within the particular interpersonal system of which it is a part, and will be helpful only insofar as it alters interpersonal behaviors, both within and outside the psychotherapy.

Most of modern interpersonal theory derives from Freud, although, ironically, Freud was much fonder of framing his models in more abstract drive and intrapsychic models. Almost despite himself, however, Freud developed an essentially interpersonal psychotherapy in which the leading ingredient was the recreation of earlier interpersonal experiences within the "transference," a context that would allow for new and more flexible interpersonal styles. It must be noted that classical psychoanalysis attempted to control the influence of the current interpersonal element of the therapy in order to avoid suggestion and to facilitate the patients' projection and resolution of internalized earlier interpersonal relationships. This emphasis has been modified in the subsequent development of psychodynamic psychotherapies which provide greater balance in their attention to past and current interpersonal relatedness, both within and outside the treatment sessions.

Freud's descriptions of universal life interpersonal experiences in childhood, and the personality styles that emerge from them, became the foundation of the psychodynamic interpersonal school of thought. This was much advanced by the work of Sullivan, who elevated the interpersonal relationship into the center of psychodynamic theory and practice and identified the transference relationship as a fully interpersonal medium of exchange (and change). Systematic research in the interpersonal soon followed and resulted in methods of systematically studying and rating interpersonal behaviors—both of the patient and of the therapist.

The research on interpersonal approaches to understanding personality and psychotherapy has been unusual in the richness of its clinical relevance. The various models developed over the last 30 years have provided methods of measuring what occurs within the psychotherapy session and determining how interpersonal behaviors may be modified. This has advanced our understanding of transference and countertransference in a way that has not been accomplished by any other empirical research method.

Lorna Smith Benjamin has been the major contributor to research on the interpersonal model and its application to clinical practice. She has developed the most clinically relevant method of assessing interpersonal styles in a manner that can be applied to patients, therapists, infants, mothers, and even monkeys. What distinguishes Dr. Benjamin (to a degree unique in my experience) is her combined excellences as a master clinician and a master researcher, and her happy integration of these viewpoints in everything she does and writes. She is one of the finest clinicians I have known and is better than perhaps anyone in our field in understanding deeply what the patient feels and why the patient is behaving in a certain way in a certain context. She is also a marvelously careful and creative researcher who is able to frame questions (and find methods of answering them) that touch most closely on why, what, and how we do what we do in the clinical situation.

Dr. Benjamin's interpersonal approach to personality and therapy provides a method that goes beyond the content of therapy to an understanding of the underlying themes. It will be equally useful to all manner of therapists (psychodynamic, cognitive, behavioral, family, group, etc.) of widely different kinds of experience and training. The interpersonal understanding can improve evaluations that last one session or therapies that last many years. This is a method that assists in every step of patient contact including the initial diagnosis, treatment planning, the conduct of the treatment, and evaluating whether the treatment's goals have been met. The book will be most readily understood by those who already have a rich clinical experience, but it is also a great way for beginners to be introduced to clinical work.

I have followed Dr. Benjamin's work closely for the past 15 years and have been profoundly influenced by it. Her approach has helped me to become more aware of the ways in which my patients' interpersonal styles "pull" for behaviors and countertransferences in me, and, reciprocally, how my ways of inter-acting "pull" for changed behavior or stalemates in them. Dr. Benjamin's method provides clear-cut predictions of how individuals will interact. This is helpful in avoiding the transference–countertransference problems that occur when we do what comes naturally.

This is a book to be read and reread many times. It is a kind of reference work that the reader will find useful over and over again at different times in the work with a given patient or as his or her clinical experience broadens with new patients. The approach is also very useful in improving one's skill as a su-pervisor—both in terms of the content it offers and also because it provides an enriched understanding of what is occurring in the supervisor–supervisee inter-personal relationship. This is a book for all seasons that I am sure will be both enlightening and enjoyable to its readers.

ALLEN FRANCES, M.D.
Duke University Medical Center
Chair, DSM-IV Task Force

Acknowledgments

Sometimes it is hard, too hard, just to go to the grocery store. The pain is everywhere, and much of it needless. I try not to look, not to see. To help, our health care system speaks of symptoms like anxiety, depression, and thought disorder. These official signs of mental disorder and related experiences like rage, fear, guilt, remorse, defeat, and disappointment drive the everyday interactions among family members and friends. In tasks as simple as shopping for food, interpersonal transactions show and make mental scars. The habits of pain are preserved and passed on from one to another, from generation to generation.

All of it makes sense, if only you can know the whole story. And little of it is necessary. If you can catch a glimpse of how it comes together, you can see how it can be changed, even how it could be prevented. I have written this book with the hope that more therapists will see and understand, and then be more effective as they seek to help those with major mental disorders.

My hope for myself is that this book will somehow facilitate my dream of starting a high-quality, low-cost psychosocial treatment center. It would specialize in research and training for helping individuals and families who suffer from major mental disorders, especially personality disorders.

Special acknowledgments to colleagues, friends, and family who have been so supportive are in order. For the healing and joy they have brought to my life, I would like especially to thank my daughters, Laureen and Linda. Their love, their goodness, their enthusiasm, and their competence in their own lives overwhelm me wonderfully. For generic help with my career, I thank Bob Carson, George Heise, Marjorie Klein, David Kupfer, and Ted Millon. For help with this book in particular, I thank Allen Frances and Seymour Weingarten. Under their firm and gentle guidance, it has been slowly shaped into better form. Allen seems to me to have been like a professional "guardian angel," swooping in now and then to read another draft, and then making incredibly wise and helpful suggestions. I have no idea how he does so much, but am grateful to be a beneficiary. Thanks too to the copyeditor, Marie Sprayberry, who has competently corrected errors in this and other projects with The Guilford Press. Her exacting attention helps me reach toward the goal of building a mosaic of pieces that consistently fit together in a synergistic whole.

I would like also to extend heartfelt appreciation to friends, colleagues, and students who commented helpfully on earlier drafts of this book. These include

Fran Friedrich, Julia Strand, Mary McGonigle, Kay McGonigle, Shawn Taylor, Margo Miles, Bill Henry, Steve Wonderlich, Ellen Frank, Marsha Linehan, Marjorie Klein, Colleen Sandor, Penny Jameson, Karen Callaway, Kelly Schloredt, and Marvin Goldfried. Gratitude is also expressed to the many patients quoted in this book for their openness and willingness to collaborate.

LORNA SMITH BENJAMIN

Key to Abbreviations
for the DSM Personality Disorders

BPD Borderline Personality Disorder
NPD Narcissistic Personality Disorder
HPD Histrionic Personality Disorder
ASP Antisocial Personality Disorder
DPD Dependent Personality Disorder
OCD Obsessive Compulsive Personality Disorder
NEG Negativistic Personality Disorder (provides new criteria for
     Passive Aggressive Personality Disorder in DSM-IV)
AVD Avoidant Personality Disorder
PAR Paranoid Personality Disorder
SOI Schizoid Personality Disorder
SZT Schizotypal Personality Disorder

These three-letter abbreviations are used throughout the book to mean either
"the diagnosis XYZ" or "a person with the diagnosis XYZ."

Contents

V. DIVERGENCES

PART ONE

BASIC CONCEPTS

1

Introduction and Overview

PROBLEMS WITH THE DSM APPROACH
TO PERSONALITY DISORDERS

A great way to come down with a case of "medical student's disease" is to read a survey of personality disorders. For example, a reader of Millon's (1982) impressive summary of each of the categories for personality disorder in the *Diagnostic and Statistical Manual of Mental Disorders*, third edition (DSM-III; American Psychiatric Association, 1980) can believe that he or she has nearly every personality disorder there is. Probably any remaining disorders can be assigned to one's spouse. The symptoms of personality disorders seem universally human. Who does not sometimes suffer from official "symptoms" of personality disorders, including idealization, devaluation, vanity, temper outbursts, boredom, seductiveness, rapidly shifting emotions, devastation in face of criticism, needs to be special or unique, failures in empathy, cruelty, infidelity, working too hard, working too little, hypervigilance, ideas of reference, odd mannerisms, wanting to be too intimate, wanting to be too distant, needing advice about little things, being too autonomous, having trouble getting started, feeling devastated when a relationship ends, being perfectionistic, being irresponsible, being too bossy, being too deferential, being withdrawn, hating being alone, wanting acceptance but fearing rejection, resenting others' control, or being critical of authorities? We all share these "symptoms" to greater or lesser degrees. The question is this: How many of these symptoms must we have, and for how long, before we become "personality-disordered"?

The present-day working definition can be found in the DSM-III-R (American Psychiatric Association, 1987) and in the DSM-IV (work in progress; American Psychiatric Association, 1991). In the former, personality traits are defined as "enduring patterns of perceiving, relating to, and thinking about the environment and oneself, exhibited in a wide range of important social and personal contexts" (1987, p. 335). Personality disorders exist when personality traits have become "inflexible and maladaptive, and cause either significant impairment in social or occupational functioning or subjective distress" (1987, p. 335). According to this official definition, "the personality disorders constitute one of the most important sources of long-term impairment in both treated and untreated populations. Nearly one in every 10 adults in the general population, and over one-half those in treated populations, may be expected to suffer from one of the personality disorders" (Merikangas & Weissman, 1986, p. 274).

To understand disorders, the tradition in medicine is to group patients together on the basis of symptoms and note whether their illnesses follow a similar course. Ideally, the grouping or diagnosis is associated with an idea about etiology, and this in turn has implications for treatment. A classical example is the diagnosis of bacterial pneumonia. The fever and other symptoms suggest (among other things) the possible presence of a pneumococcus, which may be treated by penicillin. When a syndrome has been described adequately by the medical model, then much is known about its cause, its expected course, and the available methods of treatment. The most effective methods of treatment have a logical relation to the cause. Penicillin, for example, acts directly on the cause of pneumococcal pneumonia, whereas aspirin acts on the symptom, fever. Both are helpful, but the one directed toward the cause is likely to result in a faster return to the normal condition.

Unfortunately, knowledge about causes and treatment of personality disorders is not as well developed as it is for many traditional medical problems. The current approach to psychiatric nomenclature was introduced in 1980 as the DSM-III. It was revised in 1987 as the DSM-III-R, and is again being revised at present as DSM-IV. The various editions of the DSM use the classical medical model in the description of mental disorders, known as the Kraepelinian approach. The DSM-III discarded psychoanalytic concepts, such as unconscious conflict, because they cannot be defined objectively and scientifically; instead it sought to group patients on the basis of observable symptoms. Because causes of mental disorders constitute a topic of intense and continuing controversy, no attempt was made formally to address questions of etiology in the DSM-III, DSM-III-R, or DSM-IV.[1] In an age of proliferating theories without convincing proof, the committee elected to omit theory altogether rather than attempt to select *the* correct one in the absence of empirical proof. The hope was and is that enlightened diagnostic groupings of individuals will eventually lead to clinical and research observations about pathogenesis, to valid theory, and to more effective treatment methods.

The diagnostic approach started by DSM-III succeeded in reaching its goal of improving the reliability of the definition of clinical syndromes, such as the schizophrenias, depressions, and anxiety disorders found on Axis I. However, it failed to define personality disorders on Axis II in ways that showed adequate reliability. Mellsop, Varghese, Joshua, and Hicks (1982) reported a clinical trial

---

[1]In this book the acronym DSM means DSM-III, DSM-III-R, and/or DSM-IV (draft). The DSM-III introduced the Kraepelinian approach to psychiatric diagnosis, and the other two revisions represent "fine-tuning." Distinctions among the revisions are made when necessary. These reminders about the changing standards of diagnosis can help the reader remember that the diagnostic criteria represent nothing more or less than the collective wisdom of a committee.

kappa of .41 for Axis II, while the DSM-III reported a kappa of .54 when diagnosing personality disorder.

There are at least two major reasons for the difficulty with diagnosing personality disorders. One is that defining the symptoms of personality disorders
is more challenging than defining symptoms for the clinical disorders on Axis I.
Symptoms of Axis I disorders, such as weight loss, tearfulness, anxiety, panic,
and thought disorder, are relatively easy to identify by the interview method.
Personality traits, such as vanity, inappropriate anger, dependency, and so on,
are harder to define. It is not difficult for an interviewer to ask and receive an
answer to questions appropriate for a diagnosis on Axis I: "Have you had a
change in your appetite? Do you cry a lot? Do you get the shakes?" But when
trying to diagnose a personality disorder, the interviewer cannot simply ask such
questions as "Are you vain and demanding?" or "Are you manipulative and
exploitative?" Definition of the symptoms of a personality disorder depends
largely on the evaluative opinion of the interviewer, whose view is likely to be
widely discrepant from that of the interviewee. In addition, some of the disorders include traits that might actively interfere with the flow of information.
The traits of conning, manipulation, and making oneself the center of attention
are likely to distort the diagnostic information obtained from the individual with
a personality disorder.

A second reason for the continuing controversy about the definition of
personality disorders is that many of the personality traits are considered signs
of membership in more than one category. For example, in the DSM-III-R, anger
is a symptom that is listed as a marker for several different personality disorder
categories:

> The anger item included in the DSM-III-R definition of Borderline
> Personality Disorder (BPD)[2] is this: inappropriate, intense anger or
> lack of control of anger, e.g., frequent displays of temper, constant
> anger, recurrent physical fights.
> The anger item included in the DSM-III-R definition of Histrionic Per-
> sonality Disorder (HPD) is this: expresses emotion with inappropri-
> ate exaggeration . . . has temper tantrums.
> The anger item included in the DSM-III-R definition of Narcissistic
> Personality Disorder (NPD) is this: reacts to criticism with feelings
> of rage, shame, or humiliation (even if not expressed).
> The anger item included in the DSM-III-R definition of Antisocial Per-
> sonality Disorder (ASP) is this: is irritable and aggressive, as indicated
> by repeated physical fights or assaults (not required by one's job or
> to defend someone or oneself), including spouse- or child-beating.

---

[2]As noted at the beginning of this book, three-letter abbreviations are used throughout to indicate
either "the diagnosis XYZ" or "a person with the diagnosis XYZ."

If an interviewer learns that a patient[3] has tempers, is irritable, and is aggressive, then the patient has a sign of each of these four personality disorders. When several such symptoms overlap, it becomes very difficult to make a differential diagnosis. The symptoms of anger, exploitativeness, impulsiveness, and self-centeredness all suggest the diagnoses BPD, NPD, HPD, and ASP. This overlap in symptomatology creates a *boundary* problem in the definition of personality disorders. The problem has been studied formally by Morey (1988). He asked clinicians who had treated individuals with personality disorders for at least 10 sessions to check all symptoms present from a list of the 168 possible symptoms on Axis II. DSM-III-R rules for classification indicated that 51.9% of the sample met criteria for more than one specific personality disorder. If the criterion diagnosis was NPD, 46.9% of those people also qualified for the label of BPD. Moreover, 55.6% of the HPD sample and 44.4% of the ASP sample also received a second label of BPD. Similar overlap was found for other groups of diagnostic categories. Morey's documentation of the overlap problem validated widespread clinician complaints about how hard it is to use the DSM-III and DSM-III-R to diagnose personality disorders.

After reviewing problems with unreliability and overlap, Frances and Widiger (1986) have wondered whether it is fruitless to try to use the classical medical model to diagnose personality. They suggested that it may not be possible to classify people in discrete diagnostic categories such as BPD, NPD, *or* ASP. These authors proposed that personality-disordered individuals might better be described on critically relevant underlying dimensions. Examples would be the dimensions of dominance–submission or extraversion–introversion, or the Axis II categories themselves. The latter option would allow one to "rate each patient on the extent to which he or she displays each set of maladaptive personality traits. Each patient would have a profile indicating the extent to which he or she is dependent, histrionic, schizotypic, paranoid, and so forth" (Frances & Widiger, 1986, p. 252). This version of the dimensional approach to Axis II has been implemented powerfully by others, including Theodore Millon (1982, 1986), author of the Millon Clinical Multiaxial Inventory (MCMI), and Loranger, Susman, Oldham, and Russakoff (1987), authors of the Personality Disorder Examination. Such uses of the profile method spare the clinician and the researcher the frustration of having to decide whether the patient is BPD, NPD, or ASP when he or she obviously has many symptoms in each "category." A very thoughtful consideration of the relevance of dimensional theory to classification problems appears in Skinner (1981).

One problem with the use of the present DSM categories as dimensions is

---

[3]Many psychotherapists prefer to use the word "client" rather than "patient." They reason that the word "patient" diminishes the status of the client, and inappropriately elevates the therapist's status to that of a "doctor" who understands and fixes everything. However, I use the word "patient" in this book because I like the list of synonyms for it far better than I like synonyms for the word "client." Synonyms for the word "client" include "consumer, buyer, patron, shopper, user." By contrast, synonyms for "patient" (as an adjective) include "charitable, accepting, forbearing, lenient, merciful, restrained, tolerant." I think the list for "patient" better characterizes what we need from those we seek to help.

that the usual meaning of "dimension" is changed. Ordinarily, dimensions (such as length, width, height, and time, or atomic weight and atomic numbers) are theoretically independent, or "orthogonal." The independence of dimensions provides conceptual parsimony, which is particularly important if there is an attempt to construct a theory to account for data. For example, the three theoretical concepts of distance (d), rate (r), and time (t) are related by the formula $d = rt$. These are three distinctly meaningful conceptions—(how far is it?) = (how fast do we move?) (how long does it take to get there?)—but there are only two independent ideas. Any of these three concepts is defined in terms of the other two. This is seemingly a simple observation, but the realization that time is defined only in terms of rate and distance is nonetheless one of the more unsettling implications of the theory of relativity. If the dimensions of space—length, width, and depth—were not orthogonal, the Pythagorean theorem and the formula $d = rt$ would be far more complicated. Discussions of curvature of space and time would be even more elusive. The idea is to find comparable orthogonal underlying dimensionality for describing personality disorders that will increase the clinical usefulness of diagnosis. Orthogonality in the proposed dimensions should offer simpler descriptions in personality, as it does in physics. Orthogonality should also increase the chances that the resulting nomenclature will permit development of a parsimonious, testable theory of pathogenesis and treatment.

In medicine there are several illnesses that yield the same symptoms, such as fever, headache, and joint pain. The differential diagnosis among illnesses having overlapping symptoms can be made, once the mechanisms for producing the symptoms have been identified and explained by the theory. For example, joint pain can be a result of infection, trauma, systemic disease, metabolic disorder, tumors, and so on. Medicine would be less effective if patients with joint pain were given profiles specifying the degree to which they were like people with rheumatoid arthritis, ulcerative colitis, streptococcal infection, traumatic injury, diabetic neuropathy, and so on. The comparison to medicine, where theoretical understanding reduces overlap, argues for a need for good theory about the pathogenesis and treatment of personality disorders. Good theory also should explain the difference between normality and pathology. That ability is vital when setting treatment goals for personality-disordered patients.

THE PRESENT APPROACH: AN INTRODUCTION

However, the obstacles to developing a theory that would account for the objectively observed clusters of symptoms described by the DSM are intimidating. Epstein (1987) reflected on the difficulty of adding theory to DSM-III:

> The joker in the deck is how to get the good theory. Clearly the essence of the scientific enterprise is a continuous interaction between observation and conceptualization, or, expressed otherwise, between empiricism and theory construc-

tion. There is no reason to believe that one side of the interaction is more important than the other. . . . Given good theory, it can powerfully influence good observation, which will contribute to yet better theory. But the truth of the matter is that our understanding of the nature and treatment of psychopathology is, at best, rudimentary, and we clearly do not have good theory to direct our observations. (p. 100)

The task of defining personality disorders had been undertaken many times prior to DSM-III. Previous work was published under many different headings, including psychoanalysis, the psychology of individual differences, philosophy, and literature. The present approach adds to the DSM descriptions of personality disorders aspects of psychoanalysis, interpersonal psychology, child psychology, and learning theory. The name of the approach, which permits operationalized description of interpersonal patterns and their impact on the self-concept, is Structural Analysis of Social Behavior (SASB). SASB, described in detail in Chapter 3, is a rational and empirically tested model of social interactions built on three orthogonal dimensions. It offers testable, refutable theory for understanding, on a symptom-by-symptom basis, how personality disorders described by the DSM are affected by the individual's specific social learning experiences and current social context. It is assumed that these hypothetical learning experiences interact in ultimately knowable but presently unknown ways with genetically transmitted temperamental factors.

The starting premise for the approach taken in this book is that the groupings described by the DSM represent substantial "folk wisdom." Each DSM diagnostic criterion and each casebook illustration (Spitzer, Skodol, Gibbon, & Williams, 1981; Spitzer, Gibbon, Skodol, Williams, & First, 1989) of the respective disorders can be translated into the social-interactional terms of the SASB model. To develop social-pathogenic theories for each of the DSM personality disorders, principles of the SASB model were used to infer specific early learning experiences likely to be associated with the interpersonal and intrapsychic patterns characteristic of each disorder. The SASB-based interpersonal descriptions and pathogenic hypotheses were checked and revised by using an interview method described in Chapter 4. The hypotheses have been refined and informally confirmed during the past 8 years by a spectrum of clinicians working in a variety of settings. If the present hypotheses are to achieve the status of scientific fact, they will need extended research. Since medicine itself is at the boundary of art and science, I have taken the liberty of placing the present approach at that juncture. The ideas in this book are specific enough that they can be tested and validated or refuted according to the rules of science. Nonetheless, for the purposes of this book, I assume that the use of the SASB model in the diagnosis and treatment of personality disorders is presently an art.

The SASB approach reduces the DSM boundary problems by specifying a particular interpersonal context for each of the symptoms defining the respective personality disorders. For example, BPD anger is most likely to be exhibited when the caregiver or lover is seen as neglectful and abandoning. The angry BPD wonders whether the caregiver or lover "cares and gives" enough. BPD anger is inspired by panic. It is recklessly executed to force the caregiver to provide the desperately needed attention and nurturance. By contrast, the angry HPD, functioning as both playwright and actor, will mount tantrums to force praise, admiration, and nurturance. ASP anger is very different from either BPD or HPD anger. The ASP has an anger that is cold and functional, executed to maintain or demonstrate control or distance, without remorse or regard for damage inflicted. NPDs, by contrast, feel "entitled," and become angry if their needs are not automatically filled—if the world does not "fall at their feet." Once it is known that anger is implemented in different contexts, and has different intended outcomes for different disorders, the "overlap" problem diminishes greatly. Anger suggesting panic about abandonment is consistent with the BPD diagnosis. Anger to coerce admiration is more consistent with HPD. Anger over failed entitlement raises the possibility of NPD. Remorseless anger in service of material gain or immediate pleasure is more suggestive of ASP.[4] The present thesis is that these different versions of anger arise logically from differences in early history interacting with temperamental factors.

In the chapters that follow, there is an attempt to identify interpersonal regulators for each of the symptoms defining the Axis II disorders of the DSM-III-R. For each symptom, there are speculations about social pathogenesis. The pathogenic hypotheses help generate plans for psychogenic treatment interventions that might directly address the interpersonal forces that have supported the disorder.

The approach is illustrated here by summarizing selected segments from Chapter 5 that describe the typical BPD's history, and the resulting transference patterns for BPD.

> The prototypic BPD is likely to have had unpredictably invasive and traumatic abandonment experiences. These events confused pleasure and pain, provided experiences of helplessness combined with omnipotence, and involved self-defining messages that changed rapidly from idealization to devaluation. Along with these confusing directives, independence was punished, and sickness was rewarded. The lessons provided by the developmental learning lead to the BPD's symptoms of abandonment sensitivity, rapid shifting among positions of helplessness, omnipotence, idealization, devaluation, paradoxically pleasurable self-mutilation, and personal carelessness. These attributes correspond to the symptoms of BPD as described by the DSM.[5]
>
> The traumatic abandonment experiences set the prototype for the interactional patterns so often seen between the BPD and the health care provider. The most likely transference problem is that the patient will be very active in coercing nurturance from the therapist until he or she "burns out." First the patient will bask in the joy of the therapist's nurturance, wisdom, and warmth. Then, as reality invades, it will become clear that the therapist is not going to be able to

---

[4]As an advisor to the DSM-IV Axis II work group, I have suggested that such interpersonal distinctions be used to reduce the boundary problems.

[5]An application of this approach to a person with Passive Aggressive Personality Disorder has been compared to Parallel Data Processing computer models of cognitive function (Benjamin & Friedrich, 1991).

deliver "enough." Repeated crises with overdoses, self-mutilations, and other major problems seem to show that therapy is going nowhere. The therapist begins to "withdraw"—initially by a loss of enthusiasm, reluctance to receive phone calls, to schedule extra appointments, and so on. These reactions lead to attacks on the therapist for not caring. The BPD may indignantly storm out of a session and announce that therapy is over. The withdrawals are likely to be dangerous, accompanied by dissociations, self-mutilations, and overdoses. While this occurs, the patient severely devalues the self as well as the therapist. On recovering from the episode, the BPD calls the therapist and wants to return. The stormy and dangerous departure frightens the therapist, but he or she dares not refuse lest there be a legal charge of abandonment. The BPD returns, but the therapist is distant, frightened, and resentful. He or she is likely at this stage to make jokes about BPD with colleagues, and to dread the appointments with the BPD. The BPD, of course, reads this accurately, and chastises the therapist for his or her lack of caring and hypocrisy. The therapist feels more guilty and more resentful.

It is important to reiterate that the developmental experiences interact with genetically determined temperamental factors. Not everyone who is subjected to the prototypic developmental experiences associated with BPD does in fact develop BPD. A child who was temperamentally slow and "inhibited" (Kagan, 1988) probably would not develop the full-blown interactive picture characteristic of BPD even if a prototypic BPD history existed. Genes and experiences must interact to shape interpersonal and intrapsychic habits. The process must be similar to the development of other complex human skills, such as intellectual, athletic, or musical ability. In all of these domains, genetic input sets a range of possible outcomes. Within that range, environmental experiences have major effects.

Robert Carson (1991) has proposed an apt analogy for understanding the interaction between genes and environment. He suggests that the "nature" or genetic factors compare to a computer's hardware, while the "nurture" or experiential side can be seen as the computer's software. If there is a bad disk or an erratic power supply, the computer's performance will not be reliable. Similarly, defective genes and associated erratic temperaments necessarily interfere with good interpersonal and intrapsychic functioning. On the other hand, if all the hardware is in powerful working order, but the software is primitive or defective, performance will also be limited. The hardware puts severe constraints on the software. Although this is a book about software, it is important to remember that the hardware makes a difference. The reader is asked to bear in mind that even though genetic contributions are not discussed in this book, they are powerful.

PLAN OF THE BOOK

Chapter 2 offers a brief history of relevant prior developments. Chapter 3 introduces the SASB model. Those who do not have time to learn SASB coding can simply read the first part of the chapter to get the general idea, and then skip ahead to Chapter 4. Chapter 4 describes an interviewing method and treatment approach associated with the SASB analysis. The interviewer tries to "see the world as the patient does." The purpose is to understand how the maladaptive patterns of personality disorder can be enhanced by social (but often unconscious) "reinforcement." The assumption is that the "symptoms" make adaptive sense from the perspective of the patient. Once the adaptive value of the symptoms is known, a treatment plan can be developed. The problem that encourages the symptoms must be solved in another way. The treatment approach is generic and attempts to provide guidelines for choosing among the variety of available therapy approaches. These include client-centered, psychoanalytic, gestalt, couples, group, family, paradoxical, and still other therapies.

Chapters 5 to 14 present the SASB dimensional analysis of the DSM personality disorders. The chapters are grouped according to the three DSM "clusters" of illnesses that have overlapping and related symptoms. The first to be discussed is the DSM cluster B, the "dramatic, erratic" group. Here, BPD, NPD, HPD, and ASP are considered. The second is cluster C, the "anxious, fearful" group. This includes Dependent Personality Disorders (DPD), Obsessive Compulsive Personality Disorder (OCD), Passive Aggressive Personality Disorder (recently replaced by Negativistic Personality Disorder, or NEG), and Avoidant Personality Disorder (AVD). The last is cluster A, the "odd, eccentric" group. Paranoid Personality Disorder (PAR), Schizoid Personality Disorder (SOI), and Schizotypal Personality Disorder (SZT) belong in this collection.

Each chapter follows the same outline: (1) a brief review of the literature for the disorder; (2) the DSM description of the disorder; (3) SASB-based pathogenic hypotheses for the disorder; (4) connections between the interpersonal history and the symptoms listed in the DSM; (5) an interpersonal summary of the disorder; (6) review of the DSM criteria in the light of the interpersonal modification and the empathic perspective; (7) recommended necessary and exclusionary criteria; (8) two brief case illustrations; and (9) expectable transference problems and treatment recommendations for each disorder.

The approach is briefly illustrated here by selected aspects of the analysis of BPD given in Chapter 5. The interpersonal summary of BPD given in Chapter 5 is as follows:

> *There is a morbid fear of abandonment and a wish for protective nurturance, preferably received by constant physical proximity to the rescuer (lover or caregiver). The baseline position is friendly dependency on a nurturer, which becomes hostile control if the caregiver or lover fails to deliver enough (and there is never enough). There is a belief that the provider secretly if not overtly likes dependency and neediness, and a vicious introject attacks the self if there are signs of happiness or success.*

The explication of the DSM is illustrated here by the analysis of the BPD anger criterion as it appears in Chapter 5. The DSM item appears in **bold print**.

The SASB-based interpersonal modifiers are <u>underlined</u>, and the empathic cues, written from the perspective of the BPD, are IN CAPITAL LETTERS.

inappropriate, intense anger or lack of control of anger, e.g., frequent displays of temper, constant anger, recurrent physical fights
<u>Anger is elicited when the caregiver or lover is seen as neglectful or abandoning, or there is doubt about whether the other person cares and gives enough. Anger is to control the caregiver—to make sure that he or she will provide the wished-for attention and caring.</u>
I HAVE HUGE BLOW-UPS WITH PEOPLE OVER WHETHER THEY ARE TAKING GOOD CARE OF ME.

The empathic cues that appear in CAPITAL LETTERS are selected items from the Wisconsin Personality Inventory (WISPI[6]; Klein, Benjamin, Rosenfeld, Greist, & Lohr, in press). The WISPI is a self-rating form that offers two items (presented in a randomly determined order) for every Axis II criterion. The items are written from the perspective of the rater, not the observer. Validity studies, directed by Marjorie Klein, suggest that the WISPI can improve the reliability of diagnosis of personality disorders. Correlations within diagnoses are maximized, whereas correlations between diagnoses are minimized.

Overlap among disorders is reduced by the empathic view that is written into the WISPI items. For example, NPDs would be less likely to endorse the BPD version of anger, because it would not even occur to the NPDs that others might not care about them. The item would not elicit endorsement from ASPs because they are unlikely to care whether others care. Although the empathic cues from the WISPI reduce overlap, they do not eliminate it.[7] For example, HPDs do endorse the item given above to describe BPD anger, though less often than BPDs.

The clinician can use the WISPI items presented in this book to enhance his or her empathic approach to the diagnosis of DSM personality disorders. Psychiatric residents report that they are able to imagine whether their long-term therapy patients would endorse the WISPI items for a given disorder. When they compare these guesses to the WISPI key for the disorder, they feel confident of their decision that a patient does or does not have the disorder. They report that the recommended treatment approaches for the category selected by this method are helpful. Clinician readers of this book can do the same. By reading the "DSM Descriptors Revisited" and "Necessary and Exclusionary Criteria" sections of Chapters 5–14 for the diagnoses they are considering, clinicians can make the differential diagnosis. Once the diagnosis is made, the recommended treatment approaches for that disorder should be helpful.

Chapter 15 includes a discussion of people who fall into the DSM residual

---

[6]The WISPI items were written by me, and carefully edited by Klein and her research group. Professor Klein is conducting formal validation studies of the WISPI. Interested users can write to Professor Marjorie Klein at the Department of Psychiatry, University of Wisconsin, Madison, WI 53792.

[7]The final version of the WISPI scoring program will have an algorithm that includes the recommended necessary and exclusionary conditions.

categories—Mixed Personality Disorder, and Personality Disorder Not Otherwise Specified (NOS). The thesis is that the DSM describes some commonly occurring groupings, but the Axis II categories are not exhaustive, fixed, or universal. The present approach to these residual categories is simple: *For every symptom there are reasons.* Given the requisite underlying temperament, there will be a connection between previous social experiences and the symptoms of the disorder.

Consider the DSM-III category Mixed Personality Disorder, which includes features of more than one recognized disorder. This result will be observed if one parent programs the patient for one disorder, while the other parent encourages another pattern. Suppose that the patient is male, and his mother provided the background for NPD while his father provided the abuse needed for PAR. This man is probably narcissistic in intimate relationships with women and paranoid at work in relationships with men. His diagnosis would be Mixed Personality Disorder with NPD and PAR features. Such an analysis offers a practical and rational explanation of the fact that some individuals show symptoms of more than one "disorder." The categorical system of diagnosis is neither discarded nor reified inappropriately.

Individuals with personality disorders that do not resemble any of the standard categories receive the label Personality Disorder NOS. These people probably have not had any of the "standard" social experiences. The present approach argues that they have had experiences that, along with their temperaments, can account for the patterns they present. The clinician who sees the connection between the presenting patterns and the social pathogenesis is in a better position to develop an effective treatment plan. An important goal of this book is to help the clinician with that task.

Finally, there is a brief consideration of the fact that people with personality disorders more often than not often have symptoms from Axis I. BPD, for example, sets the curve for overlap between personality disorder (Axis II) and clinical syndromes (Axis I). BPDs frequently—even typically—have depressions, thought disorder, dissociative disorder, marked alcohol and substance abuse, and various forms of the anxiety disorders. Hypotheses about possible effects of psychosocial factors on clinical syndromes are sketched briefly at the end of the book.

In sum, the purpose of this book is to translate the DSM descriptions of personality disorders into interpersonal terms that have clinical coherence. The reformulations are based on application of the SASB model to the DSM. They have been informally checked by clinical trials, and have testable pathogenic and treatment implications. The approach promises to improve reliability and clinical usefulness of the DSM descriptions of personality disorders.

2

History and Assumptions of the Approach

THE PROBLEM OF DYNAMIC ORGANIZATION

Biologists assume that the structure and function of the organism are shaped by the goal of preserving life (Darwin, 1859/1952). The biological view of infectious disease is that the body responds to the invasion of a noxious agent with a life-preserving attempt to contain, get rid of, or escape from the toxic element. Fever, pain, aches, or swollen glands—the symptoms of the disease—are correlates of defensive responses to the invasion. If this medical model of disease were to be applied to personality disorders, noxious agents would have to be identified. Then there would need to be a description of how the personality-disordered individual has tried to contain, defend against, get rid of, or escape them. There would also need to be a definition of normal personality, so there could be an assessment of whether the corrective attempts have succeeded.

If this parallel between personality disorder and medical illness is to be pursued, there needs to be some explanation of how the "maladaptive" patterns of personality disorder compare to fever, pain, or swelling of lymph nodes. Somehow a diagnosis of personality disorder must be associated with understanding of what it is *for*, how it is *adaptive*. Such a dynamic explanation of personality disorders would be true to "biology," the science of living organisms. The interpretation would differ significantly from present-day "biological" interpretations of psychiatric disorder, based on the belief that mental disorders are the result of deficient biochemistry, which induces a "breakdown." Within mainstream psychiatry, a person with mental disorder is believed to be a victim of malfunctioning genes. He or she does not have the basic equipment needed to cope adequately with life stresses. The symptoms are not seen as the direct results of efforts to adapt; rather, they are seen as the consequences of the inability to adapt.

The idea that adaptive goals or purposes need to be included in descriptions of personality has been around for a long time. Gordon Allport (1937) provided a complete, informative, and interesting survey of the concept of personality, reaching back to views developed by ancient Greeks, early philosophers, and the Christian Church. Following his summary of the variety of meanings throughout intellectual history, Allport proposed the following definition: "Personality is the *dynamic organization* within the individual of those psychophysical systems that *determine his unique adjustments* to his environment" (1937, p. 48, emphasis added). Allport gave the description of goals and purposes, which he called "dynamics," a central role in his theory of personality. Freud also gave teleology a primary role in his formulations about mental disorder. However, as noted in Chapter 1, recent versions of DSM have rejected dynamic interpretations of mental disorders. The main reason is that psychoanalytic definitions have not been amenable to testing by scientific methods.

The DSM is not alone in the decision to abandon consideration of goals or purposes when trying to explain human behavior. The large section of psychology that is based on the work of B. F. Skinner (1938) has confined itself to immediately observable, operationalizable constructs. In the early years, Skinner spoke of the person as an "empty black box." He cautioned that scientific understanding of behavior must be restricted to inferences made strictly on the basis of observed "input" to and "output" from the box. Attributing goals and purposes to the box was considered beyond the scientific pale. Recently, behavioral psychology has drifted back toward more speculation about what is inside the box, including ideas about its purposes, but not without criticism from Skinner (1990) himself.

Even the strictest adherents to Skinner's position must now come to terms with the need for dynamic concepts when trying to understand continuity and change in human behavior. The tip of the dynamic iceberg can be seen in the simplest of experiments in cognition. Experimenters glide by it, using phrases such as "deciding homunculus" (Johnston & Dank, 1986) to account for selective attention to different experimental stimuli. The appearance of such a term in experimental psychology—a branch of the discipline that places special emphasis on scientific rigor—alerts us to the need to think about underlying goals or purposes. The problem of dynamic organization must be addressed when studying human behavior in general, and personality disorders in particular.

THE PSYCHOANALYTIC VIEW

Identification of dynamic bases for personality disorders necessarily begins with the question of what drives human beings. What *are* the ultimate goals in human social interaction? Do they amount to more than physical survival? Is such a goal the "pleasure principle"? How could the principle of adaptation account for why an individual engages in persistent, inflexible, maladaptive patterns? A review of the history of thinking about this problem as it unfolded within psychoanalysis is in order, but beyond the present scope. A very brief sketch of the highlights appears here.

Sigmund Freud, the creator of psychoanalysis, held that humans are selfish and destructive, and that people need to have their primitive sexual and aggressive energy contained by threats of punishment. Freud argued that rationality is based on borrowed energy from the id. It prevails only as long as the ego can successfully figure out how to discharge the id's aggressive or sexual tensions.

Society's representatives—the parents, who have been internalized as the super-ego—insure that straightforward discharge of hostility and sexuality will not be attempted. If the ego does not find ways to discharge the primitive energy, mal-adaptive defenses will form against their expression. The associated unconscious conflicts between the need for drive discharge and what is consciously permitted are the bases of "neurosis." The nature of the personality disorder depends upon the developmental stage at which the conflict occurred.

Classical psychoanalytic treatment is directed by the cathartic model. A series of techniques designed to make the unconscious conscious (e.g., dream analy-sis, free association, hypnosis) identify early conflicts. The therapy dismantles the defenses against the unconscious, and the deflected energies are discharged constructively.

A number of different schools of psychoanalytic thought have evolved from Freud's theories. The one of greatest relevance to the present approach is the so-called "object relations" school. This perspective has been wonderfully sum-marized by Greenberg and Mitchell (1983). The developments within the object relations school that are most helpful to the present approach are (1) the emphasis on the major role of attachment in human development, and (2) the importance of differentiation to normal development.

Harry Stack Sullivan (1953) noted that an infant has a basic need for emo-tional contact, including bodily contact with other human beings. In his view, anxiety is a problem that can be acquired from the mother through "empathic linkage." Security is freedom from anxiety, and the surest routes to security are power, status, and prestige in the eyes of oneself and of others. To paraphrase Sullivan loosely, he held that love and power are the fundamental needs and that anxiety is a basic fear. This gifted clinician provided rich clinical material to dem-onstrate his theory. Sullivan emphasized the importance of trying to understand the world as the patient does, rather than looking "at" the patient from the per-spective of an outsider. His name for this therapeutic stance was "participant observer."

At the center of Sullivan's discussion of how interpersonal experience affects the development of personality is his description of the formation of the self-system. Sullivan described a complicated process for the development of self:

> I have said that the self-system begins in the organizing of experience with the mothering one's forbidding gestures, and that these forbidding gestures are refine-ments in the personification of the bad mother; this might seem to suggest that the self-system comes into being by the *incorporation* or *introjection* of the bad mother, or simply by the introjection of the mother. These terms, incorporation or introjection, have been used in this way, not in speaking of the self-system, but in speaking of the psychoanalytic superego, which is quite different from my conception of the self-system. . . . I have said that the self-system comes into being because the pursuit of general and zonal needs for satisfaction is increasingly interfered with by the good offices of the mothering one in attempting to train the young. And so the self-system, far from being anything like a function of or an identity with the mothering one, is an organization of experience for avoid-

ing increasing degrees of anxiety which are connected with the educative process. . . . The idea that one can, in some way, take in another person to become
a part of one's personality is one of the evils that comes from overlooking the
fact that between a doubtless real "external object" and a doubtless real "my
mind," there is a group of processes—the act of perceiving, understanding, and
what not—which is intercalated, which is highly subject to past experience and
increasingly subject to foresight of the neighboring future. Therefore, it would
in fact be one of the great miracles of all time if our perception of another person were, in any greatly significant number of respects, accurate or exact. (1953,
pp. 166–167)

Sullivan said that the basic tasks of psychotherapy are as follows:

(1) . . . elucidating situations in which unfortunate action is currently shown
repeatedly, so that the disordered pattern may become clear; (2) discovering
the less obvious ramifications of this inadequate and inappropriate way of life
throughout other phases of the present and the near future, including the doctor–patient relationship and the patient's expectations about it; and (3) with the
problem of inadequate development now clearly formulated, utilizing his human
abilities to explore its origins in his experience with significant people of the past.
(1953, pp. 376–377)

Sullivan's interpretations are central to the approach taken in this book.
Most important is his explicit marking of connections between the patient's adult
personality and the patient's *perceptions* of early social educational experiences.
Equally crucial is his straightforward interpretation of therapy as an exercise in
helping the patient recognize his or her patterns and expectations.

Another important object relations psychoanalyst, Margaret Mahler (1968),
cultivated the vitally important concept of "individuation" or "differentiation."
Mahler noted that the infant first attaches to the mother, then tentatively tries
out doing things separately from the mother. Separation or individuation
involves going through a rather stormy ambivalent phase, and then "making up"
with the mother. This sequence of attaching and then separating results in a stable
and friendly sense of the self as separate from the mother. Individuation unfolds
well if the mother provides adequate fondling and cuddling, and if separation is
nurtured within an atmosphere of patience, tenderness, security, and pleasure.
Mahler centered on love (attachment) and differentiation (independence),
whereas Sullivan emphasized love (emotional contact) and power as basic to the
organization of personality.

Sullivan and Mahler both saw the human being as fundamentally sociable.
Their views contrasted strongly with Freud's theory that the human is driven by
primitive, unsocialized drives such as sexuality or aggression. All agreed that the
development of personality involves an interaction between biologically determined developmental propensities and the earliest social experiences. Psychoanalytic descriptions of environmental factors usually center on what was lacking, or what was overdone, or what came at the wrong time.

Differences in beliefs about the development of personality have a profound
impact on the choice of therapeutic interventions. For example, there has been

a heated argument between Heinz Kohut and Otto Kernberg about what to do when a narcissistic patient becomes angry with the therapist (reviewed in Benjamin, 1987a, p. 64). Kohut believes that the therapist should provide the patient with a "mirroring" experience that the patient's mother failed to give. The mirroring therapist should accept the patient's anger, and even look inward to see what kind of mistake the therapist might have made. This corrective validation of self should help the patient heal. Kernberg, by contrast, believes that the therapist should not accept the anger, but should instead confront the narcissist with the fact that he or she is repeating primitive patterns. The therapist should then try to help the patient integrate the split between his or her perceptions of the good and bad therapist, as well as the split between his or her own good self and bad self.

Arguments like those between Kohut and Kernberg are difficult to resolve, because many psychoanalytic concepts are not amenable to testing by scientific methods. It is hard to assess the mental representations that result from mother–infant interactions, and to connect them to adult behaviors. In this and many other contexts, psychoanalysis has been harshly criticized for the unscientific nature of its concepts and procedures (e.g., Grunbaum, 1986). Some psychoanalytic authors have responded to such criticisms by maintaining that science is not relevant to the clinical arts. They argue that the wish to be scientific is an artifact of a mechanistic culture immersed in technology (Guntrip, 1973, pp. 25–26). Many practicing clinicians either agree with the irrelevancy argument or simply ignore the problem by conducting therapy on an "intuitive" basis.

MURRAY'S CONTRIBUTION

Because of the lack of a scientific base, psychoanalytic theory and practice were rejected by the DSM-III task force and by much of academic psychology. Nonetheless, there have been very important developments that promise to lead to methods for bringing science to psychoanalytic concepts. The chain of events began with Sullivan's interpersonal psychiatry. Greenberg and Mitchell (1983, pp. 80–81) have said that Sullivan secretly dominates much of modern psychiatry, but is rarely credited or acknowledged within psychoanalysis itself. Outside psychoanalysis, in a relatively small branch of psychology, definitions of psychopathology became ever more interpersonal. Henry A. Murray (1938) presented a comprehensive theory of personality, which he said was "guided partly by the analysts (Freud, Jung, Adler), partly by McDougall and by Lewin, and partly by our subjects—whose actions so frequently corrected our preconceptions" (p. 38). Like Allport, and like the psychoanalysts, Murray was very impressed with the underlying organizing themes of people's behavior. To parallel the analytic idea of drives, Murray presented a list of human needs:

> Primary or vicerogenic needs include Air, Water, Food, Sex, Lactation, Urination, Defecation, Harmavoidance, Noxavoidance, Heatavoidance, Coldavoidance,

Sentience, and Passivity (sleep, rest). Secondary or psychogenic needs include a group related to inanimate objects: acquisition, conservance, order, retention, and construction; a group related to people: superiority, achievement, recognition, exhibition, inviolacy, infavoidance (avoid shame, failure, ridicule), defendance (justify, resist probing), counteraction (defend honor), dominance, deference, similance (suggestible), autonomy, contrarience, aggression, abasement, blame-avoidance, affiliation, rejection, nurturance, succorance, play, cognizance (inquiring attitude), exposition. (summary based on pp. 76–83)

In addition to detailing many different kinds of drives, Murray also redefined such psychoanalytic concepts as id, ego, superego, narcissism, and ego ideal (pp. 135–141). A quotation from his account of how needs affect the personality shows Murray's predilection toward psychoanalysis:

[Needs have positive or negative or negative cathexes.] A personality is largely revealed in the objects that it cathects (values, rejects). . . . Objects can be cathected (by primary displacement), because, let us say, of their association with birthplace, nationality, parents, an unusual traumatic experience, a glamourous relationship or some other fortuitous event. Then there is secondary displacement with all the mythological imagery of the unconscious to choose from. . . . One might say that traces (images) of cathected objects in familiar settings become integrated in the mind with the needs and emotions which they customarily excite, as well as with images of preferred modes. A hypothetical compound of this sort may be called a *need integrate*, or *complex*. . . . When a need is aroused it has a tendency to seek or to avoid, as the case may be, the external objects that resemble the images with which it is integrated. Failing in this, it projects the images into the most accessible object, causing the subject to believe that the later are what is desired or feared. The thing "out there" looks like or is interpreted to be the cathected image of the need integrate. This theory accounts for the content of dreams, hallucinations, illusions and delusions. It also makes intelligible the selectivity in attention and response which individuals exhibit when confronted by a heterogeneous environment. . . . The *press* of an object is what it can *do to the subject or for the subject* —the power that it has to affect the well-being of the subject in one way or another. The cathexis of an object, on the other hand, is what it can *make the subject do*. . . . A thema is the dynamical structure of an event on a molar level. A simple thema is the combination of a particular press or action or outcome and a particular need. It deals with the general nature of the environment and the general nature of the subject's reaction. (pp. 106, 107, 110, 121, 123)

To test the validity of these concepts, Murray and his colleagues studied a group of 50 normal males. Among other things, they developed the Thematic Apperception Test (TAT) as a method for objectively measuring needs and themas, and relating them to other data about the lives of the subjects. The TAT has subsequently been used by any number of practicing clinicians seeking to prepare an assessment of unconscious organizational processes in patients. However, the scientific status of the TAT has remained equivocal, largely because subjective judgment is required to assess the meaning of the stories told in response to the TAT pictures.

THE INTERPERSONAL CIRCLE

Whether he succeeded in making a science of psychoanalysis or not, Murray systematically organized ideas about how biological drives can interact with interpersonal experiences to create a "personality." His categories of need provided the basic building blocks of the Interpersonal Circle (IPC), a monumentally important development that began with Freedman, Leary, Ossorio, and Coffey (1951). The first three authors were graduate students working with the fourth author at the University of California, Berkeley (see Freedman, 1985). The second paper in this series was published by LaForge, Leary, Naboisek, Coffey, and Freedman (1954). A subsequent very important monograph, by Leary (1957), used the IPC to propose a complete and exclusively interpersonal diagnostic system. In present-day literature, most discussions of the IPC cite the Leary monograph.

Leary's (1957) version of the IPC appears in Figure 2.1. The IPC is usually called a "circumplex," a name that comes from Guttman (1966). The mathematical equation for a circle shows that its points are defined by the underlying horizontal and vertical axes. In the case of the IPC, the underlying dimensions range from "hate" to "love" on the horizontal axis ("affiliation") and from "submission" to "dominance" on the vertical axis ("interdependence"). This means, for example, that the point "Responsible–Hypernormal" in Figure 2.1 is made up of about 50% love (horizontal axis) and 50% dominance (vertical axis). The categories in the IPC model were selected from Murray's (1938) list of needs. The creators of the IPC reduced the number of Murray's categories and arranged them so that connections would be apparent (Leary, 1957, p. 39). For example, the geometry of Figure 2.1 shows that "Responsible–Hypernormal" is close in meaning to "Cooperative–Overconventional." At the same time, "Responsible–Hypernormal" is the opposite of "Rebellious–Distrustful."

Using the categories of the IPC shown in Figure 2.1, Leary (1957, pp. 232–238) developed the Sullivanian thesis that interpersonal behavior rather than symptoms should provide the basis of psychiatric diagnosis. He suggested the following interpersonal descriptions for traditional Kraepelinian categories of personality disorder:

Octant AP: Managerial–Autocratic = Compulsive personality
Octant BC: Competitive–Narcissistic = Narcissistic, exploitative personality
Octant DE: Aggressive–Sadistic = Psychopathic personality
Octant FG: Rebellious–Distrustful = Schizoid personality
Octant HI: Self-effacing–Masochistic = Masochistic or obsessive personality
Octant JK: Docile–Dependent = Anxiety neurosis
Octant LM: Cooperative–Overconventional = Hysterical personality
Octant NO: Responsible–Hypernormal = Psychosomatic personality

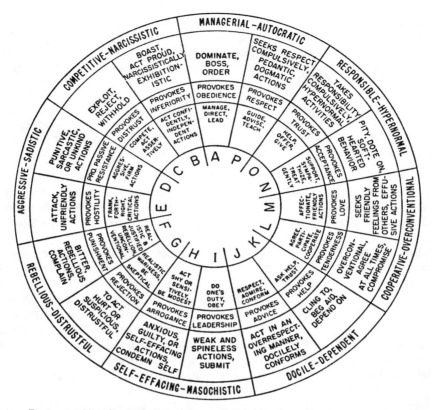

FIGURE 1. Classification of Interpersonal Behavior into Sixteen Mechanisms or Reflexes. Each of the sixteen interpersonal variables is illustrated by sample behaviors. The inner circle presents illustrations of adaptive reflexes, e.g., for the variable *A*, *manage*. The center ring indicates the type of behavior that this interpersonal reflex tends to "pull" from the other one. Thus we see that the person who uses the reflex *A* tends to provoke others to *obedience*, etc. These findings involve two-way interpersonal phenomena (what the subject does and what the "Other" does back) and are therefore less reliable than the other interpersonal codes presented in this figure. The next circle illustrates extreme or rigid reflexes, e.g., *dominates*. The perimeter of the circle is divided into eight general categories employed in *interpersonal diagnosis*. Each category has a moderate (adaptive) and an extreme (pathological) intensity, e.g., *Managerial-Autocratic*.

FIGURE 2.1. Leary's Interpersonal Circle (IPC). Art and text are reprinted by permission from Leary (1957, p. 65).

Leary was the first to make explicit connections between the medical diagnostic nomenclature and the interpersonal descriptions offered by the IPC. However, he did not persist in developing this line of thought. Instead, Leary suggested an alternative interpersonal nomenclature including such categories as "adjustment through self-effacement," "adjustment through control," and "adjustment through aggression." His recommended interpersonal diagnostic system could be applied to individuals by having them rate important figures such as spouse, child, mother, father on the Interpersonal Check List (ICL).

The ICL, written by LaForge and Suczek (cited in Leary, 1957), offers items at four levels of increasing intensity. Examples for octant AP, "Managerial–Autocratic," are as follows:

> A: 1 = able to give orders; 2 = forceful, good leader, likes responsibility; 3 = bossy, dominating, manages others; 4 = dictatorial. P: 1= well thought of; 2 = makes a good impression, often admired, respected by others; 3= always giving advice, acts important, tries to be too successful; 4 = expects everyone to admire him. (Leary, 1957, p. 456)

Level 1 represents normality, and level 4 represents the most intense and most pathological condition. A person who endorsed a few of the mild items in octant AP would be called a normal "leader" by this methodology. A person who endorsed most of the items in octant AP would be called "Managerial–Autocratic." Such an intense level of AP would correspond to compulsive personality. According to the IPC model, intensity marks the difference between normality and pathology.

Exploration of the use of the IPC for improving the diagnosis of personality has continued since Leary's early effort. Landmarks have included papers by Lorr, Bishop, and McNair (1965), Plutchik and Platman (1977), Widiger and Kelso (1983), and Kiesler (1986). Using large samples of normal subjects, Wiggins (1982) has created a carefully researched and validated version of the ICL. Wiggins and Broughton (1985) prepared a useful methodological review of applications of the IPC in personality research. Morey (1985) compared the ability of the IPC and the MCMI (Millon, 1982) to describe patients with known Axis II disorders. He concluded that people with personality disorders do differ along the IPC's control dimension, but not on the affiliation dimension:

> The primary axis along which the personality disorders vary also seems to correspond to the active–passive personality dimension which Millon (1969) identified as underlying his typology. However, the relative lack of differentiation along the Affiliation dimension is somewhat unexpected, given the predictions of some theorists that systematic variations among personality disorders would be noted in this domain as well. (Morey, 1985, p. 386)

DeJonge, van den Brink, Jansen, and Schippers (1989) replicated Morey's finding that the affiliation dimension was less important than the control dimension in distinguishing one personality disorder from another. In sum, the IPC has received significant theoretical attention as a possible way to describe personality disorders in interpersonal terms, but it has not been incorporated in medical definitions of personality disorders, nor has it received widespread clinical use. The gap between promise and accomplishment in interpersonal diagnosis has been reviewed elsewhere (McLemore & Benjamin, 1979).

One problem with the use of the IPC to define psychopathology is that it cannot describe all of the DSM personality disorders. Widiger and Frances (1985) commented:

> The antisocial personality disorder is also difficult to describe in IPC terms because the negative pole of the affiliation dimension is a mixture of hostile and detached behavior that does not adequately describe the criminal and guiltless exploitation of others. The antisocial person is neither hostile (aggressive) nor detached but can in fact be superficially friendly although disloyal, irresponsible and exploitive. This difficulty in classifying the antisocial diagnosis may lend some support to those who argue for two circumplexes to define the interpersonal domain (the footnote at this point refers to SASB). (p. 621)

It is possible that the IPC has failed to describe the personality disorders because it is incomplete. Independently of the developments in the IPC, Earl Schaefer (1965) proposed a different circumplex model of parental behavior. His circumplex has a horizontal axis that ranges from Rejection (hate) to Acceptance (love), and a vertical axis that ranges from Psychological Control to Psychological Autonomy Giving. Parental behaviors located on the Schaefer model between Psychological Control and Rejection include Satellitization, Intolerance, and Hostile Involvement. Parental behaviors plotted on Schaefer's model between Rejection and Psychological Autonomy Giving include Hostile Indifference, Indifference, and Detachment. Parental behaviors between Psychological Autonomy Giving and Acceptance include Emancipation, Encouragement of Divergence, and Acceptance of Individuation. Finally, parental behaviors located between Acceptance and Psychological Control include Loving Involvement, Protectiveness, and Intrusiveness.

Schaefer's circumplex model is similar to the IPC in that the horizontal axis ranges from love to hate. Schaefer's version differs from the IPC in that it designates Psychological Autonomy Giving as the opposite of Psychological Control (dominance), rather than submission. The validity of Schaefer's model for parenting behavior has been confirmed in many different cultures. Factor analyses of ratings of parental behavior have repeatedly conformed to the model he offered. At the same time, the validity of the IPC has also been confirmed by factor analyses.

The vertical axes of the IPC and of the Schaefer model both make intuitive sense, and each has been confirmed empirically. It is reasonable to propose, as did Leary, that submission is the opposite of dominance. Schaefer's proposal that giving autonomy provides a valid opposite of control is equally reasonable. They both correspond to accepted clinical theory. The horizontal and vertical axes of the IPC, respectively, represent Sullivan's assumption that emotional contact (love vs. hate) and power (dominance vs. submission) are basic interpersonal needs of the human being. Schaefer's model also shows a love–hate dimension on the horizontal axis, but its second (vertical) dimension includes space for individuation or differentiation (Psychological Control vs. Psychological Autonomy Giving), believed by Mahler to be so vital to normal development.

THE SASB MODEL

The model for SASB (Benjamin, 1974, 1979, 1984) accommodates both these points of view. Dominance and submission are presented in logical relation to each other, while dominance and autonomy giving appear as opposites. In effect, the SASB model includes key features of both the Leary and Schaefer versions of the interpersonal circumplex. In addition, the SASB model invokes Sullivan's hypothesis that the self-concept arises directly from interpersonal experiences with significant other people. The model is described in detail in the next chapter. It too has been validated by empirical studies. The more complex dimensionality of SASB permits adequate description of all the personality disorders listed in the DSM.

There has been an escalating chorus of criticism of the DSM decision to avoid etiology in the definition of psychopathology (e.g., Skinner, 1981; Millon, 1991; Morey, 1991; Carson, 1991). If teleology could be added to the interpersonal descriptions of personality disorders, then clinicians would have better guidelines for helping individuals change their patterns. The predictive principles of the SASB model do yield testable hypotheses about social pathogenesis, and about the dynamic underlying organization of personality disorders. Therefore, in this book, hypotheses about pathogenesis and teleology are added to the DSM definitions of personality disorders. The goals are presented as underlying wishes and fears. Successful treatment interventions must address theses underlying goals or adaptive purposes of the patterns that characterize a disorder. Specific suggestions for intervention follow the dynamic interpersonal analysis of each of the disorders.

3

The Harmonics of Therapy

"Do, re, mi, fa, so, la, ti, do."

One day early in my freshman year at Oberlin College, I came back to the dormitory and found my roommate sitting on the floor. She was huddled over an ancient record player, listening intently to organ music. "What are you doing?" I asked. "Practicing," she explained. Margaret had entered the conservatory as a highly skilled pianist planning to major in organ. She did not yet know how to play the organ, which requires, among other things, the ability to read clefs unfamiliar to piano players. At the time, Margaret was reluctant to learn to read tenor clef. Because she had perfect pitch, an astonishing memory, and other musical gifts, she could play her assignments splendidly after simply listening to recordings of great artists. There are a number of such gifted individuals—some famous, some relatively unknown—who can hear someone else perform a very complicated piece and then play it with ease. Some, like Margaret, add their own amazingly creative touch to the rendition. If musical skills are distributed normally, such very rare people must be many standard deviations above the mean.

Despite the low likelihood of a person's having the ability to acquire a complex skill primarily by imitation, the teaching of the art of psychotherapy relies heavily on modeling. Clinicians and teachers "do" psychotherapy, and students watch or read about it. They try it and talk about their cases with teachers. Through trial and error, and discussions with their supervisors, students gradually develop their own approaches. There is no universally agreed-upon "theory" of therapy. There are no therapist skills identified as essential, regardless of the "school" of therapy.

To pursue an analogy between music and psychotherapy, it is instructive to notice that the art of making music is a highly structured discipline. Professional musicians are expected to learn the basic theory of their trade. They must master an array of technical skills, including reading music, fingering techniques,

Note. A scan of pages 25 to 37 in this chapter should give the reader the background needed to follow subsequent descriptions of the personality disorders. Readers interested in generalizing the principles of the SASB model to new situations not described in this book may profit from careful reading and rereading of the entire chapter. To facilitate the interested reader's study of a number of unfamiliar but very useful concepts, an index of the SASB topics covered is provided at the end of this chapter.

developing the ability to render chords, and so on. Musical theory about the basic structure of harmonics and rhythm allows those who have an "ear" to become experts. There are texts that communicate the basics of theory and technique, and that suggest helpful exercises. Even those with extraordinary gifts expect to work hard to acquire the basic necessary skills. The musician knows that he or she will need to practice these basic skills for many years, and that some of the work is quite dreary. Nobody imagines that knowing music theory or practicing technical drills alone makes a person a musician; the training only enhances the likelihood of expertise. The final result requires the addition of the individual musician's own creativity and imagination. With the requisite technical skills, the creative musician easily makes beautiful music.

The teaching of psychotherapy may be analogous. There must be basic skills and knowable theory that relate in meaningful ways to the process of psychotherapy. If these could be identified and taught, the overall level of performance by psychotherapists should be greatly improved. The science or art of psychotherapy[1] needs a generic theory that compares at least to the musician's understanding of *do, re, mi, fa, so, la, ti, do*. There must be a way to codify the combinations of pitches and rhythms in the symphony of therapy, and to teach them to gifted students. Such knowledge could be used to train therapists' "ears" so that they could accurately hear the interpersonal "harmonics" in a moment. They might then know enough about the structure of conversation to be able to anticipate and implement the next intervention skillfully and correctly. Just as there is an overwhelming array of types of music and musical instruments, there is a tremendous variety of possible renditions of the harmonics of therapy. There is no need to worry that adding "science" or discipline to psychotherapy will make robots of the participants or otherwise compromise their creativity and uniqueness.

This book draws heavily on Sullivan's (1953) view that psychotherapy should focus intensively on patients' interactions with important others, and on how those interactions affect the self-concept. The key harmonics and rhythms of psychotherapy are in the patients' interactions with important people from their past, present, and expected future. A major thesis of this book is that primary aspects of the interpersonal harmonics and rhythms of therapy can also be recognized. A useful naming convention for identifying the harmonics of therapy is offered by the interpersonal dimensionality delineated by the SASB model, mentioned in Chapters 1 and 2. The SASB model can capture crucial, but not all, aspects of the therapy process. This model suggests that the basic elements of psychotherapy emerge from the dimensions of "interpersonal focus," "love–hate" (or, alternatively, "friendliness–hostility"), and "enmeshment–differentiation." Experienced clinicians already have an "ear" for love and hate, and for enmeshment and differentiation. The analogy to music is not exact. The argument nonetheless is that the basic SASB units, called SASB "codes" or "labels," compare to the basic pitches *do, re, mi, fa, so, la, ti, do*. Their combina-

---

[1]As noted in Chapter 1, therapy is probably both an art and a science. Music, which is an art, can also be analyzed by scientific principles of physics and of mathematics.

tions and sequences make up the harmonics and rhythms of the respective personality disorders and set the stage for the process of psychotherapy with them.

The reader is invited to learn the basic SASB "notes" of the interpersonal "scale." This skill helps the clinician identify the basic pitches and rhythms often played by individuals with personality disorders. Each disorder may be compared with a song. The BPD song is clearly identifiable, but there are passages that remind one of the HPD. Other parts of the BPD song are similar to that of the ASP. Just as any song can sound very different, depending on who is playing it and on the orchestration, presentations of the songs of the disorders will vary greatly. Think of any song—say, "Deep Purple." This composition can sound different, depending not only on the players, but on whether it is played on the organ or by a small or large orchestra; by whether the ensemble does or does not include a vocalist; by whether the interpretation is in the classical or the jazz tradition; and so on. Despite the tremendous variety of possible renditions, the melody remains recognizable. "Deep Purple" is "Deep Purple" in all these different forms. Similarly, a BPD can be recognized as a BPD in many different forms, once a clinician knows the melody, the harmonics, and the rhythm.

A clinician's knowledge of SASB labels is comparable to a musician's understanding of basic rules about harmonics and rhythm. An ability to read the SASB notes (labels) can help the clinician quickly read a patient's interpersonal and intrapsychic patterns and react appropriately. Like a musical artist, the clinician who wants to become an expert with the songs of the personality disorders needs quite an array of technical skills, plus a good interpersonal "ear." There can, of course, be clumsy renditions without the training. But when one is working with potentially suicidal or homicidal people, the consequences of "just noodling" can be quite serious.

INTERACTIONAL FOCUS ON ANOTHER PERSON

Patients A, B, C, and D

The following introductory exercise can help many readers see that they already know the basic "pitches" in the SASB language. The SASB model does nothing more or less than organize conventional clinical wisdom. In this "tuning-up" exercise, the reader is asked to consider the four types of marital relationship described for hypothetical patients A, B, C, and D. There are two steps to this exercise: (1) Find a word to characterize the patient's way of relating to his or her spouse; (2) find a phrase to characterize the interpersonal changes displayed by the descriptions from the top to the bottom of the list.

Patient A

0. Patient A murders, kills, destroys, and leaves his spouse as a useless heap.
1. Looking very mean, patient A follows his spouse and tries to hurt her.

2. Patient A rips his spouse off, tears, steals, grabs all he can from her.
3. Patient A harshly punishes and tortures his spouse, takes revenge.
4. Patient A misleads his spouse, disguises things, tries to throw her off track.
5. Patient A accuses and blames his spouse. Patient A tries to get her to believe and say she is wrong.
6. Patient A puts his spouse down, tells her that her ways are wrong and his ways are better.
7. Patient A butts in and takes over, blocks and restricts his spouse.
8. Patient A makes his spouse follow his rules and ideas of what is right and proper.
9. Patient A controls his spouse in a matter-of-fact way. He has the habit of taking charge of everything.

The reader who follows step 1 may suggest that these items describe a patient who is hostile to his spouse. Step 2 should lead to the observation that the patient is described as progressively more controlling, and less overtly hostile, from the top to the bottom of the list. Many clinicians' "ears" have learned to discern the shifts in degrees of hostility and control in these statements, even if there is no accepted language to describe them. The steps from top to bottom have gone, say, from *do* to *re* to *mi* on the musical scale. One does not need to know the names of the "notes," or to know anything about music theory, to hear the differences in pitch.

The interpersonal *do, re, mi* of this exercise is in the shifts in hostility and control that the patient shows with his spouse. The list moves from murderous attack through blaming to arbitrary control. The underlying dimensions are "hostility" and "control." The exact steps are discussed below, in association with Figure 3.2.

A second hypothetical patient is described by the next group of relational descriptions.

Patient B
0. Patient B murders, kills, destroys, and leaves her spouse as a useless heap.
1. Patient B angrily leaves her spouse out. She completely refuses to have anything to do with him.
2. Patient B angrily leaves her spouse to go without what he needs very much, even when she easily could give it to him.
3. Just when patient B is needed most, she abandons her spouse, leaves him alone with trouble.
4. Patient B ignores the facts and offers her spouse unbelievable nonsense and craziness.
5. Patient B neglects her spouse, his interests, his needs.
6. Patient B just doesn't notice or pay attention to her spouse at all.
7. Patient B forgets all about her spouse, their agreements, their plans.

8. Without concern, patient B lets her spouse do and be anything at all.
9. Patient B peacefully leaves her spouse completely on his own.

Step 1 should lead to the observation that this patient is also hostile to her spouse. But the hostility has a different quality, a different feel. Her description begins at the same murderous point, but moves stepwise in another direction. This time it is as if the notes move backwards down the scale from *do* to *ti* to *la*. Step 2 should lead to the conclusion that, from the top to bottom of the list, the descriptions change from overt attack through hostile forgetting to neutral letting go of the relationship. The stepwise progression through this hostile group of characterizations invokes increasing degrees of autonomy. The underlying dimensions are "hostility" and "autonomy giving."

Two more hypothetical patients with their spouses complete this first exercise in the training of the interpersonal ear:

Patient C
0. With gently loving tenderness, patient C connects sexually if his spouse seems to want it.
1. Patient C warmly, cheerfully invites his spouse to be in touch with him as often as she wants.
2. Patient C provides for, nurtures, takes care of his spouse.
3. Patient C lovingly looks after his spouse's interests and takes steps to protect her.
4. With much kindness and good sense, patient C figures out and explains things to his lover.
5. Patient C gets his spouse interested and teaches her how to understand and do things.
6. Patient C pays close attention to his spouse so he can figure out all of her needs and take care of everything.
7. Believing it's really for his spouse's own good, patient C checks often on her and reminds her of what should be done.
8. Believing he really knows what is best for his spouse, patient C tells her exactly what to do, be, and think.
9. Patient C controls his spouse in a matter-of-fact way. He has the habit of taking charge of everything.

The reader who follows step 1 will note that the last description in patient C's list is the same as the last in patient A's list. However, the two people are very different, because patient C is friendly to his spouse whereas patient A is hostile. Step 2 leads to the conclusion that, as in patient A's case, stepwise progression from the top to the bottom of the list invokes increasing amounts of control. Patient C's list begins with very warm sexual love and progresses through nurturance to benevolent control. The descriptions are organized by the underlying dimensions of "friendliness" and "control."

The last patient offers still another melody:

Patient D

0. With gently loving tenderness, patient D connects sexually if her spouse seems to want it.
1. Full of happy smiles, patient D lovingly greets her spouse just as he is.
2. Patient D gently, lovingly strokes and soothes her spouse without asking for anything in return.
3. Patient D likes her spouse and thinks he is fine just as he is.
4. Patient D clearly understands her spouse and likes him even when they disagree.
5. Patient D really hears her spouse, acknowledges his views even when they disagree.
6. Patient D lets her spouse speak freely and hears him even if they disagree.
7. Believing her spouse does things well, patient D leaves him to do them his own way.
8. Patient D leaves her spouse free to do and be whatever he thinks is best.
9. Patient D peacefully leaves her spouse completely on his own.

Unlike patient B, who is hostile to her spouse, this one is very friendly and loving. Patient D's description begins with the same warm and sexual love as that of patient C, but she differs from him in that she does not invoke control. Progression through the list from the top to the bottom shows increasing amounts of autonomy giving. The relational descriptions move from very warm sexual love through affirmation and understanding to comfortable emancipation. The underlying dimensions that organize this relationship are "friendliness" and "autonomy giving."

The Underlying Dimensions Describing Patients A to D

Patients A to D relate to their spouses in four very different ways. The underlying dimensions that organize the descriptions of patients A to D are shown in the top and middle parts of Figure 3.1. Hostility/hate and friendliness/love define one dimension, shown at the top of the figure by the scale that runs from left to right. The poles of this axis are named ATTACK and ACTIVE LOVE. An example of extreme attack is provided by patient A, who "murders, kills, destroys, and leaves his spouse as a useless heap." An example of extremely active loving is offered by patient C, who "With gently loving tenderness . . . connects sexually if his spouse seems to want it." The "hate–love" dimension is named "affiliation."

Enmeshment/taking control and differentiation/giving autonomy define the other dimension when focusing on another person. It is shown on the vertical line in the middle part of Figure 3.1. The poles of this dimension range from CONTROL

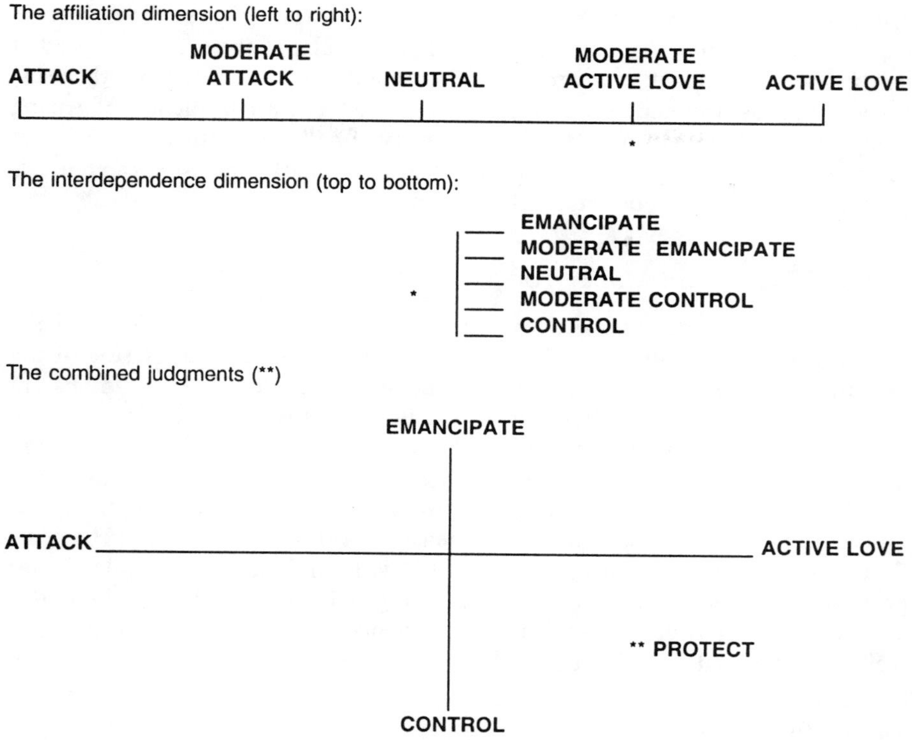

The affiliation dimension (left to right):

ATTACK	MODERATE ATTACK	NEUTRAL	MODERATE ACTIVE LOVE	ACTIVE LOVE

The interdependence dimension (top to bottom):

___ EMANCIPATE
___ MODERATE EMANCIPATE
___ NEUTRAL
___ MODERATE CONTROL
___ CONTROL

The combined judgments (**)

EMANCIPATE

ATTACK _____ ACTIVE LOVE

** PROTECT

CONTROL

FIGURE 3.1. Using dimensional judgments to classify an interaction on the "focus on other" surfaces of the SASB simplified cluster model (see Figure 3.2). *The judgments for the example given in the text, pages 33–35; **the summary.

(bottom) to EMANCIPATE (top). Extreme control is shown by patients A and C. Each "controls his spouse in a matter-of-fact way [and] has the habit of taking charge of everything." The other pole, EMANCIPATE, is illustrated by patients B and D. Each "peacefully leaves her spouse completely on his own." Again, the extreme pole of a dimension, EMANCIPATE, can apply in a hostile or in a friendly context. In itself, autonomy giving is neither "good" nor "bad." This "control–autonomy giving" dimension is called "interdependence." The method of combining these two dimensions to label an interaction is described below in the section headed "The SASB Simplified Cluster Model, Focus on Other."

Variations in the Level of Detail Provided

Conventional notation in Western music has eight basic steps: *do, re, mi, fa, so, la, ti, do.* The human ear can hear differences that are smaller than the steps that are allowed on the musical scale. There also are formal names for half steps between these standard musical intervals. Even smaller changes can be detected by the good ear. In fact, many musical instruments easily deviate from the arbitrary standards (frequencies) that define the notes. The phenomenon of getting "out of tune" is so common that before every concert the musicians must set their instruments to agree with a given standard. Similarly, the notes of an interpersonal scale can also be set at arbitrary intervals.

The SASB Quadrant Model, Focus on Other

Table 3.1 shows how the respective relational styles of these four different patients can be described in quite simple terms. Patient A is on the attack side of the affiliation dimension and on the control side of the interdependence dimension. These simple joint observations show that he uses **Hostile power**. Patient B is also hostile, but she functions in a way that is described by the independent side of the interdependence dimension. She actively ignores her spouse, and so her position is summarized in Table 3.1 as **Invoke hostile autonomy**. Patient C is on the friendly side of the affiliation dimension, and he is controlling. His position is named **Friendly influence**. Patient D is friendly and independent. Her position is summarized by the phrase **Encourage friendly autonomy**. These four combinations of affiliation and interdependence comprise the simplest SASB scale, the so-called "quadrant model."

The SASB Full Model, Focus on Other

Patients A to D are each described above by 10 sentences. These 10-sentence sketches are at the smallest intervals named by any of the SASB models. The name of this most detailed version is the SASB "full model."[2] By including the full-model descriptions of patients A, B, C, and D, Table 3.2 gives richer meaning to the four sections of Table 3.1. The numbers for the phrases in Table 3.2 match the descriptive sentences given above in the text for each patient. The numbers mark the order in which the phrases appear in the text, and they are also used later to illustrate the predictive principles of the SASB model.

Both Tables 3.1 and 3.2 are organized according to the same principles. Both show how the four relational styles are arranged according to the two underlying dimensions of affiliation and interdependence. The difference between Tables 3.2 and 3.1 is in the level of detail. The steps on the interpersonal "scale" are very large for Table 3.1, and they are very small for Table 3.2. The underlying dimensionality organizes both tables in the same way. One can begin at any place and proceed in a clockwise (or counterclockwise) direction to move incremen-

---

[2]The descriptions that appear in the text to detail the full-model entries in Tables 3.2, 3.4, and 3.6 are from the SASB Long Form INTREX questionnaires. The full model itself has the geometric shape determined by circumplex theory, rather than the simpler tabular form given in this book. For a complete exposition of the SASB models, please see Benjamin (1974, 1979, 1984).

Table 3.1. Patients A, B, C, and D, Quadrant Model

	ATTACK	ACTIVE LOVE
EMANCIPATE	B. Invoke hostile autonomy	D. Encourage friendly autonomy
CONTROL	A. Hostile power	C. Friendly influence

Note. The table depicts the two dimensions that define patients A to D with their spouses. The intersection of these dimensions suggests that patient A is abusive, patient B is rejecting and neglectful, patient C is nurturant, and patient D is harmonious. Adapted from Benjamin (1979).

tally through interpersonal space and return to the beginning.[3] The steps are very gradual in Table 3.2, and very abrupt in Table 3.1.

The SASB Simplified Cluster Model, Focus on Other

The scale used later in this book to describe the personality disorders is between these two in level of detail; it is called the "simplified cluster version"[4] of the SASB model. The section or surface of the simplified cluster model that describes focus on other is presented in Figure 3.2. This model includes the poles of each of the underlying dimensions just discussed. The left-to-right axis goes from ATTACK to ACTIVE LOVE (affiliation), and the bottom-to-top axis goes from CONTROL to EMANCIPATE (interdependence). Patients A, B, C, and D are described above in terms of the interpersonal dimensions marked by these axes. Every statement about the four patients represents a mixture or "blend" of these underlying dimensions, affiliation and interdependence.

Consider, for example, patient C. Suppose that in a family session the adolescent son is berating patient C's spouse. Imagine that this father says, "Don't you talk to your mother that way." SASB "sight reading" begins by assessing the husband's relationship to his wife[5] on the affiliation dimension, shown from left to right in Figure 3.1. In relation to his wife, patient C is clearly on the friendly side of the scale. He is definitely warm, but not extremely loving. The category marked MODERATE ACTIVE LOVE shown on the scale at the top of Figure 3.1 would

---

[3]Leisurely readers will notice that each patient's first and last description in the text overlaps with someone else's description. This overlap does not appear in Table 3.2, but could be introduced by copying nearby items numbered "9" or "0" into the cells where they are missing.

[4]The original SASB cluster models (Benjamin, 1983, 1987a) include a numbering system that is convenient for research users. That numbered system also makes it easy to connect the cluster model to the full model.

[5]SASB labeling is not restricted to any given two-person interaction in a group. All the dyads in a triangular set (e.g., husband and wife, husband and son, wife and son) can be labeled. It is also possible to label subgroups in relation to each other or to the whole group. For example, husband plus wife as a dyad can be coded in relation to the son. Any other such combination is permitted if it seems clinically important.

Table 3.2. Patients A, B, C, and D, Full Model

	ATTACK	ACTIVE LOVE
	Patient B	*Patient D*
EMANCIPATE	9. Endorse freedom	
	8. Uncaringly let go	8. Encourage separate identity
	7. Forget	7. You can do it fine
	6. Ignore, pretend not there	6. Carefully, fairly consider
	5. Neglect interests, needs	5. Friendly listen
	4. Illogical initiation	4. Show empathic understanding
	3. Abandon, leave in lurch	3. Confirm as OK as is
	2. Starve, cut out	2. Stroke, soothe, calm
	1. Angrily dismiss, reject	1. Warmly welcome
	Patient A	*Patient C*
CONTROL	0. Annihilating attack	0. Tender sexuality
	1. Approach menacingly	1. Friendly invite
	2. Rip off, drain	2. Provide for, nurture
	3. Punish, take revenge	3. Protect, back up
	4. Delude, divert, mislead	4. Sensible analysis
	5. Accuse, blame	5. Constructively stimulate
	6. Put down, act superior	6. Pamper, overindulge
	7. Intrude, block, restrict	7. Benevolently monitor, remind
	8. Enforce conformity	8. Specify what's best
		9. Manage, control

Note. The table lists phrases describing the behaviors of patients A, B, C, and D with their spouses. (Overlapping phrases—those numbered "0" and "9"— are not given in every case.) Four different types of relationships are described in the four sections of the table. Nonetheless, one can begin at any place in the table and proceed stepwise in a clockwise (or counterclockwise) direction to move incrementally through interpersonal space, returning eventually to the starting place. The reason is that the descriptions are organized by the underlying dimensions of ATTACK–ACTIVE LOVE and CONTROL–EMANCIPATE. (See the text for a more detailed explanation.) Adapted from Benjamin (1979).

apply. The single asterisk marks this judgment for patient C on the affiliation dimension.

Next, his relationship to his wife is assessed on the interdependence dimension, shown on the vertical axis in the middle of Figure 3.2. By controlling his son's attack, patient C tries to influence what is happening to his wife at this moment. He is not ordering her around, but neither is he emancipating her. As the husband exerts strong control toward his son, he is moderately controlling of his wife at this moment in the family history. The single asterisk by the category MODERATE CONTROL marks this finding.

The two decisions—that patient C shows MODERATE ACTIVE LOVE and MODERATE CONTROL—are combined to locate, SASB-code, or SASB-label the husband's interaction. The affiliation judgment is one step to the right of NEUTRAL, and the interdependence judgment is one step downward from NEUTRAL. The result is marked with a double asterisk on Figure 3.1, at a place named PROTECT. PROTECT appears between CONTROL and ACTIVE LOVE, indicating that PROTECT is made up of about 50% control and 50% love. In other words, the judgment that the husband is moderately friendly and moderately controlling of his wife amounts to

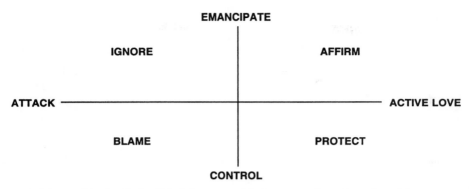

FIGURE 3.2. The SASB simplified cluster model, focus on other. The poles of the two underlying dimensions appear at the ends of the two axes. Adapted from Benjamin (1987a).

saying that he is protecting her at this moment. Descriptions for patient C that directly reflect his protective stance appear near the middle of the list given for him in the text. Consider statement 3: He "lovingly looks after his spouse's interests and takes steps to protect her."

To read "protection" accurately, the clinician needs to know only that the husband shows moderate friendliness and moderate control toward his wife. This dimensional frame of reference also allows the clinician to predict quite a bit about patient C and his marital relationship. The method is explained below in a section headed "Predictive Principles."

Inspection of Figure 3.2 also shows that BLAME appears between ATTACK and CONTROL. Its in-between position suggests that BLAME consists of about 50% attack and 50% control. One can begin at any point—say, ATTACK—and move around a circle in stepwise fashion (ATTACK, BLAME, CONTROL, PROTECT, etc.) until returning to the starting point, ATTACK. Like the musical scale, which begins with one note (*do*) and eventually returns to the same note, the "notes" of the SASB scale also come full circle.[6] When describing focus on another person, the SASB scale steps that compare[7] to *do, re, mi, fa, so, la, ti, do* are ATTACK, BLAME, CONTROL, NURTURE, ACTIVE LOVE, AFFIRM, EMANCIPATE, NEGLECT, and ATTACK.

These "notes" can be listed to sketch a "song" for each person. For example, patient C's depiction by the SASB cluster model is shown in the top half of Figure 3.3. The notes of his song are ACTIVE LOVE, PROTECT, and CONTROL. The song of patient A, sketched in the bottom half of Figure 3.3, is characterized by the notes ATTACK, BLAME, and CONTROL. Patient C always appears in the lower right-hand side of the SASB figures and tables; this placement indicates that he is in a position of benevolent control. Patient A always appears in the lower left-hand side of the figures and tables, which is a position of hostile control. All the SASB

---

[6]For mathematical reasons described elsewhere (Benjamin, 1974 1984), the SASB models are arranged in the shape of a diamond rather than a circle.

[7]Those who are informed about music theory will know that the analogy is not exact. The comparison is nonetheless useful.

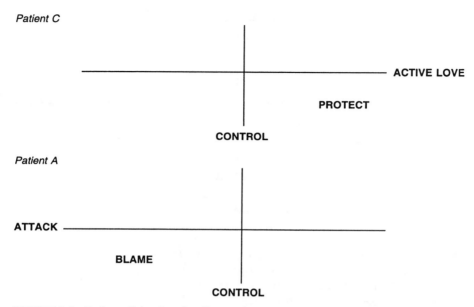

FIGURE 3.3. Patients C (top) and A (bottom) are described in terms of the SASB simplified cluster model.

models, from the simplest to the most complex, place hostility on the left, friendliness on the right, control on the bottom, and autonomy giving on the top. Among other things, the visualization of transactions in this way can help the clinician assess the context. For example, Figure 3.3 shows at a glance that both patient A and patient C control their spouses. However, the different geometry of the figures makes it clear that patient C's control has a very different meaning than patient A's control. One occurs in a benevolent context, and the other in a hostile setting.

Three SASB models (full, quadrant, and cluster) have been applied to the hypothetical patients A, B, C, and D. However, use of the models need not be restricted to patients with their spouses. The SASB labels can apply to any relationship—imaginary or real; past, present, or future. Chapters 5–14, which describe the various DSM personality disorders, are based on SASB labeling of the DSM descriptions and casebook examples showing a variety of contexts. Patient baseline positions, wishes, and fears are presented, along with likely transference problems and recommended treatment interventions. The "notes" on the SASB psychological scale, their combinations into "harmonics," and their "rhythmic progressions" define the "melodies" for each of the respective personality disorders.

One does not have to know anything about the names of notes, or about the rules of harmonics, to enjoy or even to play music. Similarly, the reader does not have to master the process of SASB labeling and its associated predictive principles to consider many of the ideas in this book. Readers who dislike figures and tables may be more comfortable at this point if they skip the balance of this chapter after glancing at Figure 3.9 on page 54. The words of Figure 3.9 will appear in subsequent analyses of the personality disorders. The reader needs to remember only two ideas from this chapter: (1) The words in Figure 3.9 are arranged on the pages according to a theory about underlying dimensionality; (2) their positions on the figure permit predictions about interpersonal interactions, and about connections between social experience and self-concept. Principles of the SASB model are used to provide interpersonal descriptions of the disorders, pathogenic hypotheses, descriptions of expected transference reactions, and therapeutic recommendations. The reader need not understand exactly how this is done. Readers who are interested in understanding the interpersonal logic behind the analyses of personality disorder that are offered in this book may read and study the balance of this chapter. Those who are not are invited now to look at Figure 3.9, which is also printed on the last page of this book, and then go directly to Chapter 4.

THE SASB LABELER'S OR CODER'S BASIC STEPS

There are only a few steps involved in using the SASB labeling system:

1. Something or someone must be relating to something or someone else. There must be two interactants or referents before SASB labeling can begin. To find such material, the clinician selects an interpersonal event that seems to summarize what is going on. Once the interpersonal clinical event has been chosen, the labeler invokes Sullivan's (1953) idea of a "participant observer." The SASB labeler successively takes the perspective of each person who is to be understood in a given context. In effect, SASB labeling teaches peripatetic empathy.

2. Next, the clinician decides whether the person to be labeled is focusing on the self or on someone else. Tables 3.1 and 3.2, and Figures 3.1, 3.2, and 3.3, present the available categories when the interpersonal focus is on someone else. In those examples, the descriptions are about what the patients are going to do (or not do) to, for, or about their spouses. They are always focusing on another person. Focus on other involves an initiation, an action that passes from an actor (a patient) to a receiver (a spouse).[8] Focus on other is prototypically characteristic of parents. Other types of focus are defined in the subsequent sections headed "Interactional Focus on the Self" and "Introjection."

---

[8]There is a formal SASB coding or labeling system that is particularly useful in research studies, but not essential to the clinician. The formal coding system does, however, make it easier to judge focus. Focus on other describes transitive action, while focus on self involves intransitive reaction. The formal SASB coding system offers a simple rule: If the patient is referent X, and the spouse is referent Y, transitive action is present whenever X is focusing on Y. For example, "I dare you" has the speaker (X) focusing on the listener (Y). On the other hand, if X is focusing on himself or herself, the interaction is intransitive. For example, "Like heck I will" has the speaker (X) focusing on himself or herself (X) as he or she interacts with Y. Once the referents X and Y are identified, the SASB labeler knows that if the transaction is about Y, it is transitive; if it is about X, it is intransitive.

3. After choosing the focus, the clinician decides how much affiliation and interdependence are present in the interaction. He or she uses scales like those presented in the horizontal (affiliation) and vertical (interdependence) alignments in Figure 3.1. Tone of voice and the context are very important in assessing affiliation and interdependence. For example, to label patient C talking to his son, one needs to hear his voice tone and see his facial expression. Those nonverbal cues help determine how hostile patient C is to his son at this moment.

4. Finally, the judgments about focus, affiliation, and interdependence are combined to find the label on the simplified cluster model. This process has been illustrated in the discussion of Figure 3.1, where patient C is shown protecting his wife. That event can be labeled again, this time in regard to the interaction between patient C and his son. Even without nonverbal cues, it is clear that the father is not friendly, and that he is quite controlling. The nonverbal cues about hostility will determine whether the final category will be in the neutral (middle) or the hostile (left-hand) region of the model. Figure 3.3 shows that the only two possibilities suggested by the judgments "control" and "not friendly" are CONTROL and BLAME. If patient C is neutral in affect when he says, "Don't talk to your mother that way," then CONTROL is the choice. On the other hand, if he is clearly angry, then BLAME better describes his way of relating to his son at the moment. BLAME is located in controlling hostile space. A number of predictions can be made about the father–son relationship from this simple exercise.

INTERACTIONAL FOCUS ON THE SELF

The Spouses of Patients A, B, C, and D

A second group of interactions described by the SASB models is called "focus on self" and reflects concern about what is being done to, for, or about the self. It refers to a condition, a state of being that is reactive to a *perceived* action coming from someone else. Focus on self is prototypically childlike, in the sense that these behaviors emerge before the parentlike group in the developmental sequence. In a mature relationship, focus on self and other should be balanced, with about half of the transactions focused on self and half on other. Focus on self is illustrated here by the spouses of patients A, B, C, and D. The examples given here are oversimplified in the sense that the patients are assigned one type of focus (i.e., focus on other), and the spouses exclusively show the other (i.e., focus on self). If a marital relationship were actually rigidly divided so that one partner was always parentlike and the other was always childlike, it would not be a mature, balanced relationship.

Spouse of Patient A
0. In great pain and rage, the spouse of patient A screams and shouts that he is destroying her.
1. The spouse of patient A is very tense, shaky, wary, fearful with him.

2. The spouse of patient A bitterly, hatefully, resentfully chooses to let his needs and wants count more than her own.
3. The spouse of patient A whines, unhappily protests, tries to defend herself from him.
4. Full of doubts and tension, the spouse of patient A sort of goes along with his views anyway.
5. To avoid patient A's disapproval, the spouse of patient A bottles up her rage and resentment and does what he wants.
6. The spouse of patient A caves in to him and does things his own way, but she sulks and fumes about it.
7. The spouse of patient A gives up, helplessly does things his way without feelings or views of her own.
8. The spouse of patient A mindlessly obeys his rules, standards, ideas about how things should be done.
9. The spouse of patient A gives in to him, yields and submits to him.

The spouse of patient A is not initiating actions that do something to, for, or about the other person, her husband. Instead, the focus is on her own condition or state in reaction to him. Clearly this spouse is not reacting to patient A in a friendly way. Progression from the top to the bottom of her list shows increasing amounts of submission. The descriptions move from intensely fearful recoil through resentful compliance to abject submission. The two dimensions underlying this group of descriptions are "reactive hostility" and "submission."

Spouse of Patient B

0. In great pain and rage, the spouse of patient B screams and shouts that she is destroying him.
1. Boiling over with rage and/or fear, the spouse of patient B tries to escape, flee, or hide from her.
2. The spouse of patient B furiously, angrily, hatefully refuses to accept her offers to help out.
3. The spouse of patient B bitterly, angrily detaches from her and doesn't ask for anything. He weeps alone about her.
4. The spouse of patient B reacts to what she says or does in strange, unconnected, unrelated ways.
5. The spouse of patient B walls himself off from her; he doesn't hear, doesn't react.
6. The spouse of patient B is too busy and alone with his "own thing" to be with her.
7. To do his or her own thing, the spouse of patient B does the opposite of what she wants.
8. The spouse of patient B goes his own separate way apart from her.
9. The spouse of patient B freely comes and goes; he does his own thing separately from her.

Like the spouse of patient A, this partner is not initiating actions that directly impinge upon the other person. This spouse's reactivity is also hostile. From the top to the bottom of the list, his group of items shows increasing amounts of autonomy taking. It progresses from intensely fearful recoil through walling off to clear separation. The dimensions underlying this group of descriptions are "hostile reactivity" and "autonomy taking."

Spouse of Patient C

0. The spouse of patient C joyfully, lovingly, very happily responds to him sexually.
1. The spouse of patient C warmly, happily stays around and keeps in touch with him.
2. The spouse of patient C warmly, comfortably accepts C's help and caregiving.
3. The spouse of patient C is trusting with him. She comfortably counts on him to come through when needed.
4. The spouse of patient C willingly accepts, goes along with his reasonable suggestions, ideas.
5. The spouse of patient C learns from him, comfortably takes advice and guidance from him.
6. The spouse of patient C trustingly depends on him to meet every need.
7. The spouse of patient C checks with him about every little thing because she cares so much about what he thinks.
8. The spouse of patient C feels, thinks, does, becomes what she thinks he wants.
9. The spouse of patient C gives in to him, yields and submits to him.

Again, there is reaction to the initiations of the partner, but clearly this spouse is friendly. Progression through the list of her items shows increasing submissiveness. The sketches move from warm sexual responsiveness through trust to strong dependency on patient C. The two underlying dimensions are "friendliness" and "submission."

Spouse of Patient D

0. The spouse of patient D joyfully, lovingly, very happily responds to her sexually.
1. The spouse of patient D is very happy, playful, joyful, delighted to be with her.
2. The spouse of patient D relaxes, lets go, enjoys, feels wonderful about being with her.
3. The spouse of patient D is joyful, happy, and very open with her.
4. The spouse of patient D expresses himself clearly in a warm and friendly way.
5. The spouse of patient D freely and openly talks with her about his innermost self.

6. The spouse of patient D is straightforward, truthful, and clear with her about his own position.
7. The spouse of patient D speaks up, clearly and firmly states his own separate position.
8. The spouse of patient D has a clear sense of who he is separately from her.
9. The spouse of Patient D freely comes and goes; he does his own thing separately from her.

Like the spouse of patient C, this one also reacts in friendly ways. Progression from the top to the bottom of the list shows increasing amounts of autonomy taking. The descriptions move from warm sexual reaction through friendly disclosure to secure self-definition. The underlying dimensions for this relationship are "friendliness" and "autonomy taking."

The Underlying Dimensions Describing the Spouses of Patients A to D

The spouses of patients A to D relate in four different ways. The underlying dimensions that organize their descriptions are shown in Figure 3.4. Reactive hostility and friendliness define one dimension, shown at the top of the page by the scale that runs from left to right. The poles of the axis are named RECOIL and REACTIVE LOVE. The spouse of patient A illustrates extreme recoil: "In great pain and rage, [she] screams and shouts that he is destroying her." An example of extreme reactive love is provided by the spouse of patient C, who "joyfully, lovingly, very happily responds to him sexually." This version of the hate–love dimension is also named "affiliation."

Submitting and taking autonomy define the other dimension, shown on the vertical line in the middle of Figure 3.4. The poles of this dimension range from SUBMIT (bottom) to SEPARATE (top). Extreme submission is shown by the spouses of patients A and C. Each "gives in . . . yields, and submits." Extreme separation is demonstrated by the spouse of patient B, who "freely comes and goes . . . does his own thing separately from her." The range from SUBMIT to SEPARATE defines the "interdependence" dimension for focus on self. The method of combining these two dimensions to label an interaction is described below in the section headed "The SASB Simplified Cluster Model, Focus on Self."

Variations in the Level of Detail Provided

The SASB Quadrant Model, Focus on Self

The reactions of all four spouses are summarized in the quadrant version of the SASB model, shown in Table 3.3. Patient A's **Hostile power** (Table 3.1) is matched by his spouse's *Hostile compliance* (Table 3.3). Patient B's **Invoke hostile autonomy** yields the spousal position *Take hostile autonomy*. Patient C's are

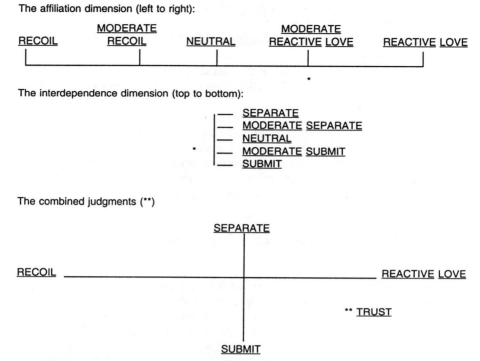

FIGURE 3.4. Using dimensional judgments to classify an interaction on the "focus on self" surface of the SASB simplified cluster model (see Figure 3.5). *The judgments; **the summary.

Friendly influence draws *Friendly acceptance,* and patient D's **Encourage friendly autonomy** is associated with *Enjoy friendly autonomy.* These "natural" pairings are reviewed later in the chapter, where the predictive principle of complementarity is discussed.

The SASB Full Model, Focus on Self

Table 3.4 combines the quadrant model of Table 3.3 with the SASB full-model descriptions for the spouses provided in the text above. Both Tables 3.3 and 3.4 are organized according to the same principles. Both show how the four relational styles are organized according to the two underlying dimensions of affiliation and interdependence. The difference between Tables 3.4 and 3.3 is in the level of detail. The steps on the interpersonal "scale" are very large for Table 3.3, and they are very small for Table 3.2. One can begin at any place in the tables and proceed stepwise in a clockwise (or counterclockwise) direction to move incrementally through interpersonal space and return eventually to the beginning.

Table 3.3. Spouses of Patients A, B, C, and D, Quadrant Model

	RECOIL	REACTIVE LOVE
SEPARATE	B. Take hostile autonomy	D. Enjoy friendly autonomy
SUBMIT	A. Hostile compliance	C. Friendly acceptance

Note. The table depicts the two dimensions that define the spouses of patients A to D. The intersection of these dimensions suggests that the spouse of patient A resentfully goes along with what he wants. The spouse of patient B refuses and angrily withdraws. The partner of patient C warmly accepts his nurturance. The spouse of patient D is secure with his own sense of self. Adapted from Benjamin (1979).

Table 3.4. Spouses of Patients A, B, C, and D, Full Model

	RECOIL	REACTIVE LOVE
	Spouse of patient B	*Spouse of patient D*
SEPARATE	9. Freely come and go	
	8. Go own separate way	8. Own identity, standards
	7. Defy, do opposite	7. Assert on own
	6. Busy with own thing	6. "Put cards on the table"
	5. Wall off, nondisclose	5. Openly disclose, reveal
	4. Noncontingent reaction	4. Clearly express
	3. Detach, weep alone	3. Enthusiastic showing
	2. Refuse assistance, care	2. Relax, flow, enjoy
	1. Flee, escape, withdraw	1. Joyful approach
	Spouse of patient A	*Spouse of patient C*
SUBMIT	0. Desperate protest	0. Ecstatic response
	1. Wary, fearful	1. Follow, maintain contact
	2. Sacrifice greatly	2. Accept caretaking
	3. Whine, defend, justify	3. Ask, trust, count on
	4. Uncomprehendingly agree	4. Accept reason
	5. Appease, scurry	5. Take in, learn from
	6. Sulk, act put upon	6. Cling, depend
	7. Apathetic compliance	7. Defer, overconform
	8. Follow rules, proper	8. Submerge into role
		9. Yield, submit, give in

Note. The table lists phrases describing the behaviors of the spouses of patients A, B, C, and D. (Overlapping phrases—those numbered "0" and "9"—are not given in every case.) Four different types of relationships are described in the four sections of the table. Nonetheless, one can begin at any place in the table and proceed stepwise in a clockwise (or counterclockwise) direction to move incrementally through interpersonal space, returning eventually to the starting place. (See the text for a more detailed explanation.) Adapted from Benjamin (1979).

The SASB Simplified Cluster Model, Focus on Self

The scale of intermediate complexity, the simplified cluster version of the SASB model for focus on self, is presented in Figure 3.5. The simplified cluster model includes the poles of each of the underlying dimensions shown in Figure 3.4. The left-to-right axis goes from RECOIL to REACTIVE LOVE, and the bottom-to-top axis goes from SUBMIT to SEPARATE. The other categories in the simplified cluster model are made up of blends of these underlying dimensions.

Consider, for example, the spouse of patient C as her husband protects her from their son's attack. Suppose that as he inhibits the son's attack, she visibly relaxes in her chair and smiles at her husband. SASB labeling begins by judging her reaction on the affiliation dimension, shown at the top of Figure 3.4. Clearly her response is friendly, so the judgment MODERATE REACTIVE LOVE would apply. The single asterisk in the figure marks this judgment for her on the affiliation dimension. Next, her response is assessed on the interdependence dimension, shown as a vertical scale in Figure 3.4. By letting him take over, she submits moderately. The judgment MODERATE SUBMIT is marked by a single asterisk on that scale.

The two decisions—that the spouse of patient C shows MODERATE REACTIVE LOVE and MODERATE SUBMIT—are combined to label her reaction to his protection. The affiliation judgment is one step to the right of NEUTRAL, and the interdependence judgment is one step downward from NEUTRAL. The result is marked with a double asterisk on Figure 3.4, at a place named TRUST. Its in-between placement suggests that TRUST is made up of about 50% submission and 50% love. Description 3 for the spouse of patient C in the text above directly reflects her trust: "[She] is trusting with him. She comfortably counts on him to come through when needed."

To read "trust" accurately, the clinician needs only to know that the wife is moderately loving and moderately submissive. This ability to read the dimen-

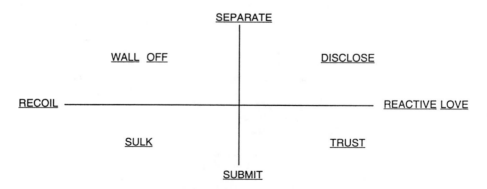

FIGURE 3.5. The SASB simplified cluster model, focus on self. The poles of the two underlying dimensions appear at the ends of the axes. Adapted from Benjamin (1987a).

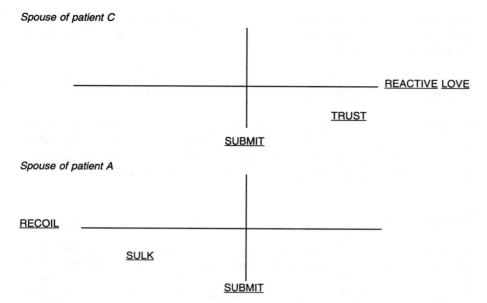

Spouse of patient C

REACTIVE LOVE

TRUST

SUBMIT

Spouse of patient A

RECOIL

SULK

SUBMIT

FIGURE 3.6. The spouses of patients C (top) and A (bottom) are described in terms of the SASB simplified cluster model.

sionality into such cues as relaxing in her chair helps the clinician see patterns that might not otherwise be apparent.

Inspection of Figure 3.5 shows that SULK appears between RECOIL and SUBMIT. Its in-between position suggests that SULK consists of about 50% recoil and 50% submission. One can begin at one place with the notes of Figure 3.5 and move stepwise in a circle, returning eventually to the starting place. For focus on self, the SASB scale steps that compare to *do, re, me, fa, so, la, ti, do* are RECOIL, SULK, SUBMIT, TRUST, REACTIVE LOVE, DISCLOSE, SEPARATE, WALL OFF, and RECOIL.

The notes for the song of patient C's spouse are sketched at the top of Figure 3.6: REACTIVE LOVE, TRUST, and SUBMIT. To identify the song, the labeler follows the same procedure described in the section headed "The SASB Labeler's or Coder's Basic Steps." In this case, the focus chosen (see step 2) is focus on self rather than focus on another. A different song comes from the spouse of patient A, shown in the bottom half of Figure 3.6. Although she too has a powerful husband, the spouse of patient A is described by the notes RECOIL, SULK, and SUBMIT.

In all the SASB figures and tables, the spouse of patient C is placed in the lower right-hand corner of the page, showing that she is in a position of friendly compliance. By contrast, the spouse of patient A is always placed in the lower left-hand side of the SASB figures and tables, showing that she is in a position of hostile submission. The visualization of patients and their spouses in the SASB space provides important information about context, and facilitates the use of the predictive principles.

PREDICTIVE PRINCIPLES

The ability to give SASB names to interpersonal positions and identify context does more than help with pattern recognition. Like *do, re, mi,* the SASB names have highly organized relationships with one another. Knowledge of that organization enables the clinician to make a number of useful predictions.

Complementarity

The principle of "complementarity" is defined if members of a dyad are matched in affiliation and interdependence and if both are focused on the same individual. For example, if patient A is focusing on his wife, and she reacts by focusing on herself, they are both focused on her. This shared attentional focus is complementarity if they also each exhibit the same amounts of affiliation and interdependence. Figures 3.3 and 3.6 show, for example, that patient A and his wife are matched in affiliation and interdependence at each possible position: His ATTACK is complemented by her RECOIL; his BLAME is matched by her SULK; and his CONTROL is paralleled by her SUBMIT.

All the possible complementary positions on the simplified cluster model are marked by the categories appearing at the same locations on Figures 3.2 and 3.5. They are as follows: ATTACK and RECOIL; BLAME and SULK; CONTROL and SUBMIT; PROTECT and TRUST; ACTIVE LOVE and REACTIVE LOVE; AFFIRM and DISCLOSE; EMANCIPATE and SEPARATE; IGNORE and WALL OFF.

The principle of complementarity applies to all versions of the SASB models. Matching squares in the quadrant models shown in Tables 3.1 and 3.3 also define complementarity. For example, patient A's **Hostile power** (lower left-hand side) matches his spouse's Hostile compliance (lower left-hand side). Patient C's **Friendly influence** (lower right-hand side) is matched by his spouse's Friendly acceptance (lower right-hand side). Similarly, matching categories on the full model define complementarity. For example, patient A's 5, **Accuse, blame,** matches his spouse's 5, Appease, scurry. Patient C's 5, **Constructively stimulate,** matches his spouse's Take in, learn from.

The principle of "complementarity" encompasses the clinical concept of "codependency." The SASB description of complementarity is more general than codependency, however, because it includes a variety of patterns in addition to the hostile enmeshment that is so often found in families having alcoholic members and said to be codependent. Complementarity includes additional ways of "matching" partners. For example, the therapist who maintains the perfect Rogerian (Rogers, 1951) position (patient D) is most likely to be complemented by the perfect client position (spouse of patient D). Neither hostile nor enmeshed, these pairs nonetheless are complementary: Each one's position enhances and enables the other's.

In the chapters to follow, the principle of complementarity is often used to connect early interpersonal learning to the interpersonal patterns that characterize the respective personality disorders. If an adult maintains the complementary positions he or she assumed in childhood, he or she "recapitulates" early patterns. The child who chronically maintains a position of SUBMIT as an adult, for instance, recapitulates his or her childhood pattern.

Complementarity can also generate what is known as "self-fulfilling prophecy." Suppose, for example, that a child named S matched parental CONTROL with chronic SUBMIT, and continues to SUBMIT to important other people as an adult. Child S may even defer to her own children, and they may well complement that deference with CONTROL. Thus, Child S, who received CONTROL from her own parents, will receive the same treatment from her own children. The characterological pattern of CONTROL will skip a generation, with child/adult S caught in between.

Moreover, the principle of complementarity is helpful in anticipating and understanding transference reactions to the therapist. A simple example of a transference problem is offered by this complementary combination: patient SULK, therapist BLAME. It is not unusual for patients to be deferential to therapists in a hostile way, and for therapists unwittingly to match that position with subtle or not-so-subtle put-downs. Henry, Schacht, and Strupp (1986) have used the formal SASB labeling system to show that if therapists are not able to resist this powerful "draw" toward hostile enmeshment, the therapy outcome is poor.

Introjection or Internalization

Introjects for the Spouses of Patients A, B, C, and D

Harry Stack Sullivan (1953) developed the idea[9] that important aspects of the self-concept derive from treating the self as one has been treated by important others. The SASB model incorporates Sullivan's idea to include a third type of focus, called "introjection" or "internalization." This third domain describes what happens if focus on other is turned inward upon the self. It is introduced here by considering the self-concepts that are predicted by the SASB model for the spouses of patients A to D.

Introject for Spouse of Patient A
0. The spouse of patient A lets herself murder, kill, destroy, and reduce herself to nothing.
1. The spouse of patient A thinks up ways to hurt and destroy herself. She is her own worst enemy.

[9]Also proposed by George Herbert Mead (1934).

2. The spouse of patient A tears away at and empties herself by greatly overburdening herself.
3. The spouse of patient A harshly punishes, tortures, "takes it out" on herself.
4. The spouse of patient A makes herself do and be things that are known not to be right for her. She fools herself.
5. The spouse of patient A accuses and blames herself until she feels guilty, bad, and ashamed.
6. The spouse of patient A puts herself down, tells herself that she has done everything wrong and that others can do better.
7. The spouse of patient A very carefully watches, holds back, and restrains herself.
8. The spouse of patient A puts all kinds of energy into making sure she follows the right standards and is proper.
9. The spouse of patient A has the habit of keeping very tight control over herself.

The spouse of patient A is turning her husband's hostile behaviors inward upon herself. From the top to the bottom of the list, this group of items shows increasing amounts of self-control. It progresses from intensely hateful self-attack through self-accusation to tight self-control. The dimensions underlying this group of descriptions are "self-attack" and "self-control."

Introject for Spouse of Patient B
0. The spouse of patient B lets himself murder, kill, destroy, and reduce himself to nothing.
1. The spouse of patient B angrily and harshly rejects himself as worthless and leaves what happens to him to fate.
2. Even if it means harming himself greatly, the spouse of patient B lets his own sickness and injury go unattended.
3. The spouse of patient B is reckless; he carelessly lets himself end up in self-destructive situations.
4. The spouse of patient B ignores and doesn't bother to know his real self.
5. The spouse of patient B neglects himself, doesn't try to develop good skills, ways of being.
6. Instead of getting around to do what he really needs to do for himself, the spouse of patient B lets himself go and just daydream.
7. The spouse of patient B just lets important personal matters, choices, thoughts, issues slip by without paying much attention.
8. The spouse of patient B lets himself drift with the moment; he has no internal direction, goals, or standards.
9. The spouse of patient B lets himself just go along with today as it is, and doesn't plan for tomorrow.

Like the spouse of patient A, this partner is hostile to himself. From the top to the bottom of the list, his group of descriptions shows increasing tendencies to let himself go. The descriptions progress from intensely hateful self-attack through neglecting the self to complete letting go of the self. The dimensions underlying this group of descriptions are "self-attack" and "self-emancipation."

Introject for Spouse of Patient C

0. The spouse of patient C tenderly, lovingly cherishes and adores herself "as is."
1. The spouse of patient C keeps herself open to connecting with people, places, or things that would be very good for her.
2. The spouse of patient C naturally and easily provides for, nurtures, and takes care of herself.
3. The spouse of patient C comfortably looks after her own interests and protects herself.
4. Because the spouse of patient C wants to help herself, she tries to figure out what is really going on within herself.
5. The spouse of patient C practices and works on developing worthwhile skills, ways of being.
6. The spouse of patient C puts a lot of energy into figuring out what she is going to need for herself and how to get it.
7. The spouse of patient C keeps an eye on herself to be sure she is doing what should and ought to be done.
8. The spouse of patient C tries very hard to make herself be like an ideal.
9. The spouse of patient C has the habit of keeping very tight control over herself.

This partner clearly is friendly to herself. From top to the bottom of the list, this group of descriptions suggests increasing amounts of self-control in a friendly context. It progresses from clear self-love through self-protection to clear self-control. The dimensions underlying this group of descriptions are "active self-love" and "self-control."

Introject for Spouse of Patient D

0. The spouse of patient D tenderly, lovingly cherishes and adores himself "as is."
1. The spouse of patient D likes himself very much and feels very good when he has a chance to be with himself.
2. The spouse of patient D gently and warmly strokes and appreciates himself for just being himself.
3. The spouse of patient D lets himself feel good about and pleased with himself just as he is.
4. The spouse of patient D understands and likes himself just as he is. He feels solid, "together."

5. The spouse of patient D comfortably lets himself hear and go by his own deepest inner feelings.
6. Knowing both his faults and strong points, the spouse of patient D comfortably lets himself be "as is."
7. The spouse of patient D freely, easily, and confidently lets himself do whatever comes naturally.
8. Without concern, the spouse of patient D just lets himself be free to turn into whatever he will.
9. The spouse of patient D lets himself just go along with today as it is, and doesn't plan for tomorrow.

Like the spouse of patient C, this partner is very friendly to himself. The descriptions show increasing amounts of autonomy giving to the self. It progresses from clear self-love through self-affirmation to letting the self be. The dimensions underlying this group of descriptions are "self-love" and "self-emancipation."

Variations in the Level of Detail Provided

The SASB Quadrant Model of the Introject. Again, the underlying dimensions can be used to create categories that vary in level of detail. Table 3.5 presents the simple quadrant version for these four spouses, which corresponds to the quadrant model in Table 3.1 (focus on other). For the spouse of patient A, the introject is *Oppress self.* For the spouse of patient B, it is *Reject self.* For the spouse of patient C, it is *Manage, cultivate self.* For the spouse of patient D, the expected introject is *Accept, enjoy self.* The respective introjects of these four spouses theoretically represent the internalization of their experiences in their marriages. For example, the spouse of patient A oppresses herself as she, in effect, adopts her husband's hostile control as her own self-talk. The spouse of patient C, who manages and cultivates herself, has turned her husband's friendly power inward upon herself. Factors affecting whose messages are internalized have yet to be identified. Attachment is likely to be one variable. If so, then the messages of parents and sexual partners will be internalized, because the attachment to these figures is normally quite strong.

The SASB Full Model of the Introject. These quadrant descriptions can be greatly enriched by appeal to the full-model descriptions listed in Table 3.6. Table 3.6 has the same structure as Tables 3.2 and 3.4. The ranges of interactions are characterized by different degrees of affiliation and interdependence. Again, hostility/hate appears on the left, and friendliness/love on the right; control is in the bottom section, and autonomy giving is in the top section. The extremes of the scales are found in Table 3.6 at the points numbered 0 (affiliation poles) or 9 (interdependence poles). Extreme hostility to the self is point 0, *Torture, annihilate self,* while extreme self-love is 0, *Love, cherish self.* Extreme control is 9, *Control, manage self,* while extreme autonomy giving is 9, *Happy-go-lucky.*

Table 3.5. Introjects for Spouses of Patients A, B, C, and D, Quadrant Model

	SELF-ATTACK	ACTIVE SELF-LOVE
SELF-EMANCIPATE	B. *Reject self*	D. *Accept, enjoy self*
SELF-CONTROL	A. *Oppress self*	C. *Manage, cultivate self*

Note. The table depicts the two dimensions that define the introjects of the spouses of patients A to D. The intersection of these dimensions suggests that the spouse of patient A has a self-critical introject. The spouse of patient B rejects and neglects himself. The partner of patient C warmly takes good care of herself. The spouse of patient D is undefended, comfortable with himself. Adapted from Benjamin (1979).

Table 3.6. Introjects for Spouses of Patients A, B, C, and D, Full Model

	SELF-ATTACK	ACTIVE SELF-LOVE
	Introject of B's spouse	*Introject of D's spouse*
SELF-EMANCIPATE	9. *Happy-go-lucky*	
	8. *Drift with the moment*	8. *Let nature unfold*
	7. *Neglect options*	7. *Let self do it, confident*
	6. *Fantasy, dream*	6. *Balanced self-accceptance*
	5. *Neglect own potential*	5. *Explore, listen to inner self*
	4. *Undefined, unknown self*	4. *Integrated, solid core*
	3. *Reckless*	3. *Protect self*
	2. *Ignore own basic needs*	2. *Stroke, soothe self*
	1. *Reject, dismiss self*	1. *Entertain, enjoy self*
	Introject of A's spouse	*Introject of C's spouse*
SELF-CONTROL	0. *Torture, annihilate self*	0. *Love, cherish self*
	1. *Menace to self*	1. *Seek best for self*
	2. *Drain, overburden self*	2. *Nurture, restore self*
	3. *Vengefully punish self*	3. *Protect self*
	4. *Decieve, divert self*	4. *Examine, analyze self*
	5. *Guilt, blame, bad self*	5. *Practice, become accomplished*
	6. *Doubt, put self down*	6. *Pamper, indulge self*
	7. *Restrain, hold back self*	7. *Benevolent eye on self*
	8. *Force propriety*	8. *Force ideal identity*
		9. *Control, manage self*

Note. The table lists phrases describing the predicted introjects of the spouses of patients A, B, C, and D. (Overlapping phrases—those numbered "0" and "9"—are not given in every case.) Four different types of self-concepts are described in the four sections of the table. Nonetheless, one can begin at any place in the table and proceed stepwise in a clockwise (or counterclockwise) direction to move incrementally through interpersonal space, returning eventually to the starting place. (See the text for a more detailed explanation.) Adapted from Benjamin (1979).

The SASB Simplified Cluster Model of the Introject.   The simplified cluster model for the introject appears in Figure 3.7. Except for the prefix SELF-, the categories on the "introject" surface of Figure 3.7 have the same names as the categories on the "focus on other" surface (Figure 3.2). ATTACK from Figure 3.2 becomes SELF-ATTACK, in Figure 3.7. BLAME becomes SELF-BLAME, CONTROL becomes SELF-CONTROL, and so on around the circumplex.

Figure 3.8 shows the predicted introjects for the spouses of patient C (top) and patient A (bottom). The figure shows that the spouse of patient C is expected to internalize his friendly influence and have a self-concept described by ACTIVE SELF-LOVE, SELF-PROTECT, and SELF-CONTROL. The spouse of patient A should internalize his hostile control to have a self-concept described as SELF-CONTROL, SELF-BLAME, and SELF-ATTACK. Again, the meaning of control is different, depending on the context. The spouse of patient C has benevolent self-control, whereas the spouse of patient A has destructive self-control.

Categories in the simplified cluster model in Figure 3.8 can be expanded by reference to the full model in Table 3.6. To illustrate, the full-model points shown in Table 3.6 that correspond to the simplified cluster model point SELF-BLAME are 3, *Vengefully punish self*; 4, *Deceive, divert self*; 5, *Guilt, blame, bad self*; 6, *Doubt, put self down.*

The classification of self-concept in terms of introjection or internalization has a number of clinical uses. For example, one DSM criterion for BPD (see Chapter 5) is as follows: "impulsiveness in at least two areas that are potentially self-damaging, e.g., spending, sex, substance use, shoplifting, reckless driving, binge eating (Do not include suicidal or self-mutilating behaviors . . .")." These behaviors are SASB-labeled as SELF-NEGLECT. The principle of internalization suggests that a BPD must have had earlier learning experiences characterized by the label IGNORE. The corresponding full model for focus on other (Table 3.2) offers

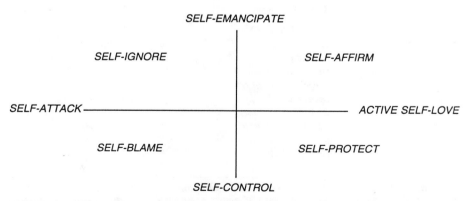

FIGURE 3.7. The SASB simplified cluster model, internalized focus. The poles of the two underlying dimensions appear at the ends of the axes. This map of the introject shows what happens if a person treats himself or herself just as important others have treated him or her. Adapted from Benjamin (1987a).

The predicted introject of the spouse of patient C

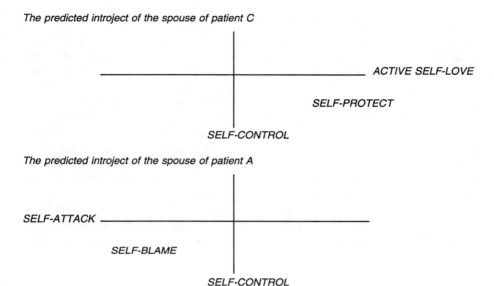

FIGURE 3.8. The predicted introjects of the spouses of patients C (top) and A (bottom) are described in terms of the SASB simplified cluster model.

more detail. The BPD has lived through the following: 3, **Abandon, leave in lurch**; 4, **Illogical initiation**; 5, **Neglect interests, needs**; 6, **Ignore, pretend not there**. The prediction that the BPD's history includes traumatic abandonment is supported by the fact that BPDs are known to be "abandonment-sensitive." That trait is so well recognized that it is reflected in another DSM criterion: "frantic efforts to avoid real or imagined abandonment (Do not include suicidal or self-mutilating behavior . . .)."

The introject organizes the adult's experience of himself or herself and others. For example, if the patient blames himself or herself, he or she is likely to see others as blaming, and to be quick to sulk. In other words, the self-concept shown in the lower left-hand side of the SASB models is associated with behaviors shown in the same locations. In this case, they all describe hostile enmeshment, and vary only in focus. If the therapist understands the relationship of the introject to interpersonal behaviors, he or she can anticipate transference problems. To give another example, it is helpful to know that the BPD has had traumatic abandonment experiences, internalizes these to be reckless with the self, and is quick to see others as abandoning. This understanding should lead the therapist to be careful about lateness, cancellations, delay in returning phone calls, and incomplete disclosure of vacation plans. The BPD is likely to label these normal therapist activities as "abandonment," and this will activate recklessness with the self. More detail for this example is provided in Chapter 5.

Complementarity and Internalization Shown on One Model

Figure 3.9 combines all three types of focus: focus on other, focus on self, and internalized focus. It depicts the complete simplified cluster model, and is thus the most important figure in this book. For reader convenience, Figure 3.9 is reproduced on the last page of the book. Further detail about the meaning of each of the points on Figure 3.9 is presented in the Appendix to this book (Table A.3).

Combining the three types of focus into one figure makes it easy for the reader to use the predictive principles. The three different types of print correspond to the three different types of focus. Items in **bold print** indicate focus on other, shown alone in Figure 3.2. <u>Underlined</u> items indicate focus on self, shown alone in Figure 3.5. Finally, the *italicized* items indicate internalized focus, shown alone in Figure 3.7. The combination of the three types of focus into one figure makes it easy to locate complementary and introjected positions. They are next to each other in Figure 3.9. For example, the complements **BLAME** and <u>SULK</u> are adjacent. The predicted internalization of **BLAME**—namely, *SELF-BLAME*—also

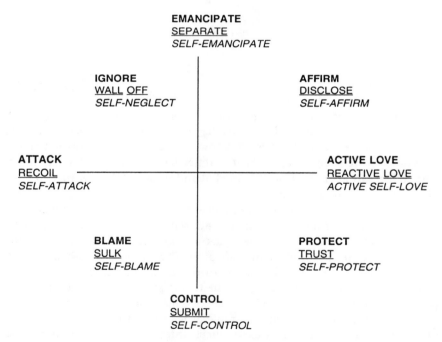

FIGURE 3.9. The SASB simplified cluster model, all three surfaces. Labels in **bold print** describe actions directed at another person (Figure 3.2, focus on other). The <u>underlined</u> labels describe reactions to another person's (perceived) initiations (Figure 3.5, focus on self). Adjacent **boldface** and <u>underlined</u> labels mark complementary pairings. Labels in *italics* show what happens if a person treats himself or herself just as important others have treated him or her (Figure 3.7, introject).

THE AFFILIATION DIMENSIONS

Focus on other

| ATTACK | MODERATE ATTACK | NEUTRAL | MODERATE ACTIVE LOVE | ACTIVE LOVE |

Focus on self

| RECOIL | MODERATE RECOIL | NEUTRAL | MODERATE REACTIVE LOVE | REACTIVE LOVE |

Introjective focus

| SELF-ATTACK | MODERATE SELF-ATTACK | NEUTRAL | MODERATE ACTIVE SELF-LOVE | ACTIVE SELF-LOVE |

FIGURE 3.10. The affiliation scales for all three types of focus.

appears at about 7:30 (in clock terms) on the map. For every type of focus, the horizontal axis shows affiliation (left = hostility/hate; right = friendliness/love). The vertical axis shows interdependence (bottom = enmeshment; top = differentiation). The three types of focus, shown in different styles of print, can be compared to octaves on the musical scale. The same structure is repeated in different ranges.

The next two figures review the underlying dimensions for each type of focus. Figure 3.10 presents the three scales for the affiliation dimension, and Figure 3.11 presents the three scales for the interdependence dimension. Once a given clinical event has been placed on Figure 3.10 and on Figure 3.11, its position on the simplified cluster model in Figure 3.9 is automatically known.

A few exercises will illustrate the connection between the affiliation and interdependence scales and the simplified cluster model of Figure 3.9. Suppose the clinician wants to label patient C as he reaches out lovingly to touch his wife without being at all invasive or patronizing. Clearly he is focusing on her, so the chosen category must be in **bold print**. The scale point in Figure 3.10 labeled ACTIVE LOVE seems appropriate for the affiliation judgment. At the moment, patient C is neither controlling nor letting his wife go. The scale point in Figure 3.11 labeled NEUTRAL seems appropriate for the interdependence judgment. The three judgments show that the final label is in bold print, at the far right-hand side, in the middle of the model. ACTIVE LOVE appears in that position on Figure 3.9.

Suppose now that patient C's wife shows with a loving smile that she accepts his loving touch. This event is about her condition or state or reaction to him, and so it represents focus on self. The affiliation in her response can be labeled REACTIVE LOVE (far right-hand side) in Figure 3.10. Her interdependence can be

THE INTERDEPENDENCE DIMENSIONS

Focus on other

— **EMANCIPATE**

— **MODERATE EMANCIPATE**

— **NEUTRAL**

— **MODERATE CONTROL**

— **CONTROL**

Focus on self

— SEPARATE

— MODERATE SEPARATE

— NEUTRAL

— MODERATE SUBMIT

— SUBMIT

Introjective focus

— *SELF-EMANCIPATE*

— *MODERATE SELF-EMANCIPATE*

— *NEUTRAL*

— *MODERATE SELF-CONTROL*

— *SELF-CONTROL*

FIGURE 3.11.   Interdependence scales for all three types of focus.

labeled NEUTRAL in Figure 3.11 (neither top nor bottom). These three-dimensional decisions (underlining, far right-hand side, neither top nor bottom) show that the final label on Figure 3.9 is REACTIVE LOVE.

For a very different example, suppose patient A tells his wife that she is a "miserable excuse for a spouse." Clearly he is focusing on her, and so the choice for this behavior must be shown in **bold print**. The affiliation selection on Figure 3.10 can be either ATTACK or MODERATE ATTACK (left-hand side). For the interdependence judgment in Figure 3.11, patient A's statement to his wife is not emancipating, and so it represents either CONTROL or MODERATE CONTROL (the bottom part of the figure). The MODERATE versions of these judgments are selected. The behavior is not close to the extremes of control and attack that are theoretically possible (they are defined by the descriptions labeled 0 and 9 in Tables 3.2, 3.4, and 3.6).

The dimensional analysis of patient A shows that the final label for this patient will be found in **bold print** (focus on other), on the left (hostile) side, at the bottom (enmeshed) part of the figure. This geometry places patient A at the space labeled BLAME on Figure 3.9. These dimensional judgments help the clinician recognize that patient A is doing more than being hostile; he is also engaged in control. It may be more important at the moment to discuss his need to control his wife than to help him "express his anger" at her. Guidelines for the use of dimensional analysis in choosing an intervention are discussed in the next chapter.

As another example, suppose that patient A's wife responds by crying and saying she is sorry, but has a very strained look on her face and seems tense. This is a reaction or state in response to him, and so the choice must be of a category that is <u>underlined</u>, indicating focus on self. Her response is not loving, and so it is on the left-hand (hostile) side of Figure 3.9. For the affiliation judgment in Figure 3.10, the choice MODERATE <u>RECOIL</u> seems close. For the interdependence judgment in Figure 3.11, we note that this spouse is not at all separate from patient A; in fact, she is falling under his influence. Her response is therefore labeled MODERATE <u>SUBMIT</u> in Figure 3.11. With these two judgments— MODERATE <u>RECOIL</u> (left-hand side of the focus on self scale of Figure 3.10) and MODERATE <u>SUBMIT</u> (bottom part of the focus on self scale of Figure 3.11)—her final label will be in the region of hostile enmeshment in Figure 3.9 (left, bottom). Inspection of Figure 3.9 shows that her response is labeled <u>SULK</u>.

It is important to remember that the words on Figure 3.9 are only summaries. They represent fairly large steps on the interpersonal scale. Smaller steps and more exact meanings are shown in Tables 3.2, 3.4, and 3.6. For example, the <u>SULK</u> of patient A's spouse can be described in more detail by appealing to Table 3.4, which is devoted to focus on self. Some of the full-model points found there that might describe this <u>SULK</u> more exactly would be 4, <u>Uncomprehendingly agree</u>; 5, <u>Appease, scurry</u>; 6, <u>Sulk, act put upon</u>. The additional information needed to make the label might help the therapist and the husband better understand her view.

Complex SASB Labels

The print types in Figures 3.10 and 3.11 must match. That is, the affiliation (Figure 3.10) and the interdependence (Figure 3.11) scales must share the same focus. **Bold** on one scale must be matched by **bold** on the other. If the two do not match, then[10] the interaction is probably complex and needs two or more labels for adequate description. Descriptions of some of the personality disorders require complex labels, while others do not. The difference between simple and complex labels is very important. For example, a BPD and an HPD share a number of features: They both are likely to try to coerce caregiving. The BPD shifts rapidly from one position to another (<u>TRUST</u> to BLAME). There can be sudden changes from bullying demandingness to sweet dependency. The HPD is better described by a complex combination of both positions simultaneously. For example, the HPD can show flirtatious dependency while at the same time flashing threats of disaster if needs are not met (<u>TRUST</u> plus BLAME). Complex

---

[10]It is assumed that the coder or labeler has not made a mistake.

labeling is discussed in more detail in subsequent chapters where complex labels are required to describe key patterns in disorders. These disorders include NPD (Chapter 6), HPD (Chapter 7), ASP (Chapter 8), OCD (Chapter 10), NEG (Chapter 11), and SZT (Chapter 14).

Enmeshment and Differentiation

Two people are "enmeshed" if they share interdependent space in complementary ways. Patient A and his spouse (hereafter referred to for brevity as "couple A") illustrate hostile enmeshment: CONTROL and SUBMIT; BLAME and SULK; and ATTACK and RECOIL. Couple C shows loving enmeshment: CONTROL and SUBMIT; PROTECT and TRUST; ACTIVE LOVE and REACTIVE LOVE.

Two people are "differentiated" if they share independent space in matching or complementary ways. Couples B and D, respectively, show hostile and friendly differentiation. Couple D shows ATTACK and RECOIL; IGNORE and WALL OFF; EMANCIPATE and SEPARATE. Couple C has a different duet: ACTIVE LOVE and REACTIVE LOVE; AFFIRM and DISCLOSE; EMANCIPATE and SEPARATE.

The varieties of enmeshment and differentiation shown by couples A to D are summarized in Figure 3.12, which combines Tables 3.1 and 3.3 to show the four types of relationships. Enmeshment and differentiation can be described in terms of the quadrant model (Figure 3.7), the cluster model, or the full model. For each version of the SASB model, as I have noted throughout, friendliness appears on the right-hand side and hostility on the left. Enmeshment is on the bottom, while differentiation is on the top.

Application of the ideas in Figure 3.12 to the introject raises the strange notions of "enmeshment with the self" and "differentiation from the self." These could be dismissed as irrelevant, but they have interesting face validity. For example, people who are engaged in oppressing themselves in all the ways listed in Table 3.6 can be seen as enmeshed with themselves in a hostile way. People who *Manage, cultivate self* can be seen as engaged in friendly self-enmeshment.

The idea of differentiation from self, implied by the top parts of the table, can also be developed by experienced clinicians who recall patients with BPD or ASP. These people show an astonishing detachment from the self, a profound recklessness, that accounts for their "conduct regardless of life"—including their own. Finally, the concept of friendly differentiation from self may be understood by people who are familiar with Tibetan Buddhism. This religion cultivates the idea (relatively unfamiliar to Westerners) of detaching from the self (and worldly interests) while still maintaining a loving connection to the self and others (e.g., Gyatso, 1984). This is loving differentiation from self.

In sum, the words "enmeshment" and "differentiation" are used throughout this book refer either to complementary relations or to internalizations. Enmeshed transactions involve control and submission, whereas differentiated transactions involve autonomy giving and taking. Enmeshment includes labels on the lower half of the models, while differentiation includes labels on the upper half of the models.

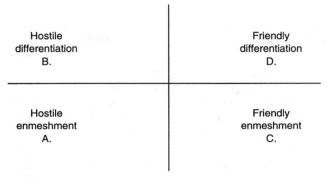

FIGURE 3.12. The four types of relationships, defined in terms of enmeshment and differentiation.

In describing enmeshment or differentiation, or when noting complementarity, it is vital to note that the focus distinction (other or self) does not necessarily convey causality. Focus on other does describe initiation or action directed toward another, whereas focus on self describes reaction, or a condition in response to the initiations of another. However, a reactor can draw out an action or initiation as easily as an actor can initiate. The observation that patient A focuses hostile control on his wife while she reacts with resentful compliance does not establish responsibility for the enmeshment. Each position facilitates the other equally. Complementarity theory holds that if one person puts down another, sulking will be the result. However, it is also true that if one partner blatantly sulks and appears too burdened, a complementary response is to criticize and act superior. The biting dog elicits fearful behavior, but the fearful person also elicits bites.

Opposites

The ability of the SASB model to define opposites permits the identification of conflicting messages. In the SASB simplified cluster model of Figure 3.2, there are four opposing positions: ATTACK versus ACTIVE LOVE, CONTROL versus EMANCIPATE, NEGLECT versus NURTURE, and BLAME versus AFFIRM. These opposites can help clinicians identify and think about different types of unconcious conflict, ambivalence, or double binds. Again, the simplified cluster model can be enriched by appeal to the full-model counterparts. Matching the numbers for the descriptions in Tables 3.2 (focus on other) and 3.4 (focus on self) allows exact opposites on the full model to be identified: One simply moves to the square located diagonally from the selected starting point, and finds the matching number. For example, description 5, Accuse, blame, in Table 3.2 is in the space of hostile control. The opposite quadrant is located on the diagonal. **Friendly lis-**

ten appears in the space of friendly autonomy giving. The exact opposite of **Accuse, blame** is therefore **Friendly listen**. If patient A constantly blames his wife, he needs to learn in couples therapy to do the opposite—namely, to listen to her point of view. He needs to learn to give up control and remain friendly as he lets her have her own different opinion.

The principle of opposition can also be helpful in predicting transference reactions. For example, the prototypical BPD alternates freely between ATTACK and ACTIVE LOVE in initiations and reactions to the therapist; these dramatic shifts are confusing to the beginner. The ability to identify and understand the roots of these opposites can help the therapist cope constructively with the sudden shifts in the BPD's behaviors. Furthermore, the principle of opposites is useful in classifying patients' wishes and fears. For example, the BPD intensely fears abandonment (NEGLECT), and desperately seeks its opposite (PROTECT). This intense wish and its opposing fear organize an amazingly large number of the interactions between the BPD and the therapist.

Similarity

"Monkey see, monkey do" is a children's saying that marks the primate tendency to imitate. Copying is a powerful mechanism in socialization. The power of imitation is demonstrated to parents who have watched their children display their own bad habits. For example, a parent may use undesired words in a moment of stress, such as slamming a finger in a car door. Such a parent is likely then to hear those same words being echoed by his or her attentive and heretofore innocent toddler. The child who imitates his or her parent is similar to the parent. The SASB principle of similarity includes, but is more general than, the clinical concept of "identification with the aggressor."

Being like someone who was important in another context is one powerful determinant of personality. The principle of similarity has a different meaning if it is shown by two people at the same time in the same interpersonal context. If two people rigidly assume the same position at the same time, the relationship is highly unstable. For example, if both people try to CONTROL, there is a power struggle. If both people SUBMIT, the relationship wobbles with uncertainty: "After you, Alfonse." "No, after you, Gaston." "What do you want to do? I don't know, what do you want to do?" "Oh, you say." "No, I can't." And so on.

Even if both members are functioning in the same "good" interpersonal position, such as AFFIRM, there is instability. For example, if each person rigidly tries to affirm the other, nobody discloses anything to be affirmed. The "affirming" relationship is unreal, and the transactions are necessarily inauthentic. On the other hand, if at least one member is able genuinely to DISCLOSE, then the other's AFFIRM creates a complementary and stable match. In an ideal personal relationship, each member is able to take each of these positions. At times, one person affirms as the other discloses. Then the roles reverse: The other affirms while the first discloses. In a therapy relationship, the roles do not reverse.

Normally, both therapist and patient focus on the patient. The therapist AFFIRMs and the patient DISCLOSEs.

Normality

Leary (1957) proposed that flexibility and moderation define "normality." A normal person is able appropriately to assume different interpersonal positions that depend on context. He or she also implements them with moderation. For example, to be in control in certain situations is normal, but always to insist on control is pathological. This reasoning led Leary and subsequent single-circumplex modelers (e.g., Kiesler, 1983) to think of distance from the center of their circumplex as an intensity dimension. Normal responses are closest to the center of the circle. Points having maximum intensity appear at the outer edges and define pathology.

Intensity can be defined on the SASB model as it is on the Leary-based circumplexes. Smaller distance from the center of the cluster model in Figure 3.9 can indicate lesser intensity. For example, suppose someone makes a passing hostile remark that does not include any discernible effort to control or distance from the target person. This can be labeled **MODERATE ATTACK** and **NEUTRAL CONTROL** on the scales in Figures 3.10 and 3.11. This means that the final label will be at the middle of the left-hand (hostile) part of the horizontal (affiliation) axis of Figure 3.9, and in the center of the vertical (interdependence) axis. This label does not correspond to any given categorical point on the SASB model. Even so, the category will be **ATTACK** because the final label is on a line that connects to the **ATTACK** category. Although **ATTACK** is usually seen as an intense event, the unusual location of this label indicates that the attack is only of moderate intensity.[11]

According to the SASB model, intensity does not define pathology. Rather, normality[12] is defined in terms of a baseline position that is qualitatively different from a pathological position. This baseline is marked by moderate degrees of enmeshment and differentiation. The normal baseline space is defined by the following combinations: **AFFIRM** and DISCLOSE; **ACTIVE LOVE** and REACTIVE LOVE; **PROTECT** and TRUST. Normal self-concepts include *SELF-AFFIRM, ACTIVE SELF-LOVE,*[13] and *SELF-PROTECT*. The highest goal for an individual in psychotherapy is to learn

---

[11]Events that yield judgments that do not end on a category given by the model are easier to study with the full SASB model (Tables 3.2, 3.4, 3.6). The reason is that the full model has 10 (rather than 3) points on the affiliation and interdependence axes. The finer resolution makes it easier to interpret any variations in intensity.

[12]"Normal" here means "ideal." One hopes that the statistical norm is close to the ideal, but it is not necessarily so.

[13]Unfortunately, *ACTIVE SELF-LOVE* has come to be associated with narcissism and exploitation of others. Chapter 6 shows that the self-love of NPD has a complex code, and occurs in an exploitative interpersonal context. Simple self-love occurs in a friendly interpersonal context.

to show these normative behaviors most of the time, while also being flexible enough to shift to any point in interpersonal space if the context requires such change.

It is vital to add that normality includes flexible responses to context. Rigid adherence to the normative baselines is not "normal." When the interpersonal context calls for other responses, including unpleasant behaviors such as BLAME or ATTACK, the normal person is able to give them. For example, in certain circumstances where there is no other alternative, a normal mother is able to ATTACK someone who threatens her child. A kidnapper or a rapist would invite ATTACK from a normal mother if she were aware of the event. This basic truth that anything can be normal under certain extraordinary contexts has long been recognized in the law, as well as in centuries-old religions (e.g., Gyatso, 1984, pp. 108–109).

If a person leaves the normative friendly baseline, then he or she may still be normal if the context is appropriate. A person who tries to maintain the friendly baseline regardless of context may be pathological. Inauthentic friendliness receives a complex SASB label. For example, consider a "friendly" therapist who rigidly affirms the views and actions of both of two embattled group therapy members. The attitude of affirming everyone is generically appropriate for a therapist. Suppose, however, that one of the members is in fact unfairly attacking the other. Suppose that this aggression also mobilizes subgroups to gang up on and scapegoat the victim. The group leader who fails to address and contain the attacks can be SASB-labeled as AFFIRM plus IGNORE plus SUBMIT in relation to the attackers. This label suggests that the therapist is affirming and deferring to the hostile group members as he or she ignores the reality of what is happening to the victim. By holding to the position of rigidly affirming all involved, the leader fails to PROTECT the victim and the integrity and safety of the group environment.[14]

The Axial Intensity Rule

Sometimes the dimensional analysis of an event yields judgments that do not fall exactly into a category given by the model (Figure 3.9). The preceding discussion suggests that this can happen if the event has low intensity. A different labeling problem arises when the dimensional analysis suggests that the event is extraordinarily intense on more than one dimension. Murder, for example, is judged by most raters to be at the endpoint of the ATTACK and the CONTROL dimensions (Figures 3.10 and 3.11). Under the usual labeling rules, murder would be plotted on Figure 3.9 at the far left and at the far bottom, in line with the category BLAME. This location in the middle of hostile interdependent space is

---

[14]This analysis by no means suggests that the leader should attack the attacker. There is no attempt to discuss principles of group therapy in this book. An interesting book on group therapy that leans heavily on SASB principles has been written by MacKenzie (1990).

dictated by the fact that each underlying dimension contributes 50% to the result. But calling murder a very intense version of BLAME does not make sense.

The "axial intensity rule"[15] solves the problem. If the judgment is that both underlying dimensions are present with extreme intensity, the result is a complex label. That complex label consists of each of the underlying dimensions themselves. Murder, then, is a complex event that includes both extreme attack and extreme control (ATTACK plus CONTROL).

The axial intensity rule applies to the friendly as well as to the hostile parts of interpersonal space. For example, the Tibetan Buddhist who successfully meditates on total detachment from an enemy while intensely loving the enemy is given a complex label: ACTIVE LOVE plus EMANCIPATE , or REACTIVE LOVE plus SEPARATE, or ACTIVE LOVE plus SEPARATE, or REACTIVE LOVE plus EMANCIPATE , depending on the nature of the meditation.

Antithesis

Application of the principle of "antithesis" should help the clinician identify the interpersonal position that is most likely to draw for the opposite of whatever is going on. For example, suppose patient A is engaged in BLAME. The opposite behavior, AFFIRM, would represent a desirable change in his way of being with his wife. The principle of antithesis suggests that the wife should engage in the complement of what she would like him to do. That complement of AFFIRM is DISCLOSE. The wife of patient A should try to tell her husband how she feels about what he is doing. She should focus on herself, not him. She should be friendly, and she should avoid enmeshment. This is the position that should have the best chance of helping him listen to her rather than blame her.

The antithesis is not hard to find. As just illustrated, the clinician first should find the opposite of the undesired behavior, and then invoke its complement. The opposite of BLAME on Figure 3.9 is AFFIRM, and the complement of AFFIRM is DISCLOSE. In sum, DISCLOSE is the antithesis of BLAME. Clinicians who teach these ideas to patients can greatly help marriages that are based on good faith, but are disrupted by bad interpersonal habits.

The Shaurette Principle

Unfortunately, the principle of antithesis is effective only with younger children and with relatively normal adults. Normality includes an ability to be flexible and to respond appropriately to the interpersonal context. Individuals with personality disorders are not likely to be able to do this; they are more likely to misperceive and to respond inappropriately to context. For example, patient A

---

[15]I am indebted to Craig Johnson, M.D., for this suggestion. Craig is a gifted psychiatrist who has made many contributions to the growth and development of SASB.

may be subject to panic attacks or severe depression if he is not in control. He may assume that if he is not in control at any given moment, then someone else must be. In effect, patient A may lack any understanding of differentiation. If so, then his wife's antithetical disclosure, which actually represents friendly autonomy, will be seen by him as a failure to submit. By his own internal logic, he may conclude that if his wife is not submitting, then she must be controlling him. That misperception that she is controlling him will make him angrier, and probably he will escalate his blaming in response to her disclosure. The principle of antithesis fails with patient A because he is not capable of understanding his wife's friendly differentiation.

With persons who have such narrow and rigid tendencies, more elaborate therapeutic planning is required. One of these more difficult, but effective, principles is called the "Shaurette principle."[16] This principle suggests that the therapist should match the hostile patient in hostile space, and then move stepwise toward the desired goal that may be set by the principle of antithesis. For example, patient A may need to be controlled by the therapist early in therapy. The therapist may have to say, "I am going to ask you to try something new and different at least while you are here. I want you to stop telling her what you don't like. Instead, I want you to . . ." (and here the therapist specifies some alternative pattern that the patient may be able to implement successfully). This therapist behavior is labeled CONTROL, which is next to patient A's BLAME on Figure 3.9. As therapy progresses, the therapist can become warmer, moving to PROTECT on Figure 3.9. This may include instructing patient A and his wife about complementarity. In addition, patient A will need to see how his rigid need to control represents a defense against the terror he experienced at the hands of his stepfather, and so on.

The next step in the desired direction is to move toward ACTIVE LOVE. Of course, ethical therapists do not engage in sexual ACTIVE LOVE. However, the therapist can show nonsexual affectionate behaviors, marked in Table 3.2 as 1, Warmly welcome and Friendly invite; 2, Stroke, soothe, calm and Provide for, nurture; and 3, Confirm as OK as is and Protect, back up.

It is vital to point out that therapist behaviors have to be genuine. If they are not, they receive a SASB complex label, and complex labels are likely to be associated with poor therapy outcomes (Henry et al., 1986). When the therapist does not feel the intense warmth for the patient described by ACTIVE LOVE, it is adequate to skip that domain and move directly to the end of the sequence, AFFIRM.

The Shaurette principle suggests that patient A should complement the therapist steps (CONTROL, PROTECT, [ACTIVE LOVE,] and AFFIRM) by making the respective changes: SUBMIT, TRUST, (REACTIVE LOVE,) and finally DISCLOSE. The

---

[16]Named after Glenn Shaurette, M.D., who organized his inpatient treatment milieu in the late 1970s and early 1980s according to the idea of matching the patient's codes or labels and moving stepwise toward the desired interpersonal goal—namely, friendly discharge from the hospital.

sequence shoud end at the desired point, friendly differentiation, as originally prescribed by the principle of antithesis. Again, for antithesis proper to work, the "tracker," the person who responds to the shifting interpersonal cues, must have few constraints on perception and response—a condition that is unlikely for individuals with a personality disorder. For these more rigid individuals, the Shaurette principle provides that the therapist moves in small steps toward the goal prescribed by the principle of antithesis.

Predictive Principles Are Neither Good nor Bad

Antithesis and the Shaurette principle are not therapeutic by definition. It is possible to use them to create psychopathology as well as to undo it. A simple illustration is provided by the child who enthusiastically shows some school work (DISCLOSE) to a destructive parent. The pathogenic parent provides the antithesis to the child's enthusiasm by criticizing the work and the child (BLAME). This parental antithesis to child disclosure encourages the child to SULK (complementary response) and to engage in SELF-BLAME (internalized response). The move thus enhances hostile enmeshment, and interferes with the development of strong self-definition (DISCLOSE), and a positive self-concept (SELF-AFFIRM).

Similarly, the Shaurette principle can be used to destroy a person's confidence. A manipulator may approach a victim in friendly ways (AFFIRM, ACTIVE LOVE, and PROTECT) and then, in stepwise fashion, move toward CONTROL, contempt (BLAME), and ATTACK. He or she may negate the victim's perception of the abusive reality (IGNORE), and then switch back to behaviors labeled as AFFIRM and ACTIVE LOVE. This is the classic cycle used by spouse batterers to hold their victims in the relationship. Of course, the victims also have their own early learning that prepares them to complement this cycle.

The SASB labels and the predictive principles function like any other body of information. If used for constructive purposes, they are very helpful and good; if used for destructive purposes, they compromise and annihilate. A major purpose of this book is to help therapists understand how the stressful behaviors of patients with personality disorders are the natural consequence of destructive experiences with earlier important people. This understanding should enhance the tolerance and steadiness that are required to work with these individuals. The next chapter shows that the dimensional analysis of the patterns of the disorders can also help therapists evaluate the effects of therapy interventions.

IF READERS ARE FEELING OVERWHELMED . . .

At this point, a reader new to SASB may feel overwhelmed by all the explanations, tables, and figures in this chapter. This is normal. A musician who can "play by ear," but who has not yet learned to read notes, also feels overwhelmed by the first reading of material that presents an overview of musical notes, chord structure, and harmonic progressions. However, with practice and rereading, the material that initially seems overwhelming can become familiar and eventually get buried in the subconscious to become "second nature." The advanced musician does not consciously name notes or chords as he or she sees them. Rather, he or she just plays them, and the underlying knowledge about structure and context adds to his or her versatility. At times, in very difficult spots, it may be necessary to stop and analyze a passage very carefully and go through it slowly until it has been mastered.

The same is true for clinicians who know the SASB labels and predictive principles. Usually a clinician is not especially aware of labeling, because that knowledge is functioning at the subconscious or even at the unconscious level. However, in very difficult sessions or situations, conscious labeling of the key events can help the clinician to understand the issues better, and consciously to choose a better treatment intervention. The reader is encouraged to reread this chapter as often as necessary, to learn better the basics of SASB coding. When he or she undertakes that exercise, the study guide that follows should be helpful.

4

The Interviewing and Treatment Methods

THE TECHNIQUES OF DYNAMIC INTERVIEWING

The clinician who can take the perspective of a BPD, an ASP, or an individual with any of the other personality disorders can learn to recognize their "songs." The method directly associated with the goal of seeing the world through the patient's eyes is called the "dynamic interview." It is outlined in Table 4.1, and an overview follows. Parts of the interview (I, II, IV) are devoted to gathering information needed to make a diagnosis in terms of the DSM. In these sections, the reasons for therapy or hospitalization are assessed, and the symptoms and their history are surveyed. The usual and customary procedures for gathering that sort of medical information are not reviewed here. Discussion in the present chapter is restricted to the sections of Table 4.1 that are less familiar (III, V, and VI).

Overview

For a dynamic assessment, the clinician attends carefully to the present and past interpersonal relationships and situations. These include the spouse, mother, father, siblings, children, work or school, therapist or health care system, the illness, the introject, and any other important situations unique to the individual. The dynamically oriented interviewer draws connections among those interpersonal relationships, the self-concept, the symptoms, and the wishes and fears. This process is not simple. Once the integration is complete, psychosocial treatment plans can be drawn that will address the psychogenic aspects of the problem patterns.

An important part of the interpersonal diagnostic procedure is to assess each relationship in terms of perceived "input," "response," and "internalization." The interviewer begins with the psychosocial situations the patient faces, and the ways in which these relate to past social learning. The impact of family, friends, coworkers, and the health care system on the patient is very important. The rationale for beginning with input is simple: It is assumed that behavior and affect correspond sensibly to the individual's perceptions. In other words,

Table 4.1. Outline of a Dynamic Assessment Interview

Date of intake, age, gender, race, marital status
Children (gender, age, where they are living, any health problems)
Occupation (is the patient presently functional?)
Spouse's occupation

I. Chief complaint
   A. Reasons for therapy or hospitalization
   B. Who brought/sent this person for therapy or hospitalization and why
   C. History of present illness
      1. Onset and course
      2. Previous hospitalizations
      3. Recent and current medications
      4. Recent and current psychotherapies

II. Current symptom status:
   A. Suicidality: Method, actual attempt
   B. Other symptoms of depression
   C. Symptoms of mania
   D. Symptoms of anxiety or panic
   E. Thought disorder
   F. Self-mutilation
   G. Enjoined awareness
   I. Drug and alcohol abuse
   J. Homicidality
   K. Legal problems
   L. Other psychiatric symptom
   M. Previous psychiatric diagnoses
   N. Diagnosed medical illnesses (Axis III): Include surgeries, other major medical events

III. Survey of present and past interpersonal circumstances:
   A. Spouse or spouse equivalent
   B. Mother or her equivalent (include attachment, discipline)
   C. Father or his equivalent (include attachment, discipline)
   D. Major siblings
   E. Children
   F. Work or school
   G. Therapist or health care system
   H. The illness itself
   I. The introject
   J. Other

IV. DSM checklist for likely diagnosis: List symptoms and give specific patient statements demonstrating the symptoms

V. Connections between present symptoms (section II) and interpersonal patterns, and early experience (section III)

VI. Treatment plan
   A. Problem input and suggested interventions
   B. Problem responses and suggested interventions
   C. Problem internalizations and suggested interventions
   D. Problem goals and suggested interventions

actions correspond to perceptions. To understand actions, a clinician must understand perceptions. For example, a jealous, paranoid husband may be irrationally controlling and critical. Nonetheless, his anxiety and anger are understandable, given that he *thinks* his wife is betraying him. Therefore, the clinician who would make a dynamic assessment must carefully assess the patient's view of his or her psychosocial world.

After clarifying how the patient sees the world, the clinician needs to assess the responses to that input. These would include both the patient's interpersonal responses and the impact on his or her self-concept. Not everyone responds the same way to the same input. For example, the jealous, paranoid husband may feel humiliated by his wife's alleged betrayal. This threat to his self-concept may lead him to become more controlling. By contrast, a depressed husband who believes his wife is unfaithful may feel self-critical and defeated. This may well lead him to a suicide attempt.

In sum, the interpersonal input, the interpersonal response, and the impact on the self-concept must be assessed. Distortions may lie in the perceptions, the responses, or the internalizations. The nature of the distortions defines the nature of the disorder. The paranoid man is very likely to distort at the input level, whereas the depressed man is less likely to inappropriately see his wife as unfaithful; his most likely distortion is in his view of himself. Regardless of where the distortions appear, the system has internal consistency. Relations among perception, response, and internalization will correspond in some way that makes sense. The patient and clinician must collaborate to find out how it all fits together.

Psychosocial treatment plans should directly address the distortions in the chain of input, response, and internalization. Plans center on the interviewer's guesses about the wishes and fears that organize the patterns of the disorder. Unfortunately, the key to the underlying wishes and fears is usually buried in the unconscious. For example the jealous, paranoid husband may consciously think that he has been very assertive with and independent of his cruel father. Unconsciously, he may be imitating his father, who chronically accused his mother of infidelity. His loyalty to his father's view of a wife may mean that in important ways he remains very attached to the father he says he hates. This analysis suggests that he needs to separate from the internal representation of his father if his marriage is to improve. This elusive factor—the unconscious wishes and fears that affect the will—can usually only be inferred in early interviews. As psychotherapy progresses, the nature of the underlying wishes and fears may become clear. The interviewer's beliefs about the organizing wishes and fears are entered in the last section of Table 4.1, under the heading "Problem goals and suggested interventions." They should be updated as more information becomes available.

The reader may say, "That makes sense. You assess the input and the response and the impact on the self-concept. Maybe the 'unconscious' does organize the patterns of the disorder. But *how* do you find connections between early learning and the present chain of input, response, and internalization? And by what logic do you identify and underlying unconscious wishes or fears? Even if you do know all of that, what does it tell you about psychosocial treatment planning?"

The answers to those important questions are sketched here in the abstract. Then, in Chapters 5 through 14, the method is illustrated concretely in the analyses of the DSM personality disorders. It is assumed that the personality-disordered individual sees and responds in ways that correspond in understandable ways to early social learning.[1] If input, response, and internalization are described by SASB codes, the clinician is more likely to see the links. The reason is that the SASB dimensional analysis focuses the clinician's attention on the most relevant features. Then the SASB predictive principles help the clinician connect input to response and internalization, and the present to the past. The logical structure of the SASB model also helps the clinician make guesses about the interpersonal wishes and fears that drive the consciously described behaviors. This composite of information—a quintessential dimensional description of characteristic patterns, of likely early learning, and of probable wishes and fears—can inform the psychosocial treatment planning. The Appendix to this book presents a summary of the interpersonal patterns characteristic of each personality disorder on Axis II of the DSM. Relevant early social learning, consequent wishes and fears, and the associated psychosocial treatment interventions are included.

Most interpersonal patterns arise through one of two mechanisms: (1) "recapitulation," or simple continuation, of patterns that were appropriate in the past; (2) "identification with," or copying of, patterns that were observed in the past. Such continuations and identifications can be traced by SASB codes. These two principles are illustrated here by the hypothetical paranoid husband and his wife. Suppose the husband's father used hostile CONTROL and BLAME on the husband's mother. The husband now does the same with his wife. This is an example of identification or imitation. Suppose the wife of the jealous husband had a controlling, demeaning mother (CONTROL, BLAME). As a child, it was natural and adaptive to complement her mother with SUBMIT, SULK. As she internalized the messages from her mother, her self-concept came to include SELF-CONTROL and SELF-BLAME. As an adult, her self-concept and hostile compliance hold her in the marriage to the jealous husband and complement or reinforce his pattern of hostile control. Her patterns illustrate the principle of recapitulation. Their respective interpersonal histories have prepared them for a miserable but stable marriage.

An Illustration

The dynamic interview that helps the clinician derive such an analysis of individual and family interactions is illustrated in the extended example that fol-

---

[1]The reader is reminded that these factors interact with temperament, the "hardware" for personality. As indicated in Chapter 1, discussion in this book is confined to the "software."

lows. The patient carried the diagnosis of BPD/multiple personality, and there had been many hospitalizations. This interview occurred during a brief hospitalization for safekeeping. She suffered from multiple suicide attempts, cutting and burning herself, drug and alcohol abuse, "losing time" in dissociative states, an array of distinct identities with different names and personalities, frightening visual hallucinations, and auditory hallucinations telling her that she was bad and should kill herself. The interview began with a thorough, empathic medical survey by the service chief of the inpatient service and ended with a dynamically oriented interpersonal interview. The medical interviewer developed a detailed history of the symptoms and treatments. There were clear time lines that established the coming and going of the depressions, the hallucinations, the dissociations, and the suicide attempts. He also reviewed the variety of treatments that she had had, as well as her responses to them. At the end of the interview, the physician assessed the patient's insight into her illness.

[I1 = medical interviewer, I2 = dynamic interviewer, P = patient.]

I1: How do you make sense of all this now?

P: I get very confused and scared. I think the personalities are here to stay and I have to learn to live with them. As far as the hallucinations go, I hope someday to be rid of them, because they are very scary and I always feel like I'm on a ledge walking a tightrope or something. The voices, I don't believe the voices are a part of me, which according to [therapist] is a part of my illness, but the voices are so much against me that I can't help wondering what it is that I did to make them hate me so much. And so it would be nice to get rid of the voices, because with them I have very little self-esteem.

I1: Let me see if I understand that. So if you had, say—there are lots of different theories about how people get to be the way they are, or why some people have some kinds of troubles and other people have other kinds and what not. Do you subscribe to any particular theory about why somebody has voices, or why somebody's personality is structured in a certain way, or . . . do you understand what I am asking?

P: I think some of it has to do with the way you're raised. I had a very painful incestuous relationship with my brother, which included being beaten on a regular basis. I think that might have something to do with the early split in my personality, but I also believe that these personalities aren't part of me. I sincerely believe that.

I1: Would you say that that's kind of like, well, are they like ghosts or something outside of you?

P: Yes.

I1: Okay. All right. I think that's all I want to ask about. Dr. B?

I2: So those personalities are really other people that kind of possess you, is that the idea?

P: Yes.

I2: Do you have a religious belief about that?

P: No. I don't.

I2: How do you account for it?

P: I feel that it sounds crazy, okay?

I2: It sounds crazy?

P: But I believe that they are people from other places that have come, and they take over and then they leave. They do whatever it is they want to do while they're here, and I think that's because I have a weak personality and they can take over.

I2: So you're just kind of a medium that . . .

P: Yes.

I2: . . . other people can use.

P: Yes.

I2: Are they from other time periods or just other places?

P: I'm not sure.

I2: Okay. So it's a sense of here you are, and these creatures come in and inhabit you and use you, and when they're done, they go.

P: Yes.

I2: You kind of tune out and don't have that much to do with it.

P: Right.

I2: And you feel helpless to change that—that's just the way it is.

P: Yes, I feel very helpless to change it.

I2: Do you remember anything like that in the earlier years? Do you remember that sort of feeling in any other context?

P: I don't think I follow you.

I2: The idea of just being—minding your own business and somebody comes by and does something to you. You don't have that much to say about it, and then they disappear.

P: Well, I never did.

I2: You never had a feeling like that?

P: I never had—as far as real people went, I never had much to say about it. People did come and use me and abuse me, and leave.

I2: What's an example?

P: My brother. When we'd get home from school, he used to sit and get me in a corner and beat me until I cried out, and if I cried out, I got slugged. And the only way to appease him was to just be quiet and let it run its course.

I2: There was nothing you could do.

P: Right.

I2: So the best thing to do would be to just kind of leave the situation psychologically, maybe.

P: Right. And that kind of thing happened a lot in my childhood.

I2: Okay. So you'd come home from school, he'd beat you, and he would say "Cry." And then if you would cry, he'd say, "You shouldn't have cried." That sort of . . .

P: Right.

I2: . . . reversal of signals?

P: Right.

I2: So there wasn't any way you could make sense of it. You were really damned if you did, and damned if you didn't. So that feeling of here's your body and somebody's going to invade it and it doesn't matter what you do. If you do, it's wrong. If you don't, it's wrong.

P: Right.

I2: And there is nothing to do except wait it out.

P: Right.

I2: Become timeless and repossess your body when he's through.

P: Yes.

I2: How do you feel about that?

P: I try not to feel about it.

The transcript offers an interpersonal interpretation of the patient's multiple personalities in terms of her childhood training. She explained to the medical interviewer that they came from outside of her (like ghosts) to take her over. She had strongly objected to her outpatient therapist's suggestion that the personalities represented a part of herself. The dynamic interviewer began by clarifying her perceived input, response, and internalization in relation to the personalities. They would take her over (CONTROL). Her response was to let that happen (SUBMIT) and to tune out (WALL OFF). Her internalization was that she "has a weak personality" (SELF-BLAME).

These patterns were connected to the past by the question "Do you remember anything like that in the earlier years?" This patient had difficulty understanding the transition question. She said, "I don't think I follow you." The interviewer repeated key features of her perceived input and response: "The idea of just being—minding your own business and somebody comes by and does something to you. You don't have that much to say about it, and then they disappear." She then offered powerful and vivid imagery of the chronic abuse that reflected that pattern and set the template for her multiple personalities.

Like the personalities, her brother would come and use (CONTROL) her and then leave. With both the brother and the personalities, she felt there was nothing she could do but tune out (WALL OFF) and let it run its course (SUBMIT). The codes of her experience of the multiple personalities were the same as the codes of her experience of abuse from her brother. Later in the interview, factors shaping the specific personalities became clearer. Other family members had been as coercive as the brother. Their various requirements for her were incompatible: In different contexts she was to be whore, angel, housekeeper, or playgirl. She developed a different personality to accommodate to each different interpersonal situation. It was not possible to integrate the different roles into a consistent personality. She was not allowed to talk about the various forms of her abuse to anyone, and she was prohibited from expressing anger or sadness. Learning to dissociate and become different people for different situations was a good way to adapt to her situation. She also learned not to trust her version of reality. The interviewer summarized:

I2: So your learning has been you can't take charge of your own body, your own mind. Others come and invade it and leave it when they're good and ready, and the only thing you can do is just wait it out.

P: Yes.

I2: And you've learned that you're not supposed to feel or think, and if you want to get along, just become someone else. And there's different demands around, so you had to become quite a few someone elses.

P: Well, that conflicts with my idea about where they come from. But it's—it's possible. I mean, I can—I can understand your flow of thought and I—it's very possible.

At this point she became willing to consider that her personalities were a part of her, not "ghosts" from outside herself. The recommended interviewing method of sharing the patient's own perspective helped to bypass her defenses and bring unconscious or preconscious patterns to awareness. The view of her illness as a survival tactic in a toxic situation contrasted dramatically with the idea that her logical circuits had failed her because of faulty genes.

Keys to Interviewing Success

It is possible to obtain much of the information listed in Table 4.1 in a single interview. However, the experience of discussing issues that are so central to the organization of the personality discussed is stressful. Following a consultative interview that addresses all the information in Table 4.1, patients usually say that they learned a lot, but that the interview was upsetting. Sometimes they forget what was said shortly thereafter. Occasionally a patient asks that a copy of the videotape of the dynamic interview be sent to his or her outpatient therapist so that they can study it together. Such an intensive and stressful one-time-only consultative interview is best conducted on an inpatient service, where there can be close monitoring afterwards. The strong affect that can be activated during such an intense examination of core issues can be addressed in a protected setting. An outpatient therapist would normally gather the information outlined in Table 4.1 over a much longer period, as the material unfolds naturally. In the outpatient mode, fewer issues are discussed at once, and the experience is less overwhelming. Affect is better controlled, and the patient can remember better what was discussed.

The therapist and patient will have greater success exploring the topics outlined in Table 4.1 if their interactive process has at least six features: (1) collaboration, (2) use of "free form" to track the unconscious, (3) the assumption that the patient makes sense, (4) interpersonal specificity, (5) avoidance of the potential to reinforce maladaptive patterns, and (6) quick correction of interviewer errors.

Collaboration

The baseline position is for the interviewer to AFFIRM the patient's views and responses. A more exact description of therapist behaviors coded AFFIRM appears in Table 3.2 (see the responses for patient D). In the context of Chapter 3, Table 3.2 illustrates the behaviors of four hypothetical patients. However, the behaviors outlined there by the SASB model can describe anyone, including therapists. Inspection of the details in Table 3.2 shows that AFFIRM does not mean that the therapist says the patient is "right" and others are "wrong." Rather, the therapist conveys that he or she is listening and hearing accurately, with benevolence and compassion. The therapist may not personally agree with the patient's view, response, or internalization, but he or she does understand how and why the patient sees it that way.

In the culture at large, and in therapy settings in particular, the enormous power of listening tends to be underestimated. For example, student physicians typically feel that "just listening" is not effective and doesn't fit their idea of how to be a doctor. Similarly, it is not unusual to hear one spouse (e.g., the wife) complain about the relative lack of communication in a marriage, while the other spouse (e.g., the husband) responds with the opinion that "just expressing feelings and listening don't do any good." A number of people believe that if a conversation is not task-oriented, and if it does not immediately result in a solution to a problem, it is a waste of time. They are mistaken. Showing that one does understand even if one does not agree with the other person's view is basic to successful human communication.

Even worse than the belief that listening is ineffective is the belief that to listen is to "give in." This attitude probably comes from the relatively common misuse of the word "listen" by parents who say to children "Listen to me," when they mean "Do exactly what I say." In these families, "Listen to me" ostensibly means "AFFIRM me." In reality, it means "SUBMIT to me." The therapist or spouse who has learned to equate listening with submission will conclude that listening gives the other person (patient, spouse) the complementary position of CONTROL. From this perspective, listeners are "losers." Those who teach that "listen" means "obey" (SUBMIT) inhibit the kind of listening (AFFIRM) that is vital to collaborative interpersonal relationships.

The dynamic interviewer does not try to CONTROL, judge, or "handle" the patient. Collaborative listening allows the interviewer to spot patterns as a mining engineer can notice a rich vein in an otherwise nondescript mountain. The interviewer can introduce the collaboration with a comment such as this: "If you're willing, I'd like to talk with you a while and see if I can see the world as you do. If I can, then I will try to make some suggestions that could be helpful to you (and your therapist). Is that all right?" If the patient agrees to that approach, the interviewer informs the inpatient that he or she will be billed for the consultation. Again, the patient is asked whether he or she is willing to continue. Often patients do not realize that they will receive bills on a fee-for-service basis while in the hospital. Similarly, outpatient therapists should make their expectations about billing and payment very clear at some point during the first interview. In outpatient work, it seems right to do that at the end of the first interview, after the patient has had a chance to see what the therapy process is like. Full disclosure about such realities, and willingness to give patients real choice and control about what happens to them, are important parts of the collaborative process.[2]

Following agreement to proceed, an appropriate opening statement is as follows: "What is your view of what you need—of what would be helpful to you?" Not surprisingly, this question usually leads promptly to the patient's perspective on his or her current situation. The interview process passes back and forth between interviewer and interviewee. It is as if there are two skilled interpersonal tennis players trying to hit the ball toward each other rather than trying to score points. The idea is to see how long they can keep the volley going, rather than to stop the process by putting the ball out of reach. The interviewer is responsible for placing every communication close to the interviewee. He or she must avoid metaphorically lobbing bricks that hurt the interviewee, or that will just lie there basically unreturnable. Clumsy "pointing out," such as "Why do you feel you have to outwit the staff?," is an example of a verbal brick.

The collaborative interviewer remains acutely aware of the patient's response throughout the interviewing processes. Tension, tears, monosyllables, and/or inordinate silences often serve as cues to ask how the patient is feeling about the interview. Sometimes it is necessary to reiterate the interview goals: "I'd like to explain that I believe that everything makes sense—that somehow it must be possible to understand why you are thinking and feeling as you do." Or: "This is just an attempt to see if we can make sense of what is going on, and if we can't do it, then we'll know this is the wrong approach." Here is still another example of interviewer dedication to the need for collaboration: "Would you rather not go along with this line of thought?" If the patient says "No, I'd rather not," the interviewer switches to another topic. It may be possible in a later context to return to the point. After becoming more familiar with the interviewer, the patient may become willing to revisit a previous difficult subject. If the interviewer is intrusive and tries to force the issue, the patient is likely to become more symptomatic.

Use of "Free Form" to Track the Unconscious

Unless facts must be gathered for administrative purposes or for crisis management, the flow of the conversation is guided by the patient's unconscious. Because the interviewer usually plays off whatever the patient says rather than controlling the transitions, large segments of the discussion can seem disorganized to an observer unfamiliar with the approach. In stark contrast to the idea that defenses will steer the dialogue away from conflicted issues, the dynamic interviewer assumes that the stream of consciousness *marks* the key issues.

The interviewer follows the tracks of the unconscious as the hound follows

---

[2]In either outpatient or inpatient settings, I am reluctant to insist on payment from unsatisfied customers. Sending accounts to collection represents failure at collaboration, and except in extraordinary circumstances, I do not recommend it.

the scent of the fox. The hound does not cut up the field into sections and search systematically. Rather, it puts its nose to the ground and follows the trail, circling back and going every which way, if that is where the scent goes. The scent is laid down by the unconscious, and the interviewer follows it using techniques like those richly illustrated by the psychoanalyst Theodore Reik (1949). In this wonderful volume, Reik described how to attend carefully to the patient's choice of metaphors, fantasies, dreams, and free associations.

The stream of consciousness, aided by interviewer queries about associative links, usually does touch on most of the points listed in Table 4.1. If it does not, at some point the interviewer may need to direct the topic with a few discontinuous questions—for example, "Tell me about your brothers and sisters," or "Did you have many friends when you were young?" or "We've talked a lot about your mother; what were things like with your father?"

The Assumption That the Patient Makes Sense

In seeking to clarify the perception of the present and its connections to the past, the dynamic interviewer *assumes that the patient makes sense*. The basic assignment is to understand the interpersonal and intrapsychic patterns in terms of where they came from and what they are for. As the interviewer engages in trying to take the patient's perspective on these matters, a natural empathy and warmth emerge.

The following case of Self-Defeating Personality Disorder (one of the "debatable" disorders covered in Appendix A of the DSM) offers another example of the value of the assumption that there are clear connections between present symptoms and early learning.

I: Why don't we start with what you would like? What do you think would be helpful to you?

P: What do I think would be helpful to me? Um, therapy. I don't know.

I: What kind of therapy?

P: Psychiatric therapy.

I: Therapy. Okay. Working on what?

P: Working on what? Oh, let's see here. A whole lot of shit, like some of the shitty thoughts I've been having. I'd like to get them out of my head, and I think the only way to do it is talk about 'em.

I: What are some of those thoughts?

P: Some of them are suicidal thoughts. Some of them are homosexual thoughts. Some of them are extreme verbal abuse to myself. Just cutting myself down. Some of 'em, I don't know. If I hear—if I'm watching TV or something and I hear about some, some crime or something, a lot of times I start verbally abusing myself. I'll tell myself that probably some sick motherfucker is going to end up in prison, and, like, I won't be able to control myself and I'll just fuckin' lose it.

I: You feel as if you might get out of control with your aggression.

P: It's not really a fantasy. It's just like verbal abuse. It's just like you'll probably turn into a murderer or a fuckin' rapist or something.

I: That's—there's more a less a voice in your head telling you that?

P: Well, it's, it's my own thoughts. But it's like an uncontrollable thought.

I: So your own mind harasses you with ugly accusations, telling you that you are homosexual, telling you that you are going to be a rapist, that you are going to be a killer. That kind of stuff.

P: Um-hum.

I: How do you feel when that happens?

P: I feel like shit.

I: What do you do about it?

P: Um, sometimes I try to fight it by negating it or saying it's not true. It's hard for me to talk about it 'cause I find it so fucking repulsive.

I: Ya. It's not a part of you that you're very comfortable with.

P: That's for sure.

I: Understatement there. This business of telling you how rotten you are and what bad, bad things are in you. Is that a familiar situation for you?

P: Myself doing it?

I: No. Somebody doing it.

P: My brother used to verbally abuse me.

I: He did? How did he do that?

P: Ya. Oh, by teasing or just name calling or sit there and rib me. You know, like, "You're a little wimp," or "You're a little fag." He'd sit there and tease me like that most of the time. He'd get to me and make me cry, or try to start a fight with me or something.

After establishing that the patient was the youngest of eight children, that this brother was 2 years older, and that the verbal abuse continued from childhood through adolescence, the interviewer asked:

I: What was done about all of this?

P: Nothing.

I: How come?

P: I don't know. I thought it was normal or something. And who was going to do anything about it?

I: What do you mean?

P: I mean, my parents couldn't stop my brother from doing it. I had low self-esteem and I bought into it. I'd try and get stronger so I could kick my brother's ass so he wouldn't be able to do it any more, but, you know, he got stronger too.

Subsequent exploration of the details of the fights clarified that this man's fears that he might hurt others, and his accusations of himself, represented identification with (ATTACK) and introjection of (SELF-ATTACK) his brother's abuse. The treatment implication was that he would need to make peace with his internal representation of his brother before he could make peace with himself.

Interpersonal Specificity

The dynamic interviewer can develop the "white heat of relevance" if he or she is constantly aware of the dimensions of interpersonal focus, love–hate, and enmeshment–differentiation. If the patient's words are so general that these dimensions cannot be identified, there is little chance that patterns and connections can be identified. Consider, for example, the following interview with a severely depressed minister who spoke in global generalities that suggested that all the world was wonderful, except for himself.

> P: Everything's fine.
> I: Everything's fine?
> P: Yes. I had a phone call from my wife last night.
> I: You had a phone call from your wife?
> P: Yes.
> I: Can you tell me more about it?
> P: She is very concerned.
> I: So I can tell better what it was like, would you mind running through it again? I mean, can you tell me what she said, and then what you said, and then what she said?
> P: She said that I was fine, and that I would be feeling better soon.
> I: She said you would be feeling better soon?
> P: Yes.
> I: What did you say then?
> P: I said, "I hope so." But I feel terrible today.
> I: How does she know what you are going to feel?
> P: I don't know.
> I: Do you get to use her crystal ball?
> P: (*Laughs*) No.
> I: Does she do that often? Does she tell you what you think and feel?
> P: Yes.

The interview continued in this vein, eventually focusing on the patient's lack of control in the marriage. At one point there was a fleeting statement of his resentment about it, but his flash of anger was quickly retracted. The staff was amazed at this glimpse of offense. Until then, this man had been adamant about the perfection and generosity of his wife and daughter in the face of his own abject worthlessness.

Without hearing the words of the conversation on the telephone, the interviewer would not have seen that the patient saw himself as subject (SUBMIT) to his wife's CONTROL. His wife's behavior (from his point of view) could be said to correspond to line 8 in the list describing patient C in Chapter 3: "Believing he (she) really knows what is best for his (her) spouse, patient C tells her (him) exactly what to do, be, and think." The patient's response to his wife's behavior could be said to correspond to line 7 in the list describing the spouse of patient A: "The spouse of patient A gives up, helplessly does things his (her) way without feelings or views of her (his) own." The implication of this highly specific view of his unremitting depression was that there should be marital therapy that would work with the imbalance of power in the relationship.

Avoidance of Affirming Destructive Patterns

The interviewer avoids either showing empathy for the symptoms of the illness itself, or focusing sharply on the task of gathering information about the symptoms.

Caution in the Use of Empathy. The interviewer needs to consider carefully what is affirmed and understood, because accurate listening is potent. Affirmation should reinforce personal strength, not deterioration. If there is warm support for and focus on pathology and suffering, that is what will be enhanced. The challenge is to provide contextually appropriate understanding and support for the suffering, so that the patient's attention can move toward coping and strength building. The therapist's task is like that of a parent who must provide security for a toddler that increases strength, not dependency. The parental attention and concern are there as a "backdrop," so that the child has the security to explore the world and develop his or her separate relationship to it. At times of special stress and challenge, parental attention to problems is intensified, but not overdone. If there is too much support offered out of context, the child becomes dependent and focused unduly on his or her fear and need (see Chapter 9).

Inadvertent reinforcement of pain and suffering through empathic focus on symptoms is not uncommon. I remember a resident who conducted a marvelously empathic interview with a severely depressed man. The resident showed great compassion for the man's despair. He clearly showed that he understood the pain in the patient's depression. The symptoms amplified noticeably during the interview. The nursing notes later indicated that the patient left the session in great despair and the depression didn't remit for days.

It is very important to meet the challenge of avoiding such subtle interviewer reinforcement of pathological patterns. The expert musician must attend to musical phrasing in exacting detail and practice technical exercises repeatedly. In an analogous way, the expert interviewer must carefully assess each of his or her tiny errors and work relentlessly toward giving true tones with exactly the right inflection. Consider the next example of a depressed, self-defeating woman who was telling her trainee therapist what would help her.

P: I have a fantasy that Dick [ex-boyfriend who had been sadistic and who repeatedly rejected her] will one day think I am wonderful.

T: You would feel good if he would like you again.

By usual and customary standards, this was a perfectly reasonable empathic reflection of the patient's position. However, careful reflection shows that the statement affirmed the patient's underlying *destructive* goal or treatment plan. The therapist underscored the patient's wish to renew her attachment to an unavailable and abusive figure. The empathic intervention was likely to elicit further elaboration on the destructive fantasy, and did nothing to help break her self-defeating pattern. A more directly constructive reflection might focus on the patient's intrapsychic process rather than on her fantasy. Consider this example: "His opinion of you affects how you feel about yourself." This response would be concrete enough that the patient could disagree with it if she thought it was wrong. If she thought it was accurate, she might take a small step in the direction of learning more about her introjection of abusive figures. This reflection would develop the "white heat of relevance."

Another example of subtle interviewer reinforcement of pathology comes from a seminar during which psychiatric residents were interviewing one another.

INTERVIEWEE: Every time there is a change in rotations, I just get nuts. For a few days I lash out all of the time, and I am just a bastard. But I've come to accept it now, and know that in a few days it will pass and I'll be better.

INTERVIEWER: You've found a way to get through the stress of rotations.

Here the interviewer also provided empathic reflection, AFFIRM. However, his "support" implicitly accepted the interviewee's adjustment as a blamer. Both interviewer and interviewee apparently agreed that there was nothing to be done but wait until it "blew over." A more constructive reflection would focus on the interviewee's pattern: "When you feel stressed, you tend to lash out." It would be important that the interviewer actually feel warm and supportive when giving this feedback. Even the slightest hostility might cause the feedback to be seen as BLAME, and the interviewee would become defensive. His statement already made it clear that he was prone to SELF-BLAME.

Further reflection suggests that the interviewee had set himself up in a "lose–lose" situation. If he were to be affirmed in what he said, it would mean that the interviewer agreed that he was a bastard. If he were challenged, then he would be likely to feel criticized. This bind might be finessed if the interviewer were to offer the recommended description of lashing out as a defense. In so doing, the interviewer would challenge the assumption that the interviewee was a bastard. "Confrontation" would become support if the interviewee did not feel criticized by the observation. If he did feel criticized, then the interviewer might invite the interviewee to contemplate the lose–lose nature of the situation. With this highly accurate labeling of the present pattern, the patient could move on to seek deeper understanding of the roots of this pattern.

Caution in Gathering Information.   The interviewer who is focused primarily on "getting information" is likely to be denied access to the unconscious. The less directive interviewer has a better opportunity to "follow the scent" of the unconscious, and to come upon important information about it. There once was a naturally occurring experiment that compared and contrasted an empathic interview with an information-centered interview. The first interviewer was a psychiatric resident who had a marvelous intuitive comprehension of the collaborative mode. With this interviewer, the patient appeared to be a very thoughtful, sincere, hard-working, responsible, but nonetheless mixed-up and very anxious young man. The patient discussed his anxiety about his engagement to marry, and made passing worried reference to a prospective father-in-law. The 20-minute interview covered his feelings of inadequacy and overwhelming anxiety on the night preceding his hospitalization. The man told the interviewer about his "experiences" with the FBI, who regularly intruded in his room and projected various obnoxious images on the walls to harass him. During this brief session, the seminar members acquired a sense of the patient's likable qualities and strengths, and had a first-hand glimpse of the patient's inner world. It was clear that he had a thought disorder, and that a working diagnosis would be Schizophrenia, Paranoid Type. But except for the strange ideas about the FBI, the patient hardly seemed different from any other young man engaged in a developmental crisis.

The format for the interviewing seminar required that following the initial 20-minute interview, the patient leave the room and the seminar members discuss the style of the trainee interviewer. The patient was to be brought back a second time to try out the group's suggestions about how to improve the interviewing style and the understanding of the patient. Normally, the leader would have instructed the trainee to explore the patient's relationship with the father-in-law. He would have been encouraged to consider possible connections among the patient's relationship with his own father and the prospective father-in-law. The connections might have helped to explain why engagement to marry was followed immediately by this psychotic episode.

During the group discussion, one of the other residents expressed displeasure and dissatisfaction with the interview, and wanted to get "more information." This second resident volunteered to do an information-oriented interview when the patient was brought back the second time, and he did so. The emphasis of the information-oriented interview was on when the anxiety and when the thought disorder first appeared. There was a survey of symptomatic changes in sleeplessness, weight loss, appetite, and so on. This part of the interview continued for 20 minutes, and considerable information of a symptomatic sort was obtained. Within just a few minutes of this second interview, the patient showed himself to be floridly psychotic, ruminating anxiously about the FBI. After the patient left the second time, the residents in the seminar discussed how interactive the interviewing process had been. They thought that the young man looked much "sicker" when confronted with a probing, information-oriented interview.

If time is limited, there is a real conflict between the need to understand dynamics (Table 4.1, sections III, V, VI) and the need to get information for the medical diagnosis (sections I, II, IV). The interviewer who must come up with a diagnosis might consider using the free-flowing mode until the last part of the interview. At that point, he or she can say that he will change the interviewing style to go through a checklist. "Blanks" in the list of needed information can then be filled in.

For report writing, the information in Table 4.1 can be organized under the following headings: "Presenting problems," "Current social circumstances," "Social history," "Diagnostic impressions," "Psychosocial treatment recommendations." The dynamic interviewer's report should make "sense" of the personality disorder in terms of past and present social perceptions. If possible, underlying unconscious goals should be included in the analysis. The treatment recommendations should flow logically from the analysis of the patient's patterns. As more information evolves in the therapy process, the treatment plan should be modified appropriately.

Quick Correction of Interviewer Errors

Interviewer errors are defined in some detail in "The Therapy Approach," below. There, five correct categories of interventions are defined and illustrated. Any intervention that is not correct is an error. Correct interventions help the patient learn new patterns, whereas errors reinforce maladaptive ones. At this point, error correction is illustrated by an example that may seem subtle to some readers. But the orchestra must tune exactly to the oboe's A; the slightest and most subtle deviations can ruin the whole effort. Similarly, the expert interviewer must have a finely tuned ear, and maintain concern for detail that may seem exotic to the outside observer. I believe that collaboration in the next example was facilitated by the highly specific reflections of the patient's perspective, the interviewer's nondemanding manner, and a willingness to correct a misunderstanding quickly.

I: How can we help you?
P: I don't want no help.
I: Does that mean you don't have any problems?
P: No, I got problems. It's just that I take care of them myself.
I: You feel that you must take care of things yourself?
P: Yup.
I: Why is that?
P: Just is. You can't trust nobody.
I: You can't count on anybody?
P: Nope.
I: Sounds like you've been disappointed.
P: Yup. Or people hurt you with their help.
I: People hurt you with their help? How did that happen?
P: My mother locked me up [in this hospital] where I could get "help."

The interview continued with an exploration of a chaotic and coercive home living situation, although the patient was afraid of betraying family secrets. It was surprising to the ward staff that collaboration was elicited so quickly from this extremely alienated patient. They had presented her for consultation because she had been very aggressive and disruptive on the ward.

It is hard to know specifically why the interview became collaborative.

Clearly the patient was not initially interested. Perhaps the early question "Does that mean you don't have any problems?" was important. Simple affirmation of the patient's statement that she did not want any help would have represented confirmation of her destructive position. On the other hand, a "confrontation" might have made the interviewer seem like a demanding mother to the patient. For example, a comment such as "You're in a psychiatric hospital and that means you must need help with *something*" would have been too powerful. The somewhat ironic question "Does that mean you don't have any problems?" showed willingness to "let her be." The interviewer "gave in" (SUBMIT) and "backed off" (EMANCIPATE), leaving the patient free to say why she was in a place to receive help and yet wanted none.

After "giving the patient her head" in this way, the interviewer persisted in trying to understand exactly how the patient felt. The error appears in the boldface line "Sounds like you've been disappointed." The interviewer assumed at the time that the patient really did want help, coded as PROTECT, but had not received it, coded as IGNORE. However, the patient corrected the reflection by adding "Or they hurt you with their help." The interviewer's acknowledgment of the patient's view of the hospital (and the home) in terms of ATTACK and BLAME conveyed that the interviewer could see the present world through the patient's eyes.

While discussing this view of hospitalization as punishment, the patient made many hostile comments about staff members and their alleged abuse of her. Except for an acknowledgment that the complaints had been heard, the interviewer showed Sullivan's (1953) "selective inattention" to these attacks on the staff (IGNORE). Exploring the accusations in any depth might have enhanced continued acting out on the ward. The patient's attention was redirected to the roots of the acting out, to the patient's current dilemmas at home. This direction enhanced the "white heat of relevance."

The reader may find it useful to reflect carefully on his or her own interview errors. My method was to force myself to write down exactly what I said in each interview during a 10-year period. I tried to do the same for patients, but paraphrased if I couldn't write fast enough. This embarrassing exercise helped me learn to say much less, and to be clearer. Ideally, the interviewer should be able to explain to himself or herself why he or she did or didn't do whatever was done or not done. Confronting oneself in writing with one's own "therapeutic" statements is an important part of therapist self-development. It compares to a musician's listening carefully to a tape recording of his or her own work.

THE THERAPY APPROACH

Overview

Very briefly, reconstructive psychotherapy based on the dynamic interview helps the patient learn to identify his or her interactive patterns, where they came from, and *what they are for*. The individual develops cognitive and affective understanding of the origins and purposes of his or her interactive patterns. He or she gradually comes to terms with the question of whether he or she *wants* to give up the old adaptations. The decision to give up old ways, the most difficult phase of therapy, may or may not be conscious. Once the decision has been made to give up old wishes or to challenge old fears, the process of learning new and better patterns can begin.

The interpretation of psychotherapy as a learning experience is not new. The history and potential of applying principles of learning to clinical problems of interest to psychoanalysts have been discussed by many, beginning with Dollard and Miller in 1950. A more recent review of the bridge between learning theory and psychoanalysis was prepared in 1980 by Marmor and Woods. Historically, learning and psychoanalytic views of personality have been placed in opposition (e.g., Mischel, 1973). Those who apply principles of learning to psychotherapy are said to be uninterested in the unconscious. Those who appeal to unconscious conflict to account for personality are alleged to have little interest in assessing the interpersonal or "situational" factors. Wachtel (1973) has noted that the "opposing" factions, the "situationalists" and the "personality theorists," need not be so far from each other. Situation variables are often equated with a learning view of personality. Person variables are usually equated in this debate with the psychoanalytic view. Both are important. The assessment of input in the present approach addresses the "situation," and the appraisal of response and internalization addresses the "personality."

The compartmentalization into input, response, and internalization is convenient. It is also an oversimplification. For example, the person's response affects the situation, and the changed situation in turn affects the person. The SASB principles of complementarity, opposition, and antithesis show how it is likely that the situation will move in the direction of self-fulfilling prophecy. The cycle is illustrated by reviewing the steps in the example of a BPD who panics over the therapist's impending vacation. Because of early traumatic abandonment experiences, the BPD sees the therapist's vacation as dangerous abandonment. The BPD defends against being left alone by trying to control and cling to the therapist/protector. The associated demanding dependency becomes too oppressive for the therapist, who withdraws in subtle ways. The BPD sees this as the dreaded abandonment, and the panic escalates. Through distorted perceptions associated with intense fears or wishes, the individual with a personality disorder rediscovers or recreates the same dilemma repeatedly. Psychoanalysts call this "repetition compulsion."

A reconstructive dynamic therapy seeks to change these repetitive maladaptive patterns (e.g., Strupp & Binder, 1984). Therapy is more effective if the therapist uses the dynamic interview and if correct treatment interventions are maximized while errors are minimized. There are five categories of correct treatment interventions: (1) interventions that facilitate collaboration between the patient and therapist; (2) interventions that help the patient recognize present and past patterns and the relationships between them; (3) interventions that block mal-adaptive patterns; (4) interventions that strengthen the patient's will to give up destructive wishes and fears; and (5) interventions that help the patient learn new, more adaptive patterns. If a therapist action does not meet one of these five conditions, it is probably an error. The five categories are arranged in approximate hierarchical order. If there is no collaboration, none of the four other conditions can be met. For example, if interpersonal patterns are not rec-ognized, then it is harder to block maladaptive ones. If the patient does not know what he or she is doing that is truly maladaptive, he or she is unlikely to "decide" to give them up. New patterns cannot be put in place if the patient still wants the old ones.

In most instances, the effect of an intervention can be assessed immedi-ately by examining the subsequent therapy process. For example, suppose the BPD is attacking the therapist for waiting too long to return a phone call. The pattern is coded ATTACK in response to the perception of IGNORE. An effective intervention will move the patient directly toward one of the five correct cat-egories—collaboration, learning about this maladaptive pattern, learning ways to block it, enhancing the will to change it, or learning about a better alterna-tive. There are many ways each of these outcomes could be implemented at any given point; all would be correct. It is more effective to emphasize the catego-ries at the top of the list early in therapy. The patient's decision to change and success in learning new patterns usually follow mastery of the earlier skills. A person with a personality disorder must first learn how to collaborate (instead of to coerce or withdraw) and to reflect thoughtfully about the self. After he or she masters these basic skills, the patient makes progress with the difficult pro-cess of giving up old habits and learning better ones.

Although the five categories of correct response are all helpful, successful reconstructions can occur even if one or more are skipped. For example, con-scious "insight" about underlying wishes and fears is not required. A man with ASP who serves in a dangerous but ultimately successful combat unit, with reliable buddies led by a kindly but tough leader, may be deeply changed. The traumatic experience may help him to develop a sense of bonding with and tol-erance for interdependence with others. This may moderate the ASP's need to dominate or maintain autonomy, and restore his natural wishes for attachment. Unfortunately, such spontaneous and natural cures are rare; they are difficult to create at will.

It is not possible to define therapy errors without having a treatment goal. And it is not possible to have a treatment goal without a definition of normal-ity. Chapter 3 defines normal behavior as characterized by friendly attachment and by moderate degrees of enmeshment and differentiation.[3] This definition is supported by a review in Chapter 2 of selected object relations theories. If the

---

[3] The discussion in Chapter 3 adds that the normal person must also be flexible enough occasion-ally to assume *any* position that may be required by the context.

patterns of a disorder involve excessive autonomy or excessive enmeshment, then the treatment plan will seek to moderate them. Patients who are too alone (ASPs, AVDs, SOIs, NEGs) need to learn about friendly, moderate enmeshment. Those who are too enmeshed must learn to differentiate. Whatever the level of interdependence, if the patterns of the disorder involve baseline hostility, this must be diminished. The person needs to learn to become friendlier.

Clinicians who believe that hostility is a basic energy and are accustomed to using the cathartic model may object to this view of therapy goals. They may ask, "What about anger? Shouldn't the normal person be able to express anger easily?" The present answer is "Not necessarily." Many relationships have been ruined by the misguided belief that expression of anger as an end in itself is healthy. The pattern analysis of personality disorders holds that anger should be interpreted in terms of whether it is in service of wishes for *control* or for *distance*. In Chapter 2, the Freudian idea of hostility as basic energy that occupies the bottom line of reality is rejected. Rather, anger is seen as a signal that the person has a problem with intimacy or distance. His or her anger is in the service of either controlling someone or distancing from someone, or both. The proper therapy plan for dealing with anger, then, is to address the enmeshment–differentiation problems that generate the anger, rather than the anger per se. (This view has been developed and illustrated at length in Benjamin, 1989.)

Reconstructive therapy can be completed by meeting once a week. It is good if there is freedom to move to twice a week when the patient wants to work more intensely. It is not necessary to meet more than twice a week, except for limited periods of crisis, when there may need to be more frequent meetings to avoid hospitalization. The patient and therapist should be sure that any increased frequency of outpatient sessions is serving to contain the suicidality or homicidality, rather than to enable crisis behaviors. The therapist's willingness to support the patient through crises should help build personal strength, and should increase the patient's ability and willingness to cope with suicidal or other dangerous impulses. If extra sessions are not clearly helping the patient contain the crisis adequately, then they are stopped. The failure shows that hospitalization is required. This rule that more frequent sessions must be associated with fewer symptoms helps guard against escalation for increased nurturance.

The therapist tries to stay right on the "white heat of relevance" all the time. Reconstructive learning therapy requires intense concentration from the therapist. I believe that psychotherapists, like airline pilots, become unsafe if they are overworked, upset, distracted, in altered states, or too tired. Every intervention should fall into one of the five classes of correct response. Each event should be assessed "on line." The therapy relationship is vital and fragile. Errors must be detected and corrected early. Continued practice of bad habits ruins the music.

The fastest possible reconstruction of a personality disorder will take at least 1 year, and the normative one 2 years or more. However, as I have learned more about how to keep the focus on major patterns relating to underlying wishes and fears, people have progressed through reconstruction with greater speed. In my eagerness to be maximally efficient, I have also frightened people away by being "too accurate." One has to find the right balance and remember that learning to play a musical instrument takes a long time too.

The Five Categories of Correct Response

For therapists who want to sharpen their skills in maintaining the "white heat of relevance," more detail about each of the five categories of correct response is now offered.

Developing a Collaborative Relationship

Without a good working relationship, a good outcome of the therapy is unlikely (Strupp, 1980, 1989; Gerstley et al., 1989). Considerable research effort is now being devoted to identifying the factors that enhance or detract from collaboration (e.g., Luborsky & Auerbach, 1985).

The Patient and the Therapist Should Collaborate against "It."   It is good to develop a contract that the patient and therapist will be "on the same side." Early in therapy it is helpful to agree that both will work to change the patterns that are not working well. If the therapist and patient agree to work together against the regressive "it," collaboration can be maintained during crises when the therapist has to confront the patient's acting out. At those times, the therapeutic interventions are directed against "it," rather than against "the patient."

For example, consider a BPD who angrily calls the therapist after a very moving session, and announces that the therapist is too hostile and the therapy is meaningless. The patient informs the therapist, "I'm quitting, and you can read all about it in the newspapers." First, the therapist takes the precautions described in a subsequent section on crisis management. Then, if the BPD has adequate ego strength, the therapist can begin to speak of "the part of you that is scared and angry about what we did in our session today." The therapist can refer separately and warmly to "the part that has decided to beat this thing and try to grow out of this mess." This reference to the original contract to collaborate against "it" can help the BPD stay strong in moments of crisis. The contract permits the therapist to be interpersonally tough and cold toward the regressive "parts," while remaining warmly and loyally supportive of the "part that wants to change." The overall idea is "It's me and you against it." "It" is the destructive parts of the past, the old patterns, and the old wishes and fears.

The "Wrong-Patient Syndrome" Cannot Be Treated.   Often the first therapy session is filled with complaints and outrage about the misdeeds of other people. Of course, there may be a strong component of reality to the complaints. The therapist must provide support and understanding to begin the collaboration. However, the patient must show some willingness to consider what he or she personally could do differently, even if others continue in their "wrong-headed" ways. People totally committed to the "wrong-patient syndrome" will not be willing to work on themselves. They come to therapy with the exclusive wish that somehow the therapist will change everyone else more to their liking. Two diagnostic groups especially likely to present with the wrong-patient syndrome are PARs and NPDs.

Collaboration requires willingness to look at one's own patterns, where they came from, what they are for, and what to do to change them. A straightforward discussion of this need helps screen out those who are unwilling to collaborate. After the first therapy session, patients with the wrong-patient syndrome will correctly decide that this is not the right therapy for them.

Court Orders for Treatment Can Interfere with Collaboration. People who come to therapy under orders of the court are often not interested in personal change. The same problem can arise in institutional treatment settings (e.g., adolescent treatment units). In these situations, the provider must offer something even if the patient does not want the treatment. The therapist and the patient do not have the luxury of saying, "Let's try this later when you feel ready." The first task in these mandated therapies is to try to create a collaborative contact. Somehow, the patient must be helped to see that there are more rewards in trying the therapy than in letting the treatment opportunity slip by.

Knowledge of likely patterns and underlying wishes and fears for the person's disorder can inspire therapist creativity in this most difficult task. For example, an ASP's need for control and autonomy can be acknowledged, and deepened by empathy with the likely reasons for it. A logically associated treatment plan can be explained. For example, the prototypic young ASP can be told, "We're sending you on a survival wilderness camping trip to try to help you have a very different experience. We'd like to help you see how in a trustworthy setting it can feel good to count on and to come through for others." The wilderness expedition should then be organized so that it will be responsive to the preferences and needs of the ASP, while also providing the vitally needed new experiences. Tough, respected, hypermasculine figures make the best leaders, and activities should be selected to enhance group collaboration and bonding. The ASP will be more comfortable if allowed maximal amounts of self-determination and control over what is happening to him or her. Of course, all of this planning also has to be within legal and ethical constraints. Program directors may need to share with institutional review boards the burden of developing guidelines that will allow the use of sometimes severe, possibly abusive sanctions. Such interventions must have a well-founded probability of having a beneficial impact on these individuals with whom ordinary procedures have clearly failed.

The Therapist Should Avoid Codependency on Patients. Some therapists may argue that it is too tough to refuse treatment for those who are unwilling to collaborate (assuming that the court is not involved). These clinicians may say that people need support and time to develop trust in the therapy relationship before confronting their own defenses. The counterargument is this: Why not devote the limited time and resources available to people who are willing to use them well? Failure to enlist the will to change and grow at the beginning risks a destructive codependency between patient and therapist.

Without a collaborative agreement to work, the possibilities for iatrogenic therapist behaviors are significant. The discussion of the dynamic interview has shown how unexamined and unframed therapist empathy can encourage the standing patterns characteristic of the disorder. Unenlighted therapist empathy can enable NPD, facilitate PAR rage, increase DPD helplessness, expedite OCD thinking, exacerbate NEG patterns, reward HPD and BPD demandingness, and so on. In Chapter 3, the idea is developed that generic codependency is described by the SASB principle of complementarity. Therapists are not immune to these powerful interpersonal forces. They are responsible for making sure that these natural proclivities facilitate constructive goals. The therapist must not deliver services that enable such patterns as entitlement, dependency, autism, or even abuse.

Patients Should Be Permitted to Sample a Few Therapists before Committing to a Specific Therapy.   Few people make a major decision such as buying a house or car, choosing a college, or accepting a job without shopping a bit. Similarly, since therapy is a major emotional and financial commitment, it is better if patients can have an initial opportunity to explore a therapist's philosophy and approach. Patients deserve a choice of therapists. This means that patients should not be faulted if they want to interview[4] two or three different therapists to make their selection. After the selected therapy has started, there should be an agreement to stick with it for at least three sessions beyond any point when the patient becomes dissatisfied. The reason is that if the therapist is actively eliciting and confronting old patterns, there will be times of discomfort and anger at the therapist. Fleeing therapy is a very natural but destructive response. The contract can be set in the first session: "After we meet a few more times, I'll ask if you want to continue with this approach. Once you decide you do wish to continue, I'll ask that you agree not to stop until you have returned at least three times to discuss why you want to stop. This will assure that we both understand the decision, and make it clear that stopping does not just represent a part of you that doesn't want to change."

A patient may tell a story that indirectly complains about the therapy, and the therapist may react by daydreaming or having a tiny edge to his or her tone

---

[4]I hesitate to share this belief here, lest already overburdened clinics be faced with even more personality-disordered patients demanding to change therapists. There is much that is good about our capitalistic system and much that is bad. In the area of mental health care, there are some unfortunate realities about restrictions on the supply of psychotherapists if people cannot afford to pay for the therapy themselves. Perhaps a solution to the problem of severe limitations on the amount of available therapist time would lie in dispensing psychotherapy in a way analogous to dissemination of food stamps. Some access to therapy would be offered to the needy and indigent, and they would have some (but certainly not total) choice over how to receive their sparse entitlements.

of voice. The patient may then leap from this minimal cue to a monumental indictment of the therapist for being angry, rejecting, or uncaring. These momentary glitches are normative in working with personality-disordered patients. In the therapy context, they can be acknowledged briefly and dealt with matter-of-factly. The therapist simply maintains concentration and gives a response in one of the five correct categories.

Negative Transference Is Destructive and Should Be Addressed Immediately. The collaborative contact is so important that negative transference must be corrected as soon as it appears. Reconstructive work cannot go forward while the patient is angry at or afraid of the therapist. Candid exploration of whatever has frightened or enraged the patient should take place soon. The therapist should be willing to disclose his or her experience of it, and to acknowledge any errors. Because the work goes faster if the patient trusts and likes the therapist, *and vice versa*, rough spots should be worked out immediately. Usually the process of resolving negative transference offers a good learning experience for the patient.

Beyond these normal temporary difficulties in the therapy relationship, there are sometimes baseline incompatibilities between patient and therapist. *Sometimes negative transference is valid.* Individuals with personality disorders habitually draw for poor interpersonal process, and too often therapists deliver it. Because the collaborative contract must be reality-based, a therapist must confront such problems personally. If the patient affects the therapist's personal vulnerabilities, a referral should be made with this simple explanation: "I think I am not the right person to work with you right now. I will try to help you find someone who may be able to help."

A therapist should be particularly careful not to accept a patient whose interpersonal patterns match the patterns of the therapist's unresolved relationships with significant others. The definition of a resolved relationship is that the therapist is now peacefully differentiated from, if not actually friendly with, old painful figures.

There Must Be Clear Potential for Bonding and Differentiation to Develop. A therapy contract should not be offered if there is no evidence that both bonding and differentiation can develop in this relationship. For example, PAR and ASP present a challenge to the bonding process. If there is not a palpable sense of potential for affection to unfold between patient and therapist, the therapy process should not be undertaken. The patient must also offer a sense of self that is strong enough for differentiation to unfold. Some BPDs seem so determined to save themselves by merging with a cosmic caregiver that it is difficult to find a core that can be expanded into a self. Individuals with Schizophrenia may be so damaged both in bonding and in differentiation that they are not treatable by this method. The topic of whether Schizophrenia can be treated by psychotherapy at all is controversial, but the idea does remain viable (McGlashan,

1983). I have only succeeded twice with the treatment of severely thought-disordered schizophrenic patients. The process was breathtakingly intense, seemed very dangerous, and had an intimacy that defies description.

Facilitating Pattern Recognition

Insight Is a Stage of Therapy, Not a Goal. The quest for the "Aha" experience—for insight into one's personality—is served well by learning about one's patterns, where they came from, and what they are for. However, such insight marks the beginning rather than the end of change. "Uncovering," "getting it out," or "understanding" is not a therapy goal in itself; it is a stage of therapy. Patients who say, "I see what I am doing, and where it came from, but that doesn't help," can be reminded that they are working with a learning model. Insight compares to learning that one's finger positions are not optimal as one plays the piano. After discovering the problem, one then has to learn something different and better. Once the patient develops insight, he or she only knows what has to be changed. Beyond insight, there are difficult stages involving the challenge of daring to change and then doing it.

Insight in psychotherapy doesn't happen all at once. It compares to insight in any complex learning situation. One can read and understand a novel or a mathematical procedure, or can learn to play a musical instrument. Then, as time and experience accumulate, new and deeper understandings of the same subject emerge. An illustration follows.

In the first interview, a woman with Self-Defeating Personality Disorder may be given a very general summary of her patterns: "It sounds like you keep getting in situations where people don't treat you well, and one result is that you feel really bad about yourself. A goal for therapy might be to find out how you learned to do that. Then you might learn how to treat yourself better and how to get yourself in situations where people are nicer to you." For a deeper level of insight, after the therapy relationship is well developed, stark realism from the therapist will not be experienced as attack. At this point, the same patterns may be described more concretely: "You keep picking abusive boyfriends because that is what you learned from your father about how men should treat you. You keep hoping that if you can be good enough and finally learn how to do things 'right,' then at last you will be loved." Still later, patient and therapist may become even more candid and discuss the patient's erotization of the abuse.

Insight about childhood changes as therapy progresses. Stabilized by a bond to the therapist, which connects the patient to the present, the patient learns to reframe old situations. The different perceptions will be accompanied by different feelings. For example, after insight, one patient saw her previously idealized long-suffering mother, now deceased, as having been fundamentally neglectful. The new affect was rage stemming from a wish to control and retrieve the rights of childhood. This rage replaced the familiar crippling feeling of guilt. Still later in therapy, the patient came to view her mother as an inadequate child without resources. The new affect for this different perception was compassionate grief, followed by detachment and acceptance of reality as it was and is.

INTREX Questionnaires Can Help Set Therapy Goals.   Patients can be introduced to a first-draft sketch of their patterns—to the first level of insight—if they rate themselves and important others on questionnaires conforming to the SASB model. The standard series of INTREX questionnaires[5] asks that each item be rated for applicability to the rater's introject at best, and at worst, to his or her relationship with a significant other person at best and at worst, to the mother when the rater was a child aged 5–10, to the father when the rater was aged 5–10, and to the mother and father's relationship with each other when the rater was at that same early age. The series may be modified as appropriate to include stepparents or significant siblings. The INTREX questionnaires have been used to validate the SASB model (Benjamin, 1974, 1984, 1988) and to study aspects of object relations in a variety of research contexts (Benjamin, 1982, 1991).

In psychotherapy, the output from program INTERP, illustrated in the INTREX user's manual (Benjamin, 1988), can be shown to the patient in order to outline the main interpersonal patterns in terms of focus, love–hate, and enmeshment–differentiation. The output can help the patient can understand that bad feelings about the self have understandable connections to perceptions of social experiences with important other people. For example, the self-defeating person described above would probably give high endorsements to the self-critical items and low endorsements to the self-approving items. She would also endorse the items depicting her father as controlling and critical. Program INTERP would connect items describing her father's hostile control to her own self-oppression. The output would also show graphically that her father and boyfriend are similar in this respect, and that she reacts to both of them with hostile compliance. The therapist can then point to the SASB model and suggest that a therapy goal may be to cultivate the opposite of these self-critical and self-negating behaviors and internalizations.

Because the questions are very straightforward, the INTREX questionnaires are worthless unless there is a collaborative contract. There is no attempt to defend against or correct for conscious or unconscious distortion or to outwit the wily rater. The only assurance of candid response is the offer of straightforward feedback for the patient's own use in self-growth.

The patient's affective and cognitive understanding of the information summarized by output from program INTERP can deepen as the therapy progresses. The perceptions or "insights" reflected in INTREX ratings or in ordinary therapy dialogue are likely to change as the therapy explorations continue. Reality is in the eyes of the beholder. Under a collaborative contract and from an adult point of view, the insightful patient will re-experience ancient perceptions and reactions to those perceptions. Stabilized by a bond to the therapist, who is a reminder of adult reality, the patient may come to see the old situations differently. The

---

[5]Available to qualified professionals from the author.

psychoanalysts describe this phase of therapy in terms of an "observing ego." The different perceptions will be accompanied by different feelings.

The Therapist Affirms the Patient's Given Affiliative Nature and Right to Change, without Validating Present Maladaptive Patterns.   The therapist affirms the patient's spirit and desire to change, to grow out of the consequences of old injuries. The therapist accepts the flaws that now exist for good and sufficient reason. However, the expectation is that these will be changed to stop harming the patient. The notion of categorical, noncontingent acceptance of the person is neither realistic nor constructive. The part of the "it" that has been targeted by both patient and therapist for change is not automatically affirmed.

This idea of accepting the patient's acting out without affirming it is especially important when handling a regressive episode involving a suicide attempt, self-mutilation, or some other form of clearly destructive old patterning. After the patient is debriefed, and both parties clearly understand what happened during the episode, the therapist can say something like this: "Okay, this is a disappointment, but it sounds like you know what set it off and how to try to do it differently next time. Overall, it seems like this sort of thing is happening less often. Let's just take it from here."

Characteristic Patterns, and Unconscious Wishes and Fears, Can Be Identified by Standard Techniques from Psychoanalysis.   Techniques from psychoanalysis, such as dream analysis, free association, tracking of the flow of the stream of consciousness (e.g., Reik, 1949), transference, countertransference, confrontation, and interpretation, can all help with pattern recognition. It is beyond the present scope to consider each of these well-known techniques. For illustrative purposes, just one is considered here.

Dream analysis can be simplified by SASB coding. The interpersonal dimensionality of the dream should compare sensibly to the dimensionality of the dreamer's everyday life. As an illustration, consider an exposition of dream analysis offered by C. G. Jung (1934/1955):

> A man who held a prominent position in the world . . . was afflicted with a sense of anxiety and insecurity and complained of dizziness sometimes resulting in nausea, of a heavy head and difficulty in breathing—this being an exact description of the symptoms of mountain-sickness. He had an unusually successful career, and had risen, with the help of ambition, industry and native talent, from a humble origin as the son of a poor peasant. . . . He had actually reached a place in life from which he could have begun his ascent into the upper regions, when suddenly his neurosis intervened. . . .
>
> The first dream was as follows: "I am once more in the small village where I was born. Some peasant boys who went to school with me are standing together in the street. I walk past them, pretending not to know them. I hear one of them, who is pointing at me, say: 'He doesn't often come back to our village.'" No tricks of interpretation are needed to recognize and to understand the allusion to the humble beginnings of the dreamer's career. The dream says quite clearly: "You forget how far down you began."

Here is the second dream: "I am in a great hurry because I am going on a journey. I hunt up my baggage, but cannot find it. Time flies, and the train will soon be leaving. Finally I succeed in getting all my things together. I hurry along the street, discover that I have forgotten a brief-case containing important papers, dash breathlessly back again, find it at last, and then run towards the station, but make hardly any headway. With a final effort I rush on to the platform only to find the train steaming out into the yards. It is very long, and runs in a curious S-shaped curve. It occurs to me that if the driver is not careful, and puts on full steam when he comes to the straight stretch, the rear coaches will still be on the curve and will be thrown over by the speed of the train. As a mater of fact the driver opens the throttle as I try to shout. The rear coaches rock frightfully, and are actually thrown off the rails. There is a terrible catastrophe. I awake in terror." (pp. 161–162)

Jung's suggestion that the "mountain-sickness" signified the dreamer's unconscious feeling that he was too high up in the world seems reasonable. That part of the analysis is not SASB-codable, because no detail is provided to explain how the patient felt about his "mountain-sickness." However, the metaphor of being "on top" of others can be coded as CONTROL. The idea that the patient suffered from an unmodulated drive toward superiority ("frantic haste to advance himself still further"; see below) was the key to Jung's interpretation. In the first dream, the dreamer walked past the boys from childhood without speaking. This behavior can be coded as IGNORE. It could be, as Jung concluded, that the boys were reproaching the dreamer for being arrogant (BLAME). However, the words of the dreamer do not support that SASB label (see lines 5 and 6 in the list describing patient A in Chapter 3). The alternate view suggested by the SASB code of the dreamer's actual statements, IGNORE, implies a need to explore the theme of guilt over abandonment. It could be that rather than feeling superior, the dreamer was worried about people he should have taken care of, but hadn't because he was so busy with his career. Perhaps he worried that there were things he should have done for them that he had not done. Maybe he was frightened by what would happen to him for doing that.

Similarly, for the analysis of the second dream, Jung commented: "It pictures the patient's frantic haste to advance himself still further. . . . He should have contented himself with his achievements, but instead he is driven by his ambition to attempt to scale heights of success for which he is not fitted" (p. 162). An SASB analysis would support Jung's interpretation if the codes of content supported the idea that the dreamer felt he had exceeded his limits and was concerned with superiority. However, the codes of his actual words again suggest that the theme was IGNORE. The patient said he had forgotten the important papers, while the negligent and preoccupied engineer ignored the needs of the people who were depending on him. The dreamer tried to find what had been forgotten, and he tried to slow things down. On the basis of the limited text available, the SASB analysis does not support Jung's conclusion that the dreamer was ambitious beyond his abilities. Rather, it suggests that the dreamer was very upset about abandoning others.

There is no way to check the accuracy of either interpretation because there are no more data. Theoretically, the SASB interpretation could be confirmed or disconfirmed by associations to the dream and by the patient's own description of his professional progress. The point is not trivial: Correct understanding is vital to correct intervening.

For ongoing cases, SASB coding of dreams, free associations, and sequences in the stream of consciousness can help identify patterns, wishes, and goals. The SASB method for encoding the dreams and associations stays close to the patient's data and links seemingly diverse themes.

Crisis Management Is Not Treatment.   The dynamic interview is not appropriate during crises when immediate life-saving support must be offered. Learning about one's patterns usually does not take place in the midst of catastrophe. Patients in emergency situations are typically deprived of the opportunity to grow. Crisis intervention is not treatment; it only preserves life so that later on, when things calm down, meaningful treatment can continue.

If the observing ego, the collaborative part of the patient, cannot be mobilized to engage in pattern analysis during the crisis, then the therapist uses standard procedures for crisis intervention. He or she must find out where the patient is, assess the danger, offer support in the form of extra appointments, or use the hospital. If the collaboration has been severely damaged, it may be necessary to call the police for detention or commitment. If these extreme measures are taken, the therapy relationship is likely to suffer major damage. But that damage is a lesser evil than a suicide or homicide.[6]

On the other hand, if the patient can maintain stability during a crisis, there is an opportunity for excellent learning. Symptoms per se are not the focus. In the chapter on HPD (Chapter 7), there is a transcript from a suicidal episode that shows how to use crisis constructively.

Hypnosis Is Not Helpful to Pattern Recognition.   Hypnosis and other such dramatically powerful techniques are not ordinarily compatible with the approach described here, because they do not directly enhance the patient's ego strength. "Information" gathered under hypnosis is of little use to the patient's collaborative part. The catharsis offered by hypnosis is not seen as a therapeutic end in itself. Hypnosis gives the interviewer much control, and individuals who are able to be hypnotized tend to be submissive. Those who are unlikely to allow themselves to be hypnotized tend to be autonomous. In short, the people who might learn good new patterns by being hypnotized do not allow it. On the other hand, those who seek hypnosis are likely to be enabling their problem patterns.

Role Plays Can Be Helpful in Understanding Patterns.   Role plays can serve to uncover patterns and to practice new responses. Patients are often brilliant

---

[6]These comments are not intended as a complete description of how to deal with a suicidal or homicidal crisis.

in their recapitulations of the role of an oppressive parent, an abusive sibling, and so on. The therapist can take the role of the patient and model a natural response ("Oh, my God, I can't take this, it's making me nuts"). He or she can then model a better alternative ("Wait a minute: First you said that you were angry with me, and now you say there never was a problem"). Such exchanges offer many advantages. The patient communicates to the therapist in vivid detail what he or she has been experiencing. Understanding is intensified. The patient has a chance to experience things from the perspective of his or her oppressor. In playing the roles of others, the patient may notice that he or she has been doing the same things to loved ones that the original oppressor did to him or her. Therapist modeling of constructive alternative responses to family dilemmas can also provide a good learning experience.

Education about Child Rearing Can Help.   Simple educational interventions also have a place. Unfortunately, many North Americans have learned about intimacy and child rearing only through defective modeling in their families of origin. Nor do movies and TV usually show constructive alternatives. Patients' difficulties with their children often result from their not knowing better ways, rather than from "bad will."

Brief discussions of patients' problems with rearing their own children serve to provide vivid and highly relevant memories of their own childhood. They can also lead to dramatic improvements in patient–child relationships. An example is offered by a man with OCD mentioned in Chapter 10. He noticed his mother telling her grandbaby that he wasn't "playing right." An educational discussion about the likely impact of the grandmother's inappropriate control on the infant helped the patient moderate his own need to control his wife and his children.

A Family Conference Can Provide a Sample of "Interpersonal Tissue." Inviting the family into individual therapy for a one-time tape-recorded conference can be extremely valuable. The conference has two stated purposes: (1) It provides a chance to act out the patient's fantasy that the family will come in, realize that everything has been a terrible mistake, apologize, fix things, and "make up." (2) An *in vivo* sample of family interactions will be recorded on tape to be studied later, to help the patient develop a more realistic and vivid understanding of family patterns. The first purpose, the realization of the fantasy, is never the outcome. The second purpose is the one that can be implemented. Such conferences are usually surprising, intense, and interesting. New perspectives sometimes emerge; if they do not, the electronic record still provides the patient with a rich lode of highly relevant information about the patterns that must be understood and integrated.

For example, a woman who had been abused by her brother hoped that the family conference would bring acknowledgment from her parents that she had been treated badly by him. Her short-term wish was that her parents would then stop insisting that she must engage in public behaviors attesting to family "togetherness." Far from loving her brother and wanting to spend time with him and his family, she was angry and wished to have nothing to do with him. In the family conference, her parents paid no attention to her explanations and requests. They repeatedly denied, undermined, undercut, changed the subject, and said "Yes, but . . ." to her attempts to describe her perception of her relationship with her brother. Having been a long-time sufferer of suicidal attacks, she said, "I just go nuts when somebody tells me I don't see, hear, and feel what I do."

After the conference, the patient listened to the audiotape with the therapist in silence. The mother, who had been idealized before the conference, was clearly heard to be undercutting and denying the patient's allegations about the brother.

P: I feel stunned when I hear this.

T: Do you feel anything else, or just renewed pain?

P: I feel stunned, confused. [She restated the patterns of the parents' not listening, and continuing the insistence that she worship her brother.] They'll never change. I feel helpless. Listening to this, I feel angry.

T: (*Long silence, because it is important to stay out of the way when a patient is processing something new.*)

P: I feel challenged, disoriented—my mother is doing a number on me here. This is like a mystery novel. I never knew it was *her.* I always thought she was fair and understanding. I was told my mother is my best friend. I have to rethink my role in the family. I listen to that and I feel again as I did when I was a child. All my life I felt that way. Now here in this safe context I can listen to it and see it clearly. Why did I ever expect anything else to happen?

A common outcome of listening to such tape recordings of *in vivo* samples of family patterns is that the patient feels less crazy because the data are so clear. Family patterns are undeniable. Reality is affirmed. Impossible fantasies are undermined. The procedure helps the patient leave old patterns behind and get on with the new generation.

Blocking Maladaptive Patterns

Patterns characteristic of personality disorders cannot be blocked at will. Patients cannot stop their maladaptive interpersonal habits on command, any more than they can stop smoking or using drugs at will. The advice "Get a grip" may work with normal individuals in crisis, but it does not work to change lifelong habits that are driven by unconscious wishes and fears.

When individuals threaten homicide or suicide, or engage in child abuse, their behaviors must be blocked forcibly by others. When such themes are discussed in therapy, the therapist has a dual role. He or she is the patient's advocate, but also has responsibilities to society at large. The therapist must be ready and willing to engage in active crisis management that blocks imminent suicide, homicide, or child abuse. These issues have been briefly mentioned earlier in the section on crisis management.

More subtle blocking of maladaptive behaviors occurs throughout therapy. Implicit blocking of maladaptive patterns occurs whenever the therapist engages in correct interventions. Maladaptive process is enjoined as the therapist enhances collaboration, teaches about maladaptive patterns, enables the will to change, or teaches new patterns.

In addition to the rare instances of coercive blocking and the many instances of implicit blocking, the therapist can actively help the patient inhibit undesired patterns for brief periods of time. This commonly happens as the patient and therapist struggle against the "it" that acts out. For example, despite their wish to change, BPDs often feel urges to cut themselves, to attack their lovers, or to overdose. At these times, they can collaborate with their therapists to resist the temptations. The basic approach is to remind such a patient that these destructive urges do make sense, given the BPD's history. The therapy plan is to "rewrite history" by working hard during sessions. Between sessions, there need to be techniques that help the BPD inhibit the urge to regress. Together, the therapist and patient can construct a list of suicide-inhibiting distractions. These may include such activities as calling a friend, reading a trashy novel, renting a video, taking a walk to a favorite place, and so on. There also has to be a backup plan, such as calling the therapist or the emergency room if these techniques do not suffice. Such distractions will only work only on a short-term basis and only if there is a trusted agreement that the underlying issues will receive full attention at the next appointment. If the collaboration between patient and therapist against "it" does not continue to grow during successive appointments, the defense of distraction will fail.

Paradoxical interventions offer another technique for blocking undesirable patterns. For example, when a patient announces a plan to kill his or her father, the therapist can say (provided that there is a strong collaborative relationship), "Well, that ought to make him love you!" Such comments serve to direct awareness to exploration of the underlying issues of pain, helplessness, and hunger for parental affirmation. It is not possible to review here principles for using paradoxical interventions. This mode is very powerful, and it is also very dangerous. Briefly, paradoxical interventions (Watzlawick, Beavin, & Jackson, 1967) always involve more than one message (described by complex SASB codes). One part of the message is in alliance with the patient, and the other is hostile to the "it." To be constructive, the target of the hostile aspects of the message must be "it," the maladaptive patterns. The target must not be the patient himself or herself. When the paradoxical message is directed at the patient's sense of reality—at the patient as a separate and decent human being—it is destructive (Bateson, Jackson, Haley, & Weakland, 1956; Wynne, Ryckoff, Day, & Hirsch, 1958).

Addressing Underlying Fears and Wishes

Underlying fears can be addressed in many ways. Conscious "insight" is not required. But somehow the patient must learn that what he or she fears is no longer a threat, or that what he or she wants is no longer wanted. An illustration of two different ways to address underlying fears is offered by a case of a child with a bath phobia, treated by psychoanalytic play therapy (Fraiberg, 1959, pp. 172–176). The analyst heard from the mother that on the day before fear of the bath began, the child had carefully watched the water disappear down the drain, and then had thrown her teddy bear in the toilet. It seemed that the child had concluded that since water disappeared down the drain, she would too. As she gave baths to various toys during play therapy, the child learned that large objects do not go down the drain with the water, and so the bath phobia disappeared.

Alternatively, this child's fear of baths might have been extinguished by the behavioral technique of desensitization. By this approach, the child also might eventually have come to understand that she would not go down the drain. Either therapy could work. Both would mitigate the child's fear that she would disappear down the drain.

Every Psychopathology Is a Gift of Love.   The path to the unconscious wishes that underlie personality disorders is built on the assumption that *every psychopathology is a gift of love*. Maladaptive patterns are driven by wishes that internalized other persons will offer love, approval, forgiveness, apologies, admiration, reparation, and so on. It may seem absurd to suggest that behaviors such as self-mutilation, or social avoidance, and depression are "acts of love." But if the world is seen from the perspective of the patient, it is not absurd. From the subjective perspective, the adaptation through disorder amounts to saying to the internalized oppressor, "I love and respect you so much I will be like you." Or "I love and respect you so much I will treat myself as you do." Or "Please know that I affirm you by my actions; love me in return." When the disorder represents an effort to come closer to the destructive figure, then successful treatment will require differentiation from that figure. A simple example of the importance of helping the patient disengage from the internal representation of a destructive but much-loved internalized person follows.

A 19-year-old woman came to the hospital following a traumatic breakup and reconciliation with her boyfriend. She had a long history of depression and drug abuse. The patient was very close to her depressed mother, a "saint" who had been beaten and then abandoned by her unfaithful alcoholic husband. The father, who had many achievements to his credit, demanded excellent school performance from the patient. He ignored the fact that she was overwhelmed with the job of managing the household and her siblings. Her mother, his ex-wife, had become nonfunctional. The father conveyed that he cared a lot about the patient. He had much to say about who and how the patient should be. However, he was not personally available to help the patient, because he was very devoted to his new wife. The patient lamented that her father "lives in his own world. If things are not his way, he doesn't let them in."

Earlier in the interview, the patient indicated that she wanted to have her father realize what a mistake he had made in leaving his first wife and children. She wanted him to return so that the happy family life of her childhood could be recreated. She ruminated angrily about all of her father's former infidelities and abuses. Toward the end of the session, the interviewer focused on her wish to recreate the family.

P: I know there's a God somewhere.

I: What do you think that God thinks about all this?

P: I don't want to know.

I: You afraid to know?

P: Yeah, kind of. I know it's okay. But I don't know how long it will be okay.

I: How long you can be forgiven? When you have to cut the mustard?

P: Yeah.

I: Well, your dad's pushed it for a long time.

P: Yeah. (*Cries*) But then again (*unintelligible*), when I was little, I asked my mom, "Mom, if Daddy dies, will he take over God's place?"

I: What did she say?

P: She just laughed at me and said "No."

I: As you're talking, I keep visualizing the story of Jack and the beanstalk. Do you know that story?

P: Kinda.

I: This little kid and this giant beanstalk. At the top of it is this monster man, very scary. The little kid ends up cutting the beanstalk down, bringing him down.

P: I just wish I could bring him back to reality at this point. Or at least to the same reality so it's a happy medium. I'm not sure that there's going to be . . .

I: Well what will his *other* wife think?

P: She hates me and I hate her. But he's chosen her for his wife.

I: Who's going to win? You or her?

P: I don't know. So far, she's won. But I haven't gave up, quite yet.

I: I see.

P: Close enough, but not all the way.

I: So leaving her to him would be a defeat for you?

P: Oh, *definitely*. Definitely. She has this thing that children or kids don't need as much nourishing as the wife. Like with her kids . . . [The patient tells a story about the new wife neglecting her own three children, and about their self-destructive behaviors.]

I: So his [new wife's son] destiny was to go down in flames to try to get her attention, but what happened was he got burned up.

P: Yeah. At least that's my opinion on it.

I: How about you? How do you interpret your getting into such trouble?

P: It might be a little bit to get attention. But all I want to do is hide. I never—I wanted what was taken from me. And I never knew how to get it back. There really is no way to get it back. It's done and over with now. It's where the pain and hurt is. . . .

I: Well, I'll tell you what I think. I think you can't fix your father. I don't think you're big enough to fix him.

P: I just wish I was. (*Cries a while*) Maybe I'll get big some day. I won't just be the big kid. I'll be the adult. I'll be able to be—I'll be able to say, "This is your corner. Stay out of mine."

I: Well, what would do that?

P: I don't know. Maybe I—I don't know. Maybe someday . . . I'll know.

[The interview was interrupted at this point by a medical student who announced that the patient had another appointment. So the interviewer focused on constructive aspects of the patient's current situation: the fact that the mom's new boyfriend was functioning for the patient "like the dad I never had"; the recent reconciliation with her own boyfriend; and the fact that the patient liked her job.]

I: Sounds like you've got some pretty good things going here. Your mom's stabilized, and she has a nice boyfriend. And you have a nice boyfriend.

P: Probably close to being the only two guys there is that I trust.

I: And you have something [the job] you'd like to do if you can get around to it on a day-to-day basis, right? So it sounds pretty good. If only you could let your father go.

P: How do I do that?

I: I think it will help if you get out your feelings—not as an end in itself—but getting out your feelings, saying to yourself, "Is he worth trashing my life over?"

P: Okay.

I: I don't think just getting the feelings out is the only work. It's get them out, and then use that to sort of assess the situation. See what's happening.

P: Please write it down so I can read it over a couple of times.

I: Okay. Is your father worth trashing your life over?

P: No.

I: You have to get that at a gut level.

P: Well, I think I don't want to lose him. I want to have my cake and eat it too.

I: Okay. But don't choke on it.

P: *I am.* There's no question but I'm choking on it.

In sum, this young woman's self-destructive pattern was clearly linked to her wish to retrieve the fantasy of a loving father. She hoped to resurrect the happy and intact family of origin that she remembered. Her drug abuse and suicidality were gifts of love. She was aware that the likelihood of getting her father back to the original family was very small, but she could not let the dream fade. She needed to learn to differentiate from her father, and to stop loving him in her self-destructive way.

The first level of expression of wishes is often hostile. For example, revenge is a common organizing wish. NEGs, BPD, AVDs, NPDs, PARs, and ASPs can all verbalize the hope that they can punish, inflict pain, wreak revenge, or torture selected others. Nonetheless, the love beneath the hostility can be uncovered if the therapist looks for it. Consider the patient who contemplates murdering his or her father. The therapist can ask, "And then what?", looking for the love beneath. The nature of the answer will vary, depending on the structure of the disorder. Maybe the patient hopes for a fantasied scene of reconciliation in heaven or hell. Maybe he or she envisions a rescued and grateful mother as the father falls in a bloody heap. Maybe the murder will realize the father's lifelong demands that the patient "grow up." The present thesis is that underneath such statements as "I hate him," there is a residue of attachment to someone important.

If patterns are maintained by underlying wishes and fears, then it follows that the turning point in the treatment of a personality disorder is the point when the patient *chooses* to give them up. A successful treatment of the personality disorder must transform the patient's will to be true to unconscious wishes and fears. The subject of will has typically not been a legitimate topic for scientific inquiry. Since music is the metaphor used in this book, the "nonscientific" concept of will should not be a problem. However, the arts of music, medicine, and psychotherapy all have scientific components. Whether the study of mental disorder is a science or an art, it remains that if mental disorder is an adaptation, the patterns must have goals. And if disorders have goals, the therapist must be free to think about and discuss them. By contrast, an auto mechanic does not have to think about the goals of the car he or she is working on. Unless a psychotherapist wants to think that he or she is fixing a broken machine, he or she needs to consider the goals and purposes of the patient. If the disorder is adaptive, then the associated wishes and fears must be addressed if the patterns of the disorder are to be changed. The most important and the most difficult task in reconstructing a personality disorder is to help the patient *decide* to give up old wishes and defy primitive fears.

If it is argued that wishes and fears organize personality disorders, then it follows that patients in some way or other choose to continue having the disorders. Recognition of that possibility should not lead to blaming patients. Patients have heard such versions of blame many times over, and changes in their patterns will not arise from repetition of old themes such as the following:

> You're just feeling sorry for yourself.
> Pull yourself together and snap out of it.
> Do you want something to feel sorry for?
> Be responsible.
> Grow up.
> You have let the devil take over.
> This is what you get for not doing as you were told.
> You never were any good.
> You must like this, or you would do something about it.

The practical therapist acknowledges that it is not known why a given individual, with some forces pushing him or her in one direction and some pushing in another, chooses to go in any one of them. The present argument is that it is realistic and effective to assume that the decision *is* in the hands of the patient. For example, an acutely suicidal patient ultimately decides to commit suicide or not. Medications can affect that decision, but they do not determine it. Therapist interventions can affect that decision, but they do not determine it. A skilled therapist knows a great deal about increasing the probabilities of blocking a suicide, but he or she does not control the "bottom line." The patient does.

Nor should families be blamed for personality disorders. Unfortunately, some psychotherapists have concluded that good therapy includes "getting out the anger" at the parents. The present view is that blaming either patients or families is likely to enhance pathological baseline patterns. Trashing patients, parents, or other important figures does not belong to one of the five categories of correct therapist response.

On the other hand, blaming "it" can block maladaptive patterns. For example, assigning responsibility to the adult member of an incestual relationship can appropriately relieve the patient of crippling guilt, and open the path to healthy differentiation. Eventually, after differentiation is well under way, the patient may be able to express genuine (not coerced) sympathy and compassion for the abusing parent in relation to his or her own dilemmas.

The Therapist Who Acknowledges Impotence Is More Effective. If the therapist recognizes his or her own impotence in confronting the patient's will, he or she will have more power to help that person choose to change. Once the patient has *decided*—either suddenly and deliberately, or slowly and less consciously—to clear away the old underbrush, the process of personal growth can begin. Through consistent supportive focus on the quintessence of interactive patterns, their roots, and their interpersonal purposes, the therapist can maximize the patient's option to decide to change.

Knowing Prototypic Wishes for the Respective Personality Disorders Is Helpful. The psychotherapist who has a good guess about the underlying wishes and fears of a disorder is more likely to discover what is driving the patterns for an individual patient. A map that shows the approximate location of buried treasure improves the chances of finding it. A "map" of the wishes likely to be found in the various personality disorders is given here.

BPD (Chapter 5): Whenever I was alone and vulnerable you raped me, as you told me it felt good. Now I need you (or your stand-in) to be with me and take care of me so that I will never be alone again.

NPD (Chapter 6): You must keep "mainlining" your unfounded opinion about how wonderful I am.

HPD (Chapter 7): You must take care of and admire me as you promised you always would.

ASP (Chapter 8): I could never count on you for anything but hassle, so I'll make sure I am always in charge or out of reach.

DPD (Chapter 9): You must take care of everything for me. You do it so well, and I do it so badly.

OCD (Chapter 10): You must love me because I have everything in perfect order.

NEG (Chapter 11): You gave the other kids all kinds of goodies, while I had to do an unfair share of the housework. Admit you were wrong and make it up to me.

AVD (Chapter 12): You reject and degrade me beyond measure, but I yearn for and await your love and acceptance.

PAR (Chapter 13): You were monstrously abusive, and now I am just like you to my loved ones. This proves I love you, so please love me.

SZT (Chapter 14): I will take care of you, but because I am supposedly so evil and powerful, I will keep my distance as I do.[7]

These prototypic statements will vary with individuals, but the general ideas are sketched as they develop in logical relation to the hypothesized pathogenic histories. As these agendas unfold in the therapy, it gradually becomes clear that the patient will have to do something to change these plans for how things should be. The BPD will have to divorce the abuser and dare to leave him to die from a broken heart. The HPD will need to risk becoming competent. The NEG will have to abandon the wish for restorative love. The OCD will have to take the risk to see whether anyone will warm up to imperfection. The ASP will have to count on somebody to come through. The DPD will have to chance trying to do it himself or herself, and trying again. And so on.

The Patient Must Be Supported in Challenging Destructive Wishes.   The preceding descriptions of organizing wishes and fears for the personality disorders may seem oversimplified. If that's all there is, one might argue, why don't people just discuss it, change it, and get on with it? The truth is that challenging these patterns invokes vulnerability comparable to a leap out the window of a tall building. Patients have little certainty that such moves can even be survived, much less that they will lead to anything better. The process of daring to risk these changes is slow and frustrating. A patient must decide when to walk on a bed of red-hot coals.

Stages of grief may follow the decision to give up the old ways and to transform the relationships with the persons (or their internalizations) associated with the wishes and fears. These stages can resemble the bereavement process described by Kübler-Ross (1969). Her theory has not been universally accepted as valid, but the stages she has described do seem to be played out to varying degrees in psychotherapy. In a sense, giving up old hopes compares to detaching from a failed love relationship. There is grief over the loss of a "loved one."

The comparison of giving up old wishes and fears to grief work is as follows. At first there is denial that there is any problem at all. Then, when it becomes clear that the present patterns, wishes and fears are not working and never will, there is angry protest or despair. One hears exclamations such as these: "Why did this have to happen to me? I can't stand it because this means I've wasted so much of my life already. Others didn't have to go through this; why did I? I don't believe this. It makes me furious." The final stage consists of reconciliation and acceptance of the need to move on.

---

[7]SOI is not included in this list because there are no known wishes associated with this diagnosis. See Chapter 14 for a discussion.

Before reconciliation and acceptance are achieved, however, the decision to change may result in panic and chaos. Patients say, in effect, "If I am not this, then I don't exist." Being in a massively new and unstructured state is typically terrifying (Kepecs, 1978). For example, one BPD had a professional degree, but had functioned marginally in her work. The problem was usually that dramatic crises with her lovers and friends took time away from work. After some time in therapy, she decided to develop new friends and to give up relating through misery and neediness. As she contemplated this new adjustment of enjoying friends and doing well at work, she could not sit still. Pacing around the therapist's office, she gave a 20-minute monologue quoting from her father and brothers: "Don't go to college. Go to teachers' college, that's what girls do. Get married and have children. That will make us happy and that will make you happy too. You think you are so smart, but you will find out you are not. You won a contest? That's a fluke. Don't worry, you couldn't do it a second time." And so on.

After delivering this monologue, the patient cried for a long time. Then, for the first time, she spoke of her feeling that her "craziness" was something she was "supposed" to do. She had not been allowed to be her strong self. That evening she asked for an emergency session because she felt she was "going crazy." During the emergency session, she discussed how terrifying it was to let go of the old ideas, and how they were "making a last stand." She spoke of the myth of Icarus, whose father gave him wax wings and warned him not to go too high, or else the sun would melt the wax on his wings. Icarus ignored the warning, flew too high, melted his wings, crashed, and died. The patient was convinced she was a modern version of Icarus and doomed. Her terror seemed untouchable until the therapist interpreted the myth as a product of a jealous introject, and suggested that myths might reflect family dynamics as easily as vice versa. When the patient reinterpreted the myth as a parallel to her own family and intrapsychic learning, she saw a chance to defy the myth and be free. Her panic had been caused by fear of defying the introjects of her father and brothers.

This transition stage is not always as dramatic and focused as in the Icarus case. Whether it is abrupt or gradual, people will say such things as this: "I don't know who I will be now. I feel very confused. I feel like I won't exist if I give up my old ways." Mysterious physical symptoms (e.g., tingles all over the body, heat flashes, shudders) are not unusual. Physical changes associated with this stage of profound reorganization are illustrated by a segment from a session with a man who had been passive aggressive. He was changing from a resentful, dependent, critical, and depressed character to a more spontaneous, enthusiastic, considerate, and nurturant person. He no longer ruminated about what people were not doing for him, and had begun to accept the positive feedback that was due for his many strengths. His boss had recently been very pleased with him.

P: I was disoriented to have [boss] treat me as a person this morning. It makes me feel so anxious. I remember experiences as a kid, dissociative episodes, like I'd be in my bedroom and my parents would have a party downstairs. I felt so extremely alone and anxious. I'd have restless legs and I'd pace the bedroom. The anxiety was unbearable, and the room would get huge and boundless, and I would feel like a tiny little thing. I walked and paced and listened to the party and tried to get oriented and I couldn't. It was very frightening. I have glimpses of that now and then. I feel that real basic anxiety . . . I'm not sure where I am, I feel really lost.

T: It sounds like you feel quite alone right now.

P: Yes.

T: And it feels like you might be at a choice point. If you can stay with the anxiety and endure it and find a new way now, you'd have a chance to change things, but there may be a strong draw to scurry back into the old patterns and deal with the anxiety in the old way. [The patient had just discussed an episode wherein he angrily screamed in an effort to get control of the family and deal with his anxiety.]

P: Do you know, my interference—the static that's always in my ear—has left. It is just *gone*. There's a real acceptance of being alone, of giving up perceiving things as I saw them as I grew up. You know, I think I might be more comfortable if you would attack me and put me down. I could be sullen and could hate you, and now with the way you are, I'm really at a loss.

T: Are you still feeling that same anxiety?

P: Yes.

T: It seems like you are in unfamiliar territory. You don't know what to expect. Maybe things feel out of control.

P: Yes, they're very out of control. I don't know what emotions will come up. I can see I'd want to retreat to discomfort and paranoia. It would be a lot safer. I feel really lost. I'm out to sea. I think I should be back home.

During this stage of lack of self-definition, the therapist's influence should be confined to helping the patient avoid regression; the therapist should not attempt to structure what to do next. Steady therapist reassurance that the disorientation or depression is a normal part of reconstructive change will stabilize patients who otherwise frequently fear that they have uncovered a basic underlying psychosis. Of course, there must be an accurate differentiation between this normative reconstructive event and a psychotic decompensation.

Facilitating New Learning

When the patient is coming out of the panic and chaos, his or her sense of self as different becomes more apparent. Besides protecting the patient against regression, the therapist functions now like a midwife or a gardener. The seed is in a good medium, and the new identity emerges. The following examples illustrate how various patients reconstructed SELF-AFFIRM.

One patient said, "I feel much better after last time. I see it so differently. I feel so differently. The expectations I had of myself were so burdensome. Now I'll just go ahead and enjoy and not worry about how I'm doing." This example shows how the affect changes with the cognition.

A patient who was no longer chronically suicidal said, "We talked about this before, but now my depression doesn't seem so mysterious. It seems clear why some scenes are so loaded. I just have to fight it out, but I don't feel there is something I don't know, like it's a total mystery." The depression lifted as the patient no longer felt helplessly victimized by her feelings.

A formerly chronically depressed patient who had learned to control her severe migraine headaches wrote, "What amazes me over and over again is the discovery, or revelation, that something I talked about or learned there [in therapy] has become a part of me, as if through some sort of osmosis some very different perspectives and feelings have become a more integral part of how I perceive and react to things." This patient's description of restructuring and introjection of the therapy process was especially direct.

After a visit to her family of origin, a patient wrote, "I used to think of childhood as freedom. But more and more it seems like the child is the trap. I need to find out what it is to be adult. Just need to keep the faith to believe things are changing and I don't have to go back. I am really interested in the changes inside me which I can feel. It's real. I don't know just what it is. It is a matter of taking it in stages. The faith that the other side is better. Before, I didn't see that at all."

Another wrote, "After all, I have felt confident in my ability to handle whatever comes up, using your principles about autonomy and control in particular, and I have been amazingly unburdened by self-doubt and depression through some rather difficult challenges."

A patient who had been chronically anxious and hypochondriacal described some stressful situations she had handled well. "A year ago I would have freaked. I would have just started eating. But now I just say, 'I did what I did and it was okay. Let it be.' I walk more slowly, more self-assuredly."

One of the more poignant and profound reflections of a BPD was this: "It is hard for me to look back and see the person I was. I have to forgive myself a little bit."

These comments, which emerged during or after the reconstructive stage, describe both the feelings and physical symptoms of changes. There was new friendliness toward the self and others. Bonding and differentiation were both facilitated in these cases.

A FINAL WORD

The reconstructive learning therapist draws from a wide range of available therapies. Techniques of psychoanalysis, experiential therapy, family therapy, group therapy, drama therapy, educational therapy, behavior therapy, gestalt therapy, and others are appropriate. *Anything* that leads to one of the five correct categories (enhances collaboration, facilitates learning about patterns, mobilizes the will, blocks maladaptive patterns, and/or teaches new patterns) is legitimate.

The following observations were made by a woman who had suffered severe physical and sexual abuse from her father and her brothers for many years. They tell the story of therapy. She survived an extended period of severe suicidal depression. Before the therapy was complete, she had to move to a distant city. Periodically she wrote of her continued learning, especially when life events renewed old injuries. When her father became gravely ill, she wrote:

> I cannot seem to imagine, envision his fear and pain without despair and hopelessness of my own. . . . I think I'm much angrier, much sadder, and maybe lonelier than at any of the moments that I acknowledged before, that there is no one there, and there never will be, that he'll never change or make good what he did to me, will never "understand." He will never even know me at all. . . . He always expects the worst and curses everything and everyone he put his hopes in. He despairs and becomes enraged over what he sees as the imminent defeat and ruination of precisely those he supposedly supports. For all his talk about faith, I don't think he has even an ounce of faith in anything except disaster, maybe death.
>
> It's not easy being here, but virtually every difficult situation becomes an object lesson in what I've learned and it never fails to be a thrill when I am able not only to react differently, but with some work, to feel differently too. . . .
>
> I'm fascinated now with the apparent fact that I've never seriously considered the possibility of just removing myself from the blows of life. . . . All sorts of positive thoughts are forcing their way into my consciousness.

Nothing is more meaningful and healing than human beings peacefully sharing an utterly undefended, starkly realistic view of themselves and others. Like this person, many patients with personality disorders are truly gifted. The rewards of watching them release themselves from their cages is matched only by the simple but profound joy of watching a toddler discover play in freshly fallen snow, or a baby happily splashing in the tub.

PART TWO

DSM CLUSTER B, THE DRAMATIC, ERRATIC GROUP

5

Borderline Personality Disorder

"My misery is your command."

REVIEW OF THE LITERATURE

The "dramatic, erratic" cluster of diagnoses in DSM includes BPD, NPD, HPD, and ASP. Individuals eligible for these labels inspire chaos both in their lives and in the professional literature. Within this group, the diagnosis of BPD holds the attentional spotlight more than the others. In the first 2 years of its existence (1987, 1988), nearly 25% of the papers in the *Journal of Personality Disorders* were specifically about BPD. Debate ranged over many topics, including diagnostic criteria, incidence and prevalence of BPD, comorbidity, and the treatment of self-mutilation and suicidality.

In addition to the overlap within DSM cluster B, BPD frequently shows "overlap" with Axis I. More often than not, these individuals suffer from depression and thought disorder. The frequency of overlap is so marked that some authors argue that BPD is itself a form of mood disorder (Akiskal et al., 1985). Others suggest that it may be related to Schizophrenia (Kety, Rosenthal, Wender, Schulsinger, & Jacobsen, 1975; Blatt & Auerbach, 1988). In the DSM-III and DSM-III-R, the overlap between BPD and these symptoms from Axis I was not addressed. The DSM-IV Axis II work group has added criteria that more specifically address the symptoms of thought and mood disorders in BPD.

A very different view comes from a psychoanalytic contingent, which holds that BPD is not a form of mood disorder or thought disorder (Kernberg, 1975, 1984; Masterson, 1975). Their view is that BPD is a unique entity. In sum, BPD may be on the borderline of Schizophrenia or of affective disorder, or it may be unique. Whatever the category, BPDs often suffer from thought disorder, affective disorder, dissociative disorder, alcohol and substance abuse, eating disorder, and a variety of the anxiety disorders. For the BPD, everything that can go wrong has gone wrong. There are disorders in every domain of function: cognition, mood, and behavior.

When all is said and done, the factor that probably accounts for the extraordinary degree of concern and interest with this group is the impact its members have on health care providers. Groves (1981, p. 259) quoted Syndenham, who wrote in 1683: "All is caprice; they love without measure those whom they soon will hate." Their passionate intensity often focuses on the therapist. Groves elaborated: "Ruthlessly dependent, they fear the very closeness they seek, and drive people away with their anger and need" (p. 259). The physician's troubled reaction is an important diagnostic sign for BPD, Groves suggested.

DSM DEFINITION OF THE DISORDER

The DSM definition provides the starting point for the present analysis. The DSM specifies that the diagnosis of BPD can be made if an individual meets five of the criteria. Here and in the following chapters, DSM-III-R items (American Psychiatric Association, 1987) appear in **bold print**. Any changes introduced by the DSM-IV (American Psychiatric Association, 1991) appear in *italics*. (The item numbering used here is that of the DSM-IV. Original numbers in the DSM-III-R appear after **bold** items, in brackets.)

A pervasive pattern of instability of mood, interpersonal relationships, and self-image, beginning by early adulthood and present in a variety of contexts, as indicated by at least *five* of the following:

A pervasive pattern of instability of interpersonal relationships, self-image, affects, and control over impulses beginning by early adulthood, and present in a variety of contexts, as indicated by at least five of the following:

(1) frantic efforts to avoid real or imagined abandonment (Do not include suicidal or self-mutilating behavior covered in [5].) [item 8 in DSM-III-R]

(2) a pattern of unstable and intense interpersonal relationships characterized by alternating between extremes of overidealization and devaluation [item 1 in DSM-III-R]

(3) marked and persistent identity disturbance manifested by uncertainty about at least two of the following: self-image, sexual orientation, long-term goals or career choice, type of friends desired, preferred values [item 6 in DSM-III-R]

identity disturbance: persistent and markedly disturbed, distorted, or unstable self-image and/or sense of self (e.g., feeling like one doesn't exist or embodies evil)

(4) impulsiveness in at least two areas that are potentially self-damaging, e.g., spending, sex, substance use, shoplifting, reckless driving, binge eating (Do not include suicidal or self-mutilating behaviors described in [5].) [item 2 in DSM-III-R]

(5) recurrent suicidal threats, gestures, or behavior, or self-mutilating behavior [item 5 in DSM-III-R]

(6) affective instability: marked shifts from baseline mood to depression, irritability, or anxiety, usually lasting a few hours and only rarely more than a few days [item 3 in DSM-III-R]

affective instability; marked reactivity of mood, e.g., intense episodic dysphoria, irritability, or anxiety, usually lasting a few hours and only rarely more than a few days

(7) chronic feelings of emptiness or boredom [item 7 in DSM-III-R]

Chronic feelings of emptiness

(8) inappropriate, intense anger or lack of control of anger, e.g., frequent displays of temper, constant anger, recurrent physical fights [item 4 in DSM-III-R]

(9) *transient, stress-related psychotic-like experiences, e.g., paranoid ideation, depersonalization, derealization, hypnogogic illusions [new item]*

Morey (1988) reported that 33.3% of a sample of 291 outpatients being treated for personality disorder qualified for the BPD label. There was substantial overlap with HPD (36.1%), AVD (36.1%), DPD (34%), PAR (32%), and NPD (30.9%).

PATHOGENIC HYPOTHESES

An important goal of this book is to offer interpersonal and intrapsychic "translations" of the criteria listed by DSM. In addition, the SASB predictive principles are used to generate hypotheses about pathogenic social factors that enhance those interpersonal and intrapsychic "symptoms." The resulting dimensional analysis of the personality disorders is used to describe expected transference reactions in psychotherapy and to recommended psychosocial treatment approaches. In the chapters that follow, this approach is repeated for each disorder in Axis II of the DSM.

I have used the following method to develop the interpersonal dimensional analyses of each of the personality disorders: (1) transforming the DSM-III-R and DSM-IV criteria into the categories of the SASB cluster model (Figure 3.9); (2) doing the same with the DSM-III and DSM-III-R casebook examples (Spitzer et al., 1981, 1989); (3) assessing the dimensionality of the behaviors and histories of clinical cases I have known; (4) identifying the predictive principles that connect[1] the SASB codes in the histories to the SASB codes of the disorders; and (5) identifying the key psychosocial transference and treatment issues implied by the dimensional analysis.

The first three steps in this procedure can be operationalized and checked[2] for reliability, but the other two cannot. I hope readers will find that the pathogenic hypotheses are useful in understanding their own patients. If they do, then

---

[1]The predictive principles were invoked by retrospective, not prospective, logic. I do not know why the individual sometimes maintains the same role through childhood (recapitulate complementarity), and sometimes changes to identify with the aggressor (invokes similarity). Similarly, I can only guess why some people in the child's world affect the introject and others do not. For this book, I have identified parallels and deduced which SASB principle must have applied. From a scientific point of view, this process is only an initial stage in formulating important research questions. In the few years remaining before I reach retirement, I hope to secure funds that will permit formal research study of the ideas in this book.

[2]My friend and colleague Marjorie H. Klein contracted with another, Laura Lynn Humphrey, to SASB-code the interpersonal descriptions as they appear in the WISPI, a personality inventory based on the present approach to the Axis II disorders. The resulting kappas were mostly above the minimally acceptable level of .60 (Hartmann, 1977).

the resulting clinical consensus can serve as an initial validating step for the overall approach.

Causality is defined if there are reliable linkages between antecedent and consequent conditions (Hume, 1748/1947). If psychosocial factors have a pathogenic role, then there needs to be a description of childhood antecedents to BPD. The social learning that sets up BPD patterns must be identified. Of course, any impact of these childhood experiences is moderated by the child's genetically given temperament. There is no attempt in this book to define the interaction between temperament and prototypical childhood experiences. That also is a very important research question.

A main thesis of this book is that the interpersonal structure of early experience is related to the interpersonal structure of the adult patterns. This book does *not* presume to offer a catalogue of generic early experiences (e.g., incest, physical abuse, or parental divorce) that can be related to adult personality disorders. Instead, the thesis is that the dimensional analysis of the individual's early experience corresponds to the interpersonal dimensionality of the adult patterns. The argument is not that specific experiences are associated with specific disorders. Rather, the specific *dimensionality* of early experiences is associated with the *dimensionality* of the various personality disorders.

Suppose, for example, that a boy defends against family chaos by spending much time alone in the woods. The code WALL OFF describes his preferred response to stress. However, as an adult he may not continue to do it by spending time in the woods; rather, the continuation of the pattern may be seen in his work habits. Perhaps he chooses to take two full-time jobs, working so much that he cannot spend time at home. Wandering in the woods as a boy and overworking as a family provider do not seem to be the same. They do have a strong link, however, because in both examples his relationship to the family is coded WALL OFF. The SASB labeling allows the clinician to see connections that might not otherwise be explicit.

The example of spending time alone in the woods is unlikely to apply to BPD. Instead, the developmental hypothesis for BPD is that the patterns were set by a painful and yet erotic incestual relationship. The assessment does not suggest that every BPD is an incest victim, or that every incest victim will become a BPD. Rather, the thesis is that any developmental experience that has the dimensionality described below for BPD will lead to characteristic adult patterns. *Incest happens to be a common, but not the only, way to generate the requisite structure for BPD.*

Readers who do not have the time to learn the SASB principles will nevertheless be able to recognize the BPD patterns. They may also find the treatment suggestions to be useful. Readers who do have time to understand the SASB labels and principles will have a tool to help extend the analysis in this chapter to cases where there was not a painful/erotic incestual relationship. Knowledge of SASB coding and the predictive principles can help clinicians see the characteristic BPD patterns in histories that did not include incest.

Table 5.1. Interpersonal Summary of BPD

History	Consequences of history
1. Chaotic, soap opera lifestyle	1. Crises sought, created; no constancy
2. Traumatic abandonment (**IGNORE** → **ATTACK**)	2. Abandonment sets off the "program" (*SELF-NEGLECT* and *SELF-ATTACK*).
Incest prototype sets the patterns:	The structure of incest is repeated:
Pain (<u>RECOIL</u>) plus love (<u>REACTIVE</u> <u>LOVE</u>)	Fuses pain and love
Helplessness (<u>SUBMIT</u>) and omnipotence (**CONTROL**)	Helpless and omnipotent (**CONTROL**)
Modeled idealization (<u>TRUST</u>, **ACTIVE LOVE**) and devaluation (**BLAME**), reckless coercion (**ATTACK**)	Idealizes (<u>TRUST</u>, **ACTIVE LOVE**) and devalues (**BLAME, ATTACK**)
3. Self-definition (<u>SEPARATE</u>), happiness (<u>REACTIVE</u> <u>LOVE</u>), were attacked.	3. Internalizes attack for doing well (*SELF-ATTACK*)
4. Sickness (<u>TRUST</u>) elicited nurturance (**PROTECT**)	4. Escalates sickness (<u>TRUST</u>) to receive care (*SELF-PROTECT*)

Summary: There is a morbid fear of abandonment and a wish for protective nurturance, preferably received by constant physical proximity to the rescuer (lover or caregiver). The baseline position is friendly dependency on a nurturer, which becomes hostile control if the caregiver or lover fails to deliver enough (and there is never enough). There is a belief that the provider secretly if not overtly likes dependency and neediness, and a vicious introject attacks the self if there are signs of happiness or success.

SASB codes of BPD baseline: **CONTROL, BLAME, ATTACK, ACTIVE LOVE,** <u>TRUST</u>, *SELF-ATTACK, SELF-NEGLECT,* and *SELF-PROTECT. Wishes:* To receive **PROTECT.** *Fears:* To receive **IGNORE.** *Necessary descriptors:* Fear of abandonment, handled by transitive coercion of protection and nurturance; self-sabotage following happiness or success. *Exclusionary descriptors:* Tolerance of aloneness on a long-term basis.

Four main features of the developmental history have been identified specifically to account for each of the BPD symptoms listed in the DSM. A summary of the hypotheses linking interpersonal history to interpersonal patterns characteristic of the disorder appears in Table 5.1. A fuller discussion of these hypotheses is provided here.

1. Chaos prevailed in the family. A disaster a day provided a template for a veritable soap opera. Examples of "routine" crises may have included terrible fights, affairs, abortions, infidelity, drunken acting out, suicide attempts, murders, imprisonment, disowning, and illicit births. Without these dramas, life was hollow, empty, and boring. The BPD often occupied center stage in all of this. Perhaps she[3] had the responsibility for keeping an explosive and dangerous alcoholic parent calm. Possibly the "privilege" associated with her unacknowledged "wifely" position made her a target of jealous other family members. Still another possible blueprint is that she was a scapegoat, being assigned responsibility for the mother's divorce from her husband (the patient's stepfather). Some-

---

[3]BPD is much more prevalent in females, perhaps because they are more often subject to incestual abuse. For this reason, I use feminine pronouns in this chapter to refer to a BPD. However, males can be incestually abused too. If their incest has the dimensionality described in this chapter, they should meet the criteria for BPD.

times the BPD was the center of the abusive incestual attentions of one or more brothers.

In a small percentage of families of BPDs, the chaos was not visible to the naked eye. The family may have appeared to be intact, but there was chaos somewhere. Perhaps there was incestual abuse by a brother, confined to the 2 hours between the time school was out and when the parents came home. Perhaps it was only in the middle of the night when the father made an incestual visit. Perhaps the chaos was only "behind closed doors," as parents argued chronically and audibly about how the birth of the BPD had ruined their lives.

Blatant or sequestered, the chaos, the high stakes, and the central role of the BPD lead her to expect and generate rapid, unpredicted change—for high stakes. Feeling empty and bored in the absence of crisis, she was drawn to trouble as an alcoholic is drawn to drink. Constancy was out of the question. The soap opera lifestyle set the stage for the "pervasive instability of mood, interpersonal relationships, and self-image" described by the DSM. Impulsiveness, angry outbursts, and shifts from idealization to devaluation were also modeled within the chaos itself.

2. The developmental history included traumatic abandonment experiences. The abandonment may have included many hours or days of being left alone without appropriate protection, companionship, or materials for constructive activities. This time was unspeakably boring and dull. An example would be the BPD's being left alone locked in a room for most of the days, while the mother was out with a boyfriend. Other possible findings in the histories of BPDs include being locked in a dark basement for alleged crimes, or being available for use in sexual or abusive religious rituals.

The isolation associated with abandonment was dangerous. There was constant danger of sudden intrusion accompanied by major abuse. For example, the child chained in the basement may have been visited unpredictably by the cult and used in sexual or religious rituals. Alternatively, older siblings may have invaded the basement to sexually abuse the child who was being punished by isolation there. Still another possible scenario is that an alcohol-dependent relative, who was supposed to be the caregiver, alternated between caring and abusing. Some BPDs were victimized by incestual attack from brothers after school, or in the evening when the parents had gone out. Another version is that aloneness in the bedroom at night made the BPD vulnerable to incestual visits from the father, as noted above.

The abuse-laden aloneness was inextricably linked with the idea that the BPD was a *bad person*. This belief may have been created by a statement to the effect that the mother left the family to go off with her new boyfriend because the BPD had been so bad. Perhaps the incestually abusing brothers conveyed the notion that the BPD was only sexual "practicing material," a convenient and altogether expendable "sexual dummy." Or maybe the idea was that the abusive rituals of the cult were performed on "deserving" victims. Perhaps the BPD was left with the abusing alcoholic relative because the other family members didn't want to take someone so despicable along with them on a vacation. Another means of making the link between "aloneness" and "bad person" might be the BPD's private belief that participation in the sequestered incest was in itself evidence for badness.

BPDs whose sexual abuse was painful are more likely to engage in self-mutilation. The reason is that there are many opportunities to confuse pleasure and pain during sexual abuse. The abuser may, for example, have been very loving during parts of the incestual attack. The "abuse" may have occurred only at the point of intercourse. The abuser may have felt loving, but the physical realities were that intercourse between a large male and a small, immature female (or anal intercourse with a small male) is painful. The jarring contrast between the loving intent of the abuser and the resulting pain for the victim is disorienting. Which message should the BPD internalize? Whereas some BPDs associate a context of erotic pleasure with pain, others "numb out," trying "not to feel." The former group will report erotization of self-mutilation. The latter are more likely to feel nothing as they self-mutilate.

The BPD's history with child abuse may also have directly instructed her in how to shift from idealization to devaluation. Early in the night visit, the father might say, "You are the light of my life; I live for these times together. Without you, I am totally lost." Then, after the incestual attack, he might say, "It's your fault. You bitch. You whore. You're filthy. Go take a shower." In a few minutes, the BPD may have gone from the peaks of idealization to the worst devaluation.

In addition, devaluation may have included injunctions against appropriate reality testing, which totally confused and disoriented the BPD. She received contradictory instruction about who she was, and about what was real and what was unreal. "Daddy hurt me. Daddy loves me and wouldn't hurt me. I am a good person. I am a bad person. Daddy adores me. Daddy is disgusted with me. He is so much bigger and I can't stop him. I can hurt Daddy if I tell. Daddy will hurt me if I tell. Daddy says it didn't hurt me. Daddy says don't cry because it feels good. Mommy says I am lying. Mommy says it didn't happen." And so on.

An incest victim, or a child at the center of a cult's rites, can at times have unacknowledged privilege and power over the perpetrator(s). This learning may have primed the BPD to interact with important figures in adulthood in ways that alternately suggest omnipotence and helplessness.

The fact that BPDs are likely to have a history of abuse has been noted by Carroll, Schaffer, Spensley, and Abramowitz (1980), and by others. But, as emphatically noted above, not all BPDs are overt incest victims, and not all incest victims are BPDs. There are many alternate versions of incest that do not set the pattern for BPD. These include incest without vaginal penetration; sexual invasion after the child is developed well enough not to be injured; incest that does not confuse pain and love; incest that does not mix helplessness and omnipotence; incest that does not involve switching from idealization to devaluation; and incestual encounters that do not disconfirm the BPD's perception of reality ("It doesn't hurt; it didn't happen").

3. Whereas physical or sexual abuse occurred when the BPD-to-be was alone and unprotected, the family norms also conveyed that autonomy was bad

and that dependency and sympathetic misery with the family were good. If the BPD wanted to find her own way in the world, she was disloyal. Such hurtful betrayal called for vengeful punishment. The message is likely to have been transmitted by direct verbal and physical attack for showing signs of happiness, competence, or self-confidence. "You think you are great because of *that*? Well, let me set the record straight. You're just a @#$@%@& kid, and when you get out in the world and try to make it without us, you'll find out what a @#$@#$@# kid you are." Another way to get the idea that autonomy was bad would be to see siblings severely abused for showing signs of independence or happiness outside the family.

The major consequence of abuse given in this context is that moves toward competence or happiness will elicit self-attack. Self-sabotage begins as soon as it becomes clear that school, a new job, a new relationship, or psychotherapy is going well. Whenever there promises to be increased health and happiness, the BPD will manifest some form of self-destruction. The undermining of self can appear as self-mutilation or suicidality, or as a precipitous decision to quit therapy, to leave a promising new relationship, to quit a good new job, or to withdraw from college. This pattern is also seen when a self-mutilative episode follows a therapy session during which patient and therapist discuss how well things have been going.

The self-sabotage can be started by one of two mechanisms:

a. The internalization of the abuser or of the jealous other parent or sibling implements revenge and inflicts pain, repeating the original experience. The BPD's goal in self-mutilating is to appease the part of the self that represents the attacker. The BPD unconsciously addresses the internalized attacker: "If you want me to feel pain, know that I do. I affirm and agree that I deserve punishment and suffering. Here is the evidence. Now you must know how much I love you, and you must love me too." This interpretation of self-mutilation as a positive act, as a "gift of love," is supported by the fact that BPDs often report they feel relieved after self-mutilation (Leibenluft, Gardner, & Cowdry, 1987). Something or someone has been pleased and appeased.

If the mutilation is not a "gift of love" to the attacker, it may be a form of self-affirmation. Some BPDs will say that self-mutilation reassures them that *something* is real. Their judgment has been undermined by shifting premises and mind-bending denials while engaged in intimate exchanges. These people find it reassuring to review the basic logic: "I cut on myself. It hurts. The hurt is real. I can find what is real. I can know it. Also, I can control it." In this way, the act of self-mutilation serves as an affirmation of reality testing.

Self-sabotage, whether it is done by physically or psychologically attacking the self, usually occurs in an orderly sequence. The prototype was carefully documented at the National Institute of Mental Health by debriefings of five self-mutilators (Leibenleaff et al., 1987). Each episode began with perceived abandonment (therapist too busy, husband inattentive, etc.). The sequence was as follows: devaluing of the defaulting caregiver, withdrawal, dissociation, devaluing of self, mutilation of self, and finally relief (see Benjamin, 1987b).

The cycle is self-perpetuating. When the BPD regresses at the brink of success, the therapist may begin to wonder about referral, or to detach in some other way. The spouse may begin to "burn out." At these signs of withdrawal, the BPD becomes more clingy and demanding, and this in turn inspires further wariness in the caregiver. The consequent shift of attentional focus away from the BPD will be seen as abandonment, and so the cycle repeats itself.

b. An alternative phenomenology accounting for the self-destruction in face of success may be this: "I am better, so you will kick me out of therapy." The idea of loss of the therapist is then read as abandonment, and the sequence just described is repeated. This alternative analyses of the consequences of improvement helps explain why events that in themselves do not imply abandonment can in fact set off the self-sabotaging sequence.

4. The BPD learns from the family that misery, sickness, and debilitation draw love and concern. Although abandonment was a major and real threat, parental nurturance nonetheless would be offered to the BPD when she was needy and miserable. BPDs will say, "The only time my mother was nice to me was when I was totally down." The adult consequence of this learning is that the BPD believes that the lover or caregiver secretly likes misery. This belief—combined with the history of receiving more nurturance when enfeebled, plus the need for self-sabotage when things are going well—sets the BPD on a course of ever-escalating symptomatology. "My misery is your command" summarizes the BPD's plan for the therapy or the marital process.

CONNECTIONS BETWEEN THE INTERPERSONAL HISTORY AND THE SYMPTOMS LISTED IN THE DSM

Not every symptom listed by the DSM is present in every case, and so not every early experience is present in every interpersonal history. If an aspect of the hypothetical history is missing, then its associated adult symptoms should also be missing. One of the case illustrations at the end of this chapter develops the point that departure from the diagnostic prototype is associated with a correspondingly different history.

The "total BPD" shows all the symptoms mentioned in the DSM. The abandonment is internalized, so that the BPD behaves very recklessly (DSM criterion 4, self-damaging impulsiveness). Internalization of neglect and its association with boring aloneness and danger lead also to feelings of emptiness, described by DSM criterion 7. Fear of abandonment, described by DSM criterion 1, comes from its association with trauma and bad personhood. The family devotion to chaos for high stakes accounts for the instability and intensity described by DSM criteria 2 and 6. The famous anger of the BPD, described in DSM criterion 8, is set off by perceived abandonment and is intended to coerce the opposite of abandonment—namely, nurturance. Self-mutilation, described in DSM criterion 5, is a replay of the abuse or an effort to appease an internalized attacker. Identity disturbance, described by DSM criterion 3, is a consequence of the internalization of objects who would attack the BPD when there were signs of differentiation or self-definition, and/or happiness. Self-sabotage amounts to self-protection from the internalized abusers. This short-circuiting of personal development comprises the BPD identity disturbance. Thought disorder, reflected in the new DSM criterion 9, may be the consequence of having reality testing negated: "What you think was hurt was pleasure. What you think happened didn't happen."

INTERPERSONAL SUMMARY OF BPD

The foregoing analysis suggests a succinct interpersonal summary for BPD:

There is a morbid fear of abandonment and a wish for protective nurturance, preferably received by constant physical proximity to the rescuer (lover or caregiver). The baseline position is friendly dependency on a nurturer, which becomes hostile control if the caregiver or lover fails to deliver enough (and there is never enough). There is a belief that the provider secretly if not overtly likes dependency and neediness, and a vicious introject attacks the self if there are signs of happiness or success.

The summary is based on the SASB codes of the BPD baseline patterns and wishes. The codes themselves, listed in Table 5.1, provide a shorthand way for identifying BPD. The baseline positions are: CONTROL, BLAME, ATTACK, ACTIVE LOVE, TRUST, SELF-ATTACK, SELF-NEGLECT, SELF-PROTECT. The wish is for PROTECT, and the fear is of IGNORE. These SASB labels are the notes of the BPD song.

The rhythm and harmonics of the BPD song are found in the sequences of interpersonal and intrapsychic response that the BPD gives and receives. The "tonic" BPD position is TRUST, and it harmonizes well with the caregiver's complementary position, PROTECT. The BPD rewards the caregiver with ACTIVE LOVE. That wonderful music is unstable, however, because the BPD is quick to perceive IGNORE. Once that happens, the BPD swings into CONTROL, BLAME, and ATTACK to try to force the return of PROTECT. These attempts to restore the tonic position are accompanied by SELF-ATTACK and reckless SELF-NEGLECT. The escalation of self-damaging behaviors and the hostile coercion of nurturance push the lover or caregiver toward the complex position of SUBMIT plus PROTECT. As the caregiver or lover complies with the demands to care and give more, the BPD takes over the relationship with the complementary position of CONTROL plus TRUST. This is especially likely to happen if the lover or caregiver responds to the BPD's BLAME with SULK and SELF-BLAME. It is not long before the lover or caregiver defensively shifts the focus back to the BPD and begins to BLAME her in one way or another. These are the harmonics and rhythms of the BPD song.

Readers who can use the SASB codes will be able to generalize the present analysis to contexts not mentioned here. For example, it is not unusual for patients to complain that their depression is getting worse. Sometimes those complaints are presented to the therapist in a way that is characteristic of BPD. To interpret a complaint about depression in this way, the therapist would need to code a patient's process as he or she describes the depression. A BPD's process with the therapist as she complains about symptoms would include the notes of the BPD song. An example would be the following:

A patient responded well to a prescription of an antidepressant (therapist **PROTECT**, patient TRUST). Then, as the depression re-emerged, the patient complained that the doctor wasn't monitoring the dosage closely enough, or that he failed to try a new wonder drug that her friend's doctor was prescribing these days (therapist **IGNORE**). The BPD disclosed reluctantly that she missed three important days of school (*SELF-NEGLECT*) and came very close to an overdose on this wrong regimen (BPD *SELF-ATTACK*, and **BLAME** the therapist). The therapist wrote a prescription for the new drug, and asked the patient to call every day to let him know how she was doing (SUBMIT plus **PROTECT**).

BPDs will abuse substances, engage in not-so-safe sex, play dangerous games with motor vehicles, and so on. They may "lose time" while engaging in these and other self-destructive activities. For a BPD, the recklessness and the losing time can be understood as "self-abandonment," or *SELF-NEGLECT*.[4] Strange as it may seem, recklessness is a form of *SELF-PROTECT*. Dissociation may have been learned during the original abuse. People who are tortured can find relief from overwhelming pain by "checking out," by leaving reality. The tendency to "lose time" when stressed is an old pattern of adaptation for BPD.

If the BPD does not escape through dissociation or altered states of consciousness accompanying drug abuse, the careless sex and so on can be seen as a version of "If you can't beat 'em, join 'em." If others have fun with the BPD's body and psyche without regard for the impact on her, she will too. In BPD, the self-injuring or self-indulgent behaviors have a quality of "socking it to oneself."

DSM DESCRIPTORS REVISITED

The DSM view of BPD has now been translated into interpersonal language, and the psychosocial learning associated with BPD patterns has been outlined. In this section, the interpersonal analysis of BPD is compared directly to the DSM. Here and in the following chapters, DSM-III-R items appear in **bold print**; any changes introduced by the DSM-IV appear in *italics*. (Again, the item numbering used is that of the DSM-IV.) The interpersonal modifiers are underlined. Items from the WISPI (discussed in Chapter 1) appear in CAPITAL LETTERS. Psychiatric residents have reported that if they read the WISPI items with a given

---

[4]Points 2, 3, 4, 5, 6, and 7 in the upper left-hand side of Table 3.6 provide a more detailed description of the meaning of *SELF-NEGLECT*.

patient in mind, they are able to imagine how the patient would answer. This "empathic cuing" helps the resident decide on the diagnosis, and this in turn provides access to the suggestions for treatment interventions.

A pervasive pattern of instability of mood, interpersonal relationships, and self-image, beginning by early adulthood and present in a variety of contexts, as indicated by at least *five* of the following:

A pervasive pattern of instability of interpersonal relationships, self-image, affects, and control over impulses beginning by early adulthood, and present in a variety of contexts, as indicated by at least five of the following:

(1) frantic efforts to avoid real or imagined abandonment (Do not include suicidal or self-mutilating behavior covered in [5].)

Quick to perceive abandonment. Sees lateness, changes in plans, vacations, absences— even if impossible to avoid—as abandonment, neglect, or rejection. Believes the "abandonment" amounts to an accusation that the subject is a "bad person."

IF SOMEONE IMPORTANT TO ME IS A FEW MINUTES LATE, I FEEL ABANDONED AND GO INTO A PANIC.

(2) a pattern of unstable and intense interpersonal relationships characterized by alternating between extremes of overidealization and devaluation

A love of intensity in relationship is shown by a desire to share very private information in great detail early in the history of the relationship. There are demands to spend large amounts of time together, and potential caregivers or lovers are idealized at the first or second meeting. However, the BPD switches easily and without reason from idealization of caregivers or lovers to devaluation. The caregiver's fall from grace is allegedly because he or she does not care enough, does not give enough, is not "there" enough. There is an ability to empathize with and nurture the caregiver, but this is accompanied by the expectation that in return, the caregiver will "be there" to fulfill a compelling dependency upon demand.

IF I LIKE SOMEONE I HAVE JUST MET, I WILL REVEAL THE MOST INTIMATE DETAILS ABOUT ALL OF MY TROUBLES RIGHT AWAY.

(3) marked and persistent identity disturbance manifested by uncertainty about at least two of the following: self-image, sexual orientation, long-term goals or career choice, type of friends desired, preferred values

identity disturbance: persistent and markedly disturbed, distorted, or unstable self-image and/ or sense of self, e.g., feeling like one doesn't exist or embodies evil

Identity disturbance is manifested by sudden changes in opinions and plans about career, sexual identity, values, and type of friends. There is a pattern of undermining self at the moment a goal is about to be realized. Examples include (1) withdrawing from school just before graduation; (2) regressing severely after a discussion about how well therapy is going; (3) behaving outrageously so that a long-sought-after good relationship is destroyed just when it was clear that the relationship could last and be good.

I HAVE A PATTERN OF DOING WELL IN SOMETHING IMPORTANT (SCHOOL, JOB, RELATIONSHIP) AND THEN SUDDENLY DROPPING IT ALTOGETHER.

(4) impulsiveness in at least two areas that are potentially self-damaging, e.g., spending, sex, substance use, shoplifting, reckless driving, binge eating (Do not include suicidal or self-mutilating behaviors described in [5].)

Impulsive behaviors are momentarily satisfying, but are also profoundly neglectful of the person's own best interests (in contrast to HPD impulsiveness, which is geared toward receiving some kind of affirmation from another person).

I RECKLESSLY GIVE IN TO URGES TO DO THINGS WHICH ARE SURE TO GET ME IN TROUBLE— LIKE GAMBLING, OVERSPENDING, SHOPLIFTING, OVEREATING, AND SO ON.

(5) recurrent suicidal threats, gestures, or behavior, or self-mutilating behavior

Set off by perceived abandonment in a predictable pattern: Perceived abandonment is followed by intense devaluation of self and of the allegedly abandoning other, and by social withdrawal. The escalating tension can be relieved temporarily by well-focused attack on the self, as in cutting, burning, overdosing, or the like. Once the suicidal ideation begins, the process that began with the interpersonal event of perceived abandonment becomes intrapsychic. Vicious internal thoughts (sometimes voices) irrationally demand that there be blood, pain, or bodily harm. There is temporary relief following that self-harm.

I LIKE TO BE INTIMATE WITH PEOPLE, AND IF I SENSE ANY REJECTION, I DELIBERATELY HURT MYSELF BY DOING SOMETHING LIKE CUTTING OR BURNING MYSELF. THEN I FEEL BETTER.

(6) affective instability: marked shifts from baseline mood to depression, irritability, or anxiety, usually lasting a few hours and only rarely more than a few days

affective instability; marked reactivity of mood, e.g., intense episodic dysphoria, irritability, or anxiety, usually lasting a few hours and only rarely more than a few days

This item is not interpersonal, and there are no interpersonal modifiers.

I CAN GET VERY ANXIOUS, DEPRESSED, OR IRRITABLE AND THEN FOR NO REASON SUDDENLY RETURN TO NORMAL.

(7) chronic feelings of emptiness or boredom

chronic feelings of emptiness

The BPD is easily bored and troubled by feelings of emptiness, and constantly seeks something interesting to do rather than just relaxing at home. The BPD seems uncomfortable if everything is calm and in order, and is often involved in a "soap opera scene." Disasters, crises, misery, horrible scenarios recur with uncanny regularity.

IF THINGS ARE GOING WELL FOR ME, IT DOESN'T TAKE MUCH TO GET ME FEELING HOLLOW, EMPTY, OR BORED.

(8) inappropriate, intense anger or lack of control of anger, e.g., frequent displays of temper, constant anger, recurrent physical fights

Anger is elicited when the caregiver or lover is seen as neglectful or abandoning, or there is doubt about whether the other person cares and gives enough. Anger is to control the caregiver—to make sure that he or she will provide the wished-for attention and caring.

I HAVE HUGE BLOW-UPS WITH PEOPLE OVER WHETHER THEY ARE TAKING GOOD CARE OF ME.

(9) transient, stress-related psychotic-like experiences, e.g., paranoid ideation, deperson-alization, derealization, hypnogogic illusions

Not interpersonal. No explicators. Codes of the thought disorder are likely to parallel codes of the prototypic abuse experience. BPD thought disorder is not associated with "weirdness," as it often is with Schizophrenia or SZT.

THERE ARE TIMES WHEN I CANNOT TELL WHAT IS REAL. I DON'T EVEN KNOW IF I AM REAL.

NECESSARY AND EXCLUSIONARY CRITERIA

The present analysis permits definition of necessary and exclusionary conditions for each personality disorder. For BPD, the recommended *necessary* descriptors are (1) a fear of abandonment that is handled by active focus on others, who are supposed to give the BPD protection and nurturance; and (2) self-sabotage for doing well or being happy. There is only one *exclusionary* consideration: long-term comfort with autonomy, as is seen in SOI, PAR, and NPD. A patient who shows such comfort cannot have the abandonment sensitivity characteristic of BPD.

Clinicians' use of these necessary and exclusionary conditions will reduce overlap with other personality disorders frequently confused with BPD. For examples, NPDs and HPDs also engage in transitive[5] coercions for nurturance, but they do not engage in internally driven self-sabotage. DPDs are also trust-ing and needy, but they do not engage in overt efforts to control the caregiver. NEGs share the BPD habit of controlling the caregiver in association with self-destructiveness. However, for BPDs self-attack is elicited by perceived abandon-ment, whereas NEGs are quite comfortable with autonomy. Like ASPs, BPDs are often careless with themselves and others. The difference in this case is that the BPDs' irresponsibility is fundamentally self-punitive, while the ASPs "sock it to others" as they engage in self-indulgent recklessness.

CASE ILLUSTRATIONS

Case 1

This 38-year-old woman entered the psychiatric system following plastic surgery to cor-rect severe facial disfigurement. There were several hospitalizations for making cuts on herself and for acute suicidality, always precipitated by therapist vacations, and accom-panied by splitting among staff members. Antidepressants were helpful in relieving her vegetative signs. On a regimen of three outpatient appointments a week, she managed to return to school and do reasonably well in selected courses. She had a number

---

[5]The distinction "transitive" and "intrasitive" is part of the formal SASB coding system mentioned in Chapter 3, footnote 8.

of personalities—some good at executive functioning, some consistently advising self-destruction and suggesting that she discontinue therapy.

There was a history of severe physical and sexual abuse by her father and by her siblings. Her mother was deceased, and her father was debilitated, and lived in a nursing home. She remained very attached to her many siblings. Unfortunately, they insisted that she was mentally inferior "trash." Her adjustment to this was to enter a make-believe world where she "lost time," did not exist, and could be "on the outside looking in."

Following her surgery, she returned home to show her siblings her accomplishment. Their response was to tell her "never to come back." She understood this to mean that she should keep her place in the family as mentally defective, ugly "trash." She felt that in their eyes, if she was an intelligent person of normal appearance, she "did not exist." As she made progress in outpatient therapy, she said it felt as if she were climbing a ladder out of a pit, but "someone always tries to pull me back down." She acknowledged that this force represented her siblings.

In retrospect, the SASB-based consultation appears to have marked a turning point in outpatient therapy. The major new idea was that if she was to get well, she must give up the dream of being affirmed by her siblings as strong, sane, smart, and socially skilled. Her challenge was to give up seeking their love and approval on their terms—namely, that she be mentally inferior, ugly, and worthless.

This patient met the following DSM criteria for BPD: (1) Her efforts to avoid abandonment were desperate. (2) She overidealized and devalued both the staff and herself. (3) Identity disturbance was salient. (4) She engaged in major self-destructive cutting on her arms and legs. (5) She was chronically suicidal. (8) She could become very angry.

This individual also fit the SASB-based interpersonal description outlined in Table 5.1. The interviewer did not "meet" her multiple personalities, but the one present in the interview was very friendly and responsive to suggestions (TRUST). That friendliness contrasted greatly with the picture drawn in her chart, which documented a proclivity for CONTROL, BLAME, and ATTACK of the staff. Her SELF-NEGLECT and SELF-ATTACK were certified by the case history. She desperately wanted acceptance (PROTECT), and she dreaded rejection and abandonment (IGNORE).

The patient's history was consistent with the pathogenic hypotheses sketched in Table 5.1: (1) Life in the family was dramatic and chaotic, and she carried this pattern into adulthood. (2) There were traumatic, frequent, chronic incestual experiences that occurred when she was left alone. Her BPD patterns were triggered by perception of abandonment. (3) She was put down by her siblings for her success, and she attacked herself for doing well. (4) Her escalation of symptoms to receive nurturance had direct and current ties to the terms set forth by her beloved siblings.

She also met the necessary interpersonal descriptors for the BPD label: (1) Abandonment sensitivity was defended against by forcing others to give nurturance. (2) There was regression after success; one hospitalization was precipitated simply by receiving an A in a difficult course.

In sum, this person met many of the criteria for BPD listed in the DSM. She also showed many of the interpersonal patterns, wishes, and fears outlined in Table 5.1. Necessary criteria were met, and the exclusionary criterion was not. Her interpersonal history and present interpersonal patterns conformed to the specified SASB dimensionality.

No nomenclature or classification system describes every case perfectly. There are always cases that do not fit the given system. Whereas the first patient conformed to the proposed interpersonal view of the DSM category for BPD, the patient in the next example deviated in a rather major way. The second case illustrates that if a BPD does not conform to the predictions, good developmental reasons can be found for the deviation. If aspects of the prototypic diagnostic example are missing, corresponding reasons for the failure can be identified.

Case 2

A woman in her 30s made cuts on her arms and abdomen whenever she was stressed by professional evaluation that she feared would result in being rejected by her female supervisor. She went numb, feeling no pain while cutting, and experienced relief afterwards. She would also binge until her stomach hurt intensely. For example, she would eat two bowls of oatmeal, one cake, one bag of cookies, and one bag of potato chips. This process could "take the place of cutting," but it was not as satisfying. She suffered from dissociative episodes and could not remember what happened for extended periods of time. She had many hospitalizations, usually for suicidality precipitated by her therapist's vacations. She had good feelings for some of her former therapists and hospitals, and anger at others for being uncaring.

Her mother was perfectionistic and competent, and maintained excellent order in the house. The patient's mother expected the patient to perform perfectly, and then claimed the daughter's successes for her own. The patient was angry with her mother and felt close to her father, who was alcoholic. During adolescence, she had assumed responsibility for trying to control his drinking, but he paid her no attention because she was not a boy. Alone after school, she suffered painful sexual abuse and beatings from an older brother on a daily basis. When she attempted to get help from her mother, she was told that she probably did something to start it.

The patient felt she had no identity. Although she had significant educational and professional accomplishments, they counted for nothing because her mother expected them anyway. Her father acknowledged nothing from a female. She felt the only way she could be unique was to be sick; this denied her mother's mandate to "be perfect."

The patient met DSM criteria for BPD in that she showed (1) sensitivity to abandonment, (3) identity disturbance, (4) binge eating, (5) self-mutilation, (7) feelings of emptiness, (8) explosive anger.

Many of the interpersonal codes (Table 5.1) were present. In her relations with the health care system and with her mother, she exhibited TRUST and AC-TIVE LOVE some of the time. CONTROL, BLAME, and ATTACK for failure to care enough appeared at other times. Her SELF-NEGLECT and SELF-ATTACK were salient. Her fear of abandonment (IGNORE) was unequivocal, and her wish for nurturance (PROTECT) was obvious. She also met the necessary and exclusionary conditions: There was abandonment sensitivity handled by transitive coercion to force nurturance, and there was some self-sabotage (but see below). Wanting to reside permanently in a hospital, she obviously was not comfortable living alone.

Her history also conformed to features 1 and 2 of Table 5.1. There was the incestual anarchy after school, and possibly also when the father was drunk. The adult consequence was that she had "islands of chaos" in the form of binges and self-mutilations. Otherwise, she functioned in the relatively orderly manner modeled and expected by her mother. She also learned to function well as she monitored and nurtured her alcoholic father. The incest attacks from her brother occurred when she was alone, but they did not include idealization or omnipotence. The adult consequences corresponded: She was abandonment-sensitive, and reckless with herself, but she did not engage in extreme idealization or devaluation.

Historical features 3 and 4 were not confirmed. In fact, the mother demanded that she be independent and competent; if she became sick, the mother attacked her for not being perfect. Accordingly, this person was very different from the prototypical BPD in that she had a college degreee in engineering. She did not become nonfunctional with BPD until shortly before she completed college. Very shortly after getting a highly paid professional job, she had to be hospitalized. She needed to stay in the hospital so long that her generous insurance benefits were exhausted. Then her mother was forced to deal with the illness in financial as well as emotional terms. In an indirect way, therefore, the mother reinforced the sickness, but not in the developmental history and not directly or willingly.

In sum, this woman met many of the DSM criteria for BPD, as well as the interpersonal codes. She was unusual, however, in that she had progressed quite far in the academic and professional world. Her interpersonal history differed from the prototypic history in corresponding ways: Her mother was highly organized, competent, and focused. The mother punished rather than encouraged disability. Accordingly, the patient was better organized and more functional than the prototypic BPD. Unfortunately, the patient ultimately used that executive ability in service of the basic BPD dynamics. She became a professional patient, adding continuous years of hospitalizations to her record.

EXPECTABLE TRANSFERENCE REACTIONS AND TREATMENT IMPLICATIONS

Transference Reactions

The traumatic abandonment experiences set the prototype for the interactional patterns so often seen between the BPD and the health care provider. The most likely transference problem is that the patient will be very active in coercing nurturance from the therapist until he or she "burns out." First the patient will bask in the joy of the therapist's nurturance, wisdom, and warmth. Then, as reality invades, it will become clear that the therapist is not going to be able to deliver "enough." Repeated crises with overdoses, self-mutilations, and other major problems seem to show that therapy is going nowhere. The therapist begins to "withdraw"—initially by a loss of enthusiasm, reluctance to receive phone calls, to schedule extra appointments, and so on. These reactions lead to attacks on the therapist for not caring. The BPD may indignantly storm out of a session and announce that therapy is over. The withdrawals are likely to be dangerous, accompanied by dissociations, self-mutilations, and overdoses. While this occurs, the patient severely devalues herself as well as the therapist. On recovering from the episode, the BPD calls the therapist and wants to return. The stormy and dangerous departure frightens the therapist, but he or she dares not refuse lest there be a legal charge of abandonment. The BPD returns, but the therapist is distant, frightened, and resentful. He or she is likely at this stage to make jokes about BPD with colleagues, and to dread the appointments with the BPD. The BPD, of course, reads this accurately, and chastises the therapist for his or her lack of caring and hypocrisy. The therapist feels more guilty and more resentful.

A variation on this cycle is that the patient starts to get better, and both patient and therapist celebrate their progress. The patient then begins to worry that the therapist will "kick her out" when she doesn't need the therapist any more. In this cycle, the result is the same: The BPD feels abandoned, deteriorates, and demands more; the therapist "burns out"; and the scenario repeats itself.

In short, whether there is progress or no progress, the BPD will feel abandoned and pursue the path of self-destruction. The reason is that she is in an intrapsychic "Catch-22." If she improves, she "undermines" herself in the eyes of her internalized jealous oppressors and abusers. They "want" her to feel pain, and they are nice only if she is broken and needy. They dictate that she reverse her progress. On the other hand, if she fails to improve, she gets rejected as "untreatable" by the therapist, who is supposed to provide protection against her internalized oppressors. This rejection will prove that she is a bad person who deserves to suffer. Whether she succeeds or fails, the BPD is programmed to self-destruct. She and the therapist are in a "lose–lose" situation.

One need not conclude that the BPD is living proof of the theory of the basic destructiveness of human nature. Rather, one can see that the BPD is trying to bond with loved ones according to ill-fated family rules and understandings. These internalizations set the BPD on a course of ever-escalating symptomatology: "My misery is your command."

As this most unfortunate cycle unfolds during the treatment of BPD, the therapist has an increasing sense of loss of control. There are amazing intrusions into his or her personal and professional life. The BPD finds many ways to "invade" the therapist's boundaries. These can include sending a romantic singing telegram to the office, "staking out" the therapist's home, calling the therapist at home at expectably inopportune hours, or showing up at places the therapist is known to frequent in his or her personal life. The BPD is able to scan the therapist's person or office to find information to use to strike directly at the therapist's most vulnerable spots. Such powerful moves toward togetherness alternate with dangerous plunges into abject helplessness, hopelessness, and grief-stricken aloneness.

The intrusions, added to the BPD's criticisms of the therapist as not caring, elicit subtle if not overt countertransference. Therapy interventions begin to have the flavor of hostile dominance. Examples may include "pointing out" the sensitivity to abandonment, or "interpreting" the BPD's need to control the therapist. Although it is the therapist's job to help the BPD learn about these patterns, "pointing out" will very likely be seen as BLAME. If so, the intervention is destructive.

The BPD's perceptiveness and knowledge of unfair rules of interpersonal play make her capable of shredding the therapist's confidence and effectiveness. Her neediness and identification with abusers drive her to ruthless extremes with the therapist. For example, a BPD may detect and appeal to the therapist's need to be seen as a loved and lovable person. She will offer presents, ask to go to dinner, bring a bottle of wine to the session, plead for hugs and kisses, draw the therapist into confessions about his or her own personal problems, and so on. If the therapist appropriately refuses to accept these offerings, he or she is called "uptight, cold, uncaring." On the other hand, if the therapist accedes to any such gestures, he or she is "dead meat" at a later point in therapy when the BPD is angry about the inevitable perceived abandonment. After desperately and skillfully pleading with the therapist to allow such intimacies, the BPD is completely capable of switching to the following: "You violated standard professional ethics when you . . . , and I am going to [see a lawyer/call your wife/tell my husband/kill myself and leave a note explaining why]." It is at this point that a therapist can really "lose it." The form that takes depends on the therapist's own patterns.

Lest this analysis be misunderstood as an example of "blaming the victim," let me say this: I firmly believe that "reality is my best friend." Telling it as it is offers the only hope for making it better. We therapists are vulnerable human beings. BPDs are victims who have learned the tactics of abuse, and they are willing to use them on caregivers. To the extent that we can embrace the truth, we are in a better position to be truly helpful. Denial, hypocrisy, and power madness only lead to more of the same. There are, for example, instances when a therapist responds to the skill and appeal of the BPD and develops a sexual relationship with her. In most cases the outcome is tragic. The sexual relationship with the therapist is a recapitulation of the original abuse. The one in the parental role, who is supposed to be the helper and protector, turns out to be an exploitative abuser. When the therapist ultimately decides to end relationship, the BPD is devastated and self-destructive. Whatever the intent, the therapist has the primary responsibility to maintain proper boundaries in the therapy re-ship. The therapist must see that the therapy relationship does not become _____l. I hope that the present candid discussion of therapist experience with the BPD is one way to help prevent such untoward outcomes.

Treatment Implications: The Five Categories of Correct Response

Chapter 4 establishes the view that therapy should help patients build the ego strength needed to recognize situations that set off regressive patterns. Patients' awareness of the roots of the destructive patterns can help them realign their unconsciously destructive goals. Once the unconscious is "on the side of health," the patients can successfully engage with the task of replacing currently maladaptive patterns with more adaptive ones.

In sum, therapy involves helping the patient learn about maladaptive patterns and their roots, make the decision to change, and learn new patterns. This view permits definition of therapist errors on a moment-to-moment basis. The five categories of correct response, described in Chapter 4, are as follows: (1) facilitating collaboration; (2) helping the patient learn about patterns; (3) blocking maladaptive patterns; (4) enabling the will to change; and (5) teaching new patterns. The interpersonal effects of any given therapist intervention can be measured by asking such questions as "How did you feel when I made that observation?" or "How did you feel after our last session? How did things go afterwards?" The content of the answers, and the coding of the therapy process while answering them, will indicate whether the intervention belongs to one of the five categories of correct response.

Facilitating Collaboration

The BPD arrives with an "empty-tank" theory of therapy. The theory behind the script "My misery is your command" is that the BPD's suffering is due to lack of nurturance and protection. In effect, the BPD promises that if (and only if) enough restorative love is available, all will go well. The inexperienced therapist, or the therapist who also subscribes to the "empty-tank" theory of development, is at risk of enabling the BPD's destructive treatment plan. Instead, the therapist should offer the BPD a contract in strength building, in terms such as the following: "This therapy can help you learn to see what your patterns are, where they came from, what they are for, and whether you want to change them. If you do want to change, then this therapy will offer help with learning new ones. Therapy is like taking music lessons. I will try to help you with this learning, but much of the work will be boring and hard. We won't be 'giving a concert in Carnegie Hall' next month. But in the end, if you have the interest and stick with the work, I believe you could learn to do quite well." This is not a false promise. BPDs often have a high level of interpersonal skill already; the proof is in the way they can disrupt whole health care systems. The problem is that BPDs use their abilities in destructive ways. They need to change their goals, and, yes, to acquire new skills too. They especially need new learning about differentiation.

The BPD may worry whether the therapist will be supportive enough when presented with this offer to help with strength building. The therapist can respond to that worry by saying something like this: "Probably I will not be supportive in the way you would like. You're right that I won't be willing to talk with you whenever you call, for however long it takes to feel better. The reason is that believe that your pattern now is to be very needy. That makes me worry that if I were to do what you want in the way you want, you would become weaker, not stronger. I would be enabling your dependency, and it's not likely you'd be helped to change your patterns."

This statement does not discharge the therapist's responsibility to provide meaningful help. A "refusal to support directly" should be clearly explained, and accompanied by positive and constructive alternatives. In the example above, once the limits have been set on nurturance, the therapist can propose an alternative to hand holding on the telephone: "What I offer instead is willingness to talk *briefly* on the phone, to help remind you of our work on strengths. The goal of that conversation is to help you get in touch with your strengths so that you can pull yourself back together. If necessary, at that time we can schedule an extra appointment to work on strength building."

Collaboration requires that the patient and therapist like each other and what they are doing. Their collaboration must be against "it," the destructive patterns. BPDs seek healing and help from wise and wonderful therapists. Therapists correspondingly want to be seen as helpful, wise, and wonderful healers. So far, so good. But when a BPD inevitably challenges this image, a therapist often is intimidated into "delivering." At that point, the therapist and patient play the BPD song, and the collaboration against "it" is lost.

The truly "wise and wonderful" therapist is wise and wonderful at strength building rather than enabling. The therapist can use the Alcoholics Anonymous (AA) model of providing generous support if the first drink is resisted, but not after it has been consumed. The BPD is addicted to empathy and nurturance, but it is vital that such support be given in the service of good functioning rather than in service of chaos, misery, and regression.

The best way to avoid transference and countertransference disasters with BPD is to keep very firm boundaries, both physical and verbal. I have come to call the recommended position "the Caribbean solution." The name came from watching a peaceful, dignified clerk in a Caribbean resort deal with an outrageously irate tourist. The man was livid about the failure of the air conditioning unit on his rented car, and was personally attacking the clerk. In response to his escalating rage and threats, she merely reiterated the facts: "I am sorry, sir. I know it is terribly inconvenient. The rental agency representative will arrive at 10 A.M., and he will either repair the air conditioning or replace the car." No matter how furious and unfair the customer got, the clerk steadfastly and warmly maintained her position, reiterating the facts.

This recommended attitude has the SASB codes SEPARATE and **AFFIRM**. No matter how lethal the verbal attacks, or how seductive the offers from the BPD, the therapist should hold to the basic terms of the therapy contract. The focus must remain on the learning that needs to be done if the BPD is to change patterns in the direction of health and strength. As the therapist maintains boundaries in this way, the BPD is very likely to complain that the therapist is "cold" and "uncaring," and "doesn't offer enough." She may seek (and may find) other therapists who do permit hugs, provide extended supportive listening on the telephone, and offer more and longer appointments. The boundary-setting therapist can respond to this peaceful termination of the present therapy (EMANCIPATE) with a welcome to return if the BPD changes her mind.

If the BPD's "executive" (the part of her that wants to get better) is not potent enough to agree to strength building, then the present therapy approach may not be appropriate. One does not usually attempt to teach violin playing to a person who has no arms, or skiing to someone without legs. Limitations on what can be learned may need to be recognized and accepted. My experience has been that people who initially decline the strength-building contract will sometimes return months or even years later, ready to work.

Facilitating Pattern Recognition

Many of the techniques listed in Chapter 4 help the BPD develop insight. These include standard techniques such as dream analysis, free association, role plays, catharsis, "regression in the service of the ego," interpretation of transference, educational assignments, and more. Anything that helps the BPD learn about her patterns (without harming herself or others) is correct.

Care must be taken that selected techniques do not serve primitive needs. For example, role plays that facilitate expressions of anger are at risk of increasing rather than decreasing hostile enmeshment with family members or their internalized representations. Use of the cathartic model to encourage expression of anger as an end in itself can be dangerous with a BPD. If expression of anger is in the service of differentiation, it is a correct therapy intervention with a BPD. Otherwise, it probably is not.

For example, in a role play, the therapist's expression of outrage at a 30-plus-year-old man's having intercourse with a 3-year-old girl can provide the perspective needed for differentiation. On the other hand, expression of that rage can also excite the BPD's wishes to "bring the abuser into line." Another result may be heightening of the wish to "hang it all up and go home to live with the abuser forever as a disabled mental patient." The therapist must constantly check the BPD's feelings, fantasies, and fears about what is being done at the moment, to make sure that the intervention is in the service of growth.

As the therapy proceeds to teach patterns of interaction, the BPD needs to have her reality testing validated (see also Linehan, 1993). After she has given specific evidence in support of the early trauma, the therapist can affirm: "It *did* hurt. It *did* happen. It *was* real. No, you don't have to take the rap all by yourself. Yes, there was pleasure in it, but that does not make you responsible for it. It makes sense that you would now feel pleasure in pain; that's what you are used to. It makes sense that you feel helpless and powerful all at once. And no, you are not filthy.

The BPD can be greatly relieved if the therapist helps her understand the connection between her early history and present symptoms. Therapist confidence that the symptoms "make sense" is reassuring. The understanding provides a helpful contrast to many BPDs' earlier experiences of being labeled as "manipulative" and "crazy."

Therapist knowledge of BPD patterns helps map out the learning task. It must not be seen as evidence of the therapist's ability to deliver infinite wisdom and help. According to the learning model, the control of growth resides within the BPD. If the information in this chapter is used within the framework of a learning model, it will not enhance destructive fantasies. An example of a destructive fantasy would be the BPD's idealization of the therapist as someone who could provide a magic cure, if only he or she would stop "withholding."

Blocking Maladaptive Patterns

The BPD can learn to recognize regressive danger if she understands that perceived abandonment sets off a chain of self destructive patterns. When she has had a self-mutilative episode with no apparent precipitant, the BPD can be helped to learn how to figure out what set it off. Therapist belief in the inherent logic of it all can inspire a collaborative exploration. The problem is to identify the event that was labeled IGNORE by the BPD.

Sometimes, the connection may not be at all obvious. For example, one BPD had an unusually severe regression when she received her engagement ring. One would not normally think of receiving an engagement ring as signifying abandonment. However, in this case, the idea of marriage was directly associated with leaving and being rejected by the jealous father. The BPD's incestual connection with him was intense. Getting married, symbolized by the ring, was an act of autonomy from the father that was worthy of severe punishment. When she got her engagement ring, the BPD both attacked her fiancé and self-mutilated. The gestures were to prove to her internalized father and her future husband-to-be that she was too mentally ill to marry. The deterioration affirmed loyalty to the old patterns, and was a "gift of love" to them.

Whenever the BPD talks about how well things are going, the therapist should anticipate and try to circumvent the expected regression. The therapist can say, "I've noticed before that as soon as we acknowledge things are going better, they seem to take a nose-dive right away." Chances are that the BPD will recognize the trend. If not, it is easy for the therapist to recount recent specific examples. In this case, the "evidence" should be given in a reflective, concerned, tentative manner rather than as an indictment. Once the BPD understands that regression in the face of success is a pattern, then the therapist can ask, "What can we do to help you avoid hurting yourself if this happens again?" In a collaborative mode, the therapist and the BPD can then work together to make a plan for averting or minimizing self-destruction. Examples of problems to be anticipated are self-mutilation, overdose, getting in a terrible fight with a new lover, missing a crucial day of work, and so on.

Urges toward self-destruction can also be treated by exploring fantasies about who would be pleased with the results of such activities. For example, the therapist can ask, "How would your mother feel if she knew how close you came to an overdose?" The answer to the question may show the BPD that her self-destructive activities are supposed to please an attacking internalized object. An escalated version of this approach is "What would your mother think or feel or do if you had succeeded in this suicide attempt?" or, "What would your father say if he could see you cutting on your thighs like that?" These efforts to elicit unconscious fantasies about the "good" consequences of self-destructive activity should have associations to early memories. The investigation should lead to a history of being attacked for doing well, or of traumatic abandonment. Recognition of the early source can help reframe the present experience so that the BPD has more choice in the present. The therapist can strengthen the BPD's will to differentiate from old attachments by asking rhetorical questions such as "Do you still love your brother enough to give him *this* [self-destructive result]?"

BPD depression, like most other depressions, is preceded by perceived helplessness (SUBMIT). That theory suggests that when depression is worse, the BPD and the therapist should seek to identify a current situation that seems to block and trap (CONTROL) the BPD. Once that is done, discussion of how to develop options and choices can be very helpful in relieving the depression. A person who sees options feels less trapped, and is less likely to remain depressed. This theme is developed at length in connection with DPD in Chapter 9.

The BPD's requests for more frequent sessions can be met with collaborative wondering about whether more sessions would nurture regressive fantasies, or whether they would intensify constructive work on patterns. An empirical approach to the question can be very effective. The therapist can say, "Let's try it the way you suggest [e.g., have more or fewer sessions—whatever was requested], and see whether or not it makes things worse. If there are episodes of self-mutilation and suicidal thoughts, we'll know the increased [or decreased] intensity of therapy contacts is wrong, and we can cut back [or resume]. On the other hand, if it works, then fine, we'll keep it there for a while." In this way, the therapist and the patient collaborate against the patient's "bad patterns." The control of the frequency of visits rests on improvement, not on deterioration.

Strengthening the Will to Give Up Maladaptive Patterns

The strengthening of the will to give up destructive wishes is another critical step. The BPD will give up self-mutilation, self-sabotage, and suicidal or homicidal acting out if she can "divorce" the internalized abusive attachment figures. The fundamental idea is that the BPD must give up the desire to be affirmed by those representations of others. This can be done by developing a "dislike" of those figures, or by developing a superseding attachment to someone who is more constructive. The relationship with the therapist can facilitate such vital change. Of course, direct attachment to the therapist would be regressive; instead, the therapist must become an important "emotional cheerleader" who helps the BPD develop good relationships in love and work.

There should be strict limits on expectations for hospitalization. A nurturant hospitalization with attributions of miracle cures may feed into regressive fantasies. BPDs long for hospitalizations that will offer constant physical proximity to their caregivers, where the "proper" sick role will be rewarded as in the past. Under the present model, hospitalization instead is only for safekeeping. It is necessary when the old patterns are dangerously out of control; this can happen after uncovering of incestual memories in therapy. It may also occur if the BPD sees the therapist as abandoning through lateness, taking a vacation, refusing extra appointments, and so on. These events are all coded by the BPD as IGNORE, and this sets off the program for self-destruction. Hospitalization may also be necessary if an event vividly reactivates a core issue. For example, a severe crisis may be precipitated if the formerly incestual father comes into the adult BPD's bedroom late at night to "look for something he misplaced." BPD does in these ways resemble Post-Traumatic Stress Disorder (Krull, 1988).

Hospitalization reflects the need for help with containing the old patterns. It should symbolize neither a "dumping" of a mess upon hospital staff, nor a promise of "resurrection." Candid discussion between the patient and therapist should clarify that hospitalization does not represent treatment of disorder per se. Within a learning model, hospitalization can be viewed by analogy to the water safety instructor who throws the drowning learner a life preserver, asking him or her to grab it. Nobody imagines that the dramatic intervention is a part of learning to swim. It merely preserves the option to take up lessons later on, when the learner is ready to continue.

With the "holding" interpretation rather than the "treatment" interpretation of hospitalization, it makes little sense for the therapist to try to conduct treatment while the BPD is hospitalized. The present model provides that the therapist should make frequent "hello" visits to assure the BPD of the therapist's interest in continuing the work together. The therapist should not do anything to reinforce the fantasy that hospitalization will provide even more and better access to therapist nurturance. Therapist enthusiasm and involvement should be keyed to strength, not regression. Many times, I have found that a BPD's crisis receded and the "need" for hospitalization disappeared after I explained this view of hospitalization.[6]

The present model also suggests that medications should be viewed as aids in controlling symptoms so that the work of learning about patterns can con-

---

[6]This view of the use of the hospital while conducting an outpatient therapy should not be taken as a dismissal of long-term inpatient treatment. Long-term hospitalizations accompanied by effective dynamic psychotherapy can have good results.

tinue. If seen in that light, medications are less likely to encourage regressive dependence on miracle cures. Medications are helpful, and sometimes necessary to make help the BPD make it through crises. But medications do not change the underlying social and intrapsychic problems in BPD.

As the therapy relationship grows strong, the BPD can internalize the therapist's compassion for the BPD as an abused child. At this point, the BPD can, as one of my patients put it, "learn to be a little bit tolerant with myself." The therapist's emotional aversion to the idea of child abuse can also be taken in by the patient. The therapist's compassion for the child and aversion to the abuse can help the patient dare to be "disloyal" to the abuser. The patient in case 1 above, for example, needed to give up her wish that her destructive siblings would approve of her accomplishments. When there is an incestual attachment to the parent, the BPD will understand such statements as "We need to work on divorcing your father."

The therapist does not assume a one-sided position. Divorce from the father may be accepted as a goal, but both therapist and patient need to remember that the regressed part of the BPD does not wish to divorce the father. This part may emerge into consciousness after a session during which "divorce" is discussed, and find ways to discredit the therapist and the therapy. The patient may act out, doing things such as telephoning the therapist and announcing that her trust fund is running so low that it is necessary to terminate therapy. Alternatively, self-destruction or direct attacks on the therapist may be used to encourage the therapist to "back off," and stop "attacking" family patterns.

Early on, the therapist can give the BPD wide latitude by making the benevolent intent toward family members very clear: "Our long-range goal is to let you be free to make your own decisions, but that doesn't mean you can't stay on good terms with your father. You don't have to confront your father about the incest unless you want to or need to. In any case, you do not have to leave him altogether. If, as you fear, he will fall apart if your relationship changes, we could try to help him by talking about it, and maybe referring him to his own therapist." As the patient becomes more differentiated from destructive internalizations, the therapist can help the patient develop compassion for the abuser. However, premature moves toward this position of sympathy for the abuser can strengthen rather than weaken the patient's dedication to psychopathology. The changes must come stepwise. A musician cannot begin with the most difficult pieces; he or she must master several levels of skill before arriving at the goal. It is not easy to maintain compassion for abusers while remaining fully aware of the suffering they have inflicted. This is particularly true for those who are victims of that abuse. Ultimately, and quite simply, the patient's task in therapy is to differentiate from and make peace with the aggressor and his or her internal representations. Learning that the aggressor has his or her own story, but that there is no sense carrying it on through the generations, is the last, very important step. The residue of child abuse need not continue through the generations.

The therapist's delight in the patient's growing strength facilitates its development. However, this can be dangerous with a BPD too. Getting better may mean being abandoned through termination. Therapists must be sensitive to that conflict, and unambivalent themselves about the inevitability of termination. I am comfortable with providing long-range constancy by asking for and receiving postcards or brief letters on important events, such as marriages, birth of children, graduation from college, and so on. Sometimes I have attended (unobtrusively and unaccompanied) important ceremonies. This provides a concrete symbolic constancy to the relationship, and evinces commitment to strength and happiness. Such promises of ongoing contact must not extend beyond these formal occasions. If they do, the regressive wishes for a cosmic merge could be encouraged.

Facilitating New Learning

The learning of new patterns is often great fun with BPDs. These people are usually very perceptive and skilled interpersonally. Once the groundwork of the preceding four steps is complete, BPDs turn their efforts in constructive directions. The results can be delightful, and the therapist's job easy. The most important training for a BPD at this stage is learning how to give and take autonomy while remaining friendly. For this purpose, the usual and customary therapy procedures for facilitating personal growth work very well.

6

Narcissistic Personality Disorder

"His Majesty the Baby."

REVIEW OF THE LITERATURE

According to Greek mythology, Narcissus was distinguished for his beauty. He was destined to have a long life, provided he never looked upon his own features. Nevertheless, Narcissius rejected the love of others and fell in love with his own reflection in the waters of a spring. He pined away, and a flower that bears his name sprang up where he died.

Freud (1914/1959) wrote:

> The word narcissism is taken from clinical terminology and was chosen by P. Nacke in 1899 to denote the attitude of a person who treats his own body in the same way as otherwise the body of a sexual object is treated; that is to say, he experiences sexual pleasure in gazing at, caressing and fondling his body, till complete gratification ensues upon these activities. (p. 30)

According to Freud, the more the libido is directed outward, the less there is for the self. The more it is deflected inward, the less there is for others. Narcissism, Freud said, can be seen in "paraphrenics who suffer from megalomania who have withdrawn their interest in people in things" (p. 31). It also, he added, is easily observed in people who are physically ill. To illustrate that point, he quoted the poet W. Busch: "Concentrated is his soul/in his jaw-tooth's aching hole" (p. 39).

Freud explained the role of narcissism in love: "We say that the human being has originally two sexual objects: himself and the woman who tends him" (1914/1959, p. 45). There are two types of object choices. The first is the narcissistic type, in which the object choice is someone like the self, what the self once was, or would like to be. The second is the anaclitic type, in which the object choice is the "woman who tends or the man who protects" (p. 47). Freud maintained that the narcissistic choice characterizes homosexuality and that the anaclitic choice is "properly speaking, characteristic of the man" (p. 45).

Freud's fixed-energy model provided that the self is depleted if the id's energy is directed outward toward another person rather than toward the self. Fortunately, if the recipient of this sexual energy loves back in return, the self is restored. On the other hand, if the love is unrequited, then the self is impoverished:

This sexual over-estimation is the origin of the peculiar state of being in love, a state suggestive of a neurotic compulsion, which is thus traceable to an impoverishment of the ego in respect of libido in favour of the love object. (p. 45). . . . He who loves has, so to speak, forfeited a part of his narcissism, which can only be replaced by his being loved. (p. 55). . . . Love in itself, in the form of longing and deprivation, lowers the self-regard; whereas to be loved, to have love returned, and to possess the beloved object, exalts it again. (p. 57)

With this analysis of the loss of self in love, Freud accounted for the intense, desperate, compulsive longing associated with sexual love.

A massive psychoanalytic literature on narcissism followed Freud's initial paper. NPD as a diagnostic entity has emerged largely from the work of the "self psychologists," Kohut (1971) and Kernberg (1984). Briefly, Kohut proposed that infantile narcissism is not replaced by adult object love, as Freud suggested. Rather, Kohut argued that narcissism is a normal adult attribute and is manifested in the mature person as humor, wisdom, and empathy. Pathological narcissism in the adult is the result of pre-Oedipal structural deficits in the self that came from deficiencies in the developmental experience.

Kernberg suggested that pathological narcissism represents a defense against paranoid projection of oral rage. According to Kernberg, narcissistic grandiosity, demandingness, and lack of empathy for others are consequences of the pathological projective process. The DSM description of NPD includes many of the features marked by each of these two important psychoanalytic theorists.

Adler (1986) noted that Kohut's and Kernberg's conceptions have very different treatment implications. For example, Kernberg suggested that when the narcissistic patient is angry at the therapist, the anger should be confronted and related to early roots. Kohut, by contrast, holds that anger toward the therapist may represent empathic failure. The therapist should acknowledge any fault and maintain the loving position of a benign parent. There has been no way of resolving the disparate theories, because the psychoanalytic approach has not provided a method of confirming or refuting its ideas.

From any theoretical perspective, it is agreed that the NPD is difficult to treat. Malin (1990) has offered a pungent summary of the behavior of the NPD:

How do we work with patients who are simply unlikable, voraciously expressing their sense of entitlement, vulnerable to the most negligible slights and perceived insensitivities, prone to withdraw and become inaccessible following the most (seemingly) harmless comments? How, moreover, do we deal with patients who are exploitative in their relationships with others, including their therapists, and who are prone to rage when the therapist fails to comment or interpret in precisely the right way? (p. 360)

DSM DEFINITION OF THE DISORDER

The DSM definition provides the starting point for the analysis. The DSM specifies that the diagnosis of NPD can be made if an individual meets five of the criteria. DSM-III-R items appear in **bold print,** and any changes introduced by the DSM-IV appear in *italics.* (As in Chapter 5, the item numbering used here is that of the DSM-IV. Original numbers in the DSM-III-R appear after **bold** items, in brackets.)

A pervasive pattern of grandiosity (in fantasy or behavior), lack of empathy, and hypersensitivity to the evaluation of others, beginning by early adulthood and present in a variety of contexts, as indicated by at least *five* **of the following:**

A pervasive pattern of grandiosity (in fantasy or behavior), need for admiration, and lack of empathy, beginning by early adulthood and present in a variety of contexts, as indicated by at least five of the following:

(1) has a grandiose sense of self-importance, e.g., exaggerates achievements and talents, expects to be noticed as "special" without appropriate achievement [item 3 in DSM-III-R]

has a grandiose sense of self-importance (e.g., exaggerates achievements and talents, expects to be recognized as superior without commensurate achievements)

(2) is preoccupied with fantasies of unlimited success, power, brilliance, beauty, or ideal love [item 5 in DSM-III-R]

(3) believes that his or her problems are unique and can be understood only by other special people [item 4 in DSM-III-R]

believes that he or she is "special" and unique and can only be understood by, or should associate with, other special or high-status people (or institutions)

(4) requires constant attention and admiration, e.g., keeps fishing for compliments [item 7 in DSM-III-R]

requires excessive admiration

(5) has a sense of entitlement: unreasonable expectation of especially favorable treatment, e.g., assumes that he or she does not have to wait in line when others must do so [item 6 in DSM-IIR]

has a sense of entitlement: unreasonable expectations of especially favorable treatment or automatic compliance with his or her expectations

(6) is interpersonally exploitative: takes advantage of others to achieve his or her own ends [item 2 in DSM-III-R]

(7) lack of empathy: inability to recognize and experience how others feel, e.g., annoyance and surprise when a friend who is seriously ill cancels a date [item 8 in DSM-III-R]

lack of empathy: unwilling to recognize or identify with the feelings and needs of others

(8) is preoccupied with feelings of envy [item 9 in DSM-III-R]

is often envious of others or believes that others are envious of him or her

(9) arrogant, haughty behaviors or attitudes [new item]

reacts to criticism with feelings of rage, shame, or humiliation (even if not expressed) [item 1 in DSM-III-R; omitted from DSM-IV]

Morey (1988) reported that 22% of a sample of 291 outpatients being treated for personality disorder qualified for the NPD label. There was substantial overlap with BPD (46.9%), HPD (53.1%), PAR (35.9%), and AVD (35.9%).

PATHOGENIC HYPOTHESES

The method of using the SASB model to develop pathogenic hypotheses has been sketched in Chapter 5. Three main features of the developmental history have been identified specifically to account for each of the NPD symptoms listed in the DSM. A summary of the hypotheses linking interpersonal history to interpersonal patterns characteristic of the disorder appears in Table 6.1. A fuller discussion of these hypotheses is provided here.

1. There was selfless, noncontingent love and adoration. An example is offered by a letter written by a grandmother to her 18-month-old grandson (quoted in Benjamin, 1987a, p. 60):

> Dear wonderful, brilliant, handsome joy of our lives, grandson Johnathon. It is we who thank you! I keep seeing your mischievous smiling face, hearing your cooing, soft (except when screaming) voice and tasting your delicious baby skin. We had such a great visit being with you and your parents. You were an angel, your parents are ideal, and your grandparents adore the whole kit and kaboodle!!! We have some great pictures of the trip. We loved it and can't wait for our next visit together. LOVE, Grandma and Grandpa.

Table 6.1. Interpersonal Summary of NPD

History	Consequences of history
1. "Selfless"(WALL OFF), noncontingent love and adoration (**ACTIVE LOVE** plus **IGNORE**)	1. Noncontingent self-love and self-adoration (*ACTIVE SELF-LOVE* plus *SELF-NEGLECT*) Insensitivity to others (**IGNORE**)
2. Submissive nurturance (SUBMIT plus **PROTECT**)	2. Arrogant (**BLAME**) expectations of noncontingent deference and caregiving Assumes **CONTROL**; takes autonomy (SEPARATE) Flies into rage (**ATTACK**) if entitlements fail
3. Implicit contempt and explicit disappointment (**BLAME**) with any evidence of imperfection	3. Self-concept degrades (*SELF-BLAME*) in the absense of noncontingent adoration, or if there evidence of imperfection

Summary: There is extreme vulnerability to criticism or being ignored, together with a strong wish for love, support, and admiring deference from others. The baseline position involves noncontingent love of self and presumptive control of others. If the support is withdrawn, or if there is any evidence of lack of perfection, the self-concept degrades to severe self-criticism. Totally lacking in empathy, these persons treat others with contempt, and hold the self above and beyond the fray.

SASB codes of NPD baseline: **CONTROL, BLAME, ATTACK**, **IGNORE**, SEPARATE, ACTIVE SELF-LOVE plus SELF-NEGLECT, and *SELF-BLAME. Wishes:* To receive **ACTIVE LOVE, PROTECT**, and SUBMIT. *Fears:* To receive **BLAME**, **IGNORE**, or **CONTROL**. *Necessary descriptors:* Grandiose sense of self-importance; entitlement. *Exclusionary descriptors:* Uncaring recklessness with self.

The letter summarizes the intense, sexual ("tasting your delicious baby skin") adoration usually found in the history of NPD. Worship of the child exceeds normal limits. "Handsome" and "brilliant" may be legitimate expectations, but they cannot be realities for an 18-month-old. If such exaggerated distortions in the parental love continue over the years, the child will internalize these attitudes and have unrealistic, intensely warm and loving feelings about himself or herself.

The adoration is not accompanied by genuine self-disclosure. The NPD is not informed about the parent's own separate feelings and needs. The lesson is apparently that the parent wants only to bask in the splendor of the NPD. This lack of parental palpability interferes with the NPD's learning that other people have needs, views, and wants of their own.

Freud (1914/1959) described a normative stage that connects such parenting and narcissism:

> If we look at the attitude of fond parents toward their children, we cannot but perceive it as a revival and reproduction of their own, long since abandoned narcissism. . . . Thus they are impelled to ascribe to the child all manner of perfections which sober observation would not confirm, to gloss over and forget all his shortcomings— . . . The child shall have things better than his parents; he shall not be subject to the necessities which they have recognized as dominating life. Illness, death, renunciation of enjoyment, restrictions on his own will, are not to touch him; the laws of nature, like those of society, are to abrogated in his favour; he is really to be the centre and the heart of creation, "His Majesty the Baby," as we once fancied ourselves to be. (p. 48)

Freud suggested that the parent's extravagant adoration of the child represents recapitulation of his or her own early developmental narcissistic stage. The parent of an NPD may be resolving his or her own disappointments in life by centering on the NPD, who, as Freud suggested, shall "have it all." This noncontingent adoration supports the child's tendency to overestimate the power of wishes and mental processes. It is a time of "omnipotence of thoughts." The "application of these grandiose premises" to the self results in megalomania (Freud, 1914/1959, p. 32).

The benevolent motives of the parent notwithstanding, the fact remains that it is destructive to continue such adoring devotion beyond infancy. The noncontingent parental adoration programs the child for NPD if continues through toddlerhood, when it is time to let the child clash with reality. The parents of the child who will be normal will allow life experience to scale back the misrepresentations of self. "His (Her) Majesty" will be dethroned by the real world. Reality-based skills can develop. The parent of the normal child teaches him or her that everyone has vulnerabilities and imperfections, strong points and weak points. Good performance comes after practice and hard work. If not given these important lessons about the real world, the child becomes "hooked" on false glory. He or she is lost—indeed, feels empty—unless there is a "mainline" feed of the familiar noncontingent praise. Without comments about how he or she affects the parent, the NPD has no idea what his or her behaviors mean to others, and thus becomes insensitive and inconsiderate.

2. The adoring parent was consistently deferential and nurturant to the NPD-in-training. For example, the worshiping grandmother just cited would ask indulgently what she could do when Johnathon was unhappy or bored. The sky seemed the only limit. His parents, by contrast, were determined to break family interpersonal habits in favor of more adaptive patterns. When Johnathon returned from subsequent visits with his grandmother, he would declare indignantly that he wanted to go back to Grandma's, and again be her "little king."

The adult consequence of such noncontingent deference and caregiving is the arrogant expectation that others will continue the tradition. The NPD is astonished if he or she does not automatically receive entitlements. At work, he or she takes it for granted that the finest space, the best equipment, and other advantages will be automatically available. The NPD's favorite indulgences should, of course, have the highest priority. If expectations are not fulfilled, rage at the offenders ensues. At home, the NPD appropriates space, time, and money with-out regard for the impact on others. The spouse's every expenditure is carefully scrutinized and controlled, but the NPD's own considerably larger purchases are not to be reviewed. Spontaneously doing one's share of menial tasks is out of the question. If not greeted with a national celebration for the smallest contribution, the NPD is astonished and enraged. If the marital partner becomes sick, the NPD is ready for divorce because the spouse is no longer of use. In brief, the NPD assumes control of others and autonomy for himself or herself, and expects others to give way. They must defer, but the NPD will come and go at will.

In an age when equity and fairness are the norm, it is natural to ask how such people can be tolerated at all. In reality, their patterns are *enabled* by complementary adoration from others. NPDs often do have talents and skills worthy of the admiration. Freud (1914/1959) offered thoughts about why narcissists seem so attractive:

> It seems very evident that one person's narcissism has a great attraction for those others who have renounced part of their own narcissism and are seeking after object love; the charm of a child lies to a great extent in his narcissism, his self-sufficiency and inaccessibility, just as does the charm of certain animals which seem not to concern themselves about us, such as cats and the large beasts of prey. It is as if we envied them their power of retaining a blissful state of mind—an unassailable libido-position which we ourselves have since abandoned. (p. 46)

Freud's explanation for tolerance of narcissism is interesting. It may account for the generic adoration given to sports heroes and movie stars. However, it does not seem adequate to interpret the behavior of spouses of NPDs. For example, husbands who abuse alcohol often have narcissistic patterns. Their wives typically enable the NPDs' patterns by trying ever harder to meet their needs. These wives often have histories of neglect and abuse, so it is hard to think of them as trying to recapture the lost bliss of infancy. An interpersonal explanation for their complementary self-defeating positions is offered later in this chapter.

3. Along with all the nurturance and adoration is an ever-present threat of a fall from grace. In the midst of her extravagant tribute, the grandmother in the letter quoted above suggested parenthetically that crying was a major flaw. She joyfully conjured up an image of his marvelous presence, but then noted that it was marred by his "screaming." Since toddlers do, after all, scream, one can see that Johnathon was not allowed normal fallibility. The NPD who is ordinary creates unbearable disappointment in the parent. Any hint of imperfection that may flit through the developmental history is devastating. The burden of being perfect is very heavy. Failure brings degradation and loss of care to the NPD. It also ruins the equilibrium of the parent, the "mirroring one" who apparently thrives on the NPD's successes. Since the narcissist's self-concept stems from internalization of unrealistic adoration, the substitution of disappointment or criticism for love is devastating. The NPD is demolished, empty, and terribly alone. He or she can "dish it out," but is not equipped to "take it."

Psychoanalysis holds that character development is set in infancy and early childhood (e.g., Greenberg & Mitchell, 1983, pp. 384–385). SASB principles that describe the more common mechanisms for maintaining continuity between childhood and adulthood are recapitulation of the original complementary position, similarity to the parent, and introjection (see Chapter 3). Sullivan (1953) noted that early interpersonal experience is not the *only* way in which character is learned. One can acquire the "software" for NPD late in life. For example, a gracious Southern woman who was a psychiatric resident feared that she was becoming narcissistic. She said, "I was waiting in line at the grocery store yesterday, and I said to myself, 'I shouldn't be waiting in line here. I am a *doctor.*'"

The rich and famous are particularly vulnerable to developing NPD in adulthood. People who receive recognition for achievements in their profession begin to pronounce on topics far afield from the work that distinguished them. Movie stars feel they are qualified to run for political offices, which are supposed to require special skills in consolidating, mobilizing, and implementing the will of very different peoples. The management skills required for good government seem patently unrelated to the ability to create an image by reading and remembering scripts. Even within the scientific professions, those who achieve a certain amount of status may feel that they no longer need to offer evidence for their positions. Again, single episodes do not create the disorder, but many repetitions of such episodes can. The public can and will deliver noncontingent adoration as well as deferential nurturance to the rich and famous. Given the right conditions, it is never too late to develop NPD.

CONNECTIONS BETWEEN THE INTERPERSONAL HISTORY AND THE SYMPTOMS LISTED IN THE DSM

The "total NPD" shows all the symptoms mentioned in the DSM. The steady diet of noncontingent love and adoration encourages behaviors that meet several of the DSM criteria. These include DSM criterion 1, grandiose sense of self-importance; DSM criterion 3, need to associate with special persons of top status; DSM criterion 2, preoccupation with fantasies of unlimited success; DSM criterion 4, need for constant attention and admiration; and the new DSM criterion 9, arrogant and haughty behaviors. The selflessness that accompanies the adoration given to the NPD enhances behaviors described by DSM criterion 7, lack of empathy. The submissive nurturance invites behaviors described by DSM criterion 6, exploitation, and DSM criterion 5, entitlement. The burden of the expectation that the NPD will be perfect makes him or her testy about threats to that image. That demand reinforces behaviors associated with DSM criterion 9, haughtiness, and DSM criterion 8, envy.

INTERPERSONAL SUMMARY OF NPD

The foregoing analysis suggests a succinct interpersonal summary for NPD:

There is extreme vulnerability to criticism or being ignored, together with a strong wish for love, support, and admiring deference from others. The baseline position involves noncontingent love of self and presumptive control of others. If the support is withdrawn, or if there is any evidence of lack of perfection, the self-concept degrades to severe self-criticism. Totally lacking in empathy, these persons treat others with contempt, and hold the self above and beyond the fray.

The summary is based on the SASB codes of the NPD baseline patterns and wishes. The codes themselves, listed in Table 6.1, provide a shorthand way to identify NPD. The baseline NPD positions are CONTROL, BLAME, ATTACK, IGNORE, SEPARATE, *ACTIVE SELF-LOVE* plus *SELF-NEGLECT* (a complex code), and *SELF-BLAME*. The wishes are to receive ACTIVE LOVE, PROTECT, and SUBMIT. The fear is of IGNORE, BLAME, or CONTROL.

The rhythm and harmonics of the NPD song are found in the sequences of interpersonal and intrapsychic response that the NPD gives and receives. The "tonic" NPD position consists of CONTROL and *ACTIVE SELF-LOVE* plus *SELF-NEGLECT*. This orientation necessarily means that the NPD IGNOREs the needs of others. His or her position harmonizes well with someone who will SUBMIT while giving him or her ACTIVE LOVE and PROTECTion. If the other person fails to do this, or if there is interference with the desire to be SEPARATE, the NPD flies into BLAME and ATTACK. Any suggestion that the NPD is not perfect is likely to lead to severe *SELF-BLAME*. These are the harmonics and rhythms of the NPD song.

Readers who can use the SASB codes will be able to generalize the present analysis to contexts not mentioned here. For example, it is not unusual for patients to complain that their depression is getting worse. Sometimes these complaints are presented to the therapist in a way that is characteristic of NPD. To interpret a complaint about depression in this way, the therapist would need to code a patient's process as he or she describes the depression. A NPD's process with the therapist as he or she complains about symptoms would include the notes of the NPD song. Consider this example:

A patient refused to try a prescription for antidepressants until he had had a complete neurological workup (**CONTROL**). He had read an article a while ago about a type of tumor associated with depression. He thought that his case was particularly interesting (*ACTIVE SELF-LOVE* plus *SELF-NEGLECT*) and expected the clinic not to charge for the diagnostic procedure (wish for **PROTECT**). They might learn something, he observed. The doctor found no evidence of a brain tumor and insisted that they begin with a brief trial of an antidepressant. The patient became enraged (**ATTACK**, **BLAME**) and said that the doctor was incompetent and inconsiderate. He would take his business elsewhere (SEPARATE). He warned the doctor and the clinic that they were lucky he wasn't suing them for negligence. He had no idea (**IGNORE**) that people in the clinic were amazed at his presumptiveness.

The baseline notes of the NPD song are compared to those of the BPD song in Table 6.2. A scan of the table shows that NPDs and BPDs share the behaviors **CONTROL, BLAME,** and **ATTACK** in relation to others. They can also be out of touch that what is best for them (*SELF-NEGLECT*). NPD features that are not shared with BPD are **IGNORE**, SEPARATE, *ACTIVE SELF-LOVE*, and *SELF-BLAME*. BPDs tend to be quite perceptive and are very good at reading how others are responding to them. BPDs also do not choose autonomy, and they are not known for self-love. Among the BPD features not shared with NPD is the willingness at times to show uncomplicated **ACTIVE LOVE** and TRUST. BPDs actively engage in *SELF-PROTECT* by trying to get others to take care of them. The NPDs simply expect others to take care of them. Finally, BPDs overtly engage in *SELF-ATTACK*, while NPDs privately degenerate to *SELF-BLAME* if their needs are not met.

The interpersonal *do, re, mi* of Table 6.2 shows exactly how these two categories overlap; it also shows how they differ. The descriptions in the tables can help the clinician make the differential diagnosis.

DSM DESCRIPTORS REVISITED

The DSM view of NPD has now been translated into interpersonal language, and the psychosocial learning associated with NPD patterns has been outlined. In this section, the interpersonal analysis of NPD is compared directly to the DSM. Again, DSM-III-R items appear in **bold print**; any changes introduced by the DSM-IV appear in *italics*. (And, again, the item numbering used is that of the DSM-IV.) The interpersonal modifiers are underlined. Items from the WISPI (discussed in Chapter 1) appear in CAPITAL LETTERS.

A pervasive pattern of grandiosity (in fantasy or behavior), lack of empathy, and hypersensitivity to the evaluation of others, beginning by early adulthood and present in a variety of contexts, as indicated by at least *five* of the following:

Table 6.2. Comparison of SASB Codes of BPD and NPD

	BPD	NPD
1. EMANCIPATE		
2. AFFIRM		
3. ACTIVE LOVE	×	
4. PROTECT		
5. CONTROL	×	×
6. BLAME	×	×
7. ATTACK	×	×
8. IGNORE		×
1. SEPARATE		×
2. DISCLOSE		
3. REACTIVE LOVE		
4. TRUST	×	
5. SUBMIT		
6. SULK		
7. RECOIL		
8. WALL OFF		
1. SELF-EMANCIPATE		
2. SELF-AFFIRM		
3. ACTIVE SELF-LOVE		×*
4. SELF-PROTECT	×	
5. SELF-CONTROL		
6. SELF-BLAME		×
7. SELF-ATTACK	×	
8. SELF-NEGELCT	×	×*

*Indicates that codes in the same column appear in complex combinations with each other.

A pervasive pattern of grandiosity (in fantasy or behavior), need for admiration, and lack of empathy, beginning by early adulthood and present in a variety of contexts, as indicated by at least five of the following:

(1) has a grandiose sense of self-importance, e.g., exaggerates achievements and talents, expects to be noticed as "special" without appropriate achievement

has a grandiose sense of self-importance (e.g., exaggerates achievements and talents, expects to be recognized as superior without commensurate achievements)

Much of the time the NPD is very pleased with himself or herself, and expects to be noticed and acknowledged as "special" without having made the appropriate substantiaive contributions. Provides grandiose and inflated reports and judgments of his or her achievements and talents —usually in a way that devalues the contributions of others. Surprised and angry if not praised lavishly for making the smallest effort on a routine communal (i.e., not of direct benefit to the self) task at work or in the home.

IT IS AMAZING HOW DIFFICULT IT IS FOR SOME PEOPLE TO APPRECIATE MY CREATIVITY.

(2) is preoccupied with fantasies of unlimited success, power, brilliance, beauty, or ideal love

Ruminates about "overdue" admiration and privilege. Compares self favorably to "other" famous or privileged people.

I OFTEN FIND MYSELF THINKING ABOUT THE LONG-OVERDUE ADMIRATION WHICH WILL COME MY WAY WHEN MY TALENTS AND SPECIAL QUALITIES ARE FULLY RECOGNIZED.

(3) believes that his or her problems are unique and can be understood only by other special people

believes that he or she is "special" and unique and can only be understood by, or should associate with, other special or high-status people (or institutions)

Insists on having only the "top" person (doctor, lawyer, hairdresser, instructor) in the area. Devalues credentials of caregiver or service provider if outcome is not to his or her liking. Associates only with persons, groups, institutions of high status.

I WILL ONLY ACCEPT SERVICE FROM THE TOP PERSON (DOCTOR, LAWYER, HAIRDRESSER, SECRETARY) IN THE FIELD.

(4) requires constant attention and admiration, e.g., keeps fishing for compliments

requires excessive admiration

Becomes angry if there is not a major "ceremony" when he or she arrives. Astonished if his or her products are not coveted and admired.

OTHER PEOPLE'S PERSONAL SHORTCOMINGS MAKE IT HARD FOR THEM TO GIVE ME THE COMPLIMENTS AND ATTENTION THAT ARE DUE ME.

(5) has a sense of entitlement: unreasonable expectation of especially favorable treatment, e.g., assumes that he or she does not have to wait in line when others must do so

has a sense of entitlement: unreasonable expectations of especially favorable treatment or automatic compliance with his or her expectations

puzzled or furious when his or her wants or needs are not automatically filled. Assumes that his or her projects, interests are so important that others should go out of their way to facilitate them

I REALLY GET IRRITATED WHEN OTHERS FAIL TO ASSIST ME IN MY VERY IMPORTANT WORK.

(6) is interpersonally exploitative: takes advantage of others to achieve his or her own ends

Expects to be given whatever he or she wants and needs, no matter what it might mean to others. This does not include active deception, but rather is a consequence of the belief that he or she is "entitled." For example, the NPD would not set out to con a "little old lady" out of her life savings; however, if she offered them, the NPD would accept such a gift without reflection about its impact on her. Will expect great dedication, overwork, and heroic performance from the people associated with him or her—without giving any thought to the impact of this pattern on their lives.

IF NECESSARY, I WILL STEP ON A FEW TOES TO MAKE SURE I GET THE SPECIAL TREATMENT I DESERVE.

(7) lack of empathy: inability to recognize and experience how others feel, e.g., annoyance and surprise when a friend who is seriously ill cancels a date

lack of empathy: unwilling to recognize or identify with the feelings and needs of others

Assumes that others are focused on and totally concerned with his or her welfare. Goes on at inappropriate length with detail about his or her own concerns. Lacks the ability to recognize that others also have feelings and needs. Oblivious that self-centered remarks may hurt others (e.g., "I am now in the relationship of a lifetime," exuberantly said to a former lover). Shows contempt and impatience with other people who talk about their own needs, problems, concerns instead of focusing on him or her.

PEOPLE CLOSE TO ME TEND TO WALLOW AROUND IN THEIR TROUBLES, AND I SHOULDN'T BE EXPECTED TO WASTE MY TIME LISTENING TO THEM.

(8) is preoccupied with feelings of envy

is often envious of others or believes that others are envious of him or her

Harshly devalues the contributions of others, particularly if they are receiving or have received acknowledgment and privilege. Thinks he or she is better than others, and more deserving of admiration or privilege than those who have it. Begrudges others their success or happiness, believing he or she deserves it more.

WHEN SOMEONE I KNOW IS PRAISED, I SPEND A LOT OF TIME THINKING ABOUT HOW MUCH MORE I DESERVE IT.

(9) arrogant, haughty behaviors or attitudes

Assumes that he or she is superior. Special privileges and extra allocations of resources are usurped under the belief that they are well deserved. There is no regard for the feelings or needs of others.

I DESERVE THE VERY BEST OF EVERYTHING.

reacts to criticism with feelings of rage, shame, or humiliation (even if not expressed) [omitted from DSM-IV]

Reacts to the smallest hint of criticism from others with an attitude of "How *dare* you," and counterattacks recklessly. Indignant if not praised enough for accomplishments, or if sympathy is not adequately empathic. Although he or she may not show it outwardly, criticism haunts and leaves him or her feeling humiliated, degraded, hollow, and empty.

IT UNDOES ME WHEN SOMEBODY DARES TO CRITICIZE ME, AND I EXPECT AN IMMEDIATE APOLOGY.

NECESSARY AND EXCLUSIONARY CRITERIA

The present analysis permits definition of necessary and exclusionary conditions for each personality disorder. For NPD, the recommended *necessary* descriptors are (1) grandiose sense of self-importance, and (2) entitlement. The self-importance and entitlement characteristic of NPD preclude recklessness with the self; thus, the "conduct regardless of self" that is seen in ASP represents an *exclusionary* condition for NPD.

CASE ILLUSTRATIONS

Kernberg (1984) described narcissism in a chapter called "Barriers to Falling and Remaining in Love." There, Kernberg suggested that narcissists cannot relate sexually at all, or else that they are promiscuous, relating only to body parts. This psychoanalyst proposed that the sexual problems of the NPD male can be attributed to unconscious envy of and greed for women. NPD men have a wish to spoil and devalue females. The autonomy that so often characterizes NPD is a defense. It represents an escape from the NPD male's projection of his own possessive greed onto women. The recommended treatment is to help such an NPD become aware of his destructiveness. The new awareness of the hostile feelings results in guilt and depression. As therapy progresses, mature appreciation of others and their feelings emerge.

Case 1

A case offered by Kernberg (1984) illustrates his ideas, and is consistent with the DSM descriptions of NPD.

> The patient originally consulted me because of intense anxiety when speaking in public and an increasingly unsatisfactory sexual promiscuity. After some sexual intimacy with a woman, he would lose all interest and move on to search for another. . . . His friends at the local university were in awe of his capacity to combine intellectual and professional success with business and financial success. . . . At first he proudly proclaimed his successes with women and what he thought were his extraordinary capacities for sexual activity and enjoyment. . . . In recent years he had frequently fantasied having intercourse with other, yet unconquered women while having intercourse with one who was already his and, therefore, on the road to devaluation. . . . Finally the patient became aware of the intensity of his envy of women, derived from his envy of and rage against his mother . . . [who had] chronically withheld from him . . . her warm and soft body while she coldly rejected his expression of love, as well as his angry demands upon her. . . . By his promiscuity he also denied the frightening dependency upon a specific woman . . . [and believed] he had a giving organ superior to any breast. . . . He [became aware] of the tendency unconsciously to spoil and destroy what he most longed for, namely understanding and interest on the part of his analyst and love as well as sexual gratification from women. [Evidence of the cure was in his increasing awareness] of how much love and dedication he received from his wife. He became deeply curious about the inside life of another human being . . . and finally realized how terribly envious he had been of his wife's independent interests. . . . He realized that by consistently depreciating her, he had made her empty and boring for him. (p. 191)

This man was interpersonally exploitative with women (DSM criterion 6), had a grandiose sense of self-importance (DSM criterion 1), required admiration (DSM criterion 4), engaged extensively in fantasies of unlimited sexual prowess (DSM criterion 2), and lacked empathy for his wife (DSM criterion 7). His marked autonomy and his devaluing contempt of others (implied by DSM criteria 5, 8, and 9) were very clear. The reference to his rage and angry demands upon his mother suggested that he might still have that pattern, so old criterion 1 from the DSM-III-R (deleted in DSM-IV) would also apply.

The case is also described by the SASB interpersonal codes (Table 6.1) of ACTIVE SELF-LOVE plus SELF-NEGLECT, **CONTROL**, SEPARATE, **BLAME**, **ATTACK**. His wish was for **ACTIVE LOVE**, but he feared his dependency on women. This could reflect a fear of loss of autonomy (SEPARATE) or of being subjected to **CONTROL**.

The pathogenic hypotheses listed in Table 6.1 cannot be tested because of the brevity of the case description. For the same reason, the interpersonal position and wishes and fears cannot be fully evaluated for this case.

Case 2

This unmarried man in his mid-20s was hospitalized while engaging in dramatic suicidal behaviors under the influence of alcohol and other drugs. He had an employment history that alternated between excellent performance with strong employer endorsement of his abilities as a writer of advertising materials, and dangerous, reckless episodes. In the latter, he disappeared for weeks; engaged in abuse of drugs, food, and "other sensory delights"; acted out pornographic fantasies with (male) prostitutes; and traveled from city to city in search of the perfect place to commit suicide. The pattern had been repeated for several hospitalizations and job histories. The most recent cycle started after he successfully completed the design for a series of advertisements for a major account, and had begun to develop a very satisfying relationship with a woman whom he thought was "wonderful." In the hospital he was a colorful character, who, among other things, set up himself as a broker among patients who wanted to sell, trade, or buy drugs.

He was raised in a matriarchy dominated by a grandmother who was devoted to Catholicism. The grandfather was described as "brilliant," "wealthy," and "artistic," but nonetheless a "nonentity" in relation to the grandmother. The patient learned to play his mother off against his grandmother to "get anything he wanted," but it was clear that the grandmother held the bottom line. In fact, the mother was banished from the home by the patient in his teens because he disapproved of her boyfriend. He said that he had a "violent temper." His grandmother strongly encouraged and endorsed his identity as a "free spirit" who stood outside the ordinary. She was quite perfectionistic, and idealized the patient as "God's perfect child." He stated that he "had no discipline," but then described an extraordinary disciplinary procedure: When he erred, he was to go to his room and "think up a punishment for himself." These assignments came often, and he became quite creative at thinking up worse and worse punishments. When told about the "*Klute* syndrome,"[1] the patient acknowledged that the nature of his pornographic

---

[1] This is discussed in more detail in the treatment section of this chapter. In the movie *Klute*, Jane Fonda plays the role of a call girl and Donald Sutherland is a detective who rescues her from a high-powered executive who is secretly committing sexual homicide. One of the many themes in the movie is that the murderer was earlier encouraged by a call girl to act out his sexual fantasies, with the observation "As long as it is only fantasy, it is okay." As the movie unfolds, it becomes clear that his behavior follows

encounters was very similar to the punishments he used to think up for himself. In both, he said his goal was to torture and demoralize himself—to feel guilty, defeated, and disgusted with himself. In short, he alternated between being an idealized, perfect child of God and being the lowest of the low. When asked what his grandmother would think about his decadent phases, he said that she probably would say something like this: "He sure is a free thinker." While in his decadent phases, he tried to live in an imaginary world, and he was angry that it "doesn't work."

The requisite number of DSM criteria applied. His exploitativeness was demonstrated by his involvement in selling drugs bought from patients on a psychiatric ward to patients on a detoxification ward (item 6). His dramatic symptoms were extraordinary and unique (item 3). He was preoccupied with fantasies about the ideal, including, most remarkably, perfection in the art of self-degradation (item 2). Entitlement was reflected in his view that life owed him more than he was getting (item 5). Interesting, charming, and sociable, he successfully cultivated his position as a center of attention throughout the hospital (item 4).

If one ignores the present interpersonal interpretation of the DSM, this patient clearly also met the DSM criteria for BPD. He had a pattern of unstable and intense interpersonal relationships (criterion 2 for BPD) and showed impulsiveness in self-damaging ways (criterion 4). Affective instability (criterion 6) and intense anger (criterion 8) were present. He also made recurrent suicide attempts (criterion 5), and had an identity disturbance (criterion 3).

Despite the overlap between the DSM diagnoses of BPD and NPD, the interpersonal diagnosis is straightforward. The patient liked to be in CONTROL. He held others, including the interviewer, in contempt (BLAME). His emphasis on his autonomy (SEPARATE) was intense, and his unusual love for himself (ACTIVE SELF-LOVE plus SELF-NEGLECT) was clear, as was his self-contempt (SELF-BLAME). His wish to be affirmed as perfect was distinct, and his fear of being controlled was outstanding. For example, he worried about whether in the recovery process outlined by AA, he would have to give up his will and lose his self to become a "nonentity. The more I get, the harder it is to run," he observed. His wildly defiant acting out and flight into sexual fantasy protected him from the fate of becoming a nonentity. He cherished the autonomy (SEPARATE) that is so dreaded by the BPD. His self-destructive activities were deliberately chosen and well orchestrated for moral purposes (SELF-BLAME). In short, he failed to meet one of the necessary criteria for BPD (fear of abandonment), and he did meet its exclusionary condition (tolerance of aloneness).

---

the fantasy. For many years I have carefully tracked the hypothesis that the SASB codes of especially rigid interpersonal patterns that do not change even after a long trial of psychotherapy are the same as the SASB codes of the favorite sexual fantasies. Much of the time the hypothesis is confirmed, and I call this parallel between SASB codes of the chief complaint and those of the favorite sexual fantasies the "*Klute* syndrome."

The necessary and exclusionary rules are not required to make this differential diagnosis between NPD and BPD. A scan of Table 6.2 reveals that he had the interpersonal behaviors predicted to overlap with BPD (CONTROL, BLAME, ATTACK, SELF-NEGLECT). He exhibited the behaviors listed for NPD but not BPD (IGNORE, SEPARATE, ACTIVE SELF-LOVE, SELF-BLAME). Finally, he did not show behaviors predicted to be present in BPD but not NPD (ACTIVE LOVE,[2] TRUST, and SELF-PROTECT).

This man's interpersonal history also showed reasonable correspondence to pathogenic predictions. His grandmother adored him, and greatly encouraged him to be special and beyond the reach of ordinary roles (hypothesis 1, Table 6.1). She also indulged him, and apparently gave him substantial control of the household (hypothesis 2). The grandmother's disappointment with his mortal sins was dramatically underscored by sending him to his bedroom to think up his own punishments (hypothesis 3).

EXPECTABLE TRANSFERENCE REACTIONS AND TREATMENT IMPLICATIONS

Transference Reactions

The men in both of the case examples above were gifted. One might say that these extraordinary people had good reason to love themselves. This association of ACTIVE SELF-LOVE with NPD raises the question of whether self-love should be viewed as normal. Many people, including therapists, believe that self-love is morally bad or pathological. Inspection of the details of the descriptions for ACTIVE SELF-LOVE that appear in Table 3.6 show that it is not necessarily narcissistic. Normal self-love is balanced and based in reality. Perfection is not involved. There is realistic acknowledgment of one's limits. There is no need elevate the self by diminishing others. Narcissistic self-love, by contrast to normal self-love, is embedded in a context of diminishing and ignoring the needs of others. Therapy with an NPD, then, need not involve exorcism of ACTIVE SELF-LOVE. Only the context in which it appears needs to change.

Narcissists seek warm support and understanding, and look forward to healing in the warm light of an admiring and high-status therapist. The transference patterns likely to emerge in the therapy relationship will include demands for support and admiration; a wish to control the therapy; rage at and disapproval of the therapist who fails to meet these needs; and a high likelihood of

---

[2]Recalling Kernberg's (1984) patient who approached many women sexually, the reader might ask why ACTIVE LOVE is not characteristic of NPD. The answer is that sexual contact is not necessarily coded ACTIVE LOVE. Table 3.2 shows that ACTIVE LOVE involves cuing on the other person and giving uncomplicated warmth. NPDs do not show this sensitivity to others. BPDs, by contrast, cue very well on other persons when in the loving state.

withdrawing from treatment at the "first bump in the road." The initial demand is that the therapist collude with rather than collaborate against "it," the patient's maladaptive patterns. A therapist should be aware that it is very easy for patient and therapist happily to affirm each other, while condemning the world. If this happens, there is little prospect for constructive change.

Treatment of NPD starts with the therapist in a bind. The patient feels entitled to adoring, warm support that, if given upon demand, will enable the continuation of the narcissistic patterns. Yet confrontation, even in the slightest degree, will be experienced as devastating criticism. It is likely that the NPD will terminate therapy before it even gets started. For example, one NPD entered a therapy group to deal with the "discovery" that his mother loved herself more than she loved him. Early on, he angrily withdrew from the group because some of the members did not agree with his choice of a favorite television program.

The definition of therapy as an opportunity to learn about one's patterns to work toward desired change is in itself an acknowledgment of imperfection. The therapy contract challenges the NPD's basic belief that he or she is not receiving adequate support and acknowledgment from the world. The therapist can use the NPD's preference to externalize by commenting on how the new learning will affect others. For example, the NPD can be told, "as you learn more about your own patterns and how to change them, you may find that you are getting better responses from others."

Treatment Implications:
The Five Categories of Correct Response

The view of therapy as a learning experience permits definition of therapist errors on a moment-to-moment basis. Therapy interventions can be evaluated in terms of whether they enhance collaboration, facilitate learning about patterns and their roots, block maladaptive patterns, enhance the will to change, or effectively encourage new patterns. The effect of interventions is assessed in terms of the actual impact on the patient, not in terms of the therapist's intention. If the effect of an intervention on NPD is rage, angry withdrawal, or regal autonomy, then the intervention is an error. The therapist using the present learning orientation is unlikely to "point out" a "resistance," because it is likely to be coded as BLAME and elicit old patterns.

Even if therapist interventions are evaluated on the basis of patient responsiveness, the patient still shares responsibility for what happens in therapy. Suppose the therapist offers substantial support and empathy, and tries to elicit the NPD's interest in changing himself or herself. If the patient unrelentingly maintains the old patterns, then it is correct for the therapist to say, "Maybe this isn't a good time to work on these things. How about taking a break from therapy, with the idea that you can come back when and if some of these ideas begin to make sense to you?" Such a stance appropriately avoids enabling already thriving patterns of entitlement and noncontingent self-approval.

Facilitating Collaboration

Collaboration in any treatment is founded on therapist empathy. Kohut (1971) noted that empathy is especially central to the treatment of NPD. According to Kohut, the narcissistic deficit in the self can be corrected if the patient can use the therapist as a "selfobject." That is, if the patient can use the therapist as an extension of the self, then he or she can internalize that experience. Through consistent empathy, the therapist provides the affirmation and soothing needed to learn self-regulation. The patient eventually internalizes this empathic affirmation of self.

Of course, with an NPD, self-affirmation seems overdone in the first place. The NPD's self approval is not balanced by an ability to see and accept defects. The crucial process of learning to tolerate one's own faults is modeled by the therapist. According to Kohut, this process is facilitated if the therapist can acknowledge an occasional minor lapse in understanding. The difference between the patient and therapist experience of the moment of therapist error creates an "optimal [level of] frustration" (p. 197). Tiny reminders of therapist fallibility and therapist acceptance of it enable the NPD to accept his or her own faults. This modeling of fallibility should not be overdone; the therapist buried in apologies will only exacerbate the NPD patterns.

Facilitating Pattern Recognition

To break patterns, there must be "confrontations" that are gentle and embedded in strong support. The phrasing of empathic statements must be carefully chosen, or they will reinforce the patterns of NPD. Some empathic statements enable old patterns, whereas others encourage insight and contribute to the potential for change. Consider, for example, the narcissistic husband who falls apart when his wife brings a complaint about him to marital therapy. One possible empathic response to this situation is this: "You have been trying so hard to make things go well, and here she just comes back with complaints." No doubt the NPD will think that this accurate reflection of his view is "right on." But SASB labels show that this version of therapist support has a significant chance of enhancing the NPD's pattern of blaming and externalizing. The reflection can be coded as BLAME. The wife is unlikely to react constructively to the implied therapist collusion with the pattern of blaming her.

Another unhelpful version of empathy is this remark: "After trying so hard to make things go well, it must be hard for you to hear her disappointment." This form of support is empathic (AFFIRM), but it is likely to validate and intensify the NPD's sense of distress. Chapter 4 contrains a discussion of the importance of trying to avoid exacerbating symptoms by offering empathy for suffering.

Still another likely error in empathy is this: "I know it will be hard, but if we are going to improve the marriage, everyone will have to be willing to look at his or her own part. Let's listen to your wife's complaint." Although the wife will probably be pleased with this reflection, the average NPD will probably feel attacked and humiliated (BLAME) by the therapist. Of course, if the therapist has great status and prestige, he or she may "get away" with such confrontations. The typical clinician is not given such latitude by the NPD.

An optimal therapist response may be as follows: "You have been trying so make things work well, and you feel just devastated to hear that they aren't going as perfectly as you thought." This response is an accurate and complete summary of the situation in terms of the NPD's dynamic organization. It demonstrates warm understanding, and still presses the edge of the NPD's awareness of important patterns.[3] In marital therapy there are ample opportunities for the NPD to learn empathy for another person, provided the process is not allowed to degenerate into a barrage of messages coded BLAME. Consistent therapist concentration on careful and supportive reflections of the complete dynamic picture helps the NPD see and change his or her patterns.

Blocking Maladaptive Patterns

Among other things, the NPD needs to learn to recognize and block the patterns of entitlement, grandiosity, and envy of others' successes. This need can be addressed if the therapist bases his or her observations about these basic patterns on knowledge of the antecedent experiences. For example, a narcissistic man who is ruminating angrily about recent acknowledgments directed toward a friend rather than himself may appreciate the following therapist comment: "Well, that will certainly make it hard for your mother at her next bridge party." Such a comment picks up on the destructive affect of the moment and draws out the connection to the originating relationship. At the moment, the NPD feels entitled to the adoration himself. He is pressured by the idea that his mother will be happy in her world if and only if the NPD is the exalted center of the universe. According to this analysis, the recommended comment presses awareness toward the source of the envy. The building awareness of the roots of the pattern should enhance the possibilities that the NPD can and will distance from the ancient contract. He will be helped if he can see that his jealousy is driven by his need to give and receive support from his internalized version of his mother.

If the primary caregiver is still living and remains emotionally centered on the NPD, then such interpretations can be very concretely based in the here and now. If not, then the understanding about the ongoing relationship with the internalized version of that person is the focus: "If your mother were still living, that sure would make it hard for her at her next bridge party." If the patient understands the present approach to therapy, the therapist can say, "That will sure make it hard for your 'internalized mother' the next time she wants to show you off." These examples attempt to enhance the NPD's will to separate from old internalizations. They try to shift the focus from the angry affect about the

---

[3]This example is from an actual case that had not progressed well until the present approach was used.

friend to the issues underlying it. As the NPD comes to realize the burden that comes with expecting noncontingent adoration, he may give up his addiction to it. He may become free to enjoy the good fortune of friends without contamination from old interpersonal contracts.

The reader is reminded that the hypotheses about underlying issues must be affirmed by the direct statements from the patient. Before the therapist makes any comments suggested by the "bridge party" example, the underlying hypothesis about the early learning should be affirmed or rejected. The check can be completed by analysis of narratives about childhood, or by fantasy or role play. For example, as the NPD rages at his friend's success, the therapist could ask, "Are you willing to explore how your pain about this might be related to your own underlying issues?" If he is willing, then the therapist can suggest, "How about using a little fantasy to see what else is going on here? What if your mother had been at your breakfast table this morning, and read about your friend in the paper? What might she say?" If the patient thinks his mother would say, "So why can't you be in the paper?", that would support the present interpretation. On the other hand, if the NPD thinks his mother would say, "That's wonderful. I always liked so-and-so. I'm so happy for him," then a reformulation of the case and the diagnosis may be in order.

The delicate art of pushing the edge of awareness for the NPD without destroying the therapy relationship is hard to describe. I have scared away many NPDs, and have only recently begun to approach mastery of the problem. Since examples can help, a second is offered here. Consider an NPD husband who is raging that his wife failed to greet him at the front door when he returned home from work last night. It is helpful if he can be reminded of the roots behind his vulnerability to such "slights." First, the therapist may try to clarify whether there are other affects, such as shame and fear, associated with the wife's failure to greet him. These may be present because of his assumption that her inattention was the result of some crime he allegedly committed. If so, the therapist can ask whether the shame or fear is a familiar feeling. The question may lead the NPD back to childhood, when his mother would withhold her usual joyful greeting if she was displeased with him. The present adult relationship with his wife may then effectively be contrasted with the early one with his mother. The NPD's wife, for example, may suffer from Self-Defeating Personality Disorder. Perhaps on the evening in question, she was trying to handle a number of responsibilities at the moment her husband arrived home. Her overwhelmed state, rather than her disappointment in her husband, might have made it impossible for her to greet him as usual. Maybe the baby was crying and dinner was burning at the time he drove up. The NPD can learn about her perspective in marital therapy. As he comes to understand her world, he can be relieved of the vulnerability that comes with needing her constant attention and approval. He may be able to drop his rage at her failures to center on him. He may learn ultimately to participate more actively in the burdens of household management. Such sharing of inglorious burdens, of course, should diminish the patterns of entitlement and undue self-importance. As the husband reduces his demands to be indulged, the wife will also need to confront her self-defeating behaviors that have enabled her husband's NPD.

NPD often coexists with alcohol and drug abuse. This may be associated with the fact that alcohol and other drugs of choice give a noncontingent feeling of dominance and well being. For a long time, alcohol has been compared in the clinical folklore to an alternately nurturant and withholding, but ultimately destructive, parent. The interpersonal dimensionality of childhood patterns can be recaptured by the alcohol and drugs. It does not follow that every case of alcohol or drug abuse is associated with NPD. Nonetheless, AA, which has a reasonable success rate, does have a philosophy that strikes at the core of the narcissistic pattern. Entitlement is confronted. Generous support is offered, but only if the person shows active efforts to confront the problem: "I am an alcoholic. Alcohol controls me. I choose not to let it." The structure of AA encourages individuals to give up the need to be in control as it simultaneously offers the opportunity to control others while they struggle to control alcohol. Implemented paradoxically, AA uses the predilection of NPDs toward control and the wish for support to block the maladaptive pattern of abusing alcohol.

Strengthening the Will to Give Up Maladaptive Patterns

The sensitive problem of enhancing the will to change can sometimes be approached in NPD (as well as in other disorders) with an idea described earlier as the "*Klute* syndrome" (see footnote 1). The idea, probably not new, is that sexual fantasies reinforce the very interactional patterns the patient needs to get rid of. I agree with the psychoanalytic position that sexuality has a major role in NPD. I disagree that there is a direct link between homosexuality and NPD. The NPD patterns of grandiosity, entitlement, and contempt for others can be seen in homosexuals, heterosexuals, or asexuals. Sexual orientation is independent of the quality of interactive patterns.

The *Klute* syndrome suggests that individuals with NPD may have sexual fantasies that parallel the interactive patterns characteristic of the disorder. A patient of Kernberg (1975, p. 193) had sadistic masturbation fantasies since childhood: "He would see himself tearing up women, torturing a group of them and then 'freeing' the one who seemed innocent, gentle, good, loving and forgiving —an ideal, ever-giving, ever-forgiving, beautiful, and inexhaustible mother surrogate." Clearly Kernberg's patient had aggressive (ATTACK) domination (CONTROL) over the women in his sexual fantasies. The wish in the fantasy was the same as the NPD wish (ACTIVE LOVE, PROTECT).

The theory of the *Klute* syndrome suggests that patients cannot change in therapy if they repeatedly have orgasms while conjuring images having the interpersonal dimensionality of the disorder. The patterns of the disorder (e.g., having aggressive control, being adored) are powerfully reinforced by such sexual practices. The implication of the *Klute* analysis is that reprogramming of sexual fantasies is necessary to achieve lasting behavioral change.

Wildly indulgent sexual bingeing was a major part of the patient's behavior in case 2. The sexual acting out was tied directly to the grandmother's disciplinary technique: She banished him to his bedroom with the message that he should please her by punishing himself. The likely linkage of masturbation to the task of self-blame while he was alone in his bedroom was not explored in the interview. However, the *Klute* syndrome was discussed with him in the abstract, and this bright man quickly understood and affirmed the need to try to link his orgasms with very different interpersonal images.

Like any powerful idea, this one can be misused. It is possible deliberately to encourage destructive sexual fantasies. Persons with NPD, ASP, or Sadistic Personality Disorder are capable of exacerbating self-destruction in persons with masochistic fantasies. Individuals with DPD, Self-Defeating Personality Disorder, and Multiple Personality Disorder are especially likely to complement the preferences of individuals with aggressive interpersonal and sexual orientations. The therapist's job is to try to help both participants in the sadomasochistic match recognize and change the destructive patterns in sexual fantasy as well as in social interactions.

Patients who want to treat themselves for the *Klute* syndrome can be instructed in basic principles of behavior therapy. The first task is to pick a new fantasy that has the desired interpersonal dimensionality. There is no particular need for the therapist to know details of the old fantasy, but it is vital to review the new one. The new fantasy "passes" if its SASB codes are in the normal range described in Chapter 3 (AFFIRM, ACTIVE LOVE, PROTECT, DISCLOSE, REACTIVE LOVE, TRUST). If the patient is in a love relationship that is primarily friendly and well balanced on the power–autonomy axis, he or she may be encouraged to abandon the need for any fantasy at all. If the relationship is already in the ideal range, no fantasy is needed; the patient can concentrate simply on the present of the relationship with the loved person.

Once an image associated with normal adjustment has been selected for reprogramming, the next step is to introduce the new image at the moment of orgasm. This will reliably ruin orgasm. But if the patient is motivated enough to change, he or she may keep trying until it does not. Then the new image is introduced earlier and earlier in the sexual sequence until the old fantasies are faded out entirely. It is not possible to describe all the ramifications of this treatment approach in the present book. Sexual reprogramming is extremely powerful and should be undertaken only with considerable caution. It appears to strike directly at the core of the organization of the personality.

Powerful though it may be, the most common response to the *Klute* program is for the patient to report that "it isn't worth it." People do not wish to sacrifice sexual pleasure for the possibility that the switch in fantasy would help them change their interpersonal patterns for the better. For those that do try the sexual reprogramming, there are usually dramatic changes, sometimes unexpected ones. Sudden "cures" have materialized. Unexpected psychoses, and quite a few divorces, have emerged precipitously. For this reason, it is a good idea to introduce the *Klute* syndrome treatment with the warning that it is very potent. The patient should agree not to make any significant life decisions or changes without first discussing them in depth for several therapy sessions.

Facilitating New Learning

Once the patient understands the patterns of NPD, and decides to give up the quest for unattainable or maladaptive goals, new learning is relatively easy. The focus of new interpersonal learning for NPD is empathy. It can effectively be taught in the context of marital therapy, but such marital therapy is not easy. Since NPDs easily form complementary relationships with individuals with Self-Defeating Personality Disorder, as noted above, marital therapy runs a high risk for blaming the self-defeating party. The NPD begins therapy convinced that his or her distress is attributable to the inadequacies of the self-defeater, who in turn is ever ready to embrace the blame the NPD offers. Therapist interventions designed only to "increase communication" or to "help the couple express affect" are very likely to do little more than enable such destructive complementarity. On the other hand, genuine collaboration against "the old patterns" can yield constructive change. Clarification of the different perspectives of loved ones can enhance the understanding of separate, equally entitled selves.

For example, therapist suggestions for allocation of goods and services in the marriage can undercut the modes of entitlement in the NPD and the undue self-sacrifice in the marital partner. The therapist may suggest that the couple seek financial counseling. Once the financial parameters are known by both partners, fairness and empathy can be built into the plans for managing money. There can be separate funds for communal business (household expenses, business expenses, and other "basics"), for marital pleasures (vacations, dinners out, visits to the theater), and separate discretionary funds for personal "self-indulgences."

Role play is another interesting way to teach empathy. For example, the NPD husband who was so furious when his wife failed to greet him at the front door can play the role of his wife at the time he arrived. This exercise may help him see that she had other things on her mind at the moment he felt so slighted. Playing the role of someone who is the target of his indignation may help him learn about his impact. In role play, there must be collaborative and benign use of the NPD's exact words and inflections. Inexact mirroring will elicit rage and withdrawal. On the other hand, consistent therapist use of all of the five correct categories of intervention will help the therapy maintain the "white heat of relevance." That focus moves the patient toward change and personal growth.

7

Histrionic Personality Disorder

"You will take care of me."

REVIEW OF THE LITERATURE

Hysteria, the clinical predecessor to HPD, inspired the development of modern psychotherapy. In 1892, Freud and Breuer described a remarkable new cathartic treatment that was effective for a variety of elusive neurological complaints. They cured contractures, neuralgias, hallucinations, and more, using the methods of hypnosis and talking therapy. In 1892, Freud reported:

> . . . when we had succeeded in bringing the exciting event to clear recollection, and had also succeeded in arousing with it the accompanying affect, and when the patient had related the occurrence in as detailed a manner as possible and had expressed his feeling in regard to it in words, the various hysterical symptoms disappeared at once, never to return. (Freud, 1892/1959, p. 28)

Freud noted that the symptoms were related directly or symbolically to earlier trauma, nearly always sexual, and concluded that "hysterical patients suffer principally from reminiscences" (1892/1959, p. 29). He explained the symptoms:

> They are all of them impressions that have failed to find an adequate discharge, either because the patient refused to deal with them for fear of distressing mental conflicts, or because (in the case of sexual impressions) he is forbidden to do so by modesty or by social circumstances, or finally because he received these impressions in a state in which his nervous system was incapable of dealing with them. (1892/1959, p. 30)

Later, Freud drew a more complicated picture of the cause of hysteria. The premise most directly pointing to the unconscious was this: "The hysterical symptom arises as a compromise between two opposing affects or instinctual trends, of which one is attempting to express a partial impulse or component of the sexual constitution, while the other tries to suppress it" (1908/1959, p. 56).

Freud's hypotheses about the cause of hysteria supported the validity of a talking therapy directed toward uncovering unconscious conflicts. He mentioned two vehicles for the curative effect of talking therapy. The first and more widely understood and applied mechanism of cure can be called the "expressive factor." Freud said that the earlier reaction to (sexual) trauma had been suppressed, and remained "attached to the memory." If that feeling was expressed fully, the memory could recede into the past, leaving few residual elements in the present: "That fading of recollection called 'forgetting' . . . tends more than anything else to absorb ideas which have lost their affective tone" (Freud, 1892/1959, p. 31). Freud's hypothesis was that trauma can be forgotten only if it is recalled to consciousness and the associated emotions are expressed fully. This idea is the basis for the immensely popular therapeutic approach used in present-day derivatives of psychoanalysis. Many practitioners of gestalt therapy (Perls, 1969), transactional analysis (Berne, 1964), and various "eclectic" psychotherapies assign extremely high therapeutic value to the act of expressing feelings as an end in itself.

A second treatment vehicle mentioned by Freud can be called a "cognitive factor." Freud wrote: "The memory of an injury to the feelings is *corrected by an objective evaluation of the facts*, consideration of one's actual worth and the like, and thus the normal man succeeds by means of associations in dissipating the accompanying affect" (1892/1959, p. 31, emphasis added). This cognitive factor has received far less attention from the present-day popular successors to psychoanalysis. It has been highlighted by other approaches that are not ordinarily seen as connected to psychoanalysis. For example, cognitive therapy (Beck, Rush, Shaw, & Emery, 1979) and rational–emotive therapy (Ellis, 1973) help the patient gain a more objective, rational, and healthful view of himself or herself.

Within mainstream psychoanalysis itself, the problem of hysteria naturally received much attention because of its central role in the construction of the etiological theory and the treatment approach. When unconscious conflicts break through into awareness, neurosis is the result; unlike character disorders, neurotic behaviors are not the quintessence of the person. The "psychoanalysis of character" grew out of observations of patient "resistances" to analytic interventions. Analysts noticed that patients' reaction to therapists' interpretations took the same form as the patients' patterns with others, and "for the same defensive purposes" (Fenichel, 1945, p. 463). In other words, there were some patients who could not be cured by release of repressed feelings in talking therapy. This group had chronic maladaptive behavior patterns that were exhibited in relation to their analysts as well as with other people in their adult lives. The manifestation of problem behaviors in the therapy process itself was called "resistance" to the therapy. A subdivision of psychoanalysis, called "ego psychology," was developed to address these problems in resistance. Within ego psychology, "personality" more than "symptom" was the topic of interest. It was no longer assumed that "that which has been warded off breaks through in an ego-alien form" (Fenichel, 1945, p. 464).

The DSM retained the psychoanalytic distinction between symptoms of hysteria that result from repression (neurosis) and chronic patterns of social interaction (personality). Syndromes belonging to the neurotic class of disorders appear in two separate DSM chapters. One is called "Dissociative Disorders (or

Hysterical Neuroses, Dissociative Type)." Examples of these disorders include Multiple Personality Disorder, Psychogenic Fugue, Psychogenic Amnesia, and Depersonalization Disorder. The other chapter on the "neurotic" version of hysteria is called "Somatoform Disorders." Examples of these disorders include Conversion Disorder (or Hysterical Neurosis, Conversion Type), Hypochondriasis (or Hypochondriacal Neurosis), Somatization Disorder, and Somatoform Pain Disorder. These two classes of disorders appear on Axis I of the DSM. They are "clinical syndromes" rather than "personality disorders." In effect, what used to be called "neurotic disorders" are now assigned to Axis I of the DSM; what used to be called "character disorders" now appear on Axis II of the DSM.

Chapter 1 of this book has reviewed the controversy surrounding Axis II. Because of the overlap problem, Widiger (1989) has suggested that it may not be appropriate to consider personality disorders as separate categories. Not only do personality disorders overlap one another, but many people with Axis II disorders also show symptoms of clinical syndromes assigned to Axis I. HPD is no exception to the tendency for people with personality disorders to qualify also for clinical syndromes. Freud's description of hysteria is now divided by the DSM into at least three "coexisting illnesses": (1) HPD (Axis II), (2) Dissociative Disorders (Axis I), and (3) Somatization Disorder (Axis I).

There are other Axis I disorders that coexist with HPD. These include anxiety that is sometimes intense enough to qualify as panic, depression, and thought disorder. In a stunningly rich summary of psychoanalytic thinking, Fenichel (1945) noted that the hysterical character has

> fear of sexuality and intense but repressed sexual strivings . . . hysterical characters have been described as persons who are inclined to sexualize all nonsexual relations, toward suggestibility, irrational emotional outbreaks, chaotic behavior, dramatization and histrionic behavior, even toward mendacity and its extreme form, pseudologia phantastica. (p. 527)

Fenichel's interpretation of the "thought disorder" in hysteria was quite sympathetic:

> Pseudologic behavior may very well be a revenge for having been deceived about sexual matters. . . . The formula may be phrased: "If it is possible to make people believe that unreal things are real, it is also possible that real things, the very memory of which is menacing, are unreal." (1945, p. 529)

In practice, HPDs seem to fall into two subtypes: those who are more flirtatious and focused on physical attractiveness, and those who are more concerned with somatic symptoms. The DSM definition emphasizes the flirtatious version for Axis II (see below). This type is also described in the DSM-III casebook illustration titled "Coquette" (Spitzer et al., 1981). There are no items in the current DSM description of HPD specifically marking the subtype that typically has "coexisting" Somatization Disorder. Curiously, the most recent casebook (Spitzer et al., 1989) provides an illustration of this type: "Suffering Lady" has many physical symptoms. The frequently observed association be-

tween the two histrionic behavioral patterns is not marked by the formal definition of HPD, but it has appeared in the casebooks.

HPD patients will vary in the degree to which they suffer from physical symptoms and the degree to which they are sexually seductive. There is, in other words,
substantial overlap between the two subtypes. The association between concern about
attractiveness and somatic symptomatology in HPD is puzzling. In some cultures,
including the one in which Freud treated persons with hysteria, being sickly in itself
was considered to be attractive in females. Femininity was marked by paleness,
vulnerability to swooning, and so on.[1] In current North American culture, Anorexia
Nervosa may represent a vestige of the connection between weakness and sexual
attractiveness. Many anorexic women starve themselves to emulate high-fashion
models. On close regard, some of the models themselves appear to be so thin that
they may be presumed to qualify for the diagnosis. But neither high-fashion models
nor women diagnosed with Anorexia Nervosa typically have HPD. They are more
likely to be highly disciplined and tightly controlled. In present-day North American culture, the association of physical illness with HPD does not appear to be
mediated by sexual attractiveness.

A genetic explanation for the association between illness and hysteria was
offered by investigators based in St. Louis (Cloninger & Guze, 1975). This psychiatric research group provided much of the impetus for the DSM's return to
Kraepelinian psychiatric diagnosis (Blashfield, 1984). Their epidemiological survey suggested that "daughters of sociopathic fathers had a significantly higher
prevalence of hysteria than did daughters of other fathers" (Cloninger & Guze,
1975, p. 27). The definition of hysteria in this pre-DSM-III research included
features now assigned to Axis I of the DSM:

> In these studies, hysteria, or Briquet's syndrome, was defined as a polysympto-
> matic disorder that is seen nearly always in females, begins early in life, and is
> characterized by a history of recurrent or chronic ill health, frequently described
> dramatically. Characteristic features of the history, most of which are seen in all
> patients, include many and varied pains, anxiety symptoms, gastrointestinal dis-
> turbances, urinary symptoms, menstrual difficulties, sexual and marital malad-
> justment, nervousness and mood disturbances, and conversion symptoms.
> (Cloninger & Guze, 1975, p. 27)

These investigators concluded that sociopathy and hysteria result from similar
(genetic) etiological factors. They wrote that "hysteria in women is a more prevalent and less deviant manifestation of the same process that causes sociopathy
in men" (Cloninger, Reich, & Guze, 1975, p. 23). Their definition of hysteria
included many physical symptoms not mentioned for HPD by the DSM. It is
not clear whether these investigators would maintain that the disorder now
defined as HPD has more to do with genes than with family interactions. Ques-

---

[1] I am indebted for this observation to an unknown but obviously perceptive woman who attended
a workshop in Portland, Oregon, in 1989.

tions about cause aside, their survey makes it clear that the "coexistence" of somatization and HPD persists, just as it did in Freud's time.

DSM DEFINITION OF THE DISORDER

The DSM definition provides the starting point for the present analysis. The DSM specifies that the diagnosis of HPD can be made if an individual meets five of the criteria. DSM-III-R items appear in **bold print,** and any changes introduced by the DSM-IV appear in *italics.* (As in earlier chapters, the item numbering used is that of the DSM-IV. Original numbers in the DSM-III-R appear after **bold** items, in brackets.)

A pervasive pattern of excessive emotionality and attention-seeking, beginning by early adulthood and present in a variety of contexts, as indicated by at least *five* **of the following:**

(1) is uncomfortable in situations in which he or she is not the center of attention [item 5 in DSM-III-R]

(2) is inappropriately sexually seductive in appearance or behavior [item 2 in DSM-III-R]

(3) displays rapidly shifting and shallow expression of emotions [item 6 in DSM-III-R]

(4) is overly concerned with physical attractiveness [item 3 in DSM-III-R]

(5) has a style of speech that is excessively impressionistic and lacking in detail, e.g., when asked to describe mother, can be no more specific than, "She was a beautiful person." [item 8 in DSM-III-R]

(6) expresses emotion with inappropriate exaggeration, e.g., embraces casual acquaintances with excessive ardor, uncontrollable sobbing on minor sentimental occasions, has temper tantrums [item 4 in DSM-III-R]

self-dramatization, theatricality, and exaggerated expression of emotion

(7) is self-centered, actions being directed toward obtaining immediate satisfaction; has no tolerance for the frustration of delayed gratification [item 7 in DSM-III-R]

is excessively intolerant of, or frustrated by, situations involving delayed gratification

(8) views relationships as possessing greater intimacy than is actually the case [new item]

manipulative suicide gestures, attempts [DSM-III item omitted from DSM-III-R and DSM-IV; I recommend restoring]

constantly seeks or demands reassurance, approval, or praise [item 1 in DSM-III-R; omitted from DSM-IV]

Morey (1988) reported that 21.6% of a sample of 291 outpatients being treated for personality disorder qualified for the HPD label. There was substantial overlap with BPD (55.6%), NPD (54%), AVD (31.7%), and DPD (30.2%).

PATHOGENIC HYPOTHESES

The method of using the SASB model to develop pathogenic hypotheses has been sketched in Chapter 5. Four main features of the developmental history have been identified specifically to account for each of the HPD symptoms listed in the DSM. A summary of the hypotheses linking interpersonal history to interpersonal patterns characteristic of the disorder appears in Table 7.1. A fuller discussion of these hypotheses is provided here.

1. The HPD was loved for his or her good looks and entertainment value. The developing HPD's self-concept in the family did not rest on competence or on signs of personal strength. Rather, the self-concept centered on how attractive, how pleasant, and how entertaining the HPD could be.

In prototypic form, the HPD is a pretty female who was admired and favored by her handsome and very interesting father. She, in turn, adored and worshiped her father. The relationship was flirtatious but not incestual. The pretty girl's relationship with her mother was competitive, and each was jealous of the other. Freud marked the tendency of children to identify with the same-sex parent and wish to marry the opposite-sex parent. In his 1909 paper on family romances, he commented:

> For a small child his parents are the first and the only authority and the source of all belief. The child's most intense and most momentous wish during these early years is to be like his parents (that is, the parent of his own sex) and to be big like his father and mother. (1909/1959, p. 74)

Freud's account of the little girl's wish to marry Daddy is quite complex. He believed that the girl's discovery that boys have penises, whereas she herself has been "mutilated," mobilizes her wish to acquire a penis for herself. "She has seen it and knows that she is without it and wants to have it" (1925/1959, p. 191).

> . . . there is no other way of putting it . . . the equation [becomes] "penis = child." She gives up her wish for a penis and puts in place of it a wish for a child: and *with this purpose in view* she takes her father as a love-object. Her mother becomes the object of her jealousy. The girl has turned into a little woman. (p. 195)

Again, the Freudian analysis is fantastic, and not easily amenable to verification or disproof by the method of interview. On the other hand, the basic observation that little boys want to marry Mommy and would like to dispense with Daddy is verifiable at the most casual level. Ordinary conversations with male toddlers reliably include declarations of intent to marry Mommy. The same is true for little girls, who frequently state that they plan to marry Daddy. The so-called Oedipal phenomenon is clear, but the reasons for it are not. The present analysis of why the HPD daughter exaggerates the common wish to marry Daddy is considerably simpler than the psychoanalytic view.

The interpersonal analysis of the Oedipal phenomenon begins with Freud's observations on the little girl's stated wishes. She wishes to be like (and maybe better than) Mommy, and to marry Daddy. This can be confirmed by listening to her talk about it. In families of girls destined for HPD, the romance between

Table 7.1. Interpersonal Summary of HPD

History	Consequences of history
1. Loved for attractiveness, entertainment value (REACTIVE LOVE) Competence (SEPARATE) was frowned upon Favored over same-sex parent	1. Very concerned with prettiness, entertainment value (REACTIVE LOVE) Avoids competence Threatened by others' dependency Contempt for same-sex persons (BLAME)
2. Appearance, charm (REACTIVE LOVE) sufficed to CONTROL caregiver	2. Self-concept centers on ability to coerce others into caregiving (CONTROL plus TRUST) via charm (REACTIVE LOVE) or BLAME.
3. "Butterfly," "as if we love each other" household demanded charm (REACTIVE LOVE) in a context of neglect (drawing complementary WALL OFF)	3. Charming, entertaining (REACTIVE LOVE) but personally inaccessible (WALL OFF)
4. Sickliness, neediness (TRUST) sufficed to CONTROL caregiver	4. Demands (CONTROL) nurturance when needy (TRUST)

Summary. There is strong fear of being ignored, together with a wish to be loved and taken care of by someone powerful, who nonetheless can be controlled through use of charm and entertainment skills. The baseline position is of friendly trust that is accompanied by a secretly disrespectful agenda of forcing delivery of the desired nurturance and love. Inappropriate seductive behaviors and manipulative suicidal attempts are examples of such coercions.

SASB codes of HPD baseline: Coercive dependency (TRUST plus CONTROL) implemented by charm (REACTIVE LOVE) that is inauthentic (WALL OFF) and backed up by BLAME. Common variations include insincere seduction (REACTIVE LOVE plus CONTROL plus WALL OFF) and manipulative suicidality (SELF-ATTACK plus TRUST plus CONTROL). *Wishes:* To receive ACTIVE LOVE and PROTECT. *Fears:* To receive IGNORE. *Necessary descriptors:* Coercive dependency. *Exclusionary descriptors:* Self-sabotage following happiness or success.

father and daughter is public. Everybody knows that the HPD is "Daddy's little sweetheart." For example, he may take her all dressed up to show off to his buddies at the poker club. Mother loses out, and the daughter becomes the "other woman" interpersonally, but not sexually. Parenthetically, in BPD, the incest taboo is smashed, and the daughter truly is the "other woman."[2]

Just as the incestual scenario is an easy way, but not the only way to generate BPD, the Oedipal scenario is an easy way but not the only way to generate HPD. Alternatively, the admiration that encourages HPD can come from grandparents, aunts, or uncles. It can be directed toward sons as well as daughters. However, if the attention and admiration are given simply for "just" being handsome or pretty, then NPD is a more likely long-range outcome. If parental concern about the child's appearance involves symbiotic investment in the parent's own self-definition, HPD is not the result. In that case, the more likely outcome is a disorder centering on identity problems. If HPD is to be the outcome, admiration for physical appearance must be accompanied by condition 2, described below.

[2]My friend and colleague Sue E. Estroff has observed that mothers of incest victims are confronted with a monumental conflict of roles: that of parent, and that of loser to the "other woman."

Because parental rewards centered on appearance, the HPD fails to learn to be competent. As adults, HPDs need and select nurturant spouses, who typically enable the incompetence by becoming "too nurturant." It is not unusual to find spouses of HPDs who not only hold down jobs, but, as the HPDs become more depressed, increasingly help with child rearing and other household tasks. An HPD's self-concept decreases as a spouse displays seemingly infinite competence in response to the escalating debility. The HPD's demanding dependency continues to accelerate, driven by the thesis put so well by one patient: "If I become independent, who will help if I get in trouble?"

Another consequence of alliance between the female HPD and Daddy is that other women, like Mommy, are treated with contempt. A female HPD is not likely initially to choose a woman psychotherapist. She knows that power and nurturance are dispensed by men; other women are "losers." But this is not always so. One HPD woman, who had adopted a lesbian lifestyle, said, "My mother was always showing me off [for good looks and skill at dancing]. Mother would make scenes over how I looked." In her family, the powerful one was the mother. The HPD was affirmed by her mother for appearance and charm (and instrumental incompetence). Those attributes were repeated in her adult love relationships with women.

2. In its prototypic form, the HPD programming is set by an adoring Daddy who dotes on his daughter, flirtatiously and admiringly doing anything and everything for her. This communicates simply that the HPD can expect submissive love contingent on charm and looks. Keeping oneself attractive gives considerable leverage with powerful others who can meet all of one's needs.

An HPD learns that physical appearance and charm are *functional*; they are used to control important others. The self-concept centers on looks and skills at entertaining, which facilitate control of an important person who will nurture and protect the HPD. The HPD's mission to charm and entertain arises from the fact that his or her sense of competence rests squarely on appearance rather than on instrumental skills. One HPD explained this version of self-definition when she said, "I look in the mirror all the time just to be sure that somebody is there." This HPD also explained her mandate to avoid competence as she observed, "I should attract people, but I shouldn't *do* anything." Another commented, "My husband is happy if I play tennis and do volunteer work, but gets very upset when I talk about going back to college." The HPD's assignment is to be "flashy," or, as still another patient put it, to be "an ornament." The HPD follows these rules: "Be attractive and charming, and those who are charmed will take care of you. You do not need to learn to do things for yourself. In fact, competence is neither attractive nor charming. Your strength is in bonding with strong providers, and the basis of that link is your attractiveness and charm. If you lose your charm, you lose your bond and your strength." The quintessence of the HPD pattern is "coercive dependency." Coquettishness is an excellent means to coerce caregiving.

The functional attractiveness of the HPD sometimes did more than elicit nurturance. It may have been important to the HPD's ability to control the father's rage at the mother. The HPD's charm and power over the father may have restricted his attacks on less favored siblings. In these cases, the HPD protected others by accepting the assignment to take care of the father when he entered his dreadfully incompetent (usually alcoholic or depressed) stages. In these more complicated family scenarios, HPD charm had very high stakes. If the HPD charmed the father out of his bad mood, he might not start a very threatening scene of uproar. If the HPD made the father feel and act better, everyone was relieved. In this way, the HPD's attractiveness gave him or her important power. Although the HPD could protect others through enlightened use of charm, rescue was not the goal. The HPD's own agenda was to take care of the parent so the parent could get better and take care of the HPD again.

Success was within reach but was not assured. The possibility of failure at this very important task of controlling a flawed caregiver made the HPD susceptible to anxiety or panic. If the HPD was not attractive or charming enough, the family situation would become dangerous. For the same reason, the HPD could also become panicked over any signs that the caregiver might be vulnerable. For example, consider the family with a father who was a stellar community figure who doted on the HPD. His very high status gave the HPD tremendous leverage in school and in the community. Meanwhile, behind closed doors at home, the father was alcoholic and often viciously attacked his wife or the children. When drunk, he would speak of his trials and tribulations out in the world. This taught the HPD to dread signs of the father's vulnerability. They signaled loss of personal nurturance and danger to other family members.

A consequence of the assignment to keep a happy mood in the family is that an HPD will orchestrate social gatherings. "I want others to be comfortable and friendly," one HPD explained. She felt compelled to carefully plan and control social events. Since skill at entertainment defines identity and provides security, the HPD requires public affirmation of these productions. The scenarios, which often have him or her in the starring role, must be applauded gratefully. Sometimes the HPD also identifies with the raging Daddy and exhibits "tempers" himself or herself. But the tempers of the HPD are not random. They too have the function of eliciting better caregiving.

The instrumental incompetence necessarily means that the HPD will be dependent, *and will be uncomfortable if anyone is dependent on him or her.* Frequently HPDs become depressed in reaction to parental responsibility. They resent the nurturance their spouses may give to the children. Such threats to loss of caregiving also lead to anger or panic that can be followed by depression.

3. The HPD's household was a shifting stage. Unpredictable changes stemmed from parental instability, perhaps associated with alcohol. In HPD families, the chaos was dramatic and "interesting," not primitive and life-threatening as in BPD families. Literature and the dramatic arts may have been central interests in the HPD family. Variations on the themes of love and power were played without constancy or depth. "My mother was a butterfly—I never could make contact with her," one HPD commented. Yet the family was supposed to be "wonderful, close, and happy." The adult consequence is to con-

tinue the pattern of superficial "as-if" social relationships that demand love from a distance.

The instability was accompanied by a demand to pretend that all was happy. Whenever a family demands that a happy face cover up chaos and ugliness, the defenses of denial and repression are encouraged. Denial and repression, in turn, are often associated with physical symptoms. The mysterious association between patterns of HPD and somatization may be strengthened, then, by threatening family conditions that must be denied and repressed.

4. The "sickly" subtype of HPD is more likely than the "coquettish" subtype to have been nurtured for being ill. These people have learned that complaints and disabilities are an effective way to elicit warm concern. Along with the forces that encourage denial, then, the families reward sickness. These two factors combine. Either encouraged to deny and repress, or nurtured for disability, or both, an HPD can embrace the sick role to the point of having Somatization Disorder. Remarkably large hospital charts chronicling dozens of surgeries and other procedures, some with slim medical justification, ensue. For this group, sickliness is a well-practiced means to coerce caregiving.

One route to HPD as described by the DSM is through physical attractiveness and charm. A second is through sickliness, and this appears with Somatization Disorder on Axis I. Presumably the choice of method depends on the interface between early social learning and constitutional tendencies. A naturally attractive child, for example, may be more vulnerable to being admired for appearance, and therefore may be more likely to use the seductive route. A constitutionally vulnerable child may be more likely to develop a sickly pattern. Some people employ both routes.

CONNECTIONS BETWEEN THE INTERPERSONAL HISTORY AND THE SYMPTOMS LISTED IN THE DSM

The "total HPD" shows all the symptoms mentioned in the DSM. Many of the items in the DSM are directly associated with self-definition as an entertainer, as a "showpiece." These include seductive behavior (item 2), overconcern with physical attractiveness (item 4), need to be the center of attention (item 1), need to be affirmed as an intimate friend by strangers (item 8), and intolerance for delay of gratification (item 7). In other words, if one is an entertainer, one must be attractive, and this is affirmed if there is applause from all who are present. The performer role also accounts for the exaggerated expressiveness (item 6), as well as the rapidly shifting and shallow emotional expression (item 3). These particular ways of performing are encouraged by the "as-if," "butterfly" household. Since competence requires focused cognitive process, the broad, unfocused cognitive style (item 5) may be a consequence of the need to cultivate incompetence to be attractive.

In an apparent effort to diminish the number of cases of HPD that also qualify for the label of BPD, the DSM-III-R and DSM-IV dropped manipulative suicidality from the list for HPD. These new definitions provide that if an HPD makes a suicide attempt, the label is likely to become BPD. My opinion is that if elimination of manipulative suicidality from the definition of HPD increased reliability, it did so at the expense of clinical validity. Many HPDs do engage in manipulative suicide attempts. My favorite example is the HPD who, in the midst of an argument with her husband, dramatically overdosed in front of him, ran into the bathroom, locked the door, and then became furious with him for taking so long to break the door down. Like most HPDs, she made the gesture "to get attention," and did not want to die.

The differences between suicidal attempts of BPDs and HPDs can often be established by asking for descriptions of perceptions and feelings before, during, and after the suicidal attempt. Suicidality in either a BPD or an HPD will be triggered by failed caregiving and perceived lack of attention. The HPD's suicidal activity will be well controlled and geared toward coercing more and better nurturance. For example, an HPD wife may take an overdose 5 minutes before her husband is due home from work. The act shows substantial trust in the reliability of his habits and in his ability to cope with an emergency. This form of suicidality is controlled and should be interpreted as an interpersonal event. By contrast, the BPD's attempt will be more reckless, autistic, and internally directed. As she struggles with her disapproving introject, she may take a dangerous overdose regardless of context and consequences.

INTERPERSONAL SUMMARY OF HPD

The foregoing analysis suggests a succinct interpersonal summary for HPD:

> *There is strong fear of being ignored, together with a wish to be loved and taken care of by someone powerful, who nonetheless can be controlled through use of charm and entertainment skills. The baseline position is of friendly trust that is accompanied by a secretly disrespectful agenda of forcing delivery of the desired nurturance and love. Inappropriate seductive behaviors and manipulative suicidal attempts are examples of such coercions.*

The summary is based on the SASB codes of the HPD baseline patterns and wishes. The codes themselves, listed in Table 7.1, provide a shorthand way to identify HPD. The baseline positions are REACTIVE LOVE, or TRUST plus CONTROL (a complex code), accompanied by detachment (WALL OFF) and backed up by BLAME. The wishes are to receive ACTIVE LOVE and PROTECT. The fear is of IGNORE.

The rhythm and harmonics of the HPD song are found in the sequences of interpersonal and intrapsychic response that the HPD gives and receives. The "tonic" HPD position is one of coercive dependency (TRUST plus CONTROL). The CONTROL is implemented through attractiveness and charm, which is made up of REACTIVE LOVE. The positions of REACTIVE LOVE and TRUST are backed up by BLAME, if necessary. One extreme version of the pattern is insincere seduction—REAC-

<u>TIVE</u> <u>LOVE</u> plus **CONTROL** plus <u>WALL</u> <u>OFF</u>. Another variation is for the control to be implemented through neediness engendered by sickness; this comprises <u>TRUST</u> plus **CONTROL**. An extreme version of this approach is manipulative suicidality, described by *SELF-ATTACK* plus <u>TRUST</u> plus **CONTROL**.

The HPD's organizing wish is to retrieve the compliant nurturance and love remembered from "the good old days" of childhood. The pattern of coercive dependency harmonizes well with someone who will comply by delivering more and better care, <u>SUBMIT</u> plus **PROTECT**. The HPD's fear is of **IGNORE**. These are the harmonics and rhythms of the HPD song.

Readers who can use the SASB codes will be able to generalize the present analysis to contexts not mentioned here. For example, it is not unusual for patients to complain that their depression is getting worse. Sometimes these complaints are presented to the therapist in a way that is characteristic of HPD. To interpret a complaint about depression in this way, the therapist would need to code the patient's process as he or she describes the depression. An HPD's process with the therapist as he or she complains about symptoms would include the notes of the HPD song. Consider this example:

> A patient arrived for an extra appointment brightly dressed and smiled as she said (<u>REACTIVE</u> <u>LOVE</u>) that she was continuing to have trouble with her depression (<u>TRUST</u>). She reminded the doctor that her husband was on the hospital board of trustees (**CONTROL**) and was very eager to see that she got better. The doctor tried hard to find the correct medication, but the vagueness of her descriptions of the symptoms (<u>WALL</u> <u>OFF</u>) made it hard to assess the problem.

The baseline notes of the HPD song are compared to those of the BPD and the NPD songs in Table 7.2. A scan of the table shows that HPD and BPD share the features **CONTROL, BLAME,** and <u>TRUST</u>. These codes reflect the coercive dependency that so clearly marks both groups. However, the coercion and dependency appear simultaneously (complex SASB code) in the HPD. By contrast, the BPD is clearly in one position and then clearly in the other. The BPD may engage in sweet <u>TRUST</u> and then switch to raw **CONTROL** or **BLAME**. The HPD will do something that simultaneously combines elements of each. Consider their different ways of asking for an extra appointment. The BPD will simply ask (<u>TRUST</u>) as soon as the idea comes to mind, and if refused will withdraw and **BLAME** the doctor for not caring. The HPD, by contrast, may plan ahead and wear a special outfit to a very tearful session; in the context of being attractive and very needy, this patient will ask for the extra appointment (<u>TRUST</u> plus **CONTROL**). These differences also appear in their suicidal behaviors. The BPD will impulsively engage in reckless suicidal action, momentarily oblivious of the consequences. The HPD will usually be sure that a reasonable possibility of rescue is ready to hand.[3]

The BPD and the HPD both want **PROTECT** and fear **IGNORE**. Their reasons are different. The BPD has life experiences that clearly associate aloneness with

---

[3]Nonetheless, suicidal threats and behaviors in HPD should also be taken very seriously. Suicidal episodes are always dangerous.

danger. The BPD has been programmed to run down a path to self-destruction whenever the possibility of aloneness arises. In contrast, the HPD has had more controlled life experiences, which have taught him or her that self-definition lies in his or her skills at charming and entertaining others. So long as he or she can be charming, somebody will make sure that all is well. The HPD's aversion to aloneness does not stem from unconscious fear of bodily harm; rather, it represents the loss of self-definition as the figure on center stage. The BPD's primitive clarity contrasts with the "higher level" of the HPD. The latter's control and contempt are masked in complex combination with neediness and attractiveness. Occasionally, this controlled picture of the HPD is marred by outbursts of temper.

Table 7.2 shows additional differences between these two groups. The BPD's warmth is active, while the HPD's is reactive (ACTIVE LOVE vs. REACTIVE LOVE). The BPD is capable of developing a more focused and lethal anger (ATTACK) and is more reckless (SELF-NEGLECT). Whereas the BPD is usually intensely enmeshed, the HPD is capable of cold distancing (WALL OFF) that is complicated by an appearance of friendliness.

HPD shares with NPD an easy willingness to CONTROL and BLAME. However, the NPD is more autonomous. The NPD is comfortable being SEPARATE, while the HPD is not. Although the HPD can show some separateness in complex codes with warm behaviors, he or she is generally warmer and more submissive than the NPD. Whereas the HPD survives by reading cues and managing others, the NPD lacks these skills. More inclined to IGNORE others, the NPD is focused only on his or her own concerns.

DSM DESCRIPTORS REVISITED

The DSM view of HPD has been translated into interpersonal language, and the psychosocial learning associated with HPD patterns has been outlined. In this section, the interpersonal analysis of HPD is compared directly to the DSM. DSM-III-R items appear in **bold print**; any changes introduced by the DSM-IV appear in *italics*. (Again, the item numbering used is that of the DSM-IV.) The interpersonal modifiers are underlined. Items from the WISPI (discussed in Chapter 1) appear in CAPITAL LETTERS.

A pervasive pattern of excessive emotionality and attention-seeking, beginning by early adulthood and present in a variety of contexts, as indicated by at least *five* of the following:

(1) is uncomfortable in situations in which he or she is not the center of attention

Commandeers the role of "the life of the party." If not the center of attention, reliably does something dramatic (e.g., makes up stories, creates a scene) to draw the focus.

AT SOCIAL GATHERINGS, I ALWAYS MANAGE TO DO SOMETHING THAT MAKES ME THE CENTER OF ATTENTION.

Table 7.2. Comparison of SASB Codes of BPD, NPD, and HPD

	BPD	NPD	HPD
1. EMANCIPATE			
2. AFFIRM			
3. ACTIVE LOVE	×		
4. PROTECT			
5. CONTROL	×	×	×*
6. BLAME	×	×	×
7. ATTACK	×	×	
8. IGNORE		×	
1. SEPARATE		×	
2. DISCLOSE			
3. REACTIVE LOVE			×*
4. TRUST	×		×*
5. SUBMIT			
6. SULK			
7. RECOIL			
8. WALL OFF			×*
1. SELF-EMANCIPATE			
2. SELF-AFFIRM			
3. ACTIVE SELF-LOVE		×*	
4. SELF-PROTECT	×		
5. SELF-CONTROL			
6. SELF-BLAME		×	
7. SELF-ATTACK	×		×*
8. SELF-NEGLECT	×	×*	

*Indicates that these codes within the same column appear in complex combinations with one another.

(2) is inappropriately sexually seductive in appearance or behavior

Characteristically emphasizes sexual attractiveness by appearance and behavior to a point beyond that appropriate for the social context. Despite intensive efforts to be seen as sexually attractive, is likely to be inaccessible rather than available sexually.

I ENJOY USING MY CHARM TO MAKE PEOPLE PASSIONATELY WANT ME AS THEIR LOVER, THOUGH I RARELY GO ALL THE WAY.

(3) displays rapidly shifting and shallow expression of emotions

Seems compelled to project an image of being attractive and charming even in contexts where others would be alienated (withdrawn or angry). On the other hand, can become suddenly angry over a minor and inadvertent "slight" to force better compliance next time.

MY SKILL AT SHOWING MY FEELINGS IN A COLORFUL WAY MAKES PEOPLE CARE FOR ME.

(4) is overly concerned with physical attractiveness

Goes to great lengths (spends excessive time, money, effort) to elicit praise and approval for being cute, lovable. Becomes angry or anxious if not praised, approved of.

I MAKE PEOPLE LIKE ME BY BEING SURE I ALWAYS LOOK MY VERY BEST.

(5) has a style of speech that is excessively impressionistic and lacking in detail, e.g., when asked to describe mother, can be no more specific than, "She was a beautiful person."

Is more interested in creating an image that is pleasantly dependent than in being personally effective. Sees use of logic and task orientation as an assignment for others, as not relevant to the self.

WHEN PEOPLE CAN'T UNDERSTAND WHAT I MEAN, THEY SHOULD APPRECIATE THE FACT THAT I AM NOT A DETAIL-ORIENTED PERSON.

(6) expresses emotion with inappropriate exaggeration, e.g., embraces casual acquaintances with excessive ardor, uncontrollable sobbing on minor sentimental occasions, has temper tantrums

self-dramatization, theatricality, and exaggerated expression of emotion

Has a sense of self as colorful, dramatic, and good at impression management. Sees self as competent at making social occasions extraordinarily interesting.

I AM A COLORFUL EMOTIONAL PERSON WITH A DRAMATIC FLAIR, AND I CAN CREATE ANY IMPRESSION I WANT.

(7) is self-centered, actions being directed toward obtaining immediate satisfaction; has no tolerance for the frustration or delayed gratification

is excessively intolerant of, or frustrated by, situations involving delayed gratification

Sees others as strong and able to provide whatever is needed whenever it is needed. Has no interest in developing competence at tasks. Counts on being attractive to someone powerful who can take care of things. Uses anger to coerce compliance if others do not immediately provide what is wanted and needed.

WHEN I NEED SOMEBODY TO TAKE CARE OF SOMETHING FOR ME, I USE MY CHARM TO GET IMMEDIATE ATTENTION.

(8) views relationships as possessing greater intimacy than is actually the case

USES FIRST NAME AND TALKS ABOUT "SPECIAL" RELATIONSHIP WHEN REFERRING TO A DOCTOR KNOWN ON A CASUAL PROFESSIONAL LEVEL. NEEDS TO BE REASSURED THAT NEW ACQUAINTANCES ARE ALREADY INTIMATE AND LIFELONG FRIENDS.

manipulative suicide gestures, attempts [DSM-III item omitted from DSM-III-R and DSM-IV; I recommend restoring]

Suicidal gestures or attempts have the interpersonal goal of making someone else do more of what is wanted or less of what is disliked. Attempts involve unquestioning trust in the person who is the perceived precipitant for the episode—for example, locking the

<u>bathroom door during a marital fight, overdosing, and then being angry because the</u>
<u>spouse took so long to break open the door.</u>

I HAVE GOTTEN SO FRUSTRATED IN AN ARGUMENT THAT I HAVE MADE A SUICIDAL SCENE IN ORDER TO
GET THE ATTENTION I NEED.

constantly seeks or demands reassurance, approval, or praise [DSM-III-R item omitted from DSM-IV]

NECESSARY AND EXCLUSIONARY CRITERIA

The present analysis permits definition of necessary and exclusionary conditions
for each personality disorder. For HPD, the recommended *necessary* descriptor
is a baseline position of coercive dependency. An *exclusionary* condition for HPD
is self-sabotage following happiness or success.

CASE ILLUSTRATIONS

Case 1

This 50-year-old married mother of four was admitted to the hospital for continuing
suicidality and a host of physical problems. The somatic complaints had, among other
things, required nearly two dozen surgeries, "always with a complication." She arrived
at the hospital with a collection of 19 different medications needed for her various disorders. Suicide represented a way to find relief from all the physical problems that she
said caused her depression.

The patient showed no signs of thought disorder other than discursiveness and a
tendency to lose her train of thought. In addition to suicidality, she suffered from anxiety, for which she had taken benzodiazapines. She was prone to fainting, and did so
during a group meeting at the hospital. Despite the suicidality, she retained a cheerful
outlook, stating that she had an ideal marriage and a perfect childhood.

The patient's husband, a very busy owner of a gas station, was extremely loving and
supportive. He "does whatever I want." She described him as helpless in the face of her
continuing suicidality and poor self-esteem. The depth of his tolerance was shown by
his response to her spending. He did not interfere with it, and simply became anxious
about how the debts would be paid. The patient said they had "beautiful sex," although
not in the past 2 years or so. The abstinence was thought to be a consequence of interference from medications for depression. The husband was frustrated by the loss of sex.
Friends had suggested that he leave the patient because of all her difficulties. He said that
he loved her and would stand by her.

The patient's father was subject to fits of temper, but not in relation to the patient.
She was certain this was because she was the only female child, and his "favorite."

The patient's mother was always cheerful, never complaining, and never angry, despite repeated provocation from the father. After one of the father's attacks on the mother, the patient remembered seeing her mother vacuuming the house with tears silently running down her cheeks. The patient hated these parental "waves," and took the role of peacemaker. To keep things calm, the patient would explain to her mother that her father "didn't mean it." Then she would explain to her father that her mother "didn't mean it." It was very difficult for the patient to be specific about the details of the parental fights, but she suggested that they had to do with money.

The mother was extremely supportive when the patient was ill. When she had stomach aches, the mother would put her in bed, make tea, give her hot water bottles, and sit on the bed with her and pat her leg. This image was so potent that it was revived during a near-death experience. In a medical emergency, the patient felt certain that her deceased mother was sitting on her bed in the usual way, patting her leg reassuringly. On the other hand, when the patient was healthy or had a success, her mother would warn against enjoying it. The mother would say, "You are beautiful and talented, but *don't let it go to your head.*" There were repeated warnings of the moral danger in enjoying achievements.

This patient met many of the DSM criteria for HPD. Her behavior in the hospital suggested that she liked to be the center of attention (item 1). Her beauty was an important part of her identity (item 4). Her emotions (depression, anxiety, anger) were intense and volatile (item 3), and she could be quite theatrical (item 6). Her cognitive style was somewhat vague (item 5). Her tendency to spend more money than was available for personal items suggested intolerance of frustration of gratification (item 7).

The interpersonal descriptions for HPD also applied to this woman. She charmed (<u>REACTIVE</u> <u>LOVE</u>) and was very well taken care of by her devoted husband, who adored her and tried to fulfill her wishes (**ACTIVE LOVE, PROTECT**). She counted on (<u>TRUST</u>) his kindness and nurturance. She could lose her temper or become more depressed if he disappointed her (**BLAME**). She was in **CONTROL**, saying that he "does whatever I want." Despite her affection and high regard for him, she was not available to him sexually (<u>WALL</u> <u>OFF</u>). She was anxious about the fact that his friends were counseling him to leave her and thus to implement her worst fear (**IGNORE**). She did not meet the exclusionary condition of self-sabotage following happiness or success.

Her interpersonal history was also consistent with the interpersonal hypotheses. She had been a beautiful child, and her father adored and clearly preferred her over her mother. Because he was so fond of her, she had more influence on the father than anyone else in the family. Her own personal competence was actively discouraged. There was a myth, perpetuated by her mother, that her childhood was "perfect." The chronic parental fighting and the father's alcoholism didn't exist. The patient was not given maternal attention unless she was sick, and then great tenderness and warmth were available to her.

In conclusion, this woman provides a prototype for HPD according to both the DSM and the interpersonal methods.

Case 2

Many of the DSM personality disorders are more likely to occur in one gender than the other. For example, BPDs and HPDs are more often female; NPDs are more often male. Reasons for these differences include differences in temperament and in gender-specific developmental experiences. Nonetheless, it is important that the clinician remain aware of the interpersonal patterns so that they also can be recognized when they occur in the "atypical" gender. Although HPDs are more often female, patient in this case was male.

This gay man in his early 30s came to the hospital for a depression that followed two major stresses: He broke up with his lover, and his father withdrew his financial support. The relationship with the lover had been very close. The two of them "would know what the other was thinking without having to discuss it." The patient liked to drop over at his house, lie down on the couch, and let the lover fix dinner. The lover, however, became concerned about the patient's dependency. He wanted the patient to "take care of himself," and said that "he needed a break" from the relationship. One day, during a fight on the phone, the friend hung up abruptly; that was the end of the love relationship.

The second stress occurred shortly before hospitalization. The patient's wealthy father discontinued his rather substantial monthly allowance. "My carefree world is no longer there," the patient explained. Although he did have a job, the loss of the allowance meant that he had to change his lifestyle. He spent several weeks at home fighting with his parents about the money. The father accepted, but was not comfortable with, the patient's gay identity. Their fighting concerned the patient's management of money and the father's apparent wish to "control how I act." The father worried that the patient was exploited by his friends and did not manage money well. The patient felt that his father "reneged on deals." The patient reported that his mother "was there" for him most of the time he was growing up. He had been a sickly, tearful infant and a shy, isolated child. Although the patient felt close to his mother, he complained that she gave priority to the father.

The patient had vegetative signs of depression. He was fond of cocaine. He reported that people at his work as a salesman said he had mood swings. "I am an emotional person. I cry at movies and things." He had many acquaintances and "shallow friendships." He described himself as a "go-out-for-fun friend. I am very generous and giving. I try to be a good host, to entertain people. Appearances are very important. I am very vain. I like to look the best. I care about myself and what I project." He added: "At a party, if I am on my own, I am bored stiff and leave soon." He worried about people taking advantage of him. He had not been a high achiever in school.

The patient met five of the DSM criteria for HPD. He needed to be the center of attention (item 1); showed rapidly shifting, shallow emotions (item 3); and was very concerned about his physical attractiveness (item 4). He embraced a description of himself as theatrical (item 6). His style of speech lacked detail (item 5). "It is odd to be so specific," he said during the interview.

He also conformed to the interpersonal interpretation of HPD that suggests a baseline position of demanding dependency. He summarized his view of his relationship with his father: "The trust I demand is the trust I give."This is the quintessential position of HPD (TRUST plus CONTROL). As his father continued to deny financial support, the patient invoked more and more BLAME. He valued his ability to charm (REACTIVE LOVE plus CONTROL) people, but was superficial in his attachments (WALL OFF). He also had the prototypic HPD wish that someone else would take care of things. IGNORE is the likely fear of HPD, and this man's depression was preceded by withdrawal of attention and support from two important figures: his lover and his father. There is no evidence that he met the exclusionary condition.

There is not enough information available on his developmental history to permit a test of the pathogenic hypotheses of Table 7.1. All that is known is that he was a sickly baby who often cried. He was shy and lonely in grade school. He was quite close to his mother, and felt that his father was demanding and critical.

An alternative diagnosis might be NPD. It appears that he felt entitled to receive support from his father, and he certainly required admiration. However, he did not have the grandiosity and noncontingent self-adoration found in NPD. He saw himself as charming and entertaining, but also felt that those skills were needed to earn the attention he sought. He did not consider himself to be superior to others. Nor was his self-concept damaged by the withdrawal of support. Rather than degenerate into self-criticism over his losses, he worked harder to restore his "sources."

The DSM-III-R casebook (Spitzer et al., 1989) offered another example of a gay male who seemed to meet criteria for both HPD and NPD. As in the present case, the addition of interpersonal descriptors permits a differential diagnosis to be made. The patient in the DSM example, "My Fan Club," was

> overly concerned with physical attractiveness, expressed emotions with inappropriate exaggeration, was uncomfortable in situations in which he was not the center of attention, and undoubtedly displayed rapidly shifting and shallow expressions of emotions. We also suspect that he had little tolerance for the frustration of delayed gratification. (Spitzer et al., 1989, p. 14)

These attributes suggested the diagnostic label of HPD. However, he was also grandiose, preoccupied with unrealistic fantasies of success, entitlements, and demands for admiration. These features suggested NPD. In the casebook, he was given a joint diagnosis of NPD and HPD.

With the addition of the present interpersonal analysis, the patient in "My Fan Club" would receive only the NPD label. He engaged in the necessary NPD condition of inappropriate self-love, and he also showed entitlement. This man *expected* deference and noncontingent nurturance, and therefore did not show the necessary HPD pattern of *coercive* dependency.

EXPECTABLE TRANSFERENCE REACTIONS AND TREATMENT IMPLICATIONS

Transference Reactions

The baseline position of demanding dependency is the most likely transference reaction in HPD. A patient is likely to attempt to insure good caregiving by dressing attractively or entertaining the therapist. Alternatively, the HPD may exhibit tears, fears, or other obvious signs of distress that continually require attention.

Over a decade ago, I had the opportunity to follow the proceedings of a psychotherapy seminar. A handsome male resident was treating an attractive young woman. Each week, the trainee would report on the preceding session; the seminar leader, who was of classical psychoanalytic persuasion, would comment. The format of the seminar provided that a group of trainees would observe one resident's individual supervision. The case material came from the therapist's progress notes. The patient knew that her case notes were the subject of this year-long seminar.

Nearly every session was devoted to narratives about the patient's many sexual adventures. They were duly reported in the seminar in substantial detail. The resident was not very active in the treatment, and functioned more like a reporter. I did not think that the patient's interpersonal patterns changed, nor that she showed enhanced self-understanding. Two weeks before the end of the seminar, the patient met a man who resembled her therapist. He had the same hair color, was of the same body build, and drove the same make of automobile. The patient discussed the similarities with her therapist. During the report to the seminar, there was much marveling about the fact that the automobiles were not only of the same make, but also of the same color. Nothing was said to the patient about the possible transference implications of her marital choice. The woman's marriage to this man was set for a week after the seminar ended, 3 weeks after she had met him. There was apparent agreement that the treatment was successful because now at last the patient would marry, whereas previously she had been unable to maintain a stable relationship.

This story delineates the endpoint of "unanalyzed" transference reaction in HPD. She used her attractiveness and charm to make a perceived caregiver agree to take care of her. Her major life choice was based on appearances. The man she planned to marry had revealed virtually nothing about himself. She acted out her wish to be taken care of by her therapist, a man who also revealed little about himself.

The story illustrates that saying nothing is not doing nothing. A blank screen is not neutral. M. Levine's "blank-trials law" (M. Levine, 1966) holds that subjects engaged in a variety of laboratory tasks will assume that their responses were correct if the experimenter says nothing. Patients in psychotherapy are also likely[4] to assume that the therapist agrees with them if he or she says nothing to the views they express. According to the blank-trials law, this patient probably believed that the therapist's silence conveyed approval of her marital choice.

The present approach would count the therapist's silence as error. Saying nothing about her marital choice facilitated the maladaptive patterns characteristic of HPD. Her decision should have been explored in depth. She should have been helped to be aware of the possibility that her marital choice represented an (inappropriate) attempt to continue the therapy work that was not yet completed. This resident made the error of being charmed, flattered, and entertained by the HPD. By following the standard "blank-screen" policy, he failed to do his job.

Recent explicit professional injunctions against sex between therapists and patients are especially good news for HPDs and BPDs. By the very nature of their disorders, they act out powerful signals that, if complemented by the therapist, are sure to destroy the therapy. Current professional sanctions provide a counterforce to the cultural factors that encourage the male therapist to become sexually attracted to needy females. I am indebted to the candor of quite a number of male psychiatry residents who, in seminars on sexuality, risked disclosure. They confided that they were aroused by women, especially attractive women, who were crying and vulnerable. The ensuing discussions in the seminars about what do about visible sexual arousal during a therapy session yielded anxiety, remorse, bravado, and resolve. The therapist needs to be aware of such vulnerabilities, and actively to resist requests to provide what the patient wants but does not need.

A major transference problem for the female therapist is that few female HPDs will even enter therapy with a woman. If they do, the therapist will be subject to constant challenge and derogation. Women are competitors and they are losers. From the HPDs' point of view, it is silly to turn to a woman to find help. Obviously there are better places to get it.

Treatment Implications: The Five Categories of Correct Response

The view of therapy as a learning experience permits definition of therapist errors on a moment-to-moment basis. Therapy interventions can be evaluated in terms of whether they enhance collaboration, facilitate learning about patterns and their roots, block maladaptive patterns, enhance the will to change, or effectively

---

[4]F. Levine and Sandeen (1985) have provided a careful and enlightening explanation of how this laboratory phenomenon can apply to psychotherapy.

encourage new patterns. The effect of interventions is assessed in terms of the actual impact on the patient, not in terms of the therapist's intention. If the effect of an intervention on HPD is to enhance demanding dependency, then the intervention is an error.

Facilitating Collaboration

The female therapist with a female HPD has the challenge of getting a viable therapy contract with a person who takes a dim view of the therapist's competence. The first task for the female therapist is to communicate accepting warmth and competent support. These are what the HPD understands. If that is successful, then the therapy can begin. The male therapist's task seems easier at first, because the contract for warmth and support comes so naturally. However, every effort must be made to build the therapeutic alliance against "it." It is important not to provide support for the dependent, needy position.

Regardless of the therapist's and patient's gender, the therapist tries to use his or her knowledge about the baseline pattern and the prototypic wishes and fears of HPD to establish a therapeutic alliance. The working contract is with the patient's observing ego, and the "enemy" is the damaging patterns. The condition of the alliance can be explored by direct questions: "How are you feeling about our work together?" "How do you feel about me?" "Would you be willing to say what you would really like from me?" When the transference reaction has been placed "on the table," a discussion of its connection with earlier history is in order. That understanding facilitates the task of learning to recognize patterns.

The patient's view of therapy must be transformed. The HPD must change from thinking that the therapist will make a fantasy come true; instead, he or she must come to view therapy as a place where personal development can be facilitated. The therapist must facilitate the change respectfully and gently.

The SASB model offers a handy way to explain the difference between therapy and the love relationship coveted by the HPD. The distinction rests on interpersonal focus. The therapist's focus is always transitive and on the patient; the patient's focus is always intransitive and on himself or herself. The therapist's state or condition should not have a major role in the therapy relationship. The patient should not spend much time focusing on the therapist rather than on himself or herself. A mature social relationship, by contrast, is balanced in interpersonal focus. In a love relationship, the therapist focuses about half the time on his or her partner, and half on himself or herself. This distinction is rather mundane, but fundamentally valid. It emphasizes the point that the therapist has interpersonal needs in a love relationship, but that these are not a part of the therapy relationship. The patient's needs and learning are the focus of the therapy relationship; the therapist's are not. The therapist's salary or billing should suffice to meet his or her needs in the therapy relationship. The clarification about focus can cut through the marriage fantasy in HPD and other disorders. It can communicate quickly that therapy is not an appropriate place to develop a viable social relationship. It also makes it clear that the therapy fees are an important part of the therapy contract. The therapist does have needs, and if they are not met by the professional contract, then there is danger that they will be met in other ways not so likely to help the HPD change his or her patterns.

Facilitating Pattern Recognition

HPDs have been programmed to believe that others must take care of instrumental tasks (money, housing, problem solving). The basic idea is that powerful others will meet these needs because the HPDs are so desirable, likable, or needy. HPDs usually have little interest in learning to think clearly, to focus effectively on a task, or to hold steady in the face of difficulty. They believe that if they become skilled at these things, nobody will take care of them any more. They will be left alone. Balancing the checkbook, learning to reduce the number of rounds of "uproar" per month, or meeting household responsibilities are tantamount to giving up their identity. If they are competent and not needy, then there is no basis for social exchange.

This devotion to a "scattered cognitive style" means that an HPD is not likely to be enthusiastic about the task of learning to recognize patterns. The HPD does not naturally have an observing ego that can help him or her stop and reflect about what is happening. The HPD is unlikely to think, "What happened just before I . . . ?" "What was I really trying to do when I . . . ?" Nonetheless, this type of cognitive focus is needed before patterns can be recognized and new patterns developed. If a female HPD makes it into a collaborative relationship with a female therapist, this stage is easier. With a female therapist, the HPD can internalize directly the therapist's modeling of benign and constructive examination of patterns. A male therapist will need to help the HPD talk about her fear that if she becomes competent, the therapist will decide she is unattractive and kick her out of therapy. If the male therapist can communicate appreciation for her strength, the female HPD can progress more rapidly.

The patient in case 1, for example, might benefit from understanding the connection between her parents' teaching and her own tendency to smile at adversity, escalate physical symptoms, and eschew success. Her father adored her feminine qualities, and her mother provided support for debilitation. She lived her life in the hope that the family of origin could be resurrected. Such insight could be useful in marking the task ahead in therapy. She would need to decide to abandon these principles, and that would take time. The patient in case 2 had a similar wish and faced a similar developmental task.

Blocking Maladaptive Patterns

Sooner or later the therapist must call the patient's attention to potentially destructive acting out based on underlying wishes and fears. For example, the patient in case 1 accepted the interviewer's suggestion that her husband and doctor should stop being so nurturant in response to her illnesses. She acknowledged that she did not like the thought of the loss of her husband's seemingly endless support. Marital sessions were recommended to help her work with her husband to use his nurturance in the service of enhancing her strength rather than her illness.

Unquestioning therapist acceptance of the patient's ways of being belies the underlying contract that the patient wants help to change. The patient is not necessarily fully informed about patterns and their reasons. Unknowing choices are not "free" choices. The therapist who supportively questions the patient's present patterns does not show "disrespect" for the patient. By providing gentle challenge, the therapist protects the patient from his or her own past. The therapist's protectiveness is manifest only in the therapy process. The idea is to expand options and enhance awareness in the light of the therapy learning. *The patient's free will is enhanced if the determinants are fully understood.* Therapist directiveness about therapy process does not mean that the therapist gives direct counsel. A therapist ordinarily does not give directions about life choices, such as "Get a divorce," "Don't marry Mr. B; he is bad for you," or "Sounds like you should quit that job." Such advice giving, no matter how much the patient pleads for or demands it, ordinarily should not be a part of therapy procedure.

The therapist does not usually block patterns by directly giving advice. The therapist normally takes active responsibility to help the patient fully understand a life choice. For example, consider the woman who married a man who drove the same kind of car her therapist drove. A better intervention would have been to help her engage in a full examination of the therapy process. She needed to be helped to consider how she felt about the therapist and the therapy. She needed to explore whether her destructive patterns were a part of her precipitous decision to marry. The patient should have been helped to articulate what she expected in the marital relationship with her husband-to-be. She should have had the opportunity to explore in the supportive therapy setting whatever evidence there was that this marriage would implement her wishes. Once she completed this review and became aware of the factors affecting her decision, she would be in a better position to make her choice. The therapist would not then object if she still wanted to marry a man she had known only 3 weeks. Perhaps, indeed, the patient had become very lucky.

Strengthening the Will to Give Up Maladaptive Patterns

A major step on the way to implementing constructive change is in developing the will to change the patterns. The possibility for change is enhanced if there is an encounter that makes the destructive wishes (or fears) totally clear. It is helpful if they can be uncovered and clearly connected in an *experiential* way to the past. The perspective that comes with connecting present problems to past problems often helps people "decide" to give up the goals that drive the patterns.

The following transcript is from an important session that directly addressed the will of an HPD to change her patterns. Her goals for therapy were to become less depressed and to be rid of debilitating panic attacks. She had been in two previous therapies.

This young mother was not shallow or "flashy," but she was outstandingly attractive. She did otherwise meet the DSM criteria for HPD. Neither psychotherapy nor medications had been helpful. Her depression appeared to be a response to perceptions of being overwhelmed. Her illness required that her husband undertake ever more of the duties of cooking, housework, and child care in addition to his job outside the home. The panic attacks, it turned out, were always preceded by some reminder of helplessness in males. The patient had been close to her father, a charismatic community leader who took very good care of her, except when he was debilitated by alcohol. Eventually his choice of alcohol destroyed his career as a doctor and his family. Scenes of helpless males reminded the patient of the loss of her nurturant and wonderful father, and sent her into a state of panic over who would take care of her.

The session started with a discussion of suicidality and the negative transference. It evolved into a discussion of the wish for nurturance, which was the basis of the suicidal feelings.

P: . . . I wanted him [husband], I asked him directly, what I wanted to know from him was if I ever felt like I was really going to do something to hurt myself, if he would do something—take me to the hospital or call somebody or just listen to it, because I was really feeling—not like I had any plans or anything, but just like I just have been trying to figure out what makes people go on and what is the reason for continuing life when you're miserable. And I look around, you know, and I see my little kids and my husband, and I keep thinking, you know, there's really got to be something wrong for someone not to . . . You know, I feel really selfish that I could even have thoughts like . . . I don't know, I'm not trying to send out hysterical red flags because I know I'm not—I don't feel like I'm suicidal. I'm just feeling like, you know, a lot of time I'd rather not continue.

T: How do you understand that, and why do you think that's happening now?

P: I don't know. It's funny because I've been thinking about it a lot today. In fact, yesterday I was really depressed about it. In fact, I called a friend of mine who has been in analysis for 10 years, and I had a long talk with her. After talking to her about how I really am feeling like for some reason this [therapy] isn't working, and I don't know why—if it's a good match or, you know, I can't tell if it really isn't a good match or if I am resisting something really big and basic. I don't know. I can't tell. I'm also very scared that you're leaving in the winter [9 months hence] and I'm feeling so undone. I'm thinking about winter being, you know, really dark and hectic and depressive anyway. I was real tempted today, I sort of all of a sudden felt better for some reason, just kind of spontaneously in the beginning of the day because I decided for a while that I had to just—I couldn't continue with this depth any more because I wasn't going to have a chance to get out of it, out of this regression or whatever, and I was going to have to just quit.

T: How do you see me responding to the regression? What is your understanding of that?

P: I guess I see you as being fairly unresponsive, but I guess what I'm feeling what I need is some—I think I need—some feeling that all this talk about meaninglessness and, you know, fearing death yet wishing that I just wouldn't wake up and all that stuff, is that I need something from you and you're not gong to give it to me. Either you're not going to give it to me, either you don't do therapy this way, and it's like I'm asking for something that I will never get from you, and that makes me feel maybe this is the wrong therapy, or this is a part of your plan to strengthen me.

T: So I'm withholding in order to toughen you up?

P: Yeah. Maybe. Or I just don't get what we're doing in here, and maybe I'm just not left-brained enough or something to learn this model.

[The discussion of the patient's unfavorable perception of the therapy continued in this vein. Then:]

T: Well, if not at the beginning of this session, I have heard you complain that I don't deal with your symptoms enough.

P: I heard that loud and clear that you don't like to deal with symptoms. I guess what scares me about it is that, you know, if I feel truly suicidal, is that a symptom?

T: What would I do? Well, I do the same thing we're doing now. Which is to take whatever is going on and try to understand it with you, and try to help you get the strength to do something different with the issue. If you are unable to—if you are suicidal, then we'll talk hospitalization. And we did one time, remember?

P: And I didn't really even feel suicidal that time. That was more like panic, you know, like out-of-control panic.

T: That's always a possibility. I prefer to understand together what it's really about. And I insist it's [hospitalization] not treatment, it's not therapy.

P: Hospitalization?

T: Right, and any emergency measures. Of course, I try to do them, but by now, if we're learning to swim here, if you're drowning, I try to jump in and pull you out and give you a life preserver or whatever, if I can. I might fail, but I'd try. And I do that, but that's not part of learning to swim. That's just what you have to do to preserve the option to later on learn to swim when you're in a better place. So, while you're bobbing up and down for the third time and sputtering, I try to be helpful, but that is not teaching you how to swim.

P: So, is that what you feel like I'm doing now? Sputtering around and bobbing up and down?

T: I'm trying to explore it with you, and I hope by the time we're finished today, you will understand this better because you haven't felt this way all along. Something has happened to change it.

P: Yeah, well the weekend . . .

[She went on to describe a monumental fight with her husband, the gist of which was that he said not only that the marriage was terrible now, but that it never had been any good. The husband was becoming very angry about her continued depression and panic attacks. The patient then went on to a discussion of her concern about whether she could handle her new job or not. Eventually the therapist summed up her position:]

T: Your husband's had it up to here with giving support and doing things for you. . . . There are demands on every front that you pull it together, and yet it seems very overwhelming because it's just too much and it's all out of control. I think it is a fundamentally depressive position to feel that helpless. You come to me hoping that I would have some wonderful magic that will give you the strength and put it together. Instead, I did this talk about helping you to learn to do it yourself, and just a few sessions ago we confronted your wish to be taken care of, to finally have a real mother. I think that's what you want from me—that I will put you in my lap and hold you and "kiss it and make it better." Believe me, if that would do it, I would love to do that. It would be great fun. What a nice way to fix all this. I would even like to fool myself that might work, because I would enjoy it so much, but I don't believe it would. And so we started to talk a few times ago about how before you started to build your strength, you would need to give up that fantasy, and I think the grief over that is what's gotten to you. The grief over the idea that there isn't going to be someone who's always going to be there like your dad was by your side, pulling the fat out of the fire and fixing things, and a mother that would make cookies and give you kisses. What a nice fantasy.

P: (*Pause for several minutes*) I can honestly say that I have never been so in touch with that wish.

T: (*Pause*) Listen, if you figure out how to realize it, let me know. Sounds good to me too.

P: I mean, intellectually, obviously I know that this is never going to happen, and it just amazes me how strong those unconscious desires are, and it's just so scary that something could be that powerful.

T: But it is.

P: I mean, I can trace it back even to being a kid and going to the infirmary for that 10 minutes to get aspirin. . . . I'm like a junkie, really. I really am. (*Pause*) And it doesn't help knowing it.

T: No. That's the trouble with a learning model. Knowing that your arm is crooked on the tennis serve doesn't make you a good server. Insight is only the first step. The hard part is giving the wish up. That's depressing.

P: And the more depressed—I know this sounds so psychoanalytic that, you know, I almost shudder to say it, but the more I get in touch with this, the more I want to crawl into bed and just like be in this dark, warm, safe place. It's just . . .

T: To sink into the depression.

P: I do. I just want to crawl in a hole.

[Patient and therapist continued to explore the wish to regress. The session ended as follows:]

P: The truth is, there's nothing that will make this go away easily. Is that what you're saying?

T: Well, if you think about it, let's say I took you in as my daughter, okay? Or marriage or something, so that I kept you with me all the time. And everything that came up, I told you exactly what to do and mostly kept trouble out of your way, made nice meals for you, didn't ask you to do anything. How does that sound?

P: Truthfully? For a while it might be okay. And then I would probably get more and more demanding until I hated myself and the whole thing.

T: Right. Exactly right. You would have very poor self-esteem, and you would become weaker and weaker.

P: Right.

Later, she wrote that the therapist "gave tremendous support via explanation, metaphors, encouragement, but [illegible] the problem and describing her intentions for dealing with it." Suicidality never came up as a topic again. The session proved to be a crucial change event because of the deep level at which the patient confronted the underlying motive for her demanding dependency. The patient did subsequently engage actively and successfully in the task of building personal strength and conquering the depression.

Facilitating New Learning

Many of the popular and well-known therapy techniques are appropriate and effective at this last stage of therapy. Warm, supportive listening continues to be vital. Techniques from a variety of other approaches can be used to build new patterns, once the "unconscious underbrush" has been cleared away.

The HPD in the transcript above, who confronted her wish to be dependent, knew how to enroll in college classes to begin to develop a sense of herself as competent. She also fully resumed her household and child care responsibilities. Once she confronted and gave up the dependency wish, she went ahead to build her strengths. This patient needed little more from the therapist.

Others need more active participation from the therapist at this last stage. Many patients use this time to re-experience adolescence. Choices about identity and lifestyle are explored. In this round, some patients have a really good time, because they have more resources available than adolescents do. On the other hand, there are many who find themselves buried under unhappy life circumstances. For these patients, digging out at this last stage is not so easy, but it can be done. The therapist needs to be a loyal and hopeful ally in the effort.

8

Antisocial Personality Disorder

"This disease is beyond my practice."

Without restraint and without any treatment worthy of the name, the psychopath continues, woe, confusion, despair, farce, and disaster, beyond any measure of these things I can convey, progressively accumulating in his social wake. (Cleckley, 1955, p. 539)

REVIEW OF THE LITERATURE

For many centuries, anyone who was caught committing a crime was held personally responsible and punished. In 1843, the *M'Naghten* rule held that persons were not responsible if, at the time of the crime, they were laboring under such a defect of reason that they did know the nature and quality of the act. Even if they did know the nature and quality of the act, they were still not responsible if they did not know it was wrong. Variations on this ruling have come and gone, including the doctrine of "irresistible impulse," offered in 1887. The irresistible-impulse rule held that criminals are not responsible if at the time of the crime they had lost the power to choose between right and wrong. In 1954, the *Durham* rule broadened tolerance even more by holding that a person was not responsible if the act was a product of a mental disease or mental defect. The *Durham* rule turned the courtroom into an arena for psychiatric gladiators. The outcome of trials depended largely on the impact of the expert witnesses. One team of psychiatrists would testify that the crime was a product of mental illness, and another group of experts would demonstrate that it was not. A recent view has reassigned some responsibility to the criminal. The rule of "diminished capacity," proposed in 1978, labels the mentally disordered criminal guilty of a lesser charge. For example, murder in the first degree by an insane person may be reduced to manslaughter because of the participant's diminished capacity for judgment. Another current variation is the finding "guilty but mentally ill." Under this view, a mentally ill person who has committed a crime is sent to a hospital first for treatment. When released as cured, the individual is then processed by the legal system.

If there is no evidence of mental illness, the convicted criminal is held responsible and duly punished. ASP (sometimes also called "sociopathy" or "psychopathy") is catalogued as a mental disorder by the DSM. Curiously, this particular mental disorder consigns the individual to full accountability in the legal system. The ASP is treated as a criminal without a mental disorder and is eligible for punishment to the fullest extent. Defense lawyers do not seek the ASP label.

The apparent contradiction between the description of ASP as a disorder and the assignment of full legal responsibility to an ASP is not so surprising. Criminal behaviors define ASP, according to DSM. It is logical that the courts have not been lenient to people who have this diagnosis. It would be circular to define a mental disorder in terms of criminal behavior, and then to excuse a person from criminal behavior because he or she has a mental disorder!

Long before the publication of DSM-III, Cleckley (1955) argued that psychopathic personality is an authentic mental disorder. In his book *The Mask of Sanity*, Cleckley identified a category of persons engaged in *self-destructive* criminal behavior. He described their characteristics and offered hypotheses about the causes of the pattern. Cleckley distinguished this disorder from ordinary criminal behavior; he decried the practice of holding individuals with psychopathic personality responsible as other criminals. Cleckley argued that although a psychopath appears sane and socially glib, the psychopath "demonstrates [an] irrationality and incompetence that is gross and obvious" (p. 19).

To make his point, Cleckley cited many instances of psychopathic "stupidity" that would not characterize a "common criminal." He observed that a psychopath will function with reckless abandon that is sure to lead to discovery. This brand of criminal will boast of criminal "achievements" in ways that inevitably lead to his or her legal downfall. Cleckley described a man who became a super salesman within his company, only to be undone by the discovery that he had been selling the product below cost. He shifted funds to hide the deficit. No professional criminal would engage in behaviors so sure to lead to detection.

Cleckley proposed a list of 16 diagnostic signs to define psychopathy. Many are found in the DSM case illustrations, if not in the DSM criteria:

1. Superficial charm and good "intelligence."
2. Absence of delusions and other signs of irrational "thinking."
3. Absence of "nervousness" or psychoneurotic manifestations.
4. Unreliability.
5. Untruthfulness and insincerity.
6. Lack of remorse or shame.
7. Inadequately motivated antisocial behavior.
8. Poor judgment and failure to learn by experience.
9. Pathologic egocentricity and incapacity for love.
10. General poverty in major affective reactions.
11. Specific loss of insight.
12. Unresponsiveness in general interpersonal relations.
13. Fantastic and uninviting behavior, with drink and sometimes without.

14. Suicide rarely carried out.
15. Sex life impersonal, trivial, and poorly integrated.
16. Failure to follow any life plan. (1955, pp. 380–381)

In contrast to the DSM, Cleckley's psychopath can be diagnosed even if the person has not been in trouble with the law. Nonetheless, the defining attributes are highly likely to lead to criminal behavior and arrest. Cleckley devoted separate chapters to describing the psychopathic personality as it appears in a businessman, a "man of the world," a gentleman, a scientist, a physician, and a psychiatrist. Interpersonal analysis of the criminal behaviors that define ASP can partially reinstate Cleckley's broader view of the disorder. The criminal behaviors can be interpreted interpersonally. For example, they manifest reckless disregard for the rights and feelings of others. That interpersonal perspective can modify the DSM's specific behavioral diagnostic criteria so that they are more amenable to dynamic analysis.

Once ASP is defined in interpersonal terms, the reasons for diagnostic overlap with other disorders become apparent. For example, disregard for others also appears in NPD. The ASP's abandonment of prudence and caution is shared with BPD, and to a lesser extent with HPD. A more detailed discussion of the overlap with other Axis II disorders appears later in this chapter. Cleckley himself was particularly concerned with the overlap between psychopathy and schizophrenia:

> The surface of the psychopath, however, all of him that can be reached by verbal exploration and direct examination, shows up as equal to or better than normal and gives no hint at all of a disorder within. Nothing about him suggests oddness, inadequacy, or moral frailty. His mask is that of robust mental health. Yet he has a disorder that often manifests itself in conduct not less seriously abnormal than that of the schizophrenic. Inwardly too, there appears to be a significant difference. Deep in the masked schizophrenic we often sense an odd, weird indifference to many of life's most urgent issues, and sometimes also bizarre, inexplicable, and unpredictable but intense emotional reactions to what seems almost irrelevant. Behind the exquisitely deceptive mask of the psychopath the emotional alteration we feel appears to be primarily one of degree, a consistent leveling of response to petty ranges, and incapacity to react with sufficient seriousness to achieve much more than pseudoexperience or quasiexperience. . . . in most psychopaths the purposiveness, the significance of all life striving and of all subjective experience are affected without obvious damage to the outer appearance or superficial reactions of the personality. (1955, pp. 437–438)

For Cleckley, the emotional detachment of the psychopath provided the strongest link between psychopathy and schizophrenia. He speculated about the causes of psychopathy and favored the idea of a neurological deficit. Like others, Cleckley was impressed that the pattern appears very early in the developmental sequence and is intractable. Such seeming total independence of family experience suggests constitutional factors (pp. 464–468). He speculated about deficiencies in the neuronal pathways that modulate affective regulation (p. 484).

Still, Cleckley mentioned possible family input. He wondered whether there was a subtle lack of affective connectedness similar to that presumed (at the time he wrote) to account for early infantile autism (pp. 470–476). However Cleckley cautioned against constructing developmental theories on the basis of interviews. He felt that the reliability of the psychopath's information is compromised by his or her tendency to tell fantasy as fact.

Cleckley's belief that psychopathic persons are neurologically impaired has received some empirical support. Their performance on neuropsychological tests has included deficits similar to those shown by brain-damaged patients. A recent exploration of this widely accepted theory was directed by Hart, Forth, and Hare (1990), who administered a battery of standard neuropsychological tests to two different samples of male prison inmates. The groups were comparable in age and educational levels (n's = 90, 167). There were no differences between prisoners who were psychopathic and those who were not. The failure to distinguish psychopathic prisoners on the basis of neurological damage was robust. It remained even after there was a correction for effects of self-reported psychopathology and substance abuse. Hart et al. concluded, "The results provide no support for traditional brain-damage explanations of psychopathy" (1990, p. 374).

Adding to the list of possible deficiencies that might account for ASP, some investigators (reviewed in Cloninger, 1978) have proposed that the disorder in males is associated with excess serum testosterone. That idea has not been confirmed by laboratory tests. Others have suggested that ASPs have a high threshold for autonomic arousal that leads to a search for "kicks." Actuarial studies have demonstrated that the incidence of ASP is greater in biological than in adoptive relatives of index cases. If there is criminality in the adoptive family, the effect is enhanced. Cloninger (1978) found greater co-occurrence of sociopathy in identical than in fraternal sets of twins.

A multifactorial model has been proposed to explain ASP (Cloninger et al., 1975; Cloninger, Christiansen, Reich, & Gottesman, 1978). The present book details hypotheses about environmental factors affecting the development of personality disorders. Nonetheless, the interactive model or multifactorial model is assumed. The balance of this chapter is devoted exclusively to an interpersonal description of ASP, and to possible interpersonal pathogenic and treatment agents.

DSM DEFINITION OF THE DISORDER

The DSM definition provides the starting point for the analysis. The DSM specifies that the diagnosis of ASP can be made if the individual meets three of the criteria in section B and four of the criteria in section C. The DSM-III-R items appear below in **bold print**. The criteria for ASP in the DSM-IV are the subject of controversy. Four different ways of defining it have been subjected to field trial (American Psychiatric Association, 1991; Hare, Hart, & Harpur, 1991). The DSM-III-R definitions comprise the first set. The second is from the *International Classification of Diseases and Related Health Problems*, 10th revision (ICD-10) list that defines "dyssocial personality disorder." The third is a set of items related to Hare's concept of psychopathy. The fourth is a shortened list from the DSM-III-R, prepared by Lee Robbins. The reliability of the DSM-III-R definition of ASP has been very good, and many are reluctant to change it. On the other hand, the length of the DSM-III-R list is cumbersome, and therefore the shortened version is viewed positively. The ICD-10 list is closer to Cleckley's original definition, but includes criteria that are difficult to define and implement reliably. The DSM is devoted to improving reliability, and so ultimate selection of the ICD-10 list for ASP seems unlikely. One ICD-10 item is "Incapacity to experience guilt and to profit from experience, particularly punishment." Another is "Very low tolerance to frustration and a low threshold for discharge of aggression, including violence." Neither the results of the field trials nor the decision of the DSM-IV work group is yet available. The SASB codes of the original and the shortened DSM-III-R lists are identical. The present interpersonal analysis is of the DSM-III-R definition. If the DSM-IV selects the shortened version, the interpersonal analysis will not change.

A. Current age at least 18.

B. Evidence of Conduct Disorder with onset before age 15, as indicated by a history of *three* or more of the following:

(1) was often truant

(2) ran away from home overnight at least twice while living in parental or parental surrogate home (or once without returning)

(3) often initiated physical fights

(4) used a weapon in more than one fight

(5) forced someone into sexual activity with him or her

(6) was physically cruel to animals

(7) was physically cruel to other people

(8) deliberately destroyed others' property (other than by fire-setting)

(9) deliberately engaged in fire-setting

(10) often lied (other than to avoid physical and sexual abuse)

(11) has stolen without confrontation of a victim on more than one occasion (including forgery)

(12) has stolen with confrontation of a victim (e.g. mugging, purse-snatching, extortion, armed robbery)

C. A pattern of irresponsible and antisocial behavior since the age of 15, as indicated by at least *four* of the following:

(1) is unable to sustain consistent work behavior, as indicated by any of the following (including similar behavior in academic settings if the person is a student):
   (a) significant unemployment for six months or more within five years when expected to work and work was available
   (b) repeated absences from work unexplained by illness in self or family
   (c) abandonment of several jobs without realistic plans for others

(2) fails to conform to social norms with respect to lawful behavior, as indicated by repeatedly performing antisocial acts that are grounds for arrest (whether arrested or not), e.g., destroying property, harassing others, stealing, pursuing an illegal occupation

(3) is irritable and aggressive, as indicated by repeated physical fights or assaults (not required by one's job or to defend someone or oneself), including spouse- or child-beating

(4) repeatedly fails to honor financial obligations, as indicated by defaulting on debts or failing to provide child support or support for other dependents on a regular basis

(5) fails to plan ahead, or is impulsive, as indicated by one or both of the following:
   (a) traveling from place to place without a prearranged job or clear goal for the period of travel or clear idea about when the travel will terminate
   (b) lack of a fixed address for a month or more

(6) has no regard for the truth, as indicated by repeated lying, use of aliases, or "conning" others for personal profit or pleasure

(7) is reckless regarding his or her own or others' personal safety, as indicated by driving while intoxicated, or recurrent speeding

(8) if a parent or guardian, lacks ability to function as a responsible parent, as indicated by one or more of the following:
   (a) malnutrition of child
   (b) child's illness resulting from lack of minimal hygiene
   (c) failure to obtain medical care for a seriously ill child
   (d) child's dependence on neighbors or nonresident relatives for food or shelter
   (e) failure to arrange for a caretaker for young child when parent is away from home.
   (f) repeated squandering, on personal items, of money required for household necessities

(9) has never sustained a totally monogamous relationship for more than one year

(10) Lacks remorse (feels justified in having hurt, mistreated, or stolen from another)

The specificity of the DSM definitions makes this diagnosis acceptable to behaviorally oriented psychologists. As a result, ASP has received far more attention than the other disorders in mainstream psychology journals such as the *Journal of Abnormal Psychology,* as well as in secondary sources (e.g., Carson & Butcher, 1992).

Despite its focus on criminal behavior, ASP shows considerable overlap with the other personality disorders. Morey (1988) reported that 6.2% of a sample of 291 outpatients being treated for personality disorder qualified for the ASP label.

There was substantial overlap with BPD (44.4%), NPD (55.6%), HPD (33.3%), and Passive Aggressive Personality Disorder (50.0%). Morey's results suggest that these individuals exhibit social interactive patterns characteristic of other personality disorders. Theodore Millon, an influential member of the DSM-III, DSM-III-R, and DSM-IV work groups, has argued vehemently against the criminally specific nature of the DSM criteria for this disorder (e.g., Millon, 1982, p. 182). Millon would add to the DSM list "hostile affectivity, assertive self-image, interpersonal vindictiveness, hyperthymic fearlessness, and malevolent projection."

PATHOGENIC HYPOTHESES

The method of using the SASB model to develop pathogenic hypotheses has been sketched in Chapter 5. Four main features of the developmental history have been identified specifically to account for each of the ASP symptoms listed in the DSM. A summary of the hypotheses linking interpersonal history to interpersonal patterns characteristic of the disorder appears in Table 8.1. A fuller description of these hypotheses is provided here.

  1. There was harsh ATTACK and gross neglect (IGNORE). Broken homes, alcoholism, violence, and dereliction of parental duty are often found in the history of ASPs. However, surveys of such variables as poverty, father absence, alcoholism, and disruptive home conditions have not convincingly demonstrated connections between these factors and ASP (e.g., Cloninger, 1978). Cleckley (1955) was not impressed with the possibility that such factors are relevant to ASP. He warned about "possibilities and probabilities of subtler environmental and personal influences which, masked by flawlessly conventional surfaces, are almost impossible to demonstrate convincingly" (p. 482).

  I would agree that such diffuse traumatic factors do not correspond uniquely to patterns observed in ASP. Once again, it is vital to note that the SASB dimensional codes of the history must correspond reasonably to the SASB codes of the adult form of the disorder. For example, parental alcoholism alone would not necessarily create ASP in the child. Alcoholism would be associated with ASP if it was consistently associated with harshness and neglect occurring in the context outlined in Table 8.1. If the alcoholism was not associated with the requisite dimensionality, then ASP would not be encouraged. For example, if a father became noncontingently loving of a son when drunk, narcissistic rather than antisocial behaviors would be encouraged. To give another example, if the father was extremely punitive while the mother was competent and supportive, the breakup of the home might *reduce* rather than increase the probability of ASP. "Broken homes" are likely to involve abandonment, but not necessarily. In disrupted homes, the children can receive adequate nurturance and loving care from the parent who remains. Moreover, a child in an intact, materially privileged home can be functionally abandoned. If the parents are totally absorbed in their work or recreational activities, they can be derelict in parental duty. The crucial

Table 8.1. Interpersonal Summary of ASP

History	Consequences of history
1. Harsh, neglectful parenting (**ATTACK, IGNORE**)	1. **IGNORES**, neglects, and is insensitive to others Pervasive detachment (<u>WALL OFF</u>) interferes with social regulation **ATTACK** is unmodulated Others are exploited (*SELF-PROTECT* plus **IGNORE**)
2. Sporadic, unmodulated parental **CONTROL, BLAME**; likely to be humiliating	2. Fiercely protects autonomy (<u>SEPARATE, WALL OFF</u>) **BLAMES** easily Likes to **CONTROL, IGNORE**
3. Inept parental caring (**ACTIVE LOVE** or **PROTECT** plus **IGNORE**)	3. Drug abuse, prostitution, crime (*SELF-PROTECT* plus *SELF-NEGLECT*) "Pseudocare" or conning (**ACTIVE LOVE** or **PROTECT** plus **IGNORE**)
4. Child **CONTROL** led family because of parental dereliction of duty	4. Control without bonding (**CONTROL** plus **IGNORE**)

Summary: There is a pattern of inappropriate and unmodulated desire to control others, implemented in a detached manner. There is a strong need to be independent, to resist being controlled by others, who are usually held in contempt. There is a willingness to use untamed aggression to back up the need for control or independence. The ASP usually presents in a friendly, sociable manner, but that friendliness is always accompanied by a baseline position of detachment. He or she doesn't care what happens to self or others.

SASB codes of ASP baseline: Uncaring aggression (**ATTACK** plus <u>WALL OFF</u>). Uncaring control (**CONTROL** plus <u>WALL OFF</u>). Controlling, uninvolved affection (**ACTIVE LOVE** or **PROTECT** plus **CONTROL** plus <u>WALL OFF</u>). Self-indulgence without protective regard for self (*SELF-PROTECT* plus *SELF-NEGLECT*), or concern about others (*SELF-PROTECT* plus **IGNORE**). **BLAMES** and is comfortable if <u>SEPARATE</u>. *Wishes:* To be given freedom (**EMANCIPATE**) or to have others <u>SUBMIT</u>. *Fears:* To receive **CONTROL**. *Necessary descriptors:* Need for control of others and autonomy for self; detachment, lack of remorse. *Exclusionary descriptors:* Fear of abandonment; entitlement; dependency.

element in the development of ASP, whether the parental home was intact or not, is that a child experienced gross interpersonal neglect at a crucial age. This would be more likely to happen in broken homes of limited economic means, but would not be restricted to these circumstances. For example, one ASP from an intact, well-to-do family commented that his parents had always taken the children along on wonderful vacations. However, the neglectful pattern was illustrated by the ocean cruises: The children had to "stay at the other end of the ship." The SASB codes may identify the elusive factors hidden beneath a veneer of social acceptability described by Cleckley.

Studies that report early experience in interpersonal detail adequate to permit SASB dimensional analysis can sometimes be used to test developmental hypotheses. For example, Pollock et al. (1990) showed that men with alcoholic fathers did not report or exhibit more antisocial behaviors than did control subjects. However, men with physical abuse histories "reported more aggressive and antisocial behaviors during a clinical interview and were rated by a clinical interviewer as more likely to act out aggression" (p. 1290). Physical

ATTACK is specific enough to code, and the Pollock et al. study suggests that it is implicated in ASP. The more general condition of having had an alcoholic parent who may or not have been physically abusive is not clearly associated with ASP. Again, the point is that tests of the relation between early experience and adult problem patterns are more informative if the specific dimensionality of that early experience and its context can be assessed.

Unmodulated aggression may also result if a child was not allowed to attach to others. People who attack recklessly have not been subject to normative social controls. Harlow and Harlow's (1962) studies of monkeys raised in social isolation showed that a primate lacking attachment will manifest unmodulated aggression in adulthood. This uncontrolled hostility can be exhibited even though the monkey has never been aggressed against by other animals. Extrapolation to humans implies that social isolation comparable to rearing in a bare wire laboratory cage may be adequate to account for poorly modulated aggression.

Still another way to learn to be brutal is to watch violent parents. If, for example, the father frequently beat the mother, the son would be likely to imitate that pattern and ATTACK others (especially sexual partners) in a detached and uncaring way. It is of more than passing interest that a careful study of assaultive male adolescents showed that they had more female than male siblings (Loeber, Weissman, & Reid, 1983). Perhaps the young males in neglectful families are more often rewarded for aggression toward sisters. Brothers may be more inclined to fight back successfully. As adults, male ASPs often show exaggerated concern with being aggressively masculine. They find subcultures that especially value their aggressiveness and unflinching willingness to attack.

Like the BPD, the ASP internalizes parental neglect and abandonment. The unthinking, unreflective "stupidity" of the ASP as described by Cleckley may simply be internalization of parental inattentiveness. For instance, nobody told the ASP, "Wear a coat today because the weather forecast is for a sudden drop in temperature." The ASP went off to school on a sunny morning and had to walk home in a snowstorm without a coat. He or she was not helped to develop a sense of how to anticipate circumstances and care for himself or herself. Not only did the ASP fail to learn self-care, but he or she also has no awareness of the needs of others (IGNORE). Complementing the early neglect from childhood, the ASP remains WALLed OFF, not attached to anyone. One result of the detachment is that his or her behaviors are unmodulated; for example, ATTACK is particularly violent. The detachment also makes it easy for the ASP to exploit others (*SELF-PROTECT* plus IGNORE).

2. In the context of overall neglect, there were unpredictable parental returns to the disciplinary role. This yielded sporadic, unmodulated parental CONTROL that was saturated with BLAME For example, a father might come home after weeks of being away and suddenly act like a stern disciplinarian with a mission to degrade. Or an alcoholic mother might get sober for a day or two and decide harshly to back up rules and regulations that had long been ignored.

The adult consequence of this sporadic parental control is that the ASP fiercely protects his or her autonomy. The ASP learns that the "mothering one" is mostly absent, and then sometimes "acts like a parent" in a bossy and degrading way. The lesson is that the best defense is to keep a distance (WALL OFF, SEPARATE). Independence is the antithesis of the dreaded arbitrary CONTROL. The ASP also identifies with the parent and becomes CONTROLing, very quick to BLAME, and insensitive to the needs of others (IGNORE).

3. Any available parental nurturance was likely to be incompetent. This parental pattern of "inept caring" has the complex SASB code PROTECT plus IGNORE "Inept caring" was illustrated poignantly in the television documentary *Streetwise* (Bell, 1986). This extraordinary video essay showed segments from the lives of mostly delinquent adolescents living in the streets of Seattle. The pattern of inept caring was illustrated by scenes of a 14-year-old prostitute and her mother, who was a hard-working but alcoholic waitress. At one point, the daughter was sitting in the restaurant where the mother worked, and the mother was serving her lunch. In the midst of ordinary chatter, the daughter said, "Ma, I think I'm pregnant." The mother softly exclaimed, "Oh, goodness!" After a brief pause, the daughter asked, "Don't you have no whipping cream?" and the mother answered, "No." That was it—no screaming, swearing, or beating, just apparent friendliness and fleeting concern. The parenting was woefully inadequate and inept.

The same pattern was repeated in a later scene, when this mother and daughter were deeply engaged in negotiations over which cosmetics her daughter could order from a catalog. The mother's focus was on how much each item cost in relation to what she could afford. There was no evidence of enlightened reflection about what it meant for a mother to be buying cosmetics for a 14-year-old prostitute. Inept caring was also suggested by the mother's worry over whether her child would survive the streets. She admired her daughter's earning capacity ("I don't make that much in a week"). But she decided to deal with the problem by waiting. The mother commented, "I think it [prostitution] is a stage she will grow out of."

This modeling of inept caring that overlooks the welfare of the other person helps the ASP learn to do the same. Sometimes this feature is combined with learning to exert inordinate control (discussed in the next section), and the ASP learns to charm and "con" others by offering wonderful "helpful" opportunities that in reality victimize. While seeming to be friendly, the ASP remains detached. He or she can offer others "help" that overrides their best interests.

The inept caring can also be internalized as SELF-PROTECT plus SELF-NEGLECT. The most advanced and hardened examples of inept caring turned inward by ASPs are drug and alcohol abuse, criminal behavior, and prostitution. In these activities, an ASP takes care of himself or herself in the sense that drugs can bring temporary good feelings. Things seem to be fine. The prostitution yields money and a type of status. The crime also leads to money and status. However, these activities also are profoundly self-destructive, both physically and socially. Consequently, the attempts at self-care are off the mark.

4. Finally, the ASP as a child had inordinate CONTROL of the family, often because of the parental dereliction of duty. Usually bright, and temperamen-

tally high in energy, ASPs-to-be "took over" since nobody else did. The control could be arbitrary, warm, or hostile. The developing ASP tried to assume responsibilities that required skills beyond his or her developmental level; he or she also had no effective models to imitate. Naturally, the "parental" functioning of the child was inept. For example, a preadolescent male might assume responsibility for getting all the siblings ready for school or for bed. His methods of "discipline" would be harsh, immoderate, and not monitored by competent parents. Without attachment, his only means of intervention would be coercive.

Inappropriate control was also shown by the daughter in *Streetwise*, who assumed inappropriate "responsibility" for the household even as her mother was present. In one sequence, the child broke into their temporary home because neither she nor her mother had a key. The daughter complained, as she surveyed the inside, "What a mess. I just cleaned up this place!" She then proceeded to "clean" by spraying Right Guard deodorant around to cope with a mess created by a neglected puppy. The mother did not engage at all in these attempts to keep the home in order. She just blamed the daughter, saying, "Well, you wanted the dog, Erin." Both retreated to their respective sleeping quarters and began to talk between rooms. The teen offered uninvited advice on love to her mother. In time, the mother's voice drifted back to the daughter: "Keep quiet! I'm drinkin'."

One adult consequence of taking an (inappropriate) parental role as a child is a continued need to control as an end in itself. An 8-year-old "parent" who has had little experience with consistent, modulated parenting has no knowledge of how to use his or her "parental" power reasonably, or of how to cue appropriately. When this pattern of inappropriate control is directed toward others in adulthood, it is recognized as harsh and exploitative.

Taken as a group, the four patterns of experience yield a person intensely devoted to implementing control and protecting autonomy. The detachment, and the underlying motivation for control and autonomy, result in an exploitative mode of interaction that can be masked by apparent friendliness. Whether exploitiveness is involved or not, there is inept, miscued caring for and about self or others. This picture of the ASP as inept with the self as well as with others contradicts the picture of the ASP as a ruthlessly self-centered, always exploitative, fundamentally "evil" criminal. I agree with Cleckley that ASP and the "common criminal" are different. However, I also believe that the "common criminal" described by Cleckley is, in effect, a person with a Mixed Personality Disorder. The combination of ASP and NPD can yield a socially exploitative and manipulative individual who, unlike the ASP, takes care of himself or herself very carefully. The diagnosis of Mixed Personality Disorder is discussed in Chapter 15. A person who shows both ASP and NPD would have had elements of the developmental experiences described for each of these disorders. Even though he or she may not qualify for the sole label of ASP, the "common criminal" still has an understandable perspective, and is not necessarily "evil."

The present interpretation of ASP received partial confirmation in a study (Benjamin, 1992) that asked carefully diagnosed psychiatric inpatients to rate themselves and others on the SASB INTREX questionnaires (described in Chapter 3). The ASPs in the study had been committed to a state hospital for rape or murder. Their ratings of their memories of childhood suggested that they had control of their households. They saw their parents as more deferential than did BPDs or normals. In most relationships rated, the ASP group endorsed far more autonomy than either of the other groups. Their self-descriptions suggested that, unlike BPDs, ASPs showed "normal" friendliness. The data set also suggested that the ASPs had failed to internalize their perceived relationship with their mothers, although they did recall behaviors that appropriately complemented the mothers' initiations. BPDs, by contrast, had internalized their primary caregivers, but the internalization was hostile. These findings of excess autonomy and control in ASP, and of poor internalization of the parent, are consistent with this finding from another study: "those whose parents supply, or can be induced to supply, discipline that is both firm and consistent are at much lower risk of becoming sociopaths in later life" (Cloninger, 1978, p. 102).

CONNECTIONS BETWEEN THE INTERPERSONAL HISTORY AND THE SYMPTOMS LISTED IN THE DSM

The "total ASP" shows all the symptoms mentioned in the DSM. Identification with abusive, attacking parents can directly encourage physical fighting (item B3), use of weapons (item B4), forcing others into sexual activity (item B5), cruelty to animals (item B6), cruelty to other people (item B7), destruction of property (item B8), stealing (items B11, B12), and assaultiveness as an adult (item C3). ASP aggressiveness is not always a consequence of having been aggressed against; it can also come from failure to attach. As noted above, in the absence of attachment, the primate does not learn to modulate aggression (Harlow & Harlow, 1962).

The ASP's need to control others can represent simple identification with parents who were uneven in their use of control, or continuation of the ASP's early habit of assuming unmodulated and inappropriate control. Improper control masked by "friendliness" is flagged by the DSM as lying (item B10, item C6). Another consequence of the unmodulated parental control and failure to provide consistent nurturance is an intense need for autonomy, a position that defends against repetition of early helplessness. This defense is exacerbated by weakness in attachment to others. The need for autonomy and weak attachment are manifested early in truancy (item B1) and running away from home (item B2). The need for autonomy interferes with the ability to accept normal social demands, and so the ASP is not able to show consistent work behavior (item C1). He or she generally fails to conform to social norms and laws (item B9, item C2).

Internalization of neglect and abandonment appears as self-abandonment. This is reflected in the DSM items that describe failure to plan ahead (item C5) and recklessness with self and others (item C7). Identification with neglecting parents means that the ASP will also fail to be a responsible parent (item C8). The parental modeling of uncaring detachment means that the ASP will probably fail to honor commitments (item C4), to sustain a monogamous relationship (item C9), and to show the compassion that is required to feel remorse (item C10).

INTERPERSONAL SUMMARY OF ASP

The foregoing analysis suggests a succinct interpersonal summary for ASP:

There is a pattern of inappropriate and unmodulated desire to control others, implemented in a detached manner. There is a strong need to be independent, to resist being controlled by others, who are usually held in contempt. There is a willingness to use untamed aggression to back up the need for control or independence. The ASP usually presents in a friendly, sociable manner, but that friendliness is always accompanied by a baseline position of detachment. He or she doesn't care what happens to self or others.

The summary is based on the SASB codes of the ASP baseline patterns and wishes. These codes are listed at the bottom of Table 8.1. The baseline ASP positions are uncaring aggression (ATTACK plus WALL OFF); uncaring control (CONTROL plus WALL OFF); affection that is controlling and detached (ACTIVE LOVE or PROTECT plus CONTROL plus WALL OFF); self-indulgence that is fundamentally reckless of self (*SELF-PROTECT* plus *SELF-NEGLECT*) and others (*SELF-PROTECT* plus IGNORE); blaming of others (BLAME); and insistence on autonomy (SEPARATE). The wishes are to be given freedom (EMANCIPATE) and to have others SUBMIT. The fear is of receiving CONTROL.

The rhythm and harmonics of the ASP song are found in the sequences of interpersonal and intrapsychic response that the ASP gives and receives. The "tonic" ASP position is uncaring control (CONTROL plus WALL OFF) and uncaring affection (ACTIVE LOVE plus WALL OFF). This is accompanied by reckless self-indulgence (*SELF-PROTECT* plus *SELF-NEGLECT*). If his or her control or autonomy is threatened, the ASP will attack without remorse (ATTACK plus WALL OFF). Detachment (WALL OFF) is present in every chord that the ASP plays. This pervasive inaccessibility is probably the aspect of ASP that reminded Cleckley of schizophrenia and of autism. The ASP position harmonizes well with someone who will SUBMIT to the ASP's CONTROL. The partner should show REACTIVE LOVE while, at the same time, being able to IGNORE the exploitation and abuse implemented by the ASP.

Readers who can use the SASB codes will be able to generalize the present analysis to contexts not mentioned here. For example, it is not unusual for patients to complain that their depression is getting worse. Sometimes these complaints are presented to the therapist in a way that is characteristic of ASP. To interpret a complaint about depression in this way, the therapist would need to code the patient's process as he or she describes the depression. An ASP's process with the therapist as he or she complains about symptoms would include the notes of the ASP song. Consider this example:

A patient insisted that the doctor prescribe Prozac. He knew the doctor was worried about misuse of this drug, which had acquired local "street value." The patient assured the doctor that he no longer had a problem with drugs (CONTROL plus WALL OFF). He said he had turned over a new leaf and only needed the drug to contain his coexisting depression so he wouldn't act out again. He noted that the doctor had special abilities to understand him. He added that he cared very much about what the doctor thought (ACTIVE LOVE plus WALL OFF); for this reason, he would not dream of betraying the doctor's trust. The patient would use the drug exactly as prescribed. Three months later, the doctor had to respond to an inquiry from the licensing board. It seemed that the patient skillfully copied the doctor's prescription. He then altered dates and dosages so that he could refill it many times at different stores in different nearby towns (SELF-PROTECT plus SELF-NEGLECT). He was dealing Prozac.

The baseline notes of the ASP song are compared to those of the BPD, NPD, and HPD songs in Table 8.2. A scan of the table shows that ASP shares with each of the other disorders in the dramatic cluster the tendency to CONTROL. ASP is similar to BPD and NPD in the disposition to ATTACK, and to indulge the self (SELF-PROTECT) in a context of SELF-NEGLECT. The ASP shares with the NPD a willingness to ATTACK and to be SEPARATE. Other than a propensity to CONTROL, the ASP only shares with the HPD the capacity to remain detached (WALL OFF) while seeming to be friendly.

The table shows that ASP is distinguished from BPD by the capacity for autonomy (SEPARATE) and the lack of TRUST. ASP is distinguished from NPD by the *actively* manipulative approaches to others (ACTIVE LOVE plus CONTROL). The NPD assumes that others will defer and is puzzled when they do not. The ASP knows he or she has to make it happen. Although both are autonomous, the ASP is less accessible (WALL OFF) than the NPD. The ASP is distinguished from the HPD by greater alienation and recklessness (ATTACK, IGNORE, SELF-NEGLECT). The HPD shows REACTIVE LOVE and TRUST, attributes not likely for the ASP.

The interpersonal *do, re, mi* of Table 8.2 shows exactly how these categories overlap and how they differ. The descriptions in the tables can help the clinician make the differential diagnoses.

DSM DESCRIPTORS REVISITED

The DSM view of ASP has now been translated into interpersonal language, and the psychosocial learning associated with ASP patterns has been outlined. In this section, the interpersonal analysis of ASP is compared directly to the DSM. DSM-III-R items appear in **bold print**. The interpersonal modifiers are underlined. Items from the WISPI (discussed in Chapter 1) appear in CAPITAL LETTERS.

Table 8.2. Comparison of SASB Codes of BPD, NPD, HPD, and ASP

	BPD	NPD	HPD	ASP
1. EMANCIPATE				
2. AFFIRM				
3. ACTIVE LOVE	×			×*
4. PROTECT				
5. CONTROL	×	×	×*	×*
6. BLAME	×	×	×	×
7. ATTACK	×	×		×*
8. IGNORE		×		×
1. SEPARATE		×		×
2. DISCLOSE				
3. REACTIVE LOVE			×*	
4. TRUST	×		×*	
5. SUBMIT				
6. SULK				
7. RECOIL				
8. WALL OFF			×*	×*
1. SELF-EMANCIPATE				
2. SELF-AFFIRM				
3. ACTIVE SELF-LOVE		×*		
4. SELF-PROTECT	×			×*
5. SELF-CONTROL				
6. SELF-BLAME		×		
7. SELF-ATTACK	×		×*	
8. SELF-NEGLECT	×	×*		×*

*Indicates that these codes within the same column appear in complex combinations with one another.

A. Current age at least 18.

B. Evidence of Conduct Disorder with onset before age 15, as indicated by a history of *three* or more of the following:

(1) was often truant

The reason was that he or she hated the controlling behaviors of a particular teacher.

BEFORE I WAS 15 YEARS OLD, I SKIPPED SCHOOL REGULARLY BECAUSE EVERYONE WAS GETTING ON MY CASE.

(2) ran away from home overnight at least twice while living in parental or parental surrogate home (or once without returning)

This happened following a fight about control. Often these children had inordinate control in the household because the parents were absent and defaulted on their duties. When a parent reappeared and tried to reassert control, the future ASP resisted this furiously and might elect to leave.

BEFORE I WAS 15 YEARS OLD, I STAYED AWAY FROM HOME OVERNIGHT MORE THAN ONCE BECAUSE MY PARENTS TOOK CONTROL OF THINGS THEY HAD NO RIGHT TO CONTROL.

(3) often initiated physical fights

The reason was to maintain dominance or to maintain distance.

WHEN I WAS A KID, I LIKED TO START PHYSICAL FIGHTS, AND DID IT TO SHOW I WAS BOSS.

(4) used a weapon in more than one fight

The weapon was used to be effective in achieving the goal of dominance or distance. It is discussed in a way that shows no attachment to or caring about the fate of a potential victim.

BEFORE I WAS 15 YEARS OLD, I USED A WEAPON IN FIGHTS IN ORDER TO BE SURE THAT I'D WIN.

(5) forced someone into sexual activity with him or her

The motivation was to control, without caring about the impact on the victim.

BEFORE I WAS 15 YEARS OLD, I FORCED SOMEONE TO HAVE SEX AND I DIDN'T GIVE A DAMN ABOUT THEIR FEELINGS.

(6) was physically cruel to animals

This was done in a social context of demonstrating control and bravado, and was marked by lack of caring about the animal.

BEFORE I WAS 15 YEARS OLD, I TORTURED ANIMALS TO SHOW HOW TOUGH AND COOL I WAS.

(7) was physically cruel to other people

Deliberately inflicted pain on others to demonstrate control.

BEFORE I WAS 15 YEARS OLD, IT DIDN'T BOTHER ME AT ALL WHEN I HAD TO HURT SOMEBODY PHYSICALLY IN ORDER TO GET MY WAY.

(8) deliberately destroyed others' property (other than by fire-setting)

Deliberately destroyed property to establish dominion.

WHEN I WAS YOUNG, I OFTEN VANDALIZED OR DESTROYED PEOPLE'S PROPERTY TO GIVE THEM A HARD TIME.

(9) deliberately engaged in fire-setting

This item is not different from item B8 for ASP. Fire setting as a syndrome is usually implemented more privately and more autistically. There was "nothing in" *secret* fire-setting for the future ASP.

WHEN I WAS YOUNG, I OFTEN VANDALIZED OR DESTROYED PEOPLE'S PROPERTY TO SHOW OFF.

(10) often lied (other than to avoid physical and sexual abuse)

Lying was a habitual survival tactic in an unpredictable, harsh world. It was done in the service of control and/or maintaining distance.

WHEN I WAS A KID, I TOLD LIES EASILY TO GET WHATEVER I NEEDED.

(11) has stolen without confrontation of a victim on more than one occasion (including forgery)

The motivation was to control, without caring about impact on others.

WHEN I WAS A KID, I JUST TOOK WHATEVER I WANTED FOR MYSELF AND LIED MY WAY OUT OF TROUBLE WHEN QUESTIONED.

(12) has stolen with confrontation of a victim (e.g. mugging, purse-snatching, extortion, armed robbery)

The reason was to control supplies, or to demonstrate ability to control to peers; implemented without caring about the victim.

WHEN I WAS A KID, I COULD WALK RIGHT UP TO SOMEBODY AND TAKE WHAT I WANTED BY FORCE.

C. A pattern of irresponsible and antisocial behavior since the age of 15, as indicated by at least *four* of the following:

(1) is unable to sustain consistent work behavior, as indicated by any of the following (including similar behavior in academic settings if the person is a student):
    (a) significant unemployment for six months or more within five years when expected to work and work was available
    (b) repeated absences from work unexplained by illness in self or family
    (c) abandonment of several jobs without realistic plans for others

These behaviors qualify as antisocial if they occur in the service of maintaining independence, of avoiding being controlled. They are implemented without caring about the consequences for the self.

WHEN SOMEBODY AT WORK GIVES ME A HARD TIME, I'LL PUNCH THE PERSON OUT, EVEN IF I GET FIRED.

(2) fails to conform to social norms with respect to lawful behavior, as indicated by repeatedly performing antisocial acts that are grounds for arrest (whether arrested or not), e.g., destroying property, harassing others, stealing, pursuing an illegal occupation

These behaviors qualify as antisocial if they are done in the service of control, or demonstrate ability to control to others. There is no regard for the impact on the victim.

THE LAW MAKES NO DIFFERENCE TO ME; I AM STRONG ENOUGH TO DO WHAT I PLEASE, AND IT WORKS JUST FINE UNLESS I'M UNLUCKY ENOUGH TO GET CAUGHT.

(3) is irritable and aggressive, as indicated by repeated physical fights or assaults (not required by one's job or to defend someone or oneself), including spouse- or child-beating

The irritability is to maintain or demonstrate control or distance (avoid being controlled). An ASP will attack to defend associates, but for the purpose of demonstrating and maintaining control over them. In the case of spouse and child beating, the attacks are to control. There is no regard for or concern about the injury inflicted, and there is no remorse.

WHEN MY LOVER OR KIDS BUG ME, I GET REAL ANGRY AND BEAT THEM UP.

(4) repeatedly fails to honor financial obligations, as indicated by defaulting on debts or failing to provide child support or support for other dependents on a regular basis

Again, this is in the service of maintaining autonomy and is done without caring about the impact on others.

I HAVE OFTEN BORROWED LARGE AMOUNTS OF MONEY THAT I NEVER MEANT TO PAY BACK.

(5) fails to plan ahead, or is impulsive, as indicated by one or both of the following:
  (a) traveling from place to place without a prearranged job or clear goal for the period of travel or clear idea about when the travel will terminate
  (b) lack of a fixed address for a month or more

These behaviors qualify as antisocial if they are motivated by the need to be independent, to avoid being controlled. They are done without regard for impact upon the self.

WHENEVER I FEEL LIKE IT, I JUST PULL UP STAKES AND HIT THE ROAD.

(6) has no regard for the truth, as indicated by repeated lying, use of aliases, or "conning" others for personal profit or pleasure

There is emphasis on the ability to control the victim in these transactions.

I CAN GET WHAT I WANT BY CONNING THE MANY IDIOTS OF THE WORLD.

(7) is reckless regarding his or her own or others' personal safety, as indicated by driving while intoxicated, or recurrent speeding

This is done in a spirit of "nobody can control me." There is no regard for consequences for self or others.

DRIVING WHEN DRUNK OR HIGH DOES NOT WORRY ME. I FIGURE WHATEVER HAPPENS, HAPPENS.

(8) if a parent or guardian, lacks ability to function as a responsible parent, as indicated by one or more of the following:
  (a) malnutrition of child
  (b) child's illness resulting from lack of minimal hygiene
  (c) failure to obtain medical care for a seriously ill child
  (d) child's dependence on neighbors or nonresident relatives for food or shelter
  (e) failure to arrange for a caretaker for young child when parent is away from home
  (f) repeated squandering, on personal items, of money required for household necessities

These behaviors qualify as antisocial if done in service of maintaining independence and unwillingness to be controlled. They are done without appropriate regard for the impact on the child. The justification for gross violation of role may be that it is good for children to have to learn to take care of themselves.

MY PARENTS LEFT ME TO MAKE IT ON MY OWN AT A VERY YOUNG AGE, AND I FIGURE THAT IS THE WAY IT SHOULD BE WITH MY KIDS TOO.

(9) has never sustained a totally monogamous relationship for more than one year

Infidelity is in a context of demonstrating independence, of controlling the new person. There is no regard for the impact on either the new or the old person.

NOBODY CAN MAKE ME STAY TIED DOWN IN A RELATIONSHIP; WHEN I WANT SOMEBODY ELSE, I JUST
GO FOR IT.

(10) lacks remorse (feels justified in having hurt, mistreated, or stolen from another)

The belief is that everyone is out to "get his (or hers)," and the main idea in life is to be
on top all the time. One stops at nothing to be sure one does not get pushed around.
One must acquire on the spot whatever is wanted. Only wimps and sissies worry about
consequences. It follows that losers deserve to lose.

MAKING SOMEBODY LOOK LIKE A PIECE OF SHIT IS GREAT SPORT.

The interpersonal analysis of ASP suggests that the "criminality" depicted
by the DSM can be characterized as inordinate autonomy taking, addiction to
control, and lack of attachment to self or others. These dimensions also describe
the "antisocial" lawyers, doctors, and politicians not diagnosable by the DSM.
Like the criminals described by the diagnostic manual, individuals within these
higher-socioeconomic-status groups misuse their positions in the service of control for control's sake. They have no regard for the impact of their actions on
other people. If either the ASP diagnosis were expressed in these interpersonal
terms *or* white-collar crimes were better defined and prosecuted, the "high-level"
ASPs could also be diagnosed using the DSM. The North American legal system
has recently shown signs of increasing interpersonal sophistication in this regard. For example, the so-called "king of junk bonds" was given a relatively harsh
sentence for manipulation of the securities market. His lawyers had argued that
his white-collar crimes were less harmful than threats of bodily harm. They were
surprised at the harshness of the sentence. The judge noted that this extremely
wealthy individual betrayed the trust of investors. The Junk Bond King apparently ignored the impact of his actions on huge numbers of persons, including
poor persons dependent on the pension funds that were diminished by his ex-
ploitations.

NECESSARY AND EXCLUSIONARY CRITERIA

The present analysis permits definition of necessary and exclusionary conditions
for each personality disorder. For ASP, the recommended *necessary* descriptors
are (1) need for control of others and autonomy for the self, and (2) attachment
failure and lack of remorse. The first pair is not directly described by the DSM;
however, if the interviewer attends to the perspective of the ASP as he or she
committed the crimes that have led to the ASP diagnosis, these dimensions should
be present. In evaluating whether the patient lacks remorse, the clinician needs
to remember that the ASP is skilled at deception. He or she may make extravagant statements of guilt and remorse and not mean them. The test of sincerity
on this point is in consistent empathic, nonexploitative behavior, shown over
an extended period.

Exclusionary conditions for ASP include entitlement, dependency, and fear of abandonment. These marks of enmeshment are unlikely to be found in the highly differentiated ASP.

CASE ILLUSTRATIONS

Case 1

The first example is of a 15-year-old male with Conduct Disorder. The diagnosis was made using criteria listed in section B of the DSM-III-R definition of ASP. Longitudinal data support the view that Conduct Disorder is very likely to persist as ASP in adulthood (Robins, 1970; Wolkind, 1974). Of course, not all adolescents with Conduct Disorder become ASPs. However, section B of the DSM definition requires that all adults labeled ASP have been conduct-disordered as adolescents.

This 15-year-old was hospitalized for an attempt to shoot his stepsister. He had two previous hospitalizations. The first, when he was a preteen, followed an attempt to shoot himself; the second emanated from an overdose. He met the criteria for Conduct Disorder through his frequent initiation of physical fighting and through continuing trouble at school, which had resulted in his suspension. He also sometimes ran away from home, and he had a record of vandalism.

This young man remembered constant parental fighting about money and his mother's infidelity. After the eventual divorce, custody shifted back and forth between parents under conditions of battle. As a child he also spent periods of time living with relatives, with friends of the family, and with his father and his stepmother. The patient's view was that he had lived "in about 16 different homes." His present stepmother suffered from depression and was unable to cope. The patient explained: "I had to more or less take over, you know, like I make sure her kids got up and off to school and stuff like that—the house kept neat and things, you know." He described the same sort of pattern with his biological mother: "She's not—I don't feel as if she's my mother, although I know she is, you know what I mean? We are more or less like a friendship that you would have up here on the hospital ward—you know, somebody you can say stuff to, but not really go to them for anything really big."

The mother did not like this situation. He explained, "She felt that she should have been treated more like a mother instead of just a friend." He explained his difficulty in shifting from the stepmother's home, where he had control, to living in his biological mother's home: ". . . but just dropping the responsibility right away and going back and not having any control over anything is hard to do, you know? 'Cause most adults don't understand that 'cause they get 18 and all of a sudden they're in control of their own lives and they have kids and they're in control of them, and I'm a kid myself and I had to be in control of a household and four other kids, and then moving back and then having all that taken away from me, you know? Adults can't understand that 'cause they've never had to give it up."

The father modeled violence. At one point after the divorce, the father's uses of battle tactics to control the mother were so dramatic that the event appeared in the local newspapers. Similarly, the patient's outbursts of aggression were reckless attempts to maintain control. The stepsister whom the patient threatened just before this hospitalization had been telling people, including the local department of social services, that the patient was abusing the younger siblings (in his role as "parent"). The patient of course disagreed with that assessment and worried that he would be taken from yet another home. He showed Cleckley's "insanity," in that he seemed totally unaware that murderous abuse of the offending stepsister was a poor defense against the accusation that he was abusing the other children. When the interviewer asked what would have happened if he had succeeded in killing his stepsister, he observed, "Well, I would have wound up in jail, but that wouldn't have bothered me." The interviewer asked, "Why not?" He responded, "I don't know why not. It just wouldn't have." In short, his impulsive aggression was in the service of control, but it was grossly maladaptive. The action seemed self-protective to him, but it was done with reckless self-abandonment and without long-range vision.

After his overdose attempt, the "concerned" parents were absorbed with blaming each other, while neglecting him. He said, "I'm sitting here laying on this table, you know, and they're stuffing this tube up my nose to pump my stomach, and they're sitting there fighting, one on each side." This young man's lack of competent parenting was also poignantly apparent in his description of his "respect" for his father:

T: What is it that you especially respect in him?

P: I'm not sure. Just, well, he's always been there for me—well, not always, but most of the time he's always tried to be, you know, and he's done things for me.

T: What are some examples?

P: Whenever I needed help, he'd always be there and help me.

T: Can you tell me how he helped? What would be an example?

P: Listening to my problems, giving his opinion on things, helping me get through it. However, he's done stuff to me too, you know, like lying to me and things like that, and not giving me the full story, but still he's—out of all the people that I trust and respect, which are very few, he's the one in the relationship, or family relationship, that has done it to me the least.

T: So he's the most trustworthy.

P: Ya, in the family situation, yes.

T: What's an example of how he's slipped, how he's betrayed you?

P: By keeping me up nights and occasionally talking to me 'til 3:00 in the morning. Getting me involved in divorce and custody situations and telling me things about my mother, and I'm not sure if any of them are true or not . . . For a while I was a straight-A student, and then when I had to start doing all these things and listening to people's problems I went down to C's and D's.

T: So you were distracted by all the family troubles.

P: Ya. Besides that, I didn't really have time to do the work either.

Technically speaking, this young man could not be diagnosed as ASP because he was not yet old enough. But he fully qualified for Conduct Disorder, a common precursor to ASP. He frequently initiated physical fighting (item B3), was truant (item B1), ran away from home (item B2), and lied (item B10). He also deliberately destroyed other's property (item B8).

His interpersonal behaviors were consistent with the description of ASP given in Table 8.1. He appropriated control as a caregiver (**PROTECT**), but was not attached to his charges (**CONTROL** plus WALL OFF). For example, his harsh **ATTACKS** on siblings as he "took care of them" were a major problem. He put the **BLAME** on others, and IGNOREd their real needs. Although he was trying to protect himself, his attack on his stepsister was reckless (*SELF-PROTECT* plus *SELF-NEGELCT*). He didn't care what happened to her or to himself. He was reluctant, but capable of going his own way alone at a very young age. His wish to control was as compelling as was his fear of being controlled.

The excerpts from the interview suggest that his history was consistent with the historical trends predicted in Table 8.1:

1. This young man's father did not directly attack his son, but he did model murderous harshness. Imitation is an alternative mechanism for learning to attack recklessly.

This boy was placed in many different homes, and this makes it likely that there was default in caregiving. However, he also was at the center of the family drama. His biological parents depended upon him as they involved him in their marital battles. This use of his time and attention failed to acknowledge his own legitimate developmental needs. For example, when he stayed up all night listening to his father, he didn't have time to do his homework. The parental "attention," intimate though it seemed, was contaminated by the ever-present counterpoint IGNORE.

2. As this young man moved from home to home, the rules changed. Often he was in control, but sometimes he was the target of harsh, arbitrary bossiness. When he lost control, he felt humiliated. He described what happened when the department of social services looked into his fights with his mother about his failure to obey: "See, my mom comes off as, you know, a nice lady. She's done everything for me, you know, that's possible, and then people always think of me as the bad guy then, so then you got a whole bunch of people coming down on your case."

3. His description of the emergency room scene following his overdose offers a prototype for inept caring. His parents could not focus on his condition even under those extreme circumstances; they had to argue over whose fault it was that he took an overdose. Similarly, his narrative about the father's "being there" for him was pathetically concrete. The father would talk to him and be with him, but only to receive and enlist the patient's support in the father's battle against the mother. The patient didn't learn to care for himself. He said that if his stepsister had died and he had been put in jail, he would not have cared.

4. This teenager's control of the family was inordinate. He regularly took charge of his stepsiblings, albeit in unmodulated ways. He nurtured the parents

and had the power to affect their destiny. For example, his testimony was very influential when the marital battles reached the courts.

Case 2

The DSM-III-R casebook (Spitzer et al., 1989) offers Cleckley's (1955) case of Tom to illustrate ASP. Following that precedent, I examine another Cleckley case here from the present point of view. Arbitrarily, I have selected the first in Cleckley's series, the case of Max. Cleckley's description of Max can be summarized as follows:

> Brought into the hospital by police at the behest of his wife, Max was boastful and verbally aggressive to the police. In the hospital, where he agreed to stay because it was acceptable as an alternative to jail (where he would have gone for forging checks), he was expansive, cordial, "a little haughty." Later, he became restless and was granted parole, but lost it for fighting. On his return to the hospital, he incited fights among other patients and glibly denied his role. When not in the hospital or prison, he would frequent "houses of joy," and brag and fight at length. He engaged in bigamy three times, but escaped legal consequences with the help of his wife, by claiming incompetency and irresponsibility. There was an episode of counterfeiting money and lavish spending. The cycle of criminal behavior, prison, hospital, and discharge against medical advice was repeated many times.

Clearly Max fit the DSM adult descriptors: He did not work consistently (item C1). He repeatedly engaged in antisocial acts that were grounds for arrest (item C2). He was notably aggressive (item C3). He had "no regard for the truth" (item C6). He was a repeat bigamist, so it is unlikely that he was totally monogamous for as long as a year (item C9). He glibly denied involvement, or simply pleaded irresponsibility, never showing remorse (item C10). Cleckley did not provide details about Max's earlier years, so the applicability of section B of the DSM definition cannot be established.

Max is also well described by the interpersonal features listed in Table 8.1. The detached hostility (ATTACK plus WALL OFF) was a baseline position. His friendly charm was fundamentally controlling and detached (ACTIVE LOVE plus CONTROL plus WALL OFF). The pattern was inherent in his exploitation of various wives and ladies of the night, not to mention the health care system. His interest in raw power (CONTROL plus IGNORE) was expressed in his pattern of bragging about his boxing ability and managing much of the time to escape real challenge and injury. Finally, his story was saturated with demonstrations of neglectful self-care (SELF-PROTECT plus SELF-NEGLECT). One of the more amusing examples described is Cleckley's description of how this talented man chose to use one of his many gifts—a flair for sculpting:

> He asked to be given a loaf of bread, stating that he would mold from it creations of great beauty and worth. On getting the bread he broke off a large chunk, placed

it in his mouth and began to chew it assiduously, apparently relishing the confusion of his observers. After proceeding for a length of time and with thoroughness that once would have met with favor from advocates of Fletcherism, he at last disgorged the mess from his mouth and with considerable dexterity set about modeling it into the figure of a cross. Soon a human form was added in the customary representation. Rosettes, intertwining leaves, garlands, and an elaborate pedestal followed. The mixture of saliva and chewed bread rapidly hardened. . . . The whole piece was skillfully and ingeniously shaped, dry, firm, and as neatly finished as if done by a machine. It was, furthermore, one of the most extravagant, florid, and unprepossessing articles that has ever met my glance. Max presented it [to Cleckley] with an air of triumph and expectancy that seemed to demand expressions of wonder and gratitude beyond reach of this ordinary man. I did my best but felt none too satisfied with my efforts. . . . For a week he worked steadily, his mouth crammed with the doughy mass, his jaws chewing deliberately, his hands nimbly shaping spewed-out hunks of the mess into various neatly finished and exact but always garish, forms. His coloring of the flowers and garlands and imitation jewels, vivid red, pale purple, sickly pink always struck a high level of the tawdry blended with the pretentious. The most gaudy atrocities of the dime store must give ground before such art. (1955, pp. 63–64)

The story shows that he used his gifts in self-neglecting ways. This incident managed to offend and charm at the same time.

Max's behavioral patterns suggest that he maintained CONTROL of and autonomy from others (SEPARATE). These are the wishes and also the necessary conditions for ASP. He greatly feared being CONTROLled. He did not meet any of the exclusionary conditions. He was not dependent, nor did he fear abandonment. He appropriated what he wanted and needed, but in a clever, active way. He did not expect his preferences automatically to be met. He simply helped himself to whatever struck his fancy.

Cleckley thought that the early social histories of his many cases of psychopathy did not show consistent patterns. If he had thought that history was important, he would have reported it. The present hypotheses about the psychosocial etiology of Max's patterns (summarized in Table 8.1) could then be tested if specific interpersonal information were available. The SASB dimensional analysis of early history may identify specific linkages between patterns in childhood and adulthood that are not apparent by the usual method of scanning for generic traumatic events (divorce, father absence, alcoholism, etc.). No information is available for Max, so the SASB developmental hypotheses cannot be tested.

EXPECTABLE TRANSFERENCE REACTIONS AND TREATMENT IMPLICATIONS

Transference Reactions

"This disease is beyond my practice," says the Doctor as he contemplates Lady Macbeth's derangement (*Macbeth*, Act V, Scene I). The quotation from Shakespeare was selected by Cleckley to express the difficulty of treating ASP effectively. The key problem is the near-impossibility of getting collaboration from the ASP, who is not at all interested in changing his or her interactive patterns. Cleckley's case of Tom, selected for the DSM-III-R casebook, spotlights a typical complication in developing collaboration. After a long history of legal and social difficulties, an experienced elderly friend of the family took Tom for an automobile ride:

> The younger man not only promised to behave from now on in an exemplary fashion, but analyzed and discussed his past in such a way that the older one found there was little that could be added. . . . The young man's appearance of sincerity in all these realizations impressed the older counselor. He spoke as the wisest and most contrite of men would speak and seemed to have a more detailed and deeper understanding of his entire situation than even the most sagacious observer could reach. . . . Before the ride was over the judicious counselor was encouraged and deeply optimistic. . . . [That evening, Tom] disappeared from his care only to show up again later in jail. (Cleckley, 1955, pp. 95–96)

Correspondingly, a kindly and attentive psychotherapist is highly likely to be "taken for a ride" by an ASP, as was this counselor who thought he was in charge. On the other hand, if the psychotherapist is harsh and unsympathetic, he or she will only prove how abusive and neglectful are those who claim to care. The fundamental inaccessibility, described by the SASB model as hostile autonomy taking, assures that these individuals are denied benevolent contact with others. Hostile autonomy taking is an ever-present theme masked in complex combination with apparently friendly positions. This confuses intimates and is totally missed by uninformed observers. The overwhelming treatment challenge with the ASP is to break through this barrier. The therapist needs to try to achieve a genuine connection, a bond with the ASP, who appears to be socialized but who is deeply alienated.

The ASP's characteristic hostile autonomy taking severely constrains the possible impact of ordinary dyadic psychotherapy. More powerful methods are required to help the ASP consider trusting another person by taking the risk of caring what happens to him or herself or others.

Treatment Implications: The Five Categories of Correct Response

The view of therapy as a learning experience permits definition of therapist errors on a moment-to-moment basis. Therapy interventions can be evaluated in terms of whether they enhance collaboration, facilitate learning about patterns and their roots, block maladaptive patterns, enhance the will to change, or effectively encourage new patterns. The effect of interventions is assessed in terms of the actual impact on the patient, not in terms of the therapist's intention.

The ASP does not respond well to individual therapy alone. I have treated only three people with this label, and I cannot discuss them because they all had legal difficulties that were well known in their community. The very different course of therapy for ASP, and the limits of my experience with this disorder, preclude discussion of the treatment in terms of the five separate categories of correct response. However, I believe that the functions described by the five categories must be met in a successful therapy.

Facilitating Collaboration, Facilitating Pattern Recognition, and Blocking Maladaptive Patterns

The ASP cannot be reached through ordinary discourse. The only recourse is either (1) to coerce the ASP into treatment, or (2) to find a way to incite the ASP to choose to undertake the change process. A court frequently attempts to implement the coercive approach by giving an ASP a choice of treatment or jail. If ordered by the court, there is a significant likelihood that the ASP will "go through the motions" of psychotherapy simply to avoid punishment.

Unfortunately, collaboration in ordinary dyadic therapy cannot be coerced and will not be chosen by the ASP. It may be possible to create alternative experiences that implement one or more of the five correct interventions. Developmental psychologists have marked the variables of dominance and warmth as crucial to the process of identification (e.g., Mussen, Conger, & Kagan, 1971, p. 359). The ASP has not had well-modulated and consistent socialization experiences with either dominance or warmth. He or she needs them.

One example of an alternative approach to ASP is offered by a milieu treatment program designed in the late 1970s and early 1980s by Dr. Glenn Shaurette at the Veterans Administration (VA) Hospital in Columbia, South Carolina. Dr. Shaurette recognized the need to meet a personality-disordered individual on his or her own terms. Those who inflexibly react from a baseline of hostility are unresponsive to ordinary helpfulness. Dr. Shaurette found a way to join the ASP in his or her initial hostile position and then progressively to move toward collaboration. He consolidated the power of the hospital setting to dominate (benevolently, but completely) the interpersonal experience of the ASP. The treatment plan assured that on any given day the ASP was confronted by the same interpersonal message from all levels of staff. The goal was to block the maladaptive ASP patterns and replace them with ones that would permit discharge.

An ASP would typically arrive on Dr. Shaurette's ward behaving in ways that could be coded WALL OFF. The ward physicians, psychologists, nurses, social workers, and others would complement this ASP hostility by leaving the ASP alone for a few days (IGNORE). Then the ward routines were explained, so that the patient learned that there were going to be rather harsh punishments for failure to comply with the behavioral therapy programs (BLAME). Patients were shown the SASB model and told that if they successfully mastered the behavior therapy treatment plan, the initial severe setting of limits would be relaxed through a series of steps. The patients could see that the plan headed stepwise (to CONTROL, PROTECT, AFFIRM) toward greater friendliness and autonomy giving by the staff. (More detail about the "Shaurette principle" is available in Chapter 3 and in Benjamin, Foster, Giat-Roberto, & Estroff, 1986.) Dr. Shaurette and his ward staff noted that ASPs were quite responsive to this highly coordinated and organized form of milieu therapy. Patients were discharged more rapidly and with better results.[1] This milieu treatment plan seems worthy of further refinement and study.

Another potentially effective way to elicit the collaboration of ASPs is to use giants of the sports world as role models. Children at risk for Conduct Disorder and subsequent ASP can be impressed by such individuals. The occasional story of the constructive impact of a superhero on a vulnerable delinquent is heart-warming. The would-be delinquent can internalize the athlete's warmth and benevolent power. The superhero's warmth is crucial to the introjective process and cannot be faked or contrived. Having an athlete talk to a group in a context where the athlete might "get points" for being so generous would probably be suspect and ineffective. The convincing connection between athlete and juvenile needs to be spontaneous, personal, and genuine. The most likely mode is for an athlete to identify on some basis with the child and sincerely want to give to him or her.

Another way to introduce warmth may be to put the ASP in a nurturant position. For example, providing kittens for any willing prison inmates may develop a basic interest in connectedness, since furry pets can provide vitally needed contact comfort (as described by Harlow & Harlow, 1962). Of course, out of compassion for the animals, this intervention requires zealous supervision until it becomes clear that the ASPs can care enough about the kittens not to abuse them. Similarly, letting ASPs assume a teaching role in any socially acceptable areas in which they have requisite skills may develop bondedness. For example, teaching kids to box or play baseball—again in a tightly supervised context—can facilitate bonding. The procedure uses the principle of complementarity to put the ASP in a position of dominance and warmth. The idea is that the dependency and trust shown by the kittens or children can draw nurturance from the ASPs. As a result, they may eventually be able to maintain a benevolent position.

A currently popular method of treating conduct-disordered adolescents is to take them on wilderness survival camping trips. The method has become controversial because of alleged mismanagement and abuse, resulting in death for some participants. Because the adventure trips are inherently interesting, challenging, and not primarily verbal, they would seem an extremely promising means of approach. It should be very helpful to identify constructive elements of the outdoor experience treatment approach and to implement them in an enlightened way with efficiency and humanity.

---

[1]Dr. Shaurette tried to implement formal research to test this idea, but before he could secure funds, he was promoted to a higher administrative position where he no longer was in charge of the inpatient service.

Recently Michael Black, a graduate student at the University of Utah and an experienced mountaineer, tried this approach and used SASB measures of self-concept to assess the results. Michael is a part-time employee of an outdoor experience program for executives known as "ABC." Borrowing from the ABC program, he offered a day of structured outdoor challenge to a group of eight adult male incest perpetrators who had been ordered by the court to undergo psychological treatment. Not formally diagnosed, the group included some individuals with ASP, some with NPD, some with NEG, and others with Mixed Personality Disorder. The SASB-based interpretation of the ABC structured outdoor experience is that it enhances bonding with others and deference to the group. Collaboration with group decision-making processes requires giving up control; carrying the decisions out requires self-discipline and personal mastery. ABC activities include "blind trust walks," "trust falls," group problem solving, and group discussions of the experiences. While problem solving, the group must figure out how to retrieve a bandana from an "acid pit." Everyone in the group must get through a "spider web" without anyone touching it. The group must also figure out how to get everyone over a 14-foot sheer wall. Mastery in the absence of control is further emphasized when blindfolded individuals must follow a rope through the forest, over rocks, and across streams, "as if it were your life."

Usually resistant and reluctant to participate in treatment, the group of perpetrators was very pleased with this experience. Measures of self-concept on the SASB INTREX questionnaires showed a significant improvement in perceived self-control in the worst state for the treatment group. Six subjects from the same population, who had been randomly assigned to a control condition of an ordinary day hike, showed no consistent changes in self-concept. The effects of the 1-day ABC treatment did not persist through a 1-month follow-up measure, however. The study needs replication and expansion, with careful diagnosis and formal coding of the patients' experiences. More careful study might permit exact measurement of the connections between the perceived dimensionality of the treatment intervention and its interpersonal and intrapsychic consequences. Subsequent replications of the study might vary the dimensionality and duration of the experiences to identify the most relevant activities, the needed amounts of each, and the proper sequencing.

The agency clinician confronted with the problem of treating large numbers of unwilling ASPs may be able to think of comparable activities. Carefully managed group therapy can offer powerful opportunities for bonding and control. Treatment plans should take advantage of special features of the local area. Activities that may facilitate bonding and interdependence should be selected.

In some cases, the family of the ASP is able and willing to participate in therapy. This can represent a powerful mode of change. It can also turn out that the family colludes deeply with the ASP's patterns. Confrontation of the interface between family patterns and the ASP's acting out can sometimes elicit collaboration. In one case, I expressed near-despair about the family interactions that supported ASP patterns. The ASP then implemented his own plan to coerce change within the family. It was a method, somewhat harsh but not clearly abusive, that never would have occurred to me. It was definitely effective in eliciting family cooperation in the treatment process.

Strengthening the Will to Give Up Maladaptive Patterns, and Facilitating New Learning

Once bonding and interdependence begin, the preconditions for collaboration have been met. At this point, the ASP may understand the self-destructive features of the exploitative lifestyle. He or she may begin to develop needed skills, such as self-care, delay of gratification, and empathy for others. It is widely believed that the patterns of ASP typically abate with increasing age. If this is true, the present analysis would suggest that such improvement should be associated with an accumulation of life experiences that encourage attachment and interdependence. It could be, for example, that ASP patterns are changed by continuing experiences with lovers and children, whose warm interdependence offers an undeniable antidote to the ASP's baseline of hostile detachment.

Like the NPD, the ASP seems especially vulnerable to the "*Klute* syndrome" (see Chapter 6). It is present if the SASB codes of the favorite sexual fantasies are identical to the SASB codes of the chief complaint. The theory is that sexual gratification is reinforcing the patterns of the "chief complaint." For example, hypermasculine and aggressive ASPs are more likely than others to have erotized violence. Some of these individuals engage in sadistic forms of sexuality. Sometimes they will speak of verbal or physical rages as generating "a high" that compares to their use of cocaine. They will explain that both cocaine and anger enhance highly pleasurable feelings of dominance and sexuality. This most extreme version of this pattern can be found in veterans of Vietnam carrying the ASP label, who speak of a "killing high." Some of these unfortunate citizens were taken from their marginal backgrounds and placed in an intensely hostile and alienating setting where everyone was the enemy—soldiers, women, children. In the military, these individuals were rewarded greatly for killing. Then they were sent back to society with their patently unusable murderous "job skills" and expected to make a new and profoundly different adjustment. For these men, and for anyone who has a *Klute* connection to ASP behaviors, no simple social intervention is likely to result in changed behavior patterns. The connection between violence and sexuality has to be broken first. The linking of erotization and violence is another factor that may account for the "irrationality" of ASP behaviors. This theme is well documented in a recent book entitled *The Seductions of Crime: Moral and Sensual Attractions in Doing Evil* (Katz, 1988).

It is not clear whether such erotization of violence is a necessary condition for ASP. It may be characteristic only of a subgroup of ASPs. Perhaps it should provide the basis for a separate diagnosis, Sadistic Personality Disorder. The category would mark arbitrary control and ruthless violence as a syndrome in itself. The highly controlled sadistic behaviors exist within populations that do not show the careless disregard of self said by Cleckley to be characteristic of ASP. For example, Satanic cults allegedly have members who function well and occupy highly respectable positions in society. It is reasonable to assume that the more violent cult members are also damaged psychologically. If studied carefully, they might be shown to have their own characteristic histories, wishes, and fears. Without requisite experiences in bonding with and empathy for others, such individuals would see little reason to give up their practices.

PART THREE

DSM CLUSTER C, THE ANXIOUS, FEARFUL GROUP

9

Dependent Personality Disorder

"So long as he (she) is there, all is well."

REVIEW OF THE LITERATURE

> Thirteen months had passed since Hedda Nussbaum was arrested along with her lover, Joel Steinberg, for the death of their six-year-old adopted daughter, Lisa. . . . It was a story of Nussbaum's almost total devotion to a man who stripped her of all human dignity. Nussbaum's first day of testimony ended with the image of a helpless and innocent child, lying comatose on a bathroom floor while her parents ignored her and freebased cocaine. Nussbaum might have saved Lisa with a phone call. But she didn't for fear of angering the man she loved, the man who left her with the fighter's face. (Hackett, McKillop, & Wang, 1988, p. 56)

The nation watched, horrified, as a grisly tale of family violence unfolded live on TV, in lurid detail. Psychiatric opinion was varied.[1] It appears that the best answer to the pressing question of why Nussbaum failed to protect her child and herself was that she suffered from DPD.

> The Dependent Personality Disorder is an outgrowth of Freud's theories of personality development and is virtually synonymous with the oral dependent character as conceptualized from Freud's paradigm by Abraham . . . and Glover. . . . such people exhibit a cluster of traits and behaviors that may be roughly characterized as follows: They are passive, dependent, submissive in interpersonal relationships (especially in relationships with authority figures) and in need of a great deal of support and reassurance from others. In addition, fear of abandonment and a relatively weak self-concept characterize these individuals. (Greenberg & Bornstein, 1988, p. 126)

The interactive pattern of DPD has generated relatively little controversy in the literature. The massive number of papers published on BPD may be inspired by the agony that this group creates among health care providers. Perhaps DPD generates relatively little interest because "everything is in control." If the most troublesome patterns garner the greatest amount of professional attention, then DPD will necessarily move to the back of the line.

Livesley, Schroeder, and Jackson (1990) recently dissected the DSM description of DPD into two distinct interpersonal dimensions: attachment and de-

---

[1]There was testimony that Nussbaum suffered from "passive dependent personality traits, depression, anxiety, psychotic disorders and infantile narcissistic tendencies" (Hackett et al., 1988, p. 61).

pendency. They wrote items representing aspects of DPD that were suggested by the literature. Then they used a well-validated method of scaling the items, and asked patients and normals to rate them. Factor analysis yielded orthogonal dependency and attachment components. The authors concluded that although dependency is well represented in the DSM, the attachment aspects of DPD are not highlighted adequately (1990, p. 139). They suggested that this personality type may be directly related to the early childhood pattern described as "insecure attachment" by Bowlby (1977). Pilkonis (1988) agrees that the DPD has insecure attachment.

DPDs have several associated Axis I disorders, most notably depression and physical complaints (Greenberg & Bornstein, 1988). Unlike the dependent pattern itself, the Axis I problems do provide a focus for extensive concern and discussion. Several studies have attempted to identify the relation between personality disorder and depression. Most report at least one associated personality subtype that resembles the DSM description of DPD. For example, Blatt (1974) identified two personality types likely to become depressed. One was characterized by "feelings of helplessness, weakness and depletion" (p. 107) and "wishes to be soothed and cared for, helped and protected" (p. 116). One of Pilkonis's (1988) prototypes for depressed personality was named "excessive dependency" and included descriptors very like those for the DSM Axis II disorder. Pilkonis's dependent and depressed prototype was summarized as follows:

> 1. Tends to be anxious and insecure because of the fear that s/he may lose an important relationship or person. 2. Tends to give up "control" to others: underestimates his/her own abilities and resources for coping. 3. Cannot take risks that might lead to the loss of a relationship (e.g. refuses to assert self with significant others, has strong inhibitions against expressing anger). 4. Relies on others for the validation of beliefs and behaviors. (1988, p. 148)

DSM DEFINITION OF THE DISORDER

The DSM definition provides the starting point for the analysis. The DSM specifies that the diagnosis of DPD can be made if an individual meets five of the criteria. DSM-III-R items appear in **bold print**, and any changes introduced by the DSM-IV appear in *italics*. (The DSM-III-R and DSM-IV item numbering is the same, except that DSM-III-R item 9 is omitted from DSM-IV.)

A pervasive pattern of dependent and submissive behavior, beginning by early adulthood and present in a variety of contexts, as indicated by at least *five* of the following:

A pervasive and excessive need to be taken care of, which leads to submissive and clinging behavior and fears of separation, beginning by early adulthood and present in a variety of contexts, as indicated by at least five of the following:

(1) is unable to make everyday decisions without an excessive amount of advice or reassurance from others

(2) allows others to make most of his or her important decisions, e.g., where to live, what job to take

encourages or allows others to assume responsibility for major areas of life

(3) agrees with people even when he or she believes they are wrong, because of fear of being rejected

has difficulty expressing disagreement with others because of fear of their anger or loss of support

(4) has difficulty initiating projects or doing things on his or her own

has difficulty independently initiating projects or doing things on his or her own (due to a lack of self-confidence in judgment or abilities rather than to lack of motivation or energy)

(5) volunteers to do things that are unpleasant or demeaning in order to get other people to like him or her

goes to excessive lengths to obtain nurturance and support from others, to the point of volunteering to do things that are unpleasant

(6) feels uncomfortable or helpless when alone, or goes to great lengths to avoid being alone

feels uncomfortable or helpless when alone, because of exaggerated fears of inability to care for himself or herself

(7) feels devastated or helpless when close relationships end

indiscriminately seeks another relationship to provide nurturance and support when a close relationship ends

(8) is frequently preoccupied with fears of being abandoned

is frequently preoccupied with fears of being left to take care of himself or herself

(9) is easily hurt by criticism or disapproval [omitted from DSM-IV]

Morey (1988) reported that 22.3% of a sample of 291 outpatients being treated for personality disorder qualified for the DPD label. There was substantial overlap with BPD (50.8%) and AVD (49.2%).

PATHOGENIC HYPOTHESES

The method of using the SASB model to develop pathogenic hypotheses has been sketched in Chapter 5. Four main features of the developmental history have been identified specifically to account for each of the DPD symptoms listed in the DSM. A summary of the hypotheses linking interpersonal history to interpersonal patterns characteristic of the disorder appears in Table 9.1. A fuller discussion of these hypotheses is provided here.

1. The DPD started the developmental cycle very well. He or she enjoyed the natural developmental sequence that begins with warm caring and intense attention. This allows a baby to bond to other human beings; the infant learns

Table 9.1. Interpersonal Summary of DPD

History	Consequences of history
1. Wonderful infancy, excellent nurturance (**PROTECT**)	1. Expects, needs caregiving, control (**PROTECT**, **CONTROL**)
2. Nurturance not stopped in time (**CONTROL, BLAME**)	2. Compliant, dependent behaviors (<u>TRUST</u>, <u>SUBMIT</u>, <u>SULK</u>)
No practicing of autonomy, competence (not <u>SEPARATE</u>)	Autonomy (<u>SEPARATE</u>) avoided at all costs
Poor self-concept by default (*SELF-BLAME*)	Sees self as inadequate (*SELF-BLAME*); tolerates **BLAME**
3. Mockery by peers (**BLAME**) for lack of competence	3. Feels inadequate, incompetent (*SELF-BLAME*)
4. Alternative history: Overt **CONTROL**, abusive (**BLAME, ATTACK**) parenting that nonetheless provided nurturance; no complex messages	4. As indicated in steps 1–3

Summary. The baseline position is of marked submissiveness to a dominant other person who is supposed to provide unending nurturance and guidance. The wish is to maintain connection to that person even if it means tolerating abuse. The DPD believes that he or she is instrumentally incompetent, and this means that he or she cannot survive without the dominant other person.

SASB codes of DPD baseline: <u>TRUST</u>, <u>SUBMIT</u>, <u>SULK</u>; *SELF-BLAME* for incompetence. *Wishes:* To receive **PROTECT, CONTROL.** *Fears:* To receive **IGNORE.** *Necessary descriptors:* Submissiveness stemming from the sense of instrumental inadequacy. *Exclusionary descriptors:* Complications of dependency (long-term comfort with autonomy; transitive demands for nurturance; intimacy only if the situation is safe; insistence on submission; scorn for authority; etc.).

that others will give what is needed, whenever it is needed. Freud (1949/1955, p. 11) called the first stage in development the "oral stage." Erikson (1959, pp. 55–61) named it the stage of "trust versus distrust." The prototypic DPD mastered this first stage very well. He or she learned to count on others because nurturance and caring were available from the beginning.

The adult DPD continues that pattern by showing trust in a selected dominant significant other person. This trust can exceed all reason, as shown by Hedda Nussbaum as she watched her dying child; she reassured herself, "No, Joel said he would take care of her" (see below).

2. The parent(s) of the DPD did not stop nurturing when it became developmentally appropriate to do so. Weaning is a vitally important developmental step. Instead of letting the toddler learn to do things on his or her own, the parent of the DPD continued to offer helpful nurturance and protectiveness. There are two common reasons for the failure to wean. First, the parent may enjoy the intimacy with the dependent child and may not want to give it up. Second, the parent may believe in the "empty-tank" theory of development; this view asserts that if a child is given enough attention and nurturance, all will be well. According to the empty-tank theory, if there is any frustration, neurotic

behaviors will follow. Under this model, the parental mandate is to take care of every need immediately, completely, and consistently.

Unfortunately, nurturance given noncontingently after infancy weakens rather than strengthens a child. What once was helpful and protective becomes raw control if it is no longer developmentally appropriate. If the helpfulness extends too far beyond the normal age of weaning, it becomes demeaning and degrading. Consider, for example, the changes in meaning of tying a child's shoes as he or she grows older. Shoe tying for a toddler is helpful and protective. Shoe tying for a first-grader, when all the other kids already know how to do it, becomes control. Shoe tying for a sixth-grader is positively demeaning and humiliating. The interpersonal dimensionality of any given action varies according to the developmental context. What is PROTECT in one context becomes CONTROL in another, and BLAME in yet another.

The SASB principle of complementarity (see Chapter 3) suggests that the consequence of relentless nurturance is dedicated submission. PROTECT inspires TRUST. CONTROL engenders SUBMIT. BLAME inspires SULK. In short, the DPD is subject to all possible forms of control and responds with all forms of submission. He or she feels inadequate. Because he or she is unable to take care of things, the DPD must depend on someone else. Being alone would leave him or her without resources to cope. He or she must be with someone competent, and he or she will tolerate abuse if that is the price of the needed caregiving.

Nussbaum summarized the developmental process and its consequences succinctly as she wrote, "[My mother] insisted on doing everything for me—putting on my socks at age 6 for example . . . My father, on the other hand, was always saying, 'Listen to me. I'm older. I know better'" (quoted in Hackett et al., 1988, p. 60). She explained why she did not telephone for medical attention as her daughter lay unconscious on the bathroom floor: "'No, Joel said he would take care of her . . .' And I didn't want to show disloyalty or distrust for him. So I didn't call" (Hackett et al., 1988, p. 58).

3. The DPD was mocked by peers for incompetence. "Sissy," "baby," "wimp," and the like are the messages from the peer group. This sense of instrumental inadequacy was internalized (*SELF-BLAME*). The DSM-III-R discarded the item from DSM-III that referred to this lack of self-confidence because it allegedly had "little diagnostic specificity." It is true that generic lack of confidence is found in many of the personality disorders. However, the sense of instrumental inadequacy is the DPD's distinctive version of poor self-concept. "I can't do it" is the starting assumption of the prototypic DPD. Nussbaum wrote, "The combination [mother plus father] made me feel like I couldn't do anything for myself and I didn't know anything. . . . I just went where I was taken" (quoted in Hackett et al., 1988, p. 60).

Developmental features 1–3 in Table 9.1 are also illustrated by the DSM-III-R casebook illustration of DPD called "Blood Is Thicker Than Water" (Spitzer et al., 1989, pp. 123–124). The DPD had been "babied and spoiled" and teased by peers for lack of assertiveness. He was unable to marry his girlfriend because his mother, with whom he lived, disapproved. He feared and admired his "domineering" mother, and felt his own judgment was poor.

4. The crucial dimension of the history of the DPD is that there is overwhelming parental control. There are no perceived options for the child other than submission. Although the DPD is submissive, he or she nonetheless has a clear sense of boundaries between self and others. Excessive protection and nurturance are not the only ways to generate submission; another is to have an overtly hostile, controlling family. One of the cases discussed later in this chapter illustrates this alternative way to generate the submissive positions characteristic of DPD. So long as there is overwhelming control, while a clear sense of self remains, DPD can be the result. If the control appears in complex combination with other messages, the simple submission characteristic of DPD does not result.

CONNECTIONS BETWEEN THE INTERPERSONAL HISTORY AND THE SYMPTOMS LISTED IN THE DSM

The "total DPD" shows all the symptoms mentioned in the DSM. The DPD's inability to make decisions or take responsibility is described by DSM items 1 and 2. The inability to initiate projects (item 4) is manifested because he or she sees no alternative; the DPD must be a part of the decisions and plans that have been made for him or her by others. The belief that someone else must take care of things lead the DPD to defer inappropriately (item 3), to allow himself or herself to be exploited or humiliated in order to maintain support (item 5), and to worry greatly about potential loss of the dominant caregiver (items 6, 7, 8, 9).

As the italicized revisions of some DSM-III-R criteria indicate (see above), the DSM-IV has implicitly restored the DSM-III criterion of poor self-concept for DPD. The lack of confidence is associated strictly with inability to perform instrumental tasks. In fact, DPDs often equate their submissiveness with "niceness" and therefore think of themselves as "good persons." DPDs do not think of themselves as evil or worthy of punishment. Their problem is just that they don't know "how." They can't. They feel unable, inadequate, helpless, inept, unequipped, and unqualified. The DPD's poor self-concept represents the internalization of the implicit or explicit contempt for his or her instrumental inadequacy, as well as a realistic appraisal of the failure to develop instrumental skills.

INTERPERSONAL SUMMARY OF DPD

The foregoing analysis suggests a succinct interpersonal summary for DPD:

The baseline position is of marked submissiveness to a dominant other person who is supposed to provide unending nurturance and guidance. The wish is to maintain connection to that person even if it means tolerating abuse. The DPD believes that he or she is instrumentally incompetent, and this means that he or she cannot survive without the dominant other person.

The summary is based on the SASB codes of the DPD baseline patterns and wishes. The codes themselves, listed in Table 9.1, provide a shorthand way to identify DPD. The baseline DPD positions are TRUST, SUBMIT, SULK, and SELF-BLAME. The wishes are to receive **PROTECT** and **CONTROL**. The fear is of IGNORE by the desperately needed caregiver.

The rhythm and harmonics of the DPD song are found in the sequences of interpersonal and intrapsychic response that the DPD gives and receives. The "tonic" DPD position is to TRUST and SUBMIT. His or her position harmonizes well with someone who will **PROTECT** and **CONTROL**. If BLAME is part of the package, that will be tolerated with SULK. Threatened loss of that important other, or any other pressure for autonomy (SEPARATE), brings the DPD to the brink of panic. His or her sense of SELF-BLAME for instrumental inadequacy paralyzes his or her willingness to try to cope. These are the harmonics and rhythms of the DPD song.

Readers who can use the SASB codes will be able to generalize the present analysis to contexts not mentioned here. For example, it is not unusual for patients to complain that their depression is getting worse. Sometimes these complaints are presented to the therapist in a way that is characteristic of DPD. To interpret a complaint about depression in this way, the therapist would need to code the patient's process as he or she describes the depression. A DPD's process with the therapist as he or she complains about symptoms would include the notes of the DPD song. Consider this example:

A patient was chronically depressed, and the doctor tried her on a new antidepressant. She did not improve and had a number of side effects, but did not mention them to the doctor. Fortunately, the doctor remembered to ask for the specific signs of side effects. The patient acknowledged the signs, and the doctor wrote a prescription for a different antidepressant. The patient was willing to acknowledge the signs of problems (SUBMIT), but she did not offer the information spontaneously. The doctor asked her why she did not say anything. She explained, "I thought that maybe they were just part of the way the drug worked (SULK). I figured you would know what was best (TRUST)."

The baseline notes of the DPD song are compared to those of the BPD, NPD, HPD, and ASP songs in Table 9.2. The interpersonal *do, re, mi* of Table 9.2 shows exactly how these categories overlap; it also shows how they differ. The descriptions in the tables can help the clinician make the differential diagnoses. A scan of the table shows that DPD is characterized by submissiveness and self-blame. DPD shares with BPD and HPD the trait of dependency. Unlike the BPD and the HPD, who are dependent only if others "deliver" in a friendly, nurturant way, the DPD complies regardless of the atmosphere. DPD shares with NPD the tendency to self-criticism, but under very different conditions. The NPD

Table 9.2. Comparison of SASB Codes of BPD, NPD, HPD, ASP, and DPD

	BPD	NPD	HPD	ASP	DPD
1. EMANCIPATE					
2. AFFIRM					
3. ACTIVE LOVE	×			×*	
4. PROTECT					
5. CONTROL	×	×	×*	×*	
6. BLAME	×	×	×	×	
7. ATTACK	×	×		×*	
8. IGNORE		×		×	
1. SEPARATE		×		×	
2. DISCLOSE					
3. REACTIVE LOVE			×*		
4. TRUST	×		×*		×
5. SUBMIT					×
6. SULK					×
7. RECOIL					
8. WALL OFF			×*	×*	
1. SELF-EMANCIPATE					
2. SELF-AFFIRM					
3. ACTIVE SELF-LOVE		×*			
4. SELF-PROTECT	×			×*	
5. SELF-CONTROL					
6. SELF-BLAME		×			×
7. SELF-ATTACK	×		×*		
8. SELF-NEGLECT	×	×*		×*	

*Indicates that these codes within the same column appear in complex combinations with one another.

will be self-critical if the required conditions of noncontingent admiration fail. The NPD can be and feel very competent under other circumstances, while the DPD always feels instrumentally inadequate. DPD is distinguished from disorders in the dramatic, erratic cluster by the fact that DPDs do not show transitive initiations toward others. The section of Table 9.2 that describes transitive initiations is completely empty for DPD. By strong contrast, all four diagnostic categories in cluster B include CONTROL and BLAME. Three of them also include ATTACK. Clearly DPD is associated with less "trouble" than are the disorders assigned to the dramatic, erratic cluster.

DSM DESCRIPTORS REVISITED

The DSM view of DPD has now been translated into interpersonal language, and the psychosocial learning associated with DPD patterns has been outlined.

In this section, the interpersonal analysis of DPD is compared directly to the DSM. DSM-III-R items appear in **bold print,** and any changes introduced by DSM-IV appear in *italics*. The interpersonal modifiers are <u>underlined</u>. Items from the WISPI (discussed in Chapter 1) appear in CAPITAL LETTERS.

A pervasive pattern of dependent and submissive behavior, beginning by early adulthood and present in a variety of contexts, as indicated by at least *five* **of the following:**

A pervasive and excessive need to be taken care of, which leads to submissive and clinging behavior and fears of separation, beginning by early adulthood and present in a variety of contexts, as indicated by at least five of the following:

(1) is unable to make everyday decisions without an excessive amount of advice or reassurance from others

<u>Thinks of self as instrumentally inadequate, and waits for strong others to preside over and guide everyday attempts to function. Seeks the opinions and guidance of others about the smallest everyday decisions.</u>

BECAUSE I DON'T TRUST MY JUDGMENT, I WAIT TO MAKE EVERYDAY DECISIONS UNTIL THE PERSON CLOSE TO ME IS THERE TO TAKE OVER.

(2) allows others to make most of his or her important decisions, e.g., where to live, what job to take

encourages or allows others to assume responsibility for major areas of life

<u>Has no respect for his or her own judgment, and waits for or asks others to take over and make major decisions for him or her.</u>

I LET PEOPLE CLOSE TO ME PLAN FOR AND TAKE CARE OF MY LIFE BECAUSE I FEEL UNABLE TO HANDLE IT MYSELF.

(3) agrees with people even when he or she believes they are wrong, because of fear of being rejected

has difficulty expressing disagreement with others because of fear of their anger or loss of support

<u>Feels so unable to function alone that he or she will agree with or go along with anything (even things that are seen as wrong), rather than risk the rejection of those to whom he or she looks to for guidance and help. Does not get appropriately angry at important others because of the fear that those others will then not be available to provide needed support and nurturance.</u>

EVEN IF I AM MISTREATED BY PEOPLE, I WILL STILL TRY TO PLEASE THEM BECAUSE I AM NOT STRONG ENOUGH TO DO THINGS ON MY OWN.

(4) has difficulty initiating projects or doing things on his or her own

has difficulty independently initiating projects or doing things on his or her own (due to a lack of self-confidence in judgment or abilities and not primarily to a lack of motivation or energy)

<u>Sees self as unable to start anything on his or her own. Waits for others to start things because of the belief that they can do things better.</u>

I NEVER START ANYTHING ON MY OWN BECAUSE OTHERS CAN DO THINGS SO MUCH BETTER.

(5) volunteers to do things that are unpleasant or demeaning in order to get other people to like him or her

goes to excessive lengths to obtain nurturance and support from others, to the point of volunteering to do things that are unpleasant

Considers his or her strongest point to be that he or she is "nice," meaning that he or she is willing to go along with what others want, even if their plans and ways are unreasonable. Believes that others like submission. Makes extraordinarily self-negating offers for personal service in an effort to become or remain connected to a powerful other.

TO GET IMPORTANT OTHERS TO LIKE ME AND TAKE CARE OF THINGS, I AGREE TO DO LITTLE FAVORS THAT SOME PEOPLE MIGHT CONSIDER TOO DEMEANING OR BENEATH THEM.

(6) feels uncomfortable or helpless when alone, or goes to great lengths to avoid being alone

feels uncomfortable or helpless when alone, because of exaggerated fears of inability to care for himself or herself

Feels so dependent on others for guidance and help with function that the idea of being alone is frightening. Just to avoid being alone, will "tag along" with important others, even if not interested in or involved in what is happening.

TO AVOID BEING ALONE, I WILL "TAG ALONG" FOR LONG PERIODS OF TIME WITH SOMEBODY I DEPEND ON, EVEN IF I AM NOT AT ALL INTERESTED IN WHAT THEY ARE DOING.

(7) feels devastated or helpless when close relationships end

indiscriminately seeks another relationship to provide nurturance and support when a close relationship ends

Sees self as unable to function without the help of an important other person, and so the loss of the connection to him or her results in total inability to function.

I BELIEVE I COULD NOT MANAGE EVEN THE SMALLEST DAILY TASKS IF I WERE TO LOSE THE PERSON CLOSEST TO ME.

(8) is frequently preoccupied with fears of being abandoned

is frequently preoccupied with fears of being left to take care of himself or herself

Sees self as so totally dependent on receiving advice and help from an important other person that there is frequent worrying about being abandoned by that person.

I WORRY A LOT OF THE TIME ABOUT LOSING THE PERSON I DEPEND UPON FOR EVERYTHING.

(9) is easily hurt by criticism or disapproval [omitted from DSM-IV]

Feels unable to do things on his or her own, and takes criticism and disapproval as evidence of total worthlessness. Needs to have the approval of others, and becomes noticeably self-critical about personal inadequacies if criticized.

I NEVER FEEL LIKE I CAN DO MUCH ANYWAY, SO IF SOMEONE IMPORTANT DOESN'T APPROVE OF ME, I COMPLETELY LOSE FAITH IN MYSELF.

NECESSARY AND EXCLUSIONARY CRITERIA

The present analysis permits definition of necessary and exclusionary conditions for each personality disorder. For DPD, the recommended *necessary* descriptor is submissiveness associated with a sense of instrumental inadequacy. Many of the personality disorders include positions of dependency (TRUST, SUBMIT, or SULK); the DPD is unique in the simplicity of his or her dependency.

Exclusionary conditions for DPD include complications of dependency. The list of complicating factors is long. To begin with, the DPD does not show the various behaviors characteristic of the cluster B disorders. The DPD does not show active, transitive anger about lack of attention or caregiving, as does the BPD. The DPD does not show the NPD's indignation about others' failure to deliver interpersonal goods and services. Nor does the DPD engage in the efforts to force approval and attention that are characteristic of the HPD; instead, the DPD "hangs out" and waits to be taken care of. Finally, the DPD certainly does not engage in openly hostile behaviors, as does the ASP.

The DPD uses the principle of complementarity to cope. His or her TRUST and SUBMIT are offered in order to receive the desired **PROTECT** and **CONTROL**. Unlike the DPD, the OCD likes to control. If the patient insists that others submit, the diagnosis of DPD is ruled out. An NEG can also relate in dependent ways; however, the NEG will criticize authorities, including providers in the health care system. By contrast, the DPD will criticize only himself or herself, not others. The distinction between DPD and AVD can be made on the basis of whether abuse will be tolerated. The DPD can be hurt by criticism, but will put up with nearly any kind of abuse just to be taken care of. The AVD, by stark contrast, disappears at the first hint of criticism. Finally, a DPD is not comfortable with long-term autonomy, as is an AVD, SOI, or SZT.

CASE ILLUSTRATIONS

Case 1

This 19-year-old man was admitted for the third time with severe depression and suicidal ideation. He had suffered from depression since he was 12 years old, when he overdosed for the first time. His first hospitalization lasted 3 months, and he received a variety of antidepressants plus a trial of electroconvulsive therapy (ECT). Nothing helped. In succeeding years, there were trials of lithium and monoamine oxidase inhibitors (MAOIs). There was no history of hallucinations or other psychotic features, though his thoughts centered on death.

The patient was presented as an example of a purely biological depression, with the comment that the family was "incredibly supportive." The staff said that family stress could not be related to this depression, because both the mother and father were kindly and concerned beyond measure. The patient agreed with the idea that his family was very caring. The following excerpts from his dynamic interview show his profoundly submissive view of himself. His idea of a treatment goal was to learn to be able to reach out more, to ask for more, and to accept more.

> T: What were the feelings you didn't deal with then, when you were 11 or 12?
> P: Well, they could range from everyday feelings of, you know, just having a bad day. I wouldn't say if I had a bad day or even if I had a good day. I wouldn't say.
> T: You wouldn't let people know what's going on.
> P: No, plus, you know, the changes that come about that time. I was entering junior high, you know, and that's a pretty big change for someone that age, and—you know, I never talked about that, never talked about my fears about that, just, you know, about that age there's a lot of other changes, entering puberty and getting used to the different environment in junior high.
> T: It sounds like you feel like you should have talked to somebody about what was going on as you matured sexually and socially, but that you didn't. Is that correct?
> P: Ya.
> T: Who should you have talked to?
> P: Um, well my parents would be the first choice . . .

> P: Well, no one knew where they were going, and they have modular scheduling in junior high and that's a big change from, you know, the regular schedule, so no one knew anything about that.
> T: What did you do?
> P: Just sort of fumbled around the first few days.
> T: What would have helped?
> P: Um, coming to people more, or . . .
> T: Who would you have come to help you with that, making your way through the halls to your classes? How could you have been helped with that?
> P: Well, something very simple. Just ask a teacher instead of walking around for 15 minutes wondering where room 102 is, you know, or asking another student.

With this DPD, there was an unusual opportunity to test an interpersonal interpretation of his depression. The family agreed to participate in a research study. The protocol required that the identified patient (P), mother (M), father (F), and a significant other person (SO) participate in a brief role play. They understood that the family patterns would be analyzed in an attempt to determine whether interactive habits have anything to do with psychiatric illness. The sessions were to be SASB-coded and related to a data bank[2] with a variety of other measures (see Benjamin, 1989). The experimental task for the family was to do a role play in response to receiving an invitation to the nursing school graduation of a cousin named Kim. The family was to assume that the identified patient did not want to attend. This family's pattern was remarkable for the kindly but relentless control mounted by both parents.

---

[2]A companion volume will eventually present the "high-tech" aspects of SASB, including validity studies, formal research coding methods, use of questionnaires and software, and interpretations of the resulting parameters.

M: See what we got in the mail today. An invitation for Kim's graduation.

P: So?

M: Well, Kim's graduating from nursing school, you know, and she's wanted to do this an awful long time. It's kind of a special occasion for Kim, and, um, the rest of us.

F: What are they doing?

M: Let's see. The invitation says, um, the graduation is at 2 on Sunday, the 15th of June, and then they're having a special party Sunday evening at their house. They are inviting relatives and some of Kim's friends. Since Kim is your cousin, I thought it might be nice if we could all go. What do you think of that?

P: Still, I don't think I want to go.

SO: Ah, you're going to see Jerry. Jerry will be there, won't he?

M: I would think so. Jerry is Kim's brother.

P: Who else is going to be there, do you know?

M: Well, I imagine Kim's grandma and grandpa—uh, Kim's boyfriend and Jerry's girlfriend and some of their closest friends.

F: You actually get along pretty good with Jerry, don't you?

P: Ya.

SO: Even though he has mono?

M: He should be recovered pretty much by then. It might, you know, it's going to be a long day, a lot of traveling, but I think it's very important to Kim. You know, she put in a lot of time and effort to get through nursing school. That means a lot to have her cousins around.

F: Sweet little Kimmy.

M: Do you have other plans that weekend, or anything else you want to do?

P: Not really.

SO: You don't have to work that weekend?

P: No. I don't think so, at least.

SO: What are you going to do? Just sit home?

P: Well, I can think of something better to do than that.

SO: Like what?

P: Just about anything.

The role play continued in that vein. Kindly, relentless pressure to conform prevailed. The parents were empathic about how going to the graduation was going to be difficult ("it's going to be a long day, a lot of traveling, but . . ."). The patient resisted the pressure to conform. This family, in contrast to others in which the identified patient had a different disorder (e.g., Bipolar Disorder, Schizoaffective Disorder, or BPD), never acknowledged that he had a different view. They did not argue or attack him for his "deviance" or oppositionalism. The family never departed from the pattern of nurturance and control.

The information provided by the interview and by the family role play suggest that this young man satisfied DSM criteria 1 and 2 for DPD: He was unable to make everyday or important decisions without help from his parents. For example, he would ask them what courses to take in college. He was also easily discouraged by any negative comments (item 9) and did not initiate projects (item 4). He was preoccupied with whether he received enough "attention" (item 8). However, he was not bothered by the idea of being alone (item 6 failed). He spent long hours by himself watching TV, refusing opportunities for peer contact. This social withdrawal was so marked that at one time he had been labeled SOI. However, the puzzle of how he could both be so dependent and so autonomous was solved by the discovery that his parents were disturbed by his withdrawal. They responded to it with increased efforts to "pay attention." He felt that normally he did not get the attention he needed. "I was odd man out," he observed. His diagnosis of depression inspired the desired increased support and attention from his parents.

He also conformed to the interpersonal description of DPD summarized in Table 9.1. His baseline position is captured by the SASB labels TRUST, SUBMIT, and SULK. This generic submissiveness appeared to stem from his belief that others held the keys to solutions to his problems. He apparently did not think that he himself was competent to solve them on his own. In the family role play, his wish to be alone was challenged relentlessly and lovingly by the family. In the interview, he clearly conveyed that he wanted the family's PROTECTion and advice (CONTROL). He disliked being IGNOREd.

However, in the family role play, he also showed some oppositionalism to that control. Playing the role of himself, he showed that he wanted to withdraw (WALL OFF). This was paralleled in his history by his predilection for withdrawing to his room to watch TV. Even though it is not marked in Table 9.1, such a conflict between withdrawal and submission is often seen in depressed persons (e.g., Pilkonis, 1988). Patients like this man, who seem dependent and yet withdrawn, present an interpersonal diagnostic dilemma: How can they need others so much and yet be comfortable being alone?

There are two possible interpersonal explanations. One, which may apply in this case, is that the withdrawal means increased rather than decreased caregiving. Another explanation for the withdrawal shown by depressed persons is that the isolation can be mounted passively and still serve as an antidote to overwhelming control (according to the SASB principle of antithesis, defined in Chapter 3). In sum, submissive and dependent individuals seek complementary control, but they also can reach a point where they try passively to escape from it.

This young man's interpersonal history is consistent with the patterns sketched in hypotheses 1 to 3 in Table 9.1. His dependent behaviors complemented the nurturant parental control so dramatically noted by the staff members in their initial presentation. He had received excellent nurturance and expected competent caregiving. He exhibited little ability to cope on his own. The interview showed that he assumed that asking his parents for help was *the* way to contend. As a child, he rarely engaged in peer play, preferring instead to watch TV at home; as a result, he did not develop the requisite social skills needed for negotiating the high school environment. At the college level, he was totally overwhelmed, unable to cope with the demands. His "withdrawal" served, paradoxically, to elicit considerable parental attention, so he did not truly meet the exclusionary condition of comfort with autonomy. Nor did he show any of the other exclusionary conditions: His demands for nurturance were indirect or intransitive. He was respectful of his parents and other authorities, and showed no signs of attempting to control them. He did not demand compliance from his significant other persons, the staff, or anyone else.

Case 2

This mother of five children had a history of repeated hospitalizations for major depression with suicidal thoughts. She had a headache for nearly a year, and was "tired of trying." She had recently been withdrawn from Xanax, and the deprivation was a stressful experience. She was unable to function, and left all the decision making to her dominant husband. He was critical, demanding, and unsympathetic. She did not contemplate challenging or leaving him because she had no idea how she could cope without him. Recently her husband had taken ill, and demanded that she take care of his daily needs. She was unable to do so.

Her history was marked by chronic and severe sexual abuse, including a gang rape by brothers and neighbors that was interrupted by her mother. The mother's response was to be furious *at her daughter*. The mother's "treatment" was to give the patient a bath in scalding water. Later, a brother began regularly abusing her sexually, and she was afraid to tell. The brother killed a pet kitten to show what would happen to her if she were to disclose the sexual activity. Her father also abused her sexually.

Just prior to her hospitalization, the patient became extremely upset when she discovered that her husband's brother was sexually abusing the children in his care. The patient's husband forbade her to report the brother-in-law. She ached for the abused children, and despaired about her husband's demand that she do nothing. The patient felt utterly trapped, helpless, and without recourse.

This case illustrates an alternative route to DPD, marked as hypothesis 4 in Table 9.1. Her abusive brother, father, and husband all engaged in arbitrary control. Her only perceived option was to submit. Her brother killed the kitten to demonstrate what would happen to her if she were to tell about the sexual abuse. By this and other forms of intimidation, she learned that her lot was just to "take it." There were no confusing, complicating messages of love. The situation was simple: She was a convenient object and a slave. The men were her masters. To them she was nothing; without them she was nothing.

This woman fit DSM criteria 2–4 for DPD because she made no decisions on her own and did not initiate projects. She deferred and demeaned herself to avoid disapproval from or abandonment by her dominant partner (DSM criteria 3, 5, 6, 8).

The interpersonal criteria described in Table 9.1 were also met in full. Her responses were exclusively submissive: TRUST, SUBMIT, and SULK. She did not lash out or demand to be taken care of; she simply maintained a dependent, needy position. Her self-concept dictated that she was unable to do otherwise. She wished to be taken care of (PROTECT), and her fear was not to be taken care of (IGNORE).

EXPECTABLE TRANSFERENCE REACTIONS AND TREATMENT IMPLICATIONS

Transference Reactions

DPDs are friendly, compliant, and apparently cooperative. The more powerful and obviously competent a therapist is, the happier a DPD is. Medications are taken, homework is completed, forms are filled out, appointments are kept, bills are paid, and everything is in good order. Despite all this evidence of good faith, the patient's patterns persist, and he or she continues to count upon the therapist to make it better. Patient and therapist are highly vulnerable to developing a codependency enabling the status quo. The patient trusts, admires, and cooperates with the therapist, and the therapist nurtures and cares for and about the patient. But nothing changes. The dependent pattern shown by the patient in case 1 is maintained between patient and therapist. This arrangement could go on indefinitely, except for the discomfort associated with the accompanying depression. Sooner or later, somebody runs out of money, patience, or both.

Treatment Implications: The Five Categories of Correct Response

Facilitating Collaboration

As noted above, the DPD has an attitude of friendly cooperativeness with the therapist, and *that is the problem*. Eliciting more and better help from the therapist is the DPD's agenda. There is no collaboration against "it," the maladaptive patterns of dependency. The quintessential therapeutic need of the DPD is to change his or her treatment plan. The DPD needs to decide to build strength rather than neediness. In effect, the DPD must somehow be encouraged to engage with the position opposite to his or her usual one: He or she must change from a baseline of SUBMIT to learn about how to be SEPARATE. The DPD is unlikely to be interested in this treatment plan.

Facilitating Pattern Recognition

The idea of being separate is seen as silly or impossible by the DPD. With their history of intense enmeshment, DPDs often have no idea what it means to be differentiated. Their view of the interpersonal world is restricted to the idea that a person either is in CONTROL or SUBMITs. The one who controls is likely to be aggressive and brutal. Although he or she needs the aggressor, the DPD does not want to identify with him or her. The DPD would rather SUBMIT and be "good."

The DPD can consider alternatives to submissiveness if he or she can learn that SEPARATE, rather than CONTROL, is the opposite of SUBMIT. The DPD needs to learn the difference between saying "I'd rather not" (SEPARATE) and saying "You have to do it my way" (CONTROL). Bossiness is the only alternative the DPD sees, and it is the unattractive position of a bully. "I'd rather not" seems impossible because of the implicit "rule" that an individual must be one up (CONTROL) or one down (SUBMIT). Saying "I'd rather not" means trying to control the other person. The idea of being SEPARATE is not a part of the picture for the DPD.

This vital distinction between assertiveness and control is central to assertiveness training (e.g., Alberti & Emmons, 1986). Assertiveness training can help the DPD learn to say "I'd rather not" without feeling as if he or she is trying to control the other person. The family role play described in Case 1 showed that the patient was in a situation where "I'd rather not" was totally ignored. Part of change comes from the patient, but changes in the family are important too.

Blocking Maladaptive Patterns

The patient in case 1 accepted the interviewer's suggestion that he might be helped to change if his parents would restrict their offers of help to times he was functioning well. The paradoxical suggestion was that the mother and father should take the DPD out to dinner only if he was *not* depressed. Up to that time, the parents would make such offers as a way of cheering him up. Although the patient said that he thought that the plan of changing the conditions for parental "attention giving" would work, he did not like it at all. The consultant's suggestion was implemented by the ward staff in a subsequent family conference. The family agreed and planned to try changing the contingencies in this way. A paradoxical plan to reward independent behaviors with satisfaction of dependency needs can break up the specific symptomatic presentation. But such short-term interventions do not constitute reconstruction, because they use rather than change the underlying wish to be taken care of. They must be followed up with interventions that help the patient change the strong wish to be dependent and to strengthen the wish to become competent.

Strengthening the Will to Give Up Maladaptive Patterns

The subtle and gradual nature of the appearance of the will to change in truly reconstructive psychotherapy of DPD cannot be summarized easily. Basically, the DPD needs to learn to recognize the patterns of dependency and to appreciate their costs and benefits in the light of the adult world. Then, of course, DPDs need to explore alternatives. The long-term therapy case summarized below illustrates how the five stages of therapy can unfold.

Facilitating New Learning

Again, learning new patterns is relatively easy for the patient, once the background work is complete. The hardest part of treating personality disorders is helping the patient collaborate against "it," the long-standing way of being. Once the patient truly sees how and why he or she interacts in this way, and faces the present-day meaning of those patterns, he or she may decide to change. If so, the implementation of new patterns is easy. Standard behavioral techniques can be very helpful. The DPD can enjoy learning how to identify and express affect, and how to communicate effectively.

A Case That Illustrates the Five Stages

This patient was in his mid-30s, still in school, and still receiving a substantial monthly allowance from his wealthy parents. He had intimate relationships with several women who liked him very much. Unfortunately for his hopes to marry, most were gay or quite a bit older than he. During the first year of therapy, it became clear that his father had favored his brothers for the role of continuing the family business. His mother, on the other hand, was extremely fond of him. When he was a child, she would take him shopping with her and then out to lunch. They would speak at length and about important and intimate matters. The patient was very fond of "hanging out" with his mother. As an adult, he made enjoyable and frequent visits home.

At least five of the DSM descriptors for DPD were applicable. The patient could not decide on a career or a mate, and was inclined to appeal to his mother and father for guidance in these matters (DSM items 1, 2). He did not express disagreement with other family members' opinions on politics and economics, though he sometimes held divergent views (item 3). He showed little initiative and refused to accept a minimum-wage job in response to his father's pressure. Instead, he volunteered to run errrands for the office of a local politician (item 5). He was devastated when an important love relationship with an older wealthy woman ended. In the years after that relationship ended, he continually tried to recapture it or to find someone equivalent (item 7).

The patient did not meet all the DPD diagnostic criteria. He did not think of himself as instrumentally inadequate. His failure to perform the specific assignment of making money had the appearance of "I won't" rather than "I can't." The patient felt entitled to a position in the family business, although he never complained overtly to his father about his disenfranchisement. Although he felt that he deserved a place in the business, he showed neither the dominant arrogance nor the autonomy of NPD. Despite his oppositional refusal to earn money, he did not have the revengeful fury and punitive masochism characteristic of NEG.

This man's developmental history was consistent with the interpersonal history for DPD described in hypotheses 1–3 in Table 9.1. There had been excellent nurturance throughout infancy and childhood. The family pattern of inordinate parental support had not been given up even in adulthood. The patient did not embrace the autonomy and competence of the male role, much to his father's distress. The patient did not internalize his father's poor opinion of him, but instead assumed that he could do his part in the family business if only his father would let him. However, he felt and acted like an incompetent follower whenever he was around his father and brothers. His expectation of and need for caregiving were the central concerns during the first year of therapy. His fear was that his father would continue to exclude him from the business, and the patient had no idea of what might then become of him.

This case illustrates that the DPD's wish to be taken care of does not need to be ferreted out by means of free association, dream analysis, and so on. Rather, the yearning for eternal nurturance is consciously embraced and steadfastly sought. The totally ego-syntonic nature of the DPD's wishes to be nurtured means that mobilizing the will to give it up is especially difficult.

Therapy was pleasant and supportive at first, and the patient saw the main problem as his father's unwillingness to let him have a major role in the family business. Difficulties with his brothers and episodic depressions all related to this theme. The collaboration against "it," the DPD pattern, had to wait until the patient had a better idea of what he was doing. He needed to reflect on what the pattern was costing him in terms of lost dignity and lost discretionary choice. The therapist was supportive and mostly reflected his perceptions and his underlying wish to be taken care of.

Slowly the patient began to learn to recognize how he interacted with others, and to compare and contrast that with his perception of patterns and values within his family of origin. He began to notice that his everyday style was very much like that of his mother. Her day was defined by the content of her calendar. Similarly, his day was defined by a never-ending series of classes and planned meetings with friends. Mother and son shared the fact that their identity was in the details of their daily schedules. Also, they were both dependent financially on his father. When not preoccupied with the family business, the son dreamed of an endowment that would free him from financial worry and leave him free to pursue the details of his daily routine. The therapist came to speak of his therapeutic plan as "the trust fund solution." The patient good-naturedly contemplated this formulation and acknowledged its accuracy, but still hesitated to change. A trust fund seemed like a fine idea to him.

As he languished in school and in his relationships, his parents threatened to reduce his monthly allowance. His dissatisfaction with his lifestyle increased. The deadlock between his parents' frustration with his dependency and his frustration with their withholding became clearer and firmer. The therapist introduced the concept of the *Klute* syndrome (described in Chapter 6). In response to the question of whether he might be eroticizing his dependent position, the patient disclosed that his sexual fantasies did involve himself in submissive positions. The thought of "fooling around" with the sexual fantasies was very threatening. He added spontaneously, "*It's easier to be submissive in school* [than in the work world that lay just ahead]."

Shortly thereafter, he received a communication from his father to the effect that he absolutely was not going to be "set up" in the family business. In the next session, the patient reported he was angry that the *Klute* discussion in therapy confronted him with something he did not like. But he added, "I know it is good." He reported a dream that he thought was a good metaphor for what was happening: "Somebody broke my bed apart. They changed it. It wasn't wrecked, just changed. I know the dream was about therapy. It was frightening. I woke up with my heart pounding."

He then reflected on his pattern of anger, which he noticed was always reactive. He entered a period of comparing himself to his father, and declared he wanted to become more active or "transitive." He began to pursue his educational goals more actively, and finally graduated from college. He tried the same new attitude in his relations with women. He said, "I realize I can do something about this. I don't have to sit around and 'take it,' just be passive." Instead of waiting for women to call, he began to take the initiative. Instead of keeping his schedule free for one favorite woman who had other boyfriends, he began actively to create his own new relationships.

Ordinary therapy dialogue continued about everyday patterns in and out of the family. From time to time, there was discussion of the *Klute* syndrome and sexual reprogramming. He had agreed to try to give up his passive fantasies and to substitute more active ones. About 9 months after the topic first came up, there was a critical session during which he was complaining that he simply was not changing enough in his life. The therapist asked about his progress with the *Klute* program. The patient protested that as he thought of more active fantasies during sex, everything was ruined. He described how much he enjoyed seeing himself in a passive, dependent, even abused position. He wondered whether he should exchange roles and imagine becoming an abuser. Although this was against his politics and morality, he thought it might work.

The therapist suggested that he apply the Shaurette principle (see Chapter 3) to his program of changing sexual fantasies. He was to begin with the switch to sadistic fantasies. Then he was to shift, changing the hostile transitive imagery in stepwise fashion toward more friendly initiations. He was to switch roles and go from the present SUBMIT and SULK to ATTACK and BLAME. Then he was to begin the transition to the desired goal, moving his sexual imagery gradually to CONTROL, to PROTECT, and finally to ACTIVE LOVE. The patient agreed to do this, and at the next therapy session announced he was having an identity crisis. He said he was losing his sense of who he was, of who and how he was going to "be" in the world.

That was the last conversation about the *Klute* syndrome. The patient continued therapy for only a few months longer. He rapidly became more assertive with his family and others. On his last visit home before termination of therapy, he stayed with friends rather than his parents. Shortly thereafter, he accepted a job that interested him greatly. Therapy terminated peacefully.

10

Obsessive Compulsive Personality Disorder

"Be ye therefore perfect, even as your Father which is in heaven is perfect."

Thus conscience does make cowards of us all;
And thus the native hue of resolution
Is sicklied o'er with the pale cast of thought;
And enterprises of great pith and moment,
With this regard their currents turn awry,
And lose the name of action.
> (*Hamlet*, Act III, Scene I)

REVIEW OF THE LITERATURE

After learning that his uncle has killed his father and wed his mother, Hamlet degrades himself for ruminating rather than taking proper retributive action. Devoted to the highest principles, and ever so harsh on himself, he is paralyzed by his inability to decide on the perfect plan. Hamlet probably does not fully qualify for the DSM label of OCD; however, he does suffer from perfectionism, harsh moral judgment of himself and others, and self-doubt.

Pollack (1987) has provided a comprehensive review of current views of OCD:

> Obsessive–compulsive individuals are inclined to procrastinate and appear indecisive. They fear mistakes and are often worried and plagued with self-doubt. They appear driven, in a hurry, harassed by unending obligations and responsibilities. They cannot leave well enough alone and make repeated abortive attempts to attain order and perfection. They stick to routines, are easily thrown by the unpredictable and unfamiliar, and are inclined to avoid and resist novelty and change. . . . Preoccupied with order, efficiency, and strict adherence to rules and regulations, they are also perceived as perfectionistic and legalistic. They are also experienced by others as stubborn, willful, stingy, withholding and unimaginative. . . . Interpersonally, obsessive–compulsive individuals are formal, to the point of appearing cold and standoffish. They are authoritarian and controlling,

perceiving relationship largely in terms of patterns of dominance and submission. While deferential and ingratiating to superiors, they may furtively rebel in passive–aggressive ways. With subordinates they may be autocratic, critical and punitive. (pp. 249–250)

The DSM defines an Obsessive Compulsive Disorder on Axis I, as well as OCD on Axis II.[1] The distinction follows the psychoanalytic tradition of distinguishing a "neurotic" or "symptomatic" form of a disorder from the "personality" or "character" form of the disorder. The description of the Axis I version lists very specific thoughts and compulsive behaviors as symptoms of a clinical syndrome. For example, there are: "ritualistic behaviors (e.g., handwashing, ordering, checking) or mental acts (e.g., praying, counting, repeating words silently) that the person feels driven to perform in response to an obsession, or according to rules that must be applied rigidly" (American Psychiatric Association, 1991a, p. H-14). The description of the Axis II version, by contrast, itemizes more general and pervasive obsessive and compulsive interactive behavior patterns. For example, there is "perfectionism that interferes with task completion, e.g., inability to complete a project because own overly strict standards are not met" (see criterion 2, below).

Freud wrote about the obsessive ideas and compulsive impulses reflected in the Axis I version of the disorder quite early (Freud, 1907/1959). Later, he provided descriptions corresponding to Axis II OCD (Freud, 1913/1959). An "anal character," as Freud and later psychoanalysts called the OCD, is a person who is orderly. He or she is tidy, punctual, meticulous, proper, frugal, obstinent, stubborn, and morally superior. The OCD will alternate between obedience and omnipotence (Fenichel, 1945, pp. 278–284). According to Fenichel, anal characters are likely to use the defenses of undoing, reaction formation, intellectualization, and isolation. They suffer from conspicuous guilt and self-criticism. In considering the relation between the compulsive character disorder and the neurosis, Fenichel commented:

> Not much is known, however, about what determines whether a compulsive character is developed simultaneously with compulsive symptoms as a part of a compulsion neurosis or whether this character structure wards off (and replaces) definite compulsive and obsessive symptoms. Both types occur. It is possible that the compulsive character without symptoms represents an arrested evolution rather than a regression. (p. 531)

The obsessive thoughts in Axis I Obsessive Compulsive Disorder can be so inappropriate that they qualify as psychotic. In fact, a relatively recent survey of inpatients concluded that "persistent obsessive–compulsive symptoms thus appear to be a powerful predictor of poor prognosis in schizophrenia" (Fenton & McGlashan, 1986, p. 437).

The Axis I and II versions of the disorder have been linked in the litera-

---

[1]For the sake of clarity and of consistency throughout the book, I use the abbreviation "OCD" to refer to Axis II Obsessive Compulsive Personality Disorder (or a person with this diagnosis) only.

ture. In practice, Axis I Obsessive Compulsive Disorder does not necessarily coexist with Axis II OCD. A recent study of 96 patients with Axis I Obsessive Compulsive Disorder (Baer et al., 1990) found that over half of the sample had a personality disorder. However, 94% received an Axis II label other than OCD: "Mixed personality disorder (personality not otherwise specified in DSM-III-R) was most frequently diagnosed (15%), followed in frequency by dependent (12%), histrionic (9%), compulsive (6%), and, with equal frequencies, schizotypal, paranoid, and avoidant personality disorders (5% each)" (1990, p. 827).

Among Axis I comorbid conditions of special interest are the eating disorders that appear nested within OCD patterns (Rothenberg, 1986). Young women with Anorexia Nervosa seek the perfect body. They assume so much self-control that they lose control of their bodies and their minds. It is easy to see the patterns of OCD in these women. They include perfectionism, excessive orderliness, devotion to mastery of detail, and stubbornness and rigidity. Interpersonally, they either comply or dominate. It is not unusual for these OCDs also to suffer from coexisting Axis I conditions of anxiety and depression.

Psychoanalytic theory holds that the central conflict behind obsessive compulsive disorders (neurotic or characterological) was introduced during toilet training. For example, the trait of obstinacy is conceived as "holding one's position," and that is equivalent to anal retentiveness. This attitude can be set early in life if the parent insists on inappropriate control of the child's bowels. Pollack (1987) reported substantial evidence in support of the clustering of OCD traits. But he added that there is little support for analytic theories about links between OCD and anal eroticism or sadism: "Consistent with the earlier reviews, there continues to be little firm empirical support for any pathogenic explanations" (1987, p. 259).

In sum, as with other personality disorders, neurotic (Axis I) and characterological (Axis II) versions of this disorder have been discussed for some time in the literature. There is a tendency for OCD to coexist with selected other Axis I and Axis II disorders. Questions about definition and etiology persist unanswered.

DSM DEFINITION OF THE DISORDER

The DSM definition provides the starting point for the analysis. The DSM specifies that the diagnosis of OCD can be made if an individual meets five of the criteria. DSM-III-R items appear in **bold print**, and any changes introduced by the DSM-IV appear in *italics*. (As in Chapters 5–7, the item numbering used here is that of the DSM-IV. Original numbers in the DSM-III-R appear after **bold** items, in brackets.)

A pervasive pattern of perfectionism and inflexibility, beginning by early adulthood and present in a variety of contexts, as indicated by at least *five* of the following:

A pervasive pattern of preoccupation with perfectionism, mental and interpersonal control, and orderliness at the expense of flexibility, openness, and efficiency, beginning by early adulthood and present in a variety of contexts, as indicated by at least five of the following:

(1) preoccupation with details, rules, lists, order, organization, or schedules to the extent that the major point of the activity is lost [item 2 in DSM-III-R]

(2) perfectionism that interferes with task completion, e.g., inability to complete a project because own overly strict standards are not met [item 1 in DSM-III-R]

(3) excessive devotion to work and productivity to the exclusion of leisure activities and friendships (not accounted for by obvious economic necessity) [item 4 in DSM-III-R]

(4) overconscientiousness, scrupulousness, and inflexibility about matters of morality, ethics, or values (not accounted for by cultural or religious identification) [item 6 in DSM-III-R]

(5) restricted expression of affection [item 7 in DSM-III-R]

limited expression of warm emotions

(6) inability to discard worn-out or worthless objects even when they have no sentimental value [item 9 in DSM-III-R]

(7) unreasonable insistence that others submit to exactly his or her way of doing things, or unreasonable reluctance to allow others to do things because of the conviction that they will not do them correctly [item 3 in DSM-III-R]

reluctant to delegate tasks or to work with others unless they submit to exactly his or her way of doing things

(8) lack of generosity in giving time, money, or gifts when no personal gain is likely to result [item 8 in DSM-III-R]

adopts a miserly spending style toward both self and others; money is viewed as something to be hoarded for future catastrophes

(9) *rigidity and stubbornness [new item]*

indecisiveness: decision making is either avoided, postponed, or protracted, e.g., the person cannot get assignments done on time because of ruminating about priorities (Do not include if indecisiveness is due to excessive need for advice or reassurance from others.) [item 5 in DSM-III-R; omitted from DSM-IV]

Morey (1988) reported that 7.9% of a sample of 291 outpatients being treated for personality disorder qualified for the OCD label. There was substantial overlap with AVD (56.5%) and NPD (30.4%).

PATHOGENIC HYPOTHESES

The method of using the SASB model to develop pathogenic hypotheses was sketched in Chapter 5. Three main features of the developmental history have been identified specifically to account for each of the OCD symptoms listed in the DSM. A summary of the hypotheses linking interpersonal history to interpersonal patterns characteristic of the disorder appears in Table 10.1. A fuller discussion of these hypotheses is provided here.

1. There was relentless coercion to perform correctly and follow the rules, regardless of the personal cost. There was relatively little warmth, and there was great emphasis on perfection and orderliness. For the OCD in training, parental demands for perfection neglected the realities of the child's developmental level. For example, one OCD in psychotherapy noticed that his mother "played" with his son, her grandchild, in an outrageously demanding and perfectionistic manner. The infant, who was only 9 months old, was managing to place colored plastic rings of different sizes on a graduated post. Grandma presided, removing the rings and rearranging them so that the sizes were graduated exactly in sequence. A more normative response would have been to express delight with the baby just for getting the rings on the post. The OCD remembered bitterly, as he watched his mother with his son, that he himself had been criticized for "not playing right."

Table 10.1. Interpersonal Summary of OCD

History	Consequences of history
1. Relentless coercion to perform, be correct, and follow the rules, regardless of the personal costs (**CONTROL** plus **IGNORE**)	1. Inconsiderate domination of others (**CONTROL** plus **IGNORE**) Perfectionism that precludes a balanced self-concept (*SELF-CONTROL* plus *SELF-NEGLECT*) Deference to authority and moral causes that is fundamentally unsociable (<u>SUBMIT</u> plus <u>WALL</u> <u>OFF</u>)
2. Judged as "horrible child"; punished for being imperfect and not rewarded for success; observed sibling punished for imperfection; responsibility without power (**BLAME**)	2. Punishes, degrades self and others for failure to be perfect (*SELF-BLAME,* **BLAME**); focuses on mistakes
3. Rules taught without personal involvement (<u>WALL</u> <u>OFF</u> and **CONTROL** plus **IGNORE**)	3. Obedient, but personally inaccessible (<u>SUBMIT</u> plus <u>WALL</u> <u>OFF</u>) Warm feelings are restrained (*SELF-CONTROL* plus **IGNORE**)

Summary: There is a fear of making a mistake or being accused of being imperfect. The quest for order yields a baseline interpersonal position of blaming and inconsiderate control of others. The OCD's control alternates with blind obedience to authority or principle. There is excessive self-discipline, as well as restraint of feelings, harsh self-criticism, and neglect of the self.

SASB codes of OCD baseline: Insensitive control (**CONTROL** plus **IGNORE**), autistic obedience and isolation (<u>SUBMIT</u> plus <u>WALL</u> <u>OFF</u>), self-negating self-control (*SELF-CONTROL* plus *SELF-NEGLECT*). Critical of self (*SELF-BLAME*) and others (**BLAME**). *Wishes:* *SELF-CONTROL* and <u>SUBMIT</u>. *Fears:* **BLAME** and loss of *SELF-CONTROL* (*SELF-EMANCIPATE*). *Necessary descriptors:* Unreasonable control; devotion to perfection. *Exclusionary descriptors:* Irresponsible behaviors; emotional excesses; contempt for authority.

The example of "not playing right" illustrates that toilet training is not the only possible target for inordinate control. In a normal household, standards of performance are not imposed until sensory–motor coordination and the central nervous system mature to the point at which demands to socialize can reasonably be met. In the second and third year of life, lessons in the proper forms of eating, evacuating, dressing, speaking, and so on begin. As parental demands escalate, the toddler experiments with complying with or defying these demands, or copying parental behaviors. Sometimes performing perfectly, sometimes showing defiance, sometimes "identifying with the aggressor," the toddler often tries the patience of the parents. A young child can become so dedicated to "proper" use of table utensils that he or she will scold his mother if the orange juice is not exactly 3 degrees northeast of the spoon every morning. The toddler's preoccupation with such irrelevant detail is both exasperating and inefficient from the point of view of the parent. In this stage, the normal toddler can manifest many of the attributes of an adult OCD. The child's experience of adult rules is probably that they are as arbitrary and nonsensical as are the rituals and fears of the OCD. Psychoanalysts have concluded (A. Freud, 1965) that such normal social patterns can become fixated or resurrected if things go awry during the developmental sequence.

The adult consequence of introjection (see Chapter 3) of the relentless parental coercion to be correct (CONTROL plus IGNORE) is an unbalanced devotion to perfection in the self and in others. The OCD dwells on his or her flaws, and strives endlessly to comply with high standards and to make himself or herself do better (SELF-CONTROL plus SELF-NEGLECT). To do this, he or she will defer inordinately to authority or principle (SUBMIT plus WALL OFF). He or she identifies with the parent and insists that others do the same (CONTROL plus IGNORE). If the family disapproved of anger, the OCD will control his or her anger. On the other hand, if the OCD identifies with an angry, morally justified parent, then the OCD too can become righteously indignant.

Harsh moralism will encourage compliance with cruel practices mounted in the name of proper training. One example is the acceptance of child abuse as a legitimate form of "discipline." Another is the following of leaders who engage in abusive control in the name of some higher cause. Groups (e.g., neo-Nazis) that engage in harsh condemnation and persecution of others provide a congenial setting for OCDs whose attachment to and empathy for others are particularly frail. On the other hand, the more benevolent, less rigid, better-adapted forms of OCD include skills especially relevant to certain professions. Examples include the practice of law, where there is a quest to identify right (legal) and wrong (illegal); the military, where obedience to and implementation of authority are crucial; and computer programming, where failure to be correct to the last detail often means total failure.

Identification with the behaviors and ideals of a cold and controlling parent is the prototypic pathway to OCD behaviors. It is not the only way to develop the OCD patterns. Another clinical finding in mothers who are OCDs is that they were neglected as children, and resolved to make up for that lack of structure in their own families. As they adopt OCD patterns, these mothers become determined to force their children to have a better-monitored and more directed childhood than they did. Unfortunately, their lack of experience with balanced parenting means that their use of power is unmoderated and out of touch with the children's developmental needs. Instead of internalizing the authoritarianism of parents, these neglected OCD mothers have usually introjected and identified with an institution that has the same interpersonal style— one that demands submission and dedication to perfection.

The parents (and institutions) that engender the OCD pattern often have highly moral goals in mind as they try to instill self-control and perfection. For example, a central part of Christian doctrine is that "God became man in order that we become God." Because God dwells within, Christians are reminded constantly to strive to reach perfection. Jesus said, "Be ye therefore perfect, even as your Father which is in heaven is perfect" (Matthew 5:48). It is not unusual to find that compliance with such high ideals is the consciously motivating force behind the OCD's demands for perfection in everyday living.

2. The OCD-to-be was punished for failure to be perfect and was given no rewards for success. The best he or she could do was to avoid criticism or punishment. If the child did the dishes, for example, there would be no comment unless an unclean spot was found somewhere. If he or she cleaned his room very well, that would not be acknowledged because it was expected. Instead of praising a basically good job, the parental white gloves would find a tiny bit of dust in an inaccessible place. There was intense focus on mistakes; there was never even temporary acknowledgment of success.

Sometimes the parents assumed that the OCD was basically a "horrible child." They believed that perfect performance could compensate for the "given" deficiencies of character. One OCD who had absorbed the lesson that children are fundamentally greedy and intolerably bothersome explained, "I was appreciated for my accomplishments, but not for my 'is-ness.'" In these households, moral culpability is assumed, and the parent sees his or her job as an exercise in beating the badness out of the child. Cruel punishments are self-righteously administered. The child is attacked to inspire compliance with high standards to compensate for basic flaws. To avoid annihilation, the child learns to make sure that everything is in order and up to snuff. This necessarily means constant control of self and others.

Still another scenario leading to the quest for perfect control is to observe less favored siblings being beaten severely for failure to perform perfectly. The OCD-to-be seeks to avoid the same fate by making no mistakes. A variation on this theme is for the future OCD to assume responsibility to keep everything and everyone in the family perfectly in order. The motivation is that a rageful alcoholic or otherwise nonfunctional parent will not be "set off."

A child who tried to impose perfection on the household to avert disaster assumed enormous responsibility with little power. The child might have tried, for example, to keep the father from killing the mother because the laundry or the dishes were dirty. The future OCD would scurry about to try to put everything in perfect order so that the father would not become angry. Perhaps some rituals and magical thoughts found in Axis I Obsessive Compulsive Disorder represent attempts to gain control when the stakes are high but the means of coping are slight. To the extent that the child was effective in controlling the home situation, such symptoms were reinforced. The success might also enhance the likelihood of the characterological version (Axis II OCD) of questing for control to implement perfection.

Focus on mistakes and self-criticism are the adult consequences of having no rewards for success and many punishments for imperfection. Uncertainty, indecision, and inability to go ahead are the consequences of needing to be perfect while expecting that there will be a flaw no matter what. Checking and rechecking, planning and replanning, the OCD is always preparing and worrying. Since success was never acknowledged, the OCD has no sense of reaching the "bottom line." There is "no rest for the wicked," no satisfaction in a job well done. The OCD finds no pleasure in his or her "is-ness."

3. In the context of strong control, there was little warmth in the household. Hugging, holding, and laughter were scarce. Affection was not modeled and may have been seen as dangerous. After all, feelings cannot always be controlled. Because of the association of rationality with control, the OCD is likely to value it highly and to "try not to feel."

The adult consequence of the lack of warmth combined with the demands for perfection is social correctness appearing in a context of personal inaccessibility. This early learning also encourages inappropriate holding back of feelings. The good news is that control was not confused with affection in the family of the OCD. There were no false displays of love. There was no enmeshment with the child, such as that appearing in the history of people with some other disorders. For the nonpsychotic OCD, it was clear that the child was separate from the parent and there was no confusion about identity. If the OCD child failed to be perfect, he or she was the one who messed up.[2] The child's failure was his or her own and did not mean that the parent was a failure.

CONNECTIONS BETWEEN THE INTERPERSONAL HISTORY AND THE SYMPTOMS LISTED IN THE DSM

The "total OCD" shows all the symptoms mentioned in the DSM. The history of coercion to be perfect, regardless of the personal consequences, leads to perfectionism that interferes with task completion (item 2) and excessive devotion to work to the exclusion of leisure (item 3). The need to control in service of

---

[2]It is difficult to describe the more lethal alternative pattern. A succinct sketch is offered in poetic form by R. D. Laing (1970): "It is bad to feel mother is cruel to me, and hence bad./ Mother is cruel to me/ but she is only being cruel to be kind/ because I thought she was cruel when/ she was cruel/ in punishing me/ because I was cruel to her/ to think she was cruel to me/ for punishing me/ for thinking she was cruel/ for punishing me/for thinking . . ." (p. 12).

perfection also leads to the OCD's insistence that others submit to his or her ways of doing things (item 7). The quest for perfection is further reflected in the judgmentalism that leads to overconscientiousness and inflexible scrupulousness item (item 4). Yet another version of the pattern of seeking complete control is the irrational need to save things in case they might be needed again (item 6). The devotion to control, the lack of warmth, and the encouraging of self-restraint in the parental home are associated with restricted expression of warmth (item 5) and miserliness (item 8).

The fact that there were harsh punishments for mistakes and no rewards for success means that the OCD is worried about making errors and has little sense of success. This fear of making mistakes and never finishing properly leads to preoccupation with details at the expense of completion of the activity (item 1). Sometimes it leads to indecisiveness stemming from rumination about priorities (old item 5 in the DSM-III-R, omitted from DSM-IV).

INTERPERSONAL SUMMARY OF OCD

The foregoing analysis suggests a succinct interpersonal summary for OCD:

> *There is a fear of making a mistake or being accused of being imperfect. The quest for order yields a baseline interpersonal position of blaming and inconsiderate control of others. The OCD's control alternates with blind obedience to authority or principle. There is excessive self-discipline, as well as restraint of feelings, harsh self-criticism, and neglect of the self.*

The summary is based on the SASB codes of the OCD baseline patterns and wishes. The codes themselves, listed in Table 10.1, provide a shorthand way to identify OCD. The baseline OCD positions are inconsiderate domination (CONTROL plus IGNORE), unfeeling adherence to authority and moral causes (SUBMIT plus WALL OFF), and imbalanced devotion to perfection (*SELF-CONTRTOL* plus *SELF-NEGLECT*). The OCD is also capable of showing indignation (BLAME) as well as self-criticism (*SELF-BLAME*). He or she fears to be the target of BLAME and to lose *SELF-CONTROL*, which is equivalent to *SELF-EMANCIPATE* (see Chapter 3). The OCD is a tragic figure. Working very hard to implement his or her wishes to be perfect, the OCD alienates those whom he or she seeks to please. The quest for perfection is lonely.

The rhythm and harmonics of the OCD song are found in the sequences of interpersonal and intrapsychic response that the OCD gives and receives. The "tonic" OCD position consists of insensitive control of others (CONTROL plus IGNORE), autistic obedience (SUBMIT plus WALL OFF), and self-negating self-control (*SELF-CONTROL* plus *SELF-NEGLECT*). This orientation necessarily means that the OCD will engage in excessive control of self and others, and will be obsequious in relation to authority. A tendency to flip from deference to arrogance is illustrated by OCD applicants to a psychiatric residency. They may be deferential and "nice" to members of the admissions committee, and subsequently prove to be overbearing and obnoxious in relation to patients and other "subordinates."

The OCD's position harmonizes well with someone who will SUBMIT easily. There is also good music when the OCD is asked to comply with plans laid down by someone with impressive authority or status. However, there will be noticeable discord with those who try to control, but who lack the requisite status. The OCD is quite ready to BLAME those who do not do their job correctly. The OCD is especially likely to do this with people who are oppositional (e.g., NEG) or disorganized (e.g., BPD). These are the harmonics and rhythms of the OCD song.

Readers who can use the SASB codes will be able to generalize the present analysis to contexts not mentioned here. For example, it is not unusual for patients to complain that their depression is getting worse. Sometimes these complaints are presented to the therapist in a way that is characteristic of OCD. To interpret a complaint about depression in this way, the therapist would need to code the patient's process as he or she describes the depression. An OCD's process with the therapist as he or she complains about symptoms would include the notes of the OCD song. Consider this example:

> A patient was very slow to recognize that he was depressed. He thought he could stay "on top of" the problem if only he could get things better organized. But the signs of depression persisted, and suddenly one day the patient admitted he was depressed. Then he was willing to take the prescription, but looked it up in the PDR to be aware of possible side effects. The depression continued. The patient sent the doctor reprints on recent studies of antidepressants and questioned the prescription. The patient expressed frustration that the right medication had not been found. He alternated between deferring to the doctor's opinion about what to do next and blaming the doctor for not doing better.

In Table 10.2, the baseline notes of the OCD song are compared to those of the songs for the disorders discussed previously. A scan of the table shows that the OCD shares CONTROL and BLAME with all disorders in the dramatic erratic cluster (BPD, NPD, HPD, and ASP). The OCD shares with the NPD, BPD, and ASP a tendency to misread or overlook his or her own social needs. Like the NPD and ASP, the OCD can also be insensitive to the needs of others. Despite these points of overlap, the OCD's great SELF-CONTROL contrasts starkly with the recklessness found in people diagnosed within cluster B.

The OCD pattern resembles the HPD's tendency to combine control with deference. With HPD, the more conspicuous feature is the agreeable dependency, whereas the control is covert. With OCD, the control is visible while the dependency is covert. It is not unusual for an OCD (male) and an HPD (female) to marry, probably because the overt messages are complementary. The OCD is ostensibly "in charge," and the HPD is instrumentally needy and dependent. Covertly, however, the HPD "runs the (emotional) show," and the OCD depends on her to meet his emotional needs.

The OCD shares with the DPD an ability to defer to others. However, unlike the DPD, who rarely initiates anything, the OCD loves to control.

The interpersonal *do, re, mi* of Table 10.2 shows how the six categories reviewed so far overlap and how they differ. The descriptions in the table can help the clinician make the differential diagnoses.

DSM DESCRIPTORS REVISITED

The DSM view of OCD has now been translated into interpersonal language, and the psychosocial learning associated with OCD patterns has been outlined. In this section, the interpersonal analysis of OCD is compared directly to the DSM. DSM-III-R items appear in **bold print**; any changes introduced by the DSM-IV appear in *italics*. Again, the item numbering used is that of the DSM-

Table 10.2. Comparison of SASB Codes of BPD, NPD, HPD, ASP, DPD, and OCD

	BPD	NPD	HPD	ASP	DPD	OCD
1. EMANCIPATE						
2. AFFIRM						
3. ACTIVE LOVE	×			×*		
4. PROTECT						
5. CONTROL	×	×	×*	×*		×*
6. BLAME	×	×	×	×		×
7. ATTACK	×	×		×*		
8. IGNORE		×		×		×*
1. SEPARATE		×		×		
2. DISCLOSE						
3. REACTIVE LOVE			×*			
4. TRUST	×		×*		×	
5. SUBMIT					×	×*
6. SULK					×	
7. RECOIL						
8. WALL OFF			×*	×*		×*
1. SELF-EMANCIPATE						
2. SELF-AFFIRM						
3. ACTIVE SELF-LOVE		×*				
4. SELF-PROTECT	×			×*		
5. SELF-CONTROL						×*
6. SELF-BLAME		×			×	×
7. SELF-ATTACK	×		×*			
8. SELF-NEGLECT	×	×*		×*		×*

*Indicates that these codes within the same column appear in complex combinations with one another.

IV.) The interpersonal modifiers are <u>underlined</u>. Items from the WISPI (discussed in Chapter 1) appear in CAPITAL LETTERS.

A pervasive pattern of perfectionism and inflexibility, beginning by early adulthood and present in a variety of contexts, as indicated by at least *five* of the following:

A pervasive pattern of preoccupation with perfectionism, mental and interpersonal control, and orderliness at the expense of flexibility, openness, and efficiency, beginning by early adulthood and present in a variety of contexts, as indicated by at least five of the following:

(1) preoccupation with details, rules, lists, order, organization, or schedules to the extent that the major point of the activity is lost

<u>Because of the need to avoid punishment for mistakes, there is excessive carefulness (shown in repetition, extraordinary attention to detail, or repeated checking). He or she is oblivious to the fact that others are greatly annoyed by the delays and inconveniences associated with this crippling perfectionism.</u>

I MAKE SURE THAT I ALWAYS FOLLOW THE RULES EXACTLY AND THAT I AM COMPLETELY PROPER.

(2) perfectionism that interferes with task completion, e.g., inability to complete a project because own overly strict standards are not met

<u>Self-talk is critical and demanding, so that he or she has to redo things again and again. This perfectionism means that the job often does not get finished, or if it is finished, it is discarded.</u>

I OFTEN GET SO INVOLVED IN MAKING EACH DETAIL OF A PROJECT SO ABSOLUTELY PERFECT THAT I NEVER FINISH.

(3) excessive devotion to work and productivity to the exclusion of leisure activities and friendships (not accounted for by obvious economic necessity)

<u>Even though there is no pressing need for more money, he or she works 12 or more hours a day, including weekends. He or she hardly ever feels there is time to take an evening or a weekend day off to go have a picnic, or just sit around. Never "wastes time." Always carries some work along to fill in little gaps in time. If he or she spends time with friends, it is likely to be only in some kind of formally organized activity (including sports). The emphasis is on perfect performance. Is very uncomfortable on vacation unless he or she has taken along something to work on.</u>

I AM A "WORKAHOLIC" WHO HAS LITTLE INTEREST IN FUN OR PLEASURE.

(4) overconscientiousness, scrupulousness, and inflexibility about matters of morality, ethics, or values (not accounted for by cultural or religious identification)

<u>Forces himself or herself and others to follow very strict and harsh standards, and is mercilessly self-critical if he or she makes a mistake. Rigidly deferential to authority and rules. Compliance with authority, rule, or principle is quite literal. No rule bending or consideration of extenuating circumstances is likely. Rigidly follows his or her moral principles. For example, he or she won't lend a dollar to a needy friend because he or she believes: "Neither a borrower or a lender be."</u>

FOLLOWING MORAL RULE IS MORE IMPORTANT THAN ANYTHING ELSE.

(5) restricted expression of affection

limited expression of warm emotions

Always turns play into a structured task—corrects an infant for not putting rings on the post in the right order; tells a toddler to ride his or her trike in a straight line; turns a baseball game into a harsh "lesson." Is stiff and formal when others would smile and be happy (e.g., greeting a lover at the airport).

I VERY CAREFULLY HOLD MYSELF BACK UNTIL I CAN BE SURE THAT WHATEVER I SAY WILL BE PERFECT.

(6) inability to discard worn-out or worthless objects even when they have no sentimental value

Likes to sort and save things, arrange them in perfect order. Loses perspective and will do this with truly worthless objects. Becomes upset if someone tries to get rid of old worthless things he or she has saved "just in case" they might be needed some day.

I CAN'T THROW AWAY OLD, PROBABLY WORTHLESS JUNK BECAUSE THERE IS THE POSSIBILITY I MIGHT NEED IT.

(7) unreasonable insistence that others submit to exactly his or her way of doing things, or unreasonable reluctance to allow others to do things because of the conviction that they will not do them correctly

reluctant to delegate tasks or to work with others unless they submit to exactly his or her way of doing things

Insists that others do things exactly as he or she wants, down to the smallest detail. For examples, there is one and only one way to mow the lawn, to wash the dishes, to wrap the garbage, to build a doghouse, and so on. Even though he or she is obviously overburdened with a job, (e.g., preparing a family meal, doing the work of three people on an assembly line), others are not allowed to help because of the belief that they won't do things correctly.

TO MAKE SURE THINGS TURN OUT RIGHT, I USUALLY INSIST THAT PEOPLE DO THINGS MY WAY.

(8) lack of generosity in giving time, money, or gifts when no personal gain is likely to result

adopts a miserly spending style toward both self and others; money is viewed as something to be hoarded for future catastrophes

Any offers of gifts (or time or money) have "strings attached." The recipient must have conformed (or is expected to conform) to the giver's ethics, rules, principles. Is not likely to give time, money, or gifts to others because of the belief that people are supposed to come up to standards, work hard, and provide for themselves. Thinks that making things too easy is "bad for character."

I DISAPPROVE OF GIFT GIVING BECAUSE IT ENCOURAGES BAD CHARACTER.

(9) *rigidity and stubbornness*

Is so concerned with having things done the one "correct" way that he or she is never able to go along with someone else's idea. Plans ahead so carefully that he or she is unwilling ever to consider changing things. Is so wrapped up in his or her own perspective that he or she is unable to acknowledge that there might be another way.

I KNOW HOW THINGS SHOULD BE DONE, AND INSIST ON MY WAY NO MATTER WHAT OTHER PEOPLE MIGHT SAY.

indecisiveness: decision making is either avoided, postponed, or protracted, e.g., the person cannot get assignments doneon time because of ruminating about priorities (Do not include if indecisiveness is due to excessive need for advice or reassurance from others.) [omitted from DSM-IV]

Never gets started on a big project (e.g., writing a term paper, building a pet cage, or repairing something in the home) because he or she can't decide on what is the perfect version. Because he or she can't decide which tasks are the most important, he or she never gets started on any of them.

OFTEN I CAN'T GET STARTED ON THINGS I SHOULD DO BECAUSE I CAN'T DECIDE ON THE RIGHT WAY.

NECESSARY AND EXCLUSIONARY CRITERIA

The present analysis permits definition of necessary and exclusionary conditions for each personality disorder. For OCD, the recommended *necessary* descriptors are unreasonable dominance and a devotion to perfection. *Exclusionary* descriptors include the irresponsible behaviors reliably found in ASPs and BPDs; the emotional excesses of HPDs and BPDs; and contempt for and defiance of authority.

CASE DESCRIPTIONS

Case 1

This married man in his mid-30s came to the hospital because of a pattern of increasing inability to function in his work as an auto mechanic or at home, and signs of depression including suicidal ideation. A large variety of medications had been tried, but none had helped significantly.

For as long as he could remember, the patient's consciousness had been dominated by his father's demanding perfectionism and intensely critical verbal assaults. When the patient was a child, his father would both affirm faith in his son's ability and criticize him for failure to implement it by perfect performance. The patient would try very hard to meet the demands, but always failed in some respect. There was no praise, and there was criticism if performance fell short. The best the patient could do was to avoid criticism. His father's words were devastating. The patient preferred spanking to his father's disapproval. Expression of feeling was not permitted. There was little affection, and the father would feel personally put down if his son cried.

The patient identified with his father and showed the same inconsiderate domination of his own children, especially his oldest son. When the patient arrived home, he regularly started yelling as soon as he got out of the car. He would criticize the children for failure to complete their chores and then would mete out punishments. His wife disapproved of the patient's militaristic attitudes and "put her foot down." She protected the children by telling them that they didn't have to do what their father said. She told the patient to "ease up," and she would do the children's chores when she felt sorry for them.

There was no joy in family life, the patient explained. His plan for family happiness was framed in perfectionistic and highly structured terms, which conformed to the dictates of the strict church to which he belonged. His vision of a "perfect family" placed the father in loving control over the children.

The patient's harsh judgment of himself was manifested in suicidal rumination. He felt that his family would be happier without him. As a child he had often thought that if his father died, they all would be better off. His fury at his father was intense, but never expressed directly. Just recently, he had found a way to express this aggression passively. The patient was working hard on a repair project at his father's business. The father was "supervising," meaning that he was offering criticism freely. After a while, the patient threatened to walk off and leave the store in disarray with the project undone if the father did not cease and desist. This assertion was successful. At the time, the patient was frightened by realizing that he wanted literally to murder his father.

This patient met the requisite number of DSM diagnostic criteria for OCD. His perfectionism interfered with task completion at work, where he performed well but slowly because of fear of mistakes; he had to go back and check things several times to be sure they were exact. At home, his idea of a perfect family caused friction between his wife and himself (DSM item 2). He was preoccupied with lists and schedules, especially those that the children should implement (DSM item 1). At home, he unreasonably insisted that others submit exactly to his way of doing things (DSM item 7). He was devoted to perfection at the expense of leisure activities and friendship (DSM item 3). It was not easy for him to show affection (DSM item 5).

The SASB interpersonal codes (Table 10.1) also describe this man. He was insensitive in his attempts to control others (CONTROL plus IGNORE). His current adaptation included abject submission to his wife (SUBMIT plus WALL OFF). He used unreasonable amounts of energy to trying to make himself be "perfect" (SELF-CONTROL plus SELF-NEGLECT). He strongly wished to be a perfect father (SELF-CONTROL) presiding over a perfect family (who would SUBMIT). His feared losing control of himself (SELF-EMANCIPATE) and murdering his father.

The pathogenic hypotheses of Table 10.1 were likewise confirmed: (1) His father was critical and demanded perfect performance regardless of context. (2) the best the patient could do was to avoid criticism; he had a sense that he was a "bad person." (3) There was no praise and no affection from this vitally important parent. The consequences of these learning experiences were also apparent: (1) The patient repeated his father's controlling and critical parenting practices with his own children; he was very deferential to the ideals and behavioral prescriptions of his authoritarian church. (2) He degraded both himself and his children for failure to be perfect. (3) He was emotionally constrained and distant. The patient met the necessary conditions for OCD of devotion to perfection and an inordinate need to control. He did not meet any of the exclusionary criteria (irresponsibility, emotional excess, or contempt for authority).

It is interesting that this man's deference to his wife was so marked that he was presented by the medical student and resident who admitted him as a DPD. At the time of admission, the patient deferred to his wife for advice and direction on nearly every matter. During the consultative interview, it became clear that he had been recently perplexed by his wife's increasing demands that he learn to cook and participate actively in housekeeping. His view of the division of labor in the household was shaped by the conventions of his church and his family of origin. He believed that the husband should be dominant and the wife's responsibility should be to tend to housekeeping. However, his wife openly criticized that model as it had been played out in his family of origin. Because he did not want to be like his father, the patient agreed to discard this traditional version of husband and wife. However, he could only imagine either being in control or deferring. This meant that if he was not to be in control as his father was, then he must be submissive as his mother was. His "dependency" represented the defeat of his hopes and the destruction of his image of the perfect family. He was depressed.

Case 2

This 59-year-old divorced mother of five came to the hospital because her therapist insisted that she do so. Ruminating suicidally, she had recently overdosed on antidepressants. However, she promptly undid the overdose with ipecac and water because she feared she did not have enough pills to make her die. She worried that she had not implemented the suicide correctly and therefore might end up as "a vegetable." She did not want treatment; she did not want to be in the hospital; she just wanted to die.

She presented with an array of vegetative signs, including weight loss, difficulty sleeping, suicidal ideation, anhedonia, irritability, and a variety of somatic difficulties. Her symptoms included headaches, urinary problems, and more. She had a history of abusing Valium. Her first depression had been successfully treated with ECT 15 years before the present episode. A second course of ECT 5 years prior had not helped. She said that her husband was the major problem then. Following the second hospitalization and series of ECT treatments, the patient said she had become very "fuzzy" mentally. She had only regained her "old" self recently, and still didn't remember as well as she did before the ECT.

A self-described perfectionist, the patient said she "made a mess of her children's lives." She dominated their days, making them clean the house repeatedly. They had to polish the furniture and scrub the bathrooms several times daily. She forbade them to touch the furniture lest they get it dirty, and so on. There was little hugging or other expressions of warmth. All energy was devoted to making everything absolutely perfect. When asked whom that was for, the patient thought it was an interesting question. After a pause, she suggested that the devotion to cleanliness was for her husband and for the church. Then she explained that she got over her compulsive neatness after the second ECT series. Unfortunately, the "improvement" yielded complaints from her husband that she was too sloppy. He wanted her to find "a middle ground" on the housecleaning question. The patient felt she had to be at one extreme or the other.

The perfectionism started in relation to her father, who also was a perfectionist. He made many demands of the patient. With little time for peer play, she had to take care of the house. She did feel resentment, as, for example, when she had to clean her brother's room. She wondered why he couldn't do it himself. Her father was very critical and backed up his demands with corporal punishments. He would "shake the daylights out of you" and "use the willow." The patient managed to avoid many beatings by trying to be perfect. She learned what would be in store if she did not perform well by seeing what happened to her brother, who was frequently beaten severely. Her father never acknowledged her work, and the patient accepted the interviewer's summary that the best she could do was to avoid punishment. There was no joy, no acknowledgment of what she tried to do. Perfection served to avoid beatings, and that was how one survived.

Like her father, her husband was demanding and verbally abusive. The patient felt that her husband controlled and exploited her. He degraded her in front of others. Her children frequently urged her to leave him, but she dutifully stayed in the marriage. Nonetheless, shortly before the onset of the current depressive episode, her husband told her he was moving in with a girlfriend. The divorce precipitated severe financial difficulty, leaving the patient with many bills and minimal resources. On the recommendation of a church leader, she had signed over the insurance benefits for her previous hospitalization to her husband. He spent the reimbursement on himself, and those bills were now her responsibility. When she was not feeling suicidal, this woman was sure she would murder her husband if she had access to him and a weapon at the same time.

The diagnostic impression was of recurrent Major Depression, and OCD. The patient showed perfectionism that made it impossible for her or her children ever to get the house clean (DSM item 2), preoccupation with organization (DSM item 1), unreasonable insistence that others submit to her way of doing things (DSM item 7), excessive devotion to housework to the exclusion of leisure activities and friendship (DSM item 3), overconscientiousness and inflexibility (DSM item 4), and restricted expression of affection (DSM item 5).

The case can also be described by the SASB interpersonal codes. The patient showed inconsiderate domination of others (CONTROL plus IGNORE) and complete deference to the perceived authority of her husband and the church (SUBMIT plus WALL OFF). She devoted herself to reaching ideals of perfection (SELF-CONTROL plus SELF-NEGLECT) and wanted others to do so as well (SUBMIT). She punished herself (SELF-BLAME) and others (BLAME) for the failure to reach them. She feared she would lose control of herself and murder her ex-husband (SELF-EMANCIPATE).

The patient's interpersonal history also conformed to the predictions in Table 10.1: (1) Her father provided relentless coercion to be correct and conform, regardless of the personal costs. (2) There were punishments for failure to be perfect, but no rewards for success. (3) There was no personal warmth within the family. The predicted consequences were also apparent: (1) She was imbalanced in her quest of perfection in herself and others; when she turned the payments for a previous hospitalization over to her husband, she complied with the authority of the church, despite his poor record in money management. (2) She degraded herself severely, including even her ability to commit suicide. (3) She was not personally accessible, warm, or spontaneous.

EXPECTABLE TRANSFERENCE REACTIONS AND TREATMENT IMPLICATIONS

Transference Reactions

The OCD in psychotherapy will want to defer to the therapist and be a "perfect patient." The OCD will be terrified if he or she thinks the therapist wants him or her to "loosen up," to express feelings, to lose self-control. There will be a conflict between the wish to defer to the therapist's wisdom and the fear of loss of self-control. It will be very hard for the OCD to freely explore the self, and to learn to identify and express affect.

One way in which the OCD may deal with this conflict may be to work harder at his or her job, so that there will be no time for therapy. A different approach may be to make detailed logs of every event that might conceivably be related to the therapy treatment plan. When it turns out that the notes and lists don't help, the OCD may become very critical of himself or herself or of the therapy. Some OCDs may try to control the therapy by insisting that the therapist provide a rationale, and data, and so on to account for every intervention. Still another transference possibility is that an OCD will bring in a set of therapy principles to which he or she subscribes, and will want the therapist to implement that selected approach, regardless of the therapist's own preferences. The choices are likely to be of approaches (e.g., hypnosis) that give the therapist substantial amounts of control. If the therapist adopts a "blank-screen" approach or a purely "Rogerian" reflective stance, the OCD will be upset about the lack of structure. He or she will be uncomfortable with approaches that emphasize openness and spontaneity.

These and other likely transference problems share the interpersonal dimensionality of inordinate control of self and others, and of abject submission to principle. Since hostility is an important correlate of control, the OCD is always on the brink of rage. OCD anger stems from the need to force things to be perfect. Some OCDs solve this problem in their lives by becoming righteously indignant, viewing their anger as justified by their role of parent or employer. Other OCDs are very constrained with their anger because their value systems prescribe that anger is evidence of imperfection.

Treatment Implications: The Five Categories of Correct Response

The view of therapy as a learning experience permits definition of therapist errors on a moment-to-moment basis. Therapy interventions can be evaluated in terms of whether they enhance collaboration, facilitate learning about patterns and their roots, block maladaptive patterns, enhance the will to change, or effectively encourage new patterns. The effect of interventions is assessed in terms of the actual impact on the patient, not in terms of the therapist's intention. If the effect of an intervention on an OCD is righteous indignation or abject submission, then the intervention is an error. The learning therapist seeks to provide structure for the OCD that can help him or her move gradually toward more openness and warmth with the self and others.

Facilitating Collaboration

Collaboration is unlikely in the context of a power struggle. OCDs will be highly enmeshed, and uneven in their attitudes about control of the therapy. Sometimes an OCD will want to take control of the therapy; at other times, he or she will want the therapist to do it. True collaboration, free of power struggles, is unlikely to emerge spontaneously. However, the OCD values rationality, and therefore can respond well to the SASB-based mapping of interpersonal patterns and of their antecedents and consequences. OCDs easily recognize themselves in terms of CONTROL, SUBMIT, and *SELF-CONTROL*. They are amazed by the SASB model's descriptions of behaviors such as AFFIRM, DISCLOSE, and *SELF-AFFIRM*. These descriptions of separateness and friendliness are to the OCD as Neptune's moon Triton is to the solar system.[3] For the highly enmeshed OCD, positions of friendly differentiation are seen as something from another universe. Given a convincing description of themselves and a reasonable explanation for how and why they developed these patterns, however, OCDs will develop an interest in collaborating. They grasp at an intellectual level the idea of friendly differentiation as the opposite of hostile control. Once this shared goal of openness and warmth has been established, the OCD can begin work on experiencing feelings and changing his or her ways of relating. The work of learning to let go is not easy.

Facilitating Pattern Recognition

Convincing exploration of connections between early learning and present difficulties is in itself supportive. The OCD needs to develop compassion and

---

[3]The details of Neptune's exotic and unfamiliar moon were first seen in August 1989 by Voyager II. Because it is so different from other parts of the solar system, Triton is thought to have been captured from a passing star.

empathy for himself or herself as a child. Couples therapy offers an especially powerful format for working with OCD patterns. Because of complementary interactive patterns, an OCD is often married to a DPD (complementary submission), an HPD (coercive dependency that may be manifest in alcoholism), an NEG (complementary dependency combined with withdrawal and the familiar judgmentalism), or a PAR who is experimenting with trust (and showing fragile, intense dependency).

The patterns in the marriage are likely to unfold with special clarity in the sexual arena. For an OCD, power struggles will dominate the sexuality. The female OCD may be unwilling and unable to give up control, and may therefore be anorgasmic. The male OCD may experience his wife's failure to submit as control. He will invoke the logic of the enmeshed character: "If I am not in control, then you must be." The therapist may soften the dichotomy in perception by noting that the spouse's sexual inaccessibility may reflect different preferences. Even if the spouse did not feel sexual last night, he or she nonetheless still loves the patient. This reframing of the spouse's reluctance in terms of differentiation rather than domination may lessen the power struggle in the marriage.

It can help to make paradoxical use of the OCD's preference for rule following. The therapist can "order" the OCD to collaborate with his or her partner to develop "rules" for dealing with the usual controversial marital topics (e.g., sex, money, and time spent together). These negotiations can help the OCD coerce himself or herself into giving up control.

Blocking Maladaptive Patterns

Explicitly sexual treatment programs can be effective if they happen to disrupt the power struggles. It is common in sexual therapy protocols for the therapist to take temporary control over who will do what to whom and when. With such interventions, the therapist takes control and necessarily disrupts the power struggle within the marriage. The prescribed sexual exercises can model and encourage more balanced interactive patterns (e.g., AFFIRM and DISCLOSE) in sexuality and elsewhere.

Because of the habitual self-restraint, the OCD needs to learn to stop obstructing feelings. Learning to experience and integrate warm affect is an important therapy goal. One OCD had an important moment of insight about the basis of her own critical self-restraint when she saw her mother refuse to give a grandchild a second can of soda. The mother explained that the child's appetite was without limit and needed to be curtailed. The patient realized that the grandchild was being given a familiar lesson: "You are fundamentally greedy and bad. Restrain your natural inclinations."

Even though recognition and expression of affect are important goals, therapists should be thoughtful about encouraging generic expression of affect. For example, the patient in case 1 had been invited by a therapist some years before hospitalization to "get in touch with his anger" about his father and about his son. The patient fled from that therapy summarily. He explained why during his later hospitalization: If he let out his rage at his father, he was likely to kill him. The patient revealed that he had to leave therapy because he did not want to go to jail.

Nonetheless, the patient was responsive to the suggestion that there be a family conference to let his father know how much he wanted to have his father's approval. The father should also know how much the patient feared his criticism. The deeper-level wish to be loved by his father was the driver of the need to be perfect. The patient's devotion to control and perfection was, at its base, an attempt at attachment. During the hospitalization, his depression seemed to lift at the thought of "improving communication" with his father. If the need to reach perfection through control can be undercut, the anger of the OCD will disappear. When the OCD no longer needs to make others be perfect, there is no need to be angry at them.

The road to discovering the underlying wish for love in OCD can be convoluted. With the patient in case 1, for example, it was also true that along with the wish to be loved, there was a wish to punish the father. The patient wanted to say, in effect, "Look what you have done to me and my family. Now you must suffer as I and we have." This wish to punish, which the patient acknowledged during the consultation, is consistent with Freud's idea of Thanatos. This perspective suggests that anyone who wants someone else to suffer must be expressing fundamental destructiveness. The present approach resists the conclusion that we are driven by a basic underlying destructive energy. Instead, the belief is that rage has evolved in the primate merely to assist with the allocation of space and of goods and supplies. But goods and supplies are wanted to care for the self and loved ones. When a patient is furious with loved ones, a wish for love often lies beneath the wish to punish. After the target of the rage suffers and takes the punishment, the wish is that he or she will then provide the long-lost love.

It is hard to see that love can drive murderous vengefulness in OCD. But the unconscious is not troubled by reality. After all, the vengefully killed loved one might behave better in an afterlife. In addition, a murder might improve the lot of those left behind. The first patient's suicidality, for example, was inspired by the "loving" idea that his family would be better off without him. The patient recalled his own vengeful wishes that his father would die so that there could be peace and happiness in his family of origin. The patient felt that his suicide would give to his children the favor his father had denied him—namely, annihilation of the oppressor. Killing himself represented killing the version of his father that lived on in the patient's behavior with his own children. Killing himself was a love gift to his present family, as well as an expression of rage at his father. Once again, *every psychopathology is a gift of love* (see also Benjamin, 1993b).

Anxiety, also frequently seen in OCD, is usually the result of fear of the inevitable failure to reach perfection. Like anger and depression, anxiety does not need expression as an end in itself. Instead, the underlying mandates to control and achieve perfection should be the therapeutic targets. If one does not need to be perfect to survive, then one doesn't have to be frightened about not being perfect.

Strengthening the Will to Give Up Maladaptive Patterns

Patients' wishes to gain the approval of a relentlessly critical parent organize many disorders. Often patients yearn for a family conference that would result in rapprochement with the inaccessible parent. I have rarely seen this universal fantasy realized in a clinical setting. Sometimes there seems to be a new understanding, but then either the patient's own internalizations or key family members undermine things. Most often, the goals have to be changed. The dream of reconciliation with the offending and otherwise alienated parent needs to be given up. When the fantasy is released, then the personality can be reorganized and permanently changed.

It is good to remember that parents have their own stories and their own reasons for what they do. If the present pathogenic theories are used to "hold court" on "bad parents," they are misused. Instead, pathogenic connections are drawn in this book to help therapists help patients see the sense in their patterns of their disorders. This understanding should be used in service of developing an adult perspective that will demonstrate how the adaptations are outdated. The patient needs to understand that the symptoms had a function once but no longer work well. Both of the patients described above needed to learn that their quest for perfection was grounded in their attempts to cope with their respective fathers. Once they could see the origins, and compare the past situation with the present, they might be better able to choose to leave the old agendas in the past. Developing empathy for the self as a child, and for the parent at that distant time, is one method of acquiring the needed perspective.

Facilitating New Learning

There are brief interventions that can help address the essentials of the OCD pattern. Beck et al.'s (1979) cognitive therapy, for example, works specifically on the narrow focus and the rigidly dichotomous cognitive style of the OCD (Shapiro, 1965). The Beck et al. treatment for Major Depression, a common Axis I covariate for OCD, includes instruction on how to give up self-criticism that is global, absolutistic, moralistic, invariant, and irreversible. The alternative is a view of self and others that is "multidimensional," relativistic, nonjudgmental, and reversible. It can include consideration of situation, time, and specific behaviors (Beck et al., 1979, p. 15). If the OCD can come to view this new cognitive style as a better version of perfection, then such constructive changes are inherently aligned with the OCD's underlying values.

Structured marital or family "playtime" can introduce normal socialization skills. However, to be effective, such "play therapy" is best presented on the basis of its inherent attractiveness. Family playtime should not be experienced by the

OCD as surrender to the wishes of the therapist or the spouse. Family games involving playful or loving body contact can speed the rehabilitation of the OCD. Female OCDs who find themselves engaged in child rearing are more likely to experience some of the needed tender body contact. Young children like to hug. They also love to have fun with activities that do not necessarily accomplish anything. In the parenting role, the OCDs can inadvertently learn about being relaxed, warm, and not always task-oriented. Therapists can take advantage of this opportunity by noting and helping the OCDs embrace this part of their child-rearing role.

Brief interventions can sometimes address selected aspects of problem patterns. However, there are no known reliable shortcuts to complete reconstructive change. It takes a long time to learn and relearn patterns of interaction in a variety of contexts. One cannot reconstruct personality by reading a good book on personality disorders, by attending a weekend encounter group, or by having an interview with a charismatic therapist. To expect significant change following such brief encounters is unreal. One does not expect to be able to learn to ski well, to play the violin, or to master any other complex skill in a brief period. Nor is there any medication that transmits interpersonal and intrapsychic skills, any more than there is a drug that will instill knowledge about how to solve differential equations. If one lacks energy, a drug can enhance it. If one is distracted by a hallucinatory voice, a drug can quiet it. If one has performance anxiety, a drug can provide beneficial calming effects. But the basic program goals of good reality testing and skilled social interactions are achieved only with care and with practice. No such reprogramming occurs until there is a will to change.

With OCD, as with many other disorders, both *transference* (relationship) and *insight* (cognitive reframing of perceptions, responses, and internalizations) are important to the change process. Insight can increase the chances that an OCD will drop the wish to control and become comfortable with fallibility. These chances are also enchanced by a benevolent experience with the psychotherapist, a caregiver who can and will accurately perceive and respond to the OCD's needs.

11

Negativistic Personality Disorder (Passive Aggressive Personality Disorder)

"Therapy is not helping."

I've been coming here a long time for help with my depression and nothing's better. I noticed on the way in here that the parking lot's filled with doctors' Mercedes. I had over $5000 in medical costs last year, and I don't make no $300 an hour or drive no Mercedes. It's a big disappointment. I was really looking forward to retirement. (Patient in a VA hospital)

REVIEW OF THE LITERATURE

The chart gets bigger with each succeeding hospitalization, and the attempts to help always fail miserably. The patient has followed the doctors' recommendations for "all different kinds of pills," but "it just made things worse." Helpless and frustrated, the patient endures the pattern that could be named the "stupid doctor [administrator, boss, parent] syndrome." The hostility is indirect. The patient is, after all, coming for appointments and complying with recommendations. He or she is not actively attacking anyone specific. Nonetheless, the message is clear that the patient suffers mightily. His or her difficulties are the result of incompetent and uninformed handling of the case by people who are more interested in their own affairs than in doing their job.

These individuals are seemingly compliant and agreeable, but ultimately oppositional and judgmental. They complain they are treated unfairly, and back the complaint up with conspicuous suffering. This interpersonal summary is easily applied to many patients. The usual response of authorities, helpers, or parents to this pattern is marginally contained fury; it will be played out differently according to the personalities of the helpers. Those who need to be in control are quick to "come down hard," and the patients, employees, or adolescents are in fact abused. Two examples of disguised abuse are implementing questionable medical procedures to cure, and issuing impossible and punitive ultimatums to passive aggressive employees.

The description Passive Aggressive Personality Disorder has been the most controversial of the DSM Axis II categories. Reliability has been disastrous. The DSM-IV, dedicated to the empirical approach to mental disorders, has replaced

266

it altogether with a new category, Negativistic Personality Disorder (NEG). The minutes of the Axis II work group meeting (American Psychiatric Association, 1991b) that announced this change read:

> *Negativistic PD.* It was determined that while there was little empirical research for this disorder, there is reason for more study and that it represented a stronger personality type than Passive Aggressive PD. Since this encompasses some of the traits of Passive Aggressive PD, the official recommendation of the Work Group is that Negativistic PD should be placed in the Appendix (where PAPD would be noted parenthetically) and Passive Aggressive PD would be dropped from DSM-IV.

As this book goes to press, a decision from the DSM-IV task force that recently reviewed the recommendations of the DSM-IV Axis II work group is available. The DSM-III-R criteria for Passive Aggressive Personality Disorder (PAG) will be replaced by the criteria for the new Negativistic Personality Disorder (NEG). However, the new category is to have the old name, Passive Aggressive, and it is to appear in the Appendix of the DSM-IV. This book uses the new name (NEG) and the new criteria. Readers are reminded that DSM-IV probably will use the old name (PAG) and the new criteria. It is still possible that the old name and the old criteria will be in the final DSM-IV. In that event, readers may need to refer to the details about the old definition of PAG presented in footnotes 2 (p. 269) and 3 (p. 275). The analysis of the character, of his or her likely developmental history, and of the treatment implications are the same, whether the final DSM-IV version is in terms of NEG, as described in this chapter, or the old Passive Aggressive Personality Disorder (compared to NEG in footnote 2).

The new DSM diagnosis of NEG is consistent with descriptions that have previously served for Passive Aggressive Personality Disorder. That name was first used in 1945 by the War Department to describe soldiers who showed "immature," helpless, passive resistance to the demands of the military (Millon, 1981; McCann, 1988). Millon objected to the decision of the DSM-III task force to define Passive Aggressive Personality Disorder largely in terms of oppositionalism and negativism. He told his colleagues (Millon, 1981, p. 245) that the definition should also include ambivalence and irritability. Passive aggressive individuals are "dependently acquiescent and assertively independent." They are irritable, are easily frustrated, and feel misunderstood and unappreciated by others. The DSM-III-R task force apparently took Millon's observations into account, and items describing the irritability and resentment were added to that revision of the DSM. The new NEG of DSM-IV adds more of Millon's views. It now includes a sense of being misunderstood and unappreciated; a tendency to "rain on every parade"; envy and resentment of those who are more fortunate; and ambivalence about dependence versus independence.

The DSM-IV definition is greatly enriched in comparison with the DSM-III's oppositional definition. It encompasses many of the traits mentioned in a recent review of Passive Aggressive Personality Disorder (McCann, 1988). The list of terms characterizing these people is long: stubbornly resistant to the fulfillment of expectation; pouting; procrastinating; inefficient and erratic in work;

gloomy and despondent; cynical, skeptical, untrusting; feeling misunderstood and unappreciated; ambivalent and conflicted over wish to express irritation; negative while needing to be agreeable and accepted by others; guilty over being dependent, but angry because of frustration over not getting needs met; impulsive; and manipulative.

Elusive though its definition may have been for recent editions of the DSM, this disorder was not created by the U.S. Army.[1] Psychoanalysts had described the pattern under the heading of "oral sadism" (Fenichel, 1945, pp. 62–66). An interpersonal translation of the psychoanalytic concept of oral sadism might begin with the observation that infants chew and bite when teeth arrive. Biting appears to relieve the pain of teeth breaking through gum tissue. It also serves the adaptive function of allowing the baby to begin to eat solid foods. The fact that the breast also gets chewed is incidental at first. Most mothers give the appropriate feedback of withdrawal when their infants bite. But some infants do not learn to sheathe their teeth, and instead become transitive in their biting of the breast. A toddler's ambivalence between trusting and taking in, and attacking the provider, usually reaps harsh punishment. The result is so predictable that the pattern of "attacking the hand that feeds" is masochistic. It is also sadistic. In persons with this disorder, the subsequent suffering is amplified to condemn the allegedly cruel and negligent caregiver. The goal of provocation and the therapist's angry countertransference were described by Reich (1949):

> . . . his provocation was an attempt to make me strict and to drive me furious. But this was only the superficial meaning of the behavior. If the deeper meaning is so often overlooked it is because of the erroneous belief that the masochist seeks punishment in itself, for the gratification of a guilt feeling. In reality it is not a matter of punishment at all, but of placing the analyst or his prototype, the parent, in a bad light, of provoking him into a behavior which would rationally justify the reproach, "You see how badly you treat me." This provocation of the analyst is, without exception, one of the great difficulties in treating any masochistic character. Without uncovering this meaning, one will not get one step further. . . . Behind the provocation there is deep disappointment in love. The provocation is directed especially against those objects who caused a disappointment, that is, objects which were loved intensely and who either actually disappointed or who did not sufficiently gratify the child's love. (pp. 223–224)

DSM DEFINITION OF THE DISORDER

The DSM definition provides the starting point for the present analysis. The DSM specifies that the diagnosis of NEG can be made if an individual meets five of the criteria. Only the DSM-IV criteria are disscussed at length in this

---

[1]Ironically, the DSM-III was explicit that the label should not be applied in certain situations, such as the military, where the pattern of indirect resistance can be adaptive. The DSM-III-R watered down the caveat: "Passive aggressive maneuvers that are used in certain situations in which assertive behavior is discouraged, or actually punished, and that are not part of a pervasive pattern of personality functioning do not warrant this diagnosis" (American Psychiatric Association, 1987 p. 357).

chapter, because changes from the DSM-III-R definition of Passive Aggressive Personality Disorder are so extensive.[2]

A pervasive pattern of passive resistance to demands for adequate social and occupational performance and negativistic attitude, beginning by early adulthood and present in a variety of contexts, as indicated by at least five of the following:

(1) passively resists fulfilling routine social and occupational tasks (e.g., behaviorally procrastinates, is inefficient)

(2) complains of being victimized, misunderstood, and unappreciated by those with whom he or she lives and works

(3) sullen, irritable, and argumentative, especially in reaction to the wishes or expectations of others

(4) unreasonably criticizes and scorns authority

(5) communicates a pervasive mix of angry and pessimistic attitudes toward numerous and diverse events (e.g., cynically notes the potentially troublesome aspects of situations that are going well)

(6) expresses envy and resentment toward those apparently more fortunate

(7) claims to be luckless, ill-starred, and jinxed in life; personal discontent is more a matter of whining and grumbling than of feeling forlorn or despairing

(8) alternates between hostile assertions of personal autonomy and independence and acting contrite and dependent

Morey (1988) reported that 12.4% of a sample of 291 outpatients being treated for personality disorder qualified for the label of Passive Aggressive Personality Disorder. There was substantial overlap with NPD (50%), BPD (36.1%), HPD (33.3%), AVD (33.3%), PAR (30.6%), and DPD (30.6%). This extraordinary degree of overlap with six other disorders suggested that the DSM-III-R characterization of Passive Aggressive Personality Disorder included features widespread among the personality disorders. The hope is that the new definition of NEG will prove to be more specific.

PATHOGENIC HYPOTHESES

The method of using the SASB model to develop pathogenic hypotheses has been sketched in Chapter 5. Three main features of the developmental history have been identified specifically to account for each of the NEG symptoms listed in the DSM. A summary of the hypotheses linking interpersonal history to inter-

---

[2]Readers who are interested in comparing them will note that DSM-III-R items 1, 3, 5, and 8 are sampled by DSM-IV item 1. DSM-III-R items 4 and 6 are represented by DSM-IV item 2. DSM-III-R items 2 and 7 are represented by DSM-IV item 3. DSM-III-R item 9 is virtually identical to DSM-IV item 4. DSM-IV items 5, 6, 7, and 8 are new, but the interpersonal patterns that are implied by the new and the old items are similar.

personal patterns characteristic of the disorder appears in Table 11.1. A fuller discussion of these hypotheses is provided here.

1. The developmental cycle started well, with nurturant parenting that built trust in the constancy and the competence of the caregivers. The consequence of the excellent beginning is that the NEG expects nurturance. One has to have had ample benefits in order to feel angry about not getting enough. A truly deprived child will not spontaneously complain about it; he or she is more likely to say something like "My mother was nice—she gave me a cookie once." The NEG, however, has "been to Paris" and is angry about being "down on the farm," where the work is hard and there is little nurturance or fun.

2. The wonderful nurturance of early infancy was abruptly withdrawn and replaced with unfair demands for performance. The prototypic experience is that the NEG was a well-cared-for firstborn who abruptly lost nurturance when a younger sibling was born: "You are a big boy (girl) now; you can dress yourself. You must also help with fixing dinner and with keeping the house clean." These demands for performance replaced the erstwhile attentive comforting. The expectations were exacting, excessive, and oblivious to the legitimate needs of the NEG. For example, in addition to the usual household duties, the NEG may have had to work long hours in the family business. It often happened that the NEG was singled out for these special assignments; siblings, for one reason or another,

Table 11.1. Interpersonal Summary of NEG

History	Consequences of history
1. Nurturant infancy (**PROTECT**)	1. Expects, feels entitled to nurturance (**PROTECT**)
2. Abrupt loss of nurturance with unfair demands for performance (**CONTROL** plus **IGNORE**)	2. Power-sensitive; sees caregiver/authorities as inconsiderate, incompetent, and neglectful (**CONTROL** plus **IGNORE**) Feels deprived; complains of unfairness; resentful and envious (SULK plus **BLAME**)
3. Harsh punishments (**ATTACK** or **BLAME**) for anger, autonomy (SEPARATE), or failure to SUBMIT and perform the tasks	3. Punitive neediness (SULK plus **BLAME**) Self-harm is an indictment of authority/caregivers (*SELF-ATTACK* plus **BLAME**) Seemingly complies, but actually resists demands to perform (SUBMIT plus WALL OFF or SEPARATE)

Summary: There is a tendency to see any form of power as inconsiderate and neglectful, together with a belief that authorities or caregivers are incompetent, unfair, and cruel. The NEG agrees to comply with perceived demands or suggestions, but fails to perform. He or she often complains of unfair treatment, and envies and resents others who fare better. His or her suffering indicts the allegedly negligent caregivers or authorities. The NEG fears control in any form and wishes for nurturant restitution.

SASB codes of NEG baseline: Compliant avoidance (SUBMIT plus WALL OFF or SEPARATE). Oppressed and envious blame (**BLAME** plus SUBMIT or SULK). Masochism that indicts (*SELF-ATTACK* plus **BLAME**). *Wishes:* To receive nurturant restitution (**PROTECT**). *Fears:* To receive **CONTROL** that is always seen as insensitive and arbitrary (plus **IGNORE**). *Necessary descriptors:* Compliant defiance of demands to perform. *Exclusionary descriptors:* Uncomplicated deference; devotion to productivity.

were excused from the excessive duties. The assignments deprived the NEG of vitally needed peer play. The differential treatment gave him or her a sense of being treated unfairly. This made the NEG resentful and envious of those (siblings) who were more fortunate (SULK plus BLAME).

The adult consequence is power sensitivity. The NEG sees authorities or caregivers as cruel, unfairly demanding, neglectful, and unfair (CONTROL plus IGNORE). The abrupt loss of nurturance and the unfairness lead the NEG to feel deprived and to complain that he or she has been treated unfairly. NEGs typically complain that they have too little money while undeserving others have too much.

3. There were very harsh punishments for the expression of anger. Understandably frustrated by the withdrawal of support, and blocked from escape to the peer group, the NEG was angry. The adult consequence is the indirect expression of anger. The DSM-IV descriptions of NEG overemphasize the expression of hostility. My own impression is that hostility is often obscured because it appears in complex combinations with other interpersonal messages. For example, an NEG may be perplexed by the therapist's treatment idea, but go along with it anyway. The silliness and uselessness of the plan will soon become "apparent" through its lack of effectiveness. Similarly, suicidal acts may be escalated because of the perceived need to escape pain and suffering, but they will also be revengeful in some way. In other words, the self is attacked, but at the same time so is someone else. The anger is not direct, and it is masochistic.

There were also harsh punishments for any forms of autonomy that interfered with parental interests. The NEG may have been encouraged to perform well in school because that reflected well on the parents. However, if he or she chose an area of performance that enabled differentiation, it was attacked. For example, one NEG was well rewarded for long hours and excellent performance on the family ranch. He was mechanically gifted and received a scholarship to go to a distant city for study in design and engineering. When he came home from school one day, the models he had built *and stored under his bed* had been crushed. His father explained, "There isn't room for them here." The NEG correctly read the message that he was not to leave home. He was to perform, but only on behalf of his father's direct interests. Demoralized and angry, he passed up the scholarship. He remained home on the ranch, embattled with his cruel father.

The consequence of punishment for autonomy is that, like anger, it must be expressed indirectly. Compliant at first, the NEG eventually burned out and gave up trying to meet all the demands. Exhausted and resentful, he or she began to develop covert ways of defying. He or she would not directly resist the parental assignments, but would take an inordinately long time to complete them. Alternatively, the job would be executed with conspicuous flaws. Not surprisingly, NEGs as a group are very likely to fall behind if not to default entirely on paying their therapy bills. The defiant–compliant pattern seems to the NEGs like the only way to cope. Inevitably, their failure to perform as adults has masochistic consequences.

CONNECTIONS BETWEEN THE INTERPERSONAL HISTORY AND THE SYMPTOMS LISTED IN THE DSM

The "total NEG" shows all the symptoms mentioned in the DSM. The cruel and neglectful parental demands result in irritability and argumentativeness when the NEG is asked to perform (DSM item 3). The NEG learns that his or her efforts are not appreciated and that he or she is treated unfairly (DSM items 2 and 6). This breeds disappointment in (DSM item 5) and disrespect for (DSM item 4) caregivers and authorities. The harsh punishments for anger and disobedience lead to indirect expressions of both (DSM items 1, 7, 8).

INTERPERSONAL SUMMARY OF NEG

The foregoing analysis suggests a succinct interpersonal summary for NEG:

There is a tendency to see any form of power as inconsiderate and neglectful, together with a belief that authorities or caregivers are incompetent, unfair, and cruel. The NEG agrees to comply with perceived demands or suggestions, but fails to perform. He or she often complains of unfair treatment, and envies and resents others who fare better. His or her suffering indicts the allegedly negligent caregivers or authorities. The NEG fears control in any form and wishes for nurturant restitution.

The summary is based on the SASB codes of the NPD baseline patterns and wishes. The codes themselves, listed in Table 11.1, provide a shorthand way to identify NEG. The baseline NEG positions are compliance that culminates in avoidance (SUBMIT plus WALL OFF or SEPARATE), resentful compliance that culminates in blame (BLAME plus SULK), and masochism that indicts the oppressor (SELF-ATTACK plus BLAME). The fear is of insensitive and arbitrary control (CONTROL plus IGNORE), and the wish is for PROTECT.

The rhythm and harmonics of the NEG song are found in the sequences of interpersonal and intrapsychic response that the NEG gives and receives. The "tonic" NEG position is one of defiant compliance (SUBMIT plus WALL OFF). This pattern of agreeing while disagreeing comprises the "passive" form of passive aggression. A more hostile version, the one marked most clearly by the DSM-IV, is compliance that blames (SULK plus BLAME). The masochistic variation includes self-destruction that blames (SELF-BLAME plus BLAME). Submission provides the loudest note. The agreeability implied by submission is accompanied by the dissonant themes of defiance and blame.

Millon (1981) and the DSM-IV Axis II work group suggest that the contradictory positions of the NEG appear at different times. I think that the NEG more often holds the two positions at the same time. The NEG knows when he or she says yes that he or she means no. The NEG knows that as he or she is suffering, he or she is also feeling that it is the oppressor's fault and that restitution is due. The NEG pattern does not involve dissociation or repression, as in Multiple Personality Disorder, where different positions appear sequentially in time. Rather, the messages of the NEG are typically complex and are delivered simultaneously.

The position of the NEG is complementary to that of the person with OCD. According to the SASB model, this defiant compliance (SUBMIT plus WALL OFF) perfectly matches the OCD's insensitive control (**CONTROL** plus **IGNORE**). Unfortunately, the OCD's baseline position of insensitive control also implements the NEG's worst fear. Ultimately, the NEG blames the OCD through suffering (*SELF-ATTACK* plus **BLAME**). The NEG's and OCD's marital choice of each other assures ongoing hostile enmeshment. These are the harmonics and rhythms of the NEG song.

Readers who can use the SASB codes will be able to generalize the present analysis to contexts not mentioned here. For example, it is not unusual for patients to complain that their depression is getting worse. Sometimes these complaints are presented to the therapist in a way that is characteristic of NEG. To interpret a complaint about depression in this way, the therapist would need to code the patient's process as he or she describes the depression. A NEG's process with the therapist as he or she complains about symptoms would include the notes of the NEG song. Consider this example:

A patient's depression had lasted for years, with multiple hospitalizations. Every approach was tried. There were courses of ECT. Many different medications, including all antidepressants, MAOIs, lithium, and even a few neuroleptics, were prescribed. Although sometimes there appeared to be initial success, nothing helped for long. The patient endured the oppression of the illness (SULK), but complained about the doctors' inability to help (**BLAME**).

His latest doctor tried the patient on a new antidepressant that was receiving trials in a research protocol. The patient agreed to participate in the research, but did not take the drug in the prescribed manner. He explained that the drug made him feel worse, and so he decided to adjust the dose himself (SUBMIT plus WALL OFF). It seemed that he was doing a little better on this drug, however, so he asked to continue in the protocol and agreed to take the drug exactly as prescribed. Two weeks later, the doctor received a call from the patient's wife saying that he was acutely suicidal and needed hospitalization. The patient said that he deferred to the doctor's research interests and took the drug exactly as prescribed (SULK plus **BLAME**); now he felt worse than ever about himself (*SELF-ATTACK* plus **BLAME**). The doctor hospitalized the patient again and took him off the research protocol.

The baseline notes of the NEG song are compared to those of the BPD, NPD, HPD, ASP, DEP, and OCD songs in Table 11.2. A scan of the table shows that NEG shares the habit of **BLAME** with BPD, HPD, NPD, ASP, and OCD. Unlike that of any of the others, however, the NEG's **BLAME** is always nested in a complex code with something else, usually compliance. The NEG shares with other members of the anxious, fearful cluster (DPD, OCD) the tendency to SUBMIT. His or her submission is exclusively hostile and resentful (SULK), while that of a DPD can be "clean" and friendly (TRUST). The NEG shares with the

Table 11.2. Comparison of SASB Codes of BPD, NPD, HPD, ASP, DPD, OCD, and NEG

	BPD	NPD	HPD	ASP	DPD	OCD	NEG
1. EMANCIPATE							
2. AFFIRM							
3. ACTIVE LOVE	×			×*			
4. PROTECT							
5. CONTROL	×	×	×*	×*		×*	
6. BLAME	×	×	×	×		×	×*
7. ATTACK	×	×		×*			
8. IGNORE		×		×		×*	
1. SEPARATE		×		×			×*
2. DISCLOSE							
3. REACTIVE LOVE			×*				
4. TRUST	×		×*		×		
5. SUBMIT					×	×*	×*
6. SULK					×		×*
7. RECOIL							
8. WALL OFF			×*	×*		×*	×*
1. SELF-EMANCIPATE							
2. SELF-AFFIRM							
3. ACTIVE SELF-LOVE		×*					
4. SELF-PROTECT	×			×*			
5. SELF-CONTROL						×*	
6. SELF-BLAME		×			×	×	
7. SELF-ATTACK	×		×*				×*
8. SELF-NEGLECT	×	×*		×*		×*	

*Indicates that these codes within the same column appear in complex combinations with one another.

HPD, ASP, and OCD an underlying hostile detachment from others (WALL OFF). Like the BPD and HPD, the NEG has overt suicidal tendencies (*SELF-ATTACK*). NEG is most easily confused with OCD; both disorders center on the pattern of hostile enmeshment. However, unlike the OCD, the NEG does not overtly control others. The NEG will not show the overt and straightforward expression of intense anger (ATTACK) that is seen in the ASP, BPD, and NPD.

The interpersonal *do, re, mi* of Table 11.2 shows exactly how these categories overlap; it also shows how they differ. The descriptions in the table can help the clinician make the differential diagnoses.

DSM DESCRIPTORS REVISITED

The DSM view of NEG has now been translated into interpersonal language, and the psychosocial learning associated with NEG patterns has been outlined.

In this section, the interpersonal analysis of NEG is compared directly to the DSM. DSM-IV items[3] appear in *italics*. The interpersonal modifiers are <u>underlined</u>. Items from the WISPI (discussed in Chapter 1) appear in CAPITAL LETTERS.

A pervasive pattern of passive resistance to demands for adequate social and occupational performance and negativistic attitude, beginning by early adulthood and present in a variety of contexts, as indicated by at least five of the following:

(1) passively resists fulfilling routine social and occupational tasks (e.g., behaviorally procrastinates, is inefficient)

<u>Accepts assignments or requests (at home, at work, or as a client) and says that he or she will begin soon, but just never gets started. "Forgets." Takes too long to do a task, or does it so badly that the contribution loses its value.</u>

JUST TO SHOW PEOPLE THEY CAN'T PRESSURE ME, I WILL MANAGE TO DO THINGS WRONG, OR FIND EXTRA THINGS THAT TAKE UP TIME.

(2) complains of being victimized, misunderstood, and unappreciated by those with whom he or she lives and works

<u>Feels comfortable about the quality and quantity of his or her performance (at home, at work, or as a client), even though others are dissatisfied. Complains that they are unfairly criticizing him or her. Says that his or her contributions have not been appreciated; unfairness has caused him or her great harm.</u>

PEOPLE WHO TELL ME I'M NOT DOING WELL ENOUGH AT WORK, HOME, OR SCHOOL ARE UNREASONABLE AND STUPID, AND DON'T REALIZE HOW MUCH I'M ALREADY DOING.

(3) sullen, irritable, and argumentative, especially in reaction to the wishes or expectations of others

<u>Resents useful suggestions from others concerning how he or she could be more productive. Will do what is asked, but it does not work out well. Often the request turns out to be "uninformed" and to do great harm to him or her.</u>

WHEN PEOPLE TRY TO FORCE ME TO DO WHAT I DON'T WANT TO DO, I GO AHEAD WITH IT, BUT ALSO TELL THEM HOW WRONG THEY ARE.

---

[3]As this book goes to press, the final name and criteria for this disorder are still being debated. If the final decision is to retain the DSM-IV revision of the old criteria for Passive Aggressive Personality Disorder, then readers will need to refer to the items defining that version. They are:

(1) procrastinates and postpones completing routine tasks that need to be done, especially those that others seek to have completed

(2) protests, without justification, that others make unreasonable demands of him or her

(3) becomes sulky, irritable, or argumentative when asked to do something he or she does not want to do

(4) unreasonably criticizes or scorns people in positions of power

(5) seems to work deliberately slowly or to do a bad job on tasks that he or she really does not want to do

(6) obstructs the efforts of others by failing to do his or her share of the work

(7) avoids obligations by claiming to have forgotten

(4) unreasonably criticizes and scorns authority

Complains that people in authority have "messed up." They have failed to deliver and have caused great inconvenience, excessive expense, or serious harm. Maintains that his or her suffering arises from the failures of the authority or caregiver. Wants confession and restitution.

USUALLY I FOLLOW THE RULES, BUT I THINK PEOPLE IN AUTHORITY ARE INCOMPETENT, UNFAIR, AND CORRUPT.

(5) communicates a pervasive mix of angry and pessimistic attitudes toward numerous and diverse events (e.g., cynically notes the potentially troublesome aspects of situations that are going well)

Looks to strong people for help, but expects to be disappointed. Complains that useful suggestions about how to make things go better (at home, at work, or as a client) are stupid, unknowing, and unreasonable.

PEOPLE WHO TRY TO BE HELPFUL USUALLY HAVE DUMB IDEAS THAT HURT RATHER THAN HELP.

(6) expresses envy and resentment toward those apparently more fortunate

Points out how others are treated with leniency and generosity while he or she is asked to do an unfair share of the work. Says that the others actually do less, but are acknowledged and rewarded more. Feels cheated and robbed of his or her due.

ALTHOUGH I DO OKAY AT WORK (OR AT SCHOOL), I DON'T GET THE PROMOTIONS (GRADES) I DESERVE.

(7) claims to be luckless, ill-starred, and jinxed in life; personal discontent is more a matter of whining and grumbling than of feeling forlorn or despairing

Agrees (at home, at work, or as a client) to do things he or she does not want to do, but complains that the assignment is unfair, or that the job or the person who requested it is "stupid." Sees control in situations that others do not see as coercive. For example, if a lover proposes living together, this is likely to be seen as an attempt to constrain.

PEOPLE MAKE UNREASONABLE DEMANDS OF ME AND DON'T FAIRLY CONSIDER MY SITUATION.

(8) alternates between hostile assertions of personal autonomy and independence and acting contrite and dependent

Simultaneously agrees and disagrees; depends and defies; counts on help and mourns the expected default.

I OFTEN ASK PEOPLE TO GIVE ME WHAT I NEED, BUT ALWAYS END UP HAVING TO TAKE CARE OF MYSELF.

NECESSARY AND EXCLUSIONARY CRITERIA

The present analysis permits definition of necessary and exclusionary conditions for each personality disorder. For NEG, the recommended *necessary* condition is the pattern of compliant defiance. The hallmark of the negativism is agreeing to perform, but not delivering. *Exclusionary* conditions for NEG include the devotion to productivity that can be found in OCD. Also, if the patient shows uncomplicated compliance, he or she does not have the NEG pattern. The NEG's words say that he or she agrees, but his or her behavior demonstrates that the answer is really no.

CASE ILLUSTRATIONS

Case 1

This 18-year-old university student suffering from polydrug overdose was transferred from a small-town hospital to a university hospital while in a coma that lasted nearly 3 days. After she was stabilized medically, she was transferred to the psychiatric unit, where the interview described below took place.

She had begun exhibiting symptoms of depression in high school. When she was in the tenth grade, she left a suicide note that involved conflict with her mother over a boyfriend. At the time, she resisted suggestions that she seek psychiatric treatment. She expressed considerable resentment that she had had to do housework when she was in high school because her mother worked. Her father had left the family years before. There were younger siblings, but they were not asked to help. She reacted to her stay on a psychiatric ward with escalating resentment and hostility.

Her history of intermittent depressive symptoms for 3 years, decreased self-esteem, decreased concentration, and a previous suicide attempt suggested the diagnosis of Dysthymic Disorder. Passive Aggressive Personality Disorder was added to her discharge summary because of her high level of ambivalence about compliance and resistance to household and school assignments.

The SASB "pond water theory" specifies that coding of a small sample of a person's patterns will reveal the structure of the character. A few "teacups" of interpersonal patterns can provide a representative sample of the whole interpersonal "pond." SASB coding can sometimes establish the diagnosis in the first few exchanges between interviewer and patient. The patient's view of the world and his or her responses to those perceptions are ready to unfold from the first moment of contact. The following interview with this patient illustrates the "pond water theory" especially well. The patient opened with cheerful denial of the seriousness of her suicide attempt. Her speech showed resentment over unfair demands from her boyfriend's parents and from her mother. Her reaction to the interviewer exhibited the baseline NEG position: She innocently complied with the interviewer's questions (SUBMIT), while simultaneously providing "evidence" that the interviewer was stupid and unable to follow the thread (BLAME). Furthermore, she managed to suggest that the interviewer was coming close to abuse by perplexing her with unfathomably obscure questions. The interviewer's exasperation is apparent in the closing line of the segment.

The fact that NEGs embrace contradictory positions (agreeing and defying; suppressing anger to comply while blaming) means that they are often illogical. NEGs often show unabashed willingness to shift logical contexts. The derailing of logic is done with such innocence and agreeableness that the listener begins to question his or her own reality testing. This patient shifted the context back and forth between the question of *whether* there was a suicide attempt and the question of *when* there was a suicide attempt. At times, she blatantly ignored what had just been said.

P: Well, see, I was going to school, and I didn't know if I wanted to go to school or anything, and my boyfriend's parents—I just assumed they wanted me to go, you know, and then after all this happened, you know, I've been talking to them and she says, "Ann, we could care less if you go to school or not." She said, "We love you anyway," so, you know . . .

T: So your boyfriend's family will accept you even if you don't go to school.

P: Ya, and I didn't think they would.

T: So that's it? [The patient, who had just been transferred from intensive care, had announced that she should go home now because everything had been worked out.]

P: Well, there was a lot of things at home that, you know, I didn't like, and I didn't want to go home, but I talked it over with my mom and I guess she's willing to, you know, meet me halfway or whatever, 'cause I had to do all the housework and everything and I didn't think that was fair. Well, I never talked it over with her and I finally did, and she said, "Well, Ann, you should have said something." You know. So.

T: You were doing too much housework at home and you wanted to drop out of school, and nobody—you were unable to discuss that with anybody, and now that you tried to kill yourself they were willing to talk and involve themselves?

P: Oh, they were always willing to talk, but I just never gave them a chance to, you know. I never asked them or anything.

T: Is that true? [The interviewer wonders whether an adolescent girl would never tell her mother that she did not want to do housework!]

P: Ya. It's true. Because I never, you know, talked to them. I just figured well, you, know, I just figured what I thought.

T: Have you ever thought of killing yourself before?

P: No, I haven't. I just figured there was no way out. And that was stupid.

T: You had never tried to kill yourself before?

P: No.

T: I heard in the history that somebody had the impression you wrote some notes when you were in the tenth grade. Is that wrong?

P: *In the tenth grade?*

T: Um-hum.

P: I don't know. I don't remember them.

T: In the eleventh grade? [The interview tries to track the shift from whether to when.]

P: I don't remember writing any notes. [The topic shifts back to the interviewer's original question about whether.]

T: At any time. [Interviewer shifts with her.]

P: No, I don't.

T: So you never thought of killing yourself before. [There is potential for an argument here. The interviewer makes sure the understanding is clear.]

P: Well, I've thought of it, but there was nothing really serious.

T: Never wrote any notes before?

P: I can't remember any, you know, if I wrote any.

T: I wonder how that story got started. That's a puzzle.

P: I don't remember any notes that I would write in high school or anything.

T: How do you feel when I ask you a question like that? That's pretty heavy. I understand you've written suicide notes before and you don't remember it. How do you feel about that? [Interviewer ignores the "bait" of circling back over the question of when, and directs the discussion to the transference interactions.]

P: I don't know.

T: You don't know how you feel about that?

P: Well, I don't. I just feel, you know, like I didn't write them. And I don't know, you know, where you got that I wrote them. [Patient is being "oppressed" by an interviewer who persists in asking irrelevant questions.]

T: Okay, so do you feel angry at me for having that wrong idea?

P: No.

T: But your view of that transaction is what? Just that, well, there must have been some mistake somewhere or what?

P: Well, you must have got it from somewhere. And I was kind of wondering where you got it from. [The patient is perplexed now by the strange interview process.]

T: Ya. Well, I understand that it's come from your family.

P: From tenth grade? [Now the question is when, not whether.]

T: Eleventh grade, any grade, it really wouldn't matter what year!

This young woman would probably meet the DSM criteria for NEG. Without doubt, she passively resisted routine tasks (item 1) and complained of being victimized and misunderstood (item 2). She also clearly resented her treatment relative to her siblings (item 6). However, her level of hostility was subdued compared to the surly character described by the DSM-IV. Despite her denials, there were subtle signs that this woman was scornful of the hospital staff (item 4) and that she was argumentative about her household assignments (item 3). Earlier definitions of Passive Aggressive Personality Disorder would probably be more appropriate for this woman, because they include characteristics indicating more successful suppression of hostility.

This patient met the interpersonal definitions of NEG very well. She complied with the interviewer's questions, but at the same time did not respond to the main points (SUBMIT plus WALL OFF). She endured the interviewing procedure while she conveyed that the interviewer was dense and possibly abusive (SULK plus BLAME]. For example, she was perplexed by the interviewer's interest in the "nonexistent" previous suicide note. She tried to endure the interviewer's apparent inability to track, and could not understand the persistent focus on an "irrelevant" point. These patterns were also apparent in the patient's perception of her world. She thought her household and educational assignments were unfair (CONTROL plus IGNORE). There was resolute resentment over the fact that she received the most burdensome household assignments. Her suicide attempt was clearly a message that she was not being listened to or treated fairly (SELF-ATTACK plus BLAME).

She wished for nurturance (**PROTECT**) from her mother and her boyfriend's family. She feared their **CONTROL**. Her style during the interview was saturated with the necessary condition of compliant defiance. She did not show the exclusionary conditions of uncomplicated deference or devotion to productivity.

This patient's history could have followed the pathogenic patterns outlined in Table 11.1. Her father had left the family when the children were quite young; the mother raised the children alone and had bouts with depression. It is reasonable to guess that the mother felt overwhelmed and turned to this oldest child for help with household duties. However, no information is available to confirm or disconfirm that prediction. Neither is there information about the family attitudes toward anger and autonomy.

Case 2

The next case was presented by hospital staff as a likely OCD. The analysis shows how the present approach helps make a clear differential diagnosis between these two related but different disorders.

This 26-year-old married man came to the hospital for treatment of his compulsive cleaning, grooming, and arranging of his body or clothing. The habit had started about 10 years ago and had worsened in the past 2 years. Sometimes he spent up to 14 hours a day "fixing" his appearance. This preoccupation interfered with his marriage to such an extent that his wife had moved out and planned divorce. He had been in outpatient therapy for the past 2 years, and had been given BuSpar, Tofranil, and Prozac. Nothing helped. Soft-spoken and unusually handsome, he had a reputation for being a very neat person. He became very upset if there was a flaw in his clothing or any other aspect of his appearance. He had dropped out of college and was unemployed.

The patient said that if he noticed an imperfection, he needed to "fix" it so that he would be perfect. Both his mother and his wife valued his good looks. He explained that the habit had gotten worse lately because he had been trying to get rid of it. He figured each episode would be the last time, so he would have to do an extra good job. Afterwards, he felt bad and did not want to face people. He thought the compulsive grooming started when he was 16 because "that is the time when social demands increase and you have to decide what your work is going to be, and you have to make big decisions. It is a time of great pressure."

The patient's wife wanted him to get a job and to be more sociable. She was especially distressed about his interpersonal distance from her. She complained that a "roommate" would be more intimate than he was. The patient was not happy in the marriage. His wife told him that the grooming was "stupid" and demanded to know why he did it. She frequently inquired in great detail about all of his activities. He felt she was judgmental. She told him that he would have to be more productive, and that he couldn't "lounge around forever." The grooming disappeared temporarily on a vacation that involved activities that each partner liked. On another vacation, it did not; this vacation was selected by his wife according to her own tastes, not his. The patient described himself as "easy." He explained that he "never said no" and always "tried to go along." If he made a suggestion that his wife did not like, he would "back off."

He grew up in a "weird" family. His father had died when he was 5, and his mother raised the children as a single parent. There was no fighting, and the patient kept quiet, mostly to himself. The mother constantly nagged about doing household jobs and homework. There were no punishments, but constant "nag, nag, nag, talk, talk, talk all the time." Sometimes his mother would complain even if he had already done the job. He would not tell her that it was already done, because then "she might think that she had control rather than that I did it on my own." He had trouble saying "thank you" because it would mean that he had complied with the wishes of the thanking person.

The patient had several features of OCD, including perfectionism (DSM item 2), preoccupation with detail (item 1), and restricted expression of affection (item 5). However, he lacked the necessary interpersonal descriptor of dominance—of insisting that others comply with his rules (item 7). Nor was he devoted to work, ethics, or morality (item 4). In sum, he was not generally engaged in the quest for perfection in himself and others. Rather, he was reactive, resistant, and withdrawn.

The descriptors for NEG were more appropriate to this patient than those for OCD. He procrastinated, as he failed to look for another job. He would do a "bad" job on things he did not want to do (DSM item 1). He sulked and complained when asked by his wife to participate in social activities, and resented suggestions that might reduce the grooming habit (item 3). He protested that his wife made unreasonable demands on him when she wanted him to find work and socialize more (item 2). He apologized for his social shortcomings, but refused to follow his wife's request to go to couples counseling to make the marriage work better by developing "communication skills" (item 8). He was subtly disrespectful and critical of doctors, bosses, and his wife (item 4).

The interpersonal descriptors summarized for NEG in Table 11.1 applied quite well to this man. The compulsive grooming itself represented compliance with the wishes of his wife and mother that his appearance be perfect. While engaged in that assignment, he managed to totally undermine their agenda of showing him off (SUBMIT plus WALL OFF). The recent exacerbation was *caused* by his wife's plan that he must give up the grooming habit (SULK plus BLAME). As he sometimes mutilated himself with excessive scrubbing, he showed that their nagging and bragging was harmful (*SELF-ATTACK* plus BLAME). His fear of CONTROL and his wish for PROTECT were clear. He showed the necessary condition of compliant defiance. He obviously did not meet the exclusionary conditions of uncomplicated deference or devotion to productivity.

There was overwhelming failure to perform. His handsome face and beautiful body—the very features that were so valued by his controllers (mother, wife)—were the medium for the debilitating symptoms. He devoted himself to maintaining a perfect appearance, and in so doing managed to resist their demands that he look for a job and be sociable. His intense compliance with their wishes that he be beautiful struck them powerless and exasperated.

EXPECTABLE TRANSFERENCE REACTIONS AND TREATMENT IMPLICATIONS

Transference Reactions

The classic NEG transference pattern is to comply (sort of) with the therapeutic recommendation, and then to declare triumphantly that it was a very poor suggestion and failed miserably. The NEG is programmed to ask for help and then both to defy it and to suffer from it. Perry and Flannery (1982) wrote that the typical patient with this disorder shows "an apparent willingness to engage in therapy, but thereafter resists and covertly sabotages the therapist's attempts to teach him or her adaptive, prosocial behaviors" (p. 164). Rather than getting better, the NEG's goal is, as Reich (1949) said of the masochist, "to place the analyst in a bad light." The failures have the purpose of saying, "See how badly you have treated me."

> "Look how miserable I am; please love me"—"You don't love me enough, you treat me badly"—"You must love me, I shall force you to; or else I'm going to annoy you." The masochistic torturing, the masochistic complaint, provocation and suffering all explain themselves on the basis of the frustration, fantasied or actual, of a demand for love which is excessive and cannot be gratified. (Reich, 1949, p. 225)

The role of retaliation in NEG was demonstrated in a recent interview with a NEG, who carried the diagnosis of recurrent Major Depression. She had had several hospitalizations for depression and suicidality. There was a history of only temporary success with a broad array of medications. The present hospitalization was precipitated by a very pleasant Saturday spent shopping and going to a movie with her boyfriend. After he left about midnight, the patient went into the bathroom, cut her wrists, and sat there watching with great satisfaction as the blood ran down her arm. Her mother came into the bathroom and, when she saw the blood, took the patient directly to the hospital.

The first half hour of the interview was devoted to developing a collaborative rather than an adversarial relationship. The patient disclosed that on the day of the shopping trip, her boyfriend had asked her to move in with him. The thought made her very anxious, because she expected that living with him would mean that she would lose control of her time and space. Her sensitivity to control had roots in her relationship with her father, a successful businessman to whom she was very attached, but who was quite harsh in his disciplinary approach.

> P: I guess I treated her [the mother] like she was dumb. I made her feel dumb, if I could.

T: Uh-huh. So if you didn't respect her properly, she'd get your dad to discipline you for sass-mouthing. Is that what we're talking about?

P: Yeah. I guess. Basically.

T: What would she—what would she be doing that you thought was dumb?

P: I think almost anything. Because of that Electra complex thing. I was in love with my dad and jealous of my mom. So I'd try to make her feel stupid or . . . Well, I don't know.

T: So you felt really close to the one who was punishing you the worst. So it was a mixed picture of a lot of love from him, and also there was that harsh discipline. And then fighting with your mom, who was jealous.

P: Yeah.

T: Could you say what you're feeling?

P: Um. I don't know. But I just remember talking to this girl and going, "I hate my mom. I mean, I hate her." And she's like, "How could you do that?" And I thought, "I've hated her all my life."

T: Um-hum. So this had been going on a long time. How does your father react after you make these suicide attempts?

P: Um. He's upset.

T: How do you know? What does he say to show his upset?

P: He talks in a certain voice. But I can tell. He's also frustrated, 'cause he can't do anything.

T: Frustrated because he can't do what?

P: He doesn't know what to do for me.

T: Um-hum. He'd like to help. How does he feel about your actively hurting yourself? Do you know?

P: Bad. Specially 'cause I used to be so perfect. I mean, pretty much together.

T: Um-hum. You were the ideal kid. So it really spoils the image that he had.

P: Yeah. I mean. 'Cause like you said, I had all these problems all my life. And then I got to ninth and tenth grade and everything was really good and he thought it was finally over. Everything's cool. And then to have this mess again.

T: Um-hum. He thought he was out of the woods, and now it's even worse.

P: Yeah.

T: Did you feel that he was very angry at you when you were messing up in high school? Or was he just worried? Or what?

P: Uh. (*Laughs*) He was a little angry. Like, end of my junior year. He was a little angry. Yeah. And um (*laughs*), but then in my senior year, I did it again. He just got used to it. He didn't really ever yell at me for my grades.

T: So he accepted that you were in charge of things, finally.

P: Yeah.

T: Much like your boyfriend has to. Does that puzzle you? My making that link?

P: Well, they occurred at different times.

T: Yeah. But the patterns that we develop can come back over and over in different relationships. So I'm thinking that you were way overcontrolled, unfairly punished. High demands for performance. And you got a real sore spot about being controlled. And about having to perform. You smile as I say that?

P: Ha. I like it. It sounds pretty neat.

T: Does it sound like an accurate description?

P: Well, yeah.

T: Okay, so you're real sensitive to being pushed around, coerced. And that came from the stuff at home, and it shows up in your love relationship. As when your boyfriend gets an apartment and wants you to move in. The theory would be that you need help with self-defining, perhaps in less reckless ways. How to keep from being overwhelmed and overcontrolled, which is a depressive position. In less reckless ways—I mean suicide is a way to keep from getting controlled, I guess. Unless you have to go back to the drawing board, as the Buddhists say. [The patient is Buddhist, whereas her father is a devout Protestant.] Then you don't have any escape. (*Very long pause*) What do you think? You look a little amused. Is that right?

P: No. That's interesting. No. I'm sure it applies.

T: Okay. The only other missing link here is the apparent pleasure that you take in hurting yourself. Is that true that you sort of enjoy it?

P: At certain times.

T: Well, to explore that, I wonder if you could recall what it felt like when you were being punished. When you were being whipped with a belt. Do you remember how you coped with that?

P: Um. I cried. Uh (*laughs*).

T: Yes, of course you cried. But people, when that happens a lot, begin to develop ideas and mental sets about how to endure it. How to get through it. (*Very long pause*)

P: Well, the only thing I can possibly think of is that—well, this would probably work. Um, if I was hurt I was glad because my dad did something. And it was a bad mark against him.

T: Um-hum. So your injury was a black mark on his record with God and others. As you hurt, that showed him to be the one that was wrong.

P: Yeah.

T: So your injury is really kind of an indictment of your oppressors?

P: It didn't feel good, though.

Then, looking around the staffing room at the nurses and doctors present, the patient denied that her suicidality had anything to do with her father. "I'm not doing it to hurt him," she declared. The interviewer retreated and suggested merely that this was an idea she might want to think and talk about in her outpatient psychotherapy. The dynamic purpose of the depression had become conscious briefly, but then it was denied or repressed.

The interview highlights the giant Catch-22 that the NEG and the therapist are in. The patient's unconscious goal is to get worse and to blame the therapist for it. He or she expects to be pushed around unfairly and not helped. If the therapist directly addresses the agenda to fail and blame, he or she humiliates the patient and inspires further negativism. If the therapist does not address the pattern, nothing different can happen. Again, the NEG will fail to get what he or she needs.

Treatment Implications: The Five Categories of Correct Response

The view of therapy as a learning experience permits definition of therapist errors on a moment-to-moment basis. Therapy interventions can be evaluated in terms of whether they enhance collaboration, facilitate learning about patterns and their roots, block maladaptive patterns, enhance the will to change, or effectively encourage new patterns. The effect of interventions is assessed in terms of the actual impact on the patient, not in terms of the therapist's intention. If the effect of an intervention on a NEG is compliant defiance or punitive neediness, then the intervention is an error.

Facilitating Collaboration

Developing a collaborative relationship with the patient is the biggest challenge in the treatment of NEG. The first condition for developing collaboration is to be aware of the likely provocative nature of the transference patterns. The therapist who has a clear understanding of the dynamics of NEG can avoid feeling personally injured and resist the draw to punish. This is very important, because the NEG has much practice in self-fulfilling prophecy. He or she expects to be injured by a negligent and cruel caregiver. His or her behavior is likely to generate "counterattack" and unfair treatment.

The knowledge that the patient's suffering is an unconscious goal must not be used to accuse the patient of enjoying or seeking misery. Such blaming would probably mean little more than that the therapist cannot bear to be ineffective. There are few disorders for which blaming is the treatment of choice.

Instead of inspiring blaming, knowledge of patterns should be used like a road map. The therapist can use this understanding of the adaptive features of disorders as a guide for travel through the patient's phenomenology. Knowing likely connections, the therapist can select statements to reflect and amplify, and knows which to ignore. The interviewer doesn't tell a patient about patterns; instead, patterns are drawn from the patient's words. The NEG in the interview above said that she was glad if she was hurt, because that meant that her father "had done something bad." The idea of revenge came from her, not the interviewer. The interviewer merely set up the conditions for that insight to emerge by accurately and empathically reflecting her experience, and then puzzling over why she found pleasure in pain. Although she quickly retracted the insight, such defensiveness is not a problem in an ongoing psychotherapy. Learning is an uneven process. A golfer, for example, may have a wonderful day rather early in his or her learning process, only to forget for many subsequent sessions. Therapist awareness and tolerance of the variation in progress are particularly vital when working with NEGs because of their exquisite sensitivity to pressure.

Instead of accusing the patient of wanting to be depressed or otherwise suffer, the therapist can describe the transference process. A typical observation would go like this: "I notice that we seem to have a pattern. Over the past 3 weeks we have developed plans together [list them] for helping you feel less depressed. Each time, something has gone wrong [reiterate what happened with each plan]. Each time, you tell me that things are worse, in a way that almost sounds like the failure is good news. Can we explore that? Can we explore how you are feeling about the process between us?" Such a review of the "failed" therapy process will elicit the expected transferential pattern of "Therapy is not helping."

The therapist should then make it clear that the message has been received: "Okay, so here you go to see this big-time therapist, and you get all of these dumb suggestions that don't work. It's the same old story all over again." If the therapist does not talk about this negative transferential pattern, the symptoms will escalate until it can no longer be "denied." When it is totally clear that the therapist has heard that he or she is stupid and unhelpful, it is time to ask whether the pattern is familiar: "Has this ever happened to you before?" The question will probably elicit reference to earlier therapies and/or job or marital situations. After clarifying the present pattern, the therapist can pursue the theme by asking for even earlier examples of a situation where someone was supposed to be helpful but messed up.

Before long, the family of origin with all of its demanding unfairness will be the topic. When that is clear, the parallel between feelings about the target parent and the therapist can be drawn. The negative transference can be scaled back by explaining that a person tends to see people in the present as he or she learned to see people in similar roles in the past. It is vital to discuss these patterns with the NEG, or the therapy will simply recapitulate them and terminate prematurely and unhappily.

Because NEGs show both sadistic and masochistic patterns, therapy with these patients is not the strong suit of either narcissistic or masochistic therapists. Much of a NEG's learning takes place in the transference. Therapy is a chance to learn to break old destructive patterns. From this perspective, negative transference is a welcome opportunity to do learning in therapy. The misperception of the therapist as an exploitative power-monger offers an opportunity to discuss the core issue.

Facilitating Pattern Recognition

As the transference unfolds, the therapist has to remain intact and steady in face of noteworthy provocation. Excerpts from a 3-year-long therapy illustrate:

> This professional man in his mid-30s came to therapy with a history of three suicide attempts, the first having been in his last year of high school. After his second attempt, he had a successful psychotherapy with a kindly older man. The patient was then able to seek and win scholarships, and make a good start on his education as a physicist. However, in one of his work assignments, he became embattled with a beloved boss who eventually fired him. A lasting depression that included another suicide attempt followed.

He received a second therapy in a training clinic, but its most helpful feature was the prescription of antidepressant medications. He presented himself for this third therapy primarily to work out his seasonal depressions. Each year, about October or November, he would slide into despair and lethargy with thoughts of shooting himself. He would not recover until the next April or May. He also recognized that he had some interpersonal habits that needed attention. He had, for example, several hundred unpaid parking tickets, and bill collectors were everyday problems. Relationships with women were easy to start, but did not last. Battles with a roommate over his lack of neatness had recently led to the decision to live alone.

He was referred for antidepressant medication, and therapy work began. At first, there was little affect in the recounting of the long and complex history. His winter depression gained momentum. *Therapy was not helping!* Along with his suicidality, there were dreams of violent attack upon the therapist, accompanied by the fear that he would be "kicked out of therapy."

After some discussion and much apprehension, a single family conference with his mother and father was held and tape-recorded. Although his mother now seemed remorseful, her candid description of her attitudes and actions during his adolescence made it astonishingly clear that he had been subject to relentless, unfeeling, neglectful control.

M: . . . When they were smaller it was real easy to cuddle 'em . . . But as they got older I think I found it lots more difficult probably than I should. I think it would've been helpful for me and for them probably to feel really, you know, loved in a physical way. . . .

P: I think I like you more these days. I can remember times when I just hated you.

M: I can believe that. I kind of hated you too.

P: Ya. You were nasty about it.

M: Ya, I sure was.

P: How come?

M: Well, I think because you rebelled against everything that I hold, held important. You know, I thought you were heading in the wrong direction. I thought your choice of friends, your choice of activities was harmful.

P: Like what?

M: [Gives complaints about his friends and activities.] So everything that I, you know, thought was important, I guess I just took it very personally, and I think you had always done well in school and that was sliding. I don't know. I just felt you were really headed, you know, in a bad direction. I think it was a combination of hurt to my pride not knowing how to handle everything like that. Because I was a child who, as I recall anyway, did everything my parents wanted me to do, and, you know, just didn't, really didn't know how to handle it. . . . I think I've always expected my kids to be perfect, and I expected more than they really were, you know, capable of. [Gives details of extremely close surveillance, even while her son was in school. This was possible because she was a friend of a teacher, who would telephone her frequently with the results of a spot check on what he was wearing, doing, saying.] And I would be the first to admit I definitely lacked a lot of parent skills that I should have had to do a better job as far as raising my family is concerned.

T: Well, there's not many places to learn that stuff.

M: No, you don't get a little bag of it when you bring the baby home. Unfortunately.

T: That might be helpful. But you mention this conflict and feeling of tension, at least on your part. I'm interested in hearing more about that, if there's any way you could put that into words.

M: Well, I think I was constantly angry.

T: You felt angry.

M: Um-hum. Again, because we lived in a small community and I felt that there was a standard—certain standards of behavior that was expected of our children, especially since, because of my husband's position [he was the mayor] . . . You know, and I think, as a result, I just expected an awful—you know, as I say, I really expected, you know, looking back I really expected perfection as I saw it, and I wasn't getting it and it made me angry.

T: And you expressed it mostly in silence, angry silence?

M: Um-hum. That's kind of the way I'd do it. Either that or I'd shout.

T: What would you shout about?

M: Well . . . cleaning up his room, I'm sure. I don't know. Coming in late. I don't remember so much as—I guess it's more just an overall impression that I remember of it, just being a really miserable time, you know, there just didn't seem to be any fun for anybody. . . . I don't think I hated you, John, but I sure hated what you were doing. I hated the things you were doing. I think I wanted you dead. I hoped you'd grow out of it. And I'm sure you—you can't believe this was, I really was concerned about, you know, the direction you were headed. I really was, you know, and as I say I think it was a time of—for me it was just a blow to my pride because all I ever wanted was to have a, you know, to be married and have children and live happily ever after, and when it wasn't working that way I guess I just really didn't know how to handle it.

The patient said that the conference rekindled his hatred for his mother. The therapy plan had been to listen to the tape to obtain a current perspective, which in turn would facilitate differentiation. However, the tape reactivated feelings from the past so vividly that it had to be put away for over a year. One immediate benefit, the patient observed, was that having seen "the real thing," he felt less afraid of and demanded of by the (female) therapist.

The patient's winter depression and suicidality continued to escalate. Unfortunately, they did not lift in the summer as they had in previous years. For the next year and a half, the patient repeatedly acted out his pattern of feeling that he was under unfair surveillance and subject to unreasonable demands. He became increasingly depressed, failing to meet his work assignments and becoming embattled with specific supervisors. He was threatened with firing, and eventually was dismissed from his job in the research department of a large firm.

The same resistant pattern emerged with the therapist in the matter of bill paying. Unfortunately, the therapist worked for a very large organization that had problems coordinating the billing process. The therapist did not have any information on the status of patient accounts until the agency decided it was necessary to send them to collection. Consequently, after a year and a half of therapy, the therapist learned that no payments had been made on the patient's very large bill. Of course, the patient expected to be severely punished and rejected. The therapist observed that he certainly was "shooting himself in the foot." He was provoking one of his few remaining supporters. He was frightened and remorseful; he was also overwhelmed with the fact that he received continued support from the therapist rather than attack. She realized that a possible decision would be to "cut losses," but decided to continue, contingent on an agreement that there would be regular (if small) payments on the account. He was able to keep this contract.

Blocking Maladaptive Patterns

The patient just described was deeply trapped in a compulsion to defy. He found a potent way of challenging the therapist to do her job well at great personal cost. The discussion about the therapy bill turned out to be critical to this therapy. When the therapist showed willingness to personally lose quite a bit and still try to be helpful, he had to change his view of the world. After this encounter, the patient began a more active collaboration with the process of looking at his patterns and their roots.

Since NEGs are so complex themselves, paradoxical interventions are dangerous. So is humor. These communications usually include negative messages that strike at the pathology, not the person. However, a NEG will see any bits of power, hostility, and neglect in a communication as personal abuse. Even if a comment is carefully nested in a benevolent context, the NEG will grasp at the most unfavorable interpretation. Instead of play in any form, work with NEGs requires enormous patience, as well as adherence to the most simple, "clean," and unequivocally friendly comments. These patients are not much fun. The therapist must perform perfectly! NEGs are more likely than others to try to sue the therapist; I could give examples, but fear to do so.

Strengthening the Will to Give Up Maladaptive Patterns

With a NEG, the third and fourth stages of therapy must be partly mastered before the second one can begin. The NEG will not look at his or her patterns until the agenda—suffering to prove the therapist abusive or incompetent—has been at least temporarily set aside. Yet recognition of patterns and their roots is a part of the process of becoming willing to give up that agenda. The stages cannot be distinctly separated in therapy with a NEG.

After the discussion about the therapy bill, the patient just described became much more curious about his distortions and overdetermined reactions to people in the present. By the beginning of the third year of therapy, his depression lifted. He became able to listen to the tape of the family session without becoming suicidal. Recognizing patterns on the tape of the family session helped him distance from his old fears and wishes. He explored his hatred of his extremely successful and much admired younger brother. He discovered he believed that his mother's goal was for him to hurt, and became acutely aware of his vengeful hopes that she would suffer as much as he did.

Still, he asked for and accepted financial help from his parents, and yearned for their love. He began to see his mother as a vulnerable human being, and decided to give up both the idea of revenge and the hope of restorative love. He realized that the family of origin is not the place to find adult love. His relationships with women improved significantly.

Facilitating New Learning

According to McCann (1988), assertiveness training is the treatment of choice for the NEG's pattern of indirect resistance. Perry and Flannery (1982) also recommend assertiveness training. They say that the goal is to teach "the ability to express anger and frustration in firm but tactful ways and tender expressions of affection and concern as well. It [assertiveness] does not include use of coercive threats or punishment to obtain one's own way" (p. 164).

Assertiveness training can directly address the NEG's basic pattern of false compliance. However, with NEG as with other personality disorders, the "obvious" intervention will not succeed until the necessary preparatory work has been completed. The NEG must give up the agenda of suffering before he or she can become open to changing his or her patterns. This is unlikely to happen until the patient learns how it all fits together. Once the preparatory work is well under way, new patterns can emerge. The case just described shows how things can change, once the groundwork is complete.

Throughout the third year of therapy, the patient continued to improve. A while after being fired, he found another job where he repeated, in a minor way, his pattern of "dereliction of duty." His was dismissed, this time without substantial reason. Probably the unfair treatment came from his reputation for inordinate delay in completing paperwork. At the next job, he was extremely successful, even beloved. He stopped therapy and continued in that job for several years. Gradually, he paid off his debts, and marveled at his accumulating bank balance. In addition to having fewer and less intense bouts with depression, he had more and more days of feeling really happy.

12

Avoidant Personality Disorder

"I just wait and see if anybody cares."

REVIEW OF THE LITERATURE

"Avoidant personality" was first described as a diagnostic category by Theodore Millon in 1969 (see Millon, 1982). AVD was recognized as a formal diagnosis in the DSM-III in 1980. Millon characterized AVDs as "*actively*, as opposed to passively, averse to social relationships" (1982, p. 298)—dysphoric, self-critical, lonely, mistrustful, fearful of humiliation, and hypersensitive. Millon suggested that his actively detached character had been previously described in the literature. He compared it to Bleuler's initial formulation of schizophrenia; to Fairbairn's schizoid character; to Kohut's narcissistic personality; to Schneider's idea of the asthenic personality; to Kretschmer's hyperaesthetic; to Fenichel's phobic character; and to Horney's detached type.

Millon was particularly concerned with the relation to schizophrenia of the actively detached avoidant personality and the passively detached schizoid personality: "The reason researchers have consistently turned up paradoxical and contradictory results in schizophrenia can be traced, in great measure, to their failure to recognize that a basic distinction exists between actively and passively detached personalities" (1982, p. 298). The contradiction, Millon said, was that some reports described schizophrenics as underaroused, undermotivated, and insensitive, whereas others described them as overaroused, overmotivated, and hypersensitive. Millon concluded that both patterns, under- and overarousal, exist, and that both are likely to be found in schizophrenics (1982, p. 297). The DSM-III task force followed his recommendation to make a distinction between active and passive detachment. They created two diagnoses corresponding, respectively, to Millon's descriptions of active and passive detachment: AVD and SOI.

Theoretical and empirical controversy followed. Livesley and West (1986) argued that DSM-III inappropriately split the Schizoid category of DSM-II into three new categories: SOI, AVD, and SZT. They noted that Millon's distinction between active and passive social withdrawal was the basis for DSM-III's distinction between SOI and AVD. These theorists observed that the distinction rested simply on the question of "whether or not there is a defect in the motivation and capacity for emotional involvement" (p. 59). They accused the DSM-

III of letting this distinction lead them to deviate inappropriately from the historically validated concept of schizoid personality. Livesey and West presented a case that illustrated Kretschmer's concept of a schizoid personality (defined by the DSM-II). The patient was caught in tension between his insensitivity on the one extreme (DSM-III's SOI), and his very great sensitivity on the other (DSM-III's AVD). These authors commented: "By separating extremes of a continuous distribution (described by Kretschmer) into distinct types, the DSM-III concepts of schizoid and avoidant personality disorders seem to be historically misconceived" (p. 61). Similar arguments appeared in Livesley, West, and Tanney (1985).

Responding to Livesley and colleagues' reviews, Akhtar (1986) used clinical opinion to defend Millon's proposal that AVD exists as a category distinct from SOI. Akhtar contended, "Avoidant personality is an ego-syntonic characterological counterpart of the phobic neurosis, just as obsessional personality is an ego-syntonic characterological counterpart of obsessional neurosis" (p. 1061). Following that line of thought, the DSM-III-R task force revised the DSM-III items. In the DSM-III-R, the AVD is "a 'phobic character,' fearful of being embarrassed, reticent in social situations, and having a tendency to exaggerate the potential difficulties of everyday life. . . . [The DSM-III-R deleted] the nonspecific item of desire for affection and acceptance" (Trull, Widiger, & Frances, 1987, pp. 770–771). This change succeeded in distinguishing AVD from SOI. Trull et al. (1987) commented that the AVD is "hypersensitive, shy, and insecure, while the schizoid patient is indifferent, aloof and cold. The differential diagnosis may in fact be a moot issue because the very small number of patients with the schizoid diagnosis found in the current study is consistent with findings from a variety of clinical settings" (p. 770).

However, this resolution of the controversy over the distinction between AVD and SOI led to a new problem: In the DSM-III-R it was difficult to distinguish between AVD and Generalized Social Phobia. The DSM-III-R defined Social Phobia as follows:

> A persistent fear of one or more situations (the social phobic situations) in which the person is exposed to possible scrutiny by others and fears that he or she may do something or act in a way that will be humiliating or embarrassing. [Examples of circumscribed fears include] fears of being unable to continue talking while speaking in public, choking on food when eating in front of others, being unable to urinate in a public lavatory, or having a hand tremble when writing in the presence of others. . . . [Examples of general fears include] fears of saying foolish things or not being able to answer questions in social situations. (American Psychiatric Association, 1987, p. 241)

The interpersonal patterns for Generalized Social Phobia are very similar to those for AVD. Both groups avoid social contact and restrain themselves because of fear of humiliation or rejection. Their overlap has been confirmed empirically (e.g., Turner, Beidel, Bordern, Stanley, & Jacob, 1991). The DSM-III-R casebook acknowledged the convergence in its discussion of "The Jerk" (Spitzer et al., 1989):

> This patient illustrates a frequent problem in diagnosing the Axis I disorder of Social Phobia, Generalized Type, in that the symptoms overlap considerably with those of Avoidant Personality Disorder. Leon has certainly displayed a pervasive pattern of social discomfort, fear of negative evaluation, and timidity through-out his life. He has no close friends, avoids activities that involve significant in-terpersonal contact, and is reticent in social situations. He undoubtedly is also easily hurt by disapproval and is probably unwilling to become involved with people unless he is certain of being liked. Therefore, we make the diagnosis of Avoidant Personality Disorder on Axis II and hope that DSM-IV will clarify the boundaries of these two disorders. (p. 55)

In addition to introducing overlap with Generalized Social Phobia, the DSM-III-R definition of AVD also resulted in overlap with DPD. Trull et al. (1987) gathered data from 84 inpatients using the Personality Interview Ques-tions structured interview method. They reported that "items for avoidant dis-order covaried with criteria for dependent disorder but not with criteria for schizoid disorder" (p. 767). Morey (1988) also found that covariance between DSM-III-R definitions of AVD and DPD was more remarkable than the overlap between SOI and SZT. In addition to the AVD-DPD overlap, Morey found that 27.1% of a sample of 291 outpatients with personality disorder could be diag-nosed as having AVD. He reported covariance between AVD and several other Axis II disorders: If the index diagnosis was AVD, 44.3% also qualified for the BPD label, 40.5% for DPD, and 39.2% for PAR. These data suggest that more than twice as many persons with dependent traits (BPD, DPD) qualify for the AVD label than persons noted for their social withdrawal (SOI and SZT).

In sum, research studies have shown that the distinction between AVD and SOI is not difficult. Because SOI is relatively rare in clinical populations, the distinction has little practical importance. However, the distinction between AVD and DPD is more problematic. The association between avoidant and depen-dent traits, and the generality of the avoidant pattern, were confirmed in the first validation study of the WISPI (Klein et al., in press). Factor analysis of a sample of 1200 individuals (300 patients, 900 nonpatients) yielded a first factor named "insecure avoidance." Thirty-six percent of its items were from the WISPI Avoidant Personality scale, while 23% were from the WISPI Dependent Person-ality scale. The items that showed the highest loading on the first factor, account-ing for 19.5% of the variance, were the following:

> I AM VERY TENSE WHEN AROUND OTHER PEOPLE BECAUSE I CAN'T BE SURE THEY WILL ACCEPT ME (LOADING = .856)
> I STAY IN THE BACKGROUND BECAUSE MY WORST FEAR IS BEING REJECTED (LOADING = .819)
> I DON'T LET PEOPLE KNOW MUCH ABOUT ME BECAUSE THEY MAY PUT ME DOWN AND REJECT ME (LOADING = .811)

The WISPI data suggest that quite a number of patients and normal individuals engage in some form of restriction of self-disclosure and social involvement because of fear of rejection, or humiliation. This interpersonal phobic pattern may not be related to schizophrenia as originally proposed by Millon. Rather, the pattern of social withdrawal to avoid rejection or humiliation that is characteristic of AVD may be a widespread pattern. Avoidance of exposure may characterize several of the Axis II disorders and the Axis I Social Phobia. The DSM-IV description of Social Phobia appears to distinguish between the Axis I and Axis II disorders on the basis of the symptoms of pervasive anxiety or panic. If these symptoms are present, Social Phobia is diagnosed.

DSM DEFINITION OF THE DISORDER

The DSM definition provides the starting point for the analysis. The DSM specifies that the diagnosis of AVD can be made if an individual meets four of the criteria. DSM-III-R items appear in **bold print,** and any changes introduced by the DSM-IV appear in *italics.* (As in several earlier chapters, the item numbering used here is that of the DSM-IV. Original numbers in the DSM-III-R appear after **bold** items, in brackets.)

A pervasive pattern of social discomfort, fear of negative evaluation, and timidity, beginning by early adulthood and present in a variety of contexts, as indicated by at least *four* **of the following:**

A pervasive pattern of social discomfort and reticence, low self-esteem, and hypersensitivity to negative evaluation, beginning by early adulthood and present in a variety of contexts, as indicated by at least four of the following:

(1) avoids social or occupational activities that involve significant interpersonal contact, e.g., refuses a promotion that will increase social demands [item 4 in DSM-III-R]

avoids social or occupational activities that involve significant interpersonal contact because of fears of criticism, disapproval, or rejection

(2) is unwilling to get involved with people unless certain of being liked [item 3 in DSM-III-R]

(3) is reticent in social situations because of a fear of saying something inappropriate or foolish, or of being unable to answer a question [item 5 in DSM-III-R]

development of intimate relationships is inhibited (despite desire for them) owing to the fear of being foolish and ridiculed, or being exposed and shamed

(4) is easily hurt by criticism or disapproval [item 1 in DSM-III-R]

preoccupation with being criticized or rejected in social situations

(5) has no close friends or confidants (or only one) other than first-degree relatives [item 2 in DSM-III-R]

has few friends despite the desire to relate to others

(6) belief that one is socially inept, personally unappealing, or inferior to others

(7) is unusually reluctant about taking personal risks or engaging in any new activities because they may prove embarrassing

occasionally has outbursts of indignant rage over alleged humiliation or slights [I recommend adding to DSM]

fears being embarrassed by blushing, crying, or showing signs of anxiety in front of other people [item 6 in DSM-III-R; omitted from DSM-IV]

exaggerates the potential difficulties, physical dangers, or risks involved in doing something ordinary but outside his or her usual routine, e.g., may cancel social plans because [he or] she anticipates being exhausted by the effort of getting there [item 7 in DSM-III-R; omitted from DSM-IV]

PATHOGENIC HYPOTHESES

The method of using the SASB model to develop pathogenic hypotheses has been sketched in Chapter 5. Four main features of the developmental history have been identified specifically to account for each of the AVD symptoms listed in the DSM. A summary of the hypotheses linking interpersonal history to interpersonal patterns characteristic of the disorder appears in Table 12.1. A fuller discussion of these hypotheses is provided here.

Table 12.1. Interpersonal Summary of AVD

History	Consequences of history
1. Loving nurturance at first (**ACTIVE LOVE, PROTECT**)	1. Wish for social contact and nurturance (**ACTIVE LOVE, PROTECT**)
2. **CONTROL** directed toward creating social image, and mockery for failures (**BLAME**)	2. Self-control to avoid embarrassment (*SELF-CONTROL*) Insecurity about self-image (*SELF-BLAME*) Extreme sensitivity to humiliation
3. Enforced autonomy associated with flaws (**BLAME** plus **IGNORE** → **ATTACK**)	3. Efforts to please while remaining walled off (<u>SULK</u> plus <u>WALL</u> <u>OFF</u>); requires safety Imitative outbursts of **BLAME**
4. Warning about outsiders; support for social withdrawal (<u>WALL</u> <u>OFF</u>)	4. Paranoid fears of outsiders (<u>RECOIL</u>); family loyalty

Summary: There is intense fear of humiliation and rejection. To avoid expected embarrassment, the AVD withdraws and carefully restrains himself or herself. He or she intensely wishes for love and acceptance, and will become very intimate with those few who pass highly stringent tests for safety. Occasionally, the AVD loses control and explodes with rageful indignation.

SASB codes of AVD baseline: <u>RECOIL</u>, <u>WALL</u> <u>OFF</u>, <u>SULK</u>, **BLAME**, *SELF-CONTROL*, *SELF-BLAME*. *Wishes:* To receive **ACTIVE LOVE**, **PROTECT**. *Fears:* To receive **BLAME** plus **IGNORE** (which equals **ATTACK**). *Necessary descriptors:* Defensive withdrawal; wishing for acceptance. *Exclusionary descriptors:* Affective detachment; avoidance of aloneness; instrumental incompetence; consistent failure to perform.

1. Like the DPD and NEG, the AVD began the developmental sequence with appropriate nurturance and social bonding. This good early experience gave him or her a base of attachment that preserved normative wishes for social contact.

2. The AVD-to-be was subject to relentless parental control on behalf of constructing an impressive and memorable social image. The opinions of others outside the family were given high value. It was clear that the AVD should carefully cultivate an admirable social image. Visible flaws were cause for great humiliation and embarrassment, not only of the individual but also of the family. The adult consequence is that the AVD is socialized to perform adequately, but is very concerned about public exposure. There is great concern about impression management, as well as strong self-control and restraint to avoid making mistakes that might be humiliating or embarrassing.

In addition to exhortations to be admirable, there was degrading mockery for any existent failures and shortcomings. If the child was overweight or physically imperfect, this flaw was the subject of continuing cruel family jokes. The adult consequence of the constant derision is that the AVD is self-critical and has a poor self-concept. The internalization of mockery and degradation makes him or her very sensitive to humiliation.

3. The humiliation was often associated with shunning, banishment, exclusion, and enforced autonomy. Because of his or her purported shortcomings, the AVD may frequently have been left at home when the family went on pleasant outings, or may have been banished or singled out in some way during major family gatherings. For example, one AVD who was overweight had to sit on the floor at family gatherings "because she might dent the furniture." Another was frequently locked in a dark basement for misbehaving. The adult consequence of such rejection is social withdrawal in anticipation of rejection and humiliation. Sometimes AVDs attempt to please, but they do it from a distance. The fact that they are well bonded means that they want to be attached and sociable. This wish conflicts with the strong fear of humiliation. As a result, these individuals want social contact, but are unwilling to reach out unless there is massive evidence that it is safe to take the risk.

I believe that the DSM should add angry outbursts to the description of AVD. Occasionally AVDs will identify with their humiliating and rejecting family members, and become quite commanding and judgmental themselves. Usually they restrain this aspect, but clinicians should be aware of AVDs' tendency to become indignant about alleged humiliations.

4. Even though the family ridiculed and rejected the AVD-to-be, the message was also that the family is the main source of support. Loyalty to the family was of paramount importance. Those outside the family were described as likely to reject the AVD. The message was this: "You are flawed and nobody out there will like you. Stay with us, where it is safe." There was no acknowledgment that the dreaded rejection from the outside world was the very pattern orchestrated within the family. One AVD's very critical mother literally wrote the patient out of her will because she would not quit telling family secrets to "that stranger," the therapist.

There is support for the theoretical idea (Kaslow, Wamboldt, Wamboldt, Anderson, & Benjamin, 1989) that the perceived resultant of intense **BLAME** combined with **IGNORE** is **ATTACK**. (See Chapter 3, Figure 3.9.) In other words, degrading and humiliating banishment is experienced as mortal attack. The complement to this intense attack is strong RECOIL and social withdrawal. The AVD's certainty that others are scrutinizing him or her and making unfavorable judgments establishes a distinctly paranoid mode of interaction. The (false) promises of safety at home encourage an uneasy dependency upon intimates.

CONNECTIONS BETWEEN THE INTERPERSONAL HISTORY AND THE SYMPTOMS LISTED IN THE DSM

The "total AVD" shows all the symptoms mentioned in the DSM. Almost all the DSM items describe one or another aspect of the avoidant defense against expected humiliation and rejection. These fears of criticism and rejection are described directly by item 4, as well as by unwillingness to be involved without guarantees of friendship (item 2); avoidance of activities that require social contact (item 1); reticence because of fear of embarrassment (item 3); feelings of inferiority (item 6); and reluctance to try something new out of fear of embarrassment (item 7). The avoidant defense combined with the injunction to be loyal to family severely restricts the number of intimate social contacts (item 5).

INTERPERSONAL SUMMARY OF AVD

The foregoing analysis suggests a succinct interpersonal summary for AVD:

There is intense fear of humiliation and rejection. To avoid expected embarrassment, the AVD withdraws and carefully restrains himself or herself. He or she intensely wishes for love and acceptance, and will become very intimate with those few who pass highly stringent tests for safety. Occasionally, the AVD loses control and explodes with rageful indignation.

The summary is based on the SASB codes of the AVD baseline patterns and wishes. The codes themselves, listed in Table 12.1, provide a shorthand way to identify AVD. The baseline AVD positions are RECOIL, WALL OFF, SULK, **BLAME**, *SELF-CONTROL,* and *SELF-BLAME.* The wishes are to receive **ACTIVE LOVE** and **PROTECT**. The fear is of **BLAME** plus **IGNORE**, and this combination is experienced as intense **ATTACK**.

The rhythm and harmonics of the AVD song are found in the sequences of interpersonal and intrapsychic response that the AVD gives and receives. The "tonic" AVD position consists of RECOIL, WALL OFF, and *SELF-BLAME.* To try to ward off attack or humiliation, the AVD will "swallow" his or her disagreement (SULK) and hold in his or her feelings (*SELF-CONTROL*). The principle of complementarity predicts that the AVD will draw for **BLAME**, **IGNORE**, and **ATTACK** from others. When the AVD occasionally loses control and engages in **BLAME**, others will increase their tendency to reject and ignore him or her. Then the complementary and reactionary attack reinforces the AVD's position of fearful withdrawal. On the other hand, the strong wish for **ACTIVE LOVE** and **PROTECT** lead the AVD to be extremely loyal to the few who pass his or her tests for interpersonal safety. These are the harmonics and rhythms of the AVD song.

Readers who can use the SASB codes will be able to generalize the present analysis to contexts not mentioned here. For example, it is not unusual for patients to complain that their depression is getting worse. Sometimes these complaints are presented to the therapist in a way that is characteristic of AVD. To interpret a complaint about depression in this way, the therapist would need to code the patient's process as he or she describes the depression. An AVD's process with the therapist as he or she complains about symptoms would include the notes of the AVD song. Consider this example:

A patient overdosed one evening on the medicine her doctor had prescribed for her persistent depression. She liked and respected him a lot. She was discovered comatose by a neighbor who wondered why her cat wouldn't stop meowing. The neighbor was the patient's only friend. It turned out that that morning her doctor had wondered aloud whether she had a personality disorder. The patient was deeply humiliated by that idea, but secretly agreed with it. She felt extremely embarrassed, and was convinced that her doctor now knew she was a completely foolish person. The next step, she believed, was that he would kick her out of therapy. It had taken her a long time to trust him, and now she was quite angry that he would reject her. However, she also knew that she would not tell him about her anger. Rather than endure the humiliation of facing him again, she decided to end it all.

The baseline notes of the AVD song are compared to those of the songs of the other Axis II disorders discussed thus far in Table 12.2. A scan of the table shows that the AVD shares with the DPD and NEG the tendency to hostile submission (SULK). The AVD shares a vulnerability to *SELF-BLAME* with the DPD, OCD, and NPD, and also shares the propensity to *SELF-CONTROL* with the OCD. The capacity to have angry outbursts (**BLAME**) is shared with all members of the dramatic, erratic cluster, as well as with the OCD and NEG. The AVD's preference to WALL OFF is straightforward; by contrast, the HPD, ASP, OCD, and NEG mask their inaccessibility by mixing it with friendliness or submission.

The interpersonal *do, re, mi* of Table 12.2 shows exactly how these categories overlap; it also shows how they differ. The descriptions in the tables can help the clinician make the differential diagnoses.

DSM DESCRIPTORS REVISITED

The DSM view of AVD has now been translated into interpersonal language, and the psychosocial learning associated with AVD patterns has been outlined. In

Table 12.2. Comparison of SASB Codes of BPD, NPD, HPD, ASP, DPD, OCD, NEG, and AVD

	BPD	NPD	HPD	ASP	DPD	OCD	NEG	AVD
1. EMANCIPATE								
2. AFFIRM								
3. ACTIVE LOVE	×			×*				
4. PROTECT								
5. CONTROL	×	×	×*	×*		×*		
6. BLAME	×	×	×	×		×	×*	×
7. ATTACK	×	×		×*				
8. IGNORE		×		×		×*		
1. SEPARATE		×		×			×*	
2. DISCLOSE								
3. REACTIVE LOVE			×*					
4. TRUST	×		×*		×			
5. SUBMIT					×	×*	×*	
6. SULK					×		×*	×
7. RECOIL								×
8. WALL OFF			×*	×*		×*	×*	×
1. SELF-EMANCIPATE								
2. SELF-AFFIRM								
3. ACTIVE SELF-LOVE		×*						
4. SELF-PROTECT	×			×*				
5. SELF-CONTROL						×*		×
6. SELF-BLAME		×			×	×		×
7. SELF-ATTACK	×		×*				×*	
8. SELF-NEGLECT	×	×*		×*		×*		

*Indicates that these codes within the same column appear in complex combinations with one another.

this section, the interpersonal analysis of NPD is compared directly to the DSM. DSM-III-R items appear in **bold print**; any changes introduced by the DSM-IV appear in *italics*. (Again, the item numbering used is that of the DSM-IV.) The interpersonal modifiers are underlined. Items from the WISPI (see Chapter 1) appear in CAPITAL LETTERS.

A pervasive pattern of social discomfort, fear of negative evaluation, and timidity, beginning by early adulthood and present in a variety of contexts, as indicated by at least *four* **of the following:**

A pervasive pattern of social discomfort and reticence, low self-esteem, and hypersensitivity to negative evaluation, beginning by early adulthood and present in a variety of contexts, as indicated by at least four of the following:

(1) avoids social or occupational activities that involve significant interpersonal contact, e.g., refuses a promotion that will increase social demands

avoids social or occupational activities that involve significant interpersonal contact because of fears of criticism, disapproval, or rejection

Expects to be degraded and humiliated by people, and so he or she refuses any assignments that might involve increased interpersonal contact and the associated likelihood of mockery, or the possibility that someone might say, "I don't want to deal with this (avoidant) person."

BECAUSE I TEND TO GET EMBARRASSED, I AVOID JOBS AND SOCIAL SITUATIONS WHICH WOULD FORCE ME TO BE MORE WITH PEOPLE.

(2) is unwilling to get involved with people unless certain of being liked

Assumes that people are going to be critical and disapproving until they can pass stringent tests proving the contrary. For example, in therapy, the AVD is withdrawn until it somehow becomes clear that the therapist can be trusted to be protective and nurturant. Expects to be rejected, and so he or she does not even try to join in group activities until and if there are repeated and generous offers of support and nurturance.

I LIKE TO BE "IN ON" THINGS, BUT ALWAYS WAIT TO JOIN UNTIL IT IS REALLY CLEAR THAT OTHERS APPROVE OF ME AND WANT ME.

(3) is reticent in social situations because of a fear of saying something inappropriate or foolish, or of being unable to answer a question

development of intimate relationships is inhibited (despite desire for them) owing to the fear of being foolish and ridiculed, or being exposed and shamed

Keeps quiet and "invisible" in social situations because of the fear that any attention would be degrading or rejecting. Expects that no matter what he or she says, it will be seen as "wrong," and so he or she says nothing.

I AM AFRAID OF APPEARING FOOLISH OR BEING EMBARRASSED, SO I KEEP QUIET AT WORK OR SCHOOL.

(4) is easily hurt by criticism or disapproval

preoccupation with being criticized or rejected in social situations

Expects to be humiliated and degraded, and so he or she has a markedly low threshold for detecting it. For example, if the caregiver is mildly annoyed, the AVD will note it, and feel very badly about himself or herself for doing whatever it was that might have preceded the annoyance. Reacts strongly to subtle cues suggestive of mockery or derision. For example, if someone is slightly disapproving or rejecting, the AVD feels extremely hurt; if he or she loses the struggle for self-control , there is likely to be an outburst of rage.

I AM VERY SENSITIVE TO AND EASILY HURT BY THE SLIGHTEST HINT OF DISAPPROVAL OR BLAME.

(5) has no close friends or confidants (or only one) other than first-degree relatives

has few friends despite the desire to relate to others

For varying reasons, throughout childhood there was interference with normal development of relations with peers, and that pattern continues in adulthood. There may be one very intimate friend, but that is the extent of social contact outside of the immediate family. Trusts only family members, or one or two intimate friends with whom there is a very intense, but not necessarily sexual, relationship.

ALTHOUGH I WOULD LIKE TO HAVE MORE GOOD FRIENDS, I HAVE VERY FEW OUTSIDE OF THE FAMILY; IT TAKES A VERY LONG TIME BEFORE I FEEL SAFE ENOUGH TO OPEN UP.

(6) fears being embarrassed by blushing, crying, or showing signs of anxiety in front of other people

belief that one is socially inept, personally unappealing, or inferior to others

Expects to be degraded or humiliated, and is very anxious about the possibility that he or she will react with blushing or crying. Expects to be mocked and seen as socially unacceptable.

I BLUSH OR CRY EASILY, AND FIND THIS SO EMBARRASSING THAT I HOLD BACK IN SOCIAL SITUATIONS.

(7) exaggerates the potential difficulties, physical dangers, or risks involved in doing something ordinary but outside his or her usual routine, e.g., may cancel social plans because [he or] she anticipates being exhausted by the effort of getting there

is unusually reluctant about taking personal risks or engaging in any new activities because they may prove embarrassing

Is so afraid of social derogation that he or she can become sick with anxiety about an upcoming social event. Marginal somatic symptoms or other poorly documented problems can become the reason for avoiding the event.

I MAY BE OVERLY CAUTIOUS, BUT I DON'T OFTEN TRY NEW SITUATIONS BECAUSE SOMETHING UNEXPECTED AND EMBARRASSING MIGHT HAPPEN.

occasionally has outbursts of indignant rage over alleged humiliation or slights [I recommend adding to DSM]

Full of a "ball of anger" about the rejection and humiliation, the AVD constantly restrains the impulse to strike back with an angry attack. If the anger is unleashed, it is delivered with great indignation at and rejection of the offender.

I HAVE MOMENTS WHEN I AM AFRAID OF LOSING CONTROL OF THE ANGER I KEEP HIDDEN WITHIN ME.

NECESSARY AND EXCLUSIONARY CRITERIA

The *necessary* conditions for AVD are defensive withdrawal out of fear of humiliation, attack, and rejection, and the wish for acceptance. *Exclusionary* criteria for AVD include the affective detachment of the SOI and the desperate attempts of the DPD or BPD to avoid aloneness. The AVD is usually competent at work, unlike the BPD, who sabotages success, and unlike the DPD, who is instrumentally inadequate.

The differential diagnosis between AVD and Social Phobia can be made interpersonally by noting whathappens in the withdrawn state. The social phobic is more likely to be accompanied by a powerful significant other person. He or she and the spouse both unhappily stay away from social events because of the phobic symptoms. By contrast, the AVD, who is less likely to be married, is content (even relieved) to stay home by himself or herself.

The AVD can be distinguished from the NEG by his or her ability to perform adequately. Both the NEG and the AVD were nurtured initially, and both were subjected to demands and harsh punishments. Both react with autonomy (and both are vulnerable to depression). A crucial difference is that the target of the demands and punishments for the NEG was work performance, whereas the targets for the AVD were social imagery and acceptability. The consequence is that the work performance of the NEG is damaged, while the ability to engage socially is fractured in the AVD.

CASE ILLUSTRATIONS

Case 1

This 35-year-old single woman was hospitalized for suicidality, and had a history of somatic complications, some of which required surgery. She had been in psychotherapy for 6 years. The present crisis followed the completely unexpected suicide of her only close friend, a woman who worked with her on a night shift. Unresponsive to antidepressants prescribed for her vegetative signs, she also had occasional panic attacks.

The patient felt that she needed to be more open to develop a support group of friends. Yet she was afraid to approach others out of a fear of humiliation and rejection. She was convinced people would think she was not good enough, and she took a very long time to trust anyone. She felt humiliated by the fact that students were present during the consultative interview.

The patient was extremely pleased that one result of this hospitalization was increased "attention" from her mother, even though their relationship was saturated with control and humiliation. The patient had not had opportunities for normal amounts of peer play. The family moved often, always "trying to find something better." Because of the constant uprooting, the patient had few friends and felt quite lonely throughout childhood.

The oldest of four, the patient began mothering her siblings when she was about 8 years old. The reason was that the mother went back to college to study plant pathology. The mother was either studying or working most of the time. The patient regularly cleaned, cooked, looked after the little ones, and helped her mother study. Her mother would ask her to read lists of concepts the mother was supposed to memorize. As the patient read the lists, the mother would criticize her pronunciation. The fancy words were difficult for the 8-year-old, and try as she might, she was "not good enough."

The mother also criticized the father for not making enough money. The mother was upset that the family could not "keep up with the Joneses." Frequently the mother would tell the patient and others in the family to "drop dead." The patient felt guilty disclosing this information to the interviewer, because the mother warned everyone not to discuss family business with outsiders. The patient said that she herself felt a "ball of anger" within her. Asked whether she could link the anger to a wish for control or for distance, she quickly answered, "Distance; it is safer." Underneath the anger was fear, even panic at the thought of being vulnerable to others' disapproval.

The patient met five of the DSM criteria for AVD. She was easily hurt by criticism or disapproval; for example, following the consultative interview, she was certain that she had been humiliated by the presence of students (item 4). She had only one close friend outside the family (item 5). The patient was unwilling to become involved with people during her hospitalization and elsewhere unless she was certain of being liked (item 2). She was generally reticent in social situations because of fear of saying something inappropriate or foolish (item 3). The patient worked a night shift to reduce social demands of her job (item 1).

The case is also described by the SASB interpersonal codes (Table 12.1). The patient's lifestyle was characterized by WALL OFF and RECOIL. Her report that she was humiliated by the interviewer can be described by SULK and BLAME. She did not express her inner "ball of anger" (*SELF-CONTROL*). Fearing BLAME and IGNORE, she was insecure about herself (*SELF-BLAME*). She wished to have friends who would provide ACTIVE LOVE and PROTECT. Her defensive withdrawal and wish for acceptance fulfilled the necessary conditions for AVD. She did not meet any of the exclusionary conditions: affective detachment, avoidance of aloneness, instrumental incompetence, or consistent failure to perform.

The pathogenic hypotheses in Table 12.1 were confirmed. The patient was comfortable with the nurturance and attention she received up to the time the mother went back to school. Concern with image in the community was the substance of the parental arguments about money. The mother's wish to better their station in life forced them to move repeatedly. Throughout, she mocked her husband and the children to exhort them to do better. The patient had to perform household duties so that the mother could go out in the world and achieve upward mobility in a somewhat exotic discipline. Unfortunately, the mother mocked the patient's efforts to comply by doing housework and helping with the mother's studies. The patient and her siblings were rejected by the mother's wish that they "drop dead." The frequent moves and excessive household duties interfered with peer contact, and thus interfered with the patient's social development. Strong injunctions against discussing important things with "strangers" encouraged her somewhat paranoid view of the world.

Case 2

This 18-year-old unmarried college student had made several overdose attempts since age 16. Following a period of significant weight loss and escalating vegetative signs, she made the present suicide attempt. She explained that she needed to "get out of everybody's hair."

She was attending college on an athletic scholarship, excelling in track and field events. When the patient went to college, she expected to be accepted and popular because she was very good in sports; unfortunately, that did not happen. The patient disliked traveling with the team because of the need to share rooms for sleeping and because she felt that nobody cared about her. Her response to the perceived rejection was to withdraw and refuse to talk to team members. Sometimes at practice or at meets, she would break down crying, and this embarrassed her greatly. She wanted very much to be included, and realized that her withdrawal only increased the alienation from her peers. Nonetheless, she held to her philosophy: "I want people to come to me so that I'm sure they want to be with me." She did not tell others when she was upset: "I just wait and see if anybody cares." During the team travel preceding the most recent overdose, the patient had been especially angry about being "left out." She said, "The whole team was against me." She expected that her teammates' reaction to her suicidal attempt would be to know that she had been very upset, and to realize that they did not "hear her."

At home, there was chronic parental battling about sex, money, and the patient. At age 16, the patient decided to move out of the home to stay with her best (and only close) friend. This resulted in uproar within the family, and the parents entered counseling. Because things got better, the patient agreed to return home; unfortunately, the improvement was short-lived, and the parental fighting resumed. Usually the father was mad that the patient was not pushing hard enough in sports, or that she was not studying hard enough. Despite the perception that her mother was much closer to her brother, the patient felt that her mother defended her. The patient would often stand at the top of the stairs to listen to the parental fights. She would make brief excursions downstairs to try to stop them. When she appeared, her father would chase her, but *stop at the bottom of the stairs*. She would then safely beat a retreat back upstairs.

The patient felt that her parents and coaches took the credit for her excellent performance in track and in academics. Her father claimed that if he had not forced her to practice, she would not have been so good. His view meant that if she did well, the credit belonged to her father; if she did poorly, the credit was hers. It was as if she could only find herself by losing herself. She believed that some people liked her *because* she was depressed. There was no point in getting better, she observed, because if she were to get better she would receive no attention at all.

The patient was very angry that her mother and father often fought bitterly, and then would show up at sporting events "all lovey-dovey." This front led friends and teachers to tell the patient how wonderfully supportive her family was. In reality, her parents repeatedly told her that she was selfish and spoiled, and thought only of herself. She tried to escape from these painful encounters by staying in her room. However, her parents objected to her withdrawal; they demanded that she be friendly with the family. She was both "chased away" and given the mandate to stay close.

This patient met four of the criteria for the diagnosis of AVD. She was preoccupied with being criticized or rejected in social situations (item 4). She had only one close friend other than first-degree relatives (item 5). She was unwilling to get involved with people unless she was certain of being liked (item 2).

She felt personally inept because of her tendency to cry in front of other team members (item 6).

The interpersonal descriptors for AVD also applied well to this person. She feared humiliation (BLAME) and rejection (IGNORE). She wanted to be loved (ACTIVE LOVE) and included (PROTECT). She was insecure (SELF-BLAME), and showed a baseline position of defensive withdrawal (RECOIL, WALL OFF), SULKing, and SELF-CONTROL. Her BLAME of team members and of her parents was overt; however, she was willing to become intimate with a few selected safe persons. Her pattern of defensive avoidance and wish for acceptance provided the necessary conditions for AVD. She did not show any of the exclusionary attributes listed in Table 12.1: She was intensely attached to her family, and so her alienation was not antisocial; she could tolerate aloneness, so she did not have HPD or BPD; DPD was ruled out by her instrumental competence; and NEG was unlikely because of her high levels of performance.

This woman had experienced some of the pathogenic features sketched in Table 12.1. She did receive nurturance and support for her athletic and academic skills. The family also had a great investment in presenting a splendid image to the community; the patient was degraded and mocked for allegedly not working hard enough at track or school, and for being "selfish and spoiled." She was further enjoined to show loyalty to the family, although there was not much emphasis on the dangers posed by outsiders. One hypothesis was not supported: Her avoidant pattern was not forced by the predicted punitive dismissals. Rather, the patient actively elected to withdraw to escape the parental battlefield. The parental fighting, however, happened to invoke a geographic rule that encouraged the AVD pattern of involvement from a distance: The parents fought downstairs within earshot while upstairs provided a safe haven. This unusual rule is compatible with AVD patterns. As the patient stood in the wings, she was intimately involved with what was going on at center stage. When she withdrew from the household at age 16, she forced her parents into therapy. This showed that her withdrawal was self-protective and powerful. Unfortunately, her peer group did not react to her withdrawal in the same way. Her pattern of keeping a distance while maintaining her focus on "center stage" was no longer adaptive.

EXPECTABLE TRANSFERENCE REACTIONS AND TREATMENT IMPLICATIONS

Transference Reactions

The prototypic AVD is reluctant to disclose much about himself or herself. Laboring under a poor self-concept, the AVD will be very cautious and will worry about whether the therapist approves of what he or she says or does. There is a tendency to hold things in, and to try to provide whatever he or she thinks the therapist wants to hear. Hypersensitive to perceived degradation and attack, the AVD will easily be injured by the therapist. Wanting nurturance intensely, the AVD is nonetheless very likely to feel degraded or put down by any therapist suggestions (e.g., "Don't you think I know to do *that*?"). The AVD will not tell the therapist that he or she feels hurt by the efforts to help. The injury may fester until the AVD "boils over" and abruptly quits therapy. If the therapist succeeds in passing the "safety test," the AVD will create a very intense and loyal therapy relationship. There is a danger that the therapist will serve well enough as the AVD's "significant other," and that social learning will thus be retarded. The therapist must figure out how to let the therapy relationship serve as a base for learning without becoming "interpersonal methadone."

Treatment Implications: The Five Categories of Correct Response

Facilitating Collaboration

The AVD's pattern is an especially intense version of the "generic" patient position. He or she wants to be accepted and loved, and "holds back" because of poor self-concept and fears of humiliation. The "generic" therapist position addresses this "generic" patient position. The AVD responds well to generous doses of "classical" therapist behaviors: accurate empathy and warm support. These must be delivered without a hint of judgmentalism or rejection. Gradually, as the AVD shares intimacies and feelings of inadequacy or guilt and shame, the therapist can provide evidence of safe haven. The therapist's benign and non-judgmental acceptance of the AVD helps the AVD begin to accept himself or herself. As the therapy relationship strengthens, the patient can begin to explore his or her patterns.

The AVD is likely to feel disloyal if he or she talks about the humiliations and abuses that were experienced in the family of origin. This belief will inhibit full participation in therapy. The family itself is likely to reinforce this reluctance by degrading or mocking the therapist, the therapy, and the patient's choice to participate. As noted earlier, one AVD's mother literally wrote the patient out of her will for refusing to quit therapy. Such pressures naturally increase the AVD's suspicions of the therapist and the therapy, and make withdrawal likely. The best antidote to this fearful attitude is for the therapist to maintain warm understanding and support.

The need for therapist warmth and protectiveness cannot be overstated for work with AVDs. The sensitivity of these patients was dramatically illustrated by the reaction of an AVD to a "confrontation" offered by a psychiatry resident I invited to sit in on the case. I had worked with the AVD for over a year to help her become comfortable enough to replace self-accusation with a bit of compassion for herself. The main arena was her relationship with her devoted but relentlessly critical mother. Just as she started to explore the possibility that her mother might be excessively critical and demanding, the resident said, "But did you ever think about your mother's point of view?" The AVD dissolved into tears and silence. After the session, I explained to the resident that his observation might have been helpful in another context, but that it was not in this one. I asked him to acknowledge to the AVD that his comment had been made without adequate familiarity with the case; I wanted him to tell her that she was taking an important step in the task of exploring her relationship with her mother. The resident refused to do this, and so I asked him not to continue with the case. I explained to the patient why he would not attend a second session. Nonetheless, it was a full 2 years before she was again able even to *mention* her mother in psychotherapy.

Facilitating Pattern Recognition

The therapist must provide uncritical support for the AVD. Helping him or her develop trust in the therapist is a vital first step. However, the therapist must also be sure that his or her giving of support does not become an end in itself. The AVD already knows how to relate to a select few people, and the therapist may simply become one of them. If this happens, the baseline avoidant pattern remains untouched. General reconstructive change will come only if the patient can learn to appreciate the impact of his or her patterns *in a way that helps him or her decide to change.*

Couples therapy can help an AVD learn about patterns and become interested in changing them. An AVD's marital or quasi-marital relationship is likely to assume a triangular form. For example, a single AVD may be "the third wheel" of a marital couple and become secretly sexually involved with one member of the couple. An AVD may have an intimate nonsexual friendship with someone who is known to be sexually involved with someone else. A married AVD may be involved in a secret extramarital affair. An AVD may have sexual intimacy with a partner who is fanatically devoted to something else—alcohol or work, for example. An AVD may develop a liaison with a heterosexual partner who turns out to be bisexual. These triangular patterns provide intimacy and assure interpersonal distance. The triangulation also provides some protection from public humiliation over rejection. For example, if a dyadic liaison within a triangle fails, there is little humiliation; everyone knows that such arrangements are precarious. This makes it easy for the AVD to withdraw.

Couples therapy may be offered initially with the more conventional side of the triangle (e.g., the AVD and spouse; the AVD and the person who the patient says is the wiser choice). The couples therapy can begin by addressing the AVD's perceived rejection by the key partner. The couples therapist can make suggestions that may improve the rejecting partner's willingness to be closer. For example, the AVD may have "ordered the spouse around" because of intense fear of being forgotten or betrayed. If the AVD can learn better ways of asking for help or reassurance, the significant other may become less likely to withdraw. For example, an AVD wife may demand that her husband pick up some groceries for dinner on his way home from work; the oppositional husband may react by being 3 hours late getting home that night. Assertiveness training can show the AVD wife how to disclose her need without "bearing down" on her husband. Better collaboration within the couple can result.

Similar interventions can be made in any of the usual marital problem areas: allocation of money, sex, time, recreational choices, household duties (e.g., cleaning, cooking, and child care), bill paying, and so on. The AVD and his or her partner need to learn that a collaborative attitude leads to better solutions. Collaboration works better than do the patterns of blaming, sulky compliance, attack, or withdrawal.

If the AVD is not involved in a relationship that offers opportunities for couples work, it is appropriate to help him or her achieve one. One AVD, who was totally isolated from contact with everyone but her mother and her father, developed her own best treatment plan: She bought a puppy, and then spent many sessions discussing the details of her interactions with the puppy. With him, she began to learn about the interface among positions of dominance, submission, contact comfort, oppositionalism, and needs for separate territory. As he matured, the dog brought her into contact with neighbors when she took him for walks. On these excursions she would proudly discuss his charms and transgressions. After a while, she began to be invited to and attend some neighborhood gatherings; eventually she hosted her own. She developed friendships with a few female friends, and finally dared to discuss her terror of dating men. Unfortunately, circumstances dictated that she move to another city and lose her psychological health care benefits. I do not know whether she succeeded in the next steps of socialization.

Blocking Maladaptive Patterns

In couples therapy with an AVD and his or her partner, it is vital that the therapist protect each partner from unrestrained "trashing." The therapist should block attempts to humiliate, and should make sure that the therapy setting is safe for learning new constructive patterns. It is not necessary and may even be destructive for the AVD to "confess" any former triangular liaisons. On the other hand, it is not appropriate for the AVD to work on improving the relationship while he or she secretly continues a triangular arrangement with someone else. The AVD may be very interested in maintaining a secret liaison because it offers a "fall-back" position in case the efforts with the key partner do not work out. The therapist needs to be clear that such an arrangement enables the chief complaint, the AVD pattern. Maintaining a secret liaison during couples therapy is comparable to trying to work with alcohol dependence while the patient is still using alcohol. Clinical wisdom dictates that the chances of success are slim under these circumstances.

Theoretically, the AVD patterns may be blocked by careful implementation of such basic behavioral interventions as desensitization to avoided social situations, and successive approximations to more sociability. Unfortunately, attempts to teach dating behaviors by a standard sequence involving progressive approximations to dating are likely to fail with an AVD. The patient's patterns are deeply rooted in unconscious loyalty to the family mandates that the AVD remain shunned and isolated. After the AVD learns in individual psychotherapy why he or she hides in the margins of interaction, he or she may become ready to explore "coming out." Eventually the AVD may reach a condition wherein he or she can benefit from straightforward behavioral interventions.

With some hesitancy, I disclose that I have the impression that AVDs like to become therapists. Perhaps this happens because a therapist has access to intimacy from a socially sanctioned safe distance. Of course, when patients attack and degrade, the AVD therapist is in a difficult spot, and becomes vulnerable to reacting with overcontrol or inappropriately invoking classical rules of therapist "distance." Assumption of the therapist role does not help an AVD change his or her patterns for the better. The therapist role sanctions the AVD patterns of highly controlled intimacy backed by "safe" distance. This trend for AVDs to become therapists could be blocked by wider acceptance of the norm that therapists undergo their own intensive psychotherapies.

Strengthening the Will to Give Up Maladaptive Patterns

The AVD's most difficult task, like that of most other personality-disordered individuals, is to decide to sacrifice the benefits of the ongoing patterns and accept the risk of developing new ones. The safety in AVD withdrawal, and the terror of venturing outward, make this step very difficult. It is not enough for the AVD to understand that he or she was humiliated for alleged basic flaws and was encouraged to stay loyal to abusive parents or siblings. Such insight does not in itself provide reassurance adequate to persuade the AVD to become more open and to risk criticism or rejection. Understanding alone is about as useful to the AVD as trying to talk a nonswimmer who nearly drowned in a shipwreck into becoming a Navy SEAL. On the other hand, the AVD can leave the protection of isolation to learn new patterns gradually if there is much reassurance in a context of competent, protective instruction.

Facilitating New Learning

Safe group therapies, meaning therapies wherein the therapist blocks "trashing" or "dumping," have considerable potential for helping the AVD learn new patterns. Controlled group therapy can provide a setting where the AVD can remain walled off until he or she feels it is safe to participate. In the context of the secure base provided by individual therapy, new skills can be developed in the group. An AVD who learns that the group can accept flaws may be able to accept himself or herself. Normal social development can follow.

PART FOUR

DSM CLUSTER A, THE ODD, ECCENTRIC GROUP

13

Paranoid Personality Disorder

"Just because you're paranoid doesn't mean everybody's not out to get you."

REVIEW OF THE LITERATURE

> Herr Senatsprasident Dr. Schreber shows no signs of confusion or of psychical inhibition, nor is his intelligence noticeably impaired. His mind is collected, his memory is excellent, he has at his disposal a very considerable store of knowledge . . . and an observer who was uninstructed upon his general condition would scarcely notice anything peculiar in this direction. (A Dr. Weber who examined Schreber, quoted by Freud, 1911/1959, p. 393)

Freud's best-known exposition of his theory of paranoia was based on the case of Dr. Schreber. Schreber was a distinguished jurist with no outward signs of disorder (as the quotation above indicates), and he had an interest in following events in the worlds of politics, science, and art. Nonetheless, Schreber suffered from delusions that he was dead and decomposing; that his body was being handled in all kinds of revolting ways; that he was the plaything of devils; and that he was being persecuted and injured by his former physician, Flechsig, whom he called a "soul-murderer."

Schreber was not only paranoid, meaning that he had a pervasive fear of harm; he also showed a form of thought disorder often found in "dementia praecox." Nonetheless, Freud proposed that paranoia "should be maintained as an independent clinical type, however frequently the picture it presents may be complicated by the presence of schizophrenic features" (1911/1959, p. 463). The distinction between paranoia and schizophrenia has been retained and expanded by the DSM, which describes three forms of paranoia. On Axis I there is (1) Delusional (Paranoid) Disorder and (2) Schizophrenia, Paranoid Type. On Axis II there is (3) PAR.[1] As usual, Axis II refers to a long-standing interactive style characteristic of the person, whereas the Axis I descriptions are more sharply focused on symptoms. If the patient's paranoia includes predominant symptoms of thought disorder, then an Axis I label is appropriate, according to DSM-III-R.

---

[1] For the sake of clarity and of consistency throughout the book, I use the abbreviation of "PAR" to refer to Axis II Paranoid Personality Disorder (or a person with this diagnosis) only.

In practice, there is substantial overlap or covariance between symptoms of paranoia as it is described on Axis I and PAR as described by Axis II. It is difficult to find a PAR who does not also have delusions approximating those described for the Axis I Delusional (Paranoid) Disorder: "nonbizarre delusion(s) (i.e., involving situations that occur in real life . . . ," characterized as "grandiose," "jealous," "persecutory," "somatic," or "unspecified" (American Psychiatric Association, 1987, pp. 202–203).

Freud proposed that paranoia be distinguished from schizophrenia, or dementia praecox (premature senility), on the basis of the time at which the developmental process goes awry. Schizophrenia (i.e., the hallucinatory features of Schreber's illness) was seen by Freud as stemming from an earlier fixation than the paranoia (Freud, 1911/1959, p. 464). His dynamic interpretation of paranoia was that it is the consequence of defenses against ego-alien homosexual wishes. Anticipating criticism for this idea, Freud commented:

> Paranoia is a disorder in which a sexual etiology is by no means obvious; on the contrary, the strikingly prominent features in the causation of paranoia, especially among males, are social humiliations and slights. But if we go into the matter only a little more deeply, we shall be able to see that the really operative factor in these social injuries lies in the part played in them by the homosexual components of affective life. (1911/1959, p. 445)

Freud was firm in his conviction, and later published a second case (1915/1959, pp. 150–161) to support his theory about the homosexual origin of paranoia. He applied it to a woman whose illness began in the midst of a heterosexual encounter.

In explaining the connection between paranoia and homosexuality, Freud suggested that the libido begins with the autoerotic choice of one's own body. The second stage involves choice of some person other than the self, but of one with similar genitals. The final stage is heterosexual object choice. Freud named the in-between stage "narcissism," and believed that a homosexual object choice represents a fixation at this stage (1911/1959, p. 446). Freud argued that the struggle to resist homosexual impulses accounts for major features of paranoia, including delusions of persecution, erotomania, jealousy, and megalomania.

Freud argued (1911/1959, pp. 448–449) that the defense of projection is central in delusions of *persecution* in paranoia. Starting with forbidden feelings of sexual attraction, there is a transformation of the feeling 'I love him' to 'I hate him.' Then the internal perceptions or feelings ('I hate him') are replaced by external perceptions ('He hates and persecutes me'). This hatred justifies hating in return. "And thus, the unconscious feeling, which is in fact the motive force, makes its appearance as though it were the consequence of an external perception: 'I do not *love* him—I *hate* him, because HE PERSECUTES ME.'" *Erotomania* is explained by this sequence: "'I do not love *him*—I love *her*. I notice that she loves me. I do not love *him*—I love *her*, because SHE LOVES ME.'"

Freud examined "alcoholic delusions of *jealousy*," starting with this observation: "We know that drink removes inhibitions and undoes the work of sublimation" (p. 450). Disappointment over a woman frequently drives a man to drink, Freud said. A man spends much time with male drinking companions who "afford him the emotional satisfaction that he has failed to get from his wife at home." Finding himself attracted to these men, the jealous alcoholic reasons: "'It is not *I* who love the man—*she* loves him', and he suspects the women in relation to all the men whom he himself is tempted to love." Delusions of jealousy in women "are exactly analogous" (p. 450), Freud insisted.

The *megalomania* characteristic of paranoia is the result of sexual overestimation of the ego (p. 451), and is also a defense against homosexuality. This time the idea is 'I do not love at all—I do not love any one.' Having no other place to go, the libido fixes on the ego and results in the same overestimation of the ego that normally one reserves for one's lover. Megalomania directly leads to the PAR's *detachment* from others. Schreber, for example, thought that the world had ended, and that other people had become "cursory contraptions."

Although Freud did not seem particularly prejudiced against homosexuals,[2] his analysis of paranoia has been used to argue that homosexuality is an illness. It is not unusual to find paranoid aspects in the personality of the homosexual, but there are other explanations. The most parsimonious alternative explanation is that homosexuals are greatly denigrated. If a homosexual was not paranoid to begin with, he or she has many opportunities to learn to be so. Colby (1977) has argued that paranoia in gays disproves rather than proves Freud's interpretation. The reasoning is that if paranoia is based on resistance to forbidden wishes, how can people who explicitly embrace homosexual impulses show symptoms that stem from defenses against them?

Freud's theory of paranoia is controversial. Again, the authors of the DSM chose to be atheoretical, and did not mark any connection between paranoia and homosexuality. After a well-publicized battle with gay rights activists, the American Psychiatric Association took a vote that established that homosexuality is not an illness (Spitzer, Williams, & Skodol, 1980, p. 152). In the DSM-III, homosexuality could only be mentioned if the patient was uncomfortable with his or her choice, and the label provided was Ego-Dystonic Homosexuality. In the DSM-III-R and DSM-IV, homosexuality appeared as a residual category without a specific label. It can be called Sexual Disorder Not Otherwise Specified (NOS) if there is "persistent and marked distress about one's sexual orientation" (American Psychiatric Association, 1987, p. 296).

Sexual and professional politics aside, the present approach is to SASB-code the interpersonal patterns that are characteristic of PAR and to use SASB principles to infer the prototypic developmental history. This history, superimposed on constitutional predisposition, predicts PAR whether the person is homosexual

---

[2]He once wrote a note to the distressed mother of a homosexual, reassuring her that everyone is bisexual. In the Schreber case, Freud commented: "Generally speaking, every human being oscillates all through his life between heterosexual and homosexual feelings, and any frustration or disappointment in the one direction is apt to drive him over into the other" (p. 428). And then, in a rarely quoted passage, Freud speculated further on the reason for Schreber's breakdown at age 51: ". . . for men as well as women are subject to a 'climacteric' and to the special susceptibility to disease which goes along with it" (p. 430).

or heterosexual, male or female. PAR is maintained by the dimensionality of the interpersonal transactions, regardless of the body parts that may be involved in sexual behavior.

A compelling description of how the social milieu can maintain or even intensify paranoid symptoms was offered by Lemert (1962). Data were obtained by exhaustive interviewing with families, work associates, employers, attorneys, police, physicians, public officials, and others. The subjects were PARs engaged as active petitioners in commitment proceedings, or already hospitalized. Lemert noted succinctly that a PAR is seen by others as having these characteristics:

1. A disregard for the values and norms of the primary group, revealed by giving priority to verbally definable values over those which are implicit, a lack of loyalty in return for confidences, and victimizing and intimidating persons in positions of weakness.
2. A disregard for the implicit structure of groups, revealed by presuming to privileges not accorded him, and the threat or actual resort to formal means for achieving his goals. (p. 6)

The organizational group response to the PAR increases the symptoms, because he or she is seen as an "ambiguous figure whose behavior is uncertain, who . . . can't be trusted because he threatens to expose informal power structures" (p. 6). The group behaviors are described in terms of the PAR's experience:

1. The spurious quality of the interaction between others and himself or between others interacting in his presence;
2. The overt avoidance of himself by others;
3. The structured exclusion of himself from interaction. (p. 6)

Lemert noted that a PAR is seen as "difficult" or "ornery," and that this perception is eventually transformed to "dangerous." People conspire to humor, evade, exclude, isolate, encapsulate, and manipulate the PAR in ways that Lemert called "morally invidious" (p. 9) and that make it difficult for the PAR to cope.

Concomitant with the magnified visibility of the paranoid individual, come distortions of his image, most pronounced in the inner coterie of exclusionists. His size, physical strength, cunning, and anecdotes of his outrages are exaggerated, with a central thematic emphasis on the fact that he is dangerous. . . . Our interpretation of this . . . is that the imputed dangerousness of the paranoid individual does not come from physical fear but from the organizational threat he presents and the need to justify collective action against him. (p. 13)

If paranoia becomes a way of life for some people, it is also true that the difficult person with grandiose and persecutory ideas may fulfill certain marginal functions in organizations and communities. One is the scapegoat function, being made the subject of humorous by-play or conjectural gossip as people "wonder what he will be up to next." In his scapegoat role, the person may help integrate primary groups within larger organizations by directing aggressions and blame towards him and thus strengthening feelings of homogeneity and consensus of group members. (p. 17)

The Lemert study offers a splendid prototype for understanding how personality disorders that begin early in development can be maintained or exacerbated by the family and community during adulthood.

DSM DEFINITION OF THE DISORDER

The DSM definition provides the starting point for the analysis. The DSM specifies that the diagnosis of PAR can be made if an individual meets five of the criteria. DSM-III-R items appear in **bold print,** and any changes introduced by the DSM-IV appear in *italics.* (As in several earlier chapters, the item numbering used here is that of the DSM-IV. Original numbers in the DSM-III-R appear after **bold** items, in brackets.)

A pervasive and unwarranted tendency, beginning by early adulthood and present in a variety of contexts, to interpret the actions of people as deliberately demeaning or threatening, as indicated by at least *four* **of the following:**

(1) expects, without sufficient basis, to be exploited or harmed by others [item 1 in DSM-III-R]

(2) questions, without justification, the loyalty or trustworthiness of friends or associates [item 2 in DSM-III-R]

(3) is reluctant to confide in others because of unwarranted fear that the information will be used against him or her [item 5 in DSM-III-R]

(4) reads hidden meanings or threatening meanings into benign remarks or events, e.g., suspects that a neighbor put out trash early to annoy him [or her] [item 3 in DSM-III-R]

(5) bears grudges or is unforgiving of insults or slights [item 4 in DSM-III-R]

tendency to bear grudges persistently, i.e., to be unforgiving of insults, injuries, or slights

(6) is easily slighted and quick to react with anger or to counterattack [item 6 in DSM-III-R]

Perceives attacks on his or her character or reputation that are not apparent to others, and is quick to react with anger or to counterattack

(7) questions, without justification, fidelity of spouse or sexual partner [item 7 in DSM-III-R]

recurrent suspicions, without justification, regarding fidelity of spouse or sexual partner

pride in rationality [DSM-III item omitted from DSM-III-R and DSM-IV; I recommend restoring]

Morey (1988) reported that 22.0% of a sample of 291 outpatients being treated for personality disorder qualified for the PAR label. There was substantial overlap with BPD (48.4%), AVD (48.4%), and NPD (35.9%). Morey's straightforward and important study demonstrates that, like many of the other disorders, PAR overlaps substantially with the other disorders. The overlap is not confined to patterns seen as "odd" or "eccentric."

PATHOGENIC HYPOTHESES

The method of using the SASB model to develop pathogenic hypotheses was sketched in Chapter 5. Four main features of the developmental history have been identified specifically to account for each of the PAR symptoms listed in the DSM. A summary of the hypotheses linking interpersonal history to interpersonal patterns characteristic of the disorder appears in Table 13.1. A fuller discussion of these hypotheses is provided here.

   1. There was sadistic, degrading, controlling parenting. Usually an abused child himself or herself, the parent of the PAR was undeniably cruel as he or she enacted an extraordinarily harsh idea of the proper role of a parent. The parental attack on the PAR-to-be was unlike the hostility arising from the chaotic modes likely to be found in the histories of the BPD and ASP. The parental hostility toward the child was likely to be stone-cold sober, and implemented with righteous indignation. The message was that the child was fundamentally bad or evil, required containment, and deserved retribution. The cruel punish-

Table 13.1. Interpersonal Summary of PAR

History	Consequences of history
1. Sadistic **ATTACK, BLAME, CONTROL**; punished for telling family secrets	1. Expects **ATTACK**, and assumes a complementary baseline of hateful withdrawal (RECOIL), nondisclosure (WALL OFF), and *SELF-CONTROL* Identifies with parent to **CONTROL**, degrade (**BLAME**), and abuse (**ATTACK**) others; strong family loyalty
2. Harsh punishment (**ATTACK**) for dependency (TRUST); attacked when accidentally hurt	2. Fierce independence (SEPARATE) Avoids intimacy unless partner can be **CONTROL**led
3. Overt and covert invidious comparisons (**BLAME**); grudges were long-lasting	3. Sensitive to exclusions and slights (**BLAME** plus **IGNORE**); carries grudges
4. Rewarded for circumscribed competence (**CONTROL**) while staying "out of the way" (WALL OFF)	4. Independent (SEPARATE), competent at tasks (CONTROL), but very withdrawn interpersonally (WALL OFF)

   Summary: There is fear that others will attack to hurt or blame. The wish is that others will affirm and understand. If affirmation fails, the hope is that others will either leave the PAR alone or submit. The baseline position is to wall off, stay separate, and tightly control the self. Angry withdrawal is easily elicited. If threatened, the PAR may attack to countercontrol or gain distance.
   SASB codes of PAR baseline: **CONTROL, BLAME, ATTACK**, RECOIL, WALL OFF, SEPARATE, and *SELF-CONTROL*. *Wishes:* To receive **AFFIRM**. If that fails, others should **EMANCIPATE** or SUBMIT. *Fears:* To receive **ATTACK, BLAME**. *Necessary descriptors:* Perception of intent to harm when it is not there. *Exclusionary descriptors:* Worry about abandonment; deference to authority.

ment was presented as totally justified, and was administered in a "rational" and "proper" manner. The severe shakings and blows with whips, belts, switches, hairbrushes, or fists were intense and repeated many times. The parent was careful to administer the punishments in ways and in "a place where the kid won't go around showing it." A sense of family pride was nourished. The PAR-to-be was admonished to be loyal to the family, not to share family "business" with outsiders.

It is of more than passing interest that Schreber's father was an esteemed physician who wrote the definitive pediatrics text of his time. Schreber's father advised parents to use incredibly cruel methods of discipline. Diabolical devices were recommended for keeping the child from masturbating or performing other unseemly acts.

The adult consequence of such harsh upbringing is that the PAR expects attack and abuse even from those close to him or her. His or her baseline position is one of fearful and hateful recoil, nondisclosure, and mistrust. The fearfulness and withdrawal are complementary to the abuse, but they also represent identification with the parents. It seems that the fearfulness of PAR is easily imitated by successive generations.[3] The parental control is likewise internalized: The PAR strongly restrains himself or herself to guard against the unexpected. The PAR also identifies with the parent's transitive hostile behaviors. He or she can be obnoxiously controlling, self-righteously judgmental, and quite willing to abuse others.

2. The PAR-to-be's abuse began in early infancy. The baby was handled harshly even at the best moments, and was beaten for crying. This was an ineffective intervention that attributed to the infant far more willfulness and ability for cognitive processing than reality warranted. The parent of the future PAR saw the infant as a "little adult" who cried to accuse the parent of doing a bad job. The crying was thought to be a command that something be done. The parent "reacted" to this perception with harsh punishment of the infant. Such inappropriate attributions to the infant or child resulted in bizarre short-circuiting of normal parenting mechanisms. If the child fell and hurt himself or herself, the parent would hit rather than comfort the child. If the child got into a scrape in the neighborhood, the parent would inquire, "What did you do to set it off?" The older crying child would be greeted with "Do you need something to cry *for*?", meaning that if the crying did not stop, there would be blows to "account" for it. Alternatively, he or she might be scolded into silence by being told, "You are too sensitive." There was no comforting for the future PAR, no rest for the "wicked."

Needless to say, the PAR quickly learned not to cry, not to be needy, not to ask for help even if sick and injured, and not to trust. He or she learned from a very early age that it is best to "stay out of the way." One explained, "If I had

[3]Fearfulness and sensitivity to danger may be preprogrammed in the primate. Baby monkeys need only see an older monkey fearing a specific kind of snake once, and the lesson is learned for a lifetime (Washburn & Hamburg, 1965). For biologically adaptive reasons, parental fearfulness and hostile mobilization may impress and inspire imitation in infants and children more than other patterns may.

a broken toy, it stayed broken; it was safer to take care of things myself." The adult consequence of such training is that PARs are extremely independent. They avoid intimacy unless they can be in control.

3. The PAR-to-be was the subject of covert and sometimes overt invidious comparisons within the family. Selected as a scapegoat for one reason or another,[4] the future PAR was known as bad, arrogant, "stuck up," stubborn, touchy, or difficult. The accusations were not of incompetence, laziness, or the like; the child's faults lay in inappropriate or excessive hostility, autonomy, or dominance. These offenses were major and "justified" the harsh and long-lasting punishment that was administered without due process. For example, one PAR had worked an entire summer to save money to go to the circus when it came to town. On the morning of the circus, her mother found a broken dish in the cupboard and asked whether she had broken it. The PAR correctly said no, whereupon the mother spanked her harshly with a hairbrush for lying and forbade her to go to the circus. The siblings were not questioned, and they went to the circus. There was no consideration of alternative explanations. The idea apparently was that the PAR was responsible for the kitchen, and if something was wrong there, obviously the PAR must have done it. Later, that PAR offended her mother with a rare critical remark. In response, the mother refused to speak for 2 years, despite the PAR's repeated apologies and attempts to undo the remark. In paranoid families, grudges are held for a long time.

Often the siblings of PARs were plainly preferred by the parents. They were conspicuously given more privileges, affection, and acknowledgment. Frequently the parents would discuss the PAR-to-be unfavorably as if he or she weren't present. The adult consequence is that the PAR is sensitive to and angry about whisperings, humiliations, and exclusions. He or she is often especially sensitive to the possibility of unequal distributions of punishments or privileges with peers, who can be seen as the functional equivalents of siblings. Like his or her family, the PAR will easily develop and carry a grudge a long time. Relatively little support from current reality is needed to sustain the PAR's belief that the world is resolutely against him or her.

Not mentioned in the DSM is the fact that PARs are also capable of a highly selective, intense intimacy. In these relationships, PARs can become very dependent and show *inordinate* trust. To those few who are seen as "on their side," PARs can maintain blind, even inappropriate loyalty.

4. The PAR was rewarded for competence at helping while "staying out of the way." If the PAR showed no needs, and instead took on specified parenting roles, the possibility of abuse was greatly reduced. The PAR is likely to have had the assignment to run the house and to do well in school. One explained: "I was rewarded for taking on Dad when he was drunk; I was Mother's guard dog." The PAR might have to do the dishes, mow the lawn, or go shopping for house-

---

[4]Some parents assign children a role very early, based on birth order, gender, physical resemblance to a hated or beloved sibling, or some other arbitrary basis. PAR and the role of scapegoat are encouraged if the child is seen by the parent as a stand-in for an earlier oppressor.

hold items, as the rest of the family played cards. Most PARs yearned for acknowl-edgment of their contributions. Greeted only with criticism and more demands, the PARs' resentment and alienation escalated year after year. As an adult, a PAR might have been expected to become a lawyer, politician, doctor, or something equally dominant. The PAR had permission and support to do well, and did. If, however, he or she ventured out of the assigned area, degradation and humili-ation awaited. It was understood that the PAR was the "bad seed." He or she might be competent, but being a good and lovable person was not within reach. Goodness and lovability were the exclusive province of others. The PAR learned to be competent and to stay separate from the mainstream.

The adult consequence is to continue this pattern. Operating from an auton-omous perch, the PAR functions well. The old pattern of not being acknowl-edged continues to inspire resentment and alienation along with fear. Usually the PAR throws fat on the fires of alienation and precipitates the dreaded attacks by his or her imperious, litigious, and headstrong demands for recognition and reparation. Lemert's (1962) description, quoted earlier, provides detail about how paranoid sensitivities are exacerbated by the adult community.

In sum, the PAR is a lonely figure, hateful and hated, frightened and fright-ening. Capable of powerful interventions, he or she stays mostly in hiding except when on righteous or vengeful missions. If schizophrenia is present, the picture is more complicated. Schreber's fluctuating boundaries among himself, God, his famous physician father, and Dr. Flechsig were characteristic of the faded dis-tinctions between parent and child often found in the world of schizophrenia. A glimpse is offered by R. D. Laing, a psychiatrist who turned to poetry to con-vey the patterns characteristic of these families. In his book *Knots*, there is a passage on the theme of good and bad that illustrates confusion in the matter of whose thoughts belong to whom:

> My mother does not love me.
> I feel bad.
> I feel bad because she does not love me
> I am bad because I feel bad
> I feel bad because I am bad
> I am bad because she does not love me
> She does not love me because I am bad. (Laing, 1970, p. 9)

Further comment on such confusion in defining the self is deferred for the moment.

CONNECTIONS BETWEEN THE INTERPERSONAL HISTORY AND THE SYMPTOMS LISTED IN THE DSM

The "total PAR" shows all the symptoms mentioned in the DSM. The history of sadistic, degrading, and controlling parenting leads the PAR to expect to be exploited and harmed (DSM item 1). He or she will see threat in benign events (item 4) and will fear personal disclosure (item 3). Identification with the parent accounts for the easily elicited rage (item 6). Having been compared unfavorably with other family members, and having served as the target of grudges, make the PAR unlikely to trust (items 2 and 7). This history also encourages grudge keeping (item 5).

The DSM does not mention that these maladaptive patterns usually occur as an island in a sea of good performance. The paranoid doctor who is rageful and suspicious at home may be kindly and beloved in his or her practice. The PAR's competence and interest in performing well are similar to those of the OCD. The long-recognized clinical covariance between PAR and OCD is not substantiated as the Axis II disorders are presently defined. Morey (1988) found only a 7.8% overlap between PAR and OCD. Restoration of the DSM-III item on pride in rationality would mark the PAR's interest in orderliness and competence, and kinship in this regard to OCD.

I believe that PARs are vulnerable to alcohol and drug abuse, including especially the "dominance drugs." Alcohol, cocaine, and amphetamines all give the user a sense of power and control. Personalities that are organized around the need to CONTROL are vulnerable to addiction. The reason is that these and related drugs easily impart the desired feeling without requiring that the user demonstrate social skills and appreciation of social complexities in way that will implement dominance in reality. In short, the "dominance drugs" offer a shortcut to power, albeit an illusry one. While using, the PAR can become uncharacteristically reckless with himself or herself; without drugs, the PAR will show strong self-control. When drug abuse is involved, then, a PAR does not reliably show self-restraint.

INTERPERSONAL SUMMARY OF PAR

The foregoing analysis suggests a succinct interpersonal summary for PAR:

There is fear that others will attack to hurt or blame. The wish is that others will affirm and understand. If affirmation fails, the hope is that others will either leave the PAR alone or submit. The baseline position is to wall off, stay separate, and tightly control the self. If threatened, the PAR will recoil in a hostile way or attack to countercontrol or gain distance.

In practice, there seem to be two stages of PAR. The earlier version encompasses a fearful, withdrawn type, and the later version adds angry, peremptory behaviors. Those in the first stage are likely to present with an Axis I anxiety disorder. In the second type, anxiety is replaced or masked by rage and indignation.

The summary is based on the SASB codes of the PAR baseline patterns and wishes. The codes themselves, listed in Table 13.1, provide a shorthand way to identify PAR. The baseline PAR positions are CONTROL, BLAME, ATTACK, RECOIL, WALL OFF, SEPARATE, and *SELF-CONTROL*. The wishes are to receive AFFIRM, but if that fails, to receive EMANCIPATE or SUBMIT. The fear is of ATTACK or BLAME.

The rhythm and harmonics of the PAR song are found in the sequences of interpersonal and intrapsychic response that the PAR gives and receives. The "tonic" PAR position consists of RECOIL, WALL OFF, and SEPARATE. This orientation draws, by the principle of complementarity, for ATTACK, IGNORE, and EMANCIPATE. The PAR's worst expectations are fulfilled if others exclude and attack him or her. When the PAR is convinced that ATTACK is imminent, he or she moves to ATTACK and BLAME in turn, to try to CONTROL the situation. The PAR really wants AFFIRM, but if that fails, the PAR will be content if others will SUBMIT or EMANCIPATE.These are the harmonics and rhythms of the PAR song.

Readers who can use the SASB codes will be able to generalize the present analysis to contexts not mentioned here. For example, it is not unusual for patients to complain that their depression is getting worse. Sometimes these complaints are presented to the therapist in a way that is characteristic of PAR. To interpret a complaint about depression in this way, the therapist would need to code the patient's process as he or she describes the depression. A PAR's process with the therapist as he or she complains about symptoms would include the notes of the PAR's song. Consider this example:

A patient refused to try a prescription for antidepressants because he felt that the medication was a sign of failure and that ultimately it would be harmful. The doctor, who was quite worried about the patient's escalating depression, reassured him that major side effects are rare. The doctor urged the patient to try the medicine for at least a few weeks. The patient became very anxious and accused the doctor of having a vested interest in the medicine. He demanded to know whether the doctor held stock in pharmaceutical companies. He knowledgeably discussed the recent literatures on antidepressant medications and on health care financing. After a lengthy discussion, the patient refused to take the medication and said that he would handle the problem on his own.

The baseline notes of the PAR song are compared to those of the songs for the other disorders discussed thus far in Table 13.2. A scan of the table shows that PAR shares with the disorders in the dramatic, erratic cluster (BPD, NPD, HPD, and ASP) the tendency to CONTROL and BLAME. The PAR's willingness to ATTACK is like that of the BPD, NPD, and ASP. The PAR's strong tendency to withdraw, shown by the joint positions RECOIL and WALL OFF, is just like that of the AVD. Finally, PAR shares with OCD the tendency to CONTROL, BLAME, and *SELF-CONTROL*; both groups are also personally inaccessible (WALL OFF). Despite the overlap, OCD and PAR are different in important ways. For example, OCDs regularly IGNORE important cues, SUBMIT to authority, *SELF-BLAME*, and *SELF-NEGLECT*, whereas PARs do not. Instead of "tuning out," PARs typically focus sharply on what is going on, maintain their own separate positions, externalize by blaming, and *SELF-PROTECT*. The differential diagnosis with BPD can be made

Table 13.2. Comparison of SASB Codes of BPD, NPD, HPD, ASP, DPD, OCD, NEG, AVD, and PAR

	BPD	NPD	HPD	ASP	DPD	OCD	NEG	AVD	PAR
1. EMANCIPATE									
2. AFFIRM									
3. ACTIVE LOVE	×			×*					
4. PROTECT									
5. CONTROL	×	×	×*	×*		×*			×
6. BLAME	×	×	×	×		×	×*	×	×
7. ATTACK	×	×		×*					×
8. IGNORE									
1. SEPARATE		×		×			×*		×
2. DISCLOSE									
3. REACTIVE LOVE			×*						
4. TRUST	×		×*		×				
5. SUBMIT				×		×*	×*		
6. SULK				×			×*	×	
7. RECOIL								×	×
8. WALL OFF			×*	×*		×*	×*	×	×
1. SELF-EMANCIPATE									
2. SELF-AFFIRM									
3. ACTIVE SELF-LOVE		×*							
4. SELF-PROTECT	×			×*					
5. SELF-CONTROL						×*		×	×
6. SELF-BLAME		×			×	×		×	
7. SELF-ATTACK	×		×*				×*		
8. SELF-NEGLECT	×	×*		×*		×*			

*Indicates that these codes within the same column appear in complex combinations with one another.

on the basis of the PAR's comfort with autonomy, in contrast with the BPD's dread of it. Comfort with autonomy also distinguishes the PAR from the AVD, who yearns to be included.

The interpersonal *do, re, mi* of Table 13.2 shows exactly how PAR and the other categories overlap; it also shows how they differ. The descriptions in the tables can help the clinician make the differential diagnoses.

DSM DESCRIPTORS REVISITED

The DSM view of PAR has now been translated into interpersonal language, and the psychosocial learning associated with PAR patterns has been outlined. In this section, the interpersonal analysis of PAR is compared to the DSM. DSM-III-R items appear in **bold print**; any changes introduced by the DSM-IV appear in *italics.* (Again, the item numbering used is that of the DSM-IV.) The interpersonal modifiers are underlined. Items from the WISPI (discussed in Chapter 1) appear in CAPITAL LETTERS.

A pervasive and unwarranted tendency, beginning by early adulthood and present in a variety of contexts, to interpret the actions of people as deliberately demeaning or threatening, as indicated by at least *four* of the following:

(1) expects, without sufficient basis, to be exploited or harmed by others

Believes that he or she could be attacked suddenly at any time, without reason, by nearly everyone, including close associates. Feels deeply and irreversibly injured by specific other persons who may hardly even be aware of him or her.

CERTAIN PEOPLE WILL TAKE UNFAIR ADVANTAGE OF ME IF GIVEN THE SLIGHTEST CHANCE.

(2) questions, without justification, the loyalty or trustworthiness of friends or associates

Is so amazed if a friend or associate shows loyalty that he or she cannot trust and believe it. Expects that if he or she gets in trouble, friends and associates will either attack him or her, or else just not notice that there is any difficulty. Is convinced on the basis of little or no evidence that friends and associates are plotting to betray or harm him or her.

I AM NOT DUMB ENOUGH TO COUNT ON OTHERS TO COME THROUGH WHEN NEEDED.

(3) is reluctant to confide in others because of unwarranted fear that the information will be used against him or her

Is secretive because he or she expects that others will use any and all personal information against him or her. Resists answering questions asked in an attempt to help, saying that details about himself or herself are "nobody's business."

WHAT I THINK AND FEEL IS NOBODY'S BUSINESS-EVEN IF OTHERS THINK THEY ARE TRYING TO BE HELPFUL.

(4) reads hidden meanings or threatening meanings into benign remarks or events, e.g., suspects that a neighbor put out trash early to annoy him [or her]

Is so sure that people are ready to injure him or her that he or she feels criticized or attacked by the most inadvertent remarks. Others feel there is nothing they can say or do that will not be seen as criticism or attack. For example, if a new acquisition (car, clothing, personal item) is admired, he or she feels that the admirer thinks he or she is selfish. If complimented on an accomplishment, the PAR feels that the other person is trying to coerce more and better performance. If there is an offer of help, the PAR takes it as criticism that he or she is not doing well enough on his or her own.

OTHERS CAN'T DECEIVE ME BECAUSE I AM SMART ENOUGH TO PICK UP SMALL SIGNS THAT GIVE THEM AWAY.

(5) bears grudges or is unforgiving of insults or slights

tendency to bear grudges persistently, i.e., to be unforgiving of insults, injuries, or slights

Small "crimes" are met with major punishments. For example, if someone was too busy to respond to a request right away, the PAR may persist for a long time in telling others how inept that person was. If it gets back to him or her that a friend or associate made an unkind remark, there is a major counterattack against that person, and the associated hostility continues for a very long time.

IF PEOPLE BETRAY ME, I MAKE SURE THEY PAY FOR IT, AND DON'T LET THEM OFF THE HOOK EASILY.

(6) is easily slighted and quick to react with anger or to counterattack

perceives attacks on his or her character or reputation that are not apparent to others, and is quick to react with anger or to counterattack

Is quick to see degradation, attack, and negation; responds with long-lasting revenge. Expects to be misunderstood and misused, so if someone shows the slightest annoyance, he or she responds with a perceptive, fierce, well-focused rage. Can attack harshly with virtually no justification because of the belief that he or she was about to be attacked by the target.

IF I SENSE THE SLIGHTEST PUT-DOWN FROM PEOPLE, I COME DOWN HARD ON THEM SO THEY WON'T BE IN ANY HURRY TO TRY THAT AGAIN.

(7) questions, without justification, fidelity of spouse or sexual partner

recurrent suspicions, without justification, regarding fidelity of spouse or sexual partner

Wants to maintain complete control of intimates because of the belief either that they will betray him or her if given the slightest opportunity, or that they will be unable to resist attempts of others to "steal" them. Constantly questions fidelity, and challenges his or her spouse's or sexual partner's whereabouts, actions, and intentions.

I HAVE TO KEEP CONTROL OF WHAT MY SPOUSE OR LOVER DOES, BECAUSE THERE ARE CERTAIN PEOPLE WHO WILL STEAL HIM OR HER IF GIVEN THE SLIGHTEST CHANCE.

pride in rationality [DSM-III item omitted from DSM-III-R and DSM-IV; I recommend restoring]

Functions well intellectually in most ways except when concerned with delusional topics. Values self-control and devalues expression of feeling.

I AM A VERY RATIONAL AND PRIVATE PERSON WHO BELIEVES THAT PEOPLE WHO LET THEIR EMOTIONS GO ARE FOOLISH.

NECESSARY AND EXCLUSIONARY CRITERIA

The present analysis permits definition of necessary and exclusionary conditions for each personality disorder. For PAR, the recommended *necessary* descriptor is the expectation of harm when it is not there. *Exclusionary* conditions include, (1) worry about abandonment (characteristic of BPD and DPD), and (2) deference to authority.

CASE ILLUSTRATIONS

Case 1

This 35-year-old married father came to the hospital to deal with his problems in concentration, saying, "My mind doesn't work the way it should. My brain and body are different—my body's there, but my mind is elsewhere." The problems with concentration had a history extending back to grade school. His early performance in school was variable, but he said, "I could do well if I put my mind to it." It also appeared that he had been anxious for a long time. He said he "couldn't sit still" in grade school.

His distractibility caused him to lose jobs because he was inattentive to matters in ways that endangered himself and others. Typically his mind drifted to thoughts about a "disgruntled employee" at a former place of employment. This man used to harass and persecute the patient. The patient believed that he was generally disliked at the former place of employment because he was efficient and worked hard. His devotion to his work as a carpenter violated the norm of taking it easy and being laid back. He said he did not fit in because his religious and political affiliations were different from those of the others.

The patient provided extensive detail to suggest that the "disgruntled employee" consistently tried to harm him with bad-mouthing and acts of destruction. Examples included letting the air out of the tires of his car and breaking windows at the patient's house. He was puzzled about why his coworker would "go to such lengths to make me miserable." The patient was also upset that the boss did nothing to investigate and curtail the abuse he suffered from this coworker.

The patient had used alcohol, cocaine, and marijuana to excess in the past. When he met his present (second) wife, all of that stopped. He had reduced his drinking to "about a six-pack a week." The patient denied homicidality, but said that he would use his gun if he caught somebody messing with his car, or if there was an intruder in his yard. This man's introject was harsh and punitive. He called himself incompetent and a "stupid shit." He deliberately deprived himself of pleasure. He said that he used to have good self-control, but that he had recently become indecisive.

The patient was presently unemployed, and had been under financial strain during the last year. His second marriage was fragile: He and his wife were "alienated." He blamed her for an earlier decision to change jobs. He was also prone to "giving her the cold shoulder" and not speaking to her for days. She hated that rejection, and tried to reconcile by giving him hugs. Sometimes that worked, but the patient said the "cold-shoulder" episodes ended only when he decided they should. He noted that his wife gave behavioral signs of being attracted to another man at her work; she denied it. The patient said that his wife was "his only friend." Besides his little daughter, whom he "spoils rotten," he trusted no one.

Providing his family with money was important to the patient, and he very much wanted to find a career that would pay him well and offer good benefits. However, he could not precisely "put a finger on what I want to do."

The patient's first marriage, which "was based on sex," ended in a violent episode.

The patient was repairing his automobile at home and had placed it on four blocks using a jack. His wife started arguing with him as he lay working under the car. In a fit of rage, she took a sledge hammer and knocked one of the blocks away so that the car fell on him. He did not remember the details, but did recall coming to consciousness after having been crushed by the car. He agreed not to press charges for her felony assault if she would simply give him a divorce without financial complications.

The patient's mother and father also were violent with him. His mother regularly spanked him for many minutes with a willow switch or a belt, and then sent him upstairs to his room. Anticipating these punishments terrified him. Eventually he learned to stuff his pants with magazines, and that helped. The mother believed that "children are mindless and irresponsible," and often called the patient and his siblings "a bunch of pigs." Nonetheless, the mother cleaned regularly and cooked well. The patient used to take her side in her arguments with his father, explaining to the father, "She's not so bad."

The father used a hairbrush, and would spank until there was crying. The goal was that the children should experience as much pain as he did. His methods of punishment could strip the children of all dignity. Once, as the mother and father fought about how dirty the children were, the father stuffed dirty underwear in the patient's mouth. As with the mother's punishments, the patient said that the terror of knowing a spanking was coming from his father was worse than the spanking itself. The father would call the patient "a stupid shit." In the father's eyes, the patient was always "screwing up"; the patient never heard about what was right, only about what was wrong. The father also frequently made unfavorable comparisons between the patient and his brothers.

There were three brothers and a sister. The boys used to terrorize the sister by using her favorite toys as targets for practice with their BB guns. The patient explained that they were acting out the role modeling by the father in relation to the mother. The boys roamed the neighborhood engaging in acts of vandalism. The patient himself feared his brothers because they would put him down and would "beat the shit out of me." The brothers still denigrated the patient because he had been the only one in the family who was successful. He had a wife, a home, a child, and (until recently), a job. Unlike the brothers, he did not abuse drugs. Now that he was failing, he believed his brothers would be elated. Making himself look bad was a way to gain their approval.

The patient qualified for the diagnosis of PAR because he met every DSM criterion. He expected to be exploited and harmed by others (item 1). He questioned trustworthiness (item 2). He was reluctant to confide (item 3). He read hidden or threatening meaning into benign remarks. In fact, the interviewer had to stop and identify the patient's perception of the interviewer as critical; only after the purpose and methods of the interview were again explained did the relationship again become collaborative (item 4). He bore grudges (item 5). He was easily slighted and quick to counterattack (item 6). He questioned his spouse's fidelity (item 7).

This man also conformed to the interpersonal description of PAR. He worried a lot that others would ATTACK, and he reacted with RECOIL, WALL OFF, and SEPARATE. He liked to CONTROL his family. He had not progressed to the PAR stage of identification with the aggressor; rather, he preferred to WALL OFF and

SEPARATE as a method of resolving conflict. It was hard for him to tell his wife what he thought and felt (*SELF-CONTROL*). He wanted to be **AFFIRM**ed, but was content with **EMANCIPATE**. He met the necessary condition of pervasive perception of intent to harm. He did not meet the exclusionary conditions of fear of aloneness or deference to authority.

His early learning included all of the factors listed in Table 13.1: (1) His parents and brothers were chronically sadistic, degrading, and controlling. (2) There were very harsh punishments, although it is not clear that they were specifically for dependency. Autonomy was encouraged, and the boys played hostile pranks on their sister as well as on others in the neighborhood. (3) There were hostile comparisons of the patient with his brothers, and the resulting jealousy and rivalry persisted through adulthood. (4) There was harsh emphasis on competence. In exhorting them to be cleaner, the mother would say that, "children are mindless and irresponsible."

In sum, this man met both the interpersonal and the DSM criteria for PAR. The brief description of his history suggests that he had many learning experiences that taught him that people close to him would try to hurt him. He learned that keeping control of things or maintaining distance was safer.

Case 2

This 40-year-old married mother of two daughters (one biological, one the child of her husband by an earlier marriage) was brought to the hospital by her husband because she was convinced that he was conspiring with his daughter (her stepdaughter) against her. More specifically, she thought there was an incestual relationship between him and this daughter. The husband said that the patient was misinterpreting his innocent conversations with his daughter. He reported that she was having similar difficulties at work, where she felt that coworkers were hostile.

The patient felt that she was right about the incest, but was caught in a bind. If she didn't press charges, she would abandon this child as she herself had been abandoned to incestual abuse. On the other hand, if she did press charges, she thought that her own biological child might be removed from the home. She was particularly fearful about this possibility, because she had lost custody of that child for a while as her first divorce was contested.

The patient was depressed, showing poor appetite, low mood, irritability, and disturbed sleep. She was not suicidal or homicidal. She said that she had always been anxious. She had a number of somatic problems, including head and neck pains (perhaps secondary to an industrial accident), asthma, ulcer, ulcerative colitis, and more. A few years prior, she had successfully completed a program for rehabilitation in alcohol and polysubstance abuse. During this hospitalization, the patient was sometimes pleasant and at other times agitated and angry. She would worry that the staff was trying to thwart her.

She had been in psychotherapy for about a year, and had recently begun exploring the psychological abuse she suffered in her first marriage. That marriage followed an intense relationship with a physically and sexually abusive boyfriend. The first husband did not physically or sexually abuse the patient. She joined him in drug and alcohol abuse, and recently felt she had realized that he had subtly damaged her ability to tell what was real. She said, "He messed with my mind." For example, he would have affairs and then accuse the patient of being unfaithful. She said, "Everything was turned around on me." Nonetheless, the patient had loved her first husband greatly. She said that for a long time, she kept trying to make that marriage work, thinking that he would get better.

She chose her second husband for his initial kindness to her. He handled all the money. The patient felt that she was the only one who initiated romantic or recreational activities, such as going on a vacation. She noted that their intimacy was mostly through fighting. Most importantly, she felt confused about whether the second husband was "messing with her mind" like her first. She said that she had told her present husband about her abusive history, and that he "used" this against her. She regretted giving him the information and tried to reassure herself, "I don't have to listen to him."

The marital debate about the alleged sexual abuse of the husband's daughter was an example of her confusion about what was real. The father and daughter denied sexual involvement. However, the patient noted that after she had a conversation with the stepdaughter about "touching in the wrong places," the child put a lock on her bedroom door. The patient sought evidence to establish the truth about the father–daughter relationship. She was also embattled with coworkers and felt unsupported by her supervisors. She wanted to quit her job, and hoped that her husband would not tell her that she had to stay on that job.

The patient had a very painful childhood, and she actively resisted remembering and talking about it: "I don't want to remember that stuff. It is too painful to remember. I don't want to go back. I want to go on." Her biological father was forcibly removed from the family because of incestual behaviors. The patient, however, denied that she was abused by her biological father and believed that she had more problems with her stepfather. He was an alcoholic and had broken her leg once; she still had a slight limp. Her stepfather, who was jealous and possessive, often "beat up" the mother, who did not fight back. The patient said that she reacted to their fights by staying "in my own little world." She was often afraid. One time her mother called from a bar, warning the patient and her siblings to get out of the house. The stepfather was allegedly coming home to shoot them.

The patient's stepfather demanded that she perform household chores. He frequently told her that she was a "lazy, no-good bitch." The other siblings had no such responsibilities and were not thus criticized. Once he tried to molest her, saying that he wanted "to see if like mother, like daughter." The patient's mother did not believe her story and so the patient ran away from home to stay with a sister. The patient was deeply hurt and had "spent a lot of years trying to figure out why my mother did not believe me."

The patient's oldest brother was very important to her. She adored him and still was very much affected by what he said and did. Despite her positive feelings for him, she said that this brother had an explosive temper. "He was mean to all of us." Once he "threw another brother to the ground and broke his arm." He often hit her and told her that she would "tell too much." She learned to keep silent and not to ask for help.

The patient met the DSM criteria for PAR. She expected to be exploited and harmed by her husband and coworkers (item 1). She questioned the loyalty or trustworthiness of her husband, coworkers, children, and hospital staff (item 2). She was reluctant to confide in her husband or in the interviewer, because of fear that the information would be used against her (item 3). She apparently read hidden threatening meanings into the benign remarks of her husband and his daughter (item 4). She said that in recent years, she bore grudges because "I am tired of everybody getting revenge on me because they thought I was trying to hurt them" (item 5). She was quick to react with anger (item 6). She questioned the fidelity of her spouse (item 7).

The patient also conformed to the interpersonal descriptors for PAR. She was quite afraid of ATTACK and BLAME. She wanted her worries about the incest and her good performance at work to be AFFIRMed. In the family she was trying hard to CONTROL a situation that perplexed her. Because she felt unable to control the home situation, she chose to WALL OFF and SEPARATE. At work, she BLAMEd her coworkers for their "laziness" and reacted with RECOIL, WALL OFF, and plans to SEPARATE. Her tendency initially to SUBMIT to both her husbands can be seen as the TRUST that PARs can show to certain intimates, but that is not marked by the DSM. Except for the angry outbursts (ATTACK) that she felt were justified, she maintained SELF-CONTROL. She showed the necessary condition for PAR of pervasive threats of harm, and she did not meet the exclusionary conditions: She was not afraid of being alone and did not defer to authority in general, although she did obey both husbands in an effort to maintain their affection.

It should be noted that the present analysis does not include an independent assessment of whether there was or was not an incestual relationship between the second husband and his daughter. Clinicians should not routinely assume that such accusations are merely the product of mental disorder. Patients should be supported in their need to explore their concerns. The therapy process can be complicated by the fact that the clinician may ethically be obligated to report possible ongoing incestual abuse. Whether this particular patient's worries about ongoing incest were valid, she could be diagnosed as having PAR because her patterns were long-standing and appeared in a number of situations. A case like this aptly illustrates the saying, "Just because you're paranoid doesn't mean everybody's not out to get you."

The patient had experienced all aspects of the interpersonal history sketched in Table 13.1: (1) She was chronically vulnerable to attack from her stepfather and probably also from her brother. (2) She was betrayed by her mother when she tried to reach out for protection from incest. Her brother threatened to harm her if she "told." The stepfather punished her severely for failure to perform household tasks. There were strong injunctions against asking for help. She was not protected, and there were harsh demands that she perform. It is unlikely that her dependent needs were met. (3) Her stepfather unfavorably compared her to her siblings (and apparently also to her mother). Grudge carrying may have been modeled. In any case, the patient herself held a lifelong grudge against her mother for not believing her about the incest. (4) The patient reacted to parental fighting by staying out of the way, by "living in her own little world."

EXPECTABLE TRANSFERENCE REACTIONS AND TREATMENT IMPLICATIONS

Transference Reactions

PARs are likely to need to control the therapy process and to be very slow to trust the therapist. The therapist can expect the PAR to be "hypersensitive" to alleged therapist criticism and to show an ever-present tendency to withdraw from therapy. At the same time, the PAR may be quite critical of the therapist. Nonetheless, it is necessary to support and affirm the PAR for quite a while. Building trust is the first priority.

Treatment Implications: The Five Categories of Correct Response

Facilitating Collaboration

The major treatment problem with PAR is the creation of a collaborative patient–therapist bond. In a sense, once there is collaboration, the paranoia has started to disappear. Accustomed to being humiliated and abused, the PAR will see the therapist as critical and judgmental, interested in finding "slip-ups," thinking that the patient is "driving him or her crazy," feeling impatient, and wanting the patient to "get out of the way." It is difficult to explore the pathogenic hypotheses, because PARs are not initially willing to discuss family matters with therapist "strangers." The PAR believes that disclosure to others betrays family, and that taking care of oneself necessarily hurts another. The PAR is caught between wanting to find safe haven from family stresses and wanting to maintain loyalty. The therapist, as a likely target of this ambivalence, needs to hold steady. The therapist should be affirming and take care never to return harshness for harshness. If, after the PAR starts to trust, the therapist becomes distracted or forgetful even once, the PAR is deeply injured; his or her developing trust may be delayed for months or years. Patience and kindness, without hints of coercion, criticism, or appeasement, are vitally needed for quite a long time in the early stages of therapy.

The process of developing collaboration is illustrated by the following interview that occurred during hospitalization of a woman with Delusional (Paranoid) Disorder. The excerpt shows how the method described in Chapter 4 can "settle" a psychotic and paranoid person into a temporarily sane state. The interviewer started with the assumption that the patient made sense. The collaboration developed as the interviewer tried to see the world as the patient did. Careful attention was given to the transference. The patient acted out the paranoid pattern in relation to the interviewer. When the interviewer used a metaphor to amplify the generic fear, the patient associated directly to relevant early history and became quite lucid. (It is helpful to know that the patient refered in her psychotic stream of associations to the fact that she had given written permission to tape-record this interview for use in teaching or research.)

T: So you want to change your planet [a response to the patient's opening comment to that effect]?

P: Sure.

T: What's wrong with this one?

P: I don't like the things that I see about a lot of them.

T: What do you . . . ?

P: Well, I see—well, I see—sometimes I see patterns that are very evil.

T: Like what?

P: You mean like examples of them?

T: Um-hum.

P: Well, some people even around us deliberately try to destroy whole cities using research techniques or teaching techniques.

T: I see. Are you feeling that I'm going to hurt you?

P: I don't know.

T: Well, what would be your concern? Do you feel . . .

P: I don't feel like I'm being surrounded and pushed in a corner, but I think that I probably have to be careful. Sometimes you brainstorm and you have ideas and you can think of all detailed methods and everything, and it falls in the wrong hands and you see it used by the wrong people.

T: Well, how might it be misused?

P: Well . . . well, you know, strains of viruses can be developed and transplanted to other portions of—of other countries, and they can be slipped into foods, and create very rapid tumors that kill people. I know people who sell aspects of their research to other people who use it for destroying some people and making—making money.

T: Do you feel . . .

P: Have you ever been slugged from the back, on the back of the neck?

T: No, have you?

P: Yes.

T: When did that happen to you?

P: Oh, when I was walking on the street, I was—I guess, you know, because—I guess what happens is sometimes the people give you drugs or they hit you on the head, and they take you places and use you for parties.

T: I get a sense that you feel extremely vulnerable, that . . .

P: Sure.

T: That you feel that you could be attacked suddenly and without warning and violently.

P: Probably not violently, 'cause people use such subtle moves now, you know. Probably I'd blow up from the inside like an alien or whatever.

T: You'd blow up from the inside like what?

P: Like an alien. I mean people use such interesting tactics to destroy people.

T: Are you feeling that I might be subtly trying to destroy you?

P: No, not at all. You just asked me how I felt in general and how I felt in my surroundings.

T: So . . .

P: And I was—if I—I'm in a thing where I read someone's mind and they're working with me and I see that they're one of the people that are doing something that I feel is very destructive, but I know, and I see that they're part of a pattern, then I—I'm afraid that they'll know that I'm reading their mind, that I know what they're doing. I don't know what to do with my intuition.

T: What is your intuition about us right now?

P: You're probably all very nice people, very socially polite. I don't know, what do you want me to say? I don't know any of you.

T: Would you like to meet everybody here?

P: Sure.

T: Okay. We can go around the room and say names and what we're doing here. I told you mine, why don't we just go around the room? [About 12 medical students and staff members introduce themselves.]

T: Okay, so that's who's here. We were talking about your sense of vulnerability, and you were worrying about being hit from behind, sudden violent attack, and also subtle attack. Is that accurate that you worry about . . .

P: That's why I am here, ya, because I couldn't sleep for a couple nights and I heard bizarre noises and that sort of things and I didn't really—I didn't have Ghostbusters' numbers to call 'em in.

T: I see, there was no help available.

P: No. I did go over to my neighbor's and just stayed there, but even there I didn't feel safe and I was awake all night.

T: I see.

P: I had this bad cold and I couldn't—I just—like I couldn't deal with the whole thing.

T: What was the being frightened about? Some unnamed someone?

P: Ya. Can you imagine being scared of someone who walks around with a plate with three green apples? You know, sort of an image, if half of them was red then it would be a Snow White story and you might take a bite of the wrong side.

T: Well, that came from the wicked mother.

P: Ya. Did it?

T: I think so.

P: Well, there might have been one around. I don't know.

T: How did you get along with your mother?

P: Well, fine. I've always had lots of mothers, though, and I've always had lots of fathers, so I left when I was 16, and that's a pretty young age to leave.

T: That's a very young age to leave. How come you left so young?

P: Well 'cause I was from a—a sort of violent and very regimented environment in which I had trouble functioning. One thing I guess I—well, my dad was violent.

T: Was he?

P: Um-hum, and I think some of it, you know, may have been personality stuff, and it's almost due to a very serious head injury when he was in an accident. They didn't know anything, you know—this is where a difficulty in balancing what people know with research and teaching and what affects people and environments have. Balancing that with your emotions and the effect that things have on you. He would sometimes line all of us up and beat us. I saw my mother thrown out of a car. I was thrown down the stairs, kicked down the stairs, kicked in the stomach. My brother's leg was broken by my dad. Sort of scary if you've been in a background for any long period of time and tried to work with it, and you don't have any physician looking after a whole situation. We had neighbors call the police and so on, and for me a lot of times my dad would wake me in the middle of the night and beat me or make me stay up all night working on things 'cause I wouldn't—'cause I hadn't, I don't know, met his expectations of what everything should, of what all should be done, or I wasn't the person he wanted me to be, and so I was from a very disrupted house in that sense. I think that, from what I've studied neurosciences since then, I understand that people who have severe brain damage do that sort of thing, and the thing is also he has no memory of any of those things he did, and when he's told it hurts the side of him that is a balanced human being so much, you know, that it's real frightening. So I guess I—I left real early 'cause I couldn't deal with that whole scene.

Following her compassionate exposition of her father's impact on her family, the patient proceeded to finish the interview without evidence of thought disorder. The transition to sanity occurred shortly after the interviewer reflected the PAR baseline position of RECOIL and asked for associations to the expected complement, ATTACK: "What was the being frightened about? Some unnamed someone?" The patient responded with a metaphor from the Snow White story about a deadly parental figure. Then the interviewer made the interpersonal implication of the symbol explicit: "Well, that came from the wicked mother." Shortly thereafter, the patient clearly described her father's frequent and violent attacks launched to force order. She spent the rest of the interview exploring how his violence and other family experiences had affected her self-concept and life choices.

The therapist is well advised to remember how hostile and litigious PARs can become. While always being kind and supportive, the therapist must be especially vigilant about not straying from professional, legal, and ethical guidelines.

One PAR began therapy by insisting on seeing the therapy notes and demanding that there be no reference to his adamantly denied alcohol use. He then insisted that the therapist take no more notes. The therapist refused to comply with the demand that there be no notes, but did reassure the patient about the confidentiality of the file. The therapist also agreed to keep note taking to a minimum, and said that from then on, notes would be taken after rather than during the sessions.

Eventually the therapy terminated because it became apparent through reports from family and the community that the patient's alcohol abuse was unremittingly severe. The therapist maintained that no constructive learning could occur until and if the patient was willing to enter an inpatient treatment program. He would need to follow it with attendance at AA (or a comparable organization) to help maintain sobriety. The patient continued to use alcohol; ultimately, this took an enormous toll on his family and work. In deteriorated condition, the patient demanded angrily to have the therapy notes. His intent was to demonstrate that the file was inadequate and that he had been exploited. The idea was that money had been paid, but service had not been rendered.

Facilitating Pattern Recognition

The PAR is likely to try to coerce the desired AFFIRM. PARs can confuse submission with affirmation. For example, one PAR was mystified that a supervisor who had just been defeated in litigation over her work assignment continued to be hostile to her. The PAR's reasoning was something like this: "I defeated you, so you must respect me. If you respect me, you must like me."

The PAR needs to learn that the expectations of attack and abusive control are understandable because they stem from early experience. Then he or she needs to appreciate that these expectations are not always appropriate because not every environment is the same. He or she must learn that hostility begets hostility. The PAR needs to understand that his or her defenses of avoidance, control, and "anticipatory retaliation" elicit attack and alienation. Major blocks in the way of this learning are the PAR's reluctance to trust the therapist, and the fear that any discussion of family interactions will elicit severe punishment for betrayal.

The PAR vitally needs tender, noncoercive holding—"contact comfort" (see Harlow, reviewed in Benjamin, 1968). Nonverbal comforting is a potential antidote to the original physical abuse. Midelfort (1957) successfully implemented this folk wisdom when he brought the infants and young children of paranoid mothers into the hospital as a part of the treatment plan. He reported that holding and hugging the babies facilitated the recovery of the mothers. Whether mothers are PARs or not, women have known for centuries that infants and children rehabilitate and resocialize. Men who now participate intimately in child rearing from the start are beginning also to reap the benefits.

The PAR's need for soothing can also be met in couples therapy if the spouse is friendly and supportive. Benevolent spousal behaviors can be highlighted, so that the PAR cannot simply dismiss or ignore them as he or she is inclined to do. This technique is especially effective in a context where the spouse has previously avoided the marital relationship by excessive work or travel. As the PAR becomes less controlling and less attacking, he or she may discover the rewards in being warmer and more playful.

Although the individual therapist cannot and should not physically hold the patient (few PARs would permit it anyway), the therapist can engage in "verbal holding." Accurate empathy, genuine affirmation of accomplishments, and understanding support of the PAR when he or she is embattled are examples. To keep the "verbal holding" constructive, and to avoid enabling continuation of PAR patterns, the therapist needs also to call the PAR's provocations to his or her attention. For example, the PAR may want to bring his or her boss into therapy, in order to have the therapist tell the boss how unreasonably critical he or she has been. The boss should become more acknowledging. Simple therapist agreement to such a plan is more likely to harm than to help. As an alternative, the therapist can say something like this: "If you would like to have your boss come to therapy, and he (she) would agree, we could use the opportunity to let him (her) know how you feel about things. We would also need to hear your boss's view, and that might possibly help us learn more about what else we should be working on in here." Such support, given in a context that also gently confronts reality, includes verbal holding. The confronting part of the support is likely to be threatening to the PAR, so the therapist needs to watch carefully for signs that indicate a need to back off. Finding the vital balance between needed affirmation and iatrogenic enabling is difficult.

A PAR needs to know that his or her feeling of vulnerability and fearfulness does not "prove" that the therapist, spouse, or boss was in fact attacking. The PAR should learn not to continue to read his or her own fearful affect as proof that others have attacking intent. Sometimes PARs benefit from learning about how fearful and vulnerable their abusers were. Abusing parents will teach their children that the world is dangerous and that disaster hovers on the brink of the next moment. Realizing that their parents also were crippled with fear can sometimes help the PAR victim separate from it.

Blocking Maladaptive Patterns

A personality-disordered individual can learn to notice that the patterns are worse when he or she has contact with the persons or situations similar to those in which the patterns were generated. For example, one PAR commented, "I am much more distant from my husband when my mother visits. I want to get rid of *that*." In this mode, the anger at family members for the abuse can be mobilized to block the maladaptive patterns that have stemmed from it. Similarly, the therapist can redirect the PAR's rage at the favored siblings by helping the patient see advantages in his or her own isolated position. The extruded PAR family member has the advantage of being less enmeshed in the destructive family system. The more favored siblings are ultimately more trapped than the scapegoated PAR. One commented, "I hate my [greatly favored] sister, but she is also my ticket to freedom. If Mother clings to her, I can leave."

Usually PARs respond well to therapist honesty, especially about transference matters. Because the PAR probably has a history of indirect condemnation in the family, any therapist discomfort is best disclosed discreetly and constructively. Suppose, for example, that the PAR rages menacingly at the therapist toward the end of a session, and then in the next session wants to know whether the therapist was frightened. An appropriate response may be something like this: "Well, yes, I was worried at the end. If that happens again, we will have to terminate the session immediately and find a way to work differently with this."

Perhaps I will need to bring in a colleague to help, and maybe we will need to meet in a different location." If asked, the therapist may indicate that the new location will be in a setting (e.g., an inpatient unit) where there are better means for helping to contain such escalating anger.

Homicidal PARs are difficult for any therapist, whether or not he or she is a target. If the therapist is a target, it is vital to diffuse the transference by bringing colleagues in on the treatment, both as consultants and as cotherapists. Correspondingly, a therapist has an obligation to be helpful to a colleague who is carrying a difficult, potentially homicidal PAR case. With homicidal patients, there needs to be constant and careful assessment of whether there are factors that indicate palpable likelihood of acting out. Some danger signs include psychosis; identification of a specific target; escalating rage; intense rumination and focusing about planned hostile action; alcohol or drug abuse; noncompliance with prescriptions for antipsychotic medication; and potential provocation by a possible target or by circumstances. If any of these is relevant, the therapist probably has a duty to warn the intended victim. Commitment should also be considered, although the disclosure will probably have a negative effect on the therapy relationship.

When a PAR (or anyone else) is abusing his or her children, the therapist may have a duty to take protective action in this situation as well. Different states have different laws and practices on child abuse. The case provider must stay abreast of and abide by current local as well as national ethical and legal guidelines. Within the limits of the law, the therapist must hold consistently to the position of supporter/protector of the patient. At the same time, the therapist needs to recognize that it is neither supportive nor protective to allow maladaptive patterns to continue without addressing them. If a PAR is abusing a child or others, I believe that the problem is ideally approached in the same way a therapist deals with suicide. At some point, if the situation becomes acute, the therapeutic alliance has to be broken and the danger disclosed to appropriate others. However, it is preferable, if possible, to continue working on the patterns and trying to change them through collaborative work in therapy. It is difficult to determine the exact point at which to make the switch from "collaborative mode" to "legal mode." The problem is that once this step has been taken, the therapy relationship will probably never again be the same. After the commitment, or after the report has been filed, the problem (suicidality, abuse) will probably recur. Then the therapy work has to continue with a disruption in the vitally important collaboration between patient and therapist.

It is unfortunate that in many states, reporting of abuse as soon as it is even mentioned in therapy is mandatory. The rule may assure that the crucial abusive situations will not be discussed, or that the therapy will compromised and terminate prematurely. There is some evidence that mandatory reporting laws have in fact driven abusers from treatment (Berlin, Malin, & Dean, 1991). My present opinion is that the laws that automatically require therapists to report should be changed. Instead, therapists might better be required to present the problem to a formally constituted panel of qualified peers. This panel should weigh the complexities and reach a consensus on the best course of action. For example, there should be an assessment of the strength of the positive aspects of the therapy relationship. If the patient trusts the therapist, and the therapist trusts the patient, the likelihood of a constructive outcome is greatly enhanced. If there is a good working relationship, if the frequency of episodes is diminishing, and if the outbursts do not result in bodily harm that requires medical attention, then the need for the therapist to consider coercive legal intervention is lessened. Therapist honesty, caring, calmness, attentiveness, and clear commitment to trying to work things out, are all extremely helpful to the PAR in crisis. If the panel cannot reach a consensus on the case, then immediate reporting may be mandated. The situation should be monitored until it is resolved satisfactorily.

If the therapy work is allowed to continue with an admitted PAR abuser, it is helpful to help the PAR recall how it felt to be abused. With the therapist's empathic support, the PAR's empathy for his or her own child can emerge. Once the PAR has consolidated sympathy for himself or herself as a child, he or she can be motivated to change some ideas about proper child rearing. A therapist who is judgmental and not able to understand the abusing PAR's position will not be able to provided the needed genuine warmth. Such a therapist runs the risk of sending complex messages coded as "helpful put-down." Arrogant, patronizing helpfulness will probably confuse the patient. It may be internalized to lower self-esteem, and may thus trigger rage or alienation.

Strengthening the Will to Give Up Maladaptive Patterns

The wish to give up the patterns of alienation, hostile control, grudge carrying, and fearfulness cannot develop until the PAR somehow feels safe to do otherwise. The PAR must become less enmeshed with the earlier controlling, attacking figures. Rehabilitative contact comfort provided by a spouse or a child, combined with the therapist's interpersonal consistency and reliability, can help. If the abusing PAR can see that he or she is acting like a hated parent, he or she may become interested in becoming different. As usual, there is ambivalence, and so the therapist has to be careful about not simply being critical of the abusive parent to support the patient. The PAR is both loyal to and identified with the abusing parent. An attack on the parent intensifies the PAR's guilt about being disloyal, and can be seen as an attack on the PAR himself or herself.

Once new, safer bases are established with the spouse and or with the therapist, the PAR may channel his or her anger in a direction that encourages separation from the earlier destructive patterns and beliefs. The PAR does not necessarily need to physically distance himself or herself from the family; the same level of contact can be maintained. What has to change is the PAR's need to be affirmed by the abusers. When the PAR is degraded and extruded, he or she needs to recognize it for what it is and not "take it to heart."

One PAR started the process of differentiation by practicing angry thoughts (not words) at her mother. If she noticed herself slipping into angry rumination at her husband or children, she would turn in fantasy to angrily dismiss her mother from her thoughts. She, like most PARs, needed to change from identification with to differentiation from the aggressor. This rechanneling of anger can be a vital change step for the PAR. It is, however, quite difficult. One profoundly PAR woman who identified with a highly successful but cruel father became much worse in the years following his death. During one session, she acknowledged that her paranoid attacks on her husband and friends were an attempt to hold her father in purgatory. If she were to sever his connection to life by giving up his ways of being, he would surely descend to hell. In a key session wherein she had a brush with recovery, she said, "Take care of yourself, Dad. You're on your own now." Most unfortunately, this PAR was not able to maintain that position and steadfastly refused any further discussion of her relationship with her father. She did not recover from her own painful hell of misery and alienation.

A fascinating alternative method for helping a PAR give up the dedication to rage is offered by Sweet and Johnson (1990). These therapists have described successful use of Buddhist meditation to help three patients dissipate intense anger. The technique, called "meditation-enhanced empathy training" (MEET), teaches empathy and other prosocial attitudes described in Buddhist sources. These therapists have used the language of the SASB model to convey Buddhist attitudes of autonomy ("detachment") combined with friendliness ("love").

One of the cases described by these authors was that of an older man with a very long history of violent paranoid fantasies. After a relatively brief treatment with MEET, he appeared at the 3-year follow-up to have maintained his significant improvement. The MEET approach warrants further research because of its dramatic success with unquestionably difficult cases, and because of its relative efficiency.

It is important to note that no discussion of family, and no insight into family origins of the patterns, are involved in MEET. Consideration of family origins of interpersonal patterns is useful only if it helps mobilize the will to change. Understanding per se does little to implement change. The rationale for discussing family is simply that accurate explication of remembered experiences can alter the old loyalties. Awareness can offer the option of changing previously unconscious wishes and fears that have been motivating and organizing the maladaptive perceptions and responses. The need to understand the early roots of the patterns of the disorder is eliminated if something or someone more compelling can replace the old destructive loyalties. New loyalty to a very steady and loving spouse or to a convincing religious orientation can sometimes suffice. In the MEET cases, the religious context, combined with strong positive transferences to the two male therapists, probably helped create more benevolent introjects.

Facilitating New Learning

As is true for every personality disorder, new learning is nested within the first four stages of therapy. Once this is mastered, any residual learning that is still needed by the last stage of therapy is relatively easy to implement. For a PAR at this last stage, excursions into the social world to test the idea that friendly approaches elicit friendly reactions are just plain fun. The marvelousness of taking in praise and friendliness is frightening but exhilarating to the PAR. The immediate rewards in confirming rather than controlling and criticizing children are compelling. The discovery that trust can be trusted lifts anxiety and offers first glimpses of peacefulness to the PAR.

14

Schizoid and Schizotypal Personality Disorders

"Accounted for, but maybe not present." (SOI)
"I need to know if I am crazy." (SZT)

SCHIZOID PERSONALITY DISORDER

Review of the Literature

> This behavior pattern manifests shyness, over-sensitivity, seclusiveness, avoidance of close or competitive relationships, and often eccentricity. Autistic thinking without loss of capacity to recognize reality is common, as are daydreaming and the inability to express hostility and ordinary aggressive feelings. These patients react to disturbing experiences and conflicts with apparent detachment. (American Psychiatric Association, 1968, p. 42)

This definition of SOI from the DSM-II was split by the DSM-III, DSM-III-R, and DSM-IV into three categories: AVD, SZT, and SOI. All three share the interpersonal attributes of withdrawal and isolation. The current SZT category is distinguished from the other two by the presence of eccentric perceptions, thoughts, and behaviors. It bears the closest resemblance to Schizophrenia, the ultimate form of social withdrawal. AVDs and SOIs do not have distorted perceptions or unusual ideas. Individuals qualifying for the AVD label are willing to be socially involved, provided they are certain of being liked. Those better described as SOIs do not want or see the need for any social contact. The distinction between AVD and SOI stems from Millon's idea that detachment can be active or passive. According to Millon (1982), SOI represents passive detachment, an inherent hyporesponsiveness. In Chapter 12, the theoretical and empirical controversy over Millon's new AVD category has been reviewed; examples suggest that AVD can be found in clinical populations. In the present chapter, SOI and SZT are considered.

Persons with SOI are rarely seen in the clinic (Pfohl, Coryell, Zimmerman, & Stangl, 1986, p. 27; Morey, 1988, p. 574). It is not altogether clear that they exist in adequate numbers to justify a place in the standard nomenclature. It is possible that persons with SOI do exist, but rarely present for help. The reasoning that led to the DSM-III, DSM-III-R, and DSM-IV versions of SOI is Millon's.[1] According to Millon (1969), three critical dimensions or "polarities" describe personality: pleasure versus pain, self versus other, and active versus passive. Pathology is the result of imbalance in any of these polarities. SOI and AVD are defined in terms of the three polarities (Millon, 1986). Neither is able to experience pain or pleasure, or to receive gratification from self or other; they differ only in whether they withdraw actively (AVD) or passively (SOI). The category of SOI evolved logically from the need to fill the theoretical space described by Millon. His theory maintains that there must be individuals who have little capacity for pleasure or pain, are unable to receive pleasure from self or others, and who function in a passive mode.

DSM Definition of the Disorder

The DSM definition provides the starting point for the analysis. The DSM specifies that the diagnosis of SOI can be made if an individual meets four of the criteria. DSM-III-R items appear in **bold print,** and any changes introduced by DSM-IV appear in *italics.* (As in several earlier chapters, the item numbering used here is that of the DSM-IV. Original numbers in the DSM-III-R appear after **bold** items, in brackets.)

A pervasive pattern of indifference to social relationships and a restricted range of emotional experience and expression, beginning by early adulthood and present in a variety of contexts, as indicated by at least *four* of the following:

A pervasive pattern of detachment from social relationships and a restricted range of expression of emotions in interpersonal settings, beginning by early adulthood and present in a variety of contexts, as indicated by at least four of the following:

(1) neither desires nor enjoys close relationships, including being part of a family [item 1 in DSM-III-R]

(2) almost always chooses solitary activities [item 2 in DSM-III-R

(3) indicates little if any desire to have sexual experiences with another person (age being taken into account) [item 4 in DSM-III-R]

little, if any, interest in having sexual experiences with another person (age being taken into account)

---

[1]Using his theory, Millon (1982) wrote the Millon Clinical Multiaxial Inventory (MCMI), a 175-item, true–false survey that defines the 11 personality disorders of DSM-III. In addition, there are nine clinical syndrome scales and one validity scale. A revision published in 1986 added measures of response sets, and two new scales for personality disorders corresponding to two of the additional patterns described in Appendix A of DSM-III-R: Sadistic Personality Disorder, and Self-Defeating Personality Disorder. Millon asserts that the MCMI is a measure of DSM-III personality disorders (Millon, 1984), but this proposition has been challenged (Widiger & Frances, 1985, 1987; Widiger & Sanderson, 1987).

(4) rarely, if ever, claims or appears to experience strong emotions, such as anger or joy [item 3 in DSM-III-R]

few, if any, activities provide pleasure

(5) has no close friends or confidants (or only one) other than first-degree relatives [item 6 in DSM-III-R]

has no close friends or confidants (or only one)

(6) is indifferent to the praise and criticism of others [item 5 in DSM-III-R]

appears indifferent to the praise or criticism of others

(7) displays constricted affect, e.g., is aloof, cold, rarely reciprocates gestures or facial expressions, such as smiles or nods [item 7 in DSM-III-R]

emotional coldness, detachment, or flattened affectivity

Morey reported that only 1.4% of his sample met criteria for the SOI diagnosis when the rules of DSM-III were used; in the same sample, the figure was increased to 11.0% when the DSM-III-R criteria were used. The major difference was that DSM-III-R removed the exclusionary rule from DSM-III that the SOI diagnosis could not be made if SZT also applied. In the DSM-III-R, a concurrent diagnosis of SZT is permitted. Using the DSM-III-R on his sample of 291 outpatients, Morey found substantial overlap between SOI and AVD (53.1%), PAR (46.9%), and SZT (37.5%).

Pathogenic Hypotheses

The method of using the SASB model to develop pathogenic hypotheses has been sketched in Chapter 5. Unfortunately, it cannot be applied intact here to SOI, for the simple reason that I have never seen a case of SOI. The developmental hypotheses for every other disorder discussed in this book have been checked against clinical experience. For SOI, the discussion is entirely theoretical, and there are no case examples.

A summary of the hypotheses that may link interpersonal history to interpersonal patterns characteristic of the disorder appears in Table 14.1. A fuller discussion of these hypotheses is provided here.

1. Perhaps an SOI would have had a home that was orderly and formal. Physical and educational needs, including training about social form, would have been met. The parents might have intended to help the child achieve adequate independent adult functioning. There would not have been other hidden or explicit agendas for the child, such as bringing fame and recognition to the family. Expectations would be confined to the fundamental idea of performing basic social roles. Life in the home would probably be colorless. The result would be that the SOI is socialized enough to perform adult roles, but remains quite detached.

2. There would probably not be much warmth, play, or social or emotional

Table 14.1. Interpersonal Summary of SOI

History	Consequences of history
1. Formal, orderly home in which physical and educational needs were met (**CONTROL**)	1. Socialized for work
2. No emotional warmth, and minimal social contact in the family or elsewhere (**IGNORE**)	2. Not sociable; comfortable with isolation (WALL OFF)
	Pushes away intimate approaches (**IGNORE**)
	Engages in fantasy (*SELF-NEGLECT*)

Summary: There are no fears of or wishes about others. The baseline position involves active and passive autonomy. Underdeveloped in social awareness and skills, the SOI nonetheless has instrumental skills, and can meet expectations of formal social roles (parent, boss, employee). He or she may be married but does not develop intimacy. There may be an active, but not necessarily bizarre, fantasy life.

SASB codes of SOI baseline: Distancing is active (**IGNORE**) and passive (WALL OFF). There is also *SELF-NEGLECT*. *Wishes:* None. *Fears:* None. *Necessary descriptors:* Social withdrawal (polythetic approach). *Exclusionary descriptors:* Strong affect; eccentricity; complex manipulative skills; concern about abandonment; wish for love and acceptance; need to control.

interaction within the family or elsewhere. The SOI would have learned mostly by modeling to withdraw to his or her room and engage in orderly, solitary, silent pursuits such as reading, stamp collecting, or building models. This identification with a withdrawn parent would also lead the SOI to expect nothing and give nothing. The SOI is, Millon says, not attached to self or others; he or she is socialized, but not sociable.

The SASB model would predict that social and emotional isolation would be associated with daydreaming. In other words, IGNORE would be internalized to become *SELF-NEGLECT*. Since there would be few complicated messages to internalize, the daydreaming need not be particularly odd or bizarre. Fantasy is not mentioned in the current DSM.

In trying to imagine whether I have ever known an SOI in any context, I recall farmers from my childhood in upstate New York. They worked long hours in the fields and barns, and came to their houses only for breakfast, dinner, supper, and sleep. They said very little to anyone at any time, but sometimes would mutter to themselves. If they spoke, they might start a sentence and not finish it. Apparently they would just drift off into their thoughts. It was not unusual to hear them talk to cows or other animals. They might laugh out loud during these "conversations." They reportedly had done well in the public educational system, but they were only marginally successful as farmers. They did read the newspaper, but never commented. At family gatherings they would fall asleep. Nowadays, I suppose, they would watch TV most of the time. Some of them were married, but they seemed not to notice their wives or children. All of them were male.

Connections between the Interpersonal History and the Symptoms Listed in the DSM

The "total SOI" should show all the symptoms mentioned in the DSM. The emphasis on instrumental adequacy in the context of social and emotional isolation should lead to all the symptoms listed for SOI. Interpersonal contact should be rare (item 2) and confidants few (item 5). Emotional skills should be atrophied: There should be a lack of desire for close relationships (item 1), indifference to praise or criticism (item 6), no interpersonal sexuality (item 3), lack of pleasure (item 4), and emotional coldness (item 7).

Interpersonal Summary of SOI

The foregoing analysis suggests a succinct interpersonal summary for SOI:

There are no fears of or wishes about others. The baseline position involves active and passive autonomy. Underdeveloped in social awareness and skills, the SOI nonetheless has instrumental skills, and can meet expectations of formal social roles (parent, boss, employee). He or she may be married but does not develop intimacy. There may be an active, but not necessarily bizarre, fantasy life.

The summary is based on the SASB codes of the baseline SOI patterns, wishes, and fears. If indeed it exists, SOI would be the only personality disorder that can directly be mapped onto a specific circumscribed area of the SASB model. The procedure of assigning personality disorders to specific areas of a circumplex was first illustrated by Leary (1957, p. 233). Leary's ideas have been developed further by Wiggins (1982, p. 212), Kiesler (1986, p. 577), and others (see Chapter 2 for further discussion). The analyses in this book suggest that personality disorders are too interpersonally complicated to be mapped directly onto the SASB model. SOI, if it exists, may be an exception. It is described simply as IGNORE, WALL OFF, and *SELF-NEGLECT*. These points are all located in the "10 o'clock region" of the SASB model (see Figure 3.9).

The rhythm and harmonics of the SOI song should be found in the sequences of interpersonal and intrapsychic response that the SOI gives and receives. The "tonic" SOI position consists of WALL OFF and IGNORE. This should call for others to do the same. A marital partner who seeks intimacy may bring the SOI for couples therapy. The SOI should be perplexed about the need. He or she also may not be particularly upset by the threat of divorce. These should be the harmonics and rhythms of the SOI song.

In each of the preceding chapters, there has been an interpersonal analysis of the different ways in which individuals with the respective disorders reacted to the need for antidepressants. With his or her comfortable distance and affective detachment, an SOI is unlikely to be depressed. If he or she were depressed, he or she would not know it. The lack of vegetative signs would not support prescription of antidepressants.

Table 14.2. Comparison of SASB Codes of BPD, NPD, HPD, ASP, DPD, OCD, NEG, AVD, PAR, SOI, and SZT

	BPD	NPD	HPD	ASP	DPD	OCD	NEG	AVD	PAR	SOI	SZT
1. EMANCIPATE											×*
2. AFFIRM											
3. ACTIVE LOVE	×			×*							
4. PROTECT											
5. CONTROL	×	×	×*	×*		×*			×		×*
6. BLAME	×	×	×	×		×	×*	×	×		
7. ATTACK	×	×		×*					×		
8. IGNORE		×		×		×*				×	
1. SEPARATE		×		×			×*		×		
2. DISCLOSE											
3. REACTIVE LOVE			×*								
4. TRUST	×		×*		×						
5. SUBMIT					×	×*	×*				×*
6. SULK					×		×*	×			
7. RECOIL								×	×		×
8. WALL OFF			×*	×*		×*	×*	×	×	×	×*
1. SELF-EMANCIPATE											
2. SELF-AFFIRM											
3. ACTIVE SELF-LOVE		×*									
4. SELF-PROTECT	×			×*							
5. SELF-CONTROL						×*		×	×		×
6. SELF-BLAME		×			×	×	×				
7. SELF-ATTACK	×		×*				×*				
8. SELF-NEGLECT	×	×*		×*		×*				×	×

*Indicates that these codes within the same column appear in complex combinations with one another.

The baseline notes of the SOI song are compared to those of the songs for the other disorders in Table 14.2. A scan of the table shows that the SOI pattern is unique in its simplicity: The SOI walls off in every way possible. There are no complex positions. The other disorders that share the three baseline codes are ASP and OCD. Like the SOI, the ASP and OCD are socially detached but functional. The SOI lacks their anger and their interest in CONTROL.

The interpersonal *do, re, mi* of Table 14.2 shows how SOI overlaps with other categories; it also shows how they differ. The descriptions can help the clinician make differential diagnoses.

DSM Descriptors Revisited

The DSM view of SOI has now been translated into interpersonal language, and the psychosocial learning presumed to be associated with SOI patterns has been outlined. In this section, the interpersonal analysis of SOI is compared directly to the DSM. DSM-III-R items appear in **bold print**; any changes introduced by the DSM-IV appear in *italics*. (Again, the item numbering used is that of the DSM-IV.) The interpersonal modifiers are underlined. Items from the WISPI (discussed in Chapter 1) appear in CAPITAL LETTERS.

A pervasive pattern of indifference to social relationships and a restricted range of emotional experience and expression, beginning by early adulthood and present in a variety of contexts, as indicated by at least *four* of the following.

A pervasive pattern of detachment from social relationships and a restricted range of expression of emotions in interpersonal settings, beginning by early adulthood and present in a variety of contexts, as indicated by at least four of the following:

(1) neither desires nor enjoys close relationships, including being part of a family

In contrast to the SZT, the SOI is interested in marrying and assuming the formal role of family member, but that does not include intimacy as shown by spending time together, disclosing, sexually attending to the spouse, and so on.

I'VE BEEN KNOWN TO READ MAGAZINES OR BOOKS AT SOCIAL GATHERINGS.

(2) almost always chooses solitary activities

Seems oblivious to others except in an instrumental sense. Just goes on with his or her role, gets tasks done, but apparently has no need for social contact.

I ALMOST ALWAYS DO THINGS ON MY OWN.

(3) indicates little if any desire to have sexual experiences with another person (age being taken into account)

little, if any, interest in having sexual experiences with another person (age being taken into account)

Is socialized, but not sociable. Role-appropriate, he or she nonetheless does not have the genuine social bonding associated with interest in sexuality.

SEXUALITY SIMPLY IS NOT IMPORTANT TO ME.

(4) rarely, if ever, claims or appears to experience strong emotions, such as anger or joy

few, if any, activities provide pleasure

Since the SOI does not attend to social cues, or have a developed sense of the subtleties of social interaction, affective reactions are rare and mild. Is truly "oblivious."

I DON'T HAVE STRONG FEELINGS ABOUT ANYONE OR ANYTHING.

(5) has no close friends or confidants (or only one) other than first-degree relatives

has no close friends or confidants (or only one)

Social contacts are restricted to those mandated by role (e.g., father, brother, partner on assembly line).

I DON'T FEEL THE NEED TO BE CLOSE TO PEOPLE OTHER THAN ONE OR TWO FAMILY MEMBERS.

(6) is indifferent to the praise or criticism of others

appears indifferent to the praise or criticism of others

Content with his or her function, and lacking interest in and skills needed for reading social cues from others, he or she is not affected by social contingencies such as praise or criticism.

I AM NEVER BOTHERED BY WHAT OTHERS THINK OF ME.

(7) displays constricted affect, e.g., is aloof, cold, rarely reciprocates gestures or facial expressions, such as smiles or nods

emotional coldness, detachment, or flattened affectivity

Formally correct, but lacks skills in sending and receiving social cues. If brought to couples therapy, for example, he or she is perplexed about what the problem might be. He or she lacks the capacity to understand the spouse's wish for more intimacy. Seems like an interpersonal "black hole"—signals disappear forever without leaving a trace.

I GET LOST IN WHAT I'M DOING AND DON'T PAY ATTENTION TO WHAT'S GOING ON AROUND ME.

Necessary and Exclusionary Criteria

All of the descriptors for SOI have to do with simple, uncomplicated social indifference and isolation. None is more crucial than another. The polythetic approach seems appropriate. No one way of walling off is *necessary* to the definition of this disorder.

The simplicity of the social withdrawal in SOI means that there are a number of *exclusionary* conditions. Any complication of the position of social withdrawal by the presence of other messages would rule out SOI. Examples would include the strong affect found in PAR, BPD, HPD, and NPD; the eccentricity of SZT; the complex manipulative skills of ASP and HPD; the concern about abandonment found in BPD and DPD; the wish for affection and acceptance seen in AVD; and the need to control seen in BPD, NPD, HPD, ASP, OCD, and PAR.

Case Illustrations

It is very difficult to find psychiatric patients who are socially withdrawn, lack interest in social contact, and are not also odd or eccentric. However, it remains true that people with this pattern would logically not define themselves as patients and be seen in a clinic or hospital. There would be little reason for SOIs to present themselves for treatment. They are socially withdrawn; do not want to make social connections; and do not suffer from anger, fear, or depression. Again, I have not seen patients who resemble the DSM-III-R or DSM-IV description of SOI. The only description of SOI offered by the DSM-III-R casebook is called "Man's Best Friend" (Spitzer et al., 1989, pp. 249–250). The patient in that example seems to be actively avoidant rather than passively detached, however. John, a 50-year-old retired policeman, came to the clinic because of a grief reaction to the death of his dog. Employed as a security guard, he was up to date on world affairs but was known by coworkers as a "loner" and a "cold fish."

> At Christmas he would buy the dog elaborate gifts, and, in return, would receive a wrapped bottle of Scotch that he bought for himself as a gift from the dog. *He believes that dogs are more sensitive and loving than people,* and he can, in return, express toward them a tenderness and emotion not possible in his relationships with people. The losses of his pets are the only events in his life that have caused him sadness. He experienced the death of his parents without emotion, and feels no regret whatever at being completely out of contact with the rest of his family. He considers himself different from other people, and regards emotionality in others with bewilderment. (Spitzer et al., 1989, p. 249; emphasis added)

The authors of the casebook note that the requisite number of DSM descriptors fit John as withdrawn and not wanting social contact. However, John's affect suggests that his isolation represented active rather than passive rejection of others ("dogs are more sensitive and loving than people"). Such views are more angry and defensive than passively hyporesponsive.

Expectable Transference Reactions and Treatment Implications

I have no data base upon which to check and refine the developmental hypotheses, and no clinical experience to use to comment on the psychosocial treatment of SOI.

SCHIZOTYPAL PERSONALITY DISORDER

Review of the Literature

In the current DSM-III-R and DSM-IV, SZT is considered to be less severe than Schizophrenia. In practice, it is often seen as the characterological parallel of Schizophrenia. In addition to separating SZT from schizophrenia, a major diagnostic dilemma has been distinguishing SZT from BPD. Both groups often include individuals who suffer from thought disorder. The issues, and the rationale for creation of the category of SZT, were presented in a paper called "Crossing the Border into Borderline Personality and Borderline Schizophrenia" by Spitzer, Endicott, and Gibbon (1979).

> Although the term "borderline" has been used in the literature as an adjective to modify a large number of terms (condition, syndrome, personality, state, character, pattern, organization, schizophrenia), it appeared to us, from a review

of the literature as well as from personal contact with current investigators interested in this area, that there are two major ways in which "borderline" is currently used that covers the range of uses. The first refers to a constellation of relatively enduring personality features of instability and vulnerability that have important treatment and outcome correlates. Examples of this use of the concept are reflected in the writings of Gunderson and Singer on the "borderline patient" and Kernberg on "borderline personality organization."

The second major use of the term is to describe certain psychopathological characteristics that are usually stable over time and are assumed to be genetically related to a spectrum of disorders including chronic schizophrenia. This usage is exemplified by the term "borderline schizophrenia" as used by Wender, Kety, Rosenthal, and their colleagues in their adoptive studies of the contribution of nature and nurture to the development of schizophrenia. (p. 17)

To determine how to distinguish BPD from SZT, Spitzer and colleagues interviewed key representatives of two points of view. One group included those believing that BPD is continuous with Schizophrenia. The other consisted of those maintaining that BPD is a unique personality disorder, not particularly related to Schizophrenia. On the basis of these interviews, two sets of items were created respectively to delineate key attributes for "unstable personality" and for SZT. The two item sets were validated by using the key theorists' clinical judgments as criteria. The sets were then cross-validated on a very large sample ($n = 800$) of members of the American Psychiatric Association. Responding clinicians were asked to select two of their own patients for the study. One subject was to "warrant a diagnosis of borderline personality, borderline personality organization, or borderline schizophrenia"; the second was to be a control subject who was "moderately to severely ill, but [did] not have a diagnosis of a psychosis nor any of the borderline categories" (Spitzer et al., 1979, p. 20).

Various statistical tests were performed to check each diagnostic item's ability to discriminate the index cases from the controls, and SZT from "unstable personality." The investigators concluded that the two types could be identified, but were not mutually exclusive: "Approximately half of the patients considered borderline will meet our criteria for both unstable and schizotypal personality" (Spitzer et al., 1979, p. 24). The results of this important study guided the definition of SZT and BPD in the DSM-III. In effect, this work established that SZT is the characterological variant of Schizophrenia. BPD may be seen as a different constellation, better conceived of as "unstable personality" (Widiger, Frances, Spitzer, & Williams, 1988, p. 792).

McGlashan (1987) studied the DSM-III definitions for these two disorders in a long-term follow-up study. Item analyses suggested that odd communication, suspicious/paranoid ideation, and social isolation were characteristic of SZT. The "core DSM-III symptoms" for BPD were, as expected, unstable relationships, impulsivity, and self-damaging acts. The same sample of patients was also used to compare these two personality disorders to Schizophrenia (McGlashan, 1986). Results suggested that the prognoses for SZT and Schizophrenia were more similar than those for SZT and BPD. McGlashan (1986) also reported, "From the perspective of follow-up, SPD [i.e., SZT] appeared related to S [Schizophrenia], but not to BPD" (p. 329).

McGlashan's (1986) study also yielded an unexpected and puzzling finding that the coexistence of SZT and Schizophrenia enhanced outcome compared to the presence of Schizophrenia alone. Usually, the coexistence of an Axis II disorder is predictive of worse outcome. McGlashan wondered, "Might character pathology serve to 'compartmentalize' or 'contain' S [Schizophrenia] pathology?" (1986, p. 333).

Controversy has continued about whether the cognitive/perceptual items (magical thinking, ideas of reference, recurrent illusions, odd speech, and suspicious/paranoid ideation) or the social/interpersonal items (social isolation, inadequate rapport, and social anxiety) are more useful in defining SZT. The arguments and data were reviewed by Widiger, Frances, and Trull (1987). These investigators concluded that the usefulness of diagnostic cues varies according to context. In a clinical population, they found that the cognitive/perceptual items were more efficient in making the diagnosis of SZT. In a clinical sample, the cognitive symptoms yielded much less overlap with the other disorders than did the social/interpersonal items.

SZTs have been successfully treated with low-dose neuroleptics (Hymowitz, Frances, Jacobsberg, Sickles, & Hoyt, 1986; Schulz, Schulz, & Wilson, 1988). The salience of the thought disorder in SZT has encouraged many researchers to agree with the idea that it is related to Schizophrenia. In further support of that view, Kendler, Masterson, Ungaro, and Davis (1984) reported that "schizophrenia-related personality disorders were significantly more common in the first-degree relatives of the schizophrenic than of the control probands. . . . These results confirm previous reports indicating a genetic link between schizophrenia and schizoid, schizotypal and paranoid personality disorders" (p. 425).

The view of SZT as closely related to Schizophrenia has reinforced the belief that at least the cognitive difficulties found in SZT, like those characteristic of Schizophrenia, arise from genetically transmitted vulnerabilities. The cognitive deficits that inspire the label of Axis I Obsessive Compulsive Disorder can also sometimes approach psychotic proportions. If this disorder is accompanied by SZT, the response to drug treatment for the thought disorder is likely to be poor (Jenike, Baer, Minichiello, Schwartz, & Carey, 1986, p. 530).

DSM Definition of the Disorder

The DSM definition provides the starting point for the analysis. The DSM specifies that the diagnosis of SZT can be made if an individual meets five of the criteria. DSM-III-R items appear in **bold print**, and any changes introduced by the DSM-IV appear in *italics*. (Again, the item numbering used here is that of the DSM-IV. Original numbers in the DSM-III-R appear after **bold** items, in brackets.)

A pervasive pattern of deficits in interpersonal relatedness and peculiarities of ideation, appearance, and behavior, beginning by early adulthood and present in a variety of contexts, as indicated by at least five of the following:

A pervasive pattern of social and interpersonal deficits marked by acute discomfort with, and reduced capacity for, close relationships as well as by cognitive or perceptual distortions and eccentricities of behavior, beginning by early adulthood and present in a variety of contexts, as indicated by at least five of the following:
[Note: These signs and symptoms should not be limited to discrete periods of mood symptomatology (e.g., depression, anxiety, anger).]

(1) ideas of reference (excluding delusions of reference) [item 1 in DSM-III-R]

(2) odd beliefs or magical thinking, influencing behavior and inconsistent with subcultural norms, e.g., superstitiousness, belief in clairvoyance, telepathy, or "sixth sense," "others can feel my feelings" (in children and adolescents, bizarre fantasies or preoccupations) [item 3 in DSM-III-R]

odd beliefs or magical thinking, which influence behavior and are inconsistent with subcultural norms (e.g., superstitiousness, belief in clairvoyance, telepathy, or "sixth sense," "others can feel my feelings"; in children and adolescents, bizarre fantasies or preoccupations)

(3) unusual perceptual experiences, e.g., illusions, sensing the presence of a force or person not actually present (e.g., "I felt as if my dead mother were in the room with me") [item 4 in DSM-III-R]

unusual perceptual experiences, including somatosensory (bodily) illusions

(4) odd speech (without loosening of associations or incoherence), e.g., speech that is impoverished, digressive, vague, or inappropriately abstract [item 7 in DSM-III-R]

odd thinking and speech (without loosening of associations or incoherence) (e.g., vague, circumstantial, metaphorical, overelaborate, or stereotyped)

(5) suspiciousness or paranoid ideation [item 9 in DSM-III-R]

(6) inappropriate or constricted affect, e.g., silly, aloof, rarely reciprocates gestures or facial expressions, such as smiles or nods [item 8 in DSM-III-R]

inappropriate or constricted affect (e.g., appears cold and aloof)

(7) odd or eccentric behavior or appearance, e.g., unkempt, unusual mannerisms, talks to self [item 5 in DSM-III-R]

behavior or appearance that is odd, eccentric, or peculiar

(8) no close friends or confidants (or only one) other than first-degree relatives [item 6 in DSM-III-R]

no close friends or confidants (or only one) other than first-degree relatives, due primarily to lack of desire, pervasive discomfort with others, or eccentricities

(9) excessive social anxiety, e.g., extreme discomfort in social situations involving unfamiliar people [item 2 in DSM-III-R]

excessive social anxiety (e.g., extreme discomfort in social situations that does not diminish with familiarity and tends to be associated with paranoid fears rather than negative judgments about self)

Morey (1988) reported that 9.3% of a sample of 291 outpatients being treated for personality disorder qualified for the SZT label. There was substantial overlap with AVD (59.3%), PAR (59.3%), SOI (44.4%), BPD (33.3%), and NPD (33.3%).

Pathogenic Hypotheses

The method of using the SASB model to develop pathogenic hypotheses was sketched in Chapter 5. Four main features of the developmental history have been identified specifically to account for each of the SZT symptoms listed in the DSM. A summary of the hypotheses linking interpersonal history to interpersonal patterns characteristic of the disorder appears in Table 14.3. A fuller discussion of these hypotheses is provided here.

1. The parent punished the child for allegedly inappropriate autonomy taking while the parent himself or herself did the same. For example, a father who was rarely home might beat the child for not staying home. The parent modeled an illogic suggesting that even when not present, he or she nonetheless "knew" something vitally important about the child (CONTROL plus WALL OFF plus EMANCIPATE). The parent undermined the child's reality testing by exhibiting the very behaviors for which he or she punished the child.

The adult consequence is that the SZT imitates the pattern of "knowing" through special channels. He or she also claims to have inordinate knowledge about and ability to influence others. The information is imparted "from a distance." For example, the SZT who claims to have a sixth sense, or telepathy, presumes to have information about events that will affect others. He or she offers it for others to use on their own behalf if they wish. For example, SZT fortune tellers do not press customers to heed the information tendered. Intimate and vital information is available if the customer sees fit. The SZT remains personally detached.

2. There was inappropriate parental reliance on the child for performance of household tasks. Life itself was at stake. For example, a daughter might have had to do all the housework and cooking, because she was told that her presence was a great stress. She was told that if she did not help out in this way, her mother might have a fatal heart attack. In effect, the child was taught that her mere existence gave her inordinate destructive power. The child also learned that if she behaved properly and did what was expected, bad outcomes could be averted. By assigning the child major responsibilities under such threatening and bizarre conditions, the parent blatantly negated and ignored the child's reality. By commanding the child to take on such important roles, the parent was inappropriately controlling and deferential (CONTROL plus SUBMIT plus IGNORE).

The principle of complementarity then predisposes the child both to defer and to control in inappropriate ways (WALL OFF plus SUBMIT plus CONTROL). This is maintained in adulthood by a paradoxical tendency to implement power through deference to certain arbitrary procedures or rituals. The SZT simulta-

Table 14.3. Interpersonal Summary of SZT

History	Consequences of history
1. From a position of autonomy, the parent blamed the child for alleged separateness (e.g., the absent father beat the child for not staying home all the time) (**BLAME** plus **IGNORE** plus <u>SEPARATE</u>)	1. From a distance, claims to "know" via mind reading, telepathy, and other special means (<u>WALL</u> <u>OFF</u> plus **CONTROL** plus **EMANCIPATE**)
2. Inappropriate reliance on the child for performance, with life itself at stake (**CONTROL** plus <u>SUBMIT</u> plus **IGNORE**)	2. Remaining separate, submits to rituals that bring control—e.g., magical rites (<u>WALL</u> <u>OFF</u> plus **CONTROL** plus <u>SUBMIT</u>)
3. Severe abuse, involving invasion of the child's personal boundaries (**ATTACK, CONTROL**)	3. Paranoid withdrawal (<u>RECOIL</u>) *SELF-CONTROL* to contain potential identification with the aggressor (**ATTACK**); somewhat permeable boundaries
4. Aloneness (<u>WALL</u> <u>OFF</u>) provided safe haven	4. Marked social withdrawal (<u>WALL</u> <u>OFF</u>) and autism (*SELF-NEGLECT*).

Summary: There is a fear of attacking, humiliating control; the wish is that others will leave the SZT alone. His or her baseline position is one of hostile withdrawal and self-neglect. The SZT believes that he or she has a capacity for magical influence that can be implemented directly (telepathy) or indirectly (control through ritual). Usually the SZT imposes these "powers" from a distance. He or she is aware of aggressive feelings, but usually restrains them.

SASB codes of SZT baseline: Delusions of autistic control (<u>WALL</u> <u>OFF</u> plus **CONTROL** plus **EMANCIPATE**, or <u>WALL</u> <u>OFF</u> plus **CONTROL** plus <u>SUBMIT</u>), <u>WALL</u> <u>OFF</u>, <u>RECOIL</u>, *SELF-NEGLECT*, and *SELF-CONTROL*. *Wishes:* To receive **EMANCIPATE**. *Fears:* To receive **BLAME** or **ATTACK**. *Necessary descriptors:* Social withdrawal; thought disorder that implies autistic control. *Exclusionary descriptors:* Fear of autonomy; proud disregard for social norms; demanding dependency.

neously remains detached. For example, the SZT who performs as a medium through which spirits communicate requires that all who are present defer to the wishes of the spirits. Participants must assume exactly the prescribed thoughts and positions, or the spirits may deny privilege and access. This is the familiar pattern from childhood of having extraordinary influence while helplessly deferring to complex and unfathomable mandates.

3. A long history of severe abuse (**ATTACK**) leads to paranoid withdrawal (<u>RECOIL</u>) in the adult SZT. He or she is usually aware of the tendency also to identify with the aggressive parent. Normally SZTs succeed in restraining themselves (*SELF-CONTROL*) and do not lash out. They are vulnerable to feeling invaded and victimized by outside forces, and consciously restrain their anger.

4. There were strong injunctions against leaving the home for peer play or other reasons. At the same time, being alone provided safe haven. Confined to the home, the SZT-to-be was allowed to spend days alone in his or her room to escape the parental "war zone." The child learned not to "bother" the abusive parent (<u>WALL</u> <u>OFF</u>). The prohibitions against leaving the home interfered with social development. The deprivation of peer play and the condition of safe haven

while alone reinforced the position of WALL OFF and encouraged the development of fantasy and other forms of SELF-NEGLECT.[2]

Connections between the Interpersonal History and the Symptoms Listed in the DSM

The "total SZT" shows all the symptoms mentioned in the DSM. Several DSM items mark thought disorders: odd beliefs or magical thinking (item 2), unusual perceptual experiences (item 3), and odd thinking and speech (item 4). The thought disorder is widely believed to be the direct consequence of flaws in the person's biochemistry. Whether genetic deficiency is the cause, the present analysis suggests that the specific form of the SZT's thought disorder is shaped by early learning. The SZT was told that he or she had great power to help or hurt. He or she was supported for being "out of the way," but couldn't achieve that through peer play. Consigned to social isolation, the SZT cultivated his or her imagination. The codes of the SZT's thought disorders are like the codes of the family experiences. The magical beliefs, unusual perceptual experiences, and patterns of odd thinking are complex mixtures of omnipotence, deference, and detachment. This extraordinarily complex view of the self in the world is associated with equally complex and "odd" affect (item 6).

The SZT's paranoia was encouraged by chronic and invasive abuse. Ideas of reference (item 1) and suspiciousness or paranoid ideation (item 5) are understandable, given the SZT's history. He or she was assigned the responsibility for the life of a parent, and at the same time was the target of severe psychological, physical, and sexual abuse. Subject to strange attributions as well as abuse in the home, the SZT never had a chance to learn normal social skills through peer play. He or she was deprived of appropriate feedback and became "odd" in behavior or appearance (item 7). The injunction against autonomy and peer play accounts for the lack of friends (item 8) and the social anxiety (item 9).

Interpersonal Summary of SZT

The foregoing analysis suggests a succinct interpersonal summary for SZT:

There is a fear of attacking, humiliating control; the wish is that others will leave the SZT alone. His or her baseline position is one of hostile withdrawal and self-neglect. The SZT believes that he or she has a capacity for magical influence that can be implemented directly (telepathy) or indirectly (control through ritual). Usually the SZT imposes these "powers" from a distance. He or she is aware of aggressive feelings, but usually restrains them.

---

[2]Please see the more detailed discussion of SELF-NEGLECT in Chapter 3 and in the Appendix (Table A.3). There, it can be seen that this way of relating to the self includes a variety of forms of self-stimulation and loss of contact with reality.

The summary is based on the SASB codes of the SZT baseline patterns and wishes. The codes themselves, listed in Table 14.3, provide a shorthand way to identify SZT. There are delusions that involve autistic control (WALL OFF plus CONTROL plus EMANCIPATE, or WALL OFF plus CONTROL plus SUBMIT). In addition, the SZT shows simple RECOIL, WALL OFF, *SELF-NEGLECT,* and *SELF-CONTROL.* The wish is to be left alone (EMANCIPATE). The fear is of BLAME or ATTACK.

The rhythm and harmonics of the SZT song are found in the sequences of interpersonal and intrapsychic response that the SZT gives and receives. The "tonic" SZT position is autistic control (WALL OFF plus CONTROL plus EMANCI-PATE). This harmonizes well with someone who will set aside the connection to reality, and defer without wanting to enmesh with the SZT (IGNORE plus SUBMIT plus SEPARATE). The believing customer of the fortune teller is an ideal example of "uninvolved deference." The other variation on the theme of autistic control is (WALL OFF plus CONTROL plus SUBMIT). Here, the SZT follows a ritual of some sort to have a desired effect. Again, the position will go well with someone who will do the same: SUBMIT to the ritual, but IGNORE both reality and the SZT personally.

The SZT is unlikely to look after himself or herself, because the early neglect has been internalized as *SELF-NEGLECT.* He or she is also less likely than the PAR to identify with the aggressor; instead, he or she will engage in *SELF-CONTROL* to restrain anger. The SZT's paranoid positions of RECOIL or WALL OFF will draw for ATTACK or IGNORE. The fearfulness, the carelessness with self, the oddness, and the constraint of anger make the SZT a very likely target for an abuser who needs to attack with impunity. These are the harmonics and the rhythms of the SZT song.

Readers who can use the SASB codes will be able to generalize the present analysis to contexts not mentioned here. For example, it is not unusual for patients to complain that their depression is getting worse. Sometimes these complaints are presented to the therapist in a way that is characteristic of SZT. To interpret a complaint about depression in this way, the therapist would need to code the patient's process as he or she describes the depression. A SZT's process with the therapist as he or she complains about symptoms would include the notes of the SZT song. Consider this example:

> A patient clearly had vegetative signs of depression, but believed them to be a consequence of the way the stars were aligned at her birth. Nonetheless, she accepted antidepressants at various times, mainly to help her control her irritability. She was not impressed by their efficacy and showed erratic compliance. She preferred treatment by acupuncture, supplemented by special herbs. Viewing a particular type of sunset also helped, she noted. The doctor wondered whether she had a thought disorder, because she believed her depression got worse when she was in the presence of certain "energy fields."

The baseline notes of the SZT song are compared to those of the songs for the other disorders in Table 14.2. A scan of the table shows that the SZT shares a number of features with the OCD. Both are interested in CONTROL that is used in complex combination with other features. Both will SUBMIT independently of social context and WALL OFF personally. The OCD will defer to rules and authority, however, whereas the SZT "submits" to his or her own idea of proper ritual and procedures. The two share a heavy investment in control and self-determination; both engage in SELF-CONTROL. The OCD is clearly interpersonal in his or her control and deference. The SZT, by contrast, implements these positions in delusional ways.

The SZT also shares many features with the PAR. Both show strong RECOIL and WALL OFF from the mainstream. Despite their alienation, both like to CONTROL others as well as themselves (SELF-CONTROL). Unlike the SZT, the PAR is likely to ATTACK others. The SZT is more capable of complex deference, while the PAR is fiercely independent.

The interpersonal analysis of Table 14.2 suggests that the SZT shares with the BPD a predilection for CONTROL and SELF-NEGLECT. They also differ greatly, in that the SZT has an autonomous baseline (RECOIL and WALL OFF) and wishes to remain EMANCIPATEd, whereas the BPD fears autonomy (IGNORE). Interpersonal analyses support the validity of the claim that the DSM-III and its successors did succeed in distinguishing SZT from BPD. SZT may still need better distinction from the Axis I disorder Schizophrenia.

The interpersonal *do, re, mi* of Table 14.2 shows exactly how the categories overlap; it also shows how they differ. The descriptions in the tables can help the clinician make the differential diagnosis.

DSM Descriptors Revisited

The DSM view of SZT has now been translated into interpersonal language, and the psychosocial learning associated with SZT patterns has been outlined. In this section, the interpersonal analysis of SZT is compared directly to the DSM. DSM-III-R items appear in **bold print**; any changes introduced by the DSM-IV appear in *italics*. (Again, the item numbering used is that of the DSM-IV.) The interpersonal modifiers are underlined. Items from the WISPI (discussed in Chapter 1) appear in CAPITAL LETTERS.

A pervasive pattern of deficits in interpersonal relatedness and peculiarities of ideation, appearance, and behavior, beginning by early adulthood and present in a variety of contexts, as indicated by at least *five* of the following:

A pervasive pattern of social and interpersonal deficits marked by acute discomfort with, and reduced capacity for, close relationships as well as by cognitive or perceptual distortions and eccentricities of behavior, beginning by early adulthood and present in a variety of contexts, as indicated by at least five of the following:
[Note: These signs and symptoms should not be limited to discrete periods of mood symptomatology (e.g., depression, anxiety, anger).]

(1) ideas of reference (excluding delusions of reference)

Feels that he or she has special powers to read, detect, predict. Emphasis is likely to be on the ability to protect self or others from harm, or to contain/punish evil forces.

THE CONNECTIONS BETWEEN SEEMINGLY UNRELATED OBJECTS OR EVENTS TELL ME ABOUT WHAT WILL HAPPEN.

(2) odd beliefs or magical thinking, influencing behavior and inconsistent with subcultural norms, e.g., superstitiousness, belief in clairvoyance, telepathy, or "sixth sense," "others can feel my feelings" (in children and adolescents, bizarre fantasies or preoccupations).

odd beliefs or magical thinking, which influence behavior and are inconsistent with subcultural norms (e.g., superstitiousness, belief in clairvoyance, telepathy, or "sixth sense," "others can feel my feelings"; in children and adolescents, bizarre fantasies or preoccupations)

In addition to possessing magical powers of influence, the SZT believes that he or she has powers of sensing—that he or she can gather data inaccessible to others. Mind reading and foreknowledge are examples. The SZT believes that he or she has magical control over others, usually presented in the context of avoiding harm and acquiring benefits—often for others rather than for the self. Sometimes the SZT will use magical ideas to constrain his or her own destructiveness, but here too the purpose is protective. The magical influence can be implemented directly (e.g., thinking that somebody will have to go to the bathroom, and then the person does), or indirectly through compliance with magical rituals (e.g., walking past a specific object three times in order to avoid a certain harmful outcome).

I CAN MAKE OTHERS DO THINGS BY JUST THINKING ABOUT IT.

(3) unusual perceptual experiences, e.g., illusions, sensing the presence of a force or person not actually present (e.g., "I felt as if my dead mother were in the room with me")

unusual perceptual experiences, including somatosensory (bodily) illusions

Despite their sense of power and of separateness from what is going on, SZTs can also feel threatened by helplessness in face of overwhelming outside forces. This weakness in the sense of self contributes to their resemblance to people with Schizophrenia. However, the SZT thought disorder usually preserves a sense of self-efficacy, a sense of magical "control" of situations that is less likely to appear in Schizophrenia.

THERE ARE TIMES WHEN I FEEL SPACY, LIKE I AM SEPARATED FROM OR OUTSIDE OF MYSELF.

(4) odd speech (without loosening of associations or incoherence), e.g., speech that is impoverished, digressive, vague, or inappropriately abstract

odd thinking and speech (without loosening of associations or incoherence) (e.g., vague, circumstantial, metaphorical, overelaborate, or stereotyped)

If the SZT feels that the interviewer is invasive, he or she will respond with speech that is not clearly bizarre, but does not really make sense.

I DON'T COMMUNICATE WELL WITH OTHERS BECAUSE I HAVE MY OWN DIFFERENT WAY OF SEEING THINGS.

(5) suspiciousness or paranoid ideation

SZT's paranoia is confined to the sense of being scrutinized and criticized, and their response is to withdraw artistically or invoke magical protections. By contrast, true PARs will show intensely hateful withdrawal or attack.

I EXPECT MOST PEOPLE TO BE CRITICAL AND DISAPPROVING OF ME.

(6) inappropriate or constricted affect, e.g., silly, aloof, rarely reciprocates gestures or facial expressions, such as smiles or nods

inappropriate or constricted affect (e.g., appears cold and aloof)

The SZT's view of events is usually reality-based, while the interpretation of them is not. The gap between event and interpretation can be shown in inappropriate affect. An example would be this response to card IX of the Rorschach: "Billowing and floating away and doing different shapes like clouds do. I love clouds. I think they're fabulous." Constricted affect and lack of reciprocity in social signals are consequences of the social anxiety described in item 9.

MY FEELINGS ARE DIFFERENT FROM OTHERS, AND I KEEP TO MYSELF.

(7) odd or eccentric behavior or appearance, e.g., unkempt, unusual mannerisms, talks to self

behavior or appearance that is odd, eccentric, or peculiar

The SZT elects to live separately, rejecting the rest of the world. In childhood this often assumed the form of watching TV excessively, listening to music alone, and so on. If the withdrawal is relatively complete over a long period of time, he or she will lose touch with social norms, and develop his or her own rules for personal hygiene, dressing, and social stereotypies.

I HAVE CERTAIN LITTLE WAYS OF DOING THINGS WHICH SOME PEOPLE THINK ARE STRANGE, BUT WHICH I THINK ARE HELPFUL.

(8) no close friends or confidants (or only one) other than first-degree relatives

no close friends or confidants (or only one) other than first-degree relatives, due primarily to lack of desire, pervasive discomfort with others, or eccentricities

The SZT has an acute sense of separateness, of being different from others. This leads to the belief that ordinary communication with others not only is undesirable, but also is not possible.

I HAVE DIFFICULTY UNDERSTANDING OTHER PEOPLE, AND THEY HAVE DIFFICULTY UNDERSTANDING ME, BECAUSE I AM SO DIFFERENT.

(9) excessive social anxiety, e.g., extreme discomfort in social situations involving unfamiliar people

excessive social anxiety (e.g., extreme discomfort in social situations that does not diminish with familiarity and tends to be associated with paranoid fears rather than negative judgments about self)

Because of the expectation of being degraded and humiliated on an irrational basis (i.e., it will happen no matter what he or she does, and he or she is perplexed about why), the SZT is extremely anxious and uncomfortable in new social situations. Prefers to be alone to avoid the experience of being seen as (and being put down for being) "strange" or different. When forced to respond in a social situation, the SZT seems perplexed; he or she is unsure of whether he knows about or can do what is appropriate.

I INTERACT WITH PEOPLE WHEN I HAVE TO, BUT OTHERWISE KEEP TO MYSELF BECAUSE I FEEL DIFFER-ENT AND JUST DON'T "FIT IN."

Necessary and Exclusionary Criteria

The present analysis permits definition of necessary and exclusionary conditions for each personality disorder. For SZT, the recommended *necessary* conditions are (1) social withdrawal and (2) the autistic control reflected in the DSM items describing thought disorder. *Exclusionary* conditions include the discomfort with autonomy found in BPD and the proud disregard for social norms shown in ASP. The SZT would like to be accepted as he or she is. SZTs, who are comfortable with autonomy, are unlikely to show the help-coercing behaviors or the demanding dependency of BPDs, DPDs, or HPDs.

It is beyond the scope of this book to discuss the overlap between Axis I and II. It may be worth noting that interpersonal analysis suggests that SZTs, who do have permeable boundaries, nonetheless are more likely than schizophrenics to maintain a sense of self that is separate from others.

Case Illustrations

Case 1

This 36-year-old divorced mother of three came to the hospital saying, "I need to know if I am crazy." Her ex-husband insisted that she was. She reasoned that if she was certified as not crazy, then her advice to her teenage daughter, about whom she was worried, would be valid.

On admission, the patient was described as delusional because she thought, for example, that her children could magically communicate where she was to her husband. She believed that she could "read people" by just looking at them. She insisted she had a "special gift for sensing" that she could not tune out. She was alleged to have heard the voices of her husband's other women in her house. She "proved" that he was having affairs in their house by citing her observation that other women's possessions were sometimes found in her husband's bedroom.

The patient responded well to antipsychotic medication while in the hospital. Previously, she had overdosed on antidepressants, and had been treated for alcohol and amphetamine abuse. She said she hated her job as a secretary, where her behavior was allegedly "erratic." She wanted to go back to school to learn to be a teacher.

The patient had been married at 18 and divorced about 2 years prior to the present hospitalization. Her husband frequently got drunk and beat her up, including "slugging, kicking, and using knives." He would often humiliate and degrade her in front of others. She learned not to cry, because if she cried when he beat her up, he would say that she did it to soften him up. Moreover, if she cried he would beat her more severely, explaining that she was trying to "cop out." A construction worker, he took jobs sporadically and "ran around on her." The patient felt that her husband had the other women in his bedroom to make her be crazy; then he could get rid of her without feeling responsible. The patient said she "hated his guts," and yet she wistfully blamed him for the breakup of the marriage. She explained that she got sick of being beaten for being unfaithful, and decided eventually to go ahead and *be* unfaithful. She regretted that her own infidelity eventually led to the divorce.

The three children lived with the patient, who worried that the youngest was acting just as she did at her age. This daughter stayed in her bedroom all the time, had no friends, and played the radio at full blast.

The patient's own developmental history was marked by neglect, exploitation, and abuse. When the patient was 4 years old, her mother was stricken by a severe heart condition. A series of surgeries served to account for the mother's dependency upon the patient from that early time. The mother would call the patient out of school to deal with family crises. In addition, the patient was responsible for all the housework and cooking, even though there were older siblings. The patient accepted the parental role because she had been persuaded by very strange "logic" from her grandfather that doing all that household work was her special assignment. He had given the patient permission to live at home with her mother only if she would take care of all the work. The "reason" was that if the patient did not take care of the household burdens, the burden of her presence would kill her mother. There was no consideration of the fact that the cleaning and shopping would have needed someone's attention even if the patient had not lived at home. Nor was there any consideration of the possibility that the patient's siblings could have shared the household burdens.

The patient's stepfather, who came into her life when she was a toddler, was abusive when drunk. He fought with her mother frequently, and the patient often withdrew to her own bedroom to get away from the hostilities. This defense was not altogether successful. In addition to her massive burden of completing all household duties, the patient also had to be a sexual partner for the stepfather. She said that he was like two people. One side, the sober one, was kind and good; the other side, the drunk one, was so awful that she tried not even to think about it. She acknowledged that she might have injuries from this major relationship, but was unwilling to discuss it. She did not want to talk about what he was like drunk, because she "didn't want that part to be real." Besides, talking about it wouldn't change him, she observed.

For most of her married years, the patient continued to live with her stepfather and mother rather than with her husband. Even after she was married, her stepfather was controlling in a bizarre way. He insisted that the *married* patient be home by dark every night, lest she meet a rapist. By marked contrast, he gave his unmarried biological daughter free rein to come and go as she pleased. The patient explained, "He loved me very much and watched over me carefully."

The patient terminated the interview prematurely, because she felt that the interviewer was touching on too many painful topics: (1) the relationship with the stepfather when he was drunk; (2) the fact that she never had a functional mother; and (3) her fear of becoming attached again following her lengthy, abusive marriage. Near tears, which she had categorically forbidden herself, she said she had "had enough for today" and left the interviewing room. This act was not hostile; the patient simply knew what she could and could not tolerate. Her defense was to withdraw physically, and the interviewer felt it was important to respect that need. The patient agreed that pursuit of these themes might be helpful in the future.

The DSM diagnosis was SZT because the patient had ideas of reference (item 1), odd beliefs (item 2), unusual perceptual experiences (item 3), few close friends or confidants (item 8), paranoid ideation (item 5), and constricted affect (item 6). She mentioned the need to restrain her anger, and did once lose control of it. She was not particularly odd in her appearance, although her clothing suggested membership in a marginal political group.

The interpersonal descriptors in Table 14.3 also fit this woman. She maintained a baseline of social withdrawal—RECOIL and WALL OFF. She believed that she had special abilities to control others magically (CONTROL plus EMANCIPATE plus WALL OFF), and attributed these same abilities to her children. She was neglectful of herself and consciously restrained her anger. She wanted to be free to come and go as she pleased, but feared attack. She fit the necessary conditions of social withdrawal and delusional beliefs in autistic control. She did not conform to any of the exclusionary conditions: She did not fear being alone or show demanding dependency; also, instead of being proud of her possible social "deviations," she worried about them and came to the hospital to learn to correct them.

Her developmental history corresponded reasonably closely to the pathogenic predictions. Her stepfather severely constrained her autonomy. Her husband, who was often absent and blatantly unfaithful, punished her severely for alleged unfaithfulness. As a child, she was responsible for maintaining the household and protecting her mother from imminent death. She was chronically subject to her drunken stepfather's incestually abusive invasions of her personal boundaries. As a child, she could find safe haven by staying "out of the way"; she also had little contact with peers. Nonetheless, she developed adequate social skills. Possibly she was helped in this by her very early marriage and her exposure to her husband's peer group.

Case 2

This 38-year-old single white female was advised by her church to seek help. She came to the hospital saying, "I want to find out all the things that have gone wrong. I don't like the way I have been." She was most bothered by her belief that evil spirits were in her apartment trying to get her to sell herself—a horrible thought that she said was "not her." Although only outpatient psychotherapy had been suggested, the patient chose inpatient hospitalization to "surprise them and show them I am better than that. I am very intelligent." Apparently the idea was that if "they" thought she needed help, she would seek the maximum and the best available.

There had been one prior hospitalization. Four years prior, there had been a trial of antidepressants, followed by psychotherapy from a social service agency for 6 months. Since childhood, the patient had suffered from grand mal seizures associated with abnormal bursts and diffuse slow waves on her electroencephalogram. Although she still experienced muscle twitching and occasional large-muscle jerking, she had not had seizures for several years.

The patient denied suicidality and did not self-mutilate. She explained that when she felt inclined to cut herself, she would "go on a picnic, look at birds, or call a friend." She said she did not hear voices, and she performed well on proverbs. However, she said that she had difficulty functioning, explaining, "My left and right brain try to separate and go in different directions. Part wants to see something, and the other part wants to name it. I can't match them up [the images of things with the names]." She was also troubled by a tendency to "misconstrue things" in the direction of feeling not listened to and put down. Indeed, at one point during this interview, the patient felt that the interviewer was "purposely misjudging" her in regard to her belief about the evil spirits in her apartment; she violently grabbed the interviewer's notes, threw them down, and left the room. A while later, she returned, apologized, and explained that she had a food allergy that interfered with her thinking. She also thought that her loss of control during the interview might have been due to her having corn for lunch. She had an emotional response to corn because her stepfather made whiskey from corn. She added that she got jaundice from carrots, just as he got jaundice from alcohol.

The patient felt very close to her stepfather, and lacked a clear sense of boundaries between herself and him. When her stepfather had surgery, the patient had extreme pain, while he felt none whatsoever. She believed she was intimately connected with others too. For example, she added that she could sense whenever something had gone wrong with relatives without having to be told. She had an out-of-body experience during an auto accident, when she "saw herself being killed." She reported that she got out of her body and looked at her mother, who was standing by the car looking past her as though she wasn't there. There were two men in black suits bending over her body. She got back into it and hoped they would forgive her, because apparently she had said "I hate you" to her mother when leaving her body. Years later, on the night her mother died, the patient felt there were evil spirits in the house because she heard furniture bumping. She was sure the spirits were evil because "angels don't make any noise." Many of these magical thoughts shared the characteristic of extreme intimacy or familiarity with others' thoughts and feelings while still retaining a separate identity.

The patient's alcoholic stepfather could not keep a job, and so the family moved frequently. She reported many episodes of sexual and physical abuse. She said that her stepfather frequently beat her and her brother while they were naked. He would rape the patient, sometimes as she was having seizures. The stepfather would order the brother to give commands to the patient (e.g., "Take off your glasses," "Do certain things"), or to say things to degrade and hurt the patient. The brother would comply because "he would be killed if he didn't."

These painful memories of her stepfather were accompanied by positive feelings and affection for him. For example, the patient loved to go to the woods with him. She said that she treasured the flowers and birds. Yet she remembered waking up in the back of the truck on the way home from the woods, "hurting awfully bad." At those times, her stepfather would laugh, look strange, speak with a different voice, and act "weird." Her mother eventually "found out" and forbade the patient to go to the woods with her stepfather. The patient was unhappy to lose these opportunities to be with him.

In addition to having the roles of victim, companion, and sexual partner, the patient also assumed a parental role with her stepfather. Sometimes she would attempt to control his drinking by pouring out his hidden bottles of whiskey. At other times, she would control him by deliberately giving him whiskey to get him drunk, so he would go to sleep and not bother anybody. Her stepfather "calmed down a lot" when he became attached to a kitten she chose. In retrospect, the patient wished she had let him choose the kitten himself. She reasoned that if her "wrong" choice of a kitten helped him so much, his own choice might have helped him even more.

The patient's mother was sick frequently, and the stepfather "pushed her around a lot." The couple frequently fought over the children. The mother's illness prevented her from leaving the stepfather. The family doctor told the mother that she was "too sick for divorce." Although the patient felt that her mother failed to protect her from the stepfather's abuse, she also said that her mother "tried to watch over me too much."

The patient did not use drugs, alcohol, or tobacco. She was not homicidal because, she explained, she stopped herself whenever she got angry. She warned that she would use martial arts if ever she were physically threatened. There was no spouse or close friends other than her church minister. As a child, playing with girls made her "dizzy and sick," she said. She had had one adult friend, but that friend betrayed her by taking the patient to a movie about incest and then "gloating off," knowing that the patient herself was an incest victim. The patient had graduated from a 2-year college, but had been unable to work long without getting fired. She described herself as outspoken on the job: "If I see something wrong, I tell them."

The patient fit the DSM diagnostic criteria for SZT because she had (2) odd beliefs and magical thinking; (3) unusual perceptual experiences; (5) suspiciousness or paranoid ideation; (6) inappropriate and constricted affect; (7) eccentricity; and (8) no close friends or confidants.

The interpersonal descriptions in Table 14.3 also apply to this woman. She was withdrawn socially (RECOIL and WALL OFF), and she was clearly delusional. The quality of her thought disorder included themes of separateness from the social world (WALL OFF) and personal choice (CONTROL). She wished for personal freedom (EMANCIPATE) and was very sensitive to humiliation (BLAME) or ATTACK. She showed the necessary baseline postions of social withdrawal and had delusions of control from a distance. She did not fear autonomy or show demanding dependency. She was willing to be assertive, but did not flout social norms; rather, she was eager to prove that she was a devoted follower of the principles of her church.

The SASB-based hypotheses for the prototypic developmental history of schizotypal personality disorder were also confirmed: (1) Her stepfather degraded and humiliated her for having the gender he disliked, though he related intensely to her femaleness. (2) Inappropriate reliance on her was suggested by her assumption of responsibility for her stepfather's drinking. She tried to protect herself and other family members from his alcoholic rages. (3) Clearly there was severe abuse. Her seizures were of unknown etiology, but one possible cause would be head trauma during the varieties of severe abuse. (4) Her abuse often involved more than one family member, so aloneness was safer for her.

Both of these cases illustrate the tendency of SZT to overlap with the diagnosis of Schizophrenia. Each showed a number of prodromal/residual symptoms of Schizophrenia: social isolation; marked impairment as a wage earner or student; inappropriate affect; odd beliefs; and unusual perceptual experiences. Neither case qualified for the diagnosis of Schizophrenia, however, because neither had known acute psychotic episodes. Nor were there frank hallucinations or regression from higher levels of functioning. Interpersonally, each of these women retained a strong sense of a separate self. This contrasts dramatically with the prototypic schizophrenic, who seems perplexed about where he or she leaves off and other important people begin.

Expectable Transference Reactions and Treatment Implications

Transference Reactions

The first task in psychotherapy with an SZT is to establish a relationship that can survive the extreme social anxiety and paranoia. The SZT will be very likely to see the therapist as attacking or humiliating, and will try to maintain distance for safety. It is also to be expected that the SZT will believe that he or she can read the therapist's mind, or influence the therapist by telepathy and other magical means. Worry that harm might befall the therapist because of his or her association with the SZT may emerge. The SZT will be vulnerable to neglecting his or her own best interests by, for example, becoming involved in or continuing with activities or relationships that may be abusive and exploitative. The partners in such relationships will be "paranoid" about the therapy and will actively interfere with it.

SZTs are more likely than individuals with other personality disorders to suffer from overt thought disorder. The thought disorder suggests to many that SZT is "hard-wired." If so, then the task of reconstructing the personality by psychosocial methods will be especially difficult, if not impossible. At a minimum, psychotherapy may help these patients learn to recognize when they are distorting reality. In this effort, they may require low-dose neuroleptics. Ordinary support and help with social learning may also be useful to SZTs. For example, to the extent that it is possible, SZTs can diminish their social withdrawal if they are supported in efforts to seek and experience less abusive love relationship(s). Straightforward counseling in getting job or professional training can be valuable. Those who have been sexually abused may be encouraged to undergo sexual rehabilitation therapy.

If reconstructive psychotherapy is attempted, it will take a very long time. The SZT will need to learn to deal with the residues of the destructive relationship with the abusive caregiver(s). The intense ambivalence and the confused reality testing will make it very difficult for the SZT to change his or her baseline interactional patterns.

Treatment Implications: The Five Categories of Correct Response

Facilitating Collaboration. The therapist can help the SZT enter a working alliance by deferring to the SZT's sensitivities. In case 1, it was important that the interviewer allowed the patient to achieve needed distance by terminating the interview early. The patient said that the conversation was too intense, and that she had "had enough for today." In addition to respecting the SZT's need for distance, the therapist should remain acutely aware of the SZT's tendency to feel humiliated. There should not be inquiry in more than one or two ways about a sensitive topic, especially if the topic is included in the SZT's delusional material. The patient in case 2, for example, believed that evil spirits were in her apartment. When the interviewer inquired about what the patient might do if the evil spirits were to prevail, she lost control of herself. The patient thought that the interviewer's questions about the delusion amounted to the accusation that she had sold out to the evil ones. Fortunately, there had been sufficient understanding before that incident that the patient was willing to return to finish the interview. Her loss of control might have been avoided if the interviewer had anticipated the extent of the patient's sensitivity and dropped the subject after a first inquiry failed to elicit an answer.

At the beginning of therapy, the therapist probably should be relaxed about the SZT's need to cancel appointments and to control the course of the sessions. If not allowed to maintain distance and control in this way, the SZT is likely to bolt from the process altogether. Gradually, the therapist can engage the SZT by ordinary skills in empathic listening, accurate mirroring, and constancy. After a while, the SZT may develop enough trust and insight to give up management by magic and come to see the benefits of agreeing to an ordinary learning contract.

In the process of learning to collaborate with the therapist, the SZT can experience and internalize nonexploitative protectiveness and nurturance. Unlike earlier caregivers, the therapist does not require caregiving himself or herself. The therapist can be totally consistent in maintaining focus and supportive attention. This very new experience is a corrective experience for the SZT.

Facilitating Pattern Recognition. The SZT needs to learn how the unrealistic assignments of responsibility in an abusive situation where he or she really was helpless predisposed him or her to the magical thinking. Those bizarre early conditions led the SZT to assume that he or she had inordinate power and influence. Paranoia and vicious self-talk can also be related to such early learning. The patient in case 2 accepted the interpretation that her fear and panic about evil spirits in her apartment followed the pattern set by her relationship with her stepfather. They wanted her to do things that were "not her"; so did he, when he was raping her. She supported the interpretation by adding that her stepfather used to take her to graveyards and tell her scary stories. He hung a skull in the playhouse he built for her. Seen in this context, her fears of evil persons taking her over and making her "sell herself" was not so strange. Her beloved stepfather would unpredictably assume an "evil" position and overtake her and make her do bad (sexual) things. He also encouraged her to share his concerns about evil spirits and death. It is not surprising that as an adult she continued to see the world in the same terms.

SZTs are usually aware of their abusive histories, and will discuss aspects of them in some detail. They often have no affect about the abuse itself. Like most victims of severe abuse, SZTs can be helped to discover affect by first being given an opportunity to express empathy and sympathy for others who have also been abused. Usually other tragic or potentially tragic figures are available for discussion. SZTs can be led back to the affect associated with their own abuse by exploring their reaction to these other people's experiences. In the context of showing compassion for others in similar situations, an SZT can begin to show the same understanding for his or her own position. As compassion for and a mature perspective on oneself grows, the willingness to be harsh on oneself diminishes.

There is danger in showing compassion and empathy for the SZT as a child. Both the therapist and the SZT are vulnerable to the parts of the SZT that remain identified with the abusers. There may be guilt, punishment, and other untoward reactions to this forbidden and traitorous activity of criticizing the abuser(s). As usual, the therapist must remain aware of such contradictory forces and remain steady in the face of the patient's changing loyalties. Sometimes the patient will identify with the aggressor. Then he or she may change and become empathic with his or her own victim position. This may be followed by anger at perceived betrayal of the abuser and guilt about the SZT's own compliance. Then the SZT may become angry at the therapist for stimulating all of this. There will be a wide range of attitudes and behaviors. The therapist should not become impatient or discouraged; it is important not to be intimidated by the kaleidoscope of intense and ever-changing feelings. If the therapist can remain benign and steady, the patient can internalize the therapist's caring and move on to the task of learning about normal socialization. The SZT needs especially to know that his or her competence can be affirmed and need not be exploited.

Blocking Maladaptive Patterns. With an SZT, as with so many other patients, the therapist has to walk a very thin line. There must be a balance between tolerating maladaptive old patterns to preserve the therapy relationship and blocking them. The SZT, like the NPD, AVD, and PAR, is especially likely to bolt from therapy at the first sign of betrayal, humiliation, or danger. The best procedure is to provide minimally threatening support at first, and then slowly to press the edges of awareness as firmly as the strength of the therapy relationship will permit.

A supportive intervention that can help the SZT consciously block psychotic thought processes is to teach him or her how to recognize when he or she distorts reality. When that happens, the SZT can be taught new self-talk that will keep him or her more based in the "here and now." Ultimately, as he or she dares to look back, the SZT can learn to understand the contribution of early learning to the unrealistic thoughts.

The therapy relationship serves as a safe base from which to explore oneself and one's relationships with others. It also provides an opportunity for learning within the therapy setting. If the patient worries that the therapist may be harmed through some magical means, that pattern can be disrupted. The therapist can acknowledge any grain of truth the fantasy may be built on, and can then express confidence that the untoward event is unlikely. For example, the SZT may worry that the therapist will become ill because of the things that have been said about the patient's abusive parent. The therapist can acknowledge that illness can strike at any time. But if it does, chances are that it will be the result of exposure to a pathogen or of genetic vulnerability, rather than of discussions during therapy. In addition, if the relationship will permit, the therapist may also encourage exploring the fear behind the fear. Perhaps the patient is terrorized by the emerging dependency on the therapist. He or she may worry that the therapist will disappear or otherwise betray the patient's trust.

Strengthening the Will to Give Up Maladaptive Patterns. The SZT's stronger sense of self suggests a better potential for response to psychotherapy than would be expected if he or she were schizophrenic. Nonetheless, the SZT still has major problems with defining his or her boundaries and with trusting others. For reconstruction to take place, the SZT must change the wish to magically protect the self and others while maintaining loyalty to early abusers.

With SZTs, as with BPDs and other victims of abuse, it can be helpful to interpret suicidal fantasies or acts in terms of their connection to underlying wishes. An example would be a paradoxical comment like this one: "Well, he [abusive father] would sure be happy to see what a good job you are doing of punishing yourself this time. This will prove that you love him and want to stay with him forever." Such an interpretation, if accurate and if given in a way that the patient can "hear," confronts the patient with the attractive features of the disorder. With fuller awareness, the patient has an opportunity for a new choice.

It is not easy to endure the psychic terror of defying the internalized wishes and fears implanted by abusers. Accurate mirroring and deep empathy can help the SZT mobilize his or her will to recover. Clear and authentic therapist understanding can be internalized by the SZT. He or she may then be able to visualize that there might be a better way to think about the self and others.

Facilitating New Learning. Because of the severity of this disorder, the suggestion that an SZT may be able to reconstruct his or her patterns is suspect. As indicated above, SZT thought disorder may represent a genetically based deficiency. If it does, one would not expect psychosocial interventions alone to be able to change the baseline patterns of SZT. The present analysis notes that there are clear parallels between the specific content of the thought disorder in SZT and the early learning experiences. It is not possible to tell whether these experiences have only shaped the disorder (which is preprogrammed by genetics), or whether they have directly instilled the disorder. Nonetheless, the connection between past social learning and the present thought disorder can help guide the psychosocial interventions, whether they aim to support the patient or to help him or her reconstruct his or her personality.

PART FIVE

DIVERGENCES

15

Category Overlap, Residual Categories, and Other Issues

"For every symptom, there are reasons."

The criteria for these [personality] disorders need further investigation to determine the extent to which they correspond to current clinical usage, the extent to which they are clustered in clinical and nonpatient populations and, ultimately, the extent to which they can be validated against external criteria: that is, course of illness, treatment response, family history, and laboratory tests. (Siever & Klar, 1986, p. 287)

THE OVERLAP PROBLEM

Thomas Widiger (e.g., Widiger, 1989) has been particularly articulate in challenging the very idea of attempting to define personality disorders as distinct categories. He has observed:

> One is obligated to choose between the two categories, yet both apply equally well. It is analogous to trying to differentiate between the borderline and the histrionic personality disorders in a patient who has equal symptomatology for both (assuming that a differential diagnosis is necessary), or trying to decide if gray is best classified as black or white. Either choice appears to be somewhat arbitrary, and this is in fact the case when one is trying to impose a categorical distinction on what is instead a dimensional variable. (1989, p. 79)

Widiger, as research coordinator for the DSM-IV, has been greatly impressed by the depth of the overlap problem. He has suggested that efforts to define personality disorders as categories should be abandoned, and that personality be defined instead in terms of profiles on underlying dimensions. Millon, who has written the most widely used and useful inventory of DSM personality disorders, the MCMI (Millon, 1982), uses the profile method to deal with the overlap problem. The MCMI provides the clinician with a profile that compares the patient's responses to each of the DSM prototypes. A patient can be above the "cutoff" on the MCMI for several disorders, such as BPD, HPD, and ASP. A categorical interpretation of this profile would suggest that the patient has three disorders and belongs in three categories: BPD, HPD, and ASP. Widiger would point out that this unwieldy conclusion is the result of thinking of personality disorders as discrete categories. By using the profile method, Millon avoids the absurd judgment that individuals who have scores above the "cutoff" on several dimensions have several different disorders.

Millon's "dimensions" in the MCMI are the Axis II disorders themselves[1] (plus some Axis I disorders). Widiger favors using dimensions derived by the method of factor analysis. Following a careful survey of the large academic literature on personality trait theory, Widiger has recently recommended that personality be described in terms of the NEO-5 Personality Inventory (Costa & McCrae, 1988). This dimensional approach describes each person in degrees of Neuroticism, Extraversion, Openness to Experience, Agreeableness, and Conscientiousness. Widiger has written:

> The empirical research favors a dimensional model for the classification and conceptualization of personality disorder pathology. The empirical research also favors the Five-Factor model for the classification of normal personality functioning. It is then only natural and reasonable to propose that personality disorders be classified and understood from the perspective of the Five-Factor model.
>
> Perhaps the only substantial limitation with a Five-Factor alternative to the DSM-III-R personality disorders is the absence of familiar treatment and clinical implications for the various dimensions and their facets. There have been many chapters, books, and articles on the treatment of the compulsive, histrionic, antisocial, schizoid, and borderline personality disorders, but very little on the treatment of excessive conscientiousness, extraversion, antagonism, introversion, and neuroticism . . . clinicians would likely have some difficulty, at least initially, in developing treatment plans with the less familiar Five-Factor trait terms. Nevertheless, it is anticipated that with additional experience and training . . . clinicians will find that it is more helpful to conceptualize treatment as involving an effort to decrease the extent to which a person is impulsive, self-conscious, mistrusting, unassertive, overly compliant, or closed to emotions within particular situations in which such tendencies are maladaptive, than to cure an avoidant, borderline, or histrionic personality disorder. (Widiger, in press)

Definition of personality disorders may be at a crossroads. One path, represented by academic psychology, leads to dimensional descriptions of personality. The other path, represented by psychiatry's DSM, leads to categories. The categorical approach has not fared well in the scientific arena. Somewhat ironically, this book advocates the DSM categorical approach even though the SASB is a dimensional model. The validity of the dimensions underlying the SASB model has been established by confirmatory factor analysis (Benjamin, 1974, 1984, 1988, draft). By using the SASB dimensional model to describe categories of personality disorder, this book invokes a hybrid model. The SASB dimensional model has been presented in Chapter 3 and applied to the DSM catego-

---

[1]Although MCMI profiles use the DSM categories as dimensions, Millon developed his concepts of the DSM disorders by using his own truly dimensional model. His theoretical model (Millon, 1969) includes these dimensions: active versus passive, pleasure versus pain, and self versus other.

ries in subsequent chapters. SASB theory has been used to make inferences[2] about social pathogenesis of the disorders and to recommend treatment interventions.

In practice, it is important to include the dimension of time when using models of social interaction. To describe ambivalence, instability, or rigidity, one needs the idea of rates of change of interpersonal positions. For example, BPDs will shift rapidly into ATTACK and BLAME of the therapist, and into SELF-ATTACK and SELF-BLAME, if a therapist appears to IGNORE them. BPDs will show the same variability if they see themselves as SEPARATE from internalized abusive figures. This "instability" of BPDs is described in very specific terms by the SASB model. In contrast to BPDs, PARs are very rigid in their response patterns. They easily see others in terms of ATTACK and BLAME, and reliably respond with RECOIL and WALL OFF. If pressed, the PARs can escalate to BLAME and ATTACK. These individuals do not vary much from this condition. The dimension of time is helpful in distinguishing the trait-like "rigidity" of PARs from the "instability" of BPDs.

The SASB-based hybrid method for defining categories of personality is consistent with the musical model introduced in Chapter 3. A "song" is a category defined by a theory that references underlying dimensions. In music, songs are defined by particular combinations of notes and rhythms (sound waves and time). This book has identified the "harmonics and rhythms" of the 11 personality disorders named by the DSM. There are rules in music about natural combinations of notes, and natural progressions among combinations of notes. Songs often follow these rules; however, deviations can give them their uniqueness. Similarly, the present analysis lists the basic notes and interactive progressions characteristic of each personality disorder.[3]

The present hybrid analysis of the DSM categories with the SASB dimensions capitalizes on the clinical wisdom in the DSM. The songs of personality disorders were noted down by experts on the DSM task forces. They were natural categories that arose from clinical experience. The DSM task forces attempted to codify the categories by the rules of science. Criteria were field-tested and revised. For many of the categories, however, the criteria did not provide independent clinicians with enough information to make reliable decisions.[4] In this

---

[2]The analysis was not entirely deductive. Frequently, clinical observations were codified, and then the operative SASB predictive principle was identified. For example, if an abused child becomes an abusive adult, the principle of similarity applies; if he or she selects an abusive partner and remains a victim, the principle of complementarity applies. For this book, the predictive principle conforming to the clinical data for a given disorder was selected. The SASB model has not been developed to a degree that would permit an *a priori* choice of which principle will apply to a given situation.

[3]As I enter the decade in which I must retire, I hope to be able to start a low-cost, high-quality research center for the treatment of personality and other severe mental disorders. In this setting, perhaps I will be able to initiate the complicated and lengthy program of research and training that is needed for an adequate test of the ideas in this book.

[4]Categories proving to be especially poor in reliability or "politically" controversial have been placed in Appendix A in recent editions of the DSM. In DSM-III-R, these included Sadistic Personality Disorder, Self-defeating Personality Disorder, and Late Luteal Phase Dysphoric Disorder. Appendix A in DSM-IV includes NEG and perhaps Self-defeating Personality Disorder. A new category, Depressive Personality Disorder, may be added to Appendix A in DSM-IV; this category is discussed in more detail later in this chapter.

book, the categories of the Axis II disorders in the DSM are assumed to have clinical construct validity. It is argued that their problems with reliability are the result of inadequate descriptions rather than of the absurdity of trying to define categories. Consider, for example, the overlapping categories BPD and HPD, mentioned by Widiger (1989) in the quotation above. Their respective features and the recommended treatment interventions have been reviewed in Chapters 5 and 7. The present review of their overlap draws on the highlights of those analyses.

Table 7.2 compares BPD and HPD, using the SASB labels or notes for their baseline positions. A scan of that table shows that both the BPD and the HPD are likely to sound notes of **CONTROL** and **BLAME**. Both offer their TRUST, and both will engage in *SELF-ATTACK*.[5] The SASB labels (plus the labels for their wishes and fears) reflect the clinical realities that both the BPD and the HPD present to the health care provider with coercive dependency. Both can be warm and friendly, and both will attack the care provider for allegedly not giving enough. Both will generate dramatic suicidal and other crises, and both will see good functioning as the route to abandonment and sure disaster. Finally, each will show suicidal behaviors following perceived failure of the nurturer to "pay attention."

Despite these powerful similarities, the interpersonal patterns, the "songs," differ in important ways. The *SELF-ATTACK* of the BPD is an intrapsychic event, while that of the HPD is combined with an interpersonal message. The BPD spins recklessly out of control, irrationally attacking the self, needing rescue but not counting on it. The HPD acts out well-timed scenarios, relatively sure of the willingness and ability of the nurturer to rescue. The BPD's suicidality is an internal, fundamentally autistic, sometimes psychotic event; the suicidality of the HPD remains interpersonal and manipulative. These differences in the patterns of suicidality illustrate the general differences in interpersonal patterns in BPD and HPD. The distinctions are not arbitrary; they have been identified by SASB labeling of the structure of actual clinical examples. Table 14.2, which compares and contrasts the baseline positions of the respective personality disorders, shows that the HPD's positions are likely to appear in complex form. The HPD mixes friendly receptiveness with control; he or she simultaneously trusts and manages the health care provider. By contrast, at any given moment, the BPD's patterns are simple. The BPD sometimes engages in simple and intense trust in the nurturing provider. Then, at the slightest hint of flawed caring, the BPD suddenly switches to devaluating murderous rage intended to coerce better caregiving. In other words, *the BPD belts out key notes in sequence, while the HPD plays a chord.* The chordlike structure of the HPD's song insures that he or she does not recklessly give up control of the self. The HPD always includes a note of attachment, even when angry or suicidal. The HPD's lesser recklessness and consistent preservation of some form of attachment make this pattern "less severe."

---

[5]In Chapter 7, I have noted that the DSM-III-R deleted suicidality from the description of HPD. This was done in an atheoretical effort to reduce overlap between BPD and HPD. I agree with the original clinician consensus of DSM-III that HPDs will engage in suicidal behaviors.

In sum, the BPD and HPD play similar but nonetheless distinct songs. In each case, the provider needs to be coerced into "giving more," but the song is not the same. Similarly, any number of popular songs about lost love may sound the same to a person not familiar with the genre. The well-trained ear will find the differences to be important. In personality disorders, the differences matter because they suggest different treatment interventions. The theoretical analyses allow transference patterns to be specified, particular issues to be targeted for intervention, and specific learning goals to be achieved.

A simple focus on behavioral symptoms or traits, such as mistrust or excessive compliance, will not often lead to successful treatment of personality disorders. The therapist who tries to decrease the impulsiveness of the BPD without addressing the motivations associated with the introject will fail. The present theory of the respective Axis II disorders suggests that psychotherapy involves quite a bit more than trying to change behaviors or traits. Implementing simple behavioral interventions can be compared to putting an ice pack on the head of a feverish patient, rather than looking for and treating the infection that is generating the fever. Traits are unlikely to change without transformation of underlying wishes and fears. A coherent theoretical view of the disorder is required to permit the patient and therapist to collaborate to make that elusive and difficult change.

A conservatory of music can greatly accelerate the musician's acquisition of professional skills by offering training in theory and encouraging mastery of technical skills. Similarly, an effective theory of personality disorders can help the therapist select and implement interventions that otherwise might require many years to learn on an intuitive basis. Like musicians, therapists need to engage in countless hours of practice that is based on relevant theory. The therapist trainee needs consistent constructive and specific help from experienced teachers.

Clinicians or researchers who want to apply the present interpersonal analysis to the DSM Axis II definitions of personality disorders may find the Appendix to this book useful. It includes the highlights of the present and historical interpersonal patterns that are associated with the DSM definitional items. Following the summaries, there is a review of specific SASB codes needed to define the respective disorders, and the recommended necessary and exclusionary conditions. The overlap problem can be both understood and minimized by using the information in the Appendix. Once the proper Axis II diagnosis has been made, the reader can turn to the corresponding chapter for detailed information on expected transference problems and recommended treatment interventions.

THE RESIDUAL CATEGORIES: MIXED PERSONALITY DISORDER AND PERSONALITY DISORDER NOT OTHERWISE SPECIFIED

Popular as they may be, the 11 "songs" presented in Chapters 5 to 14 are not the only ones there are. Other melodies and other harmonics are sung too; they happen not to be so frequent, and so the DSM task force did not include them in its catalog. Appendix A of the DSM offers an opportunity to describe and study less common or less clear patterns. But there are even more songs than those included in Appendix A. These may receive the label of Personality Disorder Not Otherwise Specified (NOS). The NOS category marks individuals who show long-standing maladaptive traits that do not resemble any of the categories for personality disorder described in the DSM. DSM-III named a special subset of the NOS category, called Mixed Personality Disorder. The Mixed category included individuals who showed less than the required number of two or more of the named Axis II disorders.

Morey (1988) noted that too many patients receive these residual labels of Mixed or NOS. The relatively poor "coverage" of the standard personality disorder categories has been seen as a failing of the nomenclature. Morey reported that over 29% of his sample of personality-disordered individuals qualified for one of these residual labels. Designers of the nomenclature face the unpleasant reality that as the definitions change to include more individuals (i.e., to increase coverage), the overlap problem becomes worse. As one problem is solved, the other is aggravated. The DSM-III-R covered more individuals, but Morey found that it also had a worse rate of overlap: Whereas the DSM-III yielded two or more diagnoses for 36.4%[6] of the patients, the DSM-III-R rules gave 51.9% of the sample two or more diagnoses. Morey concluded, "These results make apparent that the modest increase in personality disorder coverage with DSM-III-R was indeed obtained at the expense of a more substantial increase in diagnostic overlap" (1988, p. 575).

The present theory-based approach offers a method for dealing rationally with the residual categories NOS and Mixed. If a person meets criteria for Mixed Personality Disorder, then his or her history must include some of the developmental experiences discussed in the "Pathogenic Hypotheses" sections of preceding chapters. For example, a common mixture is that of PAR and NPD. The NPD part of this combination might be found in a male with a doting mother who provided experiences consistent with the development of NPD (see Chapter 6). The PAR part could have been encouraged by a cruel, jealous father who abused the child in ways that predispose an individual to PAR (see Chapter 13). The NPD should show up mostly in relation to female intimates; the PAR would be apparent in relation to male authorities. Treatment of this Mixed Personality Disorder would draw on the respective recommendations in Chapters 6 and 13.

The "common criminal" may be another example of a person with Mixed Personality Disorder. Cleckley (1955) argued that ASPs are not truly criminal types because they are far more "stupid" and reckless than the "common criminal." Unlike the ASP, the common criminal will be well organized in his or her efforts to protect himself or herself to avoid detection and punishment. The

---

[6]This result was obtained by ignoring the DSM-III exclusionary rules. If they had been observed, the DSM-III would have had even less overlap, and the differences between DSM-III and DSM-III-R would have been more marked.

Mixed label for the common (and the white-collar) criminal might mark the patterns of alienation shown by the ASP and the clever self-enhancement of the NPD. These experiences would encourage an attitude of "everyone for himself or herself." They also support the belief that what is wanted is his or hers for the taking if only detection can be avoided. (I cannot say that I have seen such a combination in practice. I have never had the opportunity of conducting an in-depth clinical interview with a "common criminal" or an "evil person.")

Case Example of Mixed Personality Disorder

The following case illustrates a mixture of BPD and OCD. This unlikely combination was made possible by a sudden change in life circumstances for the family.

This 38-year-old married white woman came to the hospital because of persistent depression, including suicidal ideation. She felt that her hospitalization meant she had failed. Her first and only serious suicide attempt had been an overdose 16 years ago, when she was in college. She promised herself then never to attempt suicide again, but had continued to engaged in suicidal rumination. She also remained prone to self-mutilation. In the current hospitalization, she was preoccupied with weight gain and nearly met criteria for Anorexia Nervosa (restricting followed by bingeing and purging).

The patient said that her marriage of a dozen years was very good because her husband was very supportive and extraordinarily patient. She did not understand why he was willing to stay with her. Her only complaint was that sometimes he procrastinated.

Her mother loomed larger than anyone else in her psyche. In brief, the mother had ignored and neglected the patient until she was a teen. Then the patient's father died and an older brother, who bullied the patient but was favored by the mother, got married. The patient was left to take care of (and, she said, "be stuck with") the mother.

The mother suddenly switched from a position of marked neglect of the patient to one of hostile intimacy. For example, before her father's death, the patient only received hand-me-down clothing from relatives. After her father died, her mother would take her shopping to get her own clothes. The mother had to go to work to support the family. Rather than ignoring the patient, the mother expected the patient to do all the housework. She had to have dinner on the table when the mother came home from work. Peer interactions during high school were discouraged because there wasn't time. The mother relentlessly criticized everything the patient did. "Can't you do anything right?" and "Are you crazy?" were common comments. The patient felt that she was a "rotten kid."

The patient was angry about her confinement to the home and the heavy assignment of household tasks. During her high school years she had more responsibility but less freedom. This seemed unfair, because as one does more work, one is supposed to have more, not fewer, privileges. The patient felt she could do nothing about her situation, and complied with her mother's demands for performance. As she thought about her helplessness, she felt sad and angry, and wanted to hurt herself. However, she believed that if her mother were to learn about the self-mutilations, she would blame the patient. The mother would say that the patient deserved to be hurt because of all the hurt she had caused.

The patient also believed that if her mother was hurt, she too was hurt. This fusion with the mother was concretely demonstrated when the patient was taking care of her mother after a surgical procedure. As the patient saw her mother in pain, she herself experienced physical pain. However, such deep caring was not reciprocated. The mother was distant from the patient except when the mother was needy.

The patient also felt close to her father. During the 9 months before he died, she was given the assignment of staying constantly with him and meeting his requests. The father would typically tell the patient to "cheer up," to keep a happy face. One of her older brothers would often pummel her. When the patient asked her father for help, he simply told them that fighting was not a good idea. The patient seemed reluctant to explore her relationship with her father, fearing that the relationship she saw as good might turn out to be not so good. For example, when the interviewer described the father as somewhat abandoning when he failed to protect her from a bullying brother, the patient objected. She said that they were close, and recalled that she gave her father backrubs during the time she was, in effect, his nursemaid. Otherwise, she remembered little about those 9 months. It is possible that there was sexual abuse, but the patient did not think so. One therapist had tried hypnosis to retrieve memories, but nothing convincing emerged. The patient remained very attached to her father, and asserted that he died because she "didn't love him enough."

The patient liked her work as a clerk in a fashionable store. However, one colleague was inappropriately critical and demanding, and reminded the patient of her mother. She apparently performed well on the job, but her mother continually pressured her to leave that job, go on to college, and then get a better job. Her mother offered to provide financial support for further education, but the patient had no interest. Her goal was to be happy and enjoy her husband and her family.

Careful examination of a self-mutilating episode in the hospital revealed the following sequence: (1) perceived rejection or abandonment when a member of the hospital staff said she should go watch TV instead of discussing a current panic attack; (2) self-criticism ("I am not worth helping. No one else cares, so I don't care"); (3) self-mutilation (she found a mirror fragment in her room and began carving on her wrist); (4) relief from anxiety ("It just went away"); and (5) a feeling of numbness ("I washed it off, and just had no feeling about it. I forgot about it"). Self-mutilation thus "closed the books" on an episode of anxiety started by perceived rejection. This is the classical sequence described for self-mutilation episodes for BPD in Chapter 5.

Before hospitalization, the patient had been engaged in outpatient psychotherapy that emphasized finding "the child within." Approaches included looking at early photographs, visualizing and nurturing herself as a child, and other methods of retrieving memories of the past to learn why she wanted to kill her "inner child." The goal was to develop a different, more constructive perspective on herself. The patient claimed that her response to these interventions was to intensify her disgust toward and disapproval of that little child, herself.

The patient was willing to discuss how her self-mutilations, poor self-esteem, and depression reflected agreement with her mother's opinion about her. As noted above, the mother called the patient "rotten," "crazy," and unable to do anything right. The patient's depressive self-talk reflected those same beliefs. Even the grief about a miscarriage was tied up with this struggle with the mother. Her mother attacked her for having a miscarriage, suggesting that it was the result of her earlier wish to adopt. Her mother had been angry that the patient was unwilling to "hold out for a baby."

There was a painful discussion about how her suicidal ruminations and self-mutilations reflected punishment inflicted for her mother and a "loving gift." The love was in this thought: "You think this is right for me? Okay, I agree. Here it is. Now do you approve of and love me for agreeing with you in this way?" The patient herself offered the observation that suicide would represent "the ultimate sacrifice" to her mother. The interviewer suggested that the patient needed to consider whether she wanted to continue showing mother her love in this way. The patient seemed quite thoughtful about this reframing of her self-destructive activities.

The diagnostic impression was of Major Depression and Mixed Personality Disorder. There were features of both OCD and BPD. The OCD traits included severe self-constraint, obedience to the mother's commands, and high levels of performance; the BPD features included self-mutilation, idealization of the father, and devaluation of the mother. The patient did not meet the requisite number of criteria for either of these Axis II categories, however. Theoretically, the BPD features stemmed from the prolonged early neglect, accompanied by physical abuse from an older sibling and possible sexual abuse from the father. The patient's addiction to pain might have been enhanced by the perception that her mother wanted her to feel pain. She was frequently abused by a sibling who was favored by the mother; if the mother thought that the sibling was wonderful, and that sibling wrought pain, then pain must be good. When the mother switched from neglect and abandonment to demanding service, the patient had an opportunity to be accepted and loved by her mother. However, when the "rules" were shifted from "Endure pain" to "Perform perfectly," this woman's patterns were shifted from the BPD song to the OCD song. Her coexisting depression was exacerbated by her view that she never could do anything right in her mother's eyes. She was helpless to change her position.

The treatment recommendation was that therapy should concentrate on helping the patient to differentiate from her mother, so that she might be free to develop an updated and more appropriate perspective on herself. Her recent recall and sympathetic treatment of "the child within" apparently elicited attack of that child from the introject. It appeared that the patient had been using the therapy exercise to act out the internalized belief system of the mother that the patient was "a rotten kid." The key to reconstruction of her personality would be in transforming this destructive introject. The patient would need to want to take better care of herself and to differentiate from her mother's destructive beliefs about her.

This reorientation might be accomplished by further development, from various perspectives, of the theme that self-destruction is a(n undesirable) form of intimacy with the mother. Toward this goal, the possibility of a conference with the mother might be considered. An effective technique might be to consider the conference as an *in vivo* sample of the relationship. A tape recording of the conference could be used later in individual therapy to help the patient develop a more objective view of her relationship with her mother (see Chapter 4). Such an exercise sometimes dramatically facilitates the differentiation process. Differentiation from a hostile parent can also be facilitated by bonding with a therapist who clearly wishes the patient well.

After differentiation from the old internalization was underway, the therapy exercise of recalling images of the "inner child" could be repeated with better results. At that point, the goal would continue to help the patient discover natural and appropriate compassion and nurturance for her "child within." When identification with the mother was weakened, the desired result of compassion and caring for the "child within" would be more likely. Without differentiation, the old introject would simply continue to attack and mock the patient for having compassion for herself.

Case Example of Personality Disorder NOS

The other residual class, Personality Disorder NOS, contains individuals whose developmental learning was substantially different from the DSM prototypes. Regional and cultural differences can produce sizable numbers of patients whose patterns may be unfamiliar to members of the DSM committees. An example of a pattern not identified by the DSM that appears to be relatively common in the southwestern United States is given below. This pattern has been seen in depressed married women coming to a hospital that serves the central and southern Rocky Mountain states. I call it the "Wizard of Oz" syndrome. Like the Wizard of Oz, these women function as vehicles for others to define and enhance their own strengths. They are assigned the identity of wife to and mother of others. Their moves are monitored and controlled by an older generation that meddles in the child rearing, often with inept or superfluous instructions. The Wizards are superhuman in their output. They may have to figure out what to do about incompatibilities among warring parties within the family, without acknowledging that a war even exists. Loyalties, plots, and triangulations abound. The peace must be kept, and the image of the family as fantastic and admirable must be preserved.

The culture is markedly male-dominant, and so the women must solve these problems indirectly. Straightforwardness is not acceptable for the female gender, whose opinions are given little inherent credibility. The mandate for secrecy and family sanctity precludes finding social support outside the family milieu. These women rarely seek psychiatric help. Their presentation at the hospital comes when they can no longer cope. Feeling overwhelmed, trapped, helpless, and without recourse, they have symptoms of severe depression.

This 28-year-old married mother of three was referred to the hospital by her mother-in-law for involuntary vomiting associated with an inability to eat and significant weight loss. Her depression had started about a year ago with the birth of her latest child during a complicated delivery.

The patient said she needed more self-understanding so that she would have more confidence in her own ideas. She said she wanted to learn to think independently and "take responsibility for herself." She relied too much on the approval of others, and was too focused on "making everybody happy." By the end of the interview, this dilemma had been reframed. She suffered from an impossible conflict between her wish for self-definition and definitive injunctions against it. Her husband's family wanted her to be like her husband's mother. If she followed the model offered, she would be completely deferential to her husband's time schedule and preferences. She would "smooth" any feathers he might ruffle, facilitate his preferences, make excuses for him, and reassure the family that everything would always be all right. On the other hand, she had ideas and plans of her own that would not be acceptable to the family.

The prototype was illustrated by the following incident. The grandfather was 2 hours late for Easter dinner. The kids were hungry and grumpy. Grandma kept everything smooth. After they finally had dinner, the children were tired and bored, and they began to fight. Grandpa pouted that it was not a nice family time. Grandma made excuses for Grandpa; tried to entertain the children; and assumed responsibility for making Grandpa, the children, and everyone else content with the "happy" family day.

This vision of male dominance seemed unfair and made the patient angry. Equal sharing of power was the better alternative, she thought. Unfortunately, she had a sister-in-law who had acted on similar beliefs. This woman had taken a more assertive stance with her own husband. The family expressed dislike and disapproval of this sister-in-law's "henpecking" behaviors. In addition, two of the patient's husband's cousins were not speaking to each other because of a fight between their respective husbands. The patient did not want to be called a "henpecker" or to cause rifts within the family.

The husband endorsed many of the beliefs held by his family of origin. He also said that he wanted to find his own separate lifestyle, together with his wife; nonetheless, when the couple argued about child rearing, the husband usually agreed with his mother. Before this hospitalization, there had been an ongoing dispute about how to handle the middle child. The patient prevailed during exacerbations of the physical symptoms associated with the complicated delivery of a new infant. After she healed physically, she was again forced to comply with the preferences of her husband and mother-in-law.

The patient's reaction to such intrusive control from the husband's family was to feel angry. She felt she had to choose between being mindlessly compliant with inept child-rearing practices and being seen as a henpecking shrew. She felt compromised, without options, overwhelmed, and depressed. It was important to avoid open conflict, so the spouses tried to read each other's minds. The ideal was always to anticipate what the other person wanted. This pattern of second-guessing resulted in a loss of a sense of what was real. The patient could not say what she wanted. She could not negotiate openly and fairly with her husband. Instead, she tried to perform the magic of creating happiness in the minds of others, regardless of reality, and without having needs or opinions of her own.

This pattern was encouraged by her learning in her own family of origin. Her mother complained bitterly about the father behind his back. The patient learned to listen to and support her mother. The mother "pretended" to be inadequate and incompetent. Because the mother was "ill," the patient had to be the mother's power, her strength. For example, the patient assumed major responsibility for a handicapped sibling. She also felt that she alone kept the family together after her father's heart attack. During this interview, she said that she was proud of how responsible she had been throughout the years. She added tearfully, however, that she would have liked to "be just one of the kids."

Discipline was not harsh, and usually involved injunctions against expressing anger at her brother. The father disciplined mostly with "guilt trips." He would say things like this: "You are ridiculous when you lose your temper." The father assumed that he could read the patient's mind, and would declare, for example, that she didn't mean it when she said she was sorry. Her parents tried to define and control her reality and affect. This pattern was repeated later by the in-laws.

The patient said that she was known to be a person who performed at a very high level. To keep everyone happy, she had to be one person for her mother, another for her father, another for her husband, and still another for her children. She herself did not exist. She felt she had disappeared mentally and emotionally, and now, as she lost weight into the anorexic range, she felt she was disappearing physically.

Along with Major Depression, the diagnosis was "Wizard of Oz" syndrome (Personality Disorder NOS). Everyone looked to the patient to provide or enhance what they were missing in themselves. Like the Wizard, she turned out to be a vulnerable figure working behind the scenes, generating wondrous illusions with smoke and mirrors. Her "identity" was to be to others what they wanted her to do for them. Her pattern does not conform to any of the DSM prototypes. This patient did not have NEG because she did actually meet demands to perform. She did not have DPD because she was skilled instrumentally and she functioned at a high level; others depended upon her. She did not present as having a conversion reaction because she was aware of and articulate about the ego-alien feelings and conflicts. Her pain on eating may have been a normal reaction to starvation. She had the perfectionistic, high-performing, self-restricting orientation of the classical anorexic, but did not concentrate her conflict on the single issue of eating. She was not a self-defeating personality because she did not choose this situation when she had better options. She didn't undermine attempts to help her or people who treated her well, and she was not pleasure-avoidant.

The treatment recommendation was to continue with individual and couples therapy. The husband had shown signs of wanting to differentiate from his family of origin; there was a chance that he would be willing to explore possibilities for a more equitable distribution of power within the marital relationship. Learning in detail about the difference between assertiveness (i.e., clearly stating one's own differing point of view) and dominance (i.e., insisting that others accept that view) could be very helpful. Assertiveness can be dignified, whereas dominance can rightfully draw the labels of "shrew" and "henpecking." The husband might be helped to be less dominant when expressing his ideas about child rearing. He could cease ordering that his ideas be implemented and leaving the scene expecting his orders to be carried out. Instead, there could be a constructive dialogue, so that each partner could come truly to understand the other's point of view. Then there might be a resolution of the dispute, with each partner comfortable about the final plan.

Such new explorations in shared understanding and equal participation in family decision making might have to be kept secret from the families of origin for a while. They would probably attack this deviation from the cultural prototype. In individual therapy, the patient might work further on developing her own identity. Deep down, she felt that she had a self, but that it was "bad" and inadequate. This feeling probably stemmed from the internalized belief that she should appear as the fantasy of others. According to that belief, any self-as-home-base orientation would be defined as "bad." Exploration of the experiences in socialization that encouraged her to accept this programming might give her the adult perspective needed to reject the demands that she be the "Wizard of Oz."

For Every Symptom There Are Reasons

Cases of Mixed Personality Disorder and Personality Disorder NOS also follow the principles developed in the "Pathogenic Hypotheses" sections in the chapters on the 11 standard disorders. There is reasonable correspondence between observed interpersonal symptoms and early learning. The basic assumption is this: "For every symptom there are reasons." The hybrid model uses SASB dimensions to describe DSM categories and assumes that social learning shapes the temperament.

If a person's temperament and social learning experiences are consistent with commonly occurring patterns, his or her disorder may conform to one of the categories of the DSM. If his or her experiences are unusual, their consequences have probably not been tabulated by the DSM committee. Some patients' social learning fails to follow any of the DSM prototypes. Nonetheless, the DSM descriptions of prototypes remain useful, so long as they describe a reasonable number of individuals in ways that are clinically meaningful. The need for the categories Mixed Personality Disorder and Personality Disorder NOS does not invalidate the validity or potential usefulness of the standard categories. Suppose, by analogy, that most people in a culture sing a group of 11 songs. If some individuals sing an altogether different song, one does not conclude that the 11 popular ones do not exist.

RELATION OF AXIS II DISORDERS TO AXIS I DISORDERS: A NEW APPROACH

The DSM-IV may introduce an "Axis I" category. The *DSM-IV Options Book* (American Psychiatric Association, 1991a) offers the following description:

New Diagnostic Categories Under Review

Depressive Personality Disorder

Interest in including a Depressive Personality Disorder in DSM-IV is prompted by support-ive (but insufficient) data from empirical studies, by the nonspecificity of the Dysthymic Disorder diagnosis, and by the recognition of "spectrum" disorders that link Axis I and Axis II. It is unlikely that this diagnosis will be included as an official diagnosis in DSM-IV, but it may appear in the Appendix. Additional field testing of these suggested criteria is being conducted, specifically with regard to examining their overlap with Dysthymic Disor-der.

A. Presence of at least ?? of the following:

(1) usual mood is dominated by dejection, gloominess, cheerlessness, joylessness, unhappi-ness

(2) prominent self-concepts center around beliefs of inadequacy, worthlessness, and low self-esteem

(3) is critical, blaming, derogatory, and punitive toward oneself

(4) is brooding and given to worry

(5) is negativistic, critical, and judgmental toward others

(6) is pessimistic

(7) is prone to feeling guilt

B. Does not occur exclusively during Major Depressive Episodes.

This proposed Axis II categoryis an attempt to solve the vexing "coexist-ence" problem. Since the appearance of DSM-III, many papers in the literature have dealt with the fact that many of the Axis II personality disorders are typi-cally accompanied by Axis I disorders. Conversely, if such Axis I symptoms as depression, anxiety, or thought disorder are accompanied by personality disor-der, the prognosis is worse than if there is no personality disorder (Docherty, Fiester, & Shea, 1986). This new diagnostic category will approach the coexist-ence problem by defining a "characterological variant" of depression.

The new category, Depressive Personality Disorder, may be analyzed for interpersonal structure in the same way as the others. The proposed descriptors include all forms of hostile enmeshment that are described by the SASB model. These have been explained in Chapter 3 (see Figure 3.12 and Tables 3.2, 3.4, and 3.6), and are reviewed in Table 15.1. The detailed descriptions of hostile enmeshment shown in Table 15.1 are summarized simply by these SASB model points (Figure 3.9): BLAME, SULK, and *SELF-BLAME*. Further detail on these and other SASB labels is provided in the Appendix to this book (Table A.3).

The interpersonal descriptions in Table 15.1 do not directly mark the depres-sive affect mentioned by the DSM-IV (e.g., "dejection, gloominess, cheerless-ness, joylessness, unhappiness, brooding, given to worry, pessimistic"). How-ever, I have argued that specific affects are associated with specific social behaviors; a first draft of an affective model appeared in Benjamin (1986, p. 632).

Table 15.1. Three Faces of Hostile Enmeshment (from Tables 3.2, 3.4, and 3.6): The SASB Labels for the DSM-IV's Description of a Possible New Category, Depressive Personality Disorder

	ATTACK
CONTROL	0. Annihilating attack
	1. Approach menacingly
	2. Rip off, drain
	3. Punish, take revenge
	4. Delude, divert, mislead
	5. Accuse, blame
	6. Put down, act superior
	7. Intrude, block, restrict
	8. Enforce conformity
	9. Manage, control
	RECOIL
SUBMIT	0. <u>Desperate protest</u>
	1. <u>Wary, fearful</u>
	2. <u>Sacrifice greatly</u>
	3. <u>Whine, defend, justify</u>
	4. <u>Uncomprehendingly agree</u>
	5. <u>Appease, scurry</u>
	6. <u>Sulk, act put upon</u>
	7. <u>Apathetic compliance</u>
	8. <u>Follow rules, proper</u>
	9. <u>Yield, submit, give in</u>
	SELF-ATTACK
SELF-CONTROL	0. *Torture, annihilate self*
	1. *Menace to self*
	2. *Drain, overburden self*
	3. *Vengefully punish self*
	4. *Deceive, divert self*
	5. *Guilt, blame, bad self*
	6. *Doubt, put self down*
	7. *Restrain, hold back self*
	8. *Force propriety*
	9. *Control, manage self*

In addition, I also believe that specific social behaviors are typically accompanied by specific cognitive styles; a corresponding model for cognition appeared in Benjamin (1986, p. 633). The first draft of the affective model would suggest that the affects associated with hostile enmeshment would be "enraged, vengeful, arrogant, forceful, hateful, fearful, humiliated, helpless." The cognitive styles associated with hostile enmeshment would be "termination, nihilistic, judgmental, sharp focus on detail, closed to experience, ruminative, constricted, overcautious, appeal to authority." Interestingly, I thought on theoretical grounds that the affects "pessimistic, bitter, uncaring, disgusted" were associated with hostile autonomy rather than with hostile enmeshment. The DSM-IV description of Depressive Personality Disorder does include the adjective "pessimistic." I do not know whether the affect model is wrong,[7] whether the DSM should drop "pessimistic," or whether the DSM should add an interpersonal item to describe hostile withdrawal to the description of the depressive personality.

Bracketing the question of whether social withdrawal and its associated affects should be included in DSM-IV Depressive Personality Disorder, the present version can be described by the SASB model points involving hostile enmeshment. The model suggests that individuals with the Depressive Personality Disorder will blame, sulk, and be self-critical. Parallels with the affect model would add that they are "enraged, vengeful, arrogant, forceful, hateful, fearful, humiliated, helpless." Parallels with the cognition model would apply the following terms to their cognitive style: "termination, nihilistic, judgmental, sharp focus on detail, closed to experience, ruminative, constricted, overcautious, appeal to authority."

The introduction of possible structural models for affect and cognitive style introduces the possibility of discussing the interpersonal structure of the Axis I clinical syndromes. These are based largely on disturbances in affect and cognition. I believe that all such disturbances have evolved together and that there is a close correspondence among them. This belief would challenge the DSM's separation of disturbances in social behavior (personality disorders) from disturbances in affect and cognition (clinical syndromes). It would suggest that characteristic interpersonal patterns are associated with characteristic affects and cognitions. The coexistence of problems in behavior, affect, and cognition would be transformed from a diagnostic conundrum to a demonstration that psychiatry and psychology do indeed study an orderly domain. Behavior, affect, and cognition have evolved together, and their coexistence is *required*.

In the future, I hope to have an opportunity to present results of analyzing the Axis I disorders with the same methods used in this book for Axis II. To illustrate how that analysis might go, here is a brief overview of the hypothetical construct "depression." In the following passage, I have not restricted the definition of depression to the variant, Depressive Personality Disorder, that appears in the DSM-IV.

> If personality and depression are hypothetical constructs, then the patient's point of view is vital to their assessment. I believe that they are valid hypothetical constructs and would like to test a predisposing model. I expect that depression follows the patient's *perception* that he or she is helpless, trapped, blocked, overwhelmed, and without recourse. I also believe that depression is likely to be manifested when there is perceived loss of an attachment object, or when there is an event that enhances self-criticism. This view of depressive predispositions has been shaped by the hypotheses of Seligman (helplessness), Blatt (self-criticism), Beck (cognitive style), Bowlby (object loss) and others (e.g., Sullivan,

[7]Paul Crits-Christoph of the University of Pennsylvania and Amy Demorst of Swarthmore College have begun to explore whether the affect model can be appropriately revised and validated.

Mischel). Some personalities are predisposed to have these perceptions ("helpless, alone, bad") and are therefore more likely to become depressed. Others are not predisposed these ways, but they still can become depressed if they find themselves in situations that are harshly critical, that are overwhelming, or that involve loss of someone or something deeply loved.

Measures of these predispositions toward helplessness, self-criticism, and sensitivity to object loss can be considered indices of aspects of "personality" that are relevant to depression. The affective depressive responses marked by DSM (weight loss, tearfulness, sleep disturbance, etc.) can be considered indicators of "depression." Both "personality" and "depression" are hypothetical constructs or entities that mean more than the measurements used to define them. This position requires that the investigator be able to think of any number of experiments that predict an association between depression and measures of helplessness, self-criticism, or object loss. Here are some examples of such predictions based on the predisposing model just described. A submissive personality will have more depressive episodes than a dominant personality. A submissive personality will become even more submissive when depressed. A self-critical person is more likely to become depressed (self-criticism is the introjective correlate of the position of resentful submission). Depressed people are more likely to be self-critical. A dominant personality subjected to situational stresses that preclude dominance is more likely to have an episode of depression. A dominant personality who is successful in maintaining dominance by social role and circumstance is less likely to have an episode. Persons sensitive to object loss are more likely to perceive rejection and to become depressed about it. If present, social withdrawal is a reaction to the depressive condition rather than a predisposing marker. Persons with DPD and with dependent, histrionic, and passive aggressive personality disorders are more likely to become depressed because they share the trait of dependency. Persons with BPD are also likely to become depressed over perceived object loss. Persons with avoidant personality disorder are vulnerable to depression because of their tendency to feel rejected and to be self-critical. Persons with narcissistic and obsessive compulsive personality disorders are vulnerable to depression because they are easily reduced to self-criticism if they are not in control and "perfect." By contrast, individuals with paranoid, antisocial, and schizoid personality disorders are resistant to depression. The reason is that they are comfortable with autonomy, and so they are neither sensitive to rejection nor dependent. Nor are they self-critical.

A person can feel helpless or self-critical or abandoned because of a predisposition, a reaction to overwhelming external circumstance, or some interaction between the two. The predisposition may be determined by genetics or experience or both. To separate the "broken brain" version of the predisposing model from the "environmentally programmed" version of the predisposing model, one would need to engage in very careful sequential analysis of the development of a person's view of himself or herself and the environment. (Benjamin, 1993a, pp. 124–125).

of the major interpretations of psychosocial aspects of depression taken from the literature correspond to hostile enmeshment. These are helplessness and self-criticism. The third, object loss, corresponds to hostile autonomy (shown in Tables 3.2, 3.4, and 3.6). The "fever" of depression can by caused by any of these three situations, given the right combination of temperament and life circumstances. The present analysis may account for why personality disorder makes the prognosis for depression worse. The predispositions to helplessness, self-criticism, and sensitivity to object loss characterize several of the personality disorders. Individuals who have these depressive orientations as a part of their personality disorder are necessarily going to be vulnerable to depression.

POSTSCRIPT FOR THERAPISTS

I hope that the reader has strengthened his or her sense that individuals with personality disorders have their reasons. Many have had painful lives, and the patterns of their disorders reflect their attempts to adjust to that pain. Unfortunately, in so doing, they often unwittingly choose to contribute to continuing the pain. The effective therapist will empathically help the patient discover how it all "fits together." This "insight," plus the power of a constructive therapy relationship, can eventually can move the patient to the edge of a vital choice point. Once there, the patient may choose to cling desperately to the familiar "safety" of the disorder. Or he or she may "take the plunge," endure the intense anxiety that often comes with giving up old ways, and slowly begin to build patterns more appropriate to the present.

Very recently I talked with a patient who was referred for consultation about her many hospitalizations, including one that lasted for 7 months:

T: What do you believe causes your depression?

P: (*Angrily*) I think it is from the post-traumatic stuff. The abuse. The death of my mother. Other stuff before that. I think it is clinical. They ruled that out with my Borderline Personality diagnosis. But the depression is there, and there is nothing I can point my finger to when I get depressed. And I can't function. It has been this way ever since I was 9 or 10 years old. It is in my genes. . . . I am also angry about the program I was in at the hospital. They say I am just manipulating when I cut on myself or overdose. They say I have to realize that and change my behaviors.

T: How can you change them?

P: I am supposed to just stop. I am told I have a choice because I have a personality disorder. Talking about feelings is just manipulative. Only behaviors count.

I hope that no reader follows this example and uses a diagnosis of personality disorder to "blame the patient." This woman felt that she had been told her label meant that her self-destructiveness was her choice and fault. The patient was engaged in a deadly power struggle with the hospital over whether her failure to improve was a question of "can't" or "won't." She described a dichotomy that I have heard many times before. Axis I disorders are not the patient's "fault," but Axis II disorders are. Axis I disorders are to be treated with sympathy and support; Axis II disorders are to be met with "tough love." No wonder this patient coveted an Axis I label in place of her diagnosis of personality disorder.

It is vital that no practicing clinician make the mistake of blaming the patient, whether the label is on Axis I or Axis II. Acceptance of a role for choice in mental disorder should never be used to scold a patient. Even though the "will" is probably a determinant of behavior, patients cannot and will not respond to coercion on that point. Only when therapy has progressed carefully, and when both insight and relationship are strong, can a patient truly stand at the edge of choice.

Consider a man learning to ski who desperately wants to carve through the giant moguls that crisscross the face of the mountain. He wants to, but he cannot. The instructor tells him how to do it well, but he cannot "put it together." There is much work to be done before he can. A number of conscious ideas must be driven into the preconscious and unconscious, because he cannot remember them all at the same time—for example, "Stay oriented down the mountain," "Absorb bumps with your knees," "Put your weight on the downhill ski," and so on. Many of the correct moves must become "second nature" before he can do what he wants to do. Some things that are unconscious must become conscious. For example, he must learn that if he is afraid, he may draw back, and that will distribute his weight improperly. Perhaps his brother is an expert and he feels he shouldn't challenge him; this belief might also interfere with learning to ski well. Before he can have the necessary attitude, he must resolve these conflicts. Then he must practice and practice.

Now imagine that the instructor says to the student, "If you don't do it right this time, it is because you choose not to." The student will not find this remark helpful. Probably he will reply, "If it is only a matter of choosing to ski the mountain well, I surely would do it." Similarly, the patient who hated her personality disorder label explained, "If I could choose not to cut on myself and overdose, I surely would."

APPENDIX

SUMMARY OF DIAGNOSTIC AND DIFFERENTIAL INDICATORS

The thesis of this book is that the DSM personality disorders can be described well by three underlying orthogonal dimensions: (1) interpersonal focus, (2) love–hate (or friendliness–hostility), and (3) enmeshment–differentiation. If the clinician uses these dimensions in attending to the patient's descriptions of the self and others, he or she will be able to recognize the respective disorders. There will be relatively little difficulty with the overlap or boundary problems discussed in Chapter 1. In this Appendix, each of the DSM personality disorders is reviewed from the perspective of the DSM and its present interpersonal translation.

The SASB model, built on the dimensions of focus, love–hate, and enmeshment–differentiation, has provided the language for the interpersonal descriptions used in this book. The characteristic baseline positions for the respective personality disorders are reviewed in Table A.1. The underlying wishes and fears that organize and maintain the interpersonal patterns, and that must be changed if behavior is to change, are reviewed in Table A.2. Tables A.1 and A.2 are based on the cluster version of the SASB model (Figure 3.9). Readers may find it useful to refer to Table A.3 for a summary of the meanings of the SASB labels.

To receive an Axis II label by the present method, the patient should meet all the necessary interpersonal conditions, and none of the exclusionary interpersonal conditions, discussed in earlier chapters and summarized in Table A.4. He or she should also meet the requisite number of DSM criteria. The discussion that follows represents "fine-tuning" of the diagnostic process. It appeals to Table A.1 to show how the categories of personality disorder can be *expected* to overlap, and marks interpersonal points of divergence. The distinctions among personality disorders can be compared to distinctions among songs. All songs can be analyzed in terms of the basic notes (*do, re, mi,* etc.) as they vary in timing and context. Related categories share important attributes, but nonetheless also have important differences.

There are good reasons to make an interpersonal diagnosis using the present method. If a patient meets the present interpersonal criteria for a given personality disorder, the treatment suggestions given in this book for that disorder should be useful. The hypotheses about the origins of the patterns and their purposes can be used to help the patient learn about his or her ways of relating to the self and others. The clinician's understanding of the patterns and their origins will allow him or her to anticipate and

394 Appendix

Table A.1. Comparison of SASB Labels for Baseline Positions

	BPD	NPD	HPD	ASP	DPD	OCD	NEG	AVD	PAR	SOI	SZT
1. EMANCIPATE											×*
2. AFFIRM											
3. ACTIVE LOVE	×			×*							
4. PROTECT											
5. CONTROL	×	×	×*	×*		×*			×		×*
6. BLAME	×	×	×	×		×	×*	×	×		
7. ATTACK	×	×		×*					×		
8. IGNORE		×		×		×*				×	
1. SEPARATE		×		×			×*		×		
2. DISCLOSE											
3. REACTIVE LOVE			×*								
4. TRUST	×		×*		×						
5. SUBMIT					×	×*	×*				×*
6. SULK					×		×*	×			
7. RECOIL								×	×		×
8. WALL OFF			×*	×*		×*	×*	×	×	×	×*
1. SELF-EMANCIPATE											
2. SELF-AFFIRM											
3. ACTIVE SELF-LOVE		×*									
4. SELF-PROTECT	×			×*							
5. SELF-CONTROL						×*		×	×		×
6. SELF-BLAME		×			×	×		×			
7. SELF-ATTACK	×		×*				×*				
8. SELF-NEGLECT	×	×*		×*		×*				×	×

*Indicates that these codes within the same column appear in complex combinations with one another.

understand transference problems. Among other things, such knowledge can help the clinician remain collaborative and nondefensive in face of the frequent provocations that come from patients with personality disorders.

The generic treatment approach has been described in Chapter 4. Briefly, the idea is that psychosocial therapy involves five more or less hierarchical stages: (1) A collaborative relationship between patient and therapist develops; (2) the patient learns to recognize his or her interpersonal and intrapsychic patterns—where the patterns came from and what they were for; (3) old, presently maladaptive patterns are blocked; (4) the will to change is mobilized; (5) new interpersonal and intrapsychic patterns are learned. The name "generic" implies that successful psychotherapies, no matter what their "school" or underlying theory, can implicitly or explicitly be described in terms of these five stages.

The last stage of psychotherapy, learning new patterns, is easiest. Relatively little has been said in this book about how to help patients learn new patterns. For that task, many well-known therapeutic techniques are useful, including facilitating expression of affect, enhancing communication skills, strengthening assertiveness, teaching self-directed behavioral management, and/or teaching better modulation of cognitive style. Unfortunately, individuals with personality disorders have acquired a reputation for being "untreatable." This pessimistic view is based on treatment failures that often result if the clinician starts the therapy by trying to teach "better ways." The classical psychoanalysts were correct in assumimg that constructive personality change cannot occur until the underlying (often unconscious) wishes and fears have been addressed. The first four steps of generic interpersonal therapy are vital to that effort to prepare for change. If they are successfully negotiated, constructive change in individuals with personality disorders is possible.

BORDERLINE PERSONALITY DISORDER

Interpersonal Summary and Transference Example

Summary: There is a morbid fear of abandonment and a wish for protective nurturance, preferably received by constant physical proximity to the rescuer (lover or caregiver). The baseline position is friendly dependency on a nurturer, which becomes hostile control if the caregiver or lover fails to deliver enough (and there is never enough). There is a belief that

Table A.2. Comparison of SASB Labels for Wishes (W) and Fears (F)

	BPD	NPD	HPD	ASP	DPD	OCD	NEG	AVD	PAR	SOI	SZT
1. EMANCIPATE				W					W		W
2. AFFIRM									W		
3. ACTIVE LOVE		W	W					W			
4. PROTECT	W	W	W		W		W	W			
5. CONTROL		F		F	W		F				
6. BLAME		F				F			F	F		F
7. ATTACK								F	F		F
8. IGNORE	F	F	F		F			F			
1. SEPARATE											
2. DISCLOSE											
3. REACTIVE LOVE											
4. TRUST											
5. SUBMIT		W		W		W			W		
6. SULK											
7. RECOIL											
8. WALL OFF											
1. SELF-EMANCIPATE						F					
2. SELF-AFFIRM											
3. ACTIVE SELF-LOVE											
4. SELF-PROTECT											
5. SELF-CONTROL						W					
6. SELF-BLAME											
7. SELF-ATTACK											
8. SELF-NEGLECT											

1. **EMANCIPATE.** 1. Without much worry, S leaves O free to do and be whatever O wants. 2. Without much concern, S gives O the freedom to do things on his/her own.
2. **AFFIRM.** 1. S lets O speak freely, and warmly tries to understand even if they disagree. 2. S likes O and tries to see his/her point of view even if they disagree.
3. **ACTIVE LOVE.** 1. S happily, gently, very lovingly approaches O, and warmly invites O to be as close as he/she would like. 2. With much love and caring, S tenderly approaches if O seems to want it.
4. **PROTECT.** 1. With much kindness, S teaches, protects, and takes care of O. 2. In a very loving way, S helps, guides, shows O how to do things.
5. **CONTROL.** 1. To keep things in good order, S takes charge of everything and makes O follow his/her rules. 2. To make sure things turn out right, S tells O exactly what to do and how to do it.
6. **BLAME.** 1. S puts O down, blames him/her, punishes him/her. 2. S tells O his/her ways are wrong and he/she deserves to be punished.
7. **ATTACK.** 1. Without worrying about the effect on O, S wildly, hatefully, destructively attacks him/her. 2. Without caring what happens to O, S murderously attacks in the worst way possible.
8. **IGNORE.** 1. Without giving it a second thought, S uncaringly ignores, neglects, abandons O. 2. Without giving it a thought, S carelessly forgets O, leaves him/her out of important things.

1. SEPARATE. 1. S knows his/her own mind and "does his/her own thing" separately from O. 2. S has a clear sense of what he/she thinks, and chooses his/her own ways separately from O.
2. DISCLOSE. 1. S clearly and comfortably expresses his/her own thoughts and feelings to O. 2. S peacefully and plainly states his/her own thoughts and feelings to O.
3. REACTIVE LOVE. 1. S relaxes, freely plays, and enjoys being with O as often as possible. 2. S is joyful and comfortable, altogether delighted to be with O.
4. TRUST. 1. S learns from O, relies upon O, accepts what he/she offers. 2. S trustingly depends on O, willingly takes in what O offers.
5. SUBMIT. 1. S thinks, does, becomes whatever O wants. 2. S defers to O and conforms to O's wishes.
6. SULK. 1. With much sulking and fuming, S scurries to do what O wants. 2. S bitterly, resentfully gives in, and hurries to do what O wants.
7. RECOIL. 1. With much fear and hate, S tries to hide from or get away from O. 2. Filled with disgust and fear, S tries to disappear, to break loose from O.
8. WALL OFF. 1. S walls him/herself off from O and doesn't react much. 2. S is closed off from O and mostly stays alone in his/her own world.

1. *SELF-EMANCIPATE.* 1. Without concern or thought, I let myself do and be whatever I feel like. 2. I let myself do whatever I feel like and don't worry about tomorrow.
2. *SELF-AFFIRM.* 1. Aware of my personal shortcomings as well as my good points, I comfortably let myself be "as is." 2. With awareness of weaknesses as well as strengths, I like and accept myself "as is."
3. *ACTIVE SELF-LOVE.* 1. I tenderly, lovingly cherish myself. 2. I very tenderly and lovingly appreciate and value myself.
4. *SELF-PROTECT.* 1. I put energy into providing for, looking after, developing myself. 2. I take good care of myself and work hard on making the most of myself.
5. *SELF-CONTROL.* 1. To make sure I do things right, I tightly control and watch over myself. 2. To become perfect, I force myself to do things correctly.
6. *SELF-BLAME.* 1. I punish myself by blaming myself and putting myself down. 2. I accuse and blame myself for being wrong or inferior.
7. *SELF-ATTACK.* 1. Without considering what might happen, I hatefully reject and destroy myself. 2. Without thought about what might happen, I recklessly attack and angrily reject myself.
8. *SELF-NEGLECT.* 1. I am recklessly neglectful of myself, sometimes completely "spacing out." 2. I carelessly let go of myself, and often get lost in an unrealistic dream world.

Note. S, self; O, other. Reprinted from Benjamin (1988; versions 1 and 2 of Short Form INTREX [SASB questionnaire] items). Copyright 1988 Lorna Smith Benjamin.

Table A.4. Summary of Necessary and Exclusionary Interpersonal Conditions

Disorder	Necessary conditions	Exclusionary conditions
BPD	Fear of abandonment, handled by transitive coercion of protection and nurturance; self-sabotage following happiness or success.	Tolerance of long-term aloneness.
NPD	Grandiose sense of self-importance; entitlement.	Uncaring recklessness with self.
HPD	Coercive dependency.	Self-sabotage following happiness or success.
ASP	Need for control of others and autonomy for self; detachment, lack of remorse.	Fear of abandonment; entitlement; dependency.
DPD	Submissiveness due to sense of instrumental inadequacy.	Complications of dependency (long-term comfort with autonomy; transitive demands for nurturance; intimacy only if the situation is safe; insistence on submission; scorn for authority; etc.).
OCD	Unreasonable control; devotion to perfection.	Irresponsible behaviors; emotional excesses; contempt for authority.
NEG	Compliant defiance of demands to perform.	Uncomplicated deference; devotion to productivity.
AVD	Defensive withdrawal; wishing for acceptance.	Affective detachment; avoidance of aloneness; instrumental incompetence; consistent failure to perform.
PAR	Perception of intent to harm when it is not there.	Worry about abandonment; deference to authority.
SOI	Social withdrawal (polythetic approach).	Anything other than simple social withdrawal.
SZT	Social withdrawal; thought disorder implying autistic control.	Fear of autonomy; demanding dependency; proud disregard for social norms.

the provider secretly if not overtly likes dependency and neediness, and a vicious introject attacks the self if there are signs of happiness or success.

These interpersonal baseline patterns, wishes, and fears are likely to appear in the therapy relationship with the BPD.[1] Consider the following example of a transference problem:

A patient responded well to a prescription of an antidepressant (therapist **PROTECT**, patient TRUST). Then, as the depression re-emerged, the patient complained that the doctor wasn't monitoring the dosage closely enough, or that he failed to try a new wonder drug that her friend's doctor was pre-

---

[1]As in the text, three-letter abbreviations are used throughout to indicate either "the diagnosis XYZ" or "a person with the diagnosis XYZ." A key to the abbreviations is provided at the beginning of this book.

scribing these days (therapist IGNORE). The BPD disclosed reluctantly that she missed three important days of school (*SELF-NEGLECT*) and came very close to an overdose on this wrong regimen (BPD *SELF-ATTACK*, and BLAME the therapist). The therapist wrote a prescription for the new drug, and asked the patient to call every day to let him know how she was doing (SUBMIT plus PROTECT).

Interpersonal Translation of the DSM

The "total BPD" shows all the symptoms mentioned in the DSM. Early abandonment is internalized, so that the BPD behaves very recklessly (DSM criterion 4, self-damaging impulsiveness).[2] Internalization of neglect and its association with boring aloneness and danger lead also to feelings of emptiness, described by DSM criterion 7. Fear of abandonment, described by DSM criterion 1, comes from its association with trauma and bad personhood. The family devotion to chaos for high stakes accounts for the instability and intensity described by DSM criteria 2 and 6. The famous anger of the BPD, described in DSM criterion 8, is set off by perceived abandonment and is intended to coerce the opposite of abandonment—namely, nurturance. Self-mutilation, described in DSM criterion 5, is a replay of the abuse or an effort to appease an internalized attacker. Identity disturbance, described by DSM criterion 3, is a consequence of the internalization of objects who would attack the BPD when there were signs of differentiation or self-definition, and/or happiness. Self-sabotage amounts to self-protection from the internalized abusers. This short-circuiting of personal development comprises the BPD identity disturbance. Thought disorder, reflected in DSM criterion 9, may be the consequence of having reality testing negated: "What you think was hurt was pleasure. What you think happened didn't happen." *The DSM requires that at least five criteria be met for a diagnosis of BPD.*

For BPD, the recommended *necessary* interpersonal descriptors are (1) a fear of abandonment that is handled by active focus on others, who are supposed to give the BPD protection and nurturance; and (2) self-sabotage for doing well or being happy. There is only one *exclusionary* consideration: long-term comfort with autonomy, as is seen in SOI, SZT, PAR, and NPD. A patient who shows such comfort cannot have the abandonment sensitivity characteristic of BPD.

Differential Diagnoses

Differential diagnoses among the categories showing at least 30% overlap with BPD according to Morey (1988) may be made as follows:

BPD and HPD (36.1%): According to Tables A.1 and A.2, these groups share the characteristics of, CONTROL, BLAME, TRUST, and *SELF-ATTACK*. Both BPD and HPD have a baseline of demanding dependency. In addition, their wishes (PROTECT) and fears

---

[2]The item numbering used throughout is that of the DSM-IV, except in the case of ASP, where only the DSM-III-R criteria are used.

(IGNORE) are the same (though the HPD also wishes for ACTIVE LOVE). A useful way to tell them apart is to look for the BPD's tendency to self-sabotage in the face of success. Each is capable of suicidal gestures triggered by perceived abandonment or inattention; however, the HPD's reaction is interpersonal and intended to coerce more services. The BPD's is more internally directed, out of touch with reality, and self-punishing.

The two categories also differ in the way with which they attempt to coerce caregiving. The HPD is usually dependent and controlling at the same time, while the BPD is more likely to assume the same positions at different points in time. In other words, the HPD usually combines TRUST with CONTROL, and simultaneously BLAMEs. By contrast, the BPD will clearly TRUST at one moment, and burst with BLAME (hostile control) in the next. This difference means that on average, the HPD is more likely implicitly to control the interpersonal process. The BPD is more at the mercy of whatever internal condition exists at the moment. The HPD's greater control means that he or she usually functions at a higher level.

BPD and AVD (36.1%): According to Tables A.1 and A.2, these two categories share the characteristic of BLAME and the wish to receive PROTECT. Marked differences occur in their willingness to be independent. The AVD's baseline positions include RECOIL and WALL OFF. The BPD will briefly show hostile withdrawal in an angry reaction to perceived abandonment, but it will not last for long, and it is not a baseline position. The key difference between these two, then, is the BPD's need to avoid aloneness versus the AVD's tolerance of it. The AVD also has more *SELF-CONTROL* than the BPD.

BPD and PAR (32%): According to Tables A.1 and A.2, these two categories share the SASB codes of CONTROL, BLAME, and ATTACK. The key difference, as with AVD, is in their response to aloneness. The PAR not only tolerates it, but actually wishes to be left alone. The BPD, in strong contrast, is panicked by aloneness. The PAR also has more *SELF-CONTROL* than the BPD.

BPD and DPD (34%): According to Tables A.1 and A.2, these two share the feature of TRUST, the wish for PROTECT, and a fear of IGNORE. An important difference is that the DPD does not coerce caregiving by CONTROL, BLAME, or ATTACK. If these aggressive behaviors are characteristic, the DPD label is ruled out.

BPD and NPD (30.9%): According to Tables A.1 and A.2, these two share four baseline codes: CONTROL, BLAME, ATTACK, and *SELF-NEGLECT*. They also have in common the wish for PROTECT and fear of IGNORE. A vital difference is that the NPD does not sabotage himself or herself when successful. Another is that the BPD has to coerce caregiving, whereas the NPD simply feels entitled and expects it. Finally, the NPD can choose to be separate, while the BPD desperately avoids being alone.

NARCISSISTIC PERSONALITY DISORDER

Interpersonal Summary and Transference Example

Summary: There is extreme vulnerability to criticism or being ignored, together with a strong wish for love, support, and admiring deference from others. The baseline position involves noncontingent love of self and presumptive control of others. If the support is with-

drawn, or if there is any evidence of lack of perfection, the self-concept degrades to severe self-criticism. Totally lacking in empathy, these persons treat others with contempt, and hold the self above and beyond the fray.

These interpersonal baseline patterns, wishes, and fears are likely to appear in the therapy relationship. Consider the following example of a transference problem:

> A patient refused to try a prescription for antidepressants until he had had a complete neurological workup (CONTROL). He had read an article a while ago about a type of tumor associated with depression. He thought that his case was particularly interesting (ACTIVE SELF-LOVE plus SELF-NEGLECT) and expected the clinic not to charge for the diagnostic procedure (wish for PROTECT). They might learn something, he observed. The doctor found no evidence of a brain tumor and insisted that they begin with a brief trial of an antidepressant. The patient became enraged (ATTACK, BLAME) and said that the doctor was incompetent and inconsiderate. He would take his business elsewhere (SEPARATE). He warned the doctor and the clinic that they were lucky he wasn't suing them for negligence. He had no idea (IGNORE) that people in the clinic were amazed at his presumptiveness.

Interpersonal Translation of the DSM

The "total NPD" shows all the symptoms mentioned in the DSM. The steady diet of noncontingent love and adoration encourages behaviors that meet several of the DSM criteria. These include DSM criterion 1, grandiose sense of self-importance; DSM criterion 3, need to associate with special persons of top status; DSM criterion 2, preoccupation with fantasies of unlimited success; DSM criterion 4, need for constant attention and admiration; and DSM criterion 9, arrogant and haughty behaviors. The selflessness that accompanies the adoration given to the NPD enhances behaviors described by DSM criterion 7, lack of empathy. The submissive nurturance invites behaviors described by DSM criterion 6, exploitation, and DSM criterion 5, entitlement. The burden of the expectation that the NPD will be perfect makes him or her testy about threats to that image. That demand reinforces behaviors associated with DSM criterion 9, haughtiness, and DSM criterion 8, envy. *The DSM requires that at least five criteria be met for a diagnosis of NPD.*

For NPD, the recommended *necessary* descriptors are (1) grandiose sense of self-importance, and (2) entitlement. The self-importance and entitlement characteristic of NPD preclude recklessness with the self; thus, the "conduct regardless of self" that is seen in ASP represents an *exclusionary* condition for NPD.

Differential Diagnoses

Differential diagnoses among the categories showing at least 30% overlap with NPD according to Morey (1988) may be made as follows:

NPD and BPD (46.9%): See the discussion of BPD and NPD, above.

NPD and HPD (53.1%). According to Tables A.1 and A.2, these two share the baseline codes of CONTROL and BLAME; both wish for ACTIVE LOVE and PROTECT, and both fear IGNORE. The HPD will not show the NPD's necessary descriptor of entitlement. Like

BPD, the HPD coerces caregiving, while the NPD expects and feels entitled to the best. The HPD is also less likely to be comfortable with aloneness than the NPD.

NPD and AVD (35.9%): According to Tables A.1 and A.2, these two categories share BLAME and *SELF-BLAME*. They also have in common the wishes for ACTIVE LOVE and PROTECT, as well as the fear of BLAME and IGNORE. They differ mostly in the NPD's willingness to show overt ATTACK and actively to dismiss others (IGNORE). By contrast, the AVD withdraws reactively, showing both RECOIL and WALL OFF. Both can show *SELF-BLAME*, but the AVD consistently has a poor self-concept. The NPD is distinctive in his or her tendency also to manifest *ACTIVE SELF-LOVE*.

NPD and PAR (35.9%): According to Tables A.1 and A.2, these two categories share the characteristics of CONTROL, BLAME, and ATTACK. Their wishes are different: The PAR seeks AFFIRM or EMANCIPATE, whereas the NPD wishes for ACTIVE LOVE and PROTECT. Both fear BLAME. They differ in the PAR's organizing tendency to see ATTACK when it is not there. The NPD is more likely to see ACTIVE LOVE or PROTECT when it is not there. While the PAR's withdrawal can be intense (RECOIL, WALL OFF), the NPD's autonomy is more often rather neutral (SEPARATE).

HISTRIONIC PERSONALITY DISORDER

Interpersonal Summary and Transference Example

Summary: There is strong fear of being ignored, together with and a wish to be loved and taken care of by someone powerful, who nonetheless can be controlled through use of charm and entertainment skills. The baseline position is of friendly trust that is accompanied by a secretly disrespectful agenda of forcing delivery of the desired nurturance and love. Inappropriate seductive behaviors and manipulative suicidal attempts are examples of such coercions.

These interpersonal baseline patterns, wishes, and fears are likely to appear in the therapy relationship. Consider the following example of a transference problem:

The patient arrived for an extra appointment brightly dressed and smiled as she said (REACTIVE LOVE) that she was continuing to have trouble with her depression (TRUST). She reminded the doctor that her husband was on the hospital board of trustees (CONTROL) and was very eager to see that she got better. The doctor tried hard to find the correct medication, but the vagueness of her descriptions of the symptoms (WALL OFF) made it hard to assess the problem.

Interpersonal Translation of the DSM

The "total HPD" shows all the symptoms mentioned in the DSM. Many of the items in the DSM are directly associated with self-definition as an entertainer, as a "showpiece." These include seductive behavior (item 2), overconcern with physical attractiveness (item 4), need to be the center of attention (item 1), need to be affirmed as an intimate friend by strangers (item 8), and intolerance for delay of gratification (item 7). In other words, if one is an entertainer, one must be attractive, and this is affirmed if there is applause from all who are present. The performer role also accounts for the exaggerated expressiveness (item 6), as well as the rapidly shifting and shallow emotional expression (item 3). These particular ways of performing are encouraged by the "as-if," "butterfly" household. Since competence requires focused cognitive process, the broad, unfocused cognitive style (item 5) may be a consequence of the need to cultivate incompetence to be attractive. *The DSM requires that at least five criteria be met for a diagnosis of HPD.*

For HPD, the recommended *necessary* descriptor is a baseline position of coercive dependency. An *exclusionary* condition for HPD is self-sabotage following happiness or success.

Differential Diagnoses

Differential diagnoses among the categories showing at least 30% overlap with HPD according to Morey (1988) may be made as follows:

HPD and BPD (55.6%): See the discussion of BPD and HPD, above.

HPD and NPD (54%): See the discussion of NPD and HPD, above.

HPD and AVD (31.7%): According to Tables A.1 and A.2, these two categories share the characteristics of BLAME and WALL OFF. They both have the wishes for ACTIVE LOVE and PROTECT, and the fear of IGNORE. The most obvious difference is that the AVD withdraws if acceptance is not forthcoming, while the HPD will coerce attention and caregiving. The HPD can typically be warm and comfortably dependent (REACTIVE LOVE and TRUST), whereas the AVD is very tense when dependent (SULK). He or she prefers to withdraw in a hostile way (RECOIL and WALL OFF).

HPD and DPD (30.2%): According to Tables A.1 and A.2, these two categories share the label of TRUST, the wish for PROTECT, and the fear of IGNORE. There are dramatic differences, however. The DPD is dependent in every possible way—TRUST, SUBMIT, and SULK. He or she will usually remain dependent, regardless of how hostile the partner becomes. The HPD, by contrast, is capable of WALL OFF, and will resist abuse by coercing better service as necessary (CONTROL, BLAME).

ANTISOCIAL PERSONALITY DISORDER

Interpersonal Summary and Transference Example

Summary: There is a pattern of inappropriate and unmodulated desire to control others, implemented in a detached manner. There is a strong need to be independent, to resist being controlled by others, who are usually held in contempt. There is a willingness to use untamed aggression to back up the need for control or independence. The ASP usually presents in a friendly, sociable manner, but that friendliness is always accompanied by a baseline position of detachment. He or she doesn't care what happens to self or others.

These interpersonal baseline patterns, wishes, and fears are likely to appear in the therapy relationship. Consider the following example of a transference problem:

A patient insisted that the doctor prescribe Prozac. He knew the doctor was worried about misuse of this drug, which had acquired local "street value." The patient assured the doctor that he no longer had a problem with drugs (**CONTROL** plus <u>WALL</u> <u>OFF</u>). He said he had turned over a new leaf and only needed the drug to contain his coexisting depression so he wouldn't act out again. He noted that the doctor had special abilities to understand him. He added that he cared very much about what the doctor thought (**ACTIVE LOVE** plus <u>WALL</u> <u>OFF</u>); for this reason, he would not dream of betraying the doctor's trust. The patient would use the drug exactly as prescribed. Three months later, the doctor had to respond to an inquiry from the licensing board. It seemed that the patient skillfully copied the doctor's prescription. He then altered dates and dosages so that he could refill it many times at different stores in different nearby towns (*SELF-PROTECT* plus *SELF-NEGLECT*). He was dealing Prozac.

Interpersonal Translation of the DSM

The "total ASP" shows all the symptoms mentioned in the DSM. Identification with abusive, attacking parents can directly encourage physical fighting (item B3), use of weapons (item B4), forcing others into sexual activity (item B5), cruelty to animals (item B6), cruelty to other people (item B7), destruction of property (item B8), stealing (items B11, B12), and assaultiveness as an adult (item C3). ASP aggressiveness is not always a consequence of having been aggressed against; it can also come from failure to attach. In the absence of attachment, the primate does not learn to modulate aggression (Harlow & Harlow, 1962).

The ASP's need to control others can represent simple identification with parents who were uneven in their use of control, or continuation of the ASP's early habit of assuming unmodulated and inappropriate control. Improper control masked by "friendliness" is flagged by the DSM as lying (item B10, item C6). Another consequence of the unmodulated parental control and failure to provide consistent nurturance is an intense need for autonomy, a position that defends against repetition of early helplessness. This defense is exacerbated by weakness in attachment to others. The need for autonomy and weak attachment are manifested early in truancy (item B1) and running away from home (item B2). The need for autonomy interferes with the ability to accept normal social demands, and so the ASP is not able to show consistent work behavior (item C1). He or she generally fails to conform to social norms and laws (item B9, item C2). *The DSM requires that at least three criteria in section B and four criteria in section C be met for a diagnosis of ASP.*

The recommended *necessary* conditions for ASP are (1) need for control of others and autonomy for the self, and (2) attachment failure and an associated lack of remorse. The first pair is not directly described by the DSM; however, if the interviewer attends to the perspective of the ASP as he or she committed the crimes that have led to the ASP diagnosis, these interpersonal dimensions should be apparent. In evaluating whether the patient lacks remorse, the clinician needs to remember that the ASP is skilled at deception. He or she may make extravagant statements of guilt and remorse and not mean them. The test of sincerity on this point is in consistent empathic, nonexploitative behavior, shown over an extended period.

Exclusionary conditions for ASP include entitlement, dependency, and fear of abandonment. These marks of enmeshment are unlikely to be found in the highly differentiated ASP.

Differential Diagnoses

Differential diagnoses among the categories showing at least 30% overlap with ASP according to Morey (1988) may be made as follows:

ASP and NPD (55.6%): According to Tables A.1 and A.2, these two categories share all possible forms of active CONTROL, including BLAME and ATTACK. They both also are comfortable with rejecting others (IGNORE) and being alone (SEPARATE). Their biggest differences are in their wishes and fears. The ASP wants to be left free (EMANCIPATE) or to have others SUBMIT; he or she fears CONTROL. The NPD, by contrast, wants ACTIVE LOVE and PROTECT as well as SUBMIT. The NPD also fears CONTROL as well as BLAME or IGNORE. The ASP does not aspire to be connected to others and prefers a detached position, whereas the NPD presumes attachment. The NPD wants warm admiration and respect, whereas the ASP does not care what others think. The ASP wants control of others, freedom for the self, and material advantage.

ASP and NEG[3] (50.0%): According to Tables A.1 and A.2, these two categories share tendencies to BLAME, WALL OFF, and SEPARATE, as well as a fear of CONTROL. Their wishes, however, are quite different. The ASP wants freedom (EMANCIPATE), while the NEG wants to receive PROTECT. The NEG is engaged in hostile enmeshment with others who are supposed to provide nurturance, whereas the ASP couldn't care less. In his or her eagerness to avoid being pushed around, the NEG can be so irresponsible that he or she can look like an ASP. But the NEG's failure to perform is the result of overdetermined resistance to authority, not lack of socialization. Unlike the ASP, the NEG can sometimes be downright compliant (SUBMIT, SULK). The NEG also is far less likely to engage in overt ATTACK or to be uninterested (IGNORE) than is the ASP. Finally, the NEG is prone to *SELF-ATTACK,* whereas the ASP is not.

ASP and BPD (44.4%): According to Tables A.1 and A.2, these two categories share the ability to show ACTIVE LOVE, CONTROL, BLAME, ATTACK, *SELF-PROTECT,* and *SELF-NEGLECT.* But their wishes are nearly opposite. The BPD is centered on receiving PROTECT and dreads receiving IGNORE. The ASP, by strong contrast, seeks to be granted independence (EMANCIPATE) and to receive SUBMIT from others. In sum, the BPD covets warm enmeshment, while the ASP treasures his or her freedom. These differences mean that the ASP will be distinguished by a preference for baseline autonomy, an exclusionary condition for the BPD diagnosis. The ASP's "friendliness" comes in complex combination with detachment. The BPD's warmth is "clean" but not stable; at the slightest hint of neglect or rejection, the BPD's friendliness is usually transformed into outright attack.

ASP and HPD (33.3%): Tables A.1 and A.2 show that these two categories combine warmth with CONTROL, BLAME, and WALL OFF. They can embody the worst of the male and female stereotypes, respectively: phony warmth and power (ASP), and phony

---

[3]Actually, Passive Aggressive Personality Disorder. See footnote 4, below.

dependency (HPD). Both suffer from underlying detachment and the tendency to "work" interpersonal agendas. Their differences are mostly in the HPD's ability to show warm dependency (REACTIVE LOVE and TRUST), and in the ASP's willingness to ruthlessly focus ATTACK on others.

DEPENDENT PERSONALITY DISORDER

Interpersonal Summary and Transference Example

Summary: The baseline position is of marked submissiveness to a dominant other person who is supposed to provide unending nurturance and guidance. The wish is to maintain connection to that person even if it means tolerating abuse. The DPD believes that he or she is instrumentally incompetent, and this means that he or she cannot survive without the dominant other person.

These interpersonal baseline patterns, wishes, and fears are likely to appear in the therapy relationship. Consider the following example of a transference problem:

A patient was chronically depressed, and the doctor tried her on a new antidepressant. She did not improve and had a number of side effects, but did not mention them to the doctor. Fortunately, the doctor remembered to ask for the specific signs of side effects. The patient acknowledged the signs, and the doctor wrote a prescription for a different antidepressant. The patient was willing to acknowledge the signs of problems (SUBMIT), but she did not offer the information spontaneously. The doctor asked her why she did not say anything. She explained, "I thought that maybe they were just part of the way the drug worked (SULK). I figured you would know what was best (TRUST)."

Interpersonal Translation of the DSM

The "total DPD" shows all the symptoms mentioned in the DSM. The DPD's inability to make decisions or take responsibility is described by DSM items 1 and 2. The inability to initiate projects (item 4) is manifested because he or she sees no alternative; the DPD must be a part of the decisions and plans that have been made for him or her by others. The belief that someone else must take care of things leads the DPD to defer inappropriately (item 3), to allow himself or herself to be exploited or humiliated in order to maintain support (item 5), and to worry greatly about potential loss of the dominant caregiver (items 6, 7, 8, 9). *The DSM requires that at least five criteria be met for a diagnosis of DPD.*

The DSM-IV has implicitly restored the DSM-III criterion of poor self-concept for DPD. The lack of confidence is associated strictly with inability to perform instrumental tasks. DPDs often equate their submissiveness with "niceness" and therefore can think of themselves as "good persons." DPDs do not think of themselves as evil or worthy of punishment. Their problem is just that they don't know "how." They can't. They feel unable, inadequate, helpless, inept, unequipped, and unqualified. The DPD's poor self-concept represents the internalization of the implicit or explicit contempt for his or her instrumental inadequacy, as well as a realistic appraisal of the failure to develop instrumental skills.

For DPD, the recommended *necessary* descriptor is submissiveness associated with a sense of instrumental inadequacy. Many of the personality disorders include positions of dependency (TRUST, SUBMIT, or SULK); the DPD is unique in the simplicity of his or her dependency.

Exclusionary conditions for DPD include complications of dependency. The list of complicating factors is long. DPD does not show the various behaviors characteristic of the cluster B disorders. The DPD does not show active transitive anger about lack of attention or caregiving, as does the BPD. The DPD does not show the NPD's indignation about others' failure to deliver interpersonal goods and services. Nor does the DPD engage in the efforts to force approval and attention that are characteristic of HPD; instead, the DPD "hangs out" and waits to be taken care of. Finally, the DPD certainly does not engage in openly hostile behaviors, as does the ASP.

The DPD uses the principle of complementarity to cope. His or her TRUST and SUBMIT are offered to receive the desired **PROTECT** and **CONTROL**. Unlike the DPD, the OCD likes to control. If the patient insists that others submit, the diagnosis of DPD is ruled out. An NEG can also relate in dependent ways; however, the NEG will criticize authorities, including providers in the health care system. By contrast, the DPD will criticize only himself or herself, not others. The distinction between DPD and AVD can be made by determining whether abuse will be tolerated. The DPD can be hurt by criticism, but will put up with nearly any kind of abuse just to be taken care of. The AVD, by stark contrast, disappears at the first hint of hostility. Finally, a DPD is not comfortable with long-term autonomy, as is an AVD, SZT, or SOI.

Differential Diagnoses

Differential diagnoses among the categories showing at least 30% overlap with DPD according to Morey (1988) may be made as follows:

DPD and BPD (50.8%): See the discussion of BPD and DPD, above.

DPD and AVD (49.2%): According to Tables A.1 and A.2, these two categories share the tendencies to SULK and *SELF-BLAME*, the wish for **PROTECT**, and the fear of IGNORE. Important differences are that the AVD is willing to **BLAME** others and to withdraw interpersonally (RECOIL and WALL OFF). The DPD is not at all autonomous or transitive (as defined in Chapter 3); he or she always reacts, and only with submission.

OBSESSIVE COMPULSIVE PERSONALITY DISORDER

Interpersonal Summary and Transference Example

Summary: There is a fear of making a mistake or being accused of being imperfect. The quest for order yields a baseline interpersonal position of blaming and inconsiderate control of others. The OCD's control alternates with blind obedience to authority or principle.

There is excessive self-discipline, as well as restraint of feelings, harsh self-criticism, and neglect of the self.

These interpersonal baseline patterns, wishes, and fears are likely to appear in the therapy relationship. Consider the following example of a transference problem:

> A patient was very slow to recognize that he was depressed. He thought he could stay "on top of" the problem if only he could get things better organized. But the signs of depression persisted, and suddenly one day the patient admitted he was depressed. Then he was willing to take the prescription, but looked it up in the PDR to be aware of possible side effects. The depression continued. The patient sent the doctor reprints on recent studies of antidepressants and questioned the prescription. The patient expressed frustration that the right medication had not been found. He alternated between deferring to the doctor's opinion about what to do next and blaming the doctor for not doing better.

Interpersonal Translation of the DSM

The "total OCD" shows all the symptoms mentioned in the DSM. The history of coercion to be perfect, regardless of the personal consequences, leads to perfectionism that interferes with task completion (item 2) and excessive devotion to work to the exclusion of leisure (item 3). The need to control in service of perfection also leads to the OCD's insistence that others submit to his or her ways of doing things (item 7). The quest for perfection is further reflected in the judgmentalism that leads to overconscientiousness and inflexible scrupulousness (item 4). Yet another version of the pattern of seeking complete control is the irrational need to save things in case they might be needed again (item 6). The devotion to control, the lack of warmth, and the encouraging of self- restraint in the parental home are associated with restricted expression of warmth (item 5) and miserliness (item 8). *The DSM requires that at least five criteria be met for a diagnosis of OCD.*

The fact that there were harsh punishments for mistakes and no rewards for success means that the OCD is worried about making errors and has little sense of success. This fear of making mistakes and never finishing properly leads to preoccupation with details at the expense of completion of the activity (item 1). Sometimes it leads to indecisiveness stemming from rumination about priorities (old item 5 in the DSM-III-R, omitted from DSM-IV).

For OCD, the recommended *necessary* descriptors are unreasonable dominance and a devotion to perfection. *Exclusionary* descriptors would include the irresponsible behaviors found in ASPs and BPDs; the emotional excesses of HPDs and BPDs; and contempt for and defiance of authority.

Differential Diagnoses

Differential diagnoses among the categories showing at least 30% overlap with OCD according to Morey (1988) may be made as follows:

OCD and AVD (56.5%): According to Tables A.1 and A.2, these two categories share tendencies to BLAME, WALL OFF, *SELF-BLAME,* and *SELF-CONTROL,* as well as fear of becoming the target of **BLAME**. Despite these similarities, they are quite different in their wishes. In brief, the OCD wants control while the AVD wants love. The OCD seeks S̲U̲B̲M̲I̲T̲ from others and tight *SELF-CONTROL*; the AVD wants to receive **ACTIVE LOVE** and **PROTECT**. These differences in wishes are associated with differences in baseline behaviors. The OCD will show overt **CONTROL** and will S̲U̲B̲M̲I̲T̲ to authority he or she respects. The AVD is more likely to be withdrawn (R̲E̲C̲O̲I̲L̲, W̲A̲L̲L̲ O̲F̲F̲) until and if there is a safe situation in which he or she can show normative attachment behaviors.

OCD and NPD (30.4%): Tables A.1 and A.2 show that these two categories share tendencies to **CONTROL**, **BLAME**, **IGNORE**, *SELF-BLAME*, and *SELF-NEGLECT*; the fear of **BLAME**; and the wish for others to S̲U̲B̲M̲I̲T̲. Additional wishes and fears, however, are divergent. For example, the NPD also wants to receive **ACTIVE LOVE** and **PROTECT** from others, while the OCD does not. The NPD fears **IGNORE**, whereas the OCD does not. Finally, the OCD fears *SELF-EMANCIPATE*, but the NPD does not feel it is essential to "keep a lid on." In short, the OCD is wrapped up in the quest for perfection, while the NPD feels he or she has already achieved it (*ACTIVE SELF-LOVE*). Comfortable with himself or herself, the NPD is willing to be S̲E̲P̲A̲R̲A̲T̲E̲, whereas the OCD is more likely to S̲U̲B̲M̲I̲T̲ to superiors.

NEGATIVISTIC PERSONALITY DISORDER (PASSIVE AGGRESSIVE PERSONALITY DISORDER)

Interpersonal Summary and Transference Example

Summary: There is a tendency to see any form of power as inconsiderate and neglectful, together with a belief that authorities or caregivers are incompetent, unfair, and cruel. The NEG agrees to comply with perceived demands or suggestions, but fails to perform. He or she often complains of unfair treatment, and envies and resents others who fare better. His or her suffering indicts the allegedly negligent caregivers or authorities. The NEG fears control in any form and wishes for nurturant restitution.

These interpersonal baseline patterns, wishes, and fears are likely to appear in the therapy relationship. Consider the following example of a transference problem:

A patient's depression lasted for years, with multiple hospitalizations. Every approach was tried. There were courses of ECT. Many different medications, including all antidepressants, MAOIs, lithium, and even a few neuroleptics, were prescribed. Although sometimes there appeared to be initial success, nothing helped for long. The patient endured the oppression of the illness (S̲U̲L̲K̲), but complains about the doctors' inability to help (**BLAME**).

His latest doctor tried the patient on a new antidepressant that was receiving trials in a research protocol. The patient agreed to participate in the research, but did not take the drug in the prescribed manner. He explained that the drug made him feel worse, and so he decided to adjust the dose himself (S̲U̲B̲M̲I̲T̲ plus W̲A̲L̲L̲ O̲F̲F̲). It seemed that he was doing a little better on this drug, however, so he asked to continue in the protocol and agreed to take the drug exactly as prescribed. Two weeks later, the doctor received a call from the patient's wife saying that he was acutely suicidal and needed hospitalization. The patient said that he deferred to the doctor's research interests and took the drug exactly as prescribed (SULK plus **BLAME**). Now he felt worse than ever about himself (*SELF-ATTACK* plus **BLAME**). The doctor hospitalized the patient again and took him off the research protocol.

Interpersonal Translation of the DSM

The "total NEG" shows all the symptoms mentioned in the DSM. Cruel and neglectful parental demands result in irritability and argumentativeness when the NEG is asked to perform (DSM item 3). The NEG learns that his or her efforts are not appreciated and that he or she is treated unfairly (DSM items 2 and 6). This breeds disappointment in (DSM item 5) and disrespect for (DSM item 4) caregivers and authorities. The harsh punishments for anger and disobedience lead to indirect expressions of both (DSM items 1, 7, 8). *The DSM requires that at least five criteria be met for a diagnosis of NEG.*

The recommended *necessary* condition is the pattern of compliant defiance. The hallmark of the negativism is agreeing to perform, but not delivering. *Exclusionary* conditions for NEG include the devotion to productivity that can be found in OCD. Also, if the patient shows uncomplicated compliance, he or she does not have the NEG pattern. The NEG's words say that he or she agrees, but his or her behavior demonstrates that the answer is really no.

Differential Diagnoses

Differential diagnoses among the categories showing at least 30% overlap with NEG[4] according to Morey (1988) may be made as follows:

NEG and NPD (50%): Tables A.1 and A.2 show that these two disorders share a willingness to **BLAME** and be SEPARATE, as well as the wish for **PROTECT** and fear of **CONTROL**. The NPD wants more: Others should SUBMIT as well as show **ACTIVE LOVE**. An important baseline difference is in the NEG's tendency to SUBMIT, even in a hostile way, and to SULK. In addition, the NPD will show overt **ATTACK** and rejection (**IGNORE**) of others, while the NEG will not. Of course, the NPD has *ACTIVE SELF-LOVE* and the NEG does not. In brief, the NPD loves himself or herself and expects others to do so too; comes and goes as he or she pleases; and is astonished and enraged if supplies are not forthcoming. The NEG, by contrast, generally feels betrayed and alienated. He or she wants restitution, expects not to get it, and dares not directly show his or her anger about it.

NEG and BPD (36.1%): Tables A.1 and A.2 suggest that these two share the baseline labels of **BLAME** and *SELF-ATTACK*, as well as the wish for **PROTECT**. There are very important differences in their fear: The BPD dreads receiving **IGNORE**, while the NEG, who is quite capable of autonomy, is exquisitely sensitive to **CONTROL**. The BPD behaves in a colorful way and shifts from position to position. The NEG shows complex combinations of submission and autonomy, friendliness and hostility. Both will blame the therapist and engage in self-sabotage through suicidal and other self-destructive acts. But the goals and the styles

---

[4]Morey actually used the category of Passive Aggressive Personality Disorder as defined in DSM-III-R, rather than NEG as newly defined in DSM-IV (and may again be named Passive Aggressive).

are different. The BPD is chaotic and passionate, trying to coerce caregiving; the NEG is surly and convoluted, resisting control and punishing defaulting caregivers.

NEG and HPD (33.3%): Tables A.1 and A.2 show that these two categories share a propensity to BLAME, WALL OFF, and *SELF-ATTACK*, and a wish for PROTECT. They differ in fears: The HPD fears IGNORE, while the NEG fears CONTROL. These differences mean that they will be upset by different events. The NEG is more likely to show *SELF-ATTACK* in reaction to perceived unfair demands to perform, while the HPD will be set off by lack of attention and nurturance. None of the NEG's positions are in the friendly part of interpersonal space. The NEG is locked in ambivalence that is described by the enmeshment–differentiation (vertical) axis of the SASB model. The HPD, by contrast, usually shows some warmth, albeit in combination with control.

NEG and AVD (33.3%): Tables A.1 and A.2 show that these two categories share the baseline labels of BLAME, SULK, and WALL OFF, and a wish for PROTECT. The NEG fears the closely related position of CONTROL, and his or her positions are usually complex. The NEG's fear of control and the wish for nurturance lead to strong ambivalence between enmeshment (SULK or BLAME) and differentiation (WALL OFF). Although the AVD also is capable of hostile enmeshment his or her baseline is less conflicted. He or she is more typically withdrawn (RECOIL, WALL OFF), and self-contained (*SELF-CONTROL* and *SELF-BLAME*). The AVD shows enmeshment only with selected people and situations. Unlike the NEG, who has closely related wishes and fears, the AVD is not ambivalent. Instead, the AVD clearly wants ACTIVE LOVE, but defensively withdraws from fear of being rejected (IGNORE) or humiliated (BLAME).

NEG and DPD (30.6%): Tables A.1 and A.2 show that these two categories overlap in SUBMIT and SULK, and in a wish for PROTECT. However, another wish of the DPD— namely, CONTROL—is the greatest fear for the NEG. Unlike the DPD, the NEG will BLAME others, SEPARATE, and WALL OFF.

NEG and PAR (30.6%): Tables A.1 and A.2 show that these two categories share a tendency to BLAME and a taste for autonomy (SEPARATE and WALL OFF). Their wishes and fears are quite different. The PAR wants freedom or deference, while the NEG wants to be taken care of. The PAR fears ATTACK and sees it when it is not there; the NEG fears CONTROL and sees it when it is not there. The NEG moves in complex ways, while the PAR is overtly hostile (ATTACK, RECOIL), exercises CONTROL, and rejects others (IGNORE). In sum, the NEG is a complicated character, ambivalent about the question of dependent enmeshment versus autonomy. The PAR is simpler: He or she fears attack, and defensively needs autonomy or control.

AVOIDANT PERSONALITY DISORDER

Interpersonal Summary and Transference Example

Summary: There is intense fear of humiliation and rejection. To avoid expected embarrassment, the AVD withdraws and carefully restrains himself or herself. He or she intensely wishes for love and acceptance, and will become very intimate with those few who pass highly stringent tests for safety. Occasionally, the AVD loses control and explodes with rageful indignation.

These interpersonal baseline patterns, wishes, and fears are likely to appear in the therapy relationship. Consider the following example of a transference problem:

A patient overdosed one evening on the medicine her doctor had prescribed for her persistent depression. She liked and respected him a lot. She was discovered comatose by a neighbor who wondered why her cat wouldn't stop meowing. The neighbor was the patient's only friend. It turned out that that morning her doctor had wondered aloud whether she had a personality disorder. The patient was deeply humiliated by that idea, but secretly agreed with it. She felt extremely embarrassed, and was convinced that her doctor now knew she was a completely foolish person. The next step, she believed, was that he would kick her out of therapy. It had taken her a long time to trust him, and now she was quite angry that he would reject her. However, she also knew that she would not tell him about her anger. Rather than endure the humiliation of facing him again, she decided to end it all.

Interpersonal Translation of the DSM

The "total AVD" shows all the symptoms mentioned in the DSM. Almost all the DSM items describe one or another aspect of the avoidant defense against expected humiliation and rejection. These fears of criticism and rejection are described directly by item 4, as well as by unwillingness to be involved without guarantees of friendship (item 2); avoidance of activities that require social contact (item 1); reticence because of fear of embarrassment (item 3); feelings of inferiority (item 6); and reluctance to try something new out of fear of embarrassment (item 7). The avoidant defense combined with the injunction to be loyal to family severely restricts the number of intimate social contacts (item 5). *The DSM requires that at least four criteria be met for a diagnosis of AVD.*

The *necessary* conditions are defensive withdrawal out of fear of humiliation, attack, and rejection, and the wish for acceptance. *Exclusionary* criteria for AVD include the affective detachment of the SOI and the desperate attempts of the DPD or BPD to avoid aloneness. The AVD is usually competent at work, unlike the BPD, who sabotages success, and unlike the DPD, who is instrumentally inadequate. The AVD can be distinguished from the NEG by his or her ability to perform adequately. Both the NEG and the AVD were both nurtured initially, and both were subjected to demands and harsh punishments. Both react with autonomy (and both are vulnerable to depression). A crucial difference is that the target of the demands and punishments for the NEG was work performance, whereas the targets for the AVD were social imagery and acceptability. The consequence is that the work performance of the NEG is damaged, while the ability to engage socially is fractured in the AVD.

Differential Diagnoses

Differential diagnoses of the categories showing at least 30% overlap with AVD according to Morey (1988) may be made as follows:

AVD and BPD (44.3%): See the discussion of BPD and AVD, above.

AVD and DPD (40.5%): See the discussion of DPD and AVD, above.

AVD and PAR (39.2%): According to Tables A.1 and A.2, these categories overlap in tendencies to BLAME, RECOIL, WALL OFF, and *SELF-CONTROL*; they also share fears of ATTACK and BLAME. However, their wishes are different. The AVD wants to receive ACTIVE LOVE and PROTECT. The PAR wants to receive AFFIRM, to be left alone (EMANCIPATE), or else to have others defer (SUBMIT). Perhaps this difference in interpersonal goals accounts for the fact that the AVD will not be so likely to ATTACK or CONTROL or to clearly SEPARATE as the PAR. In other words, these "cold" PAR behaviors will not inspire the intimacy that the AVD desires so much.

PARANOID PERSONALITY DISORDER

Interpersonal Summary and Transference Example

Summary: There is fear that others will attack to hurt or blame. The wish is that others will affirm and understand. If affirmation fails, the hope is that others will either leave the PAR alone or submit. The baseline position is to wall off, stay separate, and tightly control the self. If threatened, the PAR will recoil in a hostile way or attack to countercontrol or gain distance.

These interpersonal baseline patterns, wishes, and fears are likely to appear in the therapy relationship. Consider the following example of a transference problem:

A patient refused to try a prescription for antidepressants because he felt that the medication was a sign of failure and that ultimately it would be harmful. The doctor, who was quite worried about the patient's escalating depression, reassured him that major side effects are rare. The doctor urged the patient to try the medicine for at least a few weeks. The patient became very anxious and accused the doctor of having a vested interest in the medicine. He demanded to know whether the doctor held stock in pharmaceutical companies. He knowledgeably discussed the recent literatures on antidepressant medications and on health care financing. After a lengthy discussion, the patient refused to take the medication and said that he would handle the problem on his own.

Interpersonal Translation of the DSM

The "total PAR" shows all the symptoms mentioned in the DSM. The history of sadistic, degrading, and controlling parenting leads the PAR to expect to be exploited and harmed (DSM item 1). He or she will see threat in benign events (item 4) and will fear personal disclosure (item 3). Identification with the aggressive parent accounts for the easily elicited rage (item 6). Having been compared unfavorably with other family members, and having served as the target of grudges, make the PAR unlikely to trust (items 2 and 7). This history also encourages grudge keeping (item 5). *The DSM requires that at least four criteria be met for a diagnosis of PAR.*

For PAR, the recommended *necessary* descriptor is expectation of harm when it is not there. *Exclusionary* conditions include (1) worry about abandonment (characteristic of BPD and DPD), and (2) deference to authority.

Differential Diagnoses

Differential diagnoses among the categories showing at least 30% overlap with PAR according to Morey (1988) may be made as follows:

PAR and BPD (48.4%): See the discussion of BPD and PAR, above.

PAR and AVD (48.4%): See the discussion of AVD and PAR, above.

PAR and NPD (35.9%): See the discussion of NPD and PAR, above.

SCHIZOID PERSONALITY DISORDER

Interpersonal Summary

Summary: There are no fears of or wishes about others. The baseline position involves active and passive autonomy. Underdeveloped in social awareness and skills, the SOI nonetheless has instrumental skills, and can meet expectations of formal social roles (parent, boss, employee). He or she may be married but does not develop intimacy. There may be an active, but not necessarily bizarre, fantasy life.

As noted in Chapter 14, I do not include a transference example involving an SOI's reaction to the need for antidepressants, because such a person would be unlikely to show vegetative signs of depression or to be aware of being depressed. In any event, I have never seen a case of SOI in my practice.

Interpersonal Translation of the DSM

The "total SOI" should show all the symptoms mentioned in the DSM. The emphasis on instrumental adequacy in the context of social and emotional isolation should lead to all the symptoms listed for SOI. Interpersonal contact should be rare (item 2) and confidants few (item 5). Emotional skills should be atrophied: There should be a lack of desire for close relationships (item 1), indifference to praise or criticism (item 6), no interpersonal sexuality (item 3), lack of pleasure (item 4), and emotional coldness (item 7). *The DSM requires that at least four criteria be met for a diagnosis of SOI.*

All the descriptors for SOI have to do with simple, uncomplicated social indifference and isolation. None is more crucial than another. The polythetic approach seems appropriate. No one way of walling off is *necessary* to the definition of this disorder.

The simplicity of the social withdrawal in SOI means that there are a number of *exclusionary* conditions. Any complication of social withdrawal by the presence of other messages would rule out SOI. Examples would include the strong affect found in PAR,

BPD, HPD, and NPD; the eccentricity of the SZT; the complex manipulative skills of ASP and HPD; the concern about abandonment found in BPD and DPD; and the wish for affection and acceptance seen in AVD.

Differential Diagnoses

In Morey's (1988) study, SOI overlapped with AVD (53.1%), PAR (46.9%), and SZT (44.4%). Various forms of interpersonal withdrawal characterize these diagnoses. Lacking clinical experience with this disorder as it is defined in the DSM, I decline to comment on the "fine points" of differential diagnoses.

SCHIZOTYPAL PERSONALITY DISORDER

Interpersonal Summary and Transference Example

Summary: There is a fear of attacking, humiliating control; the wish is that others will leave the SZT alone. His or her baseline position is one of hostile withdrawal and self-neglect. The SZT believes that he or she has a capacity for magical influence that can be implemented directly (telepathy) or indirectly (control through ritual). Usually the SZT imposes these "powers" from a distance. He or she is aware of aggressive feelings, but usually restrains them.

These interpersonal baseline patterns, wishes, and fears are likely to appear in the therapy relationship. Consider the following example of a transference problem:

A patient clearly had vegetative signs of depression, but believed them to be a consequence of the way the stars were aligned at her birth. Nonetheless, she accepted antidepressants at various times, mainly to help her control her irritability. She was not impressed by their efficacy and showed erratic compliance. She preferred treatment by acupuncture, supplemented by special herbs. Viewing a particular type of sunset also helped, she noted. The doctor wondered whether she had a thought disorder, because she believed her depression got worse when she was in the presence of certain "energy fields."

Interpersonal Translation of the DSM

The "total SZT" shows all the symptoms mentioned in the DSM. Several DSM items mark thought disorders: odd beliefs or magical thinking (item 2), unusual perceptual experiences (item 3), and odd thinking and speech (item 4). The thought disorder is widely believed to be the direct consequence of flaws in the person's biochemistry. Whether genetic deficiency is the cause, the present analysis suggests that the specific form of the SZT's thought disorder is shaped by early learning. The SZT was told that he or she had great power to help or hurt. He or she was supported for being "out of the way," but couldn't achieve that through peer play. Consigned to social isolation, the SZT cultivated his or her imagination. The codes of the SZT's thought disorders are like the codes of the family experiences. The magical beliefs, unusual perceptual experiences, and patterns of odd thinking are complex mixtures of omnipotence, deference, and detachment. This extraordinarily complex view of the self in the world is associated with equally complex and "odd" affect (item 6).

The SZT's paranoia was encouraged by chronic and invasive abuse. Ideas of reference (item 1) and suspiciousness or paranoid ideation (item 5) are understandable, given the SZT's history. He or she was assigned the responsibility for the life of a parent, and at the same time was the target of severe psychological, physical, and sexual abuse. Subject to strange attributions as well as abuse in the home, the SZT never had a chance to learn normal social skills through peer play. He or she was deprived of appropriate feedback and became "odd" in behavior or appearance (item 7). The injunction against autonomy and peer play accounts for the lack of friends (item 8) and the social anxiety (item 9). *The DSM requires that at least five criteria be met for a diagnosis of SZT.*

For SZT, the recommended *necessary* conditions are (1) social withdrawal and (2) the autistic control reflected in the DSM items describing thought disorder. *Exclusionary* conditions include the discomfort with autonomy found in BPD and the proud disregard for social norms shown in ASP. The SZT would like to be accepted as he or she is. SZTs, who are comfortable with autonomy, are unlikely to show the help-coercing behaviors or the demanding dependency of BPDs, DPDs, or HPDs.

Differential Diagnoses

Differential diagnoses among the categories showing at least 30% overlap with SZT according to Morey (1988) may be made as follows:

SZT and AVD (59.3%): Tables A.1 and A.2 show that these two categories share the positions of RECOIL, WALL OFF, and *SELF-CONTROL.* They also have in common the fear of ATTACK and BLAME. Both rarely show warmth. However, the AVD wants acceptance (ACTIVE LOVE and PROTECT). The SZT is not immune to social opinion, but is content if just left alone (EMANCIPATE).

SZT and PAR (59.3%): Tables A.1 and A.2 show that these two categories share tendencies to CONTROL, WALL OFF, and *SELF-CONTROL.* Both fail to show warmth, and both fear ATTACK and BLAME. Both want to be left alone. They differ largely in the complexity of their presentations. The PAR is clear and uncomplicated; he or she will ATTACK or SEPARATE without confusion. The SZT, by contrast, is seemingly enmeshed (CONTROL or SUBMIT), but at the same time is personally and affectively inaccessible (WALL OFF). The SZT is also more reckless with and about himself or herself.[5] The detachment and the complexity of style make the SZT more vulnerable to being odd or eccentric than is the hyperattentive PAR. Oddness is not, however, a reliable differentiating index between the PAR and SZT; the PAR can get so alienated that he or she can "lose touch," too.

---

[5]I have noted in Chapter 13 that PARs are often users of "dominance drugs," such as cocaine or alcohol. PARs, who are usually self-controlled and cautious, can become quite reckless while using these drugs.

SZT and SOI (44.4%): See my inability to comment on differential diagnosis of SOI, above.

SZT and BPD (33.3%): Tables A.1 and A.2 show that these two categories share CONTROL and *SELF-NEGLECT*; their wishes and fears are different, however. The BPD wants PROTECT and fears IGNORE. The SZT has the opposite wish: He or she *wants* to be left alone. The two also differ in complexity. The BPD shows a variety of positions, but clearly and in sequence. The SZT usually moves with a complex combination of enmeshment and differentiation.

SZT and NPD (33.3%): Tables A.1 and A.2 show that these categories share CONTROL and *SELF-NEGLECT*. They both fear BLAME, but have different wishes: The NPD wants deference and nurturance, while the SZT just wants to be left alone and not criticized. The SZT is likely to control himself or herself, while the NPD loves himself or herself.

References

Adler, G. (1986). Psychotherapy of the narcissistic personality. *American Journal of Psychiatry, 143,* 430–436.

Akhtar, S. (1986). Differentiating Schizoid and Avoidant Personality Disorders. *American Journal of Psychiatry, 143,* 1061–1062.

Akiskal, H. S., Chen, S. E., Davis, G. C., Puzantian, V. R., Kashgarian, M., & Bolinger, J. M. (1985). Borderline: An adjective in search of a noun. *Journal of Clinical Psychiatry, 46,* 41–48.

Alberti, R. E., & Emmons, M. L. (1986). *The professional edition of your perfect right: A manual for assertiveness trainers.* San Luis Obispo, CA: Impact Publishers.

Allport, G. W. (1937). *Personality: A psychological interpretation.* New York: Henry Holt.

American Psychiatric Association. (1968). *Diagnostic and statistical manual of mental disorders* (2nd ed.). Washington, DC: Author.

American Psychiatric Association. (1980). *Diagnostic and statistical manual of mental disorders* (3rd ed.). Washington, DC: Author.

American Psychiatric Association. (1987). *Diagnostic and statistical manual of mental disorders* (3rd ed., rev.). Washington, DC: Author.

American Psychiatric Association. (1991a). *DSM-IV options book: Work in progress 9/1/91.* Washington, DC: Author.

American Psychiatric Association. (1991b). *DSM-IV update.* Washington, DC: Author.

Baer, L., Jenike, M. A., Ricciardi, J. N., Holland, A. D., Seymour, R. J., Minichiello, W. E., & Buttolph, M. L. (1990). Standardized assessment of personality disorders in Obsessive–Compulsive Disorders. *Archives of General Psychiatry, 47,* 826–830.

Bateson, G., Jackson, D. D., Haley, J., & Weakland, J. (1956). Toward a theory of schizophrenia. *Behavioral Science, 1,* 251–264.

Beck, A. T., Rush, A. J., Shaw, B. E., & Emery, G. (1979). *Cognitive therapy of depression.* New York: Guilford Press.

Bell, M. (Director). (1986). *Streetwise* [Videotape]. Los Angeles: LCA/New World Video.

Benjamin, L. S. (1968). Harlow's facts on affects. *Voices, 4,* 49–59.

Benjamin, L. S. (1974). Structural Analysis of Social Behavior. *Psychological Review, 81,* 392–425.

Benjamin, L. S. (1979). Structural analysis of differentiation failure. *Psychiatry: Journal for the Study of Interpersonal Processes, 42,* 1–23.

Benjamin, L. S. (1982). Use of Structural Analysis of Social Behavior (SASB) to guide interventions in therapy. In J. Anchin & D. Kiesler (Eds.), *Handbook of interpersonal psychotherapy.* Elmsford, NY: Pergamon Press.

Benjamin, L. S. (1983). *The INTREX users' manual, Part I.* Madison, WI: INTREX Interpersonal Institute.

Benjamin, L. S. (1984). Principles of prediction using Structural Analysis of Social Behavior. In R. A. Zucker, J. Aronoff, & A. J. Rabin (Eds.), *Personality and the prediction of behavior*. New York: Academic Press.

Benjamin, L. S. (1986). Adding social and intrapsychic descriptors to Axis I of DSM-III. In T. Millon & G. L. Klerman (Eds.), *Contemporary directions in psychopathology: Toward the DSM-IV*. New York: Guilford Press.

Benjamin, L. S. (1987a). Use of the SASB dimensional model to develop treatment plans for personality disorders: I. Narcissism. *Journal of Personality Disorders, 1*, 43–70.

Benjamin, L. S. (1987b). Commentary on the inner experience of the borderline self-mutilator. *Journal of Personality Disorders, 1*, 334–339.

Benjamin, L. S. (1988). *Short Form INTREX users' manual*. Madison, WI: INTREX Interpersonal Institute.

Benjamin, L. S. (1989). Interpersonal analysis of the cathartic model. In R. Plutchik & H. Kellerman (Eds.) *Emotion: Theory, research, and experience. Vol. 5*. New York: Academic Press.

Benjamin, L. S. (1991). Brief SASB-directed reconstructive learning therapy. In P. Crits-Christoph & J. P. Barber (Eds.), *Handbook of short-term dynamic psychotherapy*. New York: Basic Books.

Benjamin, L. S. (1992). An interpersonal approach to the diagnosis of Borderline Personality Disorder. In J. F. Clarkin, E. Marziali, & H. Monroe-Blum (Eds.), *Borderline personality disorder: Clinical and empirical perspectives*. New York: Guilford Press.

Benjamin, L. S. (1993a). Commentary. In M. H. Klein, D. J. Kupfer, & M. T. Shea (Eds.), *Personality and depression: A current view*. New York: Guilford Press.

Benjamin, L. S. (1993b). Every psychopathology is a gift of love. *Psychotherapy Research, 3*, 1–24.

Benjamin, L. S. (draft). A bridge between personality theory and clinical psychology. *Psychological Inquiry*.

Benjamin, L. S., Foster, S. W., Giat-Roberto, L., & Estroff, S. E. (1986). Breaking the family code: Analyzing videotapes of family interactions by SASB. In L. S. Greenberg & W. M. Pinsof (Eds.), *The psychotherapeutic process: A research handbook*. New York: Guilford Press.

Benjamin, L. S., & Friedrich, F. J. (1991). Contributions of Structural Analysis of Social Behavior (SASB) to the bridge between cognitive science and a science of object relations. In M. J. Horowitz (Ed.), *Person schemas and maladaptive behavior*. Chicago: University of Chicago Press.

Berlin, F. S., Malin, H. M., & Dean, S. (1991). Effects of statutes requiring psychiatrists to report suspected sexual abuse of children. *American Journal of Psychiatry, 148*, 449–453.

Berne, E. (1964). *Games people play*. New York: Grove Press.

Blashfield, R. K. (1984). *The classification of psychopathology: Neo-Kraepelinian and quantitative approaches*. New York: Plenum Press.

Blatt, S. J. (1974). Levels of object representation in anaclitic and introjective depression. *Psychoanalytic Study of the Child, 29*, 107–157.

Blatt, S. J., & Auerbach, J. S. (1988). Differential cognitive disturbances in three types of borderline patients. *Journal of Personality Disorders, 2*, 198–211.

Bowlby, J. (1977). The making and breaking of affectional bonds. *British Journal of Psychiatry, 130*, 201–210, 421–431.

Carroll, J., Schaffer, C., Spensley, J., & Abramowitz, S. J. (1980). Family experiences of self-mutilating patients. *American Journal of Psychiatry, 137*, 852–853.

Carson, R. (1991). Dilemmas in the pathway of the DSM-IV. *Journal of Abnormal Psychology, 100*, 302–307.

Carson, R. C., & Butcher, J. N. (1992). *Abnormal psychology and modern life* (9th ed.). New York: HarperCollins.

Cleckley, H. (1955). *The mask of sanity: An attempt to clarify some issues about the so-called psychopathic personality* (3rd ed.). St. Louis: C. V. Mosby.

Cloninger, C. R. (1978). The antisocial personality. *Hospital Practice, 13*, 97–106.

Cloninger, C. R., Christiansen, K. O., Reich, T., & Gottesman, I. (1978). Implications of sex differences in the prevalences of antisocial personality, alcoholism, and criminality for familial transmission. *Archives of General Psychiatry, 35*, 941–951.

Cloninger, C. R., & Guze, S. B. (1975). Hysteria and parental psychiatric illness. *Psychological Medicine, 5*, 27–31.

Cloninger, C. R., Reich, T., & Guze, S. B. (1975). The multifactorial model of disease transmission: III. Familial relationship between sociopathy and hysteria (Briquet's syndrome). *British Journal of Psychiatry, 127*, 23–32.

Colby, K. M. (1977). Appraisal of four psychological theories of paranoid phenomena. *Journal of Abnormal Psychology, 86*, 54–59.

Costa, P. T., & McCrae, R. R. (1988). Personality in adulthood: A six year longitudinal study of self-reports and spouse ratings on the NEO Personality Inventory. *Journal of Personality and Social Psychology, 54*, 853–863.

Darwin, C. (1952). The origin of species. In R. M. Hutchins (Ed.), *Great books of the Western world*. Chicago: Encyclopaedia Britannica. (Original work published 1859)

DeJonge, C. A. J., van den Brink, W., Jansen, J. A. M., & Schippers, G. M. (1989). Interpersonal aspects of the DSM-III Axis II: Theoretical hypotheses and empirical findings. *Journal of Personality Disorders, 3*, 135–146.

Docherty, J. P., Fiester, S. J., & Shea, T. (1986). Syndrome diagnosis and personality disorder. In A. J. Frances & R. E. Hales (Eds.), *Psychiatry update: The American Psychiatric Association annual review* (Vol. 5). Washington, DC: American Psychiatric Press.

Dollard, J., & Miller, N. E. (1950). *Personality and psychotherapy: An analysis in terms of learning, thinking, and culture*. New York: McGraw-Hill.

Ellis, A. (1973). *Humanistic psychotherapy: The rational emotive approach*. New York: Julian Press.

Epstein, S. (1987). The relative value of theoretical and empirical approaches for establishing a psychological diagnostic system. *Journal of Personality Disorders, 1*, 100–109.

Erikson, E. H. (1959). *Identity and the life cycle*. New York: International Universities Press.

Fenichel, O. (1945). *The psychoanalytic theory of neurosis*. New York: Norton.

Fenton, W. S., & McGlashan, T. H. (1986). The prognostic significance of obsessive–compulsive symptoms in schizophrenia. *American Journal of Psychiatry, 143*, 437–441.

Fraiberg, S. H. (1959). *The magic years: Understanding and handling the problems of early childhood*. New York: Scribner's.

Frances, A. J., & Widiger, T. (1986). The classification of personality disorders: An overview of problems and solutions. In A. J. Frances & R. E. Hales (Eds.), *Psychiatry update: The American Psychiatric Association annual review* (Vol. 5). Washington, DC: American Psychiatric Press.

Freedman, M. B. (1985). Symposium: Interpersonal circumplex models (1948–1983). *Journal of Personality Assessment, 49*, 622–625.

Freedman, M. B., Leary, T. F., Ossorio, A. G., & Coffey, H. S. (1951). The interpersonal dimension of personality. *Journal of Personality, 20*, 143–161.

Freud, A. (1965). *The writings of Anna Freud: Vol. 6. Normality and pathology in childhood: Assessments of development.* New York: International Universities Press.

Freud, S. (1955). The theory of instincts. In C. Thompson, M. Mazer, & E. Witenberg (Eds.), *An outline of psychoanalysis.* New York: Modern Library. (Original work published 1949)

Freud, S. (1959). Early studies on the psychical mechanisms of hysterical phenomena. In E. Jones (Ed.), *Sigmund Freud: Collected papers* (Vol. 1). New York: Basic Books. (Original work written with Breuer in 1892; first published 1940)

Freud, S. (1959). On the psychical mechanism of hysterical phenomena. In E. Jones (Ed.), *Sigmund Freud: Collected papers* (Vol. 1). New York: Basic Books. (Original work published 1893)

Freud, S. (1959). Fragment of an analysis of hysteria. In E. Jones (Ed.), *Sigmund Freud: Collected papers* (Vol. 3). New York: Basic Books. (Original work published 1905)

Freud, S. (1959). Obsessive acts and religious practices. In E. Jones (Ed.), *Sigmund Freud: collected papers* (Vol. 2). New York: Basic Books. (Original work published 1907)

Freud, S. (1959). Hysterical phantasies and their relation to bisexuality. In E. Jones (Ed.), *Sigmund Freud: Collected papers* (Vol. 2). New York: Basic Books. (Original work published 1908)

Freud, S. (1959). Family romances. In E. Jones (Ed.), *Sigmund Freud: Collected papers* (Vol. 5). New York: Basic Books. (Original work published 1909)

Freud, S. (1959). Psychoanalytic notes upon an auto-biographical account of a case of paranoia (dementia paranoides). In E. Jones (Ed.), *Sigmund Freud: Collected papers* (Vol. 3). New York: Basic Books. (Original work published 1911)

Freud, S. (1959). A predisposition to obsessional neurosis. In E. Jones (Ed.), *Sigmund Freud: Collected papers* (Vol. 2). New York: Basic Books. (Original work published 1913)

Freud, S. (1959). On narcissism: An introduction. In E. Jones (Ed.), *Sigmund Freud: Collected papers* (Vol. 4). New York: Basic Books. (Original work published 1914)

Freud, S. (1959). A case of paranoia running counter to the psychoanalytic theory of the disease. In E. Jones (Ed.), *Sigmund Freud: Collected papers* (Vol. 2). New York: Basic Books. (Original work published 1915)

Freud, S. (1959). Some psychological consequences of the anatomical distinction between the sexes. In E. Jones (Ed.), *Sigmund Freud: Collected papers* (Vol. 5). New York: Basic Books. (Original work published 1925)

Gerstley, L., McLellan, A. T., Alterman, A. I., Woody, G. E., Luborsky, L., & Prout, M. (1989). Ability to form an alliance with the therapist: A possible marker of prognosis for patients with Antisocial Personality Disorder. *American Journal of Psychiatry, 146,* 508–512.

Greenberg, J. R., & Mitchell, S. A. (1983). *Object relations in psychoanalytic theory.* Cambridge, MA: Harvard University Press.

Greenberg, R. P., & Bornstein, R. F. (1988). The dependent personality: I. Risk for physical disorders. *Journal of Personality Disorders, 2,* 126–135.

Groves, J. E. (1981). Borderline Personality Disorder. *New England Journal of Medicine, 305,* 259–262.

Grunbaum, A. (1986). What are the clinical credentials of the psychoanalytic compromise model of neurotic symptoms? In T. Millon & G. L. Klerman (Eds.), *Contemporary directions in psychopathology: Toward the DSM-IV.* New York: Guilford Press.

Guntrip, H. (1973). *Psychoanalytic theory, therapy and self.* New York: Basic Books.

Guttman, L. (1966). Order analysis of correlation matrixes. In R. B. Cattell (Ed.), *Handbook of multivariate experimental psychology.* Chicago: Rand McNally.

Gyatso, T. (1984). *Kindness, clarity and insight.* Ithaca, New York: Snow Lion.

Hackett, G., McKillop, P., & Wang, D. (1988, December 12). A tale of abuse. *Newsweek,* pp. 56–61.

Hare, R. D., Hart, S. D., & Harpur, T. J. (1991). Psychopathy and the DSM-IV criteria for Antisocial Personality Disorder. *Journal of Abnormal Psychology, 100,* 391–398.

Harlow, H. F., & Harlow, M. K. (1962). Social deprivation in monkeys. *Scientific American, 203,* 136–146.

Hart, S. D., Forth, A. E., & Hare, R. D. (1990). Performance of criminal psychopaths on selected neuropsychological tests. *Journal of Abnormal Psychology, 99,* 374–379.

Hartmann, D. P. (1977). Considerations in the choice of interobserver reliability estimates. *Journal of Applied Behavior Analysis, 10,* 103–116.

Henry, W., Schacht, T., & Strupp, H. H. (1986). Structural Analysis of Social Behavior: Application to a study of interpersonal process in differential psychotherapeutic outcome. *Journal of Consulting and Clinical Psychology, 54,* 27–31.

Hume, D. (1947). An enquiry concerning human understanding. In D. J. Bronstein, Y. H. Krikorian, & P. P. Wiener (Eds.), *Basic problems of philosophy.* Englewood Cliffs, NJ: Prentice-Hall. (Original work published 1748)

Hymowitz, P., Frances, A. J., Jacobsberg, L. B., Sickles, M., & Hoyt, R. (1986). Neuroleptic treatment of Schizotypal Personality Disorders. *Comprehensive Psychiatry, 27,* 267–271.

Jenike, M. A., Baer, L., Minichiello, W. E., Schwartz, C. E., & Carey, R. J. (1986). Concomitant Obsessive–Compulsive Disorder and Schizotypal Personality Disorder. *American Journal of Psychiatry, 143,* 530–532.

Johnston, W. A., & Dark, V. J. (1986). Selective attention. *Annual Review of Psychology, 37,* 43–76.

Jung, C. G. (1955). Dream analysis in its practical application. In C. Thompson, M. Maxer, & E. Witenberg (Eds.), *An outline of psychoanalysis.* New York: Modern Library. (Original work published 1934)

Kagan, J. (1988). The meanings of personality predicates. *American Psychologist, 43,* 614–620.

Kaslow, N., Wamboldt, F., Wamboldt, M., Anderson, R., & Benjamin, L. (1989). Interpersonal deadlock and the suicidal adolescent: An empirically based hypothesis. *American Journal of Family Therapy, 17,* 195–207.

Katz, J. (1988). *The seductions of crime: Moral and sensual attractions in doing evil.* New York: Basic Books.

Kendler, K. S., Masterson, C. C., Ungaro, R., & Davis, K. L. (1984). A family history study of schizophrenia-related personality disorders. *American Journal of Psychiatry, 141,* 424–427.

Kepecs, J. (1978). *Beyond neurosis.* Unpublished manuscript.

Kernberg, O. (1975). *Borderline conditions and pathological narcissism.* New York: Jason Aronson.

Kernberg, O. (1984). *Object relations theory and clinical psychoanalysis.* Northvale, NJ: Jason Aronson.

Kety, S. S., Rosenthal, D., Wender, P. H., Schulsinger, F., & Jacobsen, B. (1975). Mental illness in the biological and adoptive families of adopted individuals who have become schizophrenics; a preliminary report based on psychiatric interviews. In R. Fieve, P. Rosenthal, & H. Brill (Eds.), *Genetic research in psychiatry.* Baltimore: Johns Hopkins University Press.

Kiesler, D. J. (1983). The 1982 Interpersonal Circle: A taxonomy for complementarity in human transactions. *Psychological Review, 90,* 185–214.

Kiesler, D. J. (1986). The 1982 Interpersonal Circle: An analysis of DSM-III personality disorders. In T. Millon & G. L. Klerman (Eds.), *Contemporary directions in psychopathology: Toward the DSM-IV.* New York: Guilford Press.

Klein, M. K., Benjamin, L. S., Rosenfeld, R., Greist, J. H., & Lohr, M. J. (in press). The Wisconsin Personality Inventory (WISPI): Development, reliability, and validity. *Journal of Personality Disorders.*

Kohut, H. (1971). *The analysis of the self.* New York: International Universities Press.

Krull, J. (1988). *The challenge of the borderline patient.* New York: Norton.

Kübler-Ross, E. (1969). *On death and dying.* New York: Macmillan.

LaForge, R., Leary, T. F., Naboisek, H., Coffey, H. S., & Freedman, M. B. (1954). The interpersonal dimension of personality: II. An objective study of repression. *Journal of Personality, 23,* 129–153.

Laing, R. D. (1970). *Knots.* New York: Vintage Books.

Leary, T. (1957). *Interpersonal diagnosis of personality: A functional theory and methodology for personality evaluation.* New York: Ronald Press.

Leibenluft, E., Gardner, O. L., & Cowdry, R. W. (1987). The inner experience of the borderline self-mutilator. *Journal of Personality Disorders, 1,* 317–324.

Lemert, E. M. (1962). Paranoia and the dynamics of exclusion. *Sociometry, 25,* 2–20.

Levine, F., & Sandeen, E. (1985). *Conceptualization in psychotherapy: The models approach.* Hillsdale, NJ: Erlbaum.

Levine, M. (1966). Hypothesis behavior by humans during discrimination learning. *Journal of Experimental Psychology, 71,* 331–338.

Linehan, M. M. (1993). *Cognitive–behavioral therapy for Borderline Personality Disorder.* New York: Guilford Press.

Livesley, W. J., Schroeder, M. L., & Jackson, D. N. (1990). Dependent Personality Disorder and attachment problems. *Journal of Personality Disorders, 4,* 131–140.

Livesley, W. J., & West, M. (1986). The DSM-III distinction between Schizoid and Avoidant Personality Disorders. *American Journal of Psychiatry, 31,* 59–61.

Livesley, W. J., West, M., & Tanney, A. (1985). Historical comment on DSM-III Schizoid and Avoidant Personality Disorders. *American Journal of Psychiatry, 142,* 1344–1347.

Loeber, R., Weissman, W., & Reid, J. B. (1983). Family interactions of assaultive adolescents, stealers and nondelinquents. *Journal of Abnormal Child Psychology, 11,* 1–14.

Loranger, A. W., Susman, V. L., Oldham, J. M., & Russakoff, L. M. (1987). The Personality Disorder Examination: A preliminary report. *Journal of Personality Disorders, 1,* 1–13.

Lorr, M., Bishop, P. F., & McNair, D. M. (1965). Interpersonal types among psychiatric patients. *Journal of Abnormal Psychology, 70,* 468–472.

Luborsky, L., & Auerbach, A. H. (1985). The therapeutic relationship in psychodynamic psychotherapy: The research evidence and its meaning for practice. In R. E. Hales & A. J. Frances (Eds.), *Psychiatry update: The American Psychiatric Association annual review* (Vol. 4). Washington, DC: American Psychiatric Press.

MacKenzie, K. R. (1990). *Time limited group psychotherapy.* Washington, DC: American Psychiatric Press.

Mahler, M. (1968). *On human symbiosis and the vicissitudes of individuation.* New York: International Universities Press.

Malin, A. (1990). Psychotherapy of the Narcissistic Personality Disorders. In A. Tasman, S. M. Goldfinger, & C. A. Kaufmann (Eds.), *Review of psychiatry* (Vol. 9). Washington, DC: American Psychiatric Press.

Marmor, J., & Woods, S. M. (1980). *The interface between the psychodynamic and behavior therapies.* New York: Plenum Press.

Masterson, J. F. (1975). The splitting defense mechanism of the borderline adolescent: Developmental and clinical aspects. In J. Mack (Ed.), *Borderline states in psychiatry*. New York: Grune & Stratton.

McCann, J. T. (1988). Passive Aggressive Personality Disorder: A review. *Journal of Personality Disorders, 2,* 170–179.

McGlashan, T. H. (1983). Intensive individual psychotherapy of schizophrenia. *Archives of General Psychiatry, 40,* 909–920.

McGlashan, T. H. (1986). Schizotypal Personality Disorder: Chestnut Lodge Follow-Up Study, VI. Long-term follow-up perspectives. *Archives of General Psychiatry, 43,* 329–334.

McGlashan, T. H. (1987). Testing DSM-III symptom criteria for schizotypal and borderline personality disorder. *Archives of General Psychiatry, 44,* 143–148.

McLemore, C., & Benjamin, L. S. (1979). Whatever happened to interpersonal diagnosis?: A psychosocial alternative to DSM-III. *American Psychologist, 34,* 17–34.

Mead, G. H. (1934). *Mind, self and society*. Chicago: University of Chicago Press.

Mellsop, G., Varghese, M. B., Joshua, S., & Hicks, A. (1982). The reliability of Axis II of DSM-III. *American Journal of Psychiatry, 139,* 1360–1361.

Merikangas, K. R., & Weissman, M. M. (1986). Epidemiology of DSM-III Axis II personality disorders. In A. J. Frances & R. E. Hales (Eds.), *Psychiatry update: The American Psychiatric Association annual review* (Vol. 5). Washington, DC: American Psychiatric Press.

Midelfort, C. F. (1957). *The family in psychotherapy*. New York: McGraw-Hill.

Millon, T. (1969). *Modern psychopathology: A biosocial approach to maladaptive learning and functioning*. Prospect Heights, IL: Waveland Press.

Millon, T. (1981). *Disorders of personality DSM-III: Axis II*. New York: Wiley-Interscience.

Millon, T. (1982). *Millon Clinical Multiaxial Inventory manual* (2nd ed.). Minneapolis: National Computer Systems.

Millon, T. (1984). On the renaissance of personality assessment and personality theory. *Journal of Personality Assessment, 48,* 450–466.

Millon, T. (1986). A theoretical derivation of pathological personalities. In T. Millon and G. L. Klerman (Eds.), *Contemporary directions in psychopathology: Toward the DSM-IV*. New York: Guilford Press.

Millon, T. (1991). Classification in psychopathology: Rationale, alternatives, and standards. *Journal of Abnormal Psychology, 100,* 245–261.

Mischel, W. (1973). Toward a cognitive social learning reconceptualization of personality. *Psychological Review, 80,* 252–283.

Morey, L. C. (1985). An empirical comparison of interpersonal and DSM-III approaches to classification of personality disorders. *Psychiatry, 48,* 358–364.

Morey, L. C. (1988). Personality disorders in DSM-III and DSM-III-R: Convergence, coverage, and internal consistency. *American Journal of Psychiatry, 145,* 573–577.

Morey, L. C. (1991). Classification of mental disorder as a collection of hypothetical constructs. *Journal of Abnormal Psychology, 100,* 289–293.

Murray, H. A. (1938). *Explorations in personality*. New York: Oxford University Press.

Mussen, P. H., Conger, J. J., & Kagan, J. (1971). *Child development and personality* (3rd ed.). New York: Harper & Row.

Perls, F. S. (1969). *Gestalt therapy verbatim*. Lafayette, CA: Real People Press.

Perry, J. C., & Flannery, R. D. (1982). Passive aggressive personality disorder: Treatment implications of a clinical typology. *Journal of Nervous and Mental Disease, 170,* 164–173.

Pfohl, B., Coryell, W., Zimmerman, M., & Stangl, D. (1986). DSM-III personality disorders: Diagnostic overlap and internal consistency of individual DSM-III criteria. *Comprehensive Psychiatry, 27*, 21–34.

Pilkonis, P. (1988). Personality prototypes among depressives: Themes of dependency and autonomy. *Journal of Personality Disorders, 2*, 144–152.

Plutchik, R., & Platman, S. R. (1977). Personality connotations of psychiatric diagnoses. *Journal of Nervous and Mental Disease, 165*, 418–422.

Pollack, J. (1987). Obsessive compulsive personality: Theoretical and clinical perspectives and recent research findings. *Journal of Personality Disorders, 2*, 248–262.

Pollock, V. E., Briere, J., Schneider, L., Knop, J., Mednick, S. A., & Goodwin, D. W. (1990). Childhood antecedents of antisocial behavior: Parental alcoholism and physical abusiveness. *American Journal of Psychiatry, 147*, 1290–1293.

Reich, W. (1949). *Character analysis* (3rd ed.). New York: Orgone Institute Press.

Reik, T. (1949). *Listening with the third ear.* New York: Farrar, Straus.

Robins, L. N. (1970). The adult development of the antisocial child. *Seminars in Psychiatry, 2*, 420–434.

Rogers, C. R. (1951). *Client-centered therapy.* Cambridge, MA: Riverside Press.

Rothenberg, A. (1986). Eating disorder as a modern obsessive compulsive syndrome. *Psychiatry, 49*, 45–53.

Schaefer, E. S. (1965). Configurational analysis of children's reports of parent behavior. *Journal of Consulting Psychology, 29*, 552-557.

Schulz, S. C., Schulz, P. M., & Wilson, W. H. (1988). Medication treatment of Schizotypal Personality Disorder. *Journal of Personality Disorders, 2*, 1–13.

Shapiro, D. (1965). *Neurotic styles.* New York: Basic Books.

Siever, L. J., & Klar, H. K. (1986). A review of DSM-III criteria for the personality disorders. In A. J. Frances & R. E. Hales (Eds.), *Psychiatry update: The American Psychiatric Association annual review* (Vol. 5). Washington, DC: American Psychiatric Press.

Skinner, B. F. (1938). *The behavior of organisms.* New York: Appleton-Century-Crofts.

Skinner, B. F. (1990). Can psychology be a science of mind? *American Psychologist, 45*, 1206–1210.

Skinner, H. A. (1981). Toward the integration of classification theory and methods: Perspectives from psychology. *Journal of Abnormal Psychology, 90*, 68–87.

Spitzer, R. L., Endicott, J., & Gibbon, M. (1979). Crossing the border into borderline personality and borderline schizophrenia. *Archives of General Psychiatry, 36*, 17–24.

Spitzer, R. L, Gibbon, M., Skodol, A. E., Williams, J. B. W., & First, M. B. (1989). *DSM-III-R casebook.* Washington, DC: American Psychiatric Association.

Spitzer, R. L., Skodol, A. E., Gibbon, M., & Williams, J. B. W. (1981). *DSM-III casebook.* Washington, DC: American Psychiatric Association.

Spitzer, R. L., Williams, J. B. W., & Skodol, A. E. (1980). DSM-III: The major achievements and an overview. *American Journal of Psychiatry, 137*, 151–164.

Strupp, H. H. (1980). Success and failure in time-limited psychotherapy: Further evidence (comparison 4). *Archives of General Psychiatry, 37*, 947–954.

Strupp, H. H. (1989). Psychotherapy: Can the practitioner learn from the researcher? *American Psychologist, 44*, 717–724.

Strupp, H. H., & Binder, J. L. (1984). *Psychotherapy in a new key.* New York: Basic Books.

Sullivan, H. S. (1953). *The interpersonal theory of psychiatry.* New York: Norton.

Sweet, M. J., & Johnson, C. G. (1990). Enhancing empathy: The interpersonal implications of a Buddhist meditation technique. *Psychotherapy, 27*, 19–29.

Trull, T. J., Widiger, T. A., & Frances, A. (1987). Covariation of criteria sets for Avoidant,

Schizoid and Dependent Personality Disorders. *American Journal of Psychiatry, 144,* 767–771.

Turner, S. M., Beidel, D. C., Bordern, J. W., Stanley, M. A., & Jacob, R. G. (1991). Social Phobia: Axis I and II correlates. *Journal of Abnormal Psychology, 100,* 102–106.

Wachtel, P. L. (1973). Psychodynamics, behavior therapy, and the implacable experimenter: An inquiry into the consistency of personality. *Journal of Abnormal Psychology, 82,* 324–334.

Washburn, S. L., & Hamburg, D. A. (1965). The implications of primate research. In I. DeVore (Ed.), *Primate behavior: Field studies of monkeys and apes.* New York: Holt, Rinehart & Winston.

Watzlawick, P., Beavin, J. H., & Jackson, D. D. (1967). *Pragmatics of human communication.* New York: Norton.

Widiger, T. A. (1989). The categorical distinction between personality and affective disorders. *Journal of Personality Disorders, 3,* 77–91.

Widiger, T. A. (in press). The DSM-III-R categorical personality disorder diagnoses: A critique and an alternative. *Psychological Inquiry.*

Widiger, T. A., & Frances, A. J. (1985). Axis II personality disorders: Diagnostic and treatment issues. *Hospital and Community Psychiatry, 36,* 619–627.

Widiger, T. A., & Frances, A. J. (1987). Interviews and inventories for the measurement of personality disorders. *Clinical Psychology Review, 7,* 49–75.

Widiger, T. A., Frances, A. J., Spitzer, R. L., & Williams, J. B. W. (1988). The DSM-III-R personality disorders: An overview. *American Journal of Psychiatry, 145,* 786–795.

Widiger, T. A., Frances, A. J., & Trull, T. J. (1987). A psychometric analysis of the social–interpersonal and cognitive–perceptual items for the Schizotypal Personality Disorder. *Archives of General Psychiatry, 44,* 741–745.

Widiger, T. A., & Kelso, K. (1983). Psychodiagnosis of Axis II. *Clinical Psychology Review, 3,* 491–510.

Widiger, T. A., & Sanderson, C. (1987). Convergent and discriminant validity of the MCMI as a measure of the DSM-III personality disorders. *Journal of Personality Assessment, 51,* 228–241.

Wiggins, J. S. (1982). Circumplex models of interpersonal behavior in clinical psychology. In P. C. Kendall & J. N. Butcher (Eds.), *Handbook of research methods in clinical psychology.* New York: Wiley.

Wiggins, J. S., & Broughton, R. (1985). The Interpersonal Circle: A structural model for the integration of personality research. In R. Hogan & W. H. Jones (Eds.), *Perspectives in personality* (Vol. 1). Greenwich, CT: JAI Press.

Wolkind, S. N. (1974). The components of "affectionless psychopathy" in institutionalized children. *Journal of Child Psychology and Psychiatry, 15,* 215–220.

Wynne, L. C., Ryckoff, I. M., Day, J., & Hirsch, S. I. (1958). Pseudo-mutuality in the family relations of schizophrenics. *Psychiatry: Journal for the Study of Interpersonal Processes, 21,* 205–220.

Index

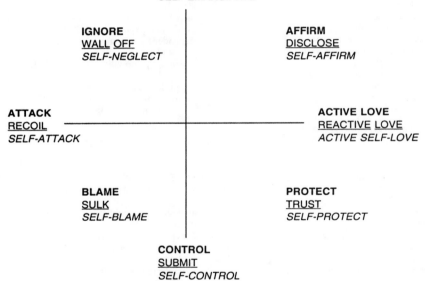

EMANCIPATE
SEPARATE
SELF-EMANCIPATE

IGNORE
WALL OFF
SELF-NEGLECT

AFFIRM
DISCLOSE
SELF-AFFIRM

ATTACK
RECOIL
SELF-ATTACK

ACTIVE LOVE
REACTIVE LOVE
ACTIVE SELF-LOVE

BLAME
SULK
SELF-BLAME

PROTECT
TRUST
SELF-PROTECT

CONTROL
SUBMIT
SELF-CONTROL

The SASB simplified cluster model, all three surfaces.